Advances in Integrated Services Digital Networks (ISDN) and Broadband ISDN

William Stallings

Advances in ISDN and Broadband ISDN

William Stallings

 IEEE Computer Society Press

The Institute of Electrical and Electronics Engineers, Inc.

Advances in Integrated Services Digital Networks (ISDN) and Broadband ISDN

William Stallings

IEEE Computer Society Press
Los Alamitos, California

Washington   •   Brussels   •   Tokyo

IEEE COMPUTER SOCIETY PRESS TUTORIAL

Library of Congress Cataloging-in-Publication Data

Stallings, William.
 Advances in integrated services digital networks (ISDN) and broadband ISDN / William
Stallings
        p.   cm.
    Includes bibliographical references.
      ISBN 0-8186-2797-2 (case). -- ISBN 0-8186-2795-6 (pbk.). -- ISBN
      0-8186-2796-4 (M/F).
    1. Integrated services digital networks.   2. Broadband communication systems. I. Title.
 TK5103.7.S72 1992   660'.2842--dc20   CIP 92-4188

Published by the
IEEE Computer Society Press
10662 Los Vaqueros Circle
PO Box 3014
Los Alamitos, CA 90720-1264

IEEE Computer Society Press Order Number 2797
Library of Congress Number 92-4188
IEEE Catalog Number 92EH0352-5
ISBN 0-8186-2796-4 (microfiche)
ISBN 0-8186-2797-2 (case)

Additional copies can be ordered from

IEEE Computer Society Press Customer Service Center 10662 Los Vaqueros Circle PO Box 3014 Los Alamitos, CA 90720-1264	IEEE Service Center 445 Hoes Lane PO Box 1331 Piscataway, NJ 08855-1331	IEEE Computer Society 13, avenue de l'Aquilon B-1200 Brussels BELGIUM	IEEE Computer Society Ooshima Building 2-19-1 Minami-Aoyama Minato-ku, Tokyo 107 JAPAN

Editorial production: Robert Werner
Technical editor: Rao Vemuri
Copy editor: Phyllis Walker
Cover designed by Joseph Daigle/Schenk-Daigle Studios
Printed in the United States of America by Braun-Brumfield, Inc.

 The Institute of Electrical and Electronics Engineers, Inc.

Preface

This tutorial is a sequel to the author's previous tutorial entitled *Integrated Services Digital Networks (ISDN)*, second edition (IEEE Computer Society Press, Los Alamitos, California, 1988). However, because this new tutorial comprises all original material and because every one of the reprinted papers is new to it, referring to it simply as a "third edition" would have been inaccurate. Instead, a new title was chosen that describes the broadened scope of this new tutorial.

Several developments have taken place since the publication of the author's previous tutorial. This new tutorial reflects these developments, which include the following:

(1) The 1988 edition of the CCITT recommendations on ISDN and on Signaling System Number 7 has been digested by industry, and products and services have emerged that are based on the standards promulgated by these recommendations.

(2) Frame relay, a major innovation of the ISDN standards effort, has achieved widespread acceptance as the technique that will replace X.25 packet switching. Frame relay is now being used in many ISDN and non-ISDN contexts.

(3) The 1990 set of interim recommendations on ISDN clarified and expanded some areas of ISDN and provided much more detail on frame relay than that provided by the 1988 recommendations.

(4) The 1990 set of interim recommendations on broadband ISDN (B-ISDN) provided the first definitive specification of B-ISDN services and protocols.

Objective

The objective of this tutorial is to provide a comprehensive introduction to ISDN and B-ISDN. The tutorial explores key topics related to ISDN and B-ISDN in the general categories of architecture and standards.

Architecture. The architecture of ISDN exploits the emerging application of digital technology to integrate voice and data transmission and to provide structured interfaces and transmissions services for the end user.

Standards. A massive effort is under way to develop standards covering the broad spectrum of protocols, architecture, and services for ISDN and B-ISDN. The 1988 recommendations and 1990 interim recommendations are products of that effort.

Intended Audience

This tutorial is intended for a broad range of readers who would benefit from an understanding of ISDN and B-ISDN concepts. This audience includes students and professionals in the fields of data processing and data communications, customers and managers involved in data communications and networking, designers, and implementers. Intended readers should have a basic, general background in the area of data communications. However, for readers who have little or no background in this area, reading the introductory material in each chapter will aid in their understanding the reprinted papers that are included therein.

Organization

This tutorial is a combination of original material and reprinted papers. It is divided into five chapters, which are described below.

Chapter 1: Integrated Services Digital Network (ISDN) Overview. This chapter introduces the concept of ISDN and provides an overview of its key concepts and areas of application.

Chapter 2: ISDN Protocols and Network Architecture. The bulk of the ISDN recommendations put forth in 1988 and 1990 deal with the user-network interface. This chapter examines the architecture and protocols that relate to that interface. In addition, it introduces a related set of recommendations that specify Signaling System Number 7 (SS7); these recommendations deal with the internal operation of ISDN.

Chapter 3: Frame Relay. Most of what constitutes ISDN is simply a repackaging of existing technologies and services, plus variations and refinements on these technologies and services. The most important original contribution of the ISDN effort is frame relay. Not only has frame relay become popular as a component of ISDN offerings, but it is being widely used in non-ISDN applications also. Since the introduction of frame relay into the 1988 ISDN recommendations, considerable progress has been made in the definition of frame relay and in its application. This chapter provides a detailed look at frame relay.

Chapter 4: Broadband ISDN (B-ISDN). This chapter introduces the latest developments in ISDN technology and standards and examines the services and architecture of B-ISDN.

Chapter 5: Asynchronous Transfer Mode (ATM) and Synchronous Optical Network/Synchronous Digital Hierarchy (SONET/SDH). Just as frame relay is the key transmission technology for ISDN, ATM is a form of packet switching that is the key transmission technology of B-ISDN. The synchronous optical network (SONET), also referred to as the "synchronous digital hierarchy (SDH)," defines a synchronous time-division multiplexing (TDM) transmission structure that is utilized both as part of B-ISDN and as a separate service. Together, these two technologies form the basis for B-ISDN transmission and switching. This chapter provides an overview and introduction to both technologies.

Glossary. The glossary includes definitions for key terms appearing in the text.

List of Acronyms. This list includes the acronyms appearing in the text.

Annotated Bibliography. This bibliography provides a guide to further reading.

Related Materials

A companion text to this new tutorial is a textbook by the author entitled *ISDN and Broadband ISDN*, second edition (The Macmillan Publishing Company, New York, New York, 1992). Intended as a textbook, it is also a reference book for professionals. The author has also prepared two videotape courses — one on ISDN and the other on B-ISDN — that are available from The Media Group, Boston University, 565 Commonwealth Avenue, Boston, Massachusetts 02215; telephone (617) 353-3217.

William Stallings
May 15, 1992

Table of Contents

List of Tables

List of Figures

Chapter 1: Integrated Services Digital Network (ISDN) Overview

The arrival of ISDN

Rapid advances in computer and communication technologies have resulted in the increasing merger of these two fields. The lines have blurred among computing, switching, and digital-transmission equipment, and the same digital techniques are being used for data, voice, and image transmissions. Merging and evolving technologies, coupled with increasing demands for the efficient and timely collection, processing, and dissemination of information, are leading to the development of integrated systems that transmit and process all types of data. The ultimate goal of this evolution is something its proponents — some of the most powerful forces in the computing and telecommunications industries — call the integrated services digital network (ISDN). ISDN will be a worldwide public telecommunications network that will replace existing public telecommunications networks. It will deliver a wide variety of services, both voice based and data based.

ISDN is defined by the standardization of user interfaces. Because it will be implemented as a set of digital switches and paths, ISDN will support a broad range of traffic types and provide value-added processing services. In practice, there will be multiple networks, implemented within national boundaries; however, from the user's point of view, there will be a single, uniformly accessible, worldwide network.

The impact of ISDN on both users and vendors will be profound. To control ISDN evolution and impact, a massive effort at standardization of user interfaces is under way. Although ISDN standards are still evolving, both the technology and the emerging implementation strategy are well understood.

Two key aspects of ISDN are universal access and user services, which are discussed below.

(1) Universal access. With standardization of the interfaces to ISDN, all ISDN-compatible equipment (for example, telephones, computer terminals, and personal computers) would be able to attach to the network anywhere in the world and connect to any other attached system. This ability would lead to extraordinary flexibility. For example, assigned telephone numbers — like US social security numbers — could be good for a lifetime. No matter where a user lived, or how often he moved, his telephone would ring when the number permanently assigned to him is dialed. In another example of the flexibility of universal access, a person, wherever he is, could reach — for instance — the nearest Holiday Inn by tapping the telephone buttons marked H-O-L-I-D-A-Y-I-N-N.

(2) User services. Two examples of user services that will be provided by implementation of ISDN are found in the medical field and the banking industry, respectively. The first example is in the medical field. A doctor maintains both a suburban office and an office at an in-town hospital. The medical records for all of his patients are kept in a database at the hospital. Suppose — with ISDN — that a patient places a call to the doctor at the hospital on a day that the doctor is at his suburban office. The call would be forwarded automatically from the hospital to the suburban office, where the incoming call would cause the telephone to ring. At the same time, the name and telephone number of the caller would be displayed on a small screen that would be part of the telephone. While the telephone is ringing, a message would be automatically sent back to the hospital to search for any records associated with this call. If a database search reveals that the caller is a patient of this doctor, the patient's medical record would be transmitted to the suburban office; the first page of that record would be displayed on a terminal screen next to the telephone by the time the receiver is picked up to answer the call. The second example is in the banking industry. Bank-by-phone services depend upon the automatic identification of the calling party; ISDN can provide such identification, while guaranteeing transaction privacy and security. In addition, ISDN will support increased — and increasingly easy-to-use — electronic funds transfer facilities, as well as rapid check clearing.

Many trends present today in the computer world are driving ISDN; these trends are part of the evolution to ISDN and will be accelerated as ISDN is implemented. Computers are being joined together, instead of being left standing alone. An estimated 30 percent of today's personal computers have communications capability, and this percentage is rising. While yesterday's corporate computer was a stand-alone device, today's business computers comprise a mix of small, medium, and large computers that can share resources (such as printers), share data, and exchange messages. Our analytical tools have sprouted wires; more and better wires are coming, and the wires will extend everywhere. Cellular radio is making communications mobile. Automobiles, taxis, and boats are becoming workstations. People can not only talk via cellular radio phones, but can also transmit data by linking up their portable computers. In the future, cellular phone/computer combinations will be developed; in time, automobiles will provide communication/computer systems as options: Any vehicle could be a unit capable of linking up to the global information network. Computers for personal use will be ubiquitous in the future; this will be especially true for students (starting with elementary school) and "knowledge workers," who deal primarily with paper documents, reports, and numbers. Soon, many office workers will have at least one workstation at the office and one at home. Furthermore, most people will own a powerful portable very personal computer (VPC) — possibly a wearable model. The hotel at which you stay may have personal computers in their rooms as amenities; some hotels already do. Computing power will be at every hand; most importantly, each computer will tap into the network.

The volume and richness of data are increasing dramatically. The first-generation personal computers have given way to the latest IBM PCs and MAC-IIs with color and high-quality graphics. New applications in the office environment are being developed that require much higher networking capacity than that of traditional office applications, and desktop image processors will soon increase network data flow by an unprecedented amount. Examples of these new applications include digital facsimile machines, document image processors, and graphics programs on personal computers. Resolutions as high as 400 dots per inch are typical for these applications. Even with compression techniques, these new applications will generate a tremendous data communications load. In addition, optical disks are beginning to reach technical maturity and are being developed toward realistic desktop capacities that exceed one gigabyte (Gbyte).

Two of the most difficult technologies to develop — voice recognition and natural-language processing — are gradually emerging from artificial-intelligence laboratories. Applications of these technologies will increase the intelligence of systems and networks. Voice recognition is the ability to recognize spoken words. Natural-language processing is the ability to extract the meaning of words and sentences. As these two technologies develop, access to information banks and databases will become increasingly easy, therefore creating a greater demand for access. A user will be able to perform a transaction or to access information with simple spoken or natural-language keyed commands. Interfacing with the worldwide network will be like talking with a very knowledgeable telephone operator, librarian, and universal expert, rolled into one. Government use of computer systems will become more efficient. (The government is the most prodigious producer and user of information in our society.) ISDN will improve and disperse access to — and help to remove incompatibilities among — different systems, so that more can be accomplished with less effort.

National and global business activities will benefit. The brokerage business has become almost a computer network unto itself, depending upon instant transmission of information and automated buy-sell orders. Banking today relies upon more than automatic tellers and computerized accounting. And banks are beginning to sell on-line information services as adjuncts to electronic banking.

Companies of all sizes are coming to depend upon telecommunications for their daily business activities. Remote data entry, electronic mail, facsimile transmission, and decision support systems are just some of the operations that rely upon communications. Multinational corporations and joint ventures between American and foreign firms depend upon quick interchange of information. Communication networks are absolutely essential for the continued globalization of trade and industry. Office buildings are being wired for intelligence. The so-called "smart building" is beginning to appear; such a building contains a network for voice, data, environmental control (of heat, humidity, and air conditioning), security (against burglary and fire), and closed-circuit TV. Many of these services generate out-of-building transmission requirements.

Electronic person-to-person interaction will increase. With electronic mail, voice mail, file transfer, document exchange, and video teleconferencing facilities, business is responding to the need for employees to interact and to avoid "telephone tag." All of these facilities generate large data communications requirements. In developed countries, fiber is rapidly replacing microwave and coaxial cable transmission paths. (Fiber, together with satellite, is appearing more gradually elsewhere.) The resulting quantum jump in capacity has permitted the planning and deployment of new applications on public and private networks.

Principles of ISDN

Standards for ISDN, called "recommendations," are being defined by the Comité Consultatif International Télégraphique et Téléphonique (CCITT) (International Consultative Committee for Telegraphy and Telephony). (This chapter explores these standards in greater detail later.) The top portion of Table 1-1, from one of the ISDN-related standards, gives the principles of ISDN from the point of view of the CCITT. Let us look at each of these principles in turn.

(1) Support of voice and nonvoice applications using a limited set of standardized facilities. This principle defines both the purpose of ISDN and the means of fulfilling this purpose. ISDN will support a variety of services related to voice communications (for example, telephone calls) and nonvoice communications (for example, digital data exchange). These services are to be provided in conformance with standards (CCITT recommendations) that specify a small number of interfaces and data transmission facilities. The benefit of standards are explored later in this chapter. For now, we simply state that — without such a limitation — a global, interconnected ISDN is virtually impossible.

(2) Support for switched and nonswitched applications. ISDN will support both circuit switching and packet switching. In addition, ISDN will support nonswitched services in the form of dedicated lines.

(3) Reliance on 64-kilobit per second (Kbps) connections. ISDN will provide circuit-switched and packet-switched connections at 64 Kbps. This reliance on 64-Kbps connections is the fundamental building block of ISDN. The rate of 64 Kbps was chosen because, at the time that it was chosen, it was the standard rate for digitized voice; hence, it was being introduced into the evolving digital networks. Although this data rate is useful, relying solely upon it is unfortunately restrictive. Future developments in ISDN will permit greater flexibility.

(4) Intelligence in the network. ISDN will provide sophisticated services beyond the simple setup of a circuit-switched call.

(5) Layered protocol architecture. The protocols being developed for user access to ISDN exhibit a layered architecture and can be mapped into something referred to as the "OSI model," where OSI stands for "open systems interconnection." This layered protocol architecture has a number of advantages, as follows:

• Standards already developed for OSI-related applications may be used on ISDN. An example is X.25 level 3 for access to packet-switching services in ISDN.

• New ISDN-related standards can be based on existing standards, reducing the cost of new implementations. An example is link access protocol-D channel (LAPD), which is based on link access protocol-balanced (LAPB).

• Standards can be developed and implemented independently for various layers and for various functions within a layer. This advantage allows for the gradual implementation of ISDN services at a pace appropriate for a given provider or a given customer base.

(6) Variety of configurations. More than one physical configuration is possible for implementing ISDN. This allows for differences in national policy, in the state of technology, and in the needs and existing equipment of the customer base.

Evolution of ISDN

Although the evolution of digital technology in telecommunications networks has been driven by the need to provide economical voice communications, the resulting network is also well suited to meet the growing variety of digital data service needs. The lower portion of Table 1-1 gives the CCITT view of the ways in which ISDN will evolve. Let us look at each of these ways in turn.

(1) Evolution from telephone integrated digital networks (IDNs). The intent is that ISDN evolve from the existing telephone IDNs. From this intent, the following two conclusions can be drawn:

• The digital technology developed for, and evolving within, existing telephone networks forms the foundation for the services to be provided by ISDN.

Table 1-1. Integrated services digital networks (ISDN) — Recommendation I.120

1	**Principles of ISDN**
1.1	The main feature of the ISDN concept is the support of a wide range of voice and non-voice applications in the same network. A key element of service integration for an ISDN is the provision of a range of services using a limited set of connection types and multipurpose user-network interface arrangements.
1.2	ISDNs support a variety of applications including both switched and non-switched connections. Switched connections in an ISDN include both circuit-switched and packet-switched connections and their concatenations.
1.3	As far as practicable, new services introduced into an ISDN should be arranged to be compatible with 64 Kbit/s switched digital connections.
1.4	An ISDN will contain intelligence for the purpose of providing service features, maintenance and network management functions. This intelligence may not be sufficient for some new services and may have to be supplemented by either additional intelligence within the network, or possibly compatible intelligence in the user terminals.
1.5	A layered protocol structure should be used for the specification of the access to an ISDN. Access from a user to ISDN resources may vary depending upon the service required and upon the status of implementation of national ISDNs.
1.6	It is recognized that ISDNs may be implemented in a variety of configurations according to specific national situations.
2	**Evolution of ISDNs**
2.1	ISDNs will be based on the concepts developed for telephone IDNs and may evolve by progressively incorporating additional functions and network features including those of any other dedicated networks such as circuit-switching and packet-switching for data so as to provide for existing and new services.
2.2	The transition from an existing network to a comprehensive ISDN may require a period of time extending over one or more decades. During this period arrangements must be developed for the interworking of services on ISDNs and services on other networks.
2.3	In the evolution towards an ISDN, digital end-to-end connectivity will be obtained via plant and equipment used in existing networks, such as digital transmission, time-division multiplex switching and/or space-division multiplex switching. Existing relevant Recommendations for these constituent elements of an ISDN are contained in the appropriate series of Recommendations of CCITT and of CCIR.
2.4	In the early stages of the evolution of ISDNs, some interim user-network arrangements may need to be adopted in certain countries to facilitate early penetration of digital service capabilities. Arrangements corresponding to national variants may comply partly or wholly with I-Series Recommendations. However, the intention is that they not be specifically included in the I-Series.
2.5	An evolving ISDN may also include at later stages switched connections at bit rates higher and lower than 64 Kbit/s.

• Although other facilities — such as third-party (not the telephone provider) packet-switched networks and satellite links — will play a role in ISDN, the telephone networks will play the dominant role.

Although packet-switching and satellite providers may be less than happy with these conclusions, the overwhelming prevalence of telephone networks dictates that these networks form the basis for ISDN.

(2) Transition of one or more decades. The evolution to ISDN will be a slow process. This is true of any migration of a complex application or set of applications from one technical base to a newer one. The introduction of ISDN services will be done in the context of existing digital facilities and existing services. There will be a period of coexistence, in which connections and perhaps protocol conversion will be needed between alternative facilities and/or services.

(3) Use of existing networks. [This item elaborates on item (2).] ISDN will provide a packet-switched service. For the time being, the interface to that service will be X.25. With the introduction of fast packet switching and more sophisticated virtual call control, a new interface may be needed in the future.

(4) Interim user-network arrangements. Primarily, the concern with interim user-network arrangements is that the lack of digital subscriber loops might delay introduction of digital services, particularly in developing countries. With the use of modems and other equipment, existing analog facilities can support at least some ISDN services.

(5) Connections at other than 64 Kbps. The 64-Kbps data rate was chosen as the basic channel for circuit switching. With improvements in voice-digitizing technology, this rate is unnecessarily high. On the other hand, this rate is too low for many digital data applications. Thus, other data rates will be needed in the future.

The details of the evolution of ISDN facilities and services will vary from one country to another — and indeed will vary from one provider to another in the same country. The above ways in which ISDN will evolve simply provide a general description, from the CCITT's point of view, of the evolution.

The user interface

Figure 1-1 is a conceptual view of ISDN features from a customer's (or user's) point of view. The user has access to ISDN by means of a local interface to a digital "pipe" of a certain bit rate. Pipes of various sizes will be available to satisfy differing needs. For example, a residential customer may require only sufficient capacity to handle a videotex terminal and a telephone. On the other hand, an office will typically wish to connect to ISDN via an on-premise digital private branch exchange (PBX); such a connection will require a much higher capacity pipe.

At any given point in time, the pipe to the user's premises has a fixed capacity, but the traffic on the pipe may be a variable mix, up to the capacity limit. Thus, a user may access packet-switched and circuit-switched services, as well as other services, in a dynamic mix of signal types and bit rates. ISDN will require rather complex control signals to instruct it how to sort out the time-multiplexed data and provide the required services. These control signals will also be multiplexed onto the same digital pipe as that for user data.

An important aspect of the interface is that the user may, at any time, employ less than the maximum capacity of the pipe; the user will be charged according to the capacity used, rather than the "connect time." This aspect will tend to lessen the value of current user design efforts that are geared to optimize circuit utilization by use of concentrators, multiplexers, packet switches, and other line-sharing arrangements.

Objectives

Activities currently under way are leading to the development of a worldwide ISDN. This effort involves national governments, data-processing and communication companies, standards organizations, and others. Certain common objectives are, by and large, shared by this disparate group. Key objectives are

• Standardization,
• Transparency,
• Separation of competitive functions,
• Leased and switched services,

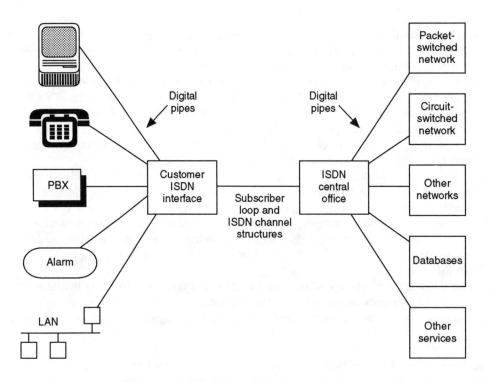

Figure 1-1. Conceptual view of ISDN features from a customer's (or user's) point of view.

- Cost-related tariffs,
- Smooth migration, and
- Multiplexed support.

Of course, additional objectives could be named; however, those listed are certainly among the most important and widely accepted, and they help to define the character of ISDN.

Standardization. Standardization is essential to the success of ISDN. Standards will provide for universal access to the network. ISDN-standard equipment can be moved from one location to another, indeed from one country to another, and be plugged into the network. The cost of such equipment will be minimized because of the competition among many vendors to provide the same type of functionality. In addition, the use of a layered protocol architecture and standardized interfaces allows users to select equipment from multiple suppliers and allows changes to be made to a configuration in a gradual, piece-by-piece fashion.

Transparency. It is also important that the digital-transmission service have the property of transparency. A service that has "transparency" is one that is independent of, and does not affect, the content of the user data to be transmitted. Transparency permits users to develop applications and protocols with the confidence that these applications and protocols will not be affected by the underlying ISDN. Once a circuit or virtual circuit has been set up, the user should be able to send information without the provider being aware of the type of information being carried. In addition, user-provided encryption techniques can be employed to provide security of user information.

Separation of competitive functions. ISDN must be defined in a way that does not preclude the separation of competitive functions from the basic digital-transmission services. Separating out functions that could be provided competitively — as opposed to those that are fundamentally part of ISDN — must be possible. In many countries, a single, government-owned entity will provide all services. Some countries desire (or require, as in the case of the United States) that certain enhanced services be offered competitively (for example, videotex and electronic mail). Competition promotes innovation and the ability to respond to and satisfy a wide range of user requirements.

Leased and switched services. ISDN should provide both leased and switched services. This will give the user the greatest range of options in configuring network services and will allow the user to optimize on the basis of cost and performance.

Cost-related tariffs. The price for ISDN services should be related to cost; it should be independent of the type of data being carried. Such a cost-related tariff will assure that one type of service is not in the position of subsidizing others. Price distinctions should be related to the cost of providing specific performance and to the functional characteristics of a service. In this way, distortions will be avoided and providers can be driven by customer need, rather than some artificial tariff structure.

Smooth migration. Because of the large installed base of telecommunications equipment in the networks, and because of customer equipment with interfaces designed for these networks, the conversion to ISDN will be gradual. Thus, for an extended period of time, the evolving ISDN must coexist with existing equipment and services. To provide for a smooth migration to ISDN, ISDN interfaces should evolve from existing interfaces, and interworking arrangements must be designed. Specific capabilities that will be needed include adapter equipment that allows pre-ISDN terminal equipment to interface to ISDN, internetwork protocols that allow data to be routed through a mixed ISDN/non-ISDN network complex, and protocol converters that allow interoperation of ISDN services and similar non-ISDN services.

Multiplexed support. To accommodate user-owned PBX and local area network (LAN) equipment, multiplexed support — in addition to low-capacity support — must be provided.

Benefits

The principal benefits of ISDN to the customer can be expressed in terms of cost savings, flexibility, and the advantages of competition among equipment vendors.

Cost savings. The integration of voice and a variety of data on a single transport system means that the user does not have to buy multiple services to meet multiple needs. The efficiencies and economies of scale of an integrated network allow these services to be offered at lower cost than if they were provided separately. Further, the user needs to bear the expense of just a single access line to these multiple services.

Flexibility. Requirements of various users can differ greatly in a number of ways: in information volume, traffic pattern, response time, and interface types. ISDN will allow the user to tailor the service purchased to actual needs to a degree not possible at present.

Competition. Advantages from competition among equipment vendors include product diversity, low price, and wide availability of services. Interface standards permit selection of terminal equipment and transport and other services from a range of competitors, without changes in equipment or use of special adapters.

Specific benefits. Specific benefits to network providers, manufacturers, and enhanced service providers are detailed below.

Network providers. Compared to customers, network providers will profit on a larger scale — but in a similar way — from the advantages of competition, including that in the areas of digital switches and digital-transmission equipment. Also, standards support universality and a larger potential market for services. Interface standards permit flexibility in selection of suppliers, consistent control-signaling procedures, and technical innovation and evolution within the network without customer involvement.

Manufacturers. Manufacturers can focus research and development on technical applications and be assured that a broad potential demand exists. In particular, the cost of developing chip implementations is justified by the size of the potential market. Specialized niches in the market create opportunities for competitive, smaller manufacturers. Significant economies of scale can be realized by manufacturers of all sizes. Interface standards assure that the manufacturer's equipment will be compatible with the equipment across the interface.

Enhanced service providers. Enhanced service providers, such as for information-retrieval or transaction-based services, will benefit from simplified user access. End users will not be required to buy special-access arrangements or terminal devices in order to gain access to particular services.

Disadvantages

Of course, any technical innovation comes with disadvantages as well as benefits. The main disadvantage in ISDN is the cost of migration. However, this cost must be seen in the context of evolving customer needs. With or without ISDN, the telecommunications offerings available to customers will change. It is hoped that the ISDN framework will at least control the cost and reduce the confusion of migration. Another potential disadvantage of ISDN is that it will retard technical innovation. The process of adopting standards is a long and complex one, with the result that by the time a standard is adopted and products are available, more advanced technical solutions have appeared. This time lag is always a problem with standards. By and large, the benefits of standards outweigh the fact that they are always at least a little way behind the state of the art.

The role of ISDN

The previous subsection presented the many potential benefits of ISDN. It is important to balance this presentation with the recognition that a number of alternatives to ISDN exist and that the reality may be that ISDN will play much less of a role than originally intended by its designers.

A paper by Carr, entitled "The Message-Makers," in the March 10, 1990, issue of *The Economist*, made a startling comparison between telex and ISDN. Ten years ago, telex dominated the text-transmission market; however, it was provided primarily as a monopoly service belonging to carriers. The telecommunications industry did little to respond to improvements in technology or to the growing sophistication of customer demands. As a result, telex failed and has been virtually replaced by the fax machine.

Similarly, ISDN was dreamed up when telephone companies still thought like utilities that provide a blanket public service. Market forces have driven telecommunications technology, products, and services beyond the slow pace of ISDN standardization, with the result that ISDN is fated to be a special service, one among a variety of alternatives for the business user. As *The Economist* put it: "ISDN is not a universal service, the next step to the future and all that jazz. If it is sold as such, it will be nothing but a disappointment to those that subscribe to it." This sober publication is not normally given to exaggeration. Indeed, it is not alone in rethinking the potential role of ISDN in the telecommunications market. ISDN was intended to be the master plan for an advanced, all-digital network and was to completely replace today's telecommunications networks. A much more modest role appears certain.

The following two key transmission characteristics of ISDN need to be kept in mind in assessing its potential role:

(1) The basic unit of switching is a 64-Kbps channel. Although it is possible to use a technique known as "subrate multiplexing" to carry multiple subchannels over a single 64-Kbps channel, all of the subchannels are carried on a single circuit between the same two endpoints. This capability has its uses, but the ability to set up circuits of less than 64 Kbps is a potentially cost-effective service not provided by ISDN. It is also possible to switch at higher data rates using a variety of higher speed channels on ISDN; however, as a practical matter, these are not being widely implemented in current ISDN offerings and in those in the pipeline. Again, the ability to set up circuits of greater than 64 Kbps is a potentially attractive service. The difficulty with the 64-Kbps channel is that its data rate is a poor compromise between the

needs of voice and data. For voice transmission, a capacity of 64 Kbps is now extravagant: High-quality voice transmission can be achieved at 32 Kbps, at 16 Kbps, and perhaps at lower values. For data transmission, 64 Kbps produces excellent response-time/throughput characteristics for many interactive applications. However, the increasing use of high-power workstations and graphics/image-processing applications makes 64 Kbps increasingly inadequate for many subscribers.

(2) The standardized primary service offered to customers operates at 1.544 megabits per second (Mbps) or 2.048 Mbps. Customers are expected to make do with these data rates until the leap — later this decade or early next century — into broadband ISDN, with data rates in the hundreds of Mbps. The ISDN data rates may be fine for public and private voice networks, but they are woefully inadequate for many users who are bringing on line high-demand image applications and ultra-high-speed LANs.

With the limitations imposed by the above transmission characteristics, ISDN must compete with a wide array of technical and packaged-network alternatives. Among the most important of these alternatives are

(1) Fractional T1. This facility is offered by carriers who provide the basic T1 (1.544-Mbps) service. Fractional T1 allows the customer to order capacity in increments of 64, 128, 256, 512, and 768 Kbps to meet the needs of specific applications.

(2) Frame-relaying bridges and routers. These products are bridges and routers that link LANs using frame relay technology. Frame relay was initially developed as an ISDN service (see Chapter 3), but many vendors are exploiting this technology independent of ISDN.

(3) Software-defined virtual networks. This facility is based on a public circuit-switched network that gives the user the appearance of a private network. The network is "software defined" in the sense that the user provides the service supplier with entries to a database used by the supplier to configure, manage, monitor, and report on the operation of the network.

(4) IEEE 802.6 metropolitan area networks (MANs). This standard uses a dual-bus architecture that appears similar to an open ring. It provides very high data rates and is intended for MAN applications.

(5) Switched Multimegabit Data Service (SMDS). This facility extends data transmission services for LANs and high-speed devices far beyond the customer's premises, but provides high-speed access without the costs associated with conventional private lines. SMDS makes use of the access protocols defined in IEEE 802.6.

Fundamentally, ISDN provides a circuit-switching service coupled with an anemic (64-Kbps access line) packet-switching service. On the one hand, this set of services must compete with the alternatives just listed to meet many customers needs. On the other hand, it is inadequate to meet a number of high-capacity requirements generated by the fast-moving pace of performance improvement in data-processing and telecommunications equipment. Put another way, ISDN is not essential, since many users are happy with existing non-ISDN solutions, and it is not responsive, given the absurdly slow pace that was evident in the development of its technical specifications. Ominously, the fate of broadband ISDN (B-ISDN) is at least partially tied to that of ISDN because of the commonality of interfaces, control-signaling schemes, and protocols.

What then is the role of ISDN? ISDN must be marketed in the context of a variety of packet-switched, circuit-switched, and dedicated services already in place. Because of the diversity of network services, ISDN cannot be imposed as was possible in the days of monopoly telecommunications. It must be marketed as a set of useful, standardized capabilities that has a — but not the — role to play in long-distance voice and data communications. ISDN can be many useful things to many people, but it won't be the universal service of which its creators dreamed. The window of opportunity was lost, if indeed it ever existed. Users listened for 10 years to the gospel of ISDN and concluded that it was oversold. Hopefully, a similar fate will not befall B-ISDN, given a once-bit, twice-shy attitude from potential customers.

Paper summary

The first paper included in this chapter, "ISDN: A Snapshot," by Wu and Livne, is a brief status report on ISDN. This paper discusses the various standards groups that are involved in the ISDN effort, looks at the current state of field trials, and summarizes existing network services and equipment offerings.

"ISDN Applications: Their Identification and Development," by Iffland, Norton, and Waxman, looks at two efforts under way to identify ISDN applications and demonstrate their benefits: the North American ISDN User's Forum and AT&T's TriVista project. This paper describes a number of specific ISDN applications.

"Southwestern Bell Telephone's ISDN Experience," by Stephenson and McGaw, describes 23 different applications that have been demonstrated over ISDN.

"Appraising PBXs with an Eye toward ISDN," by Mier, describes how major PBX vendors are supporting ISDN.

The final paper in this chapter, "ISDN: Some Current Standards Difficulties," by Thomas, uses several examples to illustrate the difficulty and complexity of the ISDN standardization process.

ISDN: A Snapshot

WILLIAM W. WU, FELLOW, IEEE, AND ADAM LIVNE, SENIOR MEMBER, IEEE

A snapshot of the present status of ISDN is presented in terms of standardization efforts, field trials and demonstrations, implementations and services, and equipment and devices. A bird's eye view of opinions and controversies as well as future trends is also given.

I. INTRODUCTION

Through the digitalization of existing telephone networks, the integration of existing and anticipated telecommunication services, the end-to-end signaling, the standardization of equipment and protocols, the integrated services digital network (ISDN) is expected to provide a single and efficient "bits' pipe", and a single standard "socket in the wall" for both voice and most non-voice communications needs, serving and connecting all the users over the globe. Also, due to this evolution, many of the existing services will be significantly enhanced and a plethora of new services, features, and applications are expected to emerge.

The participants in this gigantic task of converting the nearly 700 million lines of the existing global telephone network into the ISDN are the world's telecommunication administrations, telecommunications companies, regulatory and standardization organizations, telecommunications equipment manufacturers, research institutions and, of course, the users.

Up to now, huge investments in equipment and software developments and in other related activities have been made. It is estimated that the "hidden money" along, spent on the ISDN standardization process since its beginning in the mid-1970's, approaches the sum of 500 million dollars. In the period from 1987 until the present, over 5000 papers on ISDN related topics have been published in professional journals. Over 40 books on the subject of ISDN have been published since the late 1970's. Scores of special issues have appeared in professional society publications. People have the right to ask "what happened?"

ISDN, intended and planned to evolve gradually and in an orderly manner into a uniform and unified global telecommunication network, is not following exactly the course envisioned at its conception. All of the participants involved in ISDN evolution agree, at least in principle, on the absolute necessity of a unified approach leading to common standards, interfaces, and procedures. However, it is in putting the ISDN into practice that they differ.

In this paper we sort out some of the controversies, and we voice our own opinions in Section II. We emphasize the importance of the worldwide standardization effort and discuss the organizations that are responsible for establishing such standards in Section III.

In Section IV we sample limited recent field trials and demonstrations. We describe implementation and services in Section V. We identify available equipment and devices, including manufacturers, in Section VI. Section VII concludes with a discussion of broadband ISDN and future trends.

All discussions in this paper are intended to be indicative and not exhaustive. The purpose of such indications is to show the fact that ISDN is "for real" and is coming, even if it comes slowly. Regardless, electrical engineers as network providers, equipment manufacturers, or users need to be prepared for this eventuality.

II. OPINIONS AND CONTROVERSIES

Because of its expected global coverage, magnitude and diversification of services, and because of its potential impact on the economic and social developments, ISDN is a subject that has generated a large number of opinions, controversies, and misunderstandings. The key questions asked by those who have to make the decisions on the required investments are:

- What new services will be provided?
- What new applications will be available?
- When will a broad coverage and a "critical mass" of users be reached?
- Can the networks be maintained and operated reliably with multivendor equipment?
- To what extent will the regulators control the pricing?
- How can the potential investors assess the risk?
- When will the standardized network be realized?

Carriers, manufacturers, regulators, users, and investors address these questions in many forums and act according to their perceptions of the answers. It is our intention to focus in this section on some essentials, to argue with some published opinions, and to express concern with some of the suggestions.

It has been suggested that the scope as well as the development pace of ISDN should be user or market driven. We disagree.

First, we believe that more often than not, most of the users do not know exactly what they need or want, especially if the needs have to be estimated far into the future. Second, the exact knowledge of the new services to be available need not necessar-

Manuscript received November 29, 1990; revised January 15, 1991.

W. W. Wu is with the International Communication Systems, Stanford Telecom, Reston, VA 22090.

A. Livne is with Ministry of Communications, Tel Aviv, Israel.

IEEE Log Number 9042358.

0-8186-2797-2/92 $3.00 © 1991 IEEE

ily be the key factor driving the development of ISDN. As long as a network provides enough expandable capacity and flexible features, new and unpredicted services and applications will flourish, not only in terms of types and numbers, but also in terms of volume. Thus the ISDN market can be driven by clever and innovative technological advancements for reliable and low-cost implementations. Otherwise we would still be at the pre-telephone age. Low cost is the key driving factor for the wide acceptance of ISDN. The lower the cost, the more users. Therefore, ISDN architecture does not need to be user driven. A sensible network can create a market and increase the demand in terms of the number of its users.

The issues of network efficiency and network reliability are in the realm of network designers and implementors. Their judgments and decisions should be based on long term returns. ISDN is a network intended to integrate a very broad spectrum of services, and to provide a basis for many multimedia applications. With each service or application category, many variants should be expected. A sensible network provider or network operator should conceptually envision and realistically design and implement a universal network that is reliable, efficient, and accessible to all of the potential users. Some most recent opinions and suggestions with respect to ISDN can be found in [1]–[6].

At present, commercial ISDN services on a significant scale are provided in the U.S., Japan, France, Germany, and Singapore. On a smaller scale, ISDN are provided in Australia, U.K., Belgium, Norway, Italy, China, Spain, and Switzerland. Most of the other industrialized countries are conducting field trials, beginning initial installations, and are planning to start commercial ISDN no later than 1993.

For the less developed countries, the transition into ISDN is still a vague and remote subject and is postponed until more basic and urgent telecommunications needs are fulfilled. However, a message here for the developing countries is that during the process of providing basic communications needs, it is wise to design and implement with ISDN criteria. In the long run, telecommunication networks will not only be compatible with the outside world; they will also avoid the possibility of costly replacement equipment if and when ISDN standards are introduced.

In terms of timing when the standardized network will be realized, one outcome is certain: the sooner a half baked network is put in place, the less will it meet its orginal goal. If there must be a choice between time and completeness, we advocate completeness. Otherwise, ISDN becomes a continuous evolution process with incremental improvements at a time. The long term strategy does not necessarily agree with the general industrial economic philosophy in the U.S. Therefore, there is potential danger of an incomplete ISDN due to shortsighted commercial pressure.

Although all standardization efforts have been slow, they not only have shown a progress, but also are exerting an impact worldwide. Means to speed up the process are to show support through local, national, and international standards organizations. For the "experts" participating in these organizations, territorial interests and disputes should be minimized. They need to recognize the fact that their outputs will affect a vast industry for years to come.

III. STANDARDIZATION

Among all the controversies surrounding ISDN activities, perhaps the least controversial but significant issue is standardiza-

tion. Clear, nonambiguous, and unique standards are the key elements toward the realization of an universal network. From the network provider's viewpoint, standardization ensures users' accessibility and internetwork connectivity. From the equipment manufacturer's viewpoint, the set of standards provides equipment and software compatiblity, interchangeability, and portability. From the user's viewpoint, the standards provide a clear list of what is available and a basis for competitive and comparative shopping.

A. CCITT/ISO/IEC

To this date, there are a number of international, regional, as well as national organizations directly or indirectly responsible for ISDN standards. Among the many efforts put forward to define and to establish ISDN standards, the International Telegraph and Telephone Consultative Committee (CCITT) Study Group XVIII has been given the responsibility and has led the way in coordinating, reviewing, and adopting suggestions from other groups and organizations. Thus far SG XVIII has adopted the recommendations of the X-series from Study Group VII (data communication networks) for eventual standardization of interfaces for public data networks and protocols for packet switched networks. Other CCITT study groups such as SG I (definition and operational aspects of telegraph and user services for facsimile, teletex, videotex), SG II (telephone operation and operational services), SG XVII (digital communications over telephone networks) as well as a number of CCIR (International Radio Consultative Committee) study groups have contributed to the recommendation of ISDN standardization.

The International Organization for Standardization (ISO), representing more than 80 countries, independently exists and develops industrial standards to facilitate the international exchange of products, information systems, and services. The technical committees are concerned with computers and communications. With respect to ISDN, one of the standards developed by ISO is the reference model of Open System Interconnection (OSI), and provides the corner stone of the ISDN protocols.

Another international standardization body is the International Electrotechnical Commission (IEC) that, although a nongovernmental organization, is composed of representatives from 43 countries. The IEC has 77 Technical Committees, 128 Subcommittees, and over 650 Working Groups. Some of their activities are closely related to ISDN.

The standardization of ISDN by CCITT is based on the following three areas:

- the standardization of services offered to subscribers, so as to enable terminal equipment to be interchangeable;
- the standardization of user-network interfaces to ensure accessibility and equipment interchangeability;
- the standardization of network capabilities to the degree necessary to allow user-network and network-network interworking.

Through the Red Book published in 1984 and the Blue Book available in 1988, the I-series recommendations become the international guideline and information source with respect to ISDN [7], [8]. The I-series contains the general structure of ISDN, its definitions and terminologies, as well as general concepts, service and network capabilities, user-network and internetwork interfaces, and maintenance principles. In the I-Series, the most significant acheivement is the User/Network Interface Aspects (I.400

series) that provides clear reference configurations, simple notations, interface structures, and network access capabilities.

In addition to the I-Series, ISDN recommendations are supported by other series of CCITT's. These are the Q-Series, X-Series, V-Series, E-Series, and G-Series. The functions within each relevant series are described in Table 1 of the paper: "ISDN Standardization" by Kano *et al.* appearing in this issue.

A large amount of effort has been devoted by many experts from many countries toward the establishment of the standardization. Noticeably missing however, from either the Red or Blue books are: 1) performance criteria, 2) coding for errors, and 3) transmission media other than metallic cables and physically connected wires.

B. ANSI/ASAI/NIUF/GOSIP

The American National Standards Institute (ANSI) is the U.S. member of ISO and IEC. By consensus and judgement of the Standards Review Board, the ANSI approved over 8000 standards. A number of these standards are related to telecommunications; thus in turn, they are related to ISDN. Within ANSI, there exists the Exchange Carrier Standards Association (ECSA), known as Committee T1 that consists of six subcommittees. These subcommittees cover a large number of ISDN activities.

AT&T Adjunct/Switch Application Interface (ASAI) is a set of specifications created by AT&T for the 170 members of ISDN/Digital multiplexed Interface User's Group. This group is an association of users and equipment manufacturers formed to set common ground for ISDN products and services. ASAI incorporates CCITT recommended ISDN protocols and user/network interface standards. ASAI was designed for unix-based computers and AT&T Definity PBX's. A number of computer manufacturers in the U.S. have made their products to be compatible with ASAI.

The North American ISDN User's Forum (NIUF) was formed in 1988 by the U.S. National Institute of Standards and Technology (NIST, previously NBS). It brings together the ISDN users, operators, and implementors, providing an open forum where they speak, listen, and cooperate with each other.

The main mission of the NIUF is to provide the symbiosis between the users and implementors of ISDN, while guiding and promoting ISDN development. The Forum consists of two formal workshops: the ISDN user's workshop and the ISDN implementors workshop.

The user's workshop develops requirements for specific applications and the implementors workshop prepares application profiles, that specify the details required for the implementations and implementations agreement. The workshops are scheduled regularly and produce documents that include application requirements, implementation agreements, and conformance criteria. Although at present it is a North American forum, plans call for an international cooperation that includes other countries and international organizations in the forum.

In August 1988, the NIST in the U.S. published a standard called Government Open Systems Interconnection Profile (GOSIP) that defines a common set of data communications protocols for the acquisition of networks and services to be used by all U.S. Government agencies [9]. GOSIP is based on the international recommendations of Open System Interconnections (OSI) [10]. The GOSIP standard became effective after January 1989. It is compulsory and binding for all procurement of network products and services by the U.S. Government agencies after August 1990. Although the GOSIP standard was originally intended for

U.S. government agencies, there are indications that governments in Europe (particularly the U.K.) are attempting to adopt it for their agencies. In countries where leadership comes from the government, this standard makes a great deal of sense to promote industry.

C. CEPT/ETSI

As Europe strives for a common industry by 1993, the telecommunication entities are directly affected. ISDN was meant to be an international standard to help establish a common goal. Since the early 1980's, Europe, in general, has been very active in ISDN activities. Now, as one of the steps toward integrating Europe's disparate public networks, 24 carriers are working to support common ISDN services, standards, and applications by the end of 1993. European Commission officials portray the effort, negotiated under the auspices of a Conference European des Posted et Telecommunications (CEPT) authorities agreement in 1989, as one of the first milestones on the road to harmonizing Europe's disparate public networks.

In the CEPT memorandum of understanding, carriers from 18 countries agreed to support both Basic Rate Interface (BRI) and Primary Rate Interface (PRI) services using common European standards by 1993. The carriers also pledged to interconnect their national ISDN services via CCITT Signaling System 7 (SS7) and to support several domestic and international ISDN applications. The carriers are also later planning to supplement their ISDN BRI and PRI services with broadband ISDN services [11].

Recently, the responsibility for the regulation of standards and implementation has been transferred from CEPT to the European Telecommunications Standards Institute (ETSI), which complies closely with the CCITT ISDN standards.

IV. FIELD TRIALS AND DEMONSTRATIONS

Service, as well as economic feasiblity, of ISDN can be brought closer to reality through a series of field trials. A variety of experiments or field trials has taken place both nationally and internationally. Sample activities of ISDN field trials and demonstrations are highlighted in this section. Among all the references, the ISDN Newsletter [11] is a good source in updating the ever increasing activities, including field trials. ISDN field trials have been reported since the early 1980's [12]. Two ISDN demonstrations were performed via satellites in 1987 [13]. At present, there exist over 60 trials in the U.S. that are carried out by local exchange telephone companies, corporate network operators, as well as ISDN equipment manufacturers. For field trials beyond the boundaries of nationalities, a few ISDN items have been recently tested. The goal for telecommunications services and equipment to exist in a unified Europe beginning in 1992, in which ISDN plays a crucial role, is also discussed.

The goals of ISDN trials are stated as follows:

- define and test service architectures;
- study service capabilities;
- stimulate technology development;
- verify and extend standards;
- verify internetworking of services;
- resolve operations issues;
- stimulate network evolution planning.

The following section includes a list of field trial and demonstration highlights with detailed technical discussions omitted.

A. U.S. Activities

In the U.S., the Bell operating companies began their respective ISDN field trials early. From Bell Atlantic to Wisconsin Bell, specific tests were performed even before 1985 [12]. The following is a list of sample trials active or planned during 1989–1991.

• *The NY Six.* In New York State, through its Public Service Commission, six major users have joined the effort to support a planned ISDN trial. These six business users are: Eastman Kodak, Manufacturers Hanover, Merrill Lynch, Paine Webber, Shearson Lehman, Hutton, and Young & Rubicam. The purpose of the trial is to check how business communications may be improved by integrating voice, data, and video transmission over existing telephone lines. Specific test items include automatic retrieval of customer records, color image transmission, simultaneous computer/telephone conferencing, and data interchange.

• *The Boston Trial.* New England Telephone, NYNEX, and a number of users in the Boston area including New England Medical Center, Children's Hospital, Massachusetts General, are planning for a multimedia test of B-ISDN, starting in the spring of 1991. The test involves transmission and storage of medical information through multimedia packets such as three-dimensional imaging, voice recognition, and full-motion digitized video. The initial trial uses a small and slower switch of 1 Gb/s from Ultra Network Technologies. The test will be switched to a 80 Gb/s Fujitsu Fetex 150 in 1992. NYNEX Corporation also in cooperation with New England Telephone Company, U.S., is using a Fetex-150 SONET switch to test simultaneous transmission of voice, data, and images. The Fetex-150 can operate at up to 2.4 Gb/s with asynchronous transfer mode (ATM) switching.

• *A Saturn Test.* Siemens Information Systems, Inc. announced that the Saturn PBX has met compatibility standards for use with AT&T's ISDN PRI. The testing for Primary Rate compatibility was conducted at the AT&T test facility in Washington, DC. The AT&T PRI certification is an element of Siemens ISDN network package for Saturn systems, which also includes the Siemens CorNet networking protocol. CorNet is the Siemens Primary Rate D channel Layer 3 protocol for PBX's and provides interconnection with other ISDN PBX's and the public ISDN network.

• *An IBX Test.* InteCom, Inc., a subsidiary of Wang Laboratories, continues ISDN field trials utilizing its Integrated Business Exchange (IBX), a nonblocking digital PBX that supports simultaneous voice and data communications. This trial featured a PRI on the IBX connected to a U.S. WEST Communications and ISDN central office with an AT&T #5ESS [11].

• *The Advanced Technology Laboratories* (ATL) of Southwestern Bell provides facilities that are designed to evaluate the performance of ISDN equipment, to assist in finding solutions or specific needs and applications of the customers, and also for enabling the equipment vendors to evaluate their equipment. ATL provides the laboratory and simulated network environment to test both the proprietary features and multivendor compatibility. The equipments installed and evaluated include: AT&T, NTI, Siemens and Ericsons switches, and Telradi ISDN workstations.

• The Bell Operating Company in New England and GTE Corporation are testing and deploying high speed imaging services, such as X-rays and CAT scans, for the medical profession.

• Southwestern Bell Telephone Company and US Sprint Communications Company, both of Missouri, U.S., recently completed the successful interface between switched 56 kb/s circuits and ISDN traffic in multiples of 64 kb/s. Prior to this, with 18 000 ISDN lines, Southwestern Bell conducted tests in partic-

ipation with McDonald, Chevron, Lockheed, 3M Company, Teneco, Shell, S. Methodist University, Hayes Company, INTEL Company, DEC, CDC, Harris Company, Bellcore, and AT&T.

• In early February 1990, U.S. West Communications and IBM announced a pilot test program for the feasibility of transmitting documents from home at 19.2 kb/s and 64 kb/s with IBM's 7820 ISDN terminal adapter, which provided a BRI.

• Pacific Telesis Group of San Francisco is conducting switched multimegabit data service at Stanford University in California for medical image transmission.

• GTE is testing a satellite based image service for document retrieval while Bell Atlantic has joined with American Management Systems for the test of the terrestrial segment.

B. International Demonstrations

The international demonstrations are listed as follows.

• With compressed video at 112 kb/s by two combined B channels and a pair of 56 kb/s Switched Digital International Service (SDIS), a demonstration was conducted last year for ISDN international videoconferencing and Group IV facsimile transmission between Los Angeles and Tokyo. The participants were AT&T, Pacific Bell, KDD, and NTT. The equipments used were AT&T's SDIS and 5ESS switch, Pacific Bell's Centrex Integrated Systems, a facsimile machine by Canon, ISDN terminal adapters by Fujitsu and Hitachi, and video conferencing units by PictureTel and Kyocera. A demonstration of integrated voice, data, facsimile, and video applications with B-channel ISDN standard interfaces was conducted in early 1990 between New York, Osaka, and Tokyo by AT&T, KDD, and NTT.

• In the United Kingdom, British Telecom has conducted ISDN field trials with a Pilot System X since 1985 and with 2000 users. The trials were performed on DASS 1 and 2 protocol LAPD, on CCITT No. 7 signaling scheme, as well as on VLSI technologies. The trails took place in London, Birmingham, and Manchester. At present, BT is introducing commercial basic rate ISDN with a potential of 90 000 users over the United Kingdom by June 1991.

• Before 1986, Canada had field trials through Bell Canada such as Datapac, Datalink, Dataroute, and Envoy 100. Most recently, British Columbia (BC) Telephone, Manitoba Telephone, Alberta Government Telephones, and Edmonton Telephone have all become active in ISDN field trials. Other earlier international ISDN field trials can be found in [12], [13].

V. Implementation and Services

As will be highlighted in this section, a number of ISDN activities have progressed from field trials and demonstrations to active services. These include voice, data, and video available initially to specific countries as well as internationally. In the U.S., over 150 organizations, towns, cities, and universities had implemented ISDN services by the end of 1990. Singapore completed the ISDN basic rate telephone facilities for the whole country before 1989.

A. Accunet

Before the availability of SS Number 7, AT&T announced the Accunet switched Digital service with the collaboration of NTT, KDD, Pacific Bell, and Illinois Bell in the fall of 1990. With 90%

of all ISDN applications, including videoconference and fax, six countries can be reached through Accunet international services. These are Australia, U.K., France, Jamaica, Japan, Singapore, and U.S. By the end of 1990, 12 more countries are expected to participate in the service.

B. MICROLINK/MARCROLINK

One of the most recent strong advocates of ISDN is Australia, who not only performs ISDN trial service, but also provides ISDN equipment. Australian companies and organizations from the airline industry and banks to the Departments of Corrections and Victorian Roads have rallied behind Telecom Australia to implement MARCROLINK for primary rate and MICROLINK for basic rate trial services. The TELECOM ISDN MARCROLINK service has been available since July 1989 with 150 users in Australia. Expecting 550 users, the MICROLINK services will be available at the end of 1990.

In general, users will mainly utlized MICROLINK for integrated access to a variety of applications such as data file transfer, imaging, video, and voice applications. For example, the airline industry will trial MICROLINK for a reservation service. One MICROLINK B channel can be used to support outposted staff to a reservation database while customer calls extended from the airline system are handled on the other B channel. The D channel could be used to enhance such services as confirmation. The Victorian Roads Department will trial MICROLINK for speed detection. Speed cameras placed at strategic locations can be used to photograph data and store it on a local PC. ISDN MICROLINK will allow the transfer of this imaging information on a dial-up basis to a control location at both a 64 and a 128-kb/s transmission rate [11].

C. INS-Net

In Japan, NTT started basic rate commercial ISDN service in April 1988 with CCITT I-Series preliminary user/network interface recommendations. Since June 1989, the PRI was added to nearly 60 cities and towns and nearly 2000 subscriber lines. The service started with 3.1 kHz of speech and 65 kb/s of unrestricted circuit mode bearer service. Since then, packet mode services for both the B and D channel have been added to both BRI's and PRI's. By utilizing the D channel, supplementary services such as calling line identification, billing, and direct dialing are provided. Other planned ISDN services are discussed in [14].

Japan's domestic ISDN service, NTT's INS-Net, was launched in April 1988. At the end of April 1990, the number of subscriber lines for INS-Net 64 service was about 7500 and for INS-Net 1500 service was about 140. NTT plans to make INS-Net services available in about 1000 locations in Japan by the end of March 1991.

KDD began an International ISDN service in June of 1989, linking with AT&T of the U.S. and British Telecom of the U.K. The service has about 120 subscriber lines. Since October 1, 1989, INS-Net subscribers have also had access to the service. A link was also established with Illinois Bell. With Singapore added in 1989 and Australia in 1990, International ISDN services are now available between Japan and five other countries.

D. Numeris and Transpac

The 64-kb/s services that have been switched to the French National Packet Switching Public Data Network have been available since the fall of 1988. It was called TRANSPAC. Telecom France has had commercial ISDN services in Brittany since late 1987; the entire country will be completed to ISDN services by early 1991. As an encouragement, Telecom France has offered to pay 50% of the development costs toward new applications within the user's equipment. Such encouragement has enabled Telecom France to command an 80% premium for data service over normal voice charges. Before providing such service, France conducted field trials under the project name RENAN between Cotes du Nord and Paris. The trial consisted of file transfer, picture transmission, telecopy, and audio/videotex. Telecom France has developed ISDN, launching a service called NUMERIS in December 1987. Nationwide coverage will be completed by 1991. Telecom France has also developed ISDN applications combining text, sound, data, and image [11]. Using ALCATEL E10 switching systems, NUMERIS provides packet mode data communications on the D channel of a user access to the switching facilities. The main feature of the system is the frame-handling functions for efficient data transfer [15].

International ISDN was launched between KDD of Japan and France Telecom's NUMERIS network on April 26, 1990. The new link provides a 64-kb/s switched access for KDD's direct subscribers, or for NTT's INS-Net subscribers with international-services.

E. DBP Telekom/Telenorma

After the initiation of its ISDN pilot project in Monheim and Stuttgart sponsored by the Deutsch Bundespost, West Germany's DBP Telekom started commercial ISDN services in 40 cities in 1989, expanding to 135 cities at the end of 1990. Full coverage of ISDN service nationwide is expected by 1993. West Germany's ISDN, through DBP Telekom, also plans connections with other European PTT's. Since 1989, the pilot project involving 500 ISDN connections has been working with The Netherlands in Rotterdam. In 1990, DBP Telekom started working with British Telecom International and France Telecom for the ISDN connections. By the time this special issue appears, ISDN connections between Italy and Germany are expected to be completed [16].

After successful installation and operation for the City of Frankfurt am Main in 1989, Telenorma GmbH is under contract from Bancomer S.N.C. of Mexico City for implementing a network compound of ISDN telecommunication systems of 3500 exchanges and 8000 extensions with an expected 26 000 connecting units. The network will offer voice, PC to PC text, and video communications capabilities.

F. Singapore

The island republic of Singapore made available, in December 1989, the complete basic ISDN telephone facilities. By the end of 1990, such facilities will be connected to Australia and the U.K., in addition to Japan and the U.S.. Singapore Telecom perfomed two year field trials before establishing such operational facilities which provide not only voice, but videophone and high resolution graphics [17].

G. ISDN-2

British Telecom (BT) has set tariffs and availability for a BRI services digital network to be phased in before the end of 1993. BT offers international services to several countires. The ISDN-2 service offers 64 kb/s lines and is based on European standards. BT already has a primary rate service, ISDN30, which provides thirty 64 kb/s channels for PBX access, but is based on a proprietary signaling scheme, Digital Access Signaling System 2. ISDN-2 is the only European basic rate ISDN offering based on the International Telegraph and Telephone Consultative Committee's I.420 standard. Other European network operators, such as France Telecom and Deutsche Budespost Telekom, use national specifications. During the second half, international lines will be available to the U.S., Japan, and France. In the last phase, from January to December 1991, ISDN-2 will be available to business centers through out the U.K. In 1991, additional supplementary services will be provided and service guarantees will be introduced [11].

H. U.S. Serivces

Most ISDN services in the U.S. are provided by the Regional Bell Operating Companies (RBOC) and other private corporations.

At the end of September 1990, more than 136 major ISDN users in the U.S. were using either basic or primary rate for access [6]. Most of the switching equipments used are AT&T's 5ESS. However, Northern Telecom's DMS-100, SL-1 PBX, Siemen's Saturn III as well as AT&T's Definity have also been implemented. Northern Telecom's worldwide corporate ISDN implementation experience is described in [18].

In the U.S., Bellcore has set the goal of the "1990 Compatible ISDN." At present, the ISDN is not compatible. The equipment, protocols, and interfaces used in the trials and in the initial installations are, in many cases, nonstandard and proprietary. Bellcore's efforts and reponsibilities go beyond the RBOC's. Being assigned the mission "to see that the network is operating as one high quality network" (Judge M. Green) and being the coordinator for the communications among the participants, Bellcore appears to be in the unique position to provide specifications and recommendations that affect all the participants in the ISDN implementations.

A source of reference on user implementation strategies for ISDN is available from Frost and Sullivan Publications [19]. Papers on pre-1986 ISDN activities of technologies and implementations can be found in [20].

VI. Equipment And Devices

Aside from network strategy, standardization, and signaling schemes, digital equipment is the corner stone of ISDN implementation. As previously expressed in Section II, the timing and degree of ISDN realization mostly depend on its cost, which is contributed by the cost of network provider's equipment, test equipment, as well as the cost of user's equipments. Since devices are common components to some of the unique ISDN equipments, some new chip devices are also discussed in this section. The first ISDN interface chip was produced at AT&T in 1985 [21]. The following is a sample of recent development.

A. ISDN Switches

Digital switching architectures have evolved from mechanical and electronic, to software controlled with modular designs and high speed operations. The factors which affect switch design are network efficiency, network reliability, maintenance, and cost.

Examples of international digital switches that support SS Number 7 are: ATT's 5ESS, Northern Telecom's DMS, Siemen's EWSD, Ericson's AXE, Stromberg-Carson's DCO, U.K. GPT's System X, Alcatel's E10, Nokia's DX200, SEL's System 12, and Fujitsu's Fetex-150.

B. ISDN-CPE

The end user is an important part of ISDN development, as it was recognized early by the organizers of the North American ISDN User's Forum. The latter includes the manufacturers as well as the users. The term customer premises equipment (CPE) includes telephones, terminal adapters, ISDN PBX's, ISDN multiplexers, packet assemblers/disassemblers, controllers, and integrated voice–data workstations. From 1987 to 1990 the number of companies offering ISDN CPE has increased from 15 to over 100 [22]. Terminal adapters are used to connect a wide range of non-ISDN equipment to ISDN. At present, manufacturers who provide such equipments include AT&T, Harris, Fujitsu, NCR, NEC, IBM, Northern Telecom, Racal, Siemens, Infotron, and Universal Data Systems [23].

C. ISDN-PBX

The Private Branch Exchange (PBX) consists switching equipment used by a company or organization to provide in-house switching and access to the public network. PBX's have been daily functional work horses. ISDN-equipped PBX's are available in support of ISDN PC. In early 1989, AT&T announced the Definity PBX which included ISDN primary rate physical interfaces for connections to ISDN networks. Alcatel, Hitachi, NEC, Northern Telecom, and Siemens all plan to offer such ISDN compatible interface equipment. The reason for such offering is the potential of the PRI's which enable the PBX to access a wide variety of public and private network services and networks, such as call selection, automatic number indentification, multiservice, as well as international ISDN primary rate services. A discussion on ISDN PBX, Centrex alternatives as well as T1 networking comparison can be found in [24].

D. ISDN-PC

With respect to ISDN users of personal computers (PC), there are two choices: connecting a PC to a terminal adapter which converts non-ISDN to ISDN standards, or adding hardware and software to a PC in order to convert it to an ISDN workstation which has the capability to perform integrated voice and data applications. Although some overlapping functions exist between a terminal adapter and a PC-based workstation, the workstation is more powerful and offer features such as file transfer, data on both B channels, multitasking, and access to large storage [25].

PC terminal adapters are used to connect non-ISDN PC terminals to ISDN transports. 2B + D basic rate PC terminal adapters have provided voice capabilities. PC terminal adapters exist with IBM PC's, IBM compatibles, and Apple Macintosh. A PC terminal adapter can be purchased for less than $500, in the U.S. in 1990. For primary rate, AT&T and Rockwell/CMC have recently announced compatible equipments for Unix computers and workstations.

Natural MicroSystems Corporation announced that it has jointly developed, with NCR Corporation, an ISDN terminal adapter that allows personal computers to simultaneously handle voice and data. According to ISDN Newsletters, the product consists of a PC AT-compatible terminal adapter card that links a standard telephone and personal computer to ISDN and advanced telecommunications software. The package permits personal computer users with access to an ISDN line and an OS/2 multi-tasking environment to manage different aspects of voice and data. The adapter allows simultaneous transmission of screen images during a telephone conversion, call merging, incoming call identification, voicemail functions, prerecorded message delivery to telephone numbers contained in the computer database, and the recording of special messages for selected callers.

AT&T and MICOM Communications Corp. of Simi Valley, CA have jointly announced a new personal computer card which will make ISDN communications affordable for small and medium sized businesses and home office users. With the AT&T Personal Computer Terminal Adapter (PCTA) Model 1000, manufactured by MICOM and sold by AT&T, standard personal computers become ISDN terminals that handle both voice and data transmissions from a standard computer keyboard, according to the June 1990 issue of the ISDN Newsletter. With the PCTA card, users can originate or terminate calls on an analog touch-tone phone while simultaneously executing Prodigy or related services over the data channel. The associated software allows incoming call numbers to be displayed on the PC screen. An external power supply for the card allows calls to be received even when the PC is turned off.

Technical features of the card include an S/T (see Section VI-F) interface supporting point-to-point and passive bus configurations on AT&T's 5ESS switch. The card supports data calls over the D channel at synchronous baud rates up to 19.2 kb, while simultaneously supporting voice calls over either of the 64 kb/s B channels.

Up to three PCTA cards may be placed in a single PC with each being defined as a COM 1-4 interface, thus supporting standard COM PORT applications. The PCTA card has been designed for easy installation into PC, XT, and AT type personal computers.

NCR Corporation provides the equipment of a workstation, ISDN personal computer interface, and ISDN application software, all of which support the BRI. The NCR ISDN Workstation is an IBM Personal Computer AT-class microcomputer that runs OS/2-based software and includes NCR's new Personal Computer Terminal Adapter (PCTA) Card and OS/2-based ISDN Voice Data Manager (VDM) software. NCR's ISDN Workstation is based on the Intel Corporation 803386SX microprocessor. It runs Microsoft Corporation's OS/2 1.1 operating system and supports the Presentation Manager graphical user interface. It also has one expansion slot so it can function as a general-purpose PC or can reside on a local-area network.

An ISDN Workstation is also produced by International Computers, Ltd.'s (ICL) North American Networks Industry Division, which has been offering OS/2-based ISDN workstations since April 1988. ICL offers models with three and seven expansion slots. A new ISDN PRI board for use with IBM AT bus computers was announced by the NTI Group. This new product, the NTI 2001/PRI, is designed for ISDN Primary rate applications where maximum data throughput is critical. According to ISDN Newsletters, NTI's ISDN product is available in U.S. (AT&T publication 41449) or European (CCITT I.412) formats. The U.S. version provides maximum bandwidth utilization with either H11 bearer channel for AT&T compatibility or H12 bearer channel for European compatibility.

E. ISDN-Multiplexer

Telecom Australia and a local manufacture, Summit Communications, announced a new ISDN product called Summit System 2000 which is basically an ISDN multiplexer capable of aggregating individual 64-kb/s B channels for communication at higher bit rates. The maximum capacity of this unit is 1.856 Mb/s (29×64 kb/s). Dial-up video conferencing can be provided at 348 kb/s. A high definition image, such as X-ray picture with 10^6 bytes, can be transmitted in less than four minutes for $30. The unit supports interfaces to IEEE 802.5 (token ring) and IEEE 802.3 (ethernet) LAN with layer 3 protocols [11].

F. ISDN-Interfaces

With an ISDN terminal (TE1), there are three interface points between a user and the transmission media. The interfaces are designated as S (between a user terminal and NT2, a network termination with higher layers), T (between NT2 and NT1, a network termination with only layer 1), and U (between NT 1 and the transmission media). NT2 and NT1 may be merged as S/T. With a non-ISDN compatible terminal equipment (TE2), the interface between the equipment and a terminal adapter, in order to convert to an ISDN compatible, is denoted as R.

• Motorola produced both the S/T interface chip (MC145474) and the U interface chip (MC145472) which is a 1.2-μm technology CMOS operated at 160 kb/s. The chips conform with the ANSI T1.601 U.S. standard as well as with the international recommendation for basic rate access. The interface transceivers have an error rate of 10^{-7}.

• With hardware and software combined into a single unit, Teleos Communications Inc. and IBM jointly developed an ISDN interface called the IRX9000 ISDN Resource Exchange, which connects IBM Application System 1400 token ring local area network to CallPath 1400. Because the token ring is a 4-Mb/s interface, it is used for data communications [26].

• ISDN Technologies Corporation announced that its PRImate-PC ISDN Primary Rate Controller has met compatibility standards for use with AT&T's ISDN PRI. Compatibility testing was conducted in January 1990 at an AT&T test facility located in Englewood, CO. The PRImate-PC enables users to make and receive HO channel data calls and B-channel voice and data calls through an ISDN network using the PRI. A future version will support H11 channel data calls. The first user of the PRImate-PC is to support videoconferencing over dial-up PRI networks such as AT&T's Software Defined Data Network [11].

• British Telecom has teamed up with Mitel Semiconductor to develop a single chip ISDN U interface. The interface chip is about the same complexity as a standard 16-bit microprocessor.

G. Test Equipment

From chip sets to the complete network, preoperational systems need to be tested. In addition to the test equipment manufacturers discussed, Navtel, Hewlett Packard, Hard Engineering Atlantic Research, Digilog, Telecommunication Techniques Corporation, Federick Engineering, and Network General also produce ISDN equipment for testing.

VII. CONCLUDING REMARKS

With the limitation and inflexibility of the narrowband ISDN (N-ISDN), broadband ISDN (B-ISDN) issues for higher rate services have become prominent. For broadband services, the problem is not merely increasing the speed of the operation, it affects the compatibility of switching technology, the workability of the local loop arrangement, the availability of rate adaption, and the efficiency of bandwidth utilization. Although some basic principles of narrowband ISDN can be carried to broadband ISDN, but the technology is quite different. For example, the interconnection and transmission problems of video, HDTV, and high speed data are different from those of voice. Thus the standard 64-kb/s B channel itself, the fundamental rate of ISDN transmission, appears inadequate for wide-band services. At present, the solution is to establish the multiples of 64 kb/s for accommodation of broadband or higher rates.

With respect to B-ISDN, one of the most recent achievements in international standardization is the asynchronous transfer mode (ATM). The ATM is one of the switching and multiplexing techniques for free interconnections of packet-like transmission in high-speed networks. ATM consists of a 40-bit cell header and a 384-bit information field. The cell header, in turn, consists of the following functions: flow control, virtual path identifier, channel identifier, cell loss detection, and error control. Two interface bit rates are established for ATM: 155.520 Mb/s and 622.20 Mb/s. With simplified protocols, lower OSI layer implementation, and transmission medium independence, ATM appears most attractive. However, because of propagation delay due to higher speed, existing algorithms of flow control, methods of path and channel identifications, and schemes of error control are not necessarily directly applicable. Because of its block structure, the effectiveness or service independence of the ATM needs also to be seen.

New technological requirements are imposed upon the switch core of a local exchange for switching and transmission in B-ISDN. In terms of VLSI technology, the difference is substantial. For N-ISDN 4.0–3.0 μm technology is sufficient, however for B-ISDN 1.2–0.5 μm technology is required. It has recently been reported that the number of transistor functions for N-ISDN on the average is about 20 000 for local exchange, while 250–500 K are needed for B-ISDN [23]. Siemen's ATM experimental exchange in the BERKOM project is using switching element chip with 16 inputs and 8 outputs. Each of the 150 Mb/s switching signals has 700 000 transistor functions.

Due to a significant difference in speed between N-ISDN and B-ISDN, the switching processor capacity requirement is also different for B-ISDN. A switching matrix processor capacity with a speed of 2–4 Mb/s is sufficient for N-ISDN; but, 150–600 Mb/s are required for B-ISDN. The switch processor capacity is increased from 0.5 million instructions per second to 5.0. The memory per processor is increased from 256 kbytes for N-ISDN to 2 Mbytes for B-ISDN. In addiiton to [29], [30], some recent books [31]–[37] discuss fundamentals as well as B-ISDN.

B-ISDN has and will flourish in all related aspects from standardization to trials to equipment production. This is confirmed by recent observations at ITU meetings and carrier activities on B-ISDN [27]. As described in Section VI-D, ISDN-PC will continue to advance toward a powerful combined multiple function office facility. The deployment of personal communication with respect to ISDN will also become a reality [28].

From the present achievements for all ISDN related activities, a number of areas may be pursued in the future. In the areas of network and operation, intelligent network principles and dynamic programming approaches may be applied for more efficient and optimal solutions. In the areas of equipment and devices, mass production of reliable and low cost compatible components are the keys to the success of ISDN. In the area of standardization, speed, harmony, and sound decisions are expected.

The views and judgements expressed in this paper are solely those of the authors. They do not necessarily reflect the organizational policies.

REFERENCES

[1] P. Lewis, "Whatever Happened to ISDN?" *IEE Rev.*, Oct. 1990.
[2] H. Myerston, "ISDN—Reality falls far short of the promise," *Network World*, Nov. 5, 1990.
[3] D. Briere, "ISDN rolls out, but users are still over a barrel," *Network World*, Nov. 5, 1990.
[4] "Users and carriers differ on ISDN in Europe," Global News, *Telecommunications*, Sept. 1990.
[5] D. Gihooly, "ISDN incompatible with satellites?" *Communications Week*, Sept. 1990.
[6] T. Sweeney, "ISDN's triangle," *Communications Week*, Oct. 1990.
[7] *Integrated Services Digital Networks (ISDN)*, CCITT Recommendations of the Series I, vol. III, Fascicle III.5, 1984.
[8] *Integrated Services Digital Networks (ISDN)*, CCITT Recommendations, vol. III, Fascicle 7–9, Nov. 1988.
[9] *Government Open Systems Interconnection Profile (GOSIP)*, U.S. Federal Information Processing Standards Publ. 146, Aug. 1988.
[10] W. W. Wu, "Integrated services digital satellite networks and protocols," in *Elements of Digital Satellite Communication*. Computer Science Press, 1985, ch. 7, vol. II.
[11] P. Polishuk, *ISDN Newsletters*. Information Gatekeepers, Inc., Boston, MA, Feb.–Aug. 1990.
[12] "Special Issue on Integrated Services Digital Networks: Recommendations and Field Trials," pt. I, *IEEE J. Select. Areas Commun.*, vol. SAC-4, Nov. 1986.
[13] W. W. Wu and D. T. Tudge, "Values of ISDN attributes," in *Proc. GLOBECOM*, vol. 3, 1987.
[14] Y. Kume, "Expansion of ISDN and the impact to new media services," *ITU Telecommun. J.*, vol. 57-VI, 1990.
[15] A. Roux and F. Leclerc "Packet mode data communications in NUMERIS, the french ISDN," *IEEE Commun. Mag.*, Nov. 1990.
[16] G. Miller and J. Chalmers, "Living with chance in West Germany," *CEI*, June 1990.
[17] G. Pereira, "Singapore pushes ISDN," *The Institute*, IEEE, Dec. 1990.
[18] C. Chan and J. Eng, "Global corporate communications with integrated service digital networks," to be published.
[19] "User ISDN implementation strategies (UOO9)," Frost and Sullivan Publications, 1990.
[20] "Special Issue on Integrated Services Digital Networks: Technology and Implementation," pt. II, *IEEE J. Select. Areas Commun.*, vol. SAC-4, Nov. 1986.
[21] AT&T T7250 Units Chip, 1986 and T7112 Asynchronous Receiver/Transmitter Interface (ART1), LC1046 PCM Transceiver, 1987.
[22] W. Kanupke, "ISDN CPE—Burst on the scene," *Telephony*, July 16, 1990.
[23] J. Lilley, "ISDN switching markets," *CEI*, May 1990.
[24] R. Koenig, "How to make the PBX-to-ISDN connection," *Data Commun.*, May 1989.
[25] R. Lefkowits, "ISDN's data options," *Commun. Week* (Special Report: An Evaluation of ISDN Workstations), Sept. 17, 1990.
[26] S. Titch, "TELEOS/IBM ISDN interface," *Telephony*, Aug. 27, 1990.
[27] T. Mulqueen, "Carriers test the broadband waters," *Data Commun.*, pp. 49–64, Sept. 1990.
[28] Steele, "Deploying personal communication networks," *IEEE Commun. Mag.*, pp. 12–15, Sept. 1990.
[29] S. Minzer, "Broadband ISDN and asynchronous transfer mode (ATM)," *IEEE Commun. Mag.*, Sept. 1989.
[30] S. Minzer and D. Spears, "New directions in signaling for broadband ISDN," *IEEE Commun. Mag.*, Feb. 1989.
[31] P. Bocker, in collaboration with G. Arndt, V. Frantzen, O. Fundneider, L. Hagenhaus, H. J. Rothemel, and L. Schweizer, *ISDN*

The Integrated Services Digital Network: Concepts, Methods, System. NY: Springer-Verlag, 1988.

[32] J. Y. Hui, *Switching and Traffic Theory for Integrated Broadband Networks.* Boston, MA: Kluwer Academic, 1989.

[33] G. C. Kessler, *ISDN: Concepts, Facilities, and Services.* NY: McGraw-Hill, 1990.

[34] W. Stallings, *ISDN An Introduction.* New York, NY: St. Martins, 1989.

[35] J. M. Griffiths, Ed., *ISDN Explained: Worldwide Network and Applications Technology.* New York, NY: Wiley, 1990.

[36] K. Verma, Ed., *ISDN Systems Architecture, Technology and Applications.* Englewood Cliffs, NJ: Prentice-Hall, 1990.

[37] H. J. Heigert, *Integrated Services Digital Network-Architectures, Protocols and Services.* Reading, MA: Addison-Wesley, 1991.

William W. Wu (Fellow, IEEE), for a photograph and biography please see page 101 of this issue.

Adam Livne (Senior Member, IEEE), for a photograph and biography please see page 101 of this issue.

ISDN Applications: Their Identification and Development

Frederick C. Iffland
Glenda D. Norton
Judy M. Waxman

Reprinted from *IEEE Network Magazine*, September 1989, pages 6-11. Copyright © 1989 by The Institute of Electrical and Electronics Engineers, Inc. All rights reserved.

I n 1986, the first ISDN features were introduced in the United States. Since then, significant progress has been made in the growth of the number of customers actively using ISDN basic and primary rate interface lines. Continued successful deployment of ISDN, however, is heavily dependent on the identification and development of applications that directly relate to end-customer needs. Several efforts are underway in the telecommunications industry to identify these applications and demonstrate their benefits. Two of these are the TriVista studies sponsored by AT&T and the North American ISDN Users' Forum sponsored by the National Institute of Standards and Technology.

Almost three years ago, the deployment of Integrated Services Digital Network (ISDN) capabilities started in the United States with the ceremonial first calls and initial commercial customers. Since that time, there has been increasing recognition that service providers must demonstrate the potential economic benefits that the new technology might offer an end customer. While, as engineers, we might often like to think that technology alone is sufficient to interest customers, the hard reality is that the typical business user is in business to make money; users purchase services based upon economic benefits rather than upon pure technology.

The Federal government recognized this need, as well as the need to foster standardization of applications, and in 1988 created the North American ISDN Users' Forum (NIUF). This group, sponsored by the National Institute of Standards and Technology (NIST), is chartered with identifying and specifying end-user ISDN applications, several of which are included in this paper.

AT&T Network Systems (AT&T-NS) also recognized the need to identify ISDN applications and established a project called TriVista early in 1987. This resulted in studies of actual business customers and realizable applications for those end users. This paper presents a history of the TriVista project, including an overview of its methodologies and its major results to date.

ISDN Evolution

In the fourth quarter of 1986, the two leading central office switch vendors in the United States, Northern Telecom and AT&T Network Systems, introduced ISDN offerings. These offerings were the result of years of studies in the industry and significant input from end customers as to important needs of their businesses. However, at that time, the focus of the ISDN introduction was on the building blocks—the capabilities of the offering. The concern was focused not necessarily on how to utilize the new technology in end-user specific applications, but on reducing existing inefficiencies. For example, early "applications" included PC-to-PC file transfer, coax elimination, and improved call coverage with messaging services and electronic directory service.

While these were sufficient to stimulate limited end-customer interest, there was a growing industry recognition that more was needed to generate interest in the bulk of the end-user community and to establish standards for those emerging applications of the ISDN technology. Hence, efforts were started by the Federal government in the form of the NIUF, and by AT&T-NS with the TriVista project, to study

end-user needs and develop ISDN-based applications that would satisfy those needs.

Throughout this paper, the term "capability" will refer to a building block (hardware or software) that supports an overall implementation of a communications solution to an end-user need. We will refer to an "application" as a customized solution for a specific industry, department, or end user. Examples include patient tracking systems in the healthcare field, purchasing systems, claims processing systems in the insurance industry, and automated telemarketing systems. All these applications are based on one or more basic ISDN capabilities.

In general, end users are not concerned about specific ISDN-related capabilities such as PC-to-PC file transfer. They are concerned, though, about improving internal information flows, for example, between the nursing department and the doctors' offices in a hospital for use in applications such as patient management systems, diagnosis and treatment systems, or patient billing systems. These applications may well be composed of PC-to-PC file transfers, as well as PC screen sharing, data conferencing, incoming caller identification, and data security safeguards. To be successful, switching vendors, service providers, and third-party vendors must provide effective solutions to end users' communications needs, i.e., applications.

North American ISDN Users' Forum

Under the auspices of NIST, the North American ISDN Users' Forum (NIUF) was formed in mid-1988. The NIUF aims to provide users with the opportunity to influence the development of ISDN to reflect their needs, and to identify ISDN applications and assure their interoperability in a multi-vendor environment. Accordingly, to achieve these goals, membership in the NIUF includes both users and product and service providers. The NIUF comprises two separate groups, or workshops: the ISDN Users' Workshop (IUW) and the ISDN Implementors' Workshop (IIW). The IUW identifies, defines, and prioritizes ISDN applications, refers them to the IIW to define implementation agreements, and approves the implementation agreements as defined by the IIW. The IIW, in addition to defining implementation agreements, also provides technical advice and consultation to the IUW, addresses ISDN user application issues spanning Layers 1 through 7 of the OSI architecture, sponsors multi-vendor demonstrations and trials, addresses standards issues as required, and provides a formal liaison with appropriate organizations (e.g., OSI, COS, T1).

A number of user-initiated applications have already been approved by the NIUF. Incoming Calling Line IDentification (ICLID) is an ISDN capability that has met with great success in the marketplace and is utilized extensively in a number of approved applications by the NIUF. These applications include sales information management, customer service, and telemarketing.

Sales Information Management

In this application (NIUF Application 82001.0), order entry and order status inquiries by sales representatives are facilitated by using ISDN.

Customer Need

Sales representatives from around the country need to contact a central location both to enter orders and to check on the order and credit status of their customers. Some representatives prefer to have their inquiries handled via a data terminal session, others use an interactive voice response system, and a third group prefers to conduct a voice conversation. For those using the voice conversation option, connection to the appropriate regional representative is required.

ISDN Solution

Representatives dial in to a single 800 number, where the telephone number of the calling party is provided automatically to a sales representative's database. Based on the profile identified by the originating telephone number, the representative is then set up to conduct his or her inquiry via an interactive terminal session, a touch-tone/voice response session, or a voice conversation session. If a voice conversation is used, the calling line identification is employed again to route the call to the appropriate regional sales agent and to display the sales representative's database record for that agent.

Benefits

A single point of contact, i.e., one 800 number, is used to handle all calls, regardless of the type of session required. For voice conversations, automatic routing to the appropriate agent saves time and confusion. The automatic retrieval of the sales representative's records will save time for the agents and increase their productivity.

Customer Service

In this application (NIUF Application 840024.0), customer service agents are able to handle their calls more effectively through ISDN features.

Customer Need

Customer service agents receive incoming calls from customers and need to access account information from host computers. Sometimes it is necessary to transfer the call to a second agent who provides a different service but also needs to see the customer's account information. Currently, account history is accessed by having the agent manually input the customer's account number into a terminal connected to a host. If the call is transferred to a second agent, the same manual procedure must be repeated.

ISDN Solution

Using ISDN's ICLID feature and simultaneous voice and data connections, the customer's account record is automatically retrieved from the host computer and appears on the customer service agent's terminal screen as the agent answers the call. If it is necessary for the agent to transfer the call, the original ICLID data is passed on to the second agent, again trigger-ing the automatic appearance of the customer's records on the new agent's screen.

Benefits

Customer service agents see increased productivity when customer account information appears as they are answering the voice call. Customer satisfaction is greater with faster service. Costs will be reduced by providing a single ISDN interface to agent workstations for both voice and data, rather than the two interfaces currently in place.

Telemarketing

In this application (NIUF Application 840025.0), ICLID is used to reduce customer waiting time by triggering an automatic callback feature.

Customer Need

During peak times, telemarketing centers often receive more calls than can be handled by the agents on duty. Currently, customer calls are placed in queue by an automatic call distributor system. Customers may become impatient, hang up, and call a competing service. Telemarketing centers need a way to reduce customer waiting time without increasing their staff level.

ISDN Solution

With ISDN, the calling number, dialed number, time, and date can be recorded for each incoming call. After the calling customers wait in queue for a designated number of seconds, they will hear an announcement saying that they can hang up and be called back as soon as possible. If the caller disconnects, the callback information goes into an Automatic Callback database, which is then activated when a designated number of agents become available. The return calls are then placed automatically, with the appropriate customer records displayed on the agent's terminal.

Benefits

Customer satisfaction will increase as waiting time is reduced. As a result, customers are less likely to turn to competitive services. Agent efficiency will increase with the automatic appearance of customer records when callbacks are triggered.

TriVista Project Overview

The TriVista program was initiated by AT&T Network Systems early in 1987 to develop a base of ISDN experts, gather market information, and determine ways to apply and demonstrate ISDN technology. AT&T has worked closely with the local Telephone companies (Telcos) and their end business customers in this project. In fact, the name of TriVista actually stems from having a three-way partnership (end customer, Telco, and AT&T-NS) to determine the market for ISDN central office services. The project itself consists of several components, which include regionally distributed study teams, ISDN applications development, and ISDN marketing communications. Each of these areas plays an integral part in helping develop the market for ISDN services. The following sections further describe these activities.

Regional TriVista Team Activities

With the beginning of the TriVista effort in 1987, the primary project objective was to determine ways in which ISDN could be applied to various business and communication environments. Little information was known, initially, on how ISDN services might be applied to customers within different industries. Therefore, initial project objectives also included determining what business and communication needs existed within a variety of industries, as well as how to apply ISDN services to meet those needs. Initial studies were rather detailed and lengthy, taking six to nine months for completion. Through these studies, it was learned how to target end customers more quickly; which groups of individuals within an end customer's business were most appropriate for interviewing; which methods for analyzing the information gathered were most efficient; and how to apply ISDN technology to meet the business and communication service needs identified in the study. An entire methodology process was defined as a part of this initial data gathering. This end-customer study process has become known as the TriVista study methodology.

In 1988, the study process was streamlined by abbreviating the amount of information used to develop a solution determination and by decreasing the amount of time necessary to perform the study. As a result, more studies could be completed. Further, through training, local service providers' knowledge of the process was increased, making more studies possible. With Telco personnel driving the process, AT&T TriVista teams have moved into more of a consultative capacity. In their role of consultants, their primary area of emphasis is identification of ISDN applications and their use in building customized ISDN proposals. This process has become known as the TriVista "mini-study" process. Over 100 such studies have been completed to date in such industries as colleges and universities, manufacturing, state governments, and federal agencies.

ISDN Applications Development

Several groups at AT&T-NS and AT&T Bell Laboratories have actively identified, designed, and developed specific ISDN applications and their supporting capabilities. Since these applications are end-to-end solutions, they are frequently developed in conjunction with third-party vendors. Working relationships have been established with such third party vendors as DEC, IBM™, Wang, Teleos, Progressive Computing, Fujitsu, Baxter Healthcare, and many others. These vendors have modified their hardware and software products to take advantage of ISDN capabilities, resulting in new product prototypes and Customer Premises Equipment (CPE) products. These include products that provide functions such as recognizing ICLID and passing the information on to external databases, enhanced voice/data/video conferencing capability, Primary Rate Interface (PRI) access to cluster controllers, Basic Rate Interface (BRI) capabilities to connect to 3270-type terminals, an Integrated Voice/Data Terminal, etc. As part of this activity, vendors are invited to try their products in a live switch environment associated with the Feature Interactive Verification Environment (FIVE) in Lisle, Illinois.

Marketing Communications

An integral activity of the TriVista project has been communicating and sharing the information learned from the project through various Marketing Communications activities. These activities have included distribution of information in publications and through marketing rollout conferences, and the staging of an ISDN applications showcase at NetPower '89.

Marketing Publications

As full TriVista studies have been performed, the information has been documented in the form of non-proprietary mar-

---

™IBM is a trademark of International Business Machines Corporation.

keting guides. These guides demonstrate ways to apply the identified ISDN services to customers within a particular industry segment. An initial Single Customer Application study has been published for several industries, including a school district, a corporate headquarters, a college, an insurance company, a hospital, and a manufacturing division in a high technology area. Each publication highlights a central office solution in the form of ISDN applications—how ISDN services can enhance the way end users perform their daily work activities, therefore helping the end customer achieve its overall business objectives.

In addition to these Single Customer Application studies and as part of TriVista, AT&T has performed Industry Specific Market Analysis Research studies on a national basis. Focus groups have been used to test assumptions, which were subsequently validated on a larger scale through nationwide telephone surveys. Through the course of the market research, information is obtained that helps facilitate the understanding of end customers' communication and information management needs within a given industry on a broad basis.

These Industry Analysis studies are useful as sanity checks against the findings of the Single Customer Application studies. As with the Single Customer studies, the information from these Industry Analysis studies is being published in the form of non-proprietary marketing guides. Industry segments covered thus far include legal, primary and secondary education, corporate headquarters, and higher education. Others are planned to be released throughout 1989.

Information Rollout

Since 1987 was a "learning year," the primary method of information sharing was via the regional teams. The first TriVista "rollout of results" in the fall of 1987 was limited to an internal AT&T audience comprised of the TriVista teams. This idea of information sharing was expanded in early 1988 with another TriVista "rollout of results" customized for an audience of regional Telco marketing personnel. The rollouts shared study findings, illustrated ways to apply ISDN, and demonstrated real applications highlighting the value of ISDN services. At each of these "rollouts," demonstrations for the insurance, banking, healthcare, and education industries were displayed. Each of the demonstrations presented ISDN from an end-customer perspective, and highlighted as well the added value of using ISDN central office service. They were developed taking into account the industry-needs information gathered in the TriVista Single Customer Application studies.

NetPower '89

In 1989, this information sharing was further expanded through NetPower '89, held during March in Scottsdale, Arizona. Its emphasis on end-to-end applications helped demonstrate the value, feasibility, and, most important, immediate availability of ISDN-based solutions that address the needs of large or small business and the residence.

As in the 1988 TriVista rollouts, study findings were presented and used as a basis for developing ISDN applications. The key ingredient of NetPower was an ISDN applications showcase, which highlighted 11 AT&T-sponsored ISDN applications in specific industry segments and ISDN-related products from 54 vendors. Vendors participating included DEC, Tandem, Fujitsu, Trillium, Baxter Healthcare, Teleos and others. All the applications displayed used currently available products.

This ISDN showcase was the first time that a major central office equipment vendor had partnered with multiple CPE vendors to demonstrate ISDN-compatible products while using ISDN lines operating from a live switch. Each showcase application focused on real-world, true-to-life applications that demonstrated the value ISDN holds for businesses today—practical, available solutions. Each application operated over live ISDN lines provided by a US West Communications 5ESS® Switch. A total of 130 ISDN and 20 analog lines were utilized.

The AT&T applications were in the following areas: office automation, Management Information System (MIS) help desk, security, purchasing, residential, secondary education, higher education, publishing, legal, healthcare, and manufacturing. The first three of these are described in detail in the following sections. Each of these 11 applications was showcased to highlight the opportunities for information movement and management in the particular industry segments. These can typically be customized for specific end customer environments as required.

Office Automation

One of the application areas that has consistently shown wide market application during the TriVista studies is that of office automation. Today, all industries are making heavy investments in this area. Technologies such as facsimile, text processing, electronic mail, voice messaging, laser printers, and teleconferencing already exist in many companies. However, users are becoming increasingly interested in sharing expensive office equipment across multiple users. Hence, Local Area Networks (LANs) are springing up in more and more locations to promote sharing these resources.

However, it is also true that, in many cases, these LANs need to be interconnected to share information between departments within an entity. In many cases, document preparation is no longer the responsibility of a single organization, where authors could share their contributions across a departmental LAN. It is becoming commonplace that collaborative authors are spread across multiple departments, if not multiple geographic locations. (This paper is a good example: three authors, one in New Jersey, two in Illinois, but those two sitting two miles apart.) As data traffic increases at a rapid rate, there is a clear need for higher speeds, more flexible connectivity, and continuous availability of network solutions.

ISDN can provide answers to many of these needs. The application presented herein demonstrates a solution to the challenge of communicating among multiple authors in different locations. It is important to note that this implementation consists of available hardware and software components, that all components have been fully tested, and that all are compatible with the ISDN basic rate transport.

Customer Need

Consider the situation where the individual authors for a document are spread over four geographic locations. The team members are using a variety of personal computers with a variety of word processing packages. The team is using WordPerfect™ on an Apple Macintosh™ II personal computer and Microsoft Word™ on an IBM-compatible personal computer with MS-DOS. (Other word processing software might also be employed.) Four of the authors are in two AppleTalk™ networks and the fifth uses a stand-alone MS-DOS machine.

Without the capabilities of ISDN, the coordinating author must access each system in turn to retrieve the pieces of the final document. Generally, he or she is limited to voiceband modem speeds, most likely 1,200 b/s. If the coordinator needs to talk with the individual authors, this cannot be done simultaneously with data transmission unless a second telephone line is present or some type of nonstandard simultaneous voice/data system has been installed in that company. If there is no modem, users will resort to the U.S. mail-net system of sending floppy disks through the postal service or overnight delivery carriers.

ISDN Solution

Now consider the same situation with the authors having ISDN service. In Figure 1, the desktop publishing software is Aldus PageMaker®, Sun Microsystem's TOPS® is used to link file systems, and Farallon's Timbuktu Remote™ is used for data conferencing. The Solana R-Server™ is used to bridge to existing LANs, in this case AppleTalk. A 5ESS switch BRI ISDN line provides simultaneous voice and data capability through an AT&T 7506 or 7507 telephone set.

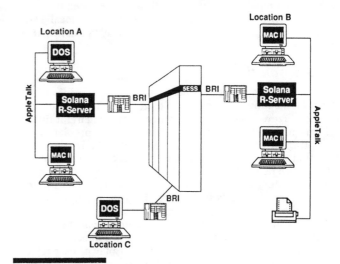

Fig. 1. Office automation.

Benefits

Data can be transmitted in the background at circuit-switched speeds of up to 64 kb/s over one B channel, while the authors maintain a voice conference call on the other B channel to discuss content, page layout, or schedules. The coordinating author can thus quickly resolve issues with the rest of the team, instead of being limited to doing this on a sequential basis. Screens of data can be reviewed and updated by all parties simultaneously. The file transfer times are now a small fraction of the voiceband alternative, as the speed has been increased by a factor of more than 50.

Data transmission speeds of 64 kb/s within a local area, i.e., a LATA, are possible today where the local exchange carrier has installed Common Channel Signalling (CCS) between the various end offices. InterLATA speeds of 56 kb/s are possible today via certain interexchange carriers. In fact, this was demonstrated over two years ago at the International Switching

®5ESS is a registered trademark of AT&T.
™WordPerfect is a trademark of WordPerfect Corporation.
™Macintosh is a trademark of Apple Computer, Inc.
™Microsoft Word is a trademark of Microsoft Corporation.
™AppleTalk is a trademark of Apple Computer, Inc.

®PageMaker is a trademark of Aldus Corporation.
®TOPS is a registered trademark of Sun Microsystems, Inc.
™Timbuktu Remote is a trademark of Farallon Computing, Inc.
™Solana R-Server is a trademark of Solana Electronics.

Symposium in Phoenix in 1987, where connections were established on a dial-up basis between Illinois and Arizona using the AT&T Accunet switched 56-kb/s network. In the future, CCS7 connectivity between the local exchange carriers and interexchange carriers will permit these speeds to increase to the full 64 kb/s.

MIS Help Desk

In today's large businesses, virtually every employee occasionally or regularly uses a computer. At one time or another, most users need help with their personal computers. If requests for help are handled inefficiently, employees become frustrated, productivity diminishes, and willingness to try anything new is lowered. If handled well, the MIS assistance center helps the whole organization achieve higher levels of computer system use, with subsequent increases in productivity.

In most current arrangements, the MIS support personnel must attempt to solve user problems solely via a voice telephone connection. Initially, the help desk is unaware of the user's particular configuration of hardware and software, nor do they typically have a trouble history for that user. Further, they do not have the ability to see the exact setup on the user's screen. Network troubles must be called in to the local Telco, resulting in an unpredictable amount of delay in clearing these troubles.

ISDN Solution

Consider the situation where the capabilities of ISDN can be combined into an application targeted at the help desk personnel. Figure 2 shows the equipment arrangement for this application. A user may have a communication problem in attempting to access an outside data network. In the ISDN solution, when the user calls the help desk with the problem, ICLID can be used to access a host database that contains the caller's history and configuration information. The Progressive Computing ISDN telAdapter™ PC card provides this access to the host. The help desk person immediately has a full set of user-related information displayed before he or she even answers the voice call using the same line as the data connection. This arrangement provides immediate display of user-related information prior to the help desk's answer of the call.

Once the user explains the details of their communication problem, the help desk person can establish a data conference call between the two personal computers (i.e., user and help desk) to verify proper parameter settings and to see the user's screen. Close-up® from Norton-Lambert is one package that supports this function. If the caller's parameters are set correctly, the help desk person can use the caller's PC software via the data conference connection to retry the connection to the external destination.

If the call attempt again fails, the help desk person can turn to the NetPartner™ network management system to test the caller's BRI loop between the switch and the user's equipment. If the problem is found in the user's D channel after performing a digital loopback test, the help desk person can enter a trouble ticket directly into the Telco's operational support system and continue to check the status of the line while the problem is being fixed. Once the problem has been cleared by the Telco, the help desk person can recheck the line and verify that all is well. The user can now proceed with his or her planned data connection.

™telAdapter is a trademark of Progressive Computing, Inc.

®Close-up is a registered trademark of Norton-Lambert Corporation.

™NetPartner is a trademark of AT&T.

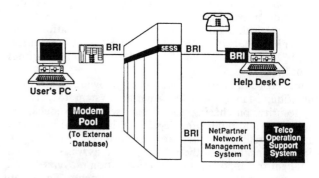

Fig. 2. MIS help desk.

Benefits

With proper support, business customers with even a basic level of computer usage can realize benefits in a number of areas. If end users' problems in using new software or hardware arrangements can be more quickly cleared, their productivity is increased. Likewise, the efficiency of the MIS personnel who are providing the assistance service can also be improved. Users will be more likely to try new software if they find it easy to deal with the MIS group providing support; the new software can improve their work by giving them new capabilities not available with the products they had purchased earlier. By increasing control of network resources via the NetPartner system, MIS personnel can monitor and reconfigure data networks in response to changing user needs. Troubleshooting becomes easier, and user troubles can be cleared faster.

Security

Lower-cost imaging technologies are now a reality. Companies are exhibiting heightened interest in enhancing textual outputs from their existing databases by adding images. This interest in imaging has direct applications in fields such as insurance claims processing, publishing, real estate, and personnel records. However, the large file sizes of captured images, typically 260K to 1,346K, can limit their distribution to high-speed LAN interconnections. These connections tend to be expensive and have limited flexibility for adding new connections or communicating with other systems.

One particular application of stored images involves allowing a security guard to retrieve a TV-quality picture from a central database to verify employee identity. If uncertainty exists, the guard requires the ability to consult a supervisor.

ISDN Solution

The guard station employs a personal computer equipped with a VEGA™ Deluxe Enhanced Graphics Adapter. HyperAccess™ is used to transfer stored files from a central personnel records database to the guard station via an ISDN circuit-switched data connection. In the personnel office, employee pictures are added to the database through the use of a personal computer equipped with a FreezeFrame™ II circuit board that allows an image to be captured and digitized in real time. This PC, also equipped with the VEGA Deluxe En-

---

™VEGA is a trademark of Video-7, Inc.

™HyperAccess is a trademark of Hilgraeve, Inc.

™FreezeFrame is a trademark of Vutek Systems, Inc.

hanced Graphics Adapter, is connected to a standard 8-mm camcorder for imaging. The guard's supervisor has an ISDN telephone equipped to display the calling party's name. This arrangement is shown in Figure 3.

When an employee arrives for work without the required ID badge, the guard can use the employee number to retrieve a TV-quality image from Personnel's central database. To aid identification, the employee's picture appears on the screen along with background information in the form of text. However, the guard cannot make a positive identification from the stored photograph because the employee has grown a beard since the original picture was taken.

With the employee data still on the screen, and using the same ISDN line, now for a voice connection, the guard calls a supervisor to assist. The supervisor, seeing the call is from one of the guard stations via the calling name display, immediately places their active call on hold and answers the guard's call. The supervisor asks the guard to verify the employee's home address, birth date, and mother's family name. When these answers match the on-screen information, the supervisor authorizes the guard to issue a temporary ID card and requests that the employee visit Personnel to obtain a new badge, with an updated picture.

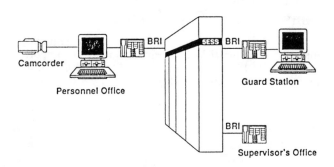

Fig. 3. Security.

Benefits

With such a system, users can quickly access and share images and text while discussing details over the phone. In this particular example, identification of the employee is made easier because the guards have all the required information available directly at their stations. The employee is allowed into the facility more quickly than under older systems. With higher file transfer speeds available to all authorized users, images can be integrated with available software the users already employ. Separate systems for text and image display are avoided by using a common high-resolution monitor. These advantages have obvious extensions to areas such as desktop publishing, where movement of draft and final copies that include full images is facilitated. Because the connection interface uses normal twisted-pair copper cabling back to the central office, relocation and installation of users is straightforward.

Summary

The work being done in the NIUF is heightening end-user awareness of potential applications using ISDN capabilities and services. It is obvious from the work thus far that many applications are both desirable and feasible.

The TriVista project activities have furthered this effort by designing, developing, and testing applications, and by stimulating Telco and end-customer interest, acceptance, and purchase of ISDN service. Through TriVista's three-way partnership, and by matching customer needs with product capabilities, customized solutions can be provided for large businesses, small businesses, and residential customers.

The activities of both the NIUF and TriVista have demonstrated a common theme: for ISDN deployment to succeed, the challenge for our telecommunications industry will be to combine our diverse products into meaningful ISDN solutions that end customers will find beneficial in their existing environments.

Biography

Frederick C. Iffland received the B.S. degree from the University of Michigan in 1969 in mathematics and the M.S. degree from the University of Chicago in 1971 in computer science.

Since joining AT&T Bell Laboratories in 1969, he has been primarily involved with the introduction of new generic programs and features, initially for the No. 1 ESS and 1A ESS systems and, starting in 1983, for the 5ESS switch. These have included areas such as toll/tandem, private networks, equal access, generic retrofits, centrex, and remote switching capabilities. During 1977–1979, he was District Manager in AT&T General Departments in the Local Switching Engineering area, where he supported the Bell Operating Companies on issues related to the No. 1 ESS switch. In late 1985, his group undertook Bell Laboratories' support of the implementation of ISDN with Illinois Bell for the McDonald's Corporation in Oak Brook, IL. In May of 1988, he assumed responsibility for the Systems Engineering group that provides technical support for the TriVista end-user studies of ISDN applications associated with the 5ESS switch.

Mr. Iffland is a member of the IEEE Communications Society.

Glenda D. Norton began her career with AT&T in 1980 in the 4ESS Switch Office Data Assembler development area. She followed this assignment by serving as Project Leader of computing services at an AT&T location providing services for over 2,500 employees. Her next assignment included marketing support for AT&T Data Systems' data networking products for several years. In 1987, she transferred to the AT&T-Bell Laboratories 5ESS Switch Systems Engineering organization. In this assignment, she provided 5ESS Switch Engineering and data communications expertise for the TriVista teams by supporting several application studies and developing the TriVista study methodology. Glenda has recently assumed the position of ISDN Market Development Manager in AT&T Network Systems, where she serves as TriVista Project Manager and Marketing Manager for AT&T's advanced communication services.

Prior to her employment with AT&T, she received an M.S. degree from DePaul University in computer engineering and an undergraduate degree from Lewis University in psychology and business administration.

Judy M. Waxman is a Senior Market Planner in the New Service Concepts group of the Marketing Organization of AT&T Network Systems in Holmdel, NJ. She joined AT&T in 1978. Her current work involves market research and new service concepts development related to ISDN and other advanced communications services. Previously, she was a member of the Industry Analysis Group, where she was responsible for environmental and strategic assessments of the network telecommunications industry. She has also served as a research specialist in long distance services and customer premises equipment in the AT&T Information Research Center. She received a B.A. degree, magna cum laude, from the University of Pennsylvania, where she was elected to membership in Phi Beta Kappa, and an M.S. degree in library science from Columbia University, where she was elected to membership in Beta Phi Mu, the national library science honor society.

Southwestern Bell Telephone's ISDN Experience

Richard W. Stephenson
Stephen A. McGaw

Southwestern Bell Telephone's (SWBT's) Integrated Services Digital Network (ISDN) experience has been heavily influenced by the realization that from a customer perspective, the most important aspects of ISDN are the applications of this technology. For that reason, this paper will focus on a description of many of the ISDN applications that SWBT has been exploring with the users of ISDN.

The ISDN architecture offers end users of the network an opportunity to transmit voice and data over a single switched fabric with performance and service characteristics that have never before been available. This paper documents several customer applications of the ISDN architecture that have been tested in SWBT's Advanced Technology Laboratory in St. Louis, MO.

These applications have been tested as a result of SWBT customer requests for support of their specific implementations of the new network. In all diagrams, Network Termination devices (NT1s) are implied for each ISDN line. The customer applications shown stress the advantages of integration, accessibility, performance, and the economics of ISDN.

Application 1: Desktop Conferencing

The desktop with ISDN has the opportunity for a truly integrated voice/data workstation capability. The capability can be realized through Personal Computers (PCs) with in-slot PC terminal adapters or through specially designed integrated workstations for ISDN. Features offered by this application allow screen sharing between workstations, automated file transfers, and the integration of voice and data communications for directory and messaging utilities.

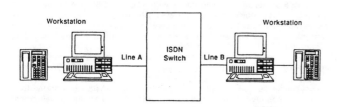

Fig. 1. Desktop conferencing.

Application Description

The workstations on Lines A and B use a circuit-switched B channel for voice communications and the other B channel for circuit-switched data applications. Data communications over the B channel are switched at 64 kb/s; however, rate adaptation methods such as DMI Mode 2, V.110, and V.120 have been implemented to support slower speeds. All signaling is accomplished over the D channel.

In some cases, the D channel is also used for X.25 packet switching in the desktop conferencing scenario at speeds of up to 9.6 kb/s. The packet capability allows for multiple concurrent sessions between the workstation and different hosts.

This article is an expanded version of a paper by the same title which appeared in the Globecom '88 (November 28–December 1, 1988, Hollywood, FL) conference records. © 1988 IEEE.

Reprinted from *IEEE Network Magazine*, September 1989, pages 25-36. Copyright © 1989 by The Institute of Electrical and Electronics Engineers, Inc. All rights reserved.

Voice features are commonly activated through the workstation keyboard for the attached telephone set. Call lists and messages are often stored in the workstation to allow the user to return calls more efficiently than with non-ISDN techniques.

Application 2: Asynchronous Protocol Conversion to SNA/SDLC

Users of asynchronous terminals and PCs frequently require access to the IBM SNA environment. To support this function with ISDN, a dial-up capability is needed, utilizing the same twisted pair as that used for voice.

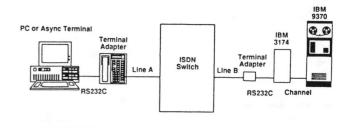

Fig. 2. Asynchronous protocol conversion to SNA/SDLC.

Application Description

The user connected to Line A has an asynchronous terminal (or a PC emulating one) attached via RS232C cable to an ISDN terminal adapter. This adapter places voice on one B channel of the Basic Rate Interface (BRI) line and data over either the other B channel or over the D channel. If the second B channel is used for data, a rate adaptation scheme is required such as V.110 or V.120.

By entering the directory number of Line B in the Line A terminal adapter, a circuit- or packet-switched data call is established between the two BRIs. The terminal adapter on Line B, using the same rate adaptation scheme used on Line A, places the data over an RS232C cable connected to an IBM 3174 controller with the Asynchronous Emulation Adapter (AEA) interface. The controller is subsequently channel-attached to the IBM 9370.

This AEA interface provides the asynchronous-to-synchronous protocol conversion at speeds of up to 38.4 kb/s. When the D channel is utilized for the data, an upper limit of

0-8186-2797-2/92 $3.00 © 1989 IEEE

9.6 kb/s is imposed. The RS232C cable standard supports speeds of up to 19.2 kb/s—thus, this would be the circuit-switched limit in the diagram shown. An identical test was performed using an IBM 7171 controller/protocol converter in place of the 3174 shown.

Application 3: VTAM INN Link Replacement

Two IBM systems are connected through a VTAM Inter-Nodal Network (INN) backbone link, which can be supported with ISDN rather than with private line circuits. This application was tested to connect to separate VTAM networks using the SNA Network Integration (SNI) facilities of VTAM.

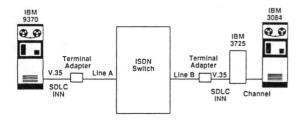

Fig. 3. VTAM INN link replacement.

Application Description

An SDLC INN interface link is connected from an IBM 9370 processor to an ISDN terminal adapter with a V.35 cable to support a 56-kb/s transmission stream. The terminal adapter (Line A) uses a circuit-switched B channel to connect to a similar B channel on Line B. This adapter is V.35-attached to an IBM 3725 front end processor, which is channel-attached to the IBM 3084 host processor. The terminal adapter on Line A is configured to automatically set up the call to Line B upon receipt of Data Terminal Ready (DTR) on the 9370 V.35 cable. The connection could also be manually set-up or run at lower speeds using a rate adaptation technique.

Application 4: Asynchronous Protocol Conversion to SNA/SDLC with Multiplexing

As stated in Application 2, asynchronous devices commonly need access capabilities to IBM SNA networks. The packet switching functionality available with ISDN allows for resources to be optimized through multiplexing several sessions across a B channel with X.25.

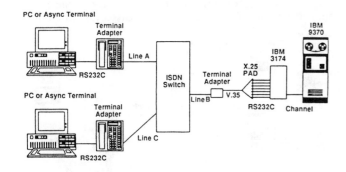

Fig. 4. Asynchronous protocol conversion to SNA/SDLC with multiplexing.

Application Description

Asynchronous terminals (or PCs emulating them) connect to ISDN terminal adapters via RS232C cable on Lines A and C. The adapters utilize one B channel for circuit-switched voice and the D channel for packet switching at 9.6 kb/s. These packet-switched sessions are aggregated across a packet-switched B channel to a terminal adapter (Line B), which passes the X.25 data on to a Packet Assembler/Disassembler (PAD) using a V.35 interface at 64 kb/s.

The PAD places each X.25 session on a separate RS232C link to the IBM 3174 (or IBM 7171) controller with the AEA interface for the protocol conversion and controller function. Since the controller no longer needs to be near the terminals, it can be channel-attached to the IBM 9370 and ports can be shared through the dial-up ISDN network.

Application 5: Remote 3174 Multiplexing via B Channel Packet

Since coaxial cable is already installed in many locations and the conversion to ISDN is evolutionary in nature, controllers will continue to require remote access capability to front end processors. The packet switching function, coupled with higher switched bandwidths available with ISDN, allow for multiple remote 3174/3274 controllers to be multiplexed for access to the front end processor. This capability makes the migration to ISDN faster and easier to justify.

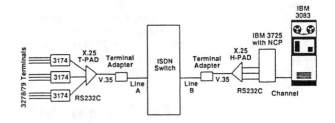

Fig. 5. Remote 3174 multiplexing via B-channel packet.

Application Description

IBM 3278/79 type terminals are connected to IBM 3174 controllers with coaxial cable. These controllers, normally remotely attached to the front end processor through modems and private lines, can have their sessions multiplexed through an X.25 PAD using a single twisted pair and a packet-switched B channel. The controllers are connected to the Terminal PAD (T-PAD) with RS232C cable. The controller communications are aggregated onto a V.35 interface, which connects to an ISDN terminal adapter. The terminal adapter passes the X.25 controller data on to the ISDN switch via a packet-switched B channel.

Line B also uses a packet-switched B channel, passing the data on to a Host PAD (H-PAD) through V.35. The H-PAD splits each controller session back out onto a separate RS232C cable connected to the IBM 3725 front end processor, which is subsequently channel-attached to the IBM 3083 host. Each controller-to-3725 connection is a permanent virtual circuit through the ISDN, so dialing is not required unless desired.

Application 6: Remote 3174 Multiplexing via B channel Packet and NPSI

As in Application 5, the packet switching function in ISDN can be used to allow multiple controllers to access an IBM 3725 front end processor remotely, eliminating costly dedicated lines. A Network packet-switched Interface (NPSI) can be implemented in the 3725 processor to eliminate the need for the H-PAD described in Application 5.

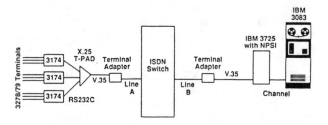

Fig. 6. Remote 3174 multiplexing via B-channel packet and NPSI.

Application Description

IBM 3278/79-type terminals are connected to IBM 3174 controllers with coaxial cable. These controllers, normally remotely attached to the front end processor through modems and private lines, can have their sessions multiplexed through an X.25 PAD using a single twisted pair and a packet-switched B channel. The controllers are connected to the T-PAD with RS232C cable. The controller communications are aggregated onto a V.35 interface which connects to an ISDN terminal adapter. The terminal adapter passes the X.25 controller on to the ISDN, switched via a packet-switched B channel.

Line B also uses a packet-switched B channel, passing the data on to the IBM 3725 front end processor, which has the NPSI software and a V.35 interface. The 3725 is thus channel-attached to the IBM 3083 host. Each controller-to-3725 connection is a permanent virtual circuit through the ISDN, so dialing is not required unless desired.

Application 7: 327X Emulation via SIM-PC, SIM-VTAM, and NPSI

Protocol conversion can take several forms. SIM-PC and SIM-VTAM, products of SIMWARE, Inc., offer yet another technique for allowing PCs access to the IBM SNA environment through ISDN.

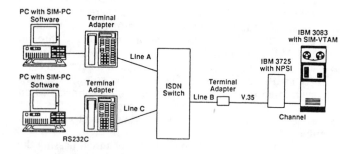

Fig. 7. 327X emulation via SIM-PC, SIM-VTAM, and NPSI.

Application Description

PCs with the SIM-PC software emulate 327X terminals across the serial communications port (RS232C) to an adjunct ISDN terminal adapter (shown in Figure 7). These terminal adapters (Lines A and C) perform the PAD function for the data to connect via D channel to a packet-switched B channel shown by Line B. The Line B terminal adapter passes the 64-kb/s packet data (multiple PC sessions) across a V.35 connec-

tion to an IBM 3725, which has the NPSI software. SIM-VTAM in the 3083 host performs the asynchronous-to-3270 protocol conversion for each PC session.

Application 8: 327X Emulation with QLLC and NPSI

Another form of 327X emulation can be achieved through the use of QLLC software in the PC, which makes the PC appear to the 3725 as an SNA PU2 with a virtual circuit speed of 9.6 kb/s.

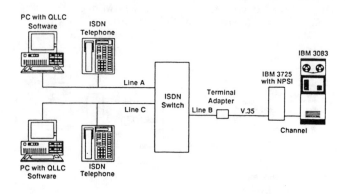

Fig. 8. 327X emulation with QLIC and NPSI.

Application Description

PCs on Lines A and C have internal ISDN terminal adapter boards and QLLC software. The QLLC software allows the PC to emulate an IBM 3274 controller and 3278 terminal, utilizing the packet-switched D channel at 9.6 kb/s to communicate with the IBM 3725 front end processor. The ISDN telephone, also shown in the picture, utilizes one B channel for voice communications.

The ISDN switch multiplexes multiple X.25 D-channel sessions onto a packet-switched B channel on Line B to a terminal adapter which has a V.35 interface (64 kb/s) with which it passes the X.25 data on to the 3725 processor. The front end processor has NPSI to perform the PAD function internally rather than using an adjunct H-PAD. The 3725, as shown, is channel-attached to the IBM 3083 host processor.

Application 9: Asynchronous Access to Private Packet-Switched Network

Companies with private packet-switched networks that are evolving toward ISDN require the interworking of the two network types to ensure complete connectivity during the evolution. An example of this requirement is displayed for connec-

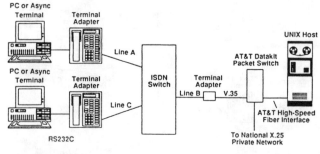

Fig. 9. Asynchronous access to private packet-switched network.

tion of ISDN to an AT&T Datakit packet switch tied into a national X.25 private network.

Application Description

Asynchronous terminals (or PCs emulating same) are connected to ISDN terminal adapters with RS232C cable for speeds of up to 9.6 kb/s over a packet-switched D channel. The PAD function is being performed within the terminal adapters on Lines A and C. Note that voice communications are being handled by the terminal adapters using a circuit-switched B channel for each line.

The ISDN switch aggregates multiple D-channel packet sessions across a packet-switched B channel on Line B terminated by a terminal adapter which passes the 64 kb/s X.25 data to the AT&T Datakit packet switch. The Datakit is connected to UNIX hosts via a proprietary fiber interface to AT&T and to a national X.25 private network. Once the session to the Datakit is established from the terminal end, a second connect sequence is initiated by the user to reach the final session destination, whether directly connected to the Datakit or on the private X.25 network.

Application 10: Asynchronous Access to UNIX Host

The flexibility of ISDN is maximized when asynchronous terminals and hosts are connected directly to the network rather than through Local Area Networks (LANs) and private networks. The dedication of 64 kb/s to each terminal for terminal-to-host communications improves the performance of each session over shared backbone LANs and modem connections.

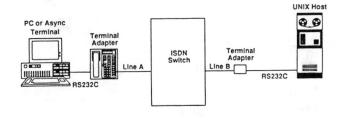

Fig. 10. Asynchronous access to UNIX host.

Application Description

Asynchronous terminals connect to stand-alone ISDN terminal adapters to make use of either a packet-switched D channel at 9.6 kb/s or a circuit-switched B channel at speeds of up to 19.2 kb/s, limited by the RS232C cable connected to them. PCs may use in-slot terminal adapters that give them the same functionality for D or B channel communications, but can transmit data at speeds of up to the full 64 kb/s through the B channel.

Line A connects to Line B in either packet or circuit mode, a decision that can be made in real time by the end user. The terminal adapter on Line B then connects to the asynchronous host with an RS232C cable. The terminal adapters on Lines A and B must use the same rate adaptation scheme to be compatible.

Application 11: Asynchronous Access to UNIX Host via PAD and X.25 Multiplexing

The multiplexing function of X.25 can be used to save on the number of ISDN lines required on the host side of the asynchronous communication application.

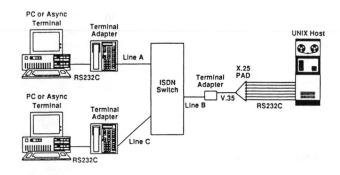

Fig. 11. Asynchronous access to UNIX host via PAD and X.25 multiplexing.

Application Description

Asynchronous terminals connect to stand-alone ISDN terminal adapters via RS232C cable to communicate over a packet-switched D channel of Lines A and C. The terminal adapter performs the PAD function for the data sessions on the terminal end. In-slot terminal adapters may be used in PCs that emulate VT-100 type terminals, also transmitting the data on the D channel at speeds of up to 9.6 kb/s.

The asynchronous host is accessed through a packet-switched B channel on Line B, which is the composite of all sessions accessing the host. The terminal adapter places the X.25 data on a 64-kb/s V.35 interface connected to a PAD, which associates each session with a separate RS232C port connected to the UNIX host. Up to 127 X.25 sessions are possible on each packet-switched B channel.

Application 12: 327X Coaxial Cable Elimination

IBM 327X terminals are normally connected to IBM 3274 controllers with coaxial cable, making moves of terminals difficult and costly. Controllers are thereby remotely attached to the front end processor via private line circuits, creating a bottleneck between controller and processor. A circuit-switched connection between 327X terminals and controllers is possible with ISDN, allowing controllers to be locally attached to host processors and reducing the expenses of terminal moves.

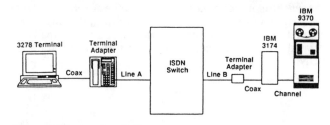

Fig. 12. 327X coaxial cable elimination.

Application Description

An IBM 3278 terminal is attached to an ISDN terminal adapter by a short segment of coaxial cable. The terminal adapter places the terminal data on a circuit-switched B channel for connection to Line B, which has an adapter converting the session data back to coaxial cable. The 3174 controller is channel attached to the IBM 9370. The circuit between terminal and controller is dialed via the terminal-end adapter.

Application 13: Extended Local Area Network with Passive Bus

A group of PCs require the capability to share disks and printers using a software package that makes the network transparent to the application. The passive bus feature allows up to six terminal devices and two voice devices to simultaneously share the same twisted pair, each being uniquely identifiable to the network.

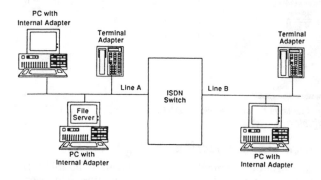

Fig. 13. Extended LAN with passive bus.

Application Description

Two PCs, each with an in-slot ISDN terminal adapter, are connected to the BRI passive bus. The ISDN adapters allow the PCs to interwork with the packet-switched D and B channels of Line A. Software running on the PCs is MS-Networks, which allows one PC to act as a file server for others on the ISDN fabric. The server PC is utilizing the packet-switched B channel, while the other PC on Line A is communicating via the D channel packet. A voice terminal adapter is also attached to Line A for use of voice features on a circuit-switched B channel.

Line B has a PC, also with an in-slot ISDN terminal adapter for access to the D channel, which similarly has a voice adapter for use of one of the B channels. The PC on Line B is also running MS-Networks, having the server on Line A defined within its software for connecting transparently through the ISDN network when the need arises.

Application 14: Asynchronous Access to Ethernet Terminal Server

Asynchronous terminals and PCs require access to Ethernet on a dial-up basis from locations distant from the LAN. This dial-up link is needed at speeds higher than those normally associated with modem connections; thus, this application for ISDN.

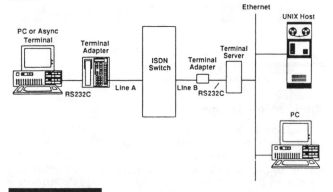

Fig. 14. Asynchronous access to Ethernet terminal server.

Application Description

A PC or asynchronous terminal is attached to an ISDN terminal adapter with an RS232C cable for access to a packet-switched D channel or circuit-switched B channel. The ISDN switch establishes the connection to Line B, through either packet or circuit, respectively, which is terminated on a terminal adapter to place the data on an RS232C interface connected to an Ethernet terminal server. The terminal server provides terminal access to hosts and other PCs directly connected to the Ethernet. In packet-switched mode, the application operates at 9.6 kb/s, while in circuit-switched mode the connection is established at 19.2 kb/s.

The preferred method of access to host processors, however, would not require the terminals to dial into the Ethernet at all. The terminals would dial into the hosts directly through ISDN as in Application 10, reserving Ethernet bandwidth for host-to-host communications and other heavy data traffic.

Application 15: Dedicated Line Replacement (64 kb/s)

For end-user environments where multiplexing is heavily embedded and host processors are required to communicate with only very specific locations, dedicated lines may be replaced with circuit-switched, 64-kb/s channels. As flexibility requirements within the network grow, processors may be moved off the point-to-point architecture and onto a real-time switched environment with ISDN direct connections.

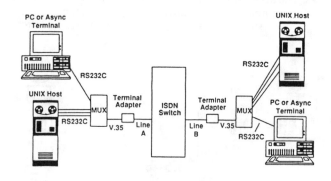

Fig. 15. Dedicated line replacement (64 kb/s).

Application Description

PCs and host processors are directly attached to a multiplexer with RS232C connections. The multiplexer statistically multiplexes the RS232C data sessions across a V.35 interface at 64 kb/s, which connects to an ISDN terminal adapter. The terminal adapter uses the ISDN circuit-switching function to connect Line A to Line B, which has a similar arrangement with a V.35 cable, a multiplexer, and multiple RS232C cables to hosts and PCs.

The evolution of this network to a more flexible alternative would provide each PC with its own ISDN line to support both voice and data (or share a passive bus between multiple PCs), and each host with an ISDN line for receipt of multiple sessions, as in Application 11.

Application 16: Asynchronous Modem Pooling (Out-Dial)

As the ISDN network evolves toward ubiquitous accessibility, interworking of circuit- and packet-switched data with modems on the analog network is required. Hosts that are connected to analog lines via modems will continue to require access from similar modem technology until they are connected to the ISDN network directly.

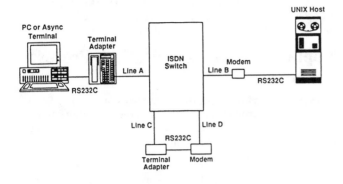

Fig. 16. Asynchronous modem pooling (out-dial).

Application Description

An asynchronous terminal (or PC with emulation software), connected to an ISDN terminal adapter with RS232C cable, uses a packet-switched D channel or circuit-switched B channel to establish a data session between Lines A and C. The terminal adapter connected to Line C answers the call and, using an RS232C interface, passes control of the attached modem to the terminal on Line A. The terminal then instructs the modem (using the ATDT command set or other modem control language) to place an analog call back through the network from Line D to Line B. When the modem on Line B answers the call, the terminal gains access to the port on the host processor.

If the terminal on Line A calls the modem pool (Lines C and D) at a higher speed than that of the modem, the terminal adapter on Line C performs a rate adaptation between the two line speeds. The modem pool also adapts to the speed of the modem on Line B.

Application 17: Asynchronous Modem Pooling (In-Dial)

As stated in Application 16, interworking between ISDN and the analog networks will be required for data communications between devices on modems and those on ISDN lines. This applies to user devices on analog lines needing access to host processors on the ISDN network as well as ISDN user devices dialing devices on the analog network.

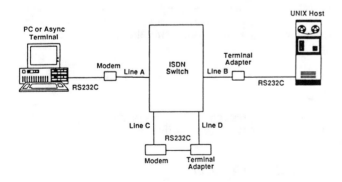

Fig. 17. Asynchronous modem pooling (in-dial).

Application Description

An asynchronous terminal or PC uses a modem to dial through the analog network from Line A to Line C. The modem on Line C connects the terminal's session to the terminal adapter on Line D through an RS232C interface. The terminal then instructs the terminal adapter to place a packet- or circuit-switched data call to the terminal adapter on Line B, which ultimately connects the terminal to the host processor.

In some cases, this two-stage dialing can be performed in one stage by assigning Line B a modem pool in-dial address, which allows the switch to route all calls to that number through the modem pool. The modem pool performs speed conversions to match the modem speed on Line A to the host port speed on Line B.

Application 18: ISDN Wide Area Networking

Interworking of ISDN with private packet-switched networks and private line networks is a requirement to ensure that businesses with existing networks will be able to migrate smoothly to an ISDN-based end-to-end network.

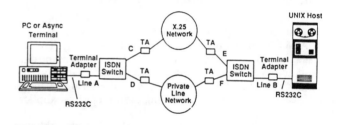

Fig. 18. ISDN wide-area networking.

Application Description

A PC or asynchronous terminal is connected to an ISDN terminal adapter via an RS232C interface, which allows the terminal to utilize the packet-switched D channel or a circuit-switched B channel to connect through ISDN to Line C for access to a private X.25 network or Line D for access to a private line network. These lines attach to ISDN terminal adapters, which use V.35 and RS232C interfaces to connect into the private network for a second stage of dialing.

The user, upon receipt of a prompt from the packet network, dials the packet address that corresponds to Line E. When Line E is reached by the calling party, the terminal adapter will prompt the user to dial a third number corresponding to Line B on the second ISDN network.

A prompt received upon connecting to Line D is actually that of the terminal adapter on Line F, the private line network appearing transparent to the connection. Upon this prompt, the user dials the ISDN number associated with Line B, connected to the host processor.

These dialing scenarios may be simplified and automated for specific applications, using dialing scripts and number translators as appropriate. Session disconnection is supported to terminate calls at each stage of the connect sequence.

Application 19: ISDN Data Gateway

Networks require addressing schemes to allow users to designate which host processor to connect their terminal session to. In ISDN, this addressing scheme is a telephone number.

These addresses are cumbersome, however, requiring users to remember many different addresses, even as those addresses change.

An approach to avoiding this addressing problem is to have connections established through the network by providing users a menu of applications, not requiring the user to know on what processors applications reside nor how to connect to them. This menuing function can be provided by a central data gateway, which establishes data calls as needed for terminals to reach remote applications.

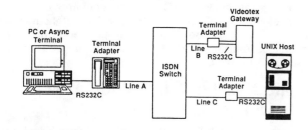

Fig. 19. ISDN data gateway.

Application Description

A terminal or PC is connected to an ISDN terminal adapter, which establishes a packet- or circuit-switched data call from Line A to Line B at 9.6 kb/s or 19.2 kb/s, respectively. The terminal adapter that completes the call on Line B places the data session across an RS232C interface to the data gateway. The data gateway provides menu screens to the terminal across ISDN, each menu item representing a different host application.

Upon selection of a menu item, the data gateway establishes a second data call across the other B channel or multiplexed on the D channel to the appropriate host processor on Line C. Either the session can be passed through the data gateway untouched, or the data gateway can perform protocol and content conversion for the terminal as data is passed on to the network.

When the data session is complete, the connection between Lines B and C is disconnected, and the session between Lines A and B remains active until the user disconnects that portion of the call.

Application 20: Gateway to AppleTalk Network

As in Application 14, remote users often require access to processors and other resources currently on LANs. The AppleTalk network is an example of a LAN that is accessible through ISDN.

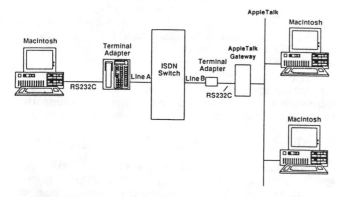

Fig. 20. Gateway to AppleTalk network.

Application Description

An Apple Macintosh is connected to an ISDN terminal adapter with RS232C cable to establish a packet- or circuit-switched data session through ISDN to Line B, which has a similar terminal adapter for connection to an AppleTalk gateway. This gateway appears as a node on the AppleTalk network to allow access to any resource on the LAN.

Application 21: Application Processor Features

ISDN allows for the continued use of existing voice features as well as the introduction of some new ones. Calling name and number identification, electronic directory services, and voice messaging are a few of these new capabilities.

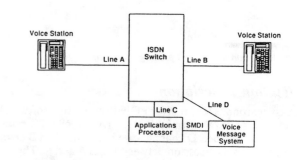

Fig. 21. Application processor features.

Application Description

An ISDN voice station connected to Line A uses the D channel for signalling and a circuit-switched B channel for voice communications. When the voice station on Line A dials the station on Line B, the ISDN switch consults the Application Processor on Line C to determine the name associated with the calling party. When this information is retrieved, the switch signals the called Line B that an incoming call from Line A's address and name is ensuing.

If Line B does not answer the call (busy or no answer), the call is forwarded to Line D, sending calling and called party information to Line C, which in turn is forwarded across a Simplified Message Desk Interface (SMDI) link to a voice message system. Upon storage of the message, a message-waiting indication is sent to Line B across the D channel from the voice message system's SMDI link and associated Line C. A similar feature is available for text messages.

Electronic directory is also available from the Application Processor, allowing the user on Line A to send D channel requests to the Application Processor connected to Line C for directory number information using the name of the required party.

Application 22: Circuit-Switched Compressed Video

Video compression techniques and ISDN have made switched video at 64 kb/s feasible for station-to-station communications.

Application Description

A video telephone/camera combination is connected via a proprietary interface to a 64-kb/s codec. The codec compresses the full motion and color image to a 64-kb/s data stream, which can be transmitted over a V.35 cable connected to an ISDN ter-

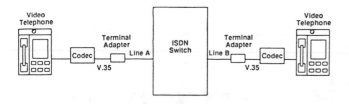

Fig. 22. Circuit-switched compressed video.

minal adapter. The terminal adapter places a B-channel circuit-switched data call, manually or automatically, to Line B, which has a similar configuration. In this configuration, voice may be compressed with the video image on the same 64-kb/s channel, or the second B channel of the ISDN line may be used to carry voice. In either case, the video connection is switched to any location that has the appropriate equipment and ISDN line.

Application 23: Ethernet LAN Bridging

End users often have Ethernet LANs at various locations that need to be bridged together for interworking of host com-

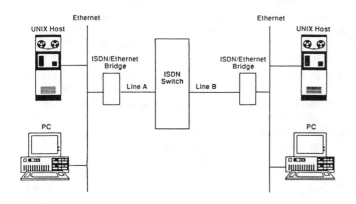

Fig. 23. Ethernet LAN bridging.

puters and for terminal access from one LAN to another. This bridging function can be performed through ISDN at 64 kb/s.

Application Description

Host processors and PCs are connected to an Ethernet LAN for local communications. An ISDN/Ethernet bridge is also connected to the LAN to allow remote access to and from other Ethernet LANs on a 64-kb/s circuit-switched basis. The connection through ISDN is established from the ISDN/Ethernet bridge on either a permanent or semipermanent basis.

Conclusion

As ISDN technology is deployed on an ever-expanding basis, the value of this technology will become more and more apparent through the applications it is able to support. It is important that equipment vendors and service providers keep the focus on the users and their perceived values in the application of ISDN. Southwestern Bell Telephone's experience with ISDN confirms that the application of this technology to provide customer focused solutions is the proper direction and priority.

Biography

Richard W. Stephenson is a graduate of Texas Tech University (B.S.E.E.). He is District Manager of Customer Applications Analysis at Southwestern Bell Telephone (SWBT), and directs the analysis group responsible for working with customers, marketing, and planning on the applications of new technologies. He was responsible for the creation and implementation of the SWBT Advanced Technology Laboratory in St. Louis, MO. He was also the initial Chairman of the ISDN Implementor's Workshop within the North American ISDN Users' Forum, which is headed by the National Institute of Standards and Technology.

Stephen A. McGaw is a graduate of Purdue University, with a B.S. in Industrial Engineering, and of Northwestern University, with an M.S. in computer science. He is Area Manager of Technology Planning at SWBT and has been responsible for applications of new technology in the telephone network since he joined two years ago. Prior to SWBT, he worked for AT&T Bell Laboratories in the Systems Engineering division on 5ESS Switching features and capabilities, with emphasis on ISDN. He also managed AT&T's technical trial of ISDN in Phoenix, AZ before joining SWBT.

(Continued from page 24)

[8]   CCITT Recommendation Q.921 (I.441), "ISDN User-Network Interface Data Link Layer Specification," 1988.
[9]   ANSI T1S1, "Frame Relaying Bearer Service: Architectural Framework and Service Description," ANSI document T1S1/88-185, Dec. 1988.
[10] ECMA TC32, "Packetized Data Transfer in Private Switching Networks," Draft Technical Report TR/PMA, ECMA/TC32/87/237, Nov. 1987.
[11] W. S. Lai, "Frame Relaying Service: An Overview," *Proc., IEEE Infocom '89*, Ottawa, Canada, Apr. 1989.
[12] IEEE Standards for Local Area Networks, "Logical Link Control," ANSI/IEEE Std. 802.2-1985, 1985.
[13] ISO Standard 8073, "Connection-Oriented Transport Protocol Specification," ISO 8073, 1986.
[14] MIL-STD 1778, "Transport Control Protocol," Defense Communications Agency, 1985.

Biography

Jim Lamont received his B.Sc. in mathematics from Queen's University, Canada, and his M.Sc. in computer science from the University of Alberta in 1980.

He joined Bell-Northern Research in 1980, participating in the development of their DPN packet-switching technology. In 1986, he moved to the Networks Technology Division, where he has been involved as a Member of Scientific Staff in various projects for high-speed data networking.

Man Him Hui received his B.Sc. from University of Hong Kong and his Ph.D. from the University of Chicago in 1973 in photophysics/photochemistry.

After continuing his research in the field at the University of Western Ontario and Canada's National Research Council, he joined Bell-Northern Research in 1977. Since then, he has been involved in the development and planning of projects on packet switching, common channel signalling, frame relaying, and LAN connectivity. He is currently managing a software development project for high-speed data networking.

By Edwin E. Mier

Appraising PBXs with an Eye Toward ISDN

Networking Professionals Need 20/20 Vision When it Comes Time to Size Up How Major PBX Vendors Are Supporting ISDN

It's 1995. After years of hype and marketing trials, the Integrated Services Digital Network is coming on-line at the local phone company. Now it's up to the corporate communications professionals to report on what's involved in shifting some or all of their operations to ISDN.

Of course, the place to start is with the tariffs to compare monthly costs. But what about existing data and telecommunications equipment? What will be involved in adapting it to ISDN? And will it be worth it?

Unfortunately, there's no simple answer. Too much still depends on just how strong customer demand for ISDN will be, a factor that will have a direct effect on the prices of ISDN equipment and adapters. Still, by looking at the current ISDN implementations and strategies of the leading PBX makers—AT&T, Northern Telecom Inc., and Rolm/IBM/Siemens—it's possible to draw a reasonably good picture of what the transition to ISDN will involve. This much is clear: Getting to ISDN from here will depend to a great extent on which PBX is the starting point.

For branch offices and small businesses linked to the public telephone network with 12 or fewer lines, the question is simple: Is it better to retain the present mode of access or replace one or more lines with ISDN basic-rate service?

For larger PBX-based sites, the issues are considerably more complex.

BACK TO BASIC RATE

If Northern Telecom's approach to ISDN basic-rate service on its DMS-100 central office switches is any indicator, access will be anything but easy.

The DMS-100, along with AT&T's 5ESS, represents most of the digital Class 5 central office switches capable of delivering ISDN service. In order to access basic-rate service, the phone company or the user (it's still unresolved) must install a device called an NT1 on the customer's premises (see Figure 1).

On the customer's side, the NT1 accepts equipment that communicates over a four-wire ISDN S/T or T interface (terminal adapters, PC plug-in boards, and so on). On the phone company side, the NT1 communicates over a single-pair U interface using 2B1Q (two binary, one quaternary) line code.

But so far, there have been no general tariff filings for ISDN basic-rate service, so it's unclear whether the NT1 will be included in the customer's monthly phone bills as a leased item (as telephones were before divestiture) or if it will be sold by local phone companies (or their unregulated equipment subsidiaries) as part of a basic-rate subscription.

Also unresolved is the cost of basic-rate service. Most analysts and phone-company sources agree that the charge for ISDN basic-rate access will be no more than about 1.5 times that of an equivalent analog telephone service loop. But this may be tough for the local telcos to sell to their state regulators. A Northern Telecom source says that the cost of an ISDN basic-rate line card, which is swapped in for an analog line card on a one-for-one basis, is five times that of the analog card.

Unfortunately, the price of the NT1 itself is also still up in the air. The devices used in ISDN basic-rate trials have all employed proprietary transmission techniques based on alternate mark inversion technology rather than 2B1Q. But the first fully compliant ISDN devices will be out soon: Semiconductor manufacturers like Motorola are busily delivering chip sets that handle 2B1Q signaling and line coding.

As noted, customers also will need new on-premises gear to tie to the NT1 over ISDN four-wire S or T interfaces. For attaching data devices, the easiest way to go will likely be a terminal adapter with a conventional EIA-232 port.

The terminal adapters that have been announced by Digital Equipment Corp., Fujitsu America Inc., General DataComm Inc., Harris Corp., Hayes Microcomputer Products Inc., IBM, and others will accommodate two to five devices plus one or more regular analog telephones (via the ubiquitous two-wire RJ-11 modular phone connection). In some cases, the devices will attach via V.35, making it possible to use a full 64-kbit/s B channel. Terminal adapters go for $1,000 to $1,500 (see "Tapping Into ISDN," April 1990).

But if customers are going to stick with conventional Touch-Tone phones and PCs and terminals communicating asynchronously at 19.2 kbit/s or less via an EIA-232 connection, there's little to be

> **If customers stick with Touch-Tone phones and async PCs and terminals there's little to be gained from ISDN basic-rate service.**

Figure 1: Upgrading to ISDN Basic Rate

Getting a line on ISDN features and services will require new and comparatively costly devices like terminal adapters, PC plug-in adapter cards, special phone sets, and NT1 links.

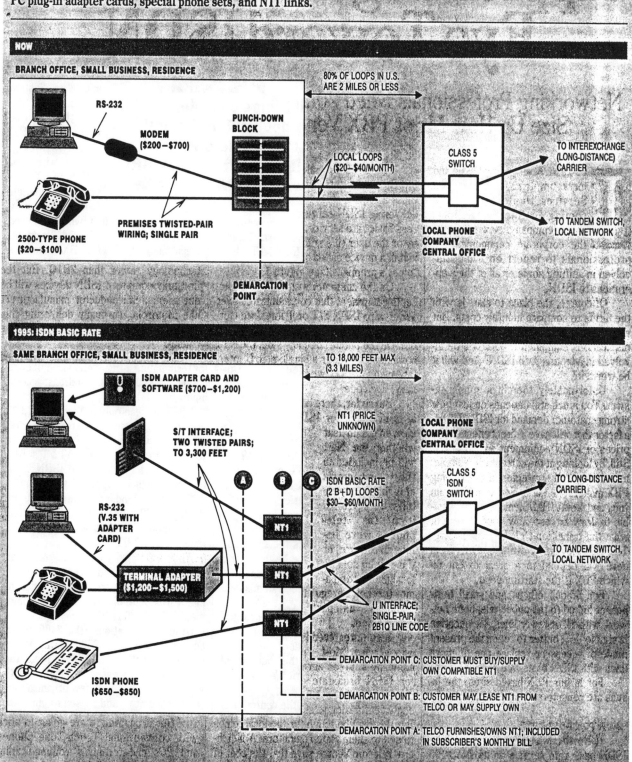

NOW

BRANCH OFFICE, SMALL BUSINESS, RESIDENCE

80% OF LOOPS IN U.S. ARE 2 MILES OR LESS

RS-232

MODEM ($200–$700)

PUNCH-DOWN BLOCK

LOCAL LOOPS ($20–$40/MONTH)

CLASS 5 SWITCH

TO INTEREXCHANGE (LONG-DISTANCE) CARRIER

PREMISES TWISTED-PAIR WIRING; SINGLE PAIR

2500-TYPE PHONE ($20–$100)

LOCAL PHONE COMPANY CENTRAL OFFICE

TO TANDEM SWITCH, LOCAL NETWORK

DEMARCATION POINT

1995: ISDN BASIC RATE

SAME BRANCH OFFICE, SMALL BUSINESS, RESIDENCE

TO 18,000 FEET MAX (3.3 MILES)

ISDN ADAPTER CARD AND SOFTWARE ($700–$1,200)

S/T INTERFACE; TWO TWISTED PAIRS; TO 3,300 FEET

NT1 (PRICE UNKNOWN)

LOCAL PHONE COMPANY CENTRAL OFFICE

RS-232 (V.35 WITH ADAPTER CARD)

Ⓐ Ⓑ Ⓒ

ISDN BASIC RATE (2 B+D) LOOPS $30–$60/MONTH

CLASS 5 ISDN SWITCH

TO LONG-DISTANCE CARRIER

NT1

TERMINAL ADAPTER ($1,200–$1,500)

NT1

NT1

TO TANDEM SWITCH, LOCAL NETWORK

U INTERFACE; SINGLE-PAIR, 2B1Q LINE CODE

ISDN PHONE ($650–$850)

DEMARCATION POINT C: CUSTOMER MUST BUY/SUPPLY OWN COMPATIBLE NT1

DEMARCATION POINT B: CUSTOMER MAY LEASE NT1 FROM TELCO OR MAY SUPPLY OWN

DEMARCATION POINT A: TELCO FURNISHES/OWNS NT1; INCLUDED IN SUBSCRIBER'S MONTHLY BILL

PBXs with ISDN

gained from using ISDN basic-rate service. Tapping into ISDN's advanced telephony features, such as automatic number identification, requires new phone sets. Similarly, boosting the speed of PC communications to 64 kbit/s requires plug-in boards and software. At the very least, a PC will need a board that provides a V.35 interface and synchronous connection— at $500 and up. Boards and software that let the PC access and use both B channels at full speed (or one B channel with a phone port) cost at least $1,000.

Northern Telecom is just one of the manufacturers offering new phones for ISDN basic-rate service. The 5309T and the 5317T work with the DMS-100 switch and retail for $650 to $850. There are some impressive features to be gained by using such phones, to be sure, but these must be weighed carefully against the significantly lower cost of regular analog phones, which start at about $20.

T1 TO PRIMARY RATE

Most communications managers will experience ISDN for the first time when they have to reconfigure a PBX to connect to an ISDN central office or directly to a long-distance carrier's central office over an ISDN primary-rate access line.

While an ISDN primary-rate interface (PRI) is virtually identical to T1 at the physical level—the same 1.544-Mbit/s signaling rate, over two pairs of wires, with the same distance constraints and repeater-spacing requirements— there are major differences at the message level.

With T1, all control and signaling is carried in the so-called robbed bits that are a part of each of the 24 subchannels. But the ISDN PRI moves all this traffic into one of the 24 subchannels, leaving the full 64-kbit/s capacity of the other 23 channels available for the user. The ISDN PRI is, at present, much more solid than the basic rate.

Primary-rate compatibility among PBX vendors and ISDN central office switches has been worked out and proven over the last year and a half. The standard against which most vendors measure their products is AT&T's primary-rate implementation on its 4ESS tandem central office switch (where long-distance carriers interface to the local telephone company).

"AT&T defined ISDN conformance procedures by publishing its specifica-

tion," acknowledges Micky Tsui, Northern Telecom's director of product line management for PBX systems (Santa Clara, Calif.). "The standard is relatively fixed, but the implementation is different from [one carrier's] service [to another's]." That means it's up to PBX vendors to support subtle differences in primary-rate implementations.

AT&T supports ISDN primary rate (along with other new features and capabilities) in the software for its recently revamped Definity line, a melding of its popular System 75 and 85 PBXs.

For System 85 users, primary-rate support is included in the Generic 2 software (along with support for AT&T's basic-rate ISDN). Actually, the basic-rate support is new; the last System 85 software (Release 2, Version 4) already accommodated the PRI.

Definity Generic 2 also involves some changes to the PBX's cache memory, increasing the system's overall call-processing capacity (see "PBX Upgrades: Forget the Forklift," March 1990). Some of this increased capacity is needed to accommodate the additional load that ISDN call-handling imposes on the system.

According to Mark Koenig, AT&T district manager for PBX product line planning (Bridgewater, N.J.), implementing an ISDN PRI on Generic 2/System 85 or Generic 1/System 75 requires only a software reconfiguration. The only additional hardware needed is the same line card that would otherwise be used for a T1 trunk. The ISDN D-channel call processing is managed by the system's central call processor.

Interestingly, Generic 1 does not support the ISDN basic-rate interface (BRI), while Generic 2 does. AT&T offers no clear reason for this, but part of the answer may be Generic 1's more limited processing power.

"In a BRI situation, the central processor has some additional things to do," acknowledges Koenig. "There's a lot of software [needed] to terminate a BRI link." How much isn't clear, but Generic 2 software represents a 20 percent to 30

percent increase over the software of System 85, says Koenig. (The Generic 1 uses an 80286 microprocessor, while Generic 2 uses a proprietary bit-slice processor, the 501CC.)

AT&T's basic-rate implementation and support apparently started with the Digital Communications Protocol (DCP) that AT&T had earlier developed for attaching its digital phone sets and terminals to System 75 and 85 PBXs.

"If you're wired for DCP," says Koenig, "you're wired for BRI." AT&T prescribes four-pair twisted-pair wiring

All things considered, it's doubtful that many customers will be clamoring to deploy BRI with their AT&T PBXs.

to each desktop, though two-pair is used for DCP. All things considered, it's doubtful that many of AT&T's PBX customers will be clamoring to deploy BRI equipment with their AT&T PBXs.

"I wouldn't encourage anyone to do it," confesses Koenig. And for good reason (see Figure 2):

□ BRI line cards have 12 ports, while DCP cards have eight. The per-port cost for terminating a BRI station is "not quite double" the cost of DCP stations, according to AT&T.

□ A BRI link can only run to about 1,900 feet using 24-gauge twisted-pair wire, compared with nearly 5,000 feet for a DCP connection. While AT&T's BRI links support the four-wire ISDN T interface, which is supposed to run up to 3,300 feet, extending it that far requires the use of 22-gauge wire. ISDN U interface support "is not available at this time," says AT&T.

□ While a Definity Generic 2 system can support both DCP and BRI stations at the same time, doing so requires different line cards and different station equipment. AT&T offers BRI equivalents to its existing DCP stations (the 7400 series supports DCP; the 7500 series is required for BRI connections). From the user's point of view, AT&T says, "both work identically." Still, few organizations would have any good reason to purchase and inventory both types.

□ Finally, there is a performance penalty exacted for deploying basic-rate ISDN on a Definity Generic 2 PBX. According to AT&T, a PBX that accommodates 10,000

PBXs with ISDN

DCP stations can handle only about 7,000 BRI stations.

Like AT&T, Northern Telecom supports the ISDN PRI interface in its basic SL-1 software, starting with the introduction early last year of Generic XII, Release 13.

Since then, Northern Telecom has shipped Release 14 and is said to be finishing Release 15. Part of the reason for these updates is changes in ISDN's primary-rate message structure.

"We're close to where X.25 was in 1976," says William Young, director of marketing for the firm's Meridian Business Systems unit (Santa Clara, Calif.), referring to the initial instability of the packet-switching interface specification of CCITT's X.25 recommendation. (X.25 was substantially revised when the second version came out in 1980, and again in 1984 with a third major revision.)

Adding primary-rate support also has increased the size and complexity of the SL-1 software, accounting for about an "additional 10 percent in terms of lines of code," says Northern Telecom's Tsui.

According to figures supplied by Northern Telecom, of the 35,000 SL-1 systems installed, nearly half are connected to at least one T1 link. And about 2,000 of those, or roughly 6 percent, are currently operating a primary-rate ISDN. (Most of these, sources say, are running from one SL-1 PBX to another SL-1 PBX; only about one in 20 are being used to access a carrier's ISDN primary-rate service.)

Northern Telecom is determined to provide one software release for the SL-1 that accommodates the ISDN primary-rate service of any telco (either local phone companies or interexchange carriers), and is close to achieving that goal.

According to Jean Poirier, group product manager for SL-1 networking at the Meridian Communications Systems division, the latest SL-1 software supports ISDN primary-rate service on AT&T's 5ESS or 4ESS (its Class 4 tandem or "toll" switch), as well as on Northern Telecom's DMS-100 and DMS-250 (Class 4) switches.

Poirier says customers still require different SL-1 software to access international primary-rate services, but he notes that "we're in the process of merging that, too." The SL-1's international primary-rate software has been checked against ISDN services provided on a wide array of foreign central office switches, including British Telecom's System 12 ISDN service; Ericsson's AXE-10 (Australia); and Siemens's EWSD switch (West Germany). Compatibility certification is expected later this year with Fujitsu's D70 central-office switches (Japan) and Alcatel's E10s (France).

MENU CONFIGURATION

An SL-1 customer in the U.S. configures the PBX for the appropriate ISDN primary-rate service simply by entering a four-letter command during installation, according to Poirier. The PBX software then automatically goes through all its ISDN modules and disables those not supported by the particular carrier's service or switch.

It's important to realize that there are subtle differences in ISDN primary-rate services even within the U.S. For instance, sources say that while AT&T, MCI, and Sprint all support automatic number identification, neither Sprint nor

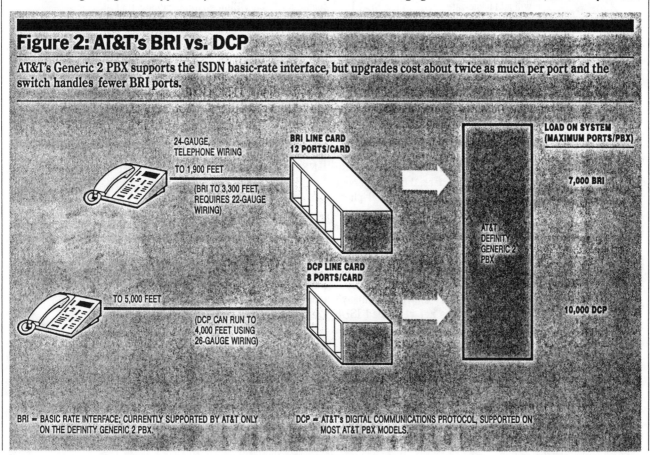

Figure 2: AT&T's BRI vs. DCP

AT&T's Generic 2 PBX supports the ISDN basic-rate interface, but upgrades cost about twice as much per port and the switch handles fewer BRI ports.

24-GAUGE, TELEPHONE WIRING TO 1,900 FEET

(BRI TO 3,300 FEET, REQUIRES 22-GAUGE WIRING)

BRI LINE CARD 12 PORTS/CARD

LOAD ON SYSTEM (MAXIMUM PORTS/PBX)

7,000 BRI

AT&T DEFINITY GENERIC 2 PBX

TO 5,000 FEET

DCP LINE CARD 8 PORTS/CARD

(DCP CAN RUN TO 4,000 FEET USING 26-GAUGE WIRING)

10,000 DCP

BRI = BASIC RATE INTERFACE; CURRENTLY SUPPORTED BY AT&T ONLY ON THE DEFINITY GENERIC 2 PBX.

DCP = AT&T's DIGITAL COMMUNICATIONS PROTOCOL; SUPPORTED ON MOST AT&T PBX MODELS.

PBXs with ISDN

MCI is expected to support call-by-call service selection in their initial service offerings, expected this summer.

While comprehensive ISDN primary-rate support is provided to SL-1 customers via the PBX software (releases earlier than Version 13 can be upgraded for a nominal charge), the customer must acquire and install a $1,700 D-channel handler card in order to run ISDN primary-rate service over any of the PBX's T1 trunk cards. One card can handle primary-rate service on up to 16 T1 trunks, provided all access the same carrier's ISDN PRI.

However, Poirier notes, "you need a different D-channel handler for each carrier's primary-rate service you are accessing [from the same SL-1 PBX]."

Northern Telecom supports ISDN basic-rate service only via its DMS-100 Class 5 central office switch—not on any of its SL-1 PBXs. The company's SL-100, which is the same as a phone company DMS-100 central office switch, supports basic-rate service in hardware. It is programmed to serve as a high-end PBX for more than 15,000 to 20,000 lines.

Whether Northern Telecom ever will add basic-rate ISDN to the SL-1 PBX line is unclear. If demand materializes for one of the biggest perceived benefits of ISDN—the ability to use any vendor's station equipment and plug into any PBX supporting the BRI—then Northern Telecom will have to add BRI support to remain competitive.

For now, though, Northern's digital station set does not meet the ISDN basic-rate specification. Resembling neither the single-wire-pair, 2B1Q U interface nor the four-wire S/T interface, the latest generation of Northern Telecom digital phone sets use a single-pair transmission and time-compression multiplexing to achieve a bandwidth of about 256 kbit/s between the switch and the set.

The No. 3 power in the U.S. PBX marketplace, Rolm Systems (now a wholly owned subsidiary of West Germany's Siemens A.G.) has not yet added ISDN support in any form to any of its CBX-II or 9750-Series of PBXs.

"The standards are basically there, but you've got to be able to do something with ISDN," says Ted Blumenstein, head of network requirements for the Rolm Co. (Unlike Rolm Systems, Rolm Co. handles the sales and service of Rolm PBXs and is jointly owned by IBM and Siemens. Both Rolm organizations currently are based in Santa Clara, Calif. However, management of Rolm Systems now is largely handled out of Siemens's U.S. headquarters in Boca Raton, Fla.). "Customers are in a learning phase," Blumenstein says. "By the end of 1990, you'll probably see enough applications [for demand to materialize]."

It is not clear what effect the acquisition of Rolm Systems by Siemens has had on ISDN development and deployment. The company maintains that primary-rate ISDN support is coming by the end of the year. However, there has been no word at all on basic-rate support.

According to Scott Augerson, director of product marketing and requirements for all of Siemens's PBX products in the U.S. (including CBXII and IBM's 9750 series), primary-rate support will be achieved on the 9751 via "an outboard ISDN adapter." This same adapter, which reportedly will handle all ISDN D-channel signaling, also will be supported on the earlier Rolm CBXII Models 8000 and 9000.

"Users won't know they're using the adapter," says Blumenstein, adding that among other functions it will deliver call-by-call selection to an ISDN primary-rate service provider. Rolm would not comment on the price of the ISDN adapter.

While AT&T, Northern Telecom, and Rolm still control the lion's share of the U.S. PBX market, there are many smaller players. Almost all of them have indicated that they plan ISDN support in one form or another. These include NEC's Business Systems Division (Melville, N.Y.), which has grown to control an estimated 9 percent of the U.S. market in the last five years.

But whether a charge-ahead deployment for ISDN is a prudent strategy for any PBX maker remains to be seen. From the users' perspective, ISDN is something that will certainly need to be addressed by U.S. communications managers—at least by 1995. But it's to be hoped that a clearer picture of ISDN service, pricing, and migration paths will emerge before then. ∎

Edwin E. Mier is president of Mier Communications Inc. (Princeton Junction, N.J.), a networking consultancy that publishes *Mier's Connections*, a series of loose-leaf guides to computer networking.

ISDN: Some Current Standards Difficulties

Does ISDN progress depend on the complicated and protracted process of standards making?

Mike W. Thomas

This year may see the long awaited "takeoff" of the ubiquitous ISDN. In a recent survey for ISDN in the US, Dataquest has forecast rapid growth at a CAGR of 80 per cent for the 1990-1994 time frame. In Europe, there have been similar projections. However, the humble user of telecommunication services might well be forgiven for being sceptical. All too often the story is the same: ISDN is delayed as the standards are not quite finished. The user might ask, "Why can't the ISDN standardization process be accelerated"? This paper will address this difficult topic by looking at some examples that serve to illustrate the complexity of this process.

It should be noted that any kind of standardization requires some consensus amongst the participants. For telecommunication standards such as ISDN, this is difficult. It is unlikely one could find a more heterogeneous collection of organizations. They have different business requirements and even political philosophies (state control led or private, regulated or

market driven, etc). Unfortunately, this leads to contradictory ISDN standards' requirements.

There are at least four different groups in every country that might be expected to have different ISDN standards requirements. First, there are customers (e.g., business users) who can use ISDN functionality to further their business objectives; second, there are service providers (e.g., PTTs and TAs) who can enhance their POTS networks with ISDN; third, there are equipment suppliers for which ISDN equipment is a new business opportunity; finally, there are regulators (e.g., FCC, Oftel) who can use ISDN standards as a way of introducing competition. This paper will also discuss how specific ISDN standardization difficulties are impacted by the different interests of these groups.

The ISDN standardization process has been in progress for over a decade. Within the CCITT — the global focal point for ISDN standardization — it is estimated that over 1000 man years have been spent at international meetings. The most recently agreed on results are for the study period 1984-1988 and are published in the so-called "Blue Book" Recommendations. In

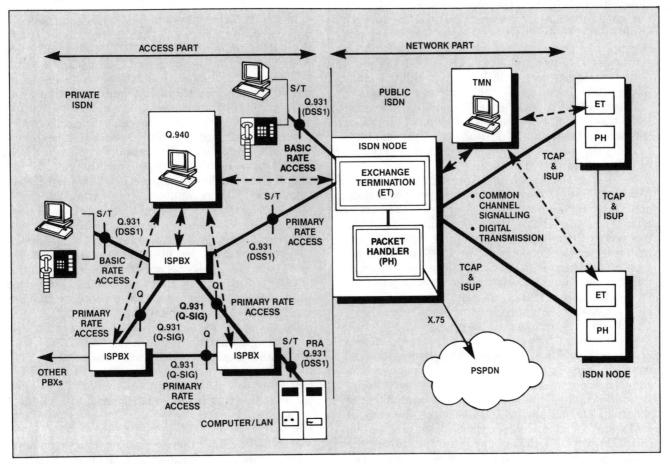

Fig. 1 CCITT ISDN functional architecture.

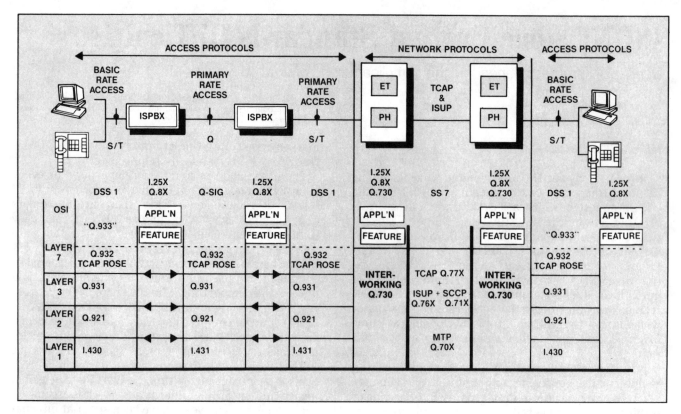

Fig. 2 CCITT ISDN protocol architecture.

these texts, ISDN standardization difficulties are identified either via options (i.e., alternative ways of doing the same function) or via areas marked "for further study", which indicates the function was either not discussed or there was not enough consensus on alternatives. Various regional (e.g., ANSI, ETSI, TTC, etc.) or national (e.g., BSI, AFNOR, DKE, NSG, etc.) standards often choose specific alternatives or options.

This can lead to incompatibilities within the same ISDN standard. For the user or the equipment supplier, this becomes a standards difficulty as equipment built to different options may not interwork in a network, or only interwork with difficulty.

ISDN standardization difficulties can be broadly placed in one of two categories: either technology constraints or nontechnology constraints. The technology constraints arise from the limitations of the technology (including software) in the context of existing networks. Remember that ISDN must evolve from the existing POTS networks. Examples of technology constraints include the U-reference point for basic rate access (BRA), the use of overlap versus enbloc signalling, and the use of stimulus versus functional signalling for featured telephony.

The nontechnology constraints arise from a mix of commercial, political, and regulatory issues. In some cases, the most active and knowledgeable participants come from organizations with monopolies to protect. Examples of nontechnology constraints include restrictions on the types of ISDN services, the issue of ONTs and VANs, and the issue of private or public ISDNs. In section 4, the difficulty in standardizing the "ring-again" feature illustrates some of these constraints.

CCITT ISDN NETWORK ARCHITECTURE

In the world of telecommunication standards, the only common architecture that has been agreed on by the global community is the CCITT ISDN architecture. In fact, the formal definition of CCITT ISDN is that it is a network architecture that provides "digital end-to-end connectivity through a limited set of network interfaces providing a wide range of service features evolving from the telephone integrated digital network to meet market needs into the twenty-first century".

This definition in itself breaks down the traditional barrier between the analogue voice world and the digital data world. No distinction is made between voice sets, PBXs, computers, workstations, or multiplexors. For the standardized basic services, all these devices process digital bit streams. Within the architecture, the higher-layer functionality and applications can be embedded in either the customer equipment or in the public network. In fact, the definition of CCITT ISDN implies that there are three architectures: a functional architecture, a protocol architecture, and a services architecture.

Details of the extent to which these architectures have been standardized are in the CCITT Blue Book Recommendations. A high-level view of the CCITT ISDN functional architecture is shown in **Figure 1**. A high-level view of the corresponding CCITT ISDN protocol architecture is shown in **Figure 2**.

CCITT ISDN Functional Architecture

The CCITT ISDN functional architecture consists of various functional entities (e.g., ETs, PHs, ISPBXs, NT1S, etc.), each of which has the capability to carry out various operations (e.g., switching, multiplexing, call processing, etc.). Functional entities are "logical" entities rather than real "physical" devices or systems. Often, a number of functional entities may be realized in one physical system.

Depending on political and regulatory constraints, these functional entities may be grouped in various ways to provide ISDN services to "users" at standardized interfaces called reference points (e.g., R, S, T, U, Q, etc.). The portion seen by the end user is sometimes called the access part of the ISDN (or, in nonstandards jargon, the private ISDN because it involves equipment which is under the control of the "user" and not the service provider).

The other portion consists of functional entities that are under the control of the service providers (e.g., PTTs and TAs). This is sometimes called the "network part" of the ISDN (or, in nonstandards jargon, the "public ISDN" because the service is generally publicly available). In general, standardized interfaces (not visible to the user) are defined between the functional entities within the network part of the ISDN.

For many years, the CCITT has undertaken the global responsibility for the standardization of the entire network part of the ISDN and much of the access part. Recently, organizations such as ISO and the IEC have started to develop standards for specific areas of the access part of the ISDN (e.g., the Q-reference point). Historically, the CCITT has been dominated by service providers (in particular the PTT monopolies). With the trend towards liberalization of service provision (particularly for nonvoice services), it is likely that some "users" will themselves become specialist "service providers" for value-added services.

This will blur the distinction between "user" and "service provider". Although this will not change the CCITT functional architecture, it may cause functional entities to migrate between the access part and the network part.

Within the access part, the important interfaces are the BRA interface (2B+D) and the primary rate access (PRA) interface (30B+D). They are defined at the S/T reference point for both terminal and integrated services PBX (ISPBX) access to the public ISDN, as well as for terminal access to an ISPBX in the private ISDN. It should be noted that PRA is also defined at the Q-reference point for interworking between ISPBXs. The protocols defined for the access part belong to the Digital Subscriber Signalling System No. 1 (DSS 1) family and are specified in the CCITT Blue Book (1988). For example, the Q.931 protocol specifies the procedures for basic ISDN calls.

Also shown is the user-network management entity, the architecture that is specified in Q.940. As much as possible, all access protocols are based on Q.931 at layer 3. This minimizes the need to develop different software and procedures for different interfaces. Moreover, as changes are made, such as new features or services, they can be applied concurrently to all interfaces. Since Q.931 PRA is used for both public and private ISDN, it means that the "user" has the choice of using either the lines between ISPBXs or interworking via the public ISDN.

Within the network part of the ISDN, a number of functional entities such as the telecommunications management network (TMN) and the ISDN node are defined. In general, for each country, the public ISDN will evolve from the existing PSTN. For many reasons,

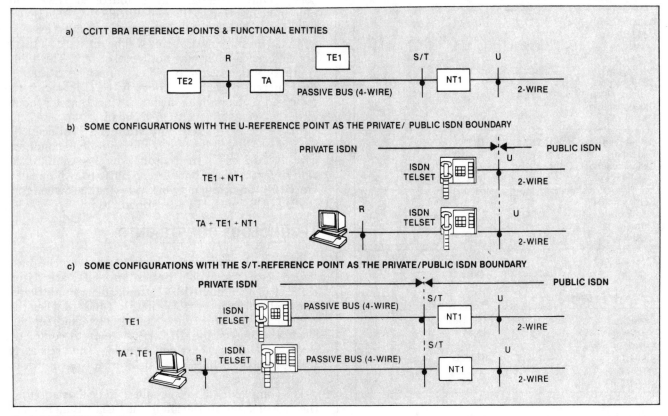

Fig. 3 CCITT ISDN BRA reference points.

every country has a different evolution path; so the standardization focus is very much on peer-to-peer communications between functional entities through the Signalling System No. 7 (SS 7) family of protocols. For functional entities with ISDN capabilities, two essential protocol sets indicated in **Figure 1** are the ISDN user part (ISUP) and the transaction capability applications protocol (TCAP).

As the ISDN evolves and functional entities migrate, it can be seen from **Figure 1** that interworking between the private ISDN and the public ISDN will be important. For example, Q.940 will need to interwork with TMN. For new services and transparent feature transport, DSS 1 will need to interwork with SS 7 to provide end-to-end networkwide services; examples include the 800 service in North America, access to public packet-switched data networks (PSPDNs), and to wide area centrex networks or virtual private networks (VPNs). These aspects can be discussed in the context of the CCITT ISDN protocol architecture.

CCITT ISDN Protocol Architecture

The CCITT ISDN protocol architecture consists of two protocol stacks, one for the "access" protocols, and one for the "network" protocols, as shown in **Figure 2** for the various reference points of the functional architecture. The diagram shows how the protocols function in a hybrid network (i.e., combination of private ISDN and public ISDN) to provide end-to-end interworking. The access protocol stack follows the OSI seven-layer model and consists of Q.931, Q.921, and I.430/431 for the first three layers. Above layer 3, the Recommendation Q.932 defines procedures to convey features and applications using TCAP and ROSE, which are defined elsewhere in ISO and CCITT standards.

In general, these map onto equivalent procedures in SS 7 to allow for end-to-end interworking. The network protocol stack (collectively known as SS 7) does not exactly follow the OSI seven-layer model as shown on the diagram. There are a large number of SS 7 protocols. The key ones for ISDN are ISUP (Q.76X), TCAP (Q.77X), and SCCP (Q.71X). Interworking between these and DSS 1 is defined in Q.730. The message of this diagram is that ISDN protocols are complex. However, the good news is end-to-end interworking is defined, and global feature transport is already defined in the CCITT Blue Book Recommendations using Q.932 and TCAP/SCCP.

In addition, a number of features or supplementary services have been partially standardized. The extent of standardization to the end of 1988 (i.e., Blue Book) is shown in **Table 1**. All that remains in most cases is protocol definitions. But this will be difficult as there are differences that may not be resolvable. This table represents the degree of global consensus after approximately 6 years of effort in CCITT standards forums. The diagram highlights the fact that it is much easier to get agreement in a small group (e.g., for DPNSS). Unfortunately, any standard produced by such a group will have only national or regional acceptability. Some of the reasons why the standardization of featured telephony is so difficult will be illustrated for the case of networkwide ring back when free (called CCBS in CCITT) described later.

TECHNOLOGY CONSTRAINTS

The rapid advances in technology over the past decade (e.g., VLSI, fiber optics, and software structures) has itself made ISDN standardization difficult. The problem is: how to formulate a standard when the technology is either uncertain or changing rapidly. Given that any standard takes 4 years to complete, does one stick with current technology (and risk early obsolescence), or does one risk intercepting unproven new technology?

The complexity of these issues can be illustrated by the lack of standardization in the CCITT Blue Book of the U-reference point. Early in the last decade, it was

TABLE 1
ISDN "FEATURES" IN CCITT BLUE BOOK

Supplementary Service	STAGE I Service Definitions	STAGE II Information Flows	STAGE III Protocols	
	1.25X	Q.8X	Q.730	Q.93X
Direct dial-in	1.251.1	Q.81.1	√	√
Multiple sub num	1.251.2	x	√	√
Calling line id pres	1.251.3	Q.81.3	√	√
Calling line id res	1.251.4	Q.81.4	√	√
Connected line id pres	1.251.5	Q.81.5	√	√
Connected line id res	1.251.6	Q.81.6	√	√
Malicious call id	x	x	√	x
Subaddressing	x	x	√	√
Call transfer	1.252.1	x	x	x
Call forward busy	1.252.2	Q.82.2	√	√
Call forward no reply	1.252.3	Q.82.2	√	√
Call forward unconditional	I.252.4	Q.82.2	√	√
Call deflection	x	x	x	x
Line hunting	I.252.6	Q.82.2	√	√
Call waiting	I.253.1	Q.83.1	x	x
Call hold	I.253.2	Q.83.2	x	x
Call completion to busy sub	x	x	?	x
Conference calling	I.254.1	x	x	x
Three party service	I.254.2	x	x	x
Closed user group	I.255.1	Q.85.1	√	x
Private numbering plan	x	x	x	x
Credit card calling	x	Q.86.1	x	x
Advice of charge	I.256.2	Q.86.2	x	x
Reverse charging	x	x	x	x
User-to-user signalling	I.257.1	Q.87.1	√	√

recognized that if ISDN was ever to be ubiquitous, it would need to use the existing two-wire subscriber loops that are designed for analogue telephones. The problem then was how to deliver ISDN BRA high-speed digital services cost-effectively over a two-wire analogue infrastructure. The key technical issue is the design of a low-power, sophisticated VLSI device that can squeeze maximum error-free bandwidth from the local loop. To be economic, however, the VLSI device must be simple and produced in large volumes.

Development of ISDN standards is constrained by commercial, political, and regulatory issues . . . .

· · · · · · · · · · · · · ·

Historically, subscriber loops vary a great deal between countries. It is not surprising then that there are at least five different standards for the U-reference point. Some countries have not yet decided whether burst mode (also called TCM, or ping pong) or echo cancelling hybrid (ECH) technology should be used at the U-interface. This is a technology trade-off issue as

TCM is less complex than ECH, but ECH has a longer reach. Thus the choice depends on the average length of subscriber loops in that country. There is a further technical trade-off for the choice of transmission encoding scheme. There is a standard for North America (2B1Q) but as yet no unique standard for either Europe (both 4B3T and 3B2T are used) or the CCITT. Again the choice depends on the characteristics of the subscriber loops.

In order to surmount the technical difficulties in developing a digital interface, the CCITT defined four separate reference points for the standardization of the BRA interface. They are:

- the R-reference point for existing standards (e.g., X.21, V.24),
- the S-reference point,
- the T-reference point (which may coincide to form the S/T-reference point),
- the U-reference point.

These reference points are shown in **Figure 3a** together with their associated functional entities (NT1, NT2, TE1, TE2, TA). The S/T-reference is a four- (or more) wire interface that is structured as a "passive bus" to support up to eight different physical devices (and 128 logical devices). This bus has two 64-kps channels (B channels) and one 16-kps data and signalling channel (D channel). In principle, B channels can be used for any service (i.e., voice or data). It

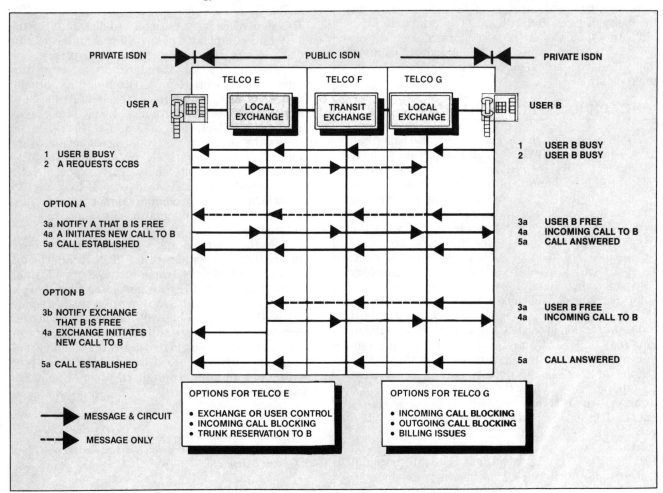

Fig. 4 Some "CCBS" options.

should be noted that currently CCITT ISDN BRA standards are fully defined only at the S/T-reference point.

A consequence of multiple reference points for BRA is that different regions have chosen different points for the boundary between private and public ISDNs. In the US, the U-reference point has been chosen, whereas in Europe, the S/T-reference point has been chosen. The result is that functional entities are realized differently as is shown in **Figures 3b** and **3c**. It should be noted that any of the **3c** configurations can also be used in **3b**, as the "user" can choose a suitable NT1.

*S*tandardization of the U-reference point depends upon the characteristics of the subscriber loop....

. . . .

In general, combining functional entities can lower the overall interface cost so that one might expect the cost of the **3a** combined TE1+NT1 in **3b** to be less than the cost of the separate TE1 and NT1 in **3c**. However, this is offset by the fact that in **3c** one unit is owned by the public ISDN and the other by the "user". Furthermore, the configuration of **3c** incorporates the flexibility of the standardized S/T interface. In principle, this should offer the user more choice. What is clear is that there is incompatibility. Lack of compatibility leads to market fragmentation and loss of economies of scale.

NONTECHNOLOGY CONSTRAINTS

The networkwide ring again feature (also called call back when free (CBWF), or call completion to busy subscriber (CCBS) is considered by many "users" to be one of the most important business communication features. The feature allows a user who attempts to call a busy subscriber to have the network monitor the busy called party. The calling user is notified when the busy called party becomes free, and upon accepting the notification, the call is placed to the subscriber. There are variations of the feature, but no technology constraints. In fact, any low-cost PC has the necessary call-processing capability to implement the feature. In CCITT over the last decade, the only visible standard is a small section in the Red Book (1980-1984) version of Q.764 (ISUP). In **Table 1**, one can see that it is one of the services that has not progressed to stage 1.

Some of the difficulties can be seen by considering a simplified view of how the CCBS feature works in a network. This is shown by means of the message sequence diagram of **Figure 4**. Also shown are the public and private ISDN boundaries.

In addition, the public ISDN may be split into telcos E, F, & G. This then represents either an international call or a national call where liberalization has occurred. Two types of message flows are involved. The solid arrows indicate that both messages and circuits (and other resources such as switching) are involved. The other arrow indicates that only messages are involved. The message sequences show two options. In option A, the user (i.e., private ISDN) has full control of the service. In option B, the telco E reserves a trunk to G before the user A fully accepts the call (user A may now be busy on another call). There is a commercial difficulty here as a telco wants to maximize the use of circuits (e.g., trunks) yet have an acceptable level of congestion.

Some telcos do not want trunk reservation (option B); others see it as essential to guarantee a path to user B. However, this means that user B must not now be busy. This means the telco G must partially block user C from making or receiving calls that CCBS has invoked. Some regulators would see this as a violation of the basic right of user C to have full control over making calls. The situation becomes more complex when the "users" are in fact entry points for private ISDN networks. The agreement here is that telco E should treat user A in the same way as it treats telco F or G. However, in some cases this would weaken the PTT monopoly.

There are other issues such as blocking user A, billing for reserved trunks, and far-end call initiation. The key point is that there is difficulty in getting a unique service definition standardized at the present time.

CONCLUSION

This paper has used examples to illustrate the difficulty and complexity of the ISDN standardization process. Given the difficulties, it is surprising that there has been any ISDN standardization. However, by common agreement, there exists today a workable global set of ISDN standards in the CCITT Blue Book that is compatible with the almost 1 billion telephones in the world. In fact, some believe that it is necessary to resist the pressures for rapid acceleration of the standards and to work instead by full consensus to get maximum global connectivity. This is perhaps the eternal standards question: does one look for full compatibility to get maximum connectivity, or does one look for minimum compatibility to encourage new functionality?

Finally, there are a number of new technical developments that will lead to future ISDN standards difficulties. These include frame relay versus ATM and the integration of ISDN with mobile/cordless telephony standards. In addition, the widespread deployment of fibre optic cable will remove some current technology constraints and blur nontechnology constraints. However, the current ISDN functional architecture, protocol architecture, and service architecture are flexible enough to cope with these challenges. □

Mike Thomas *is director of corporate networks and ISDN at Northern Telecom Europe Ltd., Maidenhead, UK.*

Chapter 2: ISDN Protocols and Network Architecture

Network architecture

Figure 2-1, based on a figure in CCITT Recommendation I.325, depicts the basic ISDN services. ISDN will support a completely new physical connecter (or interface) for users, a digital subscriber loop, and a variety of transmission services.

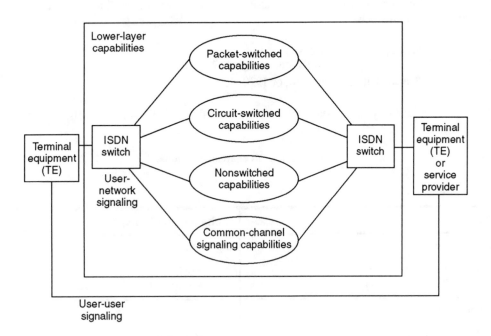

Figure 2-1. ISDN architecture.

The common physical interface provides a standardized means of attaching to the network. The same interface should be usable for the telephone and for computer and videotex terminals. Protocols are required to define the exchange of control information between the user device and the network. Provision must be made for high-speed interfaces to, for example, a digital PBX or an LAN. The interface supports a basic service consisting of three time-multiplexed channels: two at 64 Kbps and one at 16 Kbps. In addition, a primary service provides multiple 64-Kbps channels.

The subscriber loop provides the physical signal path from subscriber to the ISDN central office. This loop must support full-duplex digital transmission for both basic and primary data rates. Initially, much of the subscriber loop plant will be twisted pair. As the network evolves and grows, optical fiber will be used increasingly.

The ISDN central office connects the numerous subscriber loops to the digital network, thus providing access to a variety of lower layer (OSI layers 1 through 3) transmission functions, including packet-switched, circuit-switched, and dedicated facilities. In addition, common-channel signaling, used to control the network and provide call management, will be accessible to the user. This signaling will allow user-network control dialogue. The use of these control-signaling protocols for user-to-user dialogue is a subject for further study within the CCITT. By and large, these lower layer functions will be implemented within ISDN. In some countries with a competitive climate, some of these lower layer functions (for example, packet switching) may be provided by separate networks that may be reached by a subscriber through ISDN.

With ISDN, there will also be higher layer (OSI layers 4 through 7) functions, which will support applications such as Teletex, facsimile, and transaction processing. These functions may be implemented within ISDN, provided by separate networks, or provided by a mixture of the two.

Channels and transmission structures

Channels. The digital pipe between the central office and the ISDN subscriber will be used to carry a number of communication channels. The capacity of the pipe, and therefore the number of channels carried, may vary from user to user. The transmission structure of any access link will be constructed from the following types of channels:

- B channel, with a capacity of 64 Kbps;
- D channel, with a capacity of 16 or 64 Kbps; and
- H channel, with a capacity of 384, 1536, or 1920 Kbps.

Table 2-1 summarizes the types of data traffic to be supported on the B and D channels.

Table 2-1. ISDN channel functions.

B channel (64 Kbps)	D channel (64 Kbps)
Digitized voice	Signaling

64-Kbps pulse-code modulation
    Low bit rate (32 Kbps)
	Basic
	    Enhanced

High-speed data	Low-speed data

Packet-switched
    Circuit-switched
	Videotex
	    Teletex
	    Terminal

Other	Telemetry

Facsimile
    Slow-scan video
	Emergency services
	    Energy management

B channel. The B channel is the basic user channel. It can be used to carry digital data, digitized voice, or a mixture of lower rate traffic, including digital data and digitized voice encoded at a fraction of 64 Kbps. In the case of mixed traffic, all traffic of the B channel must be destined for the same end point; that is, the elemental unit of circuit switching is the B channel. If a B channel consists of two or more subchannels, all subchannels must be carried over the same circuit between the same subscribers. Three kinds of connections can be set up over a B channel, as follows:

- Packet-switched. The user is connected to a packet-switching node, and data are exchanged with other users via X.25.
- Circuit-switched. This connection is equivalent to switched digital service, which is available today. The user places a call, and a circuit-switched connection is established with another network user.
- Semipermanent. This connection to another user is set up by prior arrangement and does not require a call establishment protocol. It is equivalent to a leased line.

The designation of 64 Kbps as the standard user channel rate highlights a fundamental disadvantage of standardization. The rate was chosen as the most effective for digitized voice, yet the technology has progressed to the point that 32 Kbps, or even less, will produce equally satisfactory voice reproduction. To be effective, a standard must freeze the technology at some defined point. Yet by the time the standard is approved, it may already be obsolete.

D channel. The D channel serves two main purposes. First, it carries signaling information to control circuit-switched calls on associated B channels at the user interface. That is, if a user wishes to place a call on a B channel, a control message requesting the connection is sent on the D channel to the ISDN central office. The D channel is used to set up calls on all of the B channels at the customer's interface. This technique is known as "common-channel signaling," as the D channel is a common channel for providing control signals for all of the other channels. Common-channel signaling allows the other (B) channels to be used more efficiently. Secondly, in addition to its use for control signaling, the D channel may be used for packet switching or low-speed telemetry at times when no signaling information is waiting.

H channel. The H channel is provided for user information at higher bit rates. The user may use such a channel as a high-speed trunk or may subdivide the channel according to the user's own time-division multiplexing (TDM) scheme. Examples of applications include fast facsimile, video, high-speed data, high-quality audio, and multiplexed information streams at lower data rates.

Transmission structures. The preceding channel types are grouped into transmission structures that are offered as a package to the user. The best-defined structures at this time are

* The basic channel structure, referred to as "basic access," and
* The primary channel structure, referred to as "primary access."

Basic access. Basic access consists of two full-duplex 64-Kbps B channels and a full-duplex 16-Kbps D channel. The total bit rate, by simple arithmetic, is 144 Kbps. However, framing, synchronization, and other overhead bits bring the total bit rate on a basic-access link to 192 Kbps. The basic service is intended to meet the needs of most individual users, including residential subscribers and very small offices. It allows the simultaneous use of voice and several data applications, such as packet-switched access, a link to a central alarm service, facsimile, Teletex, and so on. These services could be accessed through a single, multifunction terminal or several separate terminals. In either case, a single physical interface is provided. Most existing twisted-pair local loops can support this interface.

In some cases, one or both of the B channels remain unused. This results in either a B + D or a D interface, rather than the 2B + D interface. However, to simplify the network implementation, the data rate at the interface remains at 192 Kbps. Nevertheless, for those subscribers with more modest transmission requirements, there may be a cost savings in using a reduced basic interface.

Primary access. Primary access is intended for users with greater capacity requirements, such as offices with a digital PBX or an LAN. Because of differences in the digital-transmission hierarchies used in different countries, it was not possible to get agreement on a single data rate. The United States, Canada, and Japan make use of a transmission structure based on 1.544 Mbps; this corresponds to the T1 transmission facility of AT&T. In Europe, 2.048 Mbps is the standard rate. Both of these data rates are provided as a primary interface service. Typically, the channel structure for the 1.544-Mbps rate will be 23 B channels plus one 64-Kbps D channel. For the 2.048-Mbps rate, the channel structure will be 30 B channels plus one 64-Kbps D channel. Again, it is possible for a customer with lesser requirements to employ fewer B channels, in which case the channel structure is $nB + D$, where n ranges from 1 to 23 or from 1 to 30 for the two primary services, respectively. Also, a customer with high-data-rate demands may be provided with more than one primary physical interface. In this case, a single D channel on one of the interfaces may suffice for all signaling needs, and the other interfaces may consist solely of B channels (24B or 31B).

The primary interface may also be used to support H channels. Some of these channel structures include a 64-Kbps D channel for control signaling. When no D channel is present, it is assumed that a D channel on another primary interface at the same subscriber location will provide any required signaling. The following structures are recognized for primary access:

- Primary-rate interface H0 channel structures. This interface supports multiple 384-Kbps H0 channels. The structures are 3H0 + D and 4H0 for the 1.544-Mbps interface and 5H0 + D for the 2.048-Mbps interface.
- Primary-rate interface H1 channel structures. The H11 channel structure consists of one 1536-Kbps H11 channel. The H12 channel structure consists of one 1920-Kbps H12 channel and one D channel.
- Primary-rate interface structures for mixtures of B and H0 channels. This interface consists of zero or one D channel plus any possible combination of B and H0 channels up to the capacity of the physical interface (for example, 3H0 + 5B + D and 3H0 + 6B).

Protocol architecture

The development of standards for ISDN includes, of course, the development of protocols for interaction between ISDN users and the network and for interaction between two ISDN users. Fitting these new ISDN protocols into the OSI framework would be desirable. To a great extent, this has been done; however, certain requirements for ISDN are not met within the current structure of OSI. Examples of these required functions are

- Multiple related protocols. ISDN will allow, for example, the use of a protocol on the D channel to set up, maintain, and terminate a connection on a B channel.
- Multimedia calls. ISDN will allow a call to be set up that allows information flow consisting of multiple types, such as voice, data, facsimile, and control signals.
- Multipoint connections. ISDN will allow conference calls.

These and other required functions are not directly addressed in the current OSI specification. However, the basic seven-layer framework appears valid even in the ISDN context. The issue of the exact relationship between ISDN and OSI remains one for further study.

Figure 2-2 suggests the relationship between OSI and ISDN with the seven layers of the OSI model that are shown on the left in the figure. As a network, ISDN is essentially unconcerned with user layers 4 through 7, which are end-to-end layers employed by the user for the exchange of information. Network access is concerned only with layers 1 through 3. The physical interface for basic access and primary access corresponds to OSI layer 1. Basic access and primary access are specified in Recommendations I.430 and I.431, respectively. Since the B and D channels are multiplexed over the same physical interface, Recommendations I.430 and I.431 apply to both types of channels. Above layer 1, the protocol structure differs for the two channels.

For the D channel, a new data link layer standard, LAPD, has been defined. This standard is based on high-level data link control (HDLC), modified to meet ISDN requirements. All transmission on the D channel is in the form of LAPD frames that are exchanged between the subscriber equipment and an ISDN switching element. Three applications are supported: control signaling, packet switching, and telemetry. For control signaling, a call control protocol has been defined (Recommendation I.451/Q.931). This protocol is used to establish, maintain, and terminate connections on B channels. Thus, it is a protocol between the user and the network. Above layer 3, there is the possibility for higher layer functions associated with user-to-user control signaling. These functions are a subject for further study. The D channel can also be used to provide packet-switching services to the subscriber. In this case, the X.25 level 3 protocol is used, and X.25 packets are transmitted in LAPD frames. The X.25 level 3 protocol is used to establish virtual circuits on the D channel to other users and to exchange packetized data. The final application area, telemetry, is a subject for further study.

The B channel can be used for circuit switching, semipermanent circuits, and packet switching. For circuit switching, a circuit is set up on a B channel on demand. The D-channel call control protocol is used for this purpose. Once the circuit has been set up, it may be used for data transfer between the users. Recall from Chapter 2 that a circuit-switched network provides a transparent data path between communication stations. A semipermanent circuit is a B-channel circuit that is set up by prior agreement between the connected users and the network. As with a circuit-switched connection, it provides a transparent data path between end systems. With either a circuit-switched connection or a semipermanent circuit, it appears to the connected stations that they have a direct, full-duplex link with one another. They are free to use their own formats, protocols, and frame synchronization. Hence, from the point of view of ISDN, layers 2 through 7 are neither visible nor specified. However, in addition, the CCITT has standardized Recommendation I.465/V.120, which does provide a common link control functionality for ISDN subscribers. In the case of packet switching, a circuit-switched connection is set up on a B channel between the user and a packet-switched node using the D-channel control protocol. Once the circuit has been set up on the B channel, the user employs X.25 layers 2 and 3 to establish a virtual circuit to another user over that channel and to exchange packetized data.

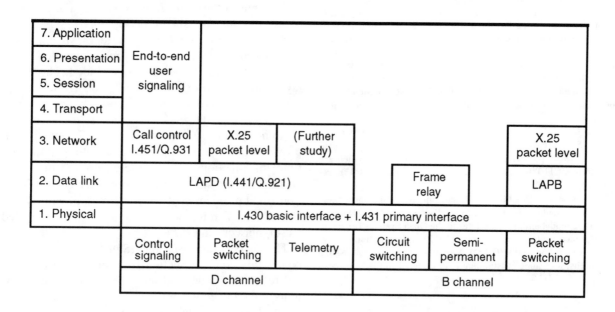

Figure 2-2. ISDN protocol architecture at the user-network interface.

Paper summary

The first paper included in this chapter, "ISDN Protocols for Connection Control," by Harman and Newman, is a detailed technical description of Recommendation I.451/Q.931, which is the call control protocol for the ISDN user-network interface.

"ISDN Computer-Aided Telephony," by Cvijan et al., examines the interface and protocol architectures to support various telephony-based applications, such as telemarketing, customer service, remote retailing, and real estate browsing.

The final paper in this chapter, "Common Channel Signaling System Number 7 for ISDN and Intelligent Networks," by Jabbari, is an in-depth, detailed look at Signaling System Number 7 (SS7).

ISDN Protocols for Connection Control

WENDY M. HARMAN AND CHERYL F. NEWMAN, MEMBER, IEEE

Abstract—The term Integrated Services Digital Network (ISDN) refers to the integration of various communication services that are transported over a single digital facility at the user–network interface. With ISDN, a user can have access to voice, circuit-switched data, or packet-switched data over one physical interface. ISDN provides communication control that allows users to request services while on a call, and to send and receive communication control messages independently of the voice, data, or video calls.

The ISDN concept has moved toward maturity over the past decade. The International Telegraph and Telephone Consultative Committee (CCITT), a technical standards organization of the United Nations, is responsible for establishing Recommendations that apply to aspects of international communication. The publication of the *Red Book* version of the ISDN Recommendations in 1985 instigated development of ISDN switches and the testing of ISDN with user trials. The ISDN Recommendations have been updated, are more complete, and include descriptions of many services. These updated ISDN Recommendations were published in the *Blue Book* version of the I-series Recommendations early in 1989.

The main focus of this paper is the description of the technical details of the ISDN access protocols for connection control. These protocols are the ISDN physical layer, link layer, and layer 3 which are documented in CCITT Recommendations I.430, I.441, and I.451, respectively.

This paper also describes other work that supports or enhances these protocols. In particular, coverage includes discussion of the ISDN protocol reference model and how it relates to the Open Systems Interconnection reference model, and a new CCITT Recommendation on service feature control on ISDN (Q.932). Possible uses of ISDN, possible evolution paths, and some outstanding issues related to ISDN are also described.

I. INTRODUCTION

THE term Integrated Services Digital Network (ISDN) refers to the integration of various communication services that are transported over a single digital facility at the user–network interface. With ISDN, a user can have access to voice, circuit-switched data, or packet-switched data over one physical interface. ISDN provides communication control that allows users to request services while on a call, and to send and receive communication control messages independently of the voice, data, or video calls.

The ISDN concept has moved toward maturity over the past decade. The International Telegraph and Telephone Consultative Committee (CCITT), a technical standards organization of the United Nations, is responsible for establishing Recommendations that apply to aspects of international communication. During the 1981–1984 CCITT study period, ISDN was first addressed in the interna-

tional arena. The complete output of this work is in the I-series Recommendations of the *Red Book* [1]. The publication of the *Red Book* version of the ISDN Recommendations instigated development of ISDN switches and the testing of ISDN with user trials. The ISDN Recommendations have been updated and are more complete during the 1985–1988 CCITT Study period and include descriptions of many services. These updated ISDN Recommendations are in the *Blue Book* version of the I-series Recommendations published early in 1989.

Only the connection control protocols over access links to ISDN are addressed in this paper. The physical layer, the link layer, and "layer 3" are included. These protocol layers are defined to work at the S and T reference points which are logically defined by network termination functions (see Fig. 1). A T reference point occurs on the customer premises after the Network Termination 1 that provides the line termination, and optionally some multiplexing functions. The S reference point occurs on the customer premises after the optional Network Termination 2 that provides switching and multiplexing functions. The S and T reference points are generally called the "user–network interface."

This paper addresses the ISDN access protocols for connection control. Section II describes the ISDN protocol reference model and how it relates to the Open Systems Interconnection reference model. Technical details of the ISDN physical layer, link layer, and layer 3 protocols are addressed in Sections III, IV, and V. A new CCITT Recommendation on control of service features associated with connections (supplementary services) on ISDN (Recommendation Q.932) is summarized in Section VI. Possible uses of ISDN and possible evolution paths are described in Section VII, Section VIII discusses some outstanding issues related to ISDN, and Section IX briefly summarizes the paper.

II. ISDN PROTOCOL REFERENCE MODEL

The overall ISDN Generic Protocol Block architecture is shown in Fig. 2, representing three types of information with parallel protocol layering. The three types of information are control, user, and management, each of which is communicated independently of the others. The logical separation of the ISDN control information from user information through all layers stems from this ISDN protocol reference model. In contrast, the Open Systems Interconnection (OSI) model [2], [3] allows the separation of control from user information, but the OSI model does not *require* such a separation.

Manuscript received July 1, 1988; revised March 1, 1989.

The authors are with Bell Communications Research, Inc., Red Bank, NJ 07701.

IEEE Log Number 8929562.

0-8186-2797-2/92 $3.00 © 1989 IEEE

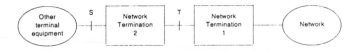

Network Termination 1: terminates the loop transmission, can perform other functions such as multiplexing
Network Termination 2 (optional): can perform functions such as switching and multiplexing

Fig. 1. *S* and *T* reference points.

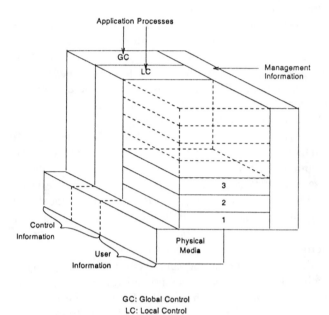

GC: Global Control
LC: Local Control

Fig. 2. Generic protocol block.

ISDN is designed to serve multiple applications, including voice, video, and data. Therefore, it is not practical for all layers to always provide functionality. While roughly modeled after OSI, the layers are explicitly not named. Adjacent layers within a type of information communicate using service primitives. However, if a layer is empty, the primitives are mapped directly onto primitives for the next nonempty layer.

In the *Blue Book* version of the ISDN protocol reference model (Recommendation I.320) [4], the concepts of local control and global control are introduced as refinements of the ISDN control information (see Fig. 2). Local control (LC) is control used between (logically) adjacent peer entities (within the same layer of protocol). Global control (GC) is used between two arbitrary peer entities where these entities are expected to be "remote" from each other. Coordination among all information types is accomplished using the management information type.

III. PHYSICAL LAYER

ISDN currently has two physical layer interface specifications, the basic rate user–network interface and the primary rate user–network interface. In both interfaces, layer primitives are defined whose primary function is to activate and deactivate the physical layer, providing service to the link layer.

The basic rate interface physical layer is defined in Recommendation I.430 [4] as 192 kbits/s with well-defined framing.[1] The most common structure on the basic rate interface provides "2*B* + *D*," two 64 kbit/s information transport channels (called *B* channels) and one 16 kbit/s packetized control and information transport channel (called a *D* channel). At least two features in the basic rate interface are worthy of note with respect to higher layer protocols and services:

1) Customer premises multipoint configurations are supported ("Passive Bus") allowing contention for the use of the local (intrapremises) transmission facility.

2) *D*-channel signaling messages are given priority over other *D*-channel messages as a matter of policy governing the interactions between Layer 2 and Layer 1.

The primary rate interface physical layer is defined in Recommendation I.431 [4] as either 1544 kbits/s or 2048 kbits/s, each of which has well-defined framing. The most common structures on the primary rate access interface are "23*B* + *D*" and "30*B* + *D*," respectively, where the *D* channel is 64 kbits/s. On the primary rate interface, only point-to-point configurations of terminating equipment are supported, and no priority scheme exists on *D*-channel messaging.

IV. LINK LAYER

The purpose of the ISDN Link Access Procedure on the *D* channel (LAPD) is to provide the OSI layer 2 functionality of guaranteeing data integrity of information passed by layer 3 over the ISDN user–network interface. The general aspects of the ISDN user–network interface link layer are described in Recommendations I.440 (duplicated in Q.920) [5], including the layer services expected from the physical layer and provided to the network layer with the associated primitives. The link layer service is based on OSI's Data Link Layer Service [2], providing efficient and timely data transfer, link synchronization, error detection and correction, flow control, frame sequencing, and addressing for multiplexing.

Link layer procedures for LAPD are given in Recommendation I.441 (duplicated in Q.921) [5]. LAPD evolved from a basis in the Recommendation X.25 layer 2 protocol called LAPB [6]. In particular, the ISDN LAPD protocol supports multiple Layer 3 entities and multiple terminal equipments on one interface using octets of addressing via Data Link Connection Identifiers (DLCI's). DLCI's have two octets, the Service Access Point Identifier (SAPI) in the high-order octet, and the Terminal Endpoint Identifier (TEI) in the low-order octet. LAPD supports multiple frame operation with modulo 128 for point-to-point information transfer associated with most call control. Unacknowledged information procedures in LAPD handle broadcast information transfer for initial call setup to a passive bus from the network. Fig. 3 shows the

[1]Line format is not part of the user–network interface since line formats operate between Network Termination 1 and the Network (see Fig. 1).

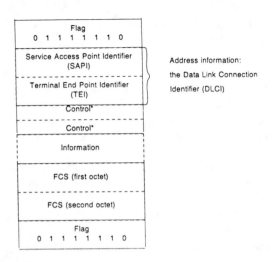

```
              Flag
         0  1  1  1  1  1  1  0
  - - - - - - - - - - - - - - - -
  Service Access Point Identifier
             (SAPI)                      Address information:
  - - - - - - - - - - - - - - - -
  Terminal End Point Identifier          the Data Link Connection
             (TEI)                       Identifier (DLCI)
  - - - - - - - - - - - - - - - -
            Control*
  - - - - - - - - - - - - - - - -
            Control*
  - - - - - - - - - - - - - - - -
           Information
  - - - - - - - - - - - - - - - -
          FCS (first octet)
  - - - - - - - - - - - - - - - -
         FCS (second octet)
  - - - - - - - - - - - - - - - -
              Flag
         0  1  1  1  1  1  1  0
```

*Unacknowledged operation - one octet
Multiple frame operation   - two octets for frames with sequence numbers
                           - one octet for frames without sequence numbers

Fig. 3. LAPD information frame structure.

LAPD information frame structure that carries the layer 3 protocol information in the Information octets.

Currently, there are four values of SAPI defined for use (all others are reserved):

- SAPI = 0: used for signaling,
- SAPI = 1: reserved for packet communications using I.451 (Q.931) call control procedures,
- SAPI = 16: used for packet communications conforming to X.25 level 3 procedures, and
- SAPI = 63: used for layer 2 management procedures.

Thus, in most implementations, for D-channel X.25 information transfer, X.25 layer 3 procedures are indicated at the data link layer by a SAPI value of 16. Those X.25 frames are routed based on recognition of this layer 2 SAPI to an X.25 packet handling function.

V. LAYER 3

Recommendation I.450 (duplicated in Q.930) [7] describes general aspects of the ISDN layer 3 protocol.[2] This Recommendation explains the services expected from the data link layer by layer 3, and lists the peer functions of the layer 3, for example, network connection control and conveying user-to-network and network-to-user information.

The layer 3 protocol, specified in Recommendation I.451 (duplicated in Q.931) [7], is the key to ISDN call control. The layer 3 procedures deal with

- circuit-switched calls where the services are described in Recommendation I.231 [8] (type "C"),
- packet-switched calls based on Recommendation I.462 (X.31) [6][3] where the services are described in Recommendation I.232 [8] (type "P"), and

---

[2] Again, the ISDN protocols do not strictly adhere to OSI, so this protocol is not called a "network layer."

[3] Procedures described in I.462 (X.31) provide ISDN access control for calls providing X.25 service.

- user signaling connections, also known as user-to-user signaling not associated with a circuit-switched call (type "S"). No service descriptions are provided for these connections in the current I-series Recommendations.

In addition, link restart procedures for an entire DLCI have layer 3 messages and procedures defined (type 'G' for global).

Messages for call control and their applicability by call type are listed in Table I.

Layer 3 messages are comprised of information elements. Fig. 4 shows the four information elements that appear in each layer 3 message in the same order: Protocol discriminator, Length of call reference value, Call reference value, and Message type information elements. In the general message structure, these common information elements have the following functions:

- *Protocol discriminator:* Distinguishes messages for ISDN user–network call control from other messages (for example, X.25).

- *Call reference value:* Identifies the call request or facility registration/cancellation request at the local user–network interface to which the particular message applies. The call reference does not have end-to-end significance across ISDN's. Two special cases are noteworthy. First is the case where the message has no third octet (that is, technically the message has no call reference octet), and the second octet (length of call reference value) is all zeros. This case is referred to as the all-zero (dummy) call reference value and is reserved for Q.932 supplementary service procedures which will be discussed in Section VI. The second case is the global call reference, used for link restart procedures, which has a meaningful second octet in a message (giving a nonzero call reference length), but the numerical value of the call reference itself is zero, triggering applicability of the message to all call references associated with the DLCI.

- *Message type:* Identifies the function of the message being sent. These are the messages listed in Table I.

Within this overall structure, some messages are pivotal in basic call control for computer communications: SETUP, CONNECT, DISCONNECT, and RELEASE.

Each of these messages will be described in Section V-A. Section V-B treats some of their key information elements, while Table II contains a brief summary of all the information elements associated directly with call control. Table III lists those information elements associated with control of features (supplementary services). Typical message sequences for 64 kbit/s unrestricted calling appear in Section V-C.

A. Message Contents

Message contents for certain key call control messages provide insight into the detail of the control a user can exert over an ISDN connection.

1) SETUP Message Contents: The SETUP message is sent by the calling user to the network and by the network to the called user to initiate call establishment for bearer

TABLE I
MESSAGES FOR CALL CONTROL

Message	Applicability			
	C	P	S	G
Call establishment messages				
ALERTING	yes	yes	yes	no
CALL PROCEEDING	yes	yes	yes	no
CONNECT	yes	yes	yes	no
CONNECT ACKNOWLEDGE	yes	yes	yes	no
PROGRESS	yes	yes	no	no
SETUP	yes	yes	yes	no
SETUP ACKNOWLEDGE	yes	no	yes	no
Call information phase messages:				
SUSPEND	yes	no	no	no
SUSPEND ACKNOWLEDGE	yes	no	no	no
SUSPEND REJECT	yes	no	no	no
RESUME	yes	no	no	no
RESUME ACKNOWLEDGE	yes	no	no	no
RESUME REJECT	yes	no	no	no
USER INFORMATION	yes	no	yes	no
Call clearing messages:				
DISCONNECT	yes	yes	no	no
RELEASE	yes	yes	yes	no
RELEASE COMPLETE	yes	yes	yes	no
RESTART	no	no	no	yes
RESTART ACKNOWLEDGE	no	no	no	yes
Miscellaneous messages:				
CONGESTION CONTROL	yes	no	yes	no
FACILITY	yes	no	no	no
INFORMATION	yes	no	yes	no
NOTIFY	yes	no	no	no
STATUS	yes	yes	yes	yes
STATUS INQUIRY	yes	yes	yes	no

C - circuit
P - packet
S - signaling
G - global reset

Protocol discriminator			
0	0	0	0	Length of call reference value (in octets)
Call reference value			
0	Message type		
Other information elements as required			

Fig. 4. General message organization example.

TABLE II
SUMMARY OF INFORMATION ELEMENT USES

Information Element Identification	Use
Bearer capability	Transport specification
Call state	Error recovery
Called party number	Network destination addressing
Called party subaddress	Full destination addressing
Calling party number	Network source addressing
Calling party subaddress	Full source addressing
Cause	Reasons for a message and diagnostics
Channel identification	Specification controlled channel
Congestion level	Signaling service congestion indication
Display	Sending network-to-user ASCII information
End-to-end transit delay	End-to-end delay selection
High layer compatibility	End-to-end layer 4-7 descriptions
Information rate	Throughput class indication
Keypad facility	Sending user-to-network ASCII information
Low layer compatibility	End-to-end layer 1-3 descriptions
More data	Indication of blocks of end-to-end user information
Notification indicator	Unacknowledged network-to-user information
Packet layer binary parameters	Listing requested layer 3 parameter values
Packet layer window size	Window value
Packet size	Maximum packet size
Progress indicator	Interworking between networks
Redirecting number	Number from which call diversion occurs
Repeat indicator	Indication of prioritized, repeated information elements
Restart indicator	Identification of class of facility for restart
Segmented message	Indication of overall message too long for one frame
Sending complete	Indication of end of called party number
Signal	Triggering of special indications, such as tones
Transit delay selection and indication	Transit network delay selection
Transit network selection	Designation of desired transport networks
User-user	Transmission of user-to-user unrestricted information

TABLE III
SUPPLEMENTARY SERVICE CONTROL RELATED INFORMATION ELEMENTS

Call identity
Date/time
Facility
Feature activation
Feature indication
Invoke component
Network-specific facilities
Return error component
Return result component
Switchhook

services (fundamental transport services such as speech). As such, the message has information associated with the end-to-end establishment of a call ("global" significance). Associated with that establishment, other information related to features (called "supplementary services" such as call waiting) may also be included. That information may, for example, be of local significance only.

Table IV summarizes the use of information elements in the SETUP message:
- information element name,
- direction in which the messages flow (network to user, user to network, or both),
- an indication of whether the information element is mandatory or optional, and
- indications of applicability [circuit-switched calling (C), I.462 (X.31)-based packet-switched calling (P), user signaling calling (S)].

The order of the information elements in Table IV is the order in which they would appear in an actual SETUP message. The rules for using the optional information elements are detailed in I.451 (Q.931).

2) CONNECT Message Contents: The CONNECT message is sent by the called user to the network and by the network to the calling user to indicate call acceptance for circuit-switched calls (type C) and for user signaling calls (type S). Thus, for these connections, CONNECT has global significance. For I.462 (X.31) packet-switched calls, CONNECT has only local significance, signifying acceptance of the access connection to the packet network. CONNECT messages, depending on the application, can have the following information elements in addition to the common header information elements (Fig. 4):
- Channel identification,
- Facility,
- Progress indicator,
- Display,
- Signal,
- Switchhook,
- Feature activation,
- Feature indication,
- Low layer compatibility,
- User–user.

3) DISCONNECT Message Contents: For circuit-switched calls, the DISCONNECT message is sent by the user to request the network to clear an end-to-end con-

TABLE IV
SETUP MESSAGE CONTENTS

Information Element	Direction	Usage	Applicability
Protocol discriminator	both	Mandatory	C,P,S
Call reference	both	Mandatory	C,P,S
Message type	both	Mandatory	C,P,S
Sending complete	both	Optional	C,S
Repeat indicator	both	Optional	C
Bearer capability	both	Mandatory	C,P,S
Channel identification	both	Optional	C,P,S
Facility	both	Optional	C
Progress indicator	both	Optional	C,P
Network specific facilities	both	Optional	C,S
Display	n→u	Optional	C,P,S
Keypad facility	u→n	Optional	C,S
Signal	n→u	Optional	C
Switchhook	u→n	Optional	C
Feature activation	u→n	Optional	C
Feature indication	n→u	Optional	C
Information rate	n→u	Optional	P
End-end transit delay	n→u	Optional	P
Transit delay selection and indication	n→u	Optional	P
Packet layer binary parameters	n→u	Optional	P
Packet layer window size	n→u	Optional	P
Packet size	n→u	Optional	P
Calling party number	both	Optional	C,P,S
Calling party subaddress	both	Optional	C,P,S
Called party number	both	Optional	C,P,S
Called party subaddress	both	Optional	C,P,S
Transit network selection	u→n	Optional	C,S
Redirecting number	n→u	Optional	P
Low layer compatibility	both	Optional	C,S
High layer compatibility	both	Optional	C,S
User-user	both	Optional	C,P,S

nection or is sent by the network to indicate that the end-to-end connection is cleared. For these connections, DISCONNECT has global significance. For I.462 (X.31)-based packet-switched calls, the DISCONNECT message has local significance only and is sent by the user to request the network to clear an access connection or is sent by the network to the user to indicate that the access connection has been cleared. The DISCONNECT message has no applicability in user signaling calls. DISCONNECT messages, depending on the application, can have the following information elements in addition to the common header information elements (Fig. 4):

- Cause,
- Facility,
- Progress indicator,
- Display,
- Signal,
- Feature indication,
- User-user.

4) RELEASE Message Contents: For all call types, the RELEASE message is sent by the user or the network to indicate that the receiving equipment should release the channel and prepare to release the call reference after sending a RELEASE COMPLETE message as a local RELEASE acknowledgment. For circuit-switched calls, the RELEASE message also indicates that the equipment sending the message has disconnected the channel, thus providing a local acknowledgment for the DISCONNECT message. For I.462 (X.31) packet-switched calls, when channel negotiation is used to establish the terminating channel to deliver the X.25 call, the RELEASE message is sent by the network to the user to indicate that the X.25

call itself has been delivered on either the *D* channel or an existing, active channel, and that the network intends to release the call reference used to negotiate the channel.

RELEASE messages, depending on the application, can have the following information elements in addition to the common header information elements (Fig. 4):

- Cause,
- Facility,
- Display,
- Signal,
- Feature indication,
- User-user.

B. Key Information Elements

The messages outlined above are constructed from information elements, some of which have functions that are intuitive from their names (see Tables II and III). Several are not so intuitive, including the Bearer capability information element used in the SETUP message (see Table IV), a backbone element in call control that will be described in detail. Several other important information elements will be discussed as well, namely, Calling and Called party number, Calling and Called party subaddress, Cause, Channel identification, High layer compatibility, User-user, and Information rate.

1) Bearer Capability Information Element: The Bearer capability informtaion element indicates a requested fundamental transport service, called a "bearer service" (I.231 and I.232) to be provided by the network. In addition, the Bearer capability information element contains detailed information on protocol options at each layer to construct the desired service. The network is expected to *use*[4] the bearer capability information, for example, in call routing. Fig. 5 lists the contents of the Bearer capability information element. The remainder of Section V-B1) describes the details of the Bearer capability information element, as shown in Fig. 5. The first two octets of the Bearer capability information element show some common aspects with all other information elements: the information element identifier and the length of the information element.

The third octet contains a coding standard indication. In addition, the third octet has the information transfer capability, stating that the associated call can be handled as one of the following: speech, 3.1 kHz audio, 7 kHz audio, unrestricted digital information, restricted digital information, or video. These transfer capabilities are frequently referred to as bearer services and are described in detail in Recommendations I.231 [8] and I.232 [8].

Octets 4, 4a, and 4b describe different aspects of the information transfer. Recognized transfer modes in octet 4 are circuit mode or packet mode. Also in octet 4, information transfer rates describe the bandwidth allocated to the circuit call (namely, 64 kbits/s, 2 × 64 kbits/s, 384

---

[4]This is in contrast to several other information elements whose contents the network effectively ignores.

							Octet
Bearer capability Information element identifier							Octet 1
Length of the bearer capability contents							2
1 ext	coding standard	information transfer capability					3
0/1 ext	transfer mode	information transfer rate					4
0/1 ext	structure		configuration	establishment			4a
1 ext	symmetry	information transfer rate (destination → origination)					4b
0/1 ext	0	1	user information layer 1 protocol				5
0/1 ext	synch/ asynch	negot	user rate				5a V.110/V.120
0/1 ext	intermediate rate	NIC on Tx	NIC on Rx	Flow control on Tx	Flow control on Rx	0	5b V.110 only
0/1 ext	Hdr/ no Hdr	Multi frame support	Mode	LLI negot	As'nor/ As'nee	In/Out band negot / 0	5b V.120 only
0/1 ext	number of stop bits	number of data bits	Parity				5c V.110/V.120
1 ext	duplex mode	modem type					5d V.110/V.120
1 ext	1	0	user information layer 2 protocol				6
1 ext	1	1	user information layer 3 protocol				7

Fig. 5. Bearer capability information element contents.

kbits/s, 1536 kbits/s, and 1920 kbits/s). For packet calls, information transfer rate is only a place holder. All octets *after* octet 4 are optional, with information supplied, as necessary, by defaults or by the user under circumstances detailed in I.451 (Q.931).

"Structure," contained in octet 4a, provides information on synchronization:
• explicit invocation of 8 kHz integrity, indicating the timing for framing;
• explicit invocation of service data unit integrity, indicating frame delimiting done by flags;
• default choice, governed by transfer mode choice:
—for circuit mode: 8 kHz integrity;
—for packet mode: service data unit integrity;
• explicit statement of unstructured.

Currently, the remainder of octet 4a and octet 4b only supports point-to-point configurations with on-demand establishment providing bidirectional symmetric transfer. Network implications for asymmetric and unidirectional traffic are for further study.

Octet 5 is used to indicate the coding rule followed for the information transfer capability (for example, Recommendation G.711 [9] for speech, Recommendation I.462 (X.31) for flag stuffing, Recommendation V.120 [10] for asynchronous rate adaption, Recommendation V.110 [10] for synchronous rate adaption, or non-CCITT standardized rate adaption). Rate adaption is the process by which user information streams encoded according to earlier (pre-ISDN) Recommendations become transferable on an ISDN channel. Multiple techniques have been standardized (in X.31 in [6], and in V.110 and V.120 both in [10]), with the choice depending on the type of application.

Octet 5a includes synchronous/asynchronous indicators that can be used for ambiguous coding indications, and negotiation indications that are used with the V.110 standard. Octet 5a also contains the user rate showing the base rate from which rate adaption occurs. Octet 5b deals with details of the chosen rate adaption technique and takes two forms, one used with V.110 (synchronous rate adaption) and the other used with V.120 (asynchronous rate adaption). For example, "NIC on Tx" is Network Independent Clock on Transmission, and "LLI negot" simply asks whether or not the default Logical Link Identifier will be used. Octets 5c and 5d contain, for both V.110 and V.120 use, number of stop bits, number of data bits, parity information, indication of half or full duplex, and modem type indication (based on network-specific support).

Octet 6 covers layer 2 use (I.441 (Q.921) or layer 2 of X.25). Similarly, octet 7 indicates layer 3 use, either I.451 (Q.931) or layer 3 of X.25.

2) Other Important Information Elements: Many other information elements gain importance in various contexts, including Calling/Called party number information elements, Calling/Called party subaddress information elements, Cause information element, Channel identification information element, High layer compatibility information element, User–user information element, and Information rate information element. Important aspects of each are discussed in this section. Information elements not discussed are not as important to understanding the fundamental functions of I.451 (Q.931).

Calling/Called party number information elements identify the subnetwork address of the origination and destination of the call. The most striking feature of these information elements is the inclusion of the numbering plan identification field, allowing indication of different numbering plans (for example, Recommendation X.121 [11] for Public Data Networks and E.164 [12] for the ISDN era).

Calling/Called party subaddress information elements include 20 octets for the subaddress. In addition, these information elements also have a *type* of subaddress indicator, allowing either Network Service Access Point (NSAP) (X.213 [2]) addresses or user-specified values (for example, four digit Private Branch Exchange extension number). Thus, subaddresses are defined by the users and can be used to address individual communicating end points (for example, specific terminals) or groups of end points (for example, sets of terminals).

The *Cause* information element provides the reason for generating the associated message and diagnostic information, and also the "location" of the cause originator. "Location" may be, for example, a local private network, a local public network, or somewhere unidentifiable beyond an interworking point. Cause information may be one of the 52 values (ranging from "normal call

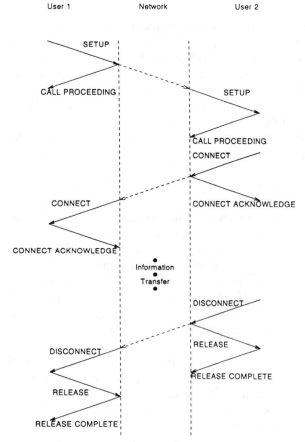

Fig. 6. Typical example message sequence for call control.

clearing'' to ''protocol error, unspecified'') from those specified in the I.451 (Q.931) code set or any others specified in standardized code sets.

The *Channel identification* information element allows identification of an information *channel* (for example, a *B* channel) whose connections are to be controlled by I.451 (Q.931) procedures on a separate *D* channel. The information channel may be in the same ISDN interface as the controlling *D* channel or in a separate interface. The information element contains a field for use in identifying a separate information channel interface, if needed. Channel choices may be either exclusive or negotiable as indicated in the information element.

The *High layer compatibility* information element supplies the type terminal that is on the user side of an S/T interface. The network transports this information transparently end-to-end. In particular, telematic terminals (defined by CCITT [13]–[16]) can be specified using this information element. Identified telematic terminals support telephony, facsimile (groups 2 and 3), facsimile (group 4), teletex, videotex, mixed mode communication (text and facsimile), message handling, and telex.

The *User–user* information element conveys up to 128 octets of information between ISDN end users. The network does not interpret contents of this information element. Presence of this information element helps support the OSI network service [2] across an ISDN.

Most information elements dealing with I.462 (X.31) packet communications are used at the destination interface when negotiating the channel on which to terminate an incoming X.25 call. Some X.25 call request packet contents are mapped into I.451 (Q.931) information elements for inclusion in terminating SETUP message. One of those information elements is the *Information rate* information element, containing throughput class information.

C. Typical Message Sequences for Call Control

For circuit-switched, on-demand 64 kbit/s unrestricted service, Fig. 6 depicts a typical minimum call control message sequence with information transfer phase. In this figure, SETUP, CONNECT, DISCONNECT, and RELEASE messages have already been introduced. CALL PROCEEDING, CONNECT ACKNOWLEDGE, and RELEASE COMPLETE messages are local acknowledgments for those messages.

VI. SUPPLEMENTARY SERVICES CONTROL

Recommendation Q.932 [7] is a new Recommendation for the *Blue Book*, containing generic procedures for the control of ISDN supplementary services. Supplementary services provide additional capabilities to be used in conjunction with telecommunications services (in a Recommendation I.451 (Q.931) context, bearer capability). Supplementary services cannot be offered to a customer on a standalone basis. Desirable connection control-oriented supplementary services are hold and conferencing. Thus, the Q.932 procedures are carefully interleaved with those for I.451 (Q.931).

Q.932 identifies three major methods by which supplementary services may be controlled, namely,
- Keypad,
- Feature key management, and
- Functional.

The first two methods are classed as ''stimulus,'' where individual keystrokes (Keypad) or button pressing (Feature key management) are used to trigger service operation. Such operation is seen to entail little more than, in effect, identifying the service request to the network. Terminals that operate essentially like today's voice telephones are envisioned to use these methods.

For service requests entailing more complicated invocation or activation or for terminals that have a means of supporting more than simple button pressing/keypad operation, ''functional'' methods are envisioned. For data applications, most interest focuses around these functional methods, which are currently least defined. The intention, as stated in Q.932, is to use a message, FACILITY, and a Facility information element to accomplish the service activation (desire for the service to start), invocation (service actually used), and deactivation. The functional methods are adapted from the OSI Remote Operations [2], [3].

Despite their inclusion in the *Blue Book*, the functional methods described in Q.932 are still evolving and will be studied further in the 1989–1992 CCITT study period.

VII. USES AND EVOLUTION

Current uses for ISDN are built around the bearer services, which are themselves evolving, along with their control capabilities.

A. Uses

With ISDN, a user can have access to voice, circuit-switched data, packet-switched data, or video over one interface. The ISDN protocols for connection control and a variety of protocol supported applications have been tested and verified in several recent trials of ISDN.

The Bearer capability information element in I.451 (Q.931) was described in detail in Section V-B1) of this paper, including its use in selecting some of the standard bearer services [8]. Several standard ISDN bearer services currently support data communication applications in ISDN environments. The virtual call and permanent virtual circuit bearer services support X.25 packet-switched services via I.462 (X.31) interface control. 64 kbit/s unrestricted bearer services support circuit-switched, transparent transmission at 64 and 56 kbits/s. Support for transparent private lines has not been the subject of detailed service standards but has been emulated and tested in ISDN trials. The 3.1 kHz audio bearer service supports voice band data circuit-switched point-to-point calling.

User data applications that use these ISDN transport capabilities include: file transfer, billing applications, PC networking, simultaneous voice and data, remote computer access, high-speed facsimile, electronic mail, LAN interconnection via ISDN, and wide area networks. Voice applications using these transport capabilities include 7 kHz (high-quality) audio, encrypted voice, and "plain" voice.

In addition, the fact that the ISDN protocol reference model and the I.451 (Q.931) protocol implementation supports much of the OSI network service leads to other network capabilities that are very useful in data applications. In particular, ISDN calling number delivery and user-to-user signaling in conjunction with call control have many applications in data communications, including use in security screening. Furthermore, the ISDN user-to-user signaling supplementary services can also be used over the D channel in association with a circuit-switched call active on the B channel.

B. Evolution

To date, Recommendation I.451 (Q.931) control procedures have been developed to handle circuit-mode, point-to-point, on-demand, bidirectional symmetric calls for 64 kbit/s calls using B-channel access on either basic rate or primary rate interfaces. For packet mode, the current I.451 (Q.931) procedures primarily handle the establishment of local B channels accessing packet switches,

supporting X.25 call control once the access has been established. Recommendation I.451 (Q.931) is approaching stability for control of these narrowband connections.

Thus, areas of extension to I.451 (Q.931), that are likely for standards activity in the 1989–1992 CCITT study period are in two major areas.

1) $H0$ (384 kbit/s) and $H1$ (1.536 Mbit/s and 1.920 Mbit/s) end-to-end circuit-mode, on-demand, bidirectional symmetric calls are to be defined further with primary rate access interfaces. Also, a use will be defined for $H0$ and $H1$ channels to access packet switches to carry some form of virtual call/permanent virtual circuit service.

2) Diverse needs of the data communications market have spurred exploratory work on additional packet bearer services during the 1985–1988 CCITT study period, leading to I.122 [8], a framework description for further work on some select packet bearer services. The proposed packet services all use I.451 (Q.931) call control over the local access. The differences between these packet services are in the data transfer phase of the services.

In addition, Recommendation Q.932 (or related Recommendations) will have explicit procedures to handle specific, key supplementary services such as hold and conferencing.

VIII. ISSUES

To date, work on ISDN protocols has been primarily devoted to connection establishment and ongoing control. Little work has been done on the issue of assuring that the terminal equipments connected to the ISDN will be able to communicate intelligibly. Particularly in the computer communication world, the variety of end systems and terminal equipment brings the need for intelligible interconnection to the forefront. Several ideas (such as directory numbers, subaddressing, and mandatory high-layer compatibility) have been proposed for helping to resolve the resultant problems; however, compatibility is still an open issue.

In addition, broadband applications will require a streamlined protocol for ordinary activities and will demand higher performance criteria. Such a broadband protocol may be a new development since it must be optimized for high-speed data of the sort envisioned for wide-area LAN interconnections and video transport. In broadband applications, multimedia, multipoint communications are likely to be common. Making such communications easy and simultaneously meeting on-demand performance criteria provides new requirements on a communications control protocol [17]. However, since existing applications are also likely to be used on broadband interfaces, many of the lessons learned from the development of ISDN may be of use in the specification of protocols for broadband.

IX. SUMMARY

To date, work on ISDN connection control has developed a protocol architecture and a set of control protocols handling various types of circuit and packet calls. These are detailed in this paper. In addition, work has been done on a set of generic protocols for handling supplementary service control.

Future work for protocols dealing with direct extensions to those detailed in this paper will cover $H0$ and $H1$ channel control and additional packet bearer services.

Extensions to I.451 (Q.931)-based connection control per se are unlikely to handle terminal compatibility or broadband. Terminal compatibility for data uses will require stronger tie-ins with OSI, and broadband may require an entirely new protocol architecture. Both these issues are likely to be studied extensively by CCITT over the next four years.

REFERENCES

[1] CCITT, *Red Book*, vol. III, fascicle III.5, "Integrated Services Digital Network (ISDN)," Recommendations of the I-series, Geneva, Switzerland, 1985.
[2] CCITT, *Blue Book*, vol. VIII, fascicle VIII.4, "Data communication networks: Open Systems Interconnection (OSI)—Model and notation, service definition," Recommendations X.200-X.219, Geneva, Switzerland, 1989.
[3] CCITT, *Blue Book*, vol. VIII, fascicle VIII.5, "Data communication networks: Open Systems Interconnection (OSI)—Protocol specification, conformance testing," Recommendations X.220-X.290, Geneva, Switzerland, 1989.
[4] CCITT, *Blue Book*, vol. III, fascicle III.8, "Integrated Services Digital Network (ISDN)—Overall network aspects and function, user-network interface," Recommendations I.310-I.470, Geneva, Switzerland, 1989.
[5] CCITT, *Blue Book*, vol. VI, fascicle VI.10, "Digital access signalling system, Network layer," Recommendations Q.920-Q.921, Geneva, Switzerland, 1989.
[6] CCITT, *Blue Book*, vol. VIII, fascicle VIII.2, "Data communication networks: Services and facilities interfaces," Recommendations X.2-X.32, Geneva, Switzerland, 1989.
[7] CCITT, *Blue Book*, vol. VI, fascicle VI.11, "Digital access signalling system, network layer, user-network management," Recommendations Q.930-Q.940, Geneva, Switzerland, 1989.
[8] CCITT, *Blue Book*, vol. III, fascicle III.7, "Integrated Services Digital Network (ISDN)—General characteristics and service aspects," Recommendations I.110-I.254, Geneva, Switzerland, 1989.
[9] CCITT, *Blue Book*, vol. III, fascicle III.4, "General aspects of digital transmission systems: Terminal equipments," Recommendations G.700-G.722, Geneva, Switzerland, 1989.
[10] CCITT, *Blue Book*, vol. VIII, fascicle VIII.1, "Data communication over the telephone network," Series V Recommendations, Geneva, Switzerland, 1989.
[11] CCITT, *Blue Book*, vol. VIII, fascicle VIII.3, "Data communication networks: Transmission, signalling and switching, network aspects, maintenance and administrative arrangements," Recommendations X.40-X.181, Geneva, Switzerland, 1989.
[12] CCITT, *Blue Book*, vol. II, fascicle II.2, "Telephone network and ISDN—Operation, numbering, routing, and mobile service," Recommendations E.100-E.300, Geneva, Switzerland, 1989.
[13] CCITT, *Blue Book*, vol. VII, fascicle VII.3, "Terminal equipment and protocols for telematic services," Recommendations T.0-T.63, Geneva, Switzerland, 1989.
[14] CCITT, *Blue Book*, vol. VII, fascicle VII.5, "Terminal equipment and protocols for telematic services," Recommendations T.65-T.101, T.150-T.390, Geneva, Switzerland, 1989.
[15] CCITT, *Blue Book*, vol. VII, fascicle VII.6, "Terminal equipment and protocols for telematic services," Recommendations T.400-T.418, Geneva, Switzerland, 1989.
[16] CCITT, *Blue Book*, vol. VII, fascicle VII.7, "Terminal equipment and protocols for telematic services," Recommendations T.431-T.564, Geneva, Switzerland, 1989.
[17] S. E. Minzer and D. R. Spears, "New directions in signaling for broadband ISDN," *IEEE Commun. Mag.*, vol. 27, Feb. 1989.

Wendy M. Harman received the B.S. degree in operations research and industrial engineering from Cornell University, Ithaca, NY, in 1982, and the M.S.E. degree in industrial and operations engineering from the University of Michigan, Ann Arbor, in 1983.

In October 1983 she joined Bell Laboratories, proceeding in January 1984 to Bellcore, where she is currently a member of the Technical Staff in the Intelligent Network Planning Division. Her work has included several areas of network planning functions, including work on X.25 packet protocols and Integrated Services Digital Network (ISDN) services and protocols. She has been an active participant in X.25 packet standards committees, and has also been a technical leader in ISDN standards committees, T1D1 in the United States and CCITT Study Group XVIII internationally. She has had experience in implementation of ISDN protocols on a system used to test integrated voice and data services. Currently, her primary interests are in the area of network architectures and implementation of services on Intelligent Networks.

Cheryl F. Newman (M'75) received the B.S., M.S., and Ph.D. degrees in electric engineering from Cornell University, Ithaca, NY, in 1970, 1972, and 1975, respectively.

In October 1974 she joined Bell Laboratories, proceeding in January 1984 to Bellcore, where she is currently a member of the Technical Staff in Integrated Services Planning. Her work has taken her into several areas of network planning functions, including transmission facility network planning, special services planning, and local switching network planning. Currently, her primary interests lie in the area of message handling, directory, and related services as they might be offered on an Integrated Services Digital Network (ISDN) with Intelligent Network elements. Other interests are in multimedia services on ISDN. As part of her work, since 1984, she has been participating in ISDN standards committees, T1S1 in the United States and CCITT Study Group XVIII internationally.

ISDN Computer-Aided Telephony

Reprinted from *IEEE Network Magazine*, January 1991, pages 46-53. Copyright © 1991 by The Institute of Electrical and Electronics Engineers, Inc. All rights reserved.

Zarko Cvijan
Anthony E. Brock
Frank P. Corr
Joi D. Grieg
John E. Kuras
Thomas Schick

The Integrated Services Digital Network (ISDN) is no longer just a technology in search of applications [1] [2]. Users, vendors, and carriers are working together to make ISDN the basis for a growing number of applications such as telemarketing, customer service, real estate browsing, and remote retailing [3–6]. These applications are being enabled on evolving ISDN-based platforms. Proper architecting of such platforms is required to allow applications to keep pace with changing needs. As ISDN goes through a number of evolutionary phases (see Figure 1), this architecting will be one of the main challenges faced by the platform developers during the 1990s.

Today, ISDN has gained its initial acceptance in new platforms, often implemented as separate islands. The use of ISDN started with trials of network adapters and has progressed to exploratory user applications integrating some voice, data, and image functions. This, in turn, is causing the industry focus to shift to applications and their Application Programming Interfaces (APIs). Existing data APIs, such as Network Basic Input Output System (NetBIOS), are being used with some modifications to enable applications that require ISDN call control [7] [8]. In addition, new functionally richer telephony APIs are being introduced, including IBM's CallPath Services Architecture.

During the 1990s, countrywide ISDNs will expand information movement and management. Telephony and data APIs will coexist to enable the development of applications that utilize ISDN-unique call control as well as voice, data and image communications. Multivendor environments for these applications will include Open Systems Interconnection (OSI) and unique vendor architectures like IBM Systems Network Architecture (SNA). We envision that the CallPath Services Architecture will allow future use of ISDN in applications that require telephony under Systems Application Architecture (SAA).

By the year 2001, proven ISDN-based platforms will support worldwide communications. These platforms will include interconnections of public and private ISDNs, and allow bridging to Broadband ISDN (BISDN). Based on user needs for multimedia applications, a common API will evolve from the separate telephony and data APIs. With a common API architected within the OSI framework, ISDN computer-aided telephony applications will be pervasive and support innovative business solutions.

ISDN-Based Platforms

To enable various user applications, ISDN-based platforms will be implemented in different forms, depending on customer networking requirements. Figure 2 shows an example of one such platform consisting of the following components:

- ISDN backbone based on Signaling System No. 7 (SS7) interconnections used for countrywide or worldwide communications, which may bridge to non-ISDN SS7 backbones
- Switches supporting ISDN or non-ISDN access services
- Private Branch Exchanges (PBXs) with ISDN and non-ISDN access, providing a wide range of telephony functions
- Local Area Networks (LANs) using ISDN for wide-area communications
- Hosts that support telephony and other applications in different operating environments with appropriate APIs

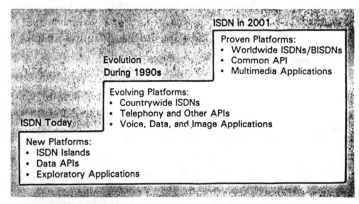

Fig. 1. Evolving ISDN-based platforms.

- Personal Computers (PCs) as user workstations for voice, data, and image communications and personalized telephony services
- Telephones used by clients calling for a service or agents providing a service
- Fax devices using ISDN for image communications.

ISDN access links can provide the following logical channels:

- D-channel at 16 kb/s or 64 kb/s, which is used for signaling, as well as X.25 packet data transmission
- B-channel at 64 kb/s, which provides the bearer capabilities for integrated voice, data, and image communications
- H-channels, which are structured as multiples of B-channels to provide higher bandwidth using H0 = 6 Bs at 384 kb/s, H11 = 24 Bs at 1,536 kb/s, or H12 = 30 Bs at 1,920 kb/s

These channels, which are logically multiplexed on a single ISDN access link, can be provided as either a Basic Rate Interface (BRI) (= 2B+D) or a Primary Rate Interface (PRI) (= 23B+D, 30B=D, or xB+yH+D).

0-8186-2797-2/92 $3.00 © 1991 IEEE

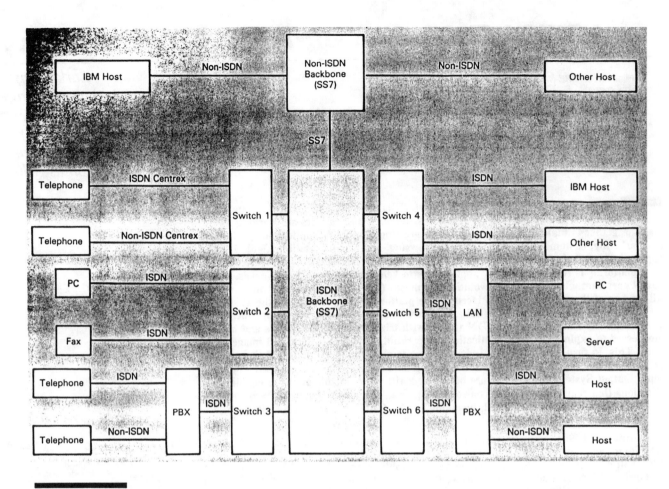

Fig. 2. ISDN-based platform for computer-aided telephony.

Telephony API and Modes

A telephony API provides a programming interface for applications that may use computer-switch telephony communications. This interface allows an application program to invoke a set of telephony services such as call establishment, transfer, and progress monitoring. In a properly architected platform, a telephony API provides consistent functions across different systems. From a customer's perspective, the importance of such an API lies in enabling the development of new applications while protecting the existing investment in hardware and software.

API service primitives give an application the ability to invoke functions such as call setup, answer, transfer, and disconnect. Complementary to these functions, computer-switch protocols are specified for computer-aided telephony, which can be supported in either the first-party or third-party mode of operation (see Figure 3).

In the first-party mode, a single computer-switch link supports telephony control and voice, data, or image communications. The computer-aided telephony functions are invoked directly by the application process for its own use.

In the third-party mode, separate telephony and communications links are used. The computer-aided telephony functions are invoked indirectly by a computer that acts as the third party for the communicating entities. These entities may include telephones, terminals, and computers, which are used for voice, data, or image communications in a given application.

Formats and Protocols for ISDN

With ISDN, computer-aided telephony can be supported in the first-party or third-party mode. Figure 4 illustrates the first-party mode support for which ISDN is suitable because of its multiple logical channels on a single access link. This involves the use of the D-channel signaling to support the following ISDN-based functions:

- Basic call control such as setup and disconnect, as specified by International Consultative Committee for Telephone and Telegraph (CCITT) Recommendation Q.931.
- Supplementary services suitable for telephony and supported in accordance with CCITT Recommendations Q.931 and Q.932. These include services like Calling Line Identification (CLID) and Call Transfer (CT).
- Bearer services such as voice, 3.1 kHz audio for voiceband data, 64 kb/s unrestricted data, and packet data.
- Teleservices that combine bearer services and application functions, which may include switch-based telephony, fax, or teletex.

On an ISDN access link, Q.931 and Q.932 protocols are used at layer 3. A layer 7 protocol may also be used as required to provide computer-switch functions complementary to ISDN access services. Since Q.931 and Q.932 protocols are or will be supported in computers, PBXs, and central office switches, they will facilitate the implementation of multivendor platforms. With ISDN-based lower-layer architecture, computer-aided telephony functions such as CLID and CT can be provided on a worldwide basis.

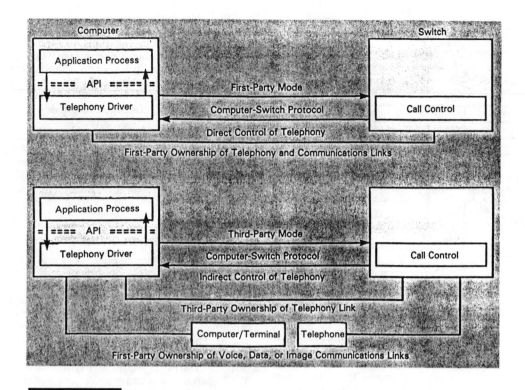

Fig. 3. Computer-aided telephony operation modes.

IBM's CallPath Services Architecture will provide for the future mapping of different computer-switch protocols, including Q.931/Q.932 layer 3 protocols. This mapping may also be provided for the future standard layer 7 protocols: Switch-Computer Applications Interface (SCAI), defined by the American National Standards Institute (ANSI) [10]; and Computer Supported Telephony Applications (CSTA), defined by the European Computer Manufacturers Association (ECMA) [11].

When a BRI or PRI link is used in the first-party mode, the D-channel facilitates computer-aided telephony. The associated B/H-channels support voice, data, or image communications. This ISDN-unique access link structure provides the basis for many innovative user applications.

ISDN Driver Architecture

With telephony and other APIs, ISDN access can be controlled through a driver architected within the OSI framework [13] [14]. This driver consists of mutually supportive D-channel and B/H-channel parts. An application process uses these parts through the API primitives for ISDN-based call management, voice, data, or image communications, bandwidth management, and network management. Support of these functions may involve driving the D-channel and B/H-channel protocol stacks in various environments (see Figure 5).

The D-channel part of the ISDN driver supports an exchange of service primitives with the telephony entity of the application process. It also interacts with the Q.931 and Q.932 components for the purpose of exchanging layer 3 protocol messages with the switch. The D-channel can also support X.25 packet data transmission in accordance with CCITT Recommendation X.31 [15].

The B/H-channel part of the ISDN driver enables voice, data, and image communications. Data communications may

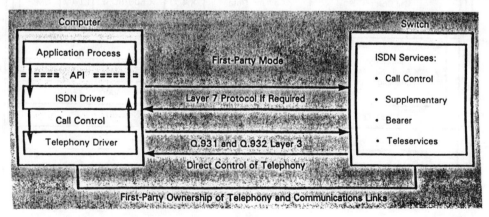

Fig. 4. Computer-switch ISDN access formats and protocols.

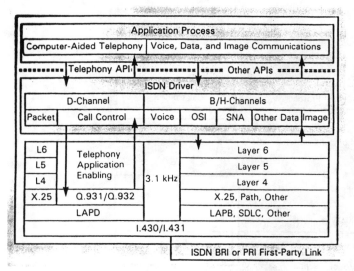

Fig. 5. ISDN D-channel and B/H-channel architecture.

use OSI, SNA, and other protocol stacks, including X.25 on a B-channel. Voice support may include 3.1 kHz audio for Dual Tone Multifrequency (DTMF) touch-tone telephone access, which may be required by some applications. Image transmission is also possible using the bandwidth of B/H-channels.

OSI and NetBIOS Environments

Figure 6 illustrates a possible structure for OSI and NetBIOS protocol stacks on B/H-channels. The OSI stacks may include X.400 for messaging, X.500 for directory services using the Remote Operation Service Element (ROSE) procedure, File Transfer Access Management (FTAM), and Common Management Information Protocol (CMIP).

NetBIOS may use B/H-channels for data and provide an extension for telephony functions on the D-channel. The early use of this API is attractive because of its simplicity [16] as well as a large number of its LAN-based applications. However, the NetBIOS telephony support is limited. Hence, functionally richer telephony APIs, such as IBM's CallPath Services Architecture, are being introduced to provide enhanced telephony functions for user applications.

The North American ISDN Users' Forum (NIUF) is encouraging an OSI-based framework for enabling ISDN applications in accordance with its charter to drive the interoperability of multivendor products [4] [12]. With a common ISDN-based lower-layer architecture, users expect heterogeneous computers and switches to coexist in their networks.

SAA/SNA Environments

With the CallPath Services API and SAA Common Programming Interface—Communications (CPI-C) [10], we envision future integration of telephony, data, and image applications within the framework conceptualized in Figure 7. This integration can include an expansion of the CallPath Services Architecture to provide a D-channel driver in the first-party mode. This architectural concept assumes that the complementary use of the B/H-channel driver part is in compliance with SAA CPI-C. Additionally, if this expansion is done, ISDN-based image communications under SAA may be supported via IBM's Image Object Content Architecture (IOCA) [17]. Thus, there is the possibility for future development of integrated applications using ISDN under SAA/SNA.

To allow an orderly introduction of telephony applications under SAA, IBM's CallPath Services Architecture will provide consistent and functionally rich API service primitives across multiple systems in various operating environments; support standardized computer-switch formats and protocols or, in the interim, accommodate agreed upon unique formats and proto-

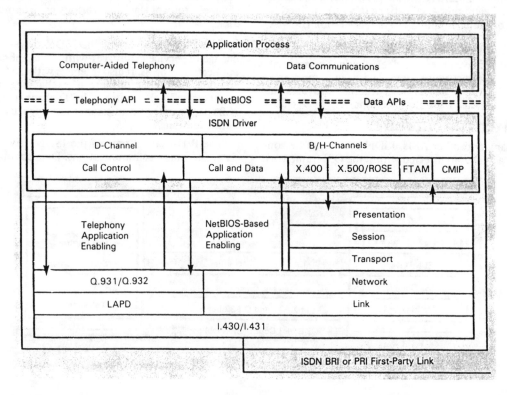

Fig. 6. ISDN driver architecture for OSI and other applications.

cols for switches from different vendors; allow multiple switches and computers to be interconnected using different networks; and make applications portable between systems in order to protect the customer's investment in hardware and software.

User Applications

Telephony applications can be provided today without ISDN. With ISDN access from offices and homes on a country-wide or worldwide basis, computer-aided telephony applications will be enhanced in many business solutions, including:

- Telemarketing desks
- Customer service desks
- Real estate browsing access
- Retail sales and shipment agencies
- Wholesale agencies
- Integrated telephone and computer-based message desks
- Desk videoconferencing
- Financial service transactions
- Credit checking service transactions
- Government service inquiries
- Health care service inquiries
- Medical records access
- Legal agencies
- Consulting agencies
- Accounting agencies
- Advertising agencies
- Education agencies
- Technical design reviews

Customers are evaluating ISDN against the existing voice and data networks currently used for computer-aided telephony. An analysis by the NIUF shows that ISDN-based incoming call management can enhance existing, and enable new, applications [3] [4]. Exploratory applications being developed in France have demonstrated the possible use of ISDN for LAN-based image server access [5] [6]. A brief description of these two types of early applications follows.

Incoming Call Management

A telemarketing or customer service application can use CLID for automatic number identification and CT for automatic call distribution on an ISDN-based platform, as conceptualized in Figure 8. Such an application assumes service interaction of Client Workstations (CWs), which may be telephones or PCs; Agent Workstations (AWs), which are assumed to be PCs; and a host-based Client Knowledge Database (CKD), which processes client calls and files based on required client-agent service interaction.

In this application example, ISDN can potentially satisfy client-agent communications on a worldwide basis, with CWs and AWs located in offices or at homes. With ISDN and non-ISDN access support, new CW devices can be introduced and existing devices migrated in a given user application.

ISDN can significantly enhance incoming call management with Q.931/Q.932-based call control. This standard control makes CLID and CT services available worldwide for global user applications. Multiple B-channels and ISDN fast call

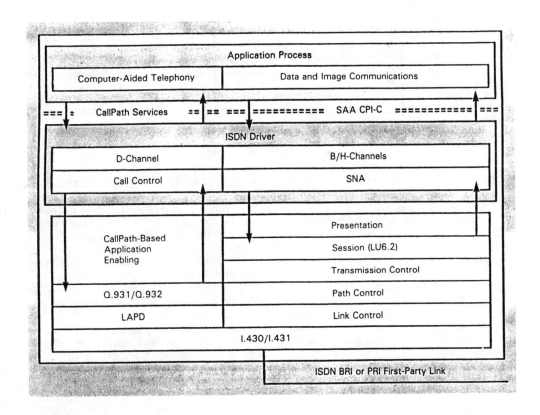

Fig. 7. Framework for ISDN-based applications under SAA/SNA.

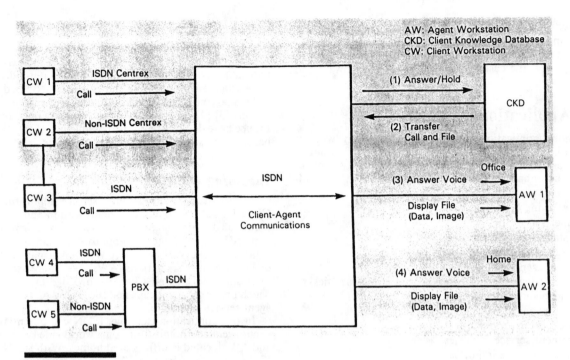

Fig. 8. *ISDN-based platform for incoming call management.*

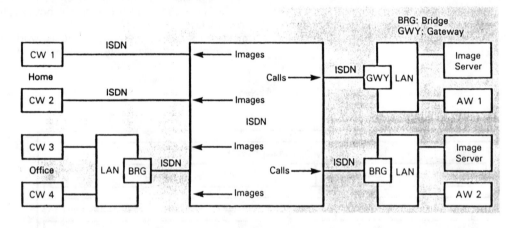

Fig. 9. *ISDN-based platform for LAN-based image server access.*

setup allow for a coordinated call and file transfer to an AW. B/H-channel bandwidth allows data and image files to be used by the CKD and AWs. By proper selection of service primitives, it is possible to customize telephony functions for a CW, AW, or the CKD, which can help satisfy the customer's changing business needs.

Today, incoming call management is widely used with the existing telephone networks. With ISDN, it will be possible to enhance the existing, and enable new, applications based on the advanced telephony functions. This includes globalization of applications such as telemarketing, which will be increasingly important in the international economy of the 1990s. Using ISDN access services in such applications will enable customers to gain a competitive advantage in their business through countrywide or worldwide information movement and management [13].

Image Server Access

Transmission speeds of switched B/H-channels ranging from 64 kb/s to 1,920 kb/s create new potentials for image applications, especially in business solutions that involve agents

working at home or in geographically distant branch offices. LAN-based image server access via ISDN is suitable for applications such as real estate browsing and remote retailing. LANs may be connected to ISDN, using gateways or bridges to provide a platform for wide-area communications (see Figure 9).

With ISDN, LAN-based image server access allows images of houses and sales items to be rapidly downloaded to CWs in response to client calls made from homes or offices. CLID may be used for access security or billing, and CT may be used to transfer a call to an AW if the client requires service assistance from an agent.

The need for LAN-based communications via ISDN, which is not limited to image transmission, will significantly contribute to the widespread acceptance of ISDN-based platforms. Switched B/H-channels will often prove to be more economical than dedicated high speed links. In addition, the bandwidth of these channels can be dynamically controlled to satisfy changing service requirements in a given user application.

Towards The Year 2001

To become a proven platform for multimedia applications, ISDN must successfully complete its evolution. ISDN nodes

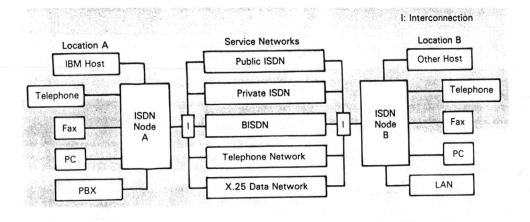

Fig. 10. ISDN access and interconnection evolution.

will evolve during the 1990s to support access by various hosts and devices and provide interconnections to different service networks (see Figure 10).

User requirements will drive the melding of telephony and other APIs. These requirements will be directed at improving the application programming efficiency and allowing the integration of voice, data, image. and video applications. Through this user-driven process, a common API will emerge to facilitate the development of multimedia applications within the OSI framework. Q.931 and Q.932 protocols will provide a lower-layer base for multivendor platforms. These platforms will include interconnections of public and private ISDNs. The increased bandwidth required for some platforms will necessitate bridging to BISDNs supporting transmission speeds of 150 Mb/s or higher. This bridging will include necessary API enhancements to accommodate future BISDN services.

Summary

ISDN computer-aided telephony requires properly architected platforms to satisfy changing application needs during the 1990s. Proper architecting necessitates the use of functionally rich and consistent telephony APIs, such as IBM's CallPath Services Architecture. Other APIs are also needed to support integrated applications. The coexistence of telephony and other APIs must be accommodated in the ISDN driver architecture to make efficient use of D-channel signaling and voice, data, or image communications on the associated B/H-channels. This driver may support OSI, SNA, X.25, or other protocol stacks in the same computer using a single ISDN access link. For ISDN-based telephony under SAA, we foresee a future expansion of the CallPath Services Architecture and the complementary use of CPI-C. Applications being currently explored show that significant benefits can be realized using incoming call management and LAN-based image server access via ISDN. We envision that by the year 2001, a common API will facilitate multimedia applications on multivendor platforms architected within the OSI framework. These platforms will support interconnections of public and private ISDNs and bridging to BISDNs. In this environment, ISDN computer-aided telephony will be used to provide innovative solutions in many customer business applications.

Acknowledgments

The authors wish to acknowledge the valuable contributions to this article by the following reviewers: Vince Carey— Communications Systems (Resarch Triangle Park); Jim Cockrum—Communications Systems (Santa Clara); Bruce Forsyth— IBM Canada Ltd. (Toronto); Tom Hunter—Communications Systems (Research Triangle Park); Jane Munn—Communications Systems (Santa Clara); and Mike Ryan—Communications Systems (Research Triangle Park). Their knowledge in the wide-ranging topics addressed by this article allowed us to successfully respond to the challenging theme, "Where will OSI and ISDN be in the year 2001?"

References

[1] K. Martersteck, "ISDN Delivers the '90s Technology Today," *AT&T Tech.*, vol. 5, no. 1, 1990.

[2] G. L. Zielinski, "ISDN Technology—Serving Industry Today," *AT&T Tech.*, vol. 5, no. 1, 1990.

[3] NIUF/CM-90-01, "Incoming Call Management Application Profile," Draft 3.2, Mar. 1990.

[4] NIUF, Book 7, *List of User Applications*, Nov. 1989.

[5] M. Zulke and S. Chopard, "ISDN Applications in France," *IEEE Telecommun.*, Mar. 1990.

[6] O. Lubliner, "ISDN Development in France," *Telecommun.*, July 1989.

[7] E. M. Hindin, "Hayes Unveils ISDN API, Which Could Become Standard," *Data Commun.*, Feb. 1990.

[8] P. Berkowitz, "Attention Shoppers: Please Proceed To ISDN For Access," *Telephone Eng. and Mngmt.*, June 1990.

[9] IBM SC26-4399-1, "Systems Application Architecture, Common Programming Interface Communications," Oct. 1988.

[10] R. Jepson, "Switch-Computer Applications Interface," ANSI/T1S1.1/89-511, Sept. 1989.

[11] ECMA/TC32-TG11/89, "Computer Supported Telephony Applications," 3rd Draft TR/CSTA, Sept. 1989.

[12] NIUF, "Application Software Interface (ASI) Users Manual," ASI IIW, July 1989.

[13] R. T. Roca, "ISDN Architecture," *AT&T Tech. J.*, Dec. 1988.

[14] CCITT Recommendations X.200–X.219, "Data Communications Networks Open Systems Interconnection (OSI)," *Blue Book*, 1989.

[15] CCITT Recommendation X.31, "Support of Packet Mode Terminal Equipment by an ISDN," Mar. 1988.

[16] IBM S68X-2270, "NetBIOS Application Development Guide," Apr. 1987.

[17] IBM SC31-6805-0, "Image Object Content Architecture Reference," Jan. 1990.

[18] I. Toda, "Migration to Broadband ISDN," *IEEE Commun. Mag.*, Apr. 1990.

[19] W. Stallings, "CCITT Standards Foreshadow Broadband ISDN," *IEEE Telecommun.*, Apr. 1990.

[20] C. L. Wong and R. Wood, Implementation of ISDN, *BNR Telesis*. vol 3. 1986.

[21] B. McNinch, "Screen-Based Telephony," *IEEE Commun. Mag*. Apr 1990.

Biography

Zarko Cvijan is a Staff Development Analyst in Distributed Software Products (DSP) in Toronto, Canada, which is part of the Programming Systems Line of Business. His current involvement in DSP strategy and architecture activities focuses on enabling multimedia distributed application, including ISDN-based platforms. Before joining IBM's Canada Laboratory in 1986, he worked for Bell Canada, where his work included Dataroute and Datapac planning, coordination of SHARE OSI/X.25 activities, and consulting on Datex-P in Germany. He received the B.Sc. degree in electrical engineering from the University of Belgrade, Yugoslavia, in 1966. He is a member of the Association of Professional Engineers of Ontario.

Anthony E. Brock is a Staff Engineer working for the IBM Application Business Systems Line of Business at its facility in Rochester, Minnesota. He is a telecommunications specialist and has held various technical positions in product development, systems architecture, and product planning. He is currently assigned to a market support position for a recently announced ISDN product that works with the IBM AS/400 System. He received a Bachelor of Administration degree in Business Administration from the University of Iowa in 1977. He is a member of the Association for Computing Machinery.

Frank P. Corr is a Senior Technical Staff Member in the IBM Communication Systems Line of Business at Research Triangle Park (RTP), North Carolina. He has written papers on error control, modem design, air traffic control, and packet networks. His three patents are in adaptive error control and multiplexing, with a first-level patent award from IBM. He received his B.E.E. from Manhattan College in 1954, his Master of Engineering from Yale University in 1957, and his doctorate in electrical engineering from Yale in 1960. He is a member of Sigma Xi, Eta Kappa Nu, and the IEEE.

Joi D. Grieg is a Senior Planner working for the IBM Corporation Communication Systems Line of Business supporting the Hursley ISDN Products Group in the U.K. She is located in Gaithersburg, Maryland. She has held a number of marketing, technical, and management positions in the Washington, D.C. metropolitan area. She is currently responsible for U.S. application activities for the Hursley ISDN Products Group. She received a Bachelor of Arts degree from San Francisco State University in 1975 and a Master of Business Administration degree from University of California at Berkeley in 1977.

John E. Kuras is a Senior Engineer working for the IBM Corporation Communication Systems Line of Business at its facility in RTP, North Carolina. He has held a number of technical positions at IBM's development facilities in Kingston, New York, and RTP. He is currently a member of the ISDN Systems Group in RTP. He received a Bachelor of Engineering degree from Pratt Institute, Brooklyn, New York, in 1969 and a Master of Science in electrical engineering from Syracuse University in 1975. He is a member of the Association for Computing Machinery, the Tau Beta Pi Engineering Honor Society, and the Eta Kappa Nu Electrical Engineering Honor Society.

Thomas Schick is a Senior Programmer working for the IBM Corporation in RTP, North Carolina. Most of his career has been devoted to different advanced technology activities, especially in the area of communications. He has concentrated on computer system design considerations, including office systems, in which he introduced several architectures, one of which is called Document Interchange Architecture (DIA). He has received several IBM awards, including a Second Level Invention Achievement Award. He joined IBM in 1960 after receiving a B.A. degree from Hofstra University. He has written several papers, one of which was presented at the IEEE Globecom '84 Conference. That paper and his most recent work have been in the area of voice and data integration, an aspect of which is the subject of this article.

Common Channel Signalling System Number 7 for ISDN and Intelligent Networks

BIJAN JABBARI, SENIOR MEMBER, IEEE

Common channel signalling system number 7, defined by the CCITT Recommendations, is a key element in supporting a large number of applications in telecommunications networks ranging from call control in the interconnection of the exchanges of an integrated services digital network to intelligent networks and mobile telephony services. The traditional methods of inband signalling and other common channel signalling methods in telecommunication networks have given way to an overlay network using a more capable, layered signalling system number 7 protocol. The emerging networks using high capacity packet switches provide a vehicle for reliable transport of circuit-related information between the exchanges for setup and release of calls and reduce the connection setup time significantly. They also provide an opportunity to distribute the network database resources. In this paper, we describe various functional parts of the signalling system number 7 and the underlying concepts. The unique attributes of the lower and higher functional layers are discussed. We present applications of signalling system number 7 both for call control and for transaction services. The signalling transfer point is a major component of common channel signalling systems which makes signalling networks possible. Using the lower layers of the protocol, it provides routing capability for signalling messages between the exchange offices and access of these exchange offices to the network databases. We discuss the performance parameters associated with the signalling transfer point, and finally examine its implementations.

I. INTRODUCTION

A. Signalling

In establishing a call which involves interconnection of multiple switching nodes throughout the path from an origin to destination points in a communication network, addressing, and control information need to be conveyed among the switches. This information is referred to as *signalling* and is used in selecting a path, providing information on the status of the users and resources, or performing the necessary network supervision and charging functions.

The signalling between the two points in a network is comprised of the signalling originated at the two user points (referred to as access signalling), delivered to the network access nodes, and signalling within the backbone network. Security and additional functionality are the two main reasons for separating the backbone signalling from access signalling. Our focus in this paper will be on the signalling within the backbone network which

is often called trunk signalling as it relates to interconnections of the trunks (links between the switches).

One way in which signalling can take place is to seize one of the trunks connecting the switching node to the adjacent switch and then transfer the signalling over this trunk. That is, signalling and conversation take place over the same channel. This is referred to as *inband signalling* and fits the early generation of switches (the electromechanical switch). Typically signalling is conveyed by using a combination of two frequencies. For example, in one such method called MF signalling, each digit is signalled by nearly 100 ms of two tones (approximately 50 ms on, 50 ms off). Inband signalling is slow and susceptible to errors.

Another way is to use separate channels dedicated for signalling between the two switching nodes. This is referred to as *common channel signalling* and fits today's stored program switches. Common channel signalling has its roots in the early days of telephony in which the manual switch operators used a separate path to communicate with each other on which trunks to interconnect [1].

The first CCITT common channel signalling recommendation, referred to as *CCITT No. 6* was introduced for international signalling in 1972. It was designed for low speed links where each link would handle over 200 trunks. It was not a layered protocol and not flexible. In 1976, AT&T introduced Common Channel Interoffice Signalling (CCIS), which was based on CCITT No. 6 adapted to suit the national long haul network. The bit structure of CCIS is different from CCITT No. 6. Signalling information is carried by signal units (SU's), 28 bits long, including 8 bits for error check. Signalling messages must be broken into several SU's. CCITT No. 6 and CCIS have become obsolete and are being replaced by Signalling System Number 7 (SS No. 7). The early work was reported in CCITT Yellow Books in 1980 with further modifications and enhancements in Red Books [2] and [3] and Blue Books in 1984 and 1988, respectively.

The common channel signalling network can be viewed as a packet switched network overlaid on the trunking network, as presented in Fig. 1. In this figure, the exchanges correspond to the Signalling Points (SP's) in the common channel signalling network which are connected via the packet switches known as the Signalling Transfer Points (STP's). The origination and destination exchanges will establish a path, link by link, by sending and receiving messages through this packet switched network to and from the transit exchanges (see Fig. 2).

There are a number of benefits gained by using a common channel signalling approach. First, there is a significant reduction

Manuscript received June 12, 1990; revised August 27, 1990. This work was supported in part by MCI Telecommunications and by Contel Technology Center.

B. Jabbari is with the Department of Electrical and Computer Engineering, George Mason University, Fairfax, VA 22030-4444.

IEEE Log Number 9040848.

Reprinted from the *Proceedings of the IEEE*, Volume 79, Number 2, February 1991, pages 155-169. Copyright © 1991 by The Institute of Electrical and Electronics Engineers, Inc. All rights reserved.

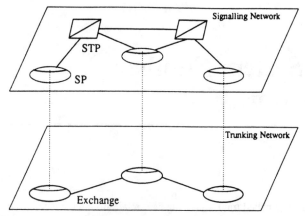

Fig. 1. Conceptual diagram for trunk and signalling networks.

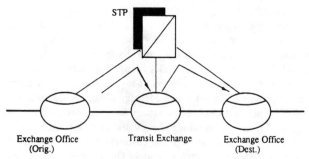

Fig. 2. Flow of messages in establishing a circuit-switched connection.

in connection setup time for the links between the exchanges, as compared to the inband signalling method being practiced. This reduced connection setup time will shorten the total time to establish a path between the two end-users after sending the last digit of the address of the called party (this is sometimes referred to as the *post dial delay*). As the time to setup or disconnect the trunks is considered to be the overhead associated with a call, this reduction in connection setup time will result in a more efficient usage of trunks.

Second, the existence of a signalling path separated from the user information path facilitates call control prior to and during the conversation and provides additional signalling capability, flexibility and security, as compared to inband signalling. For example, by sending interrogation signals to the destination exchange via the signalling network, the originating exchange may gain information regarding the status of the called party or destination resources, prior to making any connections. Or, additional information regarding the calling party can be passed through the signalling network to the destination exchange. The additional signalling capability results in new call features.

Third, by interconnecting the network databases to the signalling network we gain the capability for introducing a spectrum of new services. The data transport capability of the signalling network can be further extended to support network management, billing, test and maintenance, and therefore to provide an opportunity to an integrated transport approach for reliable and efficient means of call control for circuit-switching, network database access and network management, and network processing. This integration would replace the dedicated facilities and use of other protocols and is therefore expected to bring network economy.

Last but not least, availability of a worldwide standard for signalling protocols would result in a more simplified interconnection of networks and facilitate access to their remote databases.

B. ISDN and Common Channel Signalling

Basic call processing within the existing backbone networks or the transit nodes of the Integrated Service Digital Networks (ISDN) requires use of SS No. 7. (Only ISDN service in a very limited form of isolated exchanges does not require the use of the SS No. 7.) For two switches of an ISDN network to exchange signalling information, the communication has to take place using the SS No. 7 protocol. Therefore, regional, national, or international support of ISDN will only be possible if the switches in these networks are equipped with SS No. 7 capability.

C. Intelligent Networks

The introduction of centralized on-line real-time databases to control new services in telecommunications networks has provided an initial framework for intelligent networks [8]. The local exchange and interexchange carriers in the U.S. are beginning to deploy these services [27]. Several architectures have been defined to provide intelligent network services with rapid service introduction and greater flexibility in design and deployment [9]-[11].

One of the main features of intelligent networks is the use of Signalling System No. 7 as the transport vehicle for intelligent network signalling. Examples of intelligent network services include Alternate Billing Service [12], Freephone or Toll-free (800 Service in the U.S.), and Private Virtual Network (PVN) Service. Although, currently, other network access protocols (like X.25) along with proprietary transaction servers are being used in some networks to provide such services, the SS No. 7 protocol is replacing them rapidly.

D. Other Applications

Signalling in mobile telephony is another important area of applications of SS No. 7. The Mobile Telecommunication Switching Offices (MTOS's) may be connected via a dedicated SS No. 7 network for transport of signaling between exchanges and especially to provide a uniform procedure for roaming services (i.e., cellular phone services outside of mobile subscriber's local serving area) between different areas. The nationwide cellular network in the UK (Racal Vodaphone) represents one such implementation [13].

Broadband ISDN [14]-[15] is another area which may initially use SS No. 7. However, significant work is required to determine the signalling requirements, optimum signalling architecture, and the relation of service control to connection control, especially in view of emerging heterogeneous services.

E. Outline of the Paper

In this paper, we continue by considering the general functional structure of the Signalling System No. 7 protocol within the frame of the Open Systems Interconnection (OSI) layered model. Then we consider each functional layer and examine the capability that a particular layer provides along with the message formats and the procedures. We will pay attention to the relation of a particular layer with its users and service providers, and the way messages are formatted. Our objective is to provide a clear understanding of the operation of the protocol. Therefore, at times we may deviate slightly from the specifications, although throughout the paper an attempt has been made to be compatible with the CCITT Recommendations. Throughout the discussion, we report the areas of difference between the CCITT Recommendations and the American National Standards Institute (ANSI) standards. Also, the areas which have not been clearly defined or appear likely to be removed from the specification have not been discussed, nor do they appear graphically. We provide a discussion on major performance issues, however, we avoid any modeling of the performance parameters at this time. Finally, we consider the implementation of the signalling transfer points, and describe representative implemented architectures.

II. SIGNALLING SYSTEM NO. 7 PROTOCOL

A. Signalling System Functional Structure

The Signalling System No. 7 (SS No. 7) protocol functional division, as defined in the CCITT Blue Books, is based on a common signalling transport capability referred to as the Message Transfer Part (MTP) and its users (see Fig. 3). The elements of

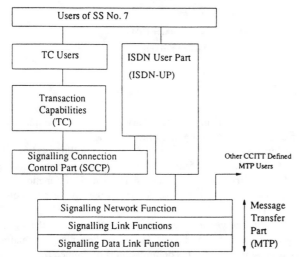

Fig. 3. Signalling system No. 7 functional structure according to CCITT blue books.

this functional division, as described in this paper, are: Call control MPT users: Telephone User Part (TUP)[1] and other MTP users (e.g., Data User Part (DUP), and ISDN User Part (ISDN-UP)); Signalling Connection Control Part (SCCP); SCCP users which include ISDN User Part (ISDN-UP)[2] and Transaction Capabilities (TC); and TC users which include Application Service Elements (ASE's).

B. SS No. 7 Layering and the OSI Reference Model

Although the work in CCITT for the definition of the SS No. 7 protocol started prior to the availability of the OSI reference model defined by the International Standards Organization (ISO), significant efforts have been made to bring the OSI structure into the SS No. 7 protocol. The result of the early attempts appeared in the SS No. 7 layering defined in the CCITT Red Books (Q series Recommendations), and the subsequent conforming to the layering has been described in the CCITT Blue Books [4]–[6].

Figure 4 presents the functional layering of the SS No. 7 in relation to the OSI reference model. The MTP provides reliable transport capability of information in a *connectionless* mode (i.e., no logical connection prior to transfer of information; also known

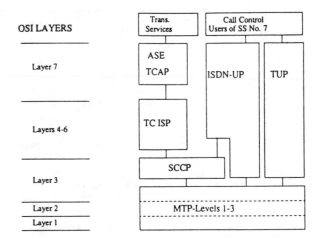

Fig. 4. Functional layering of the SS No. 7 protocol and the OSI model.

as a datagram mode of communication) between the two locations of MTP users. One of the functions of the SCCP is to provide virtual circuit capability. The MTP in conjunction with the SCCP, referred to as Network Service Part (NSP) provides both connection-oriented and connectionless services. The NSP functionality aligns with the layers 1–3 of the OSI reference model (i.e., the physical, data link, and network layers).

The NSP is used by both the ISDN-UP and the TC. The ISDN-UP provides the OSI layers 4 through 7 functionality for call control application services. The OSI layers 4 through 7 provide the end-to-end communication functionality, independent of the network (i.e., transport, session, presentation and application layers). The TC consists of the Intermediate Service Part (ISP) and the Transaction Capability Application Part (TCAP). The TC ISP provides layers 4 through 6 and the TCAP provides layer 7 services to the application process.

C. Signalling Network Components

The components of a signalling network are: Signalling Points (SP's) and Signalling Links (SL's). Examples of SP's are Service Switching Points (SSP's), Service Control Points (SCP's), and Signalling Transfer Points (STP's). SP's are signalling network nodes which originate, terminate, or route the signalling messages. The SSP's [16] are exchange offices and are associated with call processing and communicating with application databases. The SCP's incorporate the intelligence of the network by their database control. The STP's are high capacity packet switches which route and transport signalling messages among SP's. The SL's are used to provide communication paths among SSP's, STP's, and SCP's.

A signalling link set consists of a number of signalling links used as a module that interconnect two SP's. *Signalling route* refers to the predetermined path between originating and terminating SP's passing through STP's. *Signalling route set* consists of all the signalling routes between an originating point and a destination point traversed by a message through the signalling network.

III. MESSAGE TRANSFER PART (MTP)

The MTP is the basic building block for reliable connectionless transport of signalling information within a signalling network. Furthermore, it provides the signalling network management capability in case of failure. The MTP consists of the three elements described as follows.

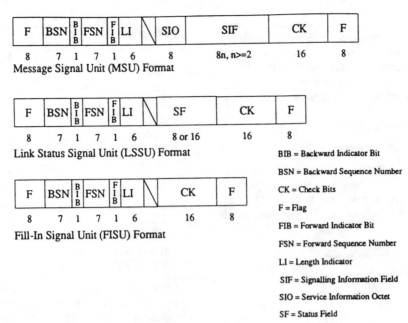

F	BSN	B I B	FSN	F I B	LI	\	SIO	SIF	CK	F
8	7	1	7	1	6		8	8n, n>=2	16	8

Message Signal Unit (MSU) Format

F	BSN	B I B	FSN	F I B	LI	\	SF	CK	F
8	7	1	7	1	6		8 or 16	16	8

Link Status Signal Unit (LSSU) Format

F	BSN	B I B	FSN	F I B	LI	\	CK	F
8	7	1	7	1	6		16	8

Fill-In Signal Unit (FISU) Format

BIB = Backward Indicator Bit

BSN = Backward Sequence Number

CK = Check Bits

F = Flag

FIB = Forward Indicator Bit

FSN = Forward Sequence Number

LI = Length Indicator

SIF = Signalling Information Field

SIO = Service Information Octet

SF = Status Field

Fig. 5. Signal unit formats: MSU, LSSU, and FISU [4,] fig. 3/Q.703].

A. Signalling Data Link

The signalling data link functions are associated with the physical, electrical, and functional characteristics of the signalling path. The signalling data link consists of a full-duplex transparent digital channel operating normally at the bit rate of 64 Kbps[3] and exclusively dedicated to the use of SS No. 7. The transmission path may be based on terrestrial or satellite facilities or a combination of the two. The interface requirements when the digital channel is derived from 1.544 Mbps or 2.048 Mbps digital paths are defined in [17] (for the electrical characteristics) and in [18]-[20] (for the functional characteristics, e.g., for the frame structure).

B. Signalling Link

The physical path, provided by the signalling data link, requires functions and procedures as described in the OSI Layer 2 to provide reliable transfer of signalling information between the two signalling points directly interconnected by that signalling data link. The protocol data unit is referred to as the *signal unit* (also known as frame) and consists of the variable length signalling messages originated at the higher layers and the signalling link control information. Depending on the functionality of the signal unit, three types of signal units can be identified. These signal units are referred to as Message Signal Unit (MSU), Link Status Signal Unit (LSSU), and Fill-In Signal Unit (FISU) and their message formats are presented in Fig. 5. The MSU is a signal unit which carries the signalling information from the signalling link user. The LSSU carries the status indication of the signalling link. The FISU carries only the signalling link functional information and is transmitted when there are no other signal units available for transmission and the functional information (error checking, positive and negative acknowledgements, and sequence numbering) is needed. Sending FISU's assists in determining the

link quality and taking the necessary actions (for example layer 3 management functions) in a timely manner.

A functional block diagram of the signalling link is shown in Fig. 6. The functions of the signalling link and the corresponding fields are discussed below. The fields and their functions are somewhat different from those defined in the LAP-B protocol of X.25 [21].

1) Delimitation and Alignment of Signal Units: As the signalling information has a variable length, its beginning and ending needs to be indicated. This delimitation is performed by a unique bit pattern (01111110) called the *flag* at the start and end of a signal unit. The closing flag of a signal unit is normally the opening flag of the subsequent signal unit. The flag should not be imitated within any other part of the signal unit. Zero insertion and deletion is used to prevent the flag imitation. In this operation, prior to transmission, a zero is inserted in the bit stream after every five consecutive 1 s. At the receiving end, the original bit pattern is restored by deletion of each zero followed directly by five consecutive 1 s after flag detection and removal.

2) Alignment of Signal Units: Alignment is lost either when a disallowed bit pattern due to delimitation (i.e., more than six consecutive 1 s) is received or when a certain maximum length of a signal unit (minimum and maximum of a signal unit is 6 and 279) is exceeded.

3) Error Detection: Prior to delimitation of signalling information, 16 check bits (denoted by CK in Fig. 5) are appended to the end of the bit stream for detection of transmission errors. The generation of the check bits is performed using the *modified cyclic redundancy codes* with the well-known generator polynomial $x^{16} + x^{12} + x^5 + 1$ (bit pattern 10001000000100001). At the receiving point, the received signal unit, after applying the delimitation function, deletion of the inserted zeros and separation of check bits (i.e., the bit stream starting after the opening flag up to the beginning of the check bits) is examined using the received check bits and the same generator polynomial to detect any errors in the signal unit. If presence of any errors within the signal unit is detected, the signal unit is discarded and error condition is indicated.

4) Error Correction: The signalling link employs the retrans-

---

[3]In North America, the standard bit rate may initially be 56 Kbps and will evolve to 64 Kbps. The CCITT Recommendation includes the possibility of using lower bit rates, however for call control the minimum bit rate is specified as 4.8 kbps. Analog channels with modem may also be used.

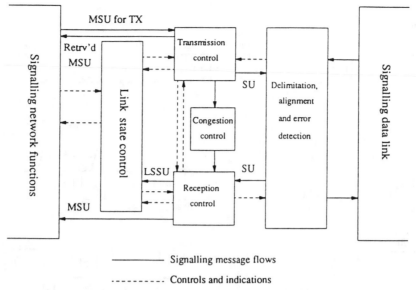

 (Note: remove)

Fig. 6. Signalling link functional block diagram [4, fig. 7/Q.703].

mission methods for correction of the received signal units in corrupt form. Two methods of retransmission are defined: the *basic method* and the *preventive cyclic retransmission* (PCR) method. The basic method is used in signalling links using terrestrial facilities with one-way propagation delay of less than 15 ms, whereas the PCR method applies to signalling links (or one signalling link within a link set) using transmission facilities with propagation delay of 15 ms or greater (e.g., satellite).[4]

The basic method uses both positive and negative acknowledgements, whereas in the PCR method only positive acknowledgements are present. A positive acknowledgement indicates correct receipt of a signal unit. In either retransmission method, a copy of the signal unit being transmitted is maintained in a retransmission buffer at the sending end until a positive acknowledgement for that signal unit is received from the other end and the message in the retransmission buffer is discarded.

The basic method employs the well-known *go-back-n* approach [22] for retransmission. That is, if a negative acknowledgment is received from the other end indicating the receipt of a specific signal unit in corrupt form, that signal unit and all subsequent signal units are retransmitted. Due to the fact that there is no negative acknowledgment in the PCR method when no new signal units are to be transmitted, the previously transmitted signal units which have not yet been positively acknowledged are cyclically retransmitted.

5) Sequence Numbering: Sequence numbering is used to identify and control the sequence of the signal units and for acknowledgment functions. The *Forward Sequence Number*, the 7-bit FSN field in the signal unit, represents the sequence number of the MSU. Similarly, the *Backward Sequence Number*, the 7-bit BSN field in the signal unit, represents the sequence number of an MSU being acknowledged. Each successive MSU increments the last assigned FSN value by 1 using modulo 128. At any time, no more than 127 MSU's may be unacknowledged. Any signal unit other than MSU, i.e., LSSU's and FISU's carries the FNS associated with the last MSU transmitted.

A positive acknowledgment may be sent for correct reception

of one or more MSU's, in which case the receiving point assigns the FSN value of the MSU accepted last to the BSN of the subsequent signal unit. An FISU may be the next signal unit when no MSU's are available at the receiving point to carry the assigned BSN value. Timers are also used to indicate the excessive delay in acknowledgments.

The Forward Indication Bit (FIB) and Backward Indication Bit (BIB) are used to indicate retransmission and negative acknowledgement, respectively. To transmit a negative acknowledgement for a transmitted signal unit, the BIB value of the transmitted signal unit is inverted and maintained in subsequent signal units until another negative acknowledgement is to be sent in which case the BIB is inverted again. The BSN associated with the negative acknowledgement is taken from the FSN field of the last accepted MSU. The retransmissions are indicated by inverting the FIB value upon beginning of retransmission. This inversion is maintained in subsequent signal units until another negative acknowledgement is received.

Figure 7 shows the association of FSN and FIB in one direction together with the BSN and the BIB of the other direction for each direction of MSU flow. Two cases without and with errors have been presented here to demonstrate the changes.

6) Length Indicator: The length indicator (LI) is used to determine the three types of signal units. The length indicator with a value of zero designates the signal unit as FISU. A value of one or two indicates the signal unit as LSSU and any value greater than two indicates the signal unit as MSU. The value of the length indicator represents the number of octets between the end of the LI and beginning of the check bits. When the number of octets exceeds the maximum number presented by the LI, the LI is set to 63.

7) Signalling Information Field and Service Information Octet: The Signalling Information Field (SIF) and the Service Information Octet (SIO) are presented in the MSU and use the functionality provided by the signalling link. The SIO is one octet and the SIF consists of an integer number of octets between 2 and 272.

8) Status Field: This is a one or two octets field for link status indication carried by LSSU. Six different status indications have been defined which include Out of Alignment, Normal, Emergency, Out of Service, Processor Outage, and Busy (B) status.

[4]In the ANSI standards, the basic and PCR methods apply to signalling links (or one signaling link within a link set) established using terrestrial transmission means and via satellites, respectively.

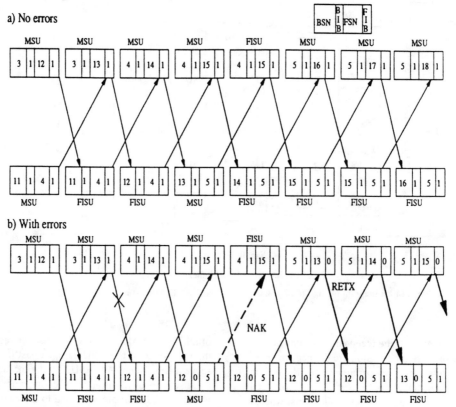

Fig. 7. The association of FSN and FIB, and BSN and BIB of the two directions.

The status indications above are used in initial alignment of the signal link, processor outage, and flow control.

9) Initial Alignment: Upon the first initialization of a link (activation), status information between the two signalling points is exchanged for a specified proving period. This procedure also applies to alignment in restoring a link following its failure. By examining the signal units during the proving, the two end points of the link validate whether the link can carry signal units correctly. The proving period is specified as 2^{16} and 2^{12} octets transmission time for normal and emergency, repectively.

10) Signalling Error Rate Monitoring: The function of signalling error rate monitor is to estimate the signal unit error rate either during the time a link is in service, in which case it provides one of the criteria for taking the link out of service, or during initial alignment.

11) Processor Outage: Processor outage refers to situations occurring at functional layers higher than layer two, where signalling messages cannot be transferred to these layers. One example is the failure of a central processor, which does not necessarily affect all signalling links at a signalling point.

12) Signalling Link Flow Control: When congestion occurs and is detected at the receiving end of a signalling point, the receiving end periodically transmits an SIB (status indication busy) signal to the other end at an interval T5 (80–120 ms). The first receipt of SIB triggers a timer (T6) (3–6 s). When congestion is ceased, the receiving point stops sending SIB and resumes the normal operation [23]. On the other hand, if the timer T6 expires, the link is declared failed.

C. Signalling Network Functions

The MTP signalling network functions have two purposes. First, they define the protocols for reliable transfer of signalling messages between the nodes of the signalling network, and second, they provide the necessary management actions and procedures to reconfigure the routing of messages through the signalling network in the case of failure and congestion. The two classes of functions are referred to as *signalling message handling* and *signalling network management* and are discussed as follows (see Fig. 8). The MTP signalling network functions reside on top of the MTP signalling link functionality and provide services to the MTP users (SCCP, ISDN-UP, and TUP). The format associated with the signalling network functions (the payload of MSU) is provided in Fig. 9 and the functions of each element are discussed here.

1) Signalling Message Handling: Signalling message handling functions include *message routing*, *message distribution*, and *message discrimination*. These functions are necessary to transport a message between two users of MTP over a signalling link or a route (successive signalling links). The segments SIF and SIO incorporate the signalling message handling functions and the user information. The protocol part includes a *routing label* which consists of the user part information plus the addresses of the origination and destination points of the message as well as the routing information. These are referred to as Originating Point Code (OPC), Destination Point Code (DPC), and Signalling Link Selection (SLS), respectively. SLS is used to perform load sharing among a multiplicity of signalling links. The SIO includes a Service Indicator (SI) and a SubService Field (SSF). The SI (4 bits) is used for message distribution (e.g., to a user part such as SCCP, ISDN-UP, etc.) or to support the signalling network management at the destination point (or, in some circumstances for routing). The SSF (4 bits) includes a two bit field (the two most significant bits) referred to as the network indicator and distinguishes between the national and international message types (for example, the label sizes).

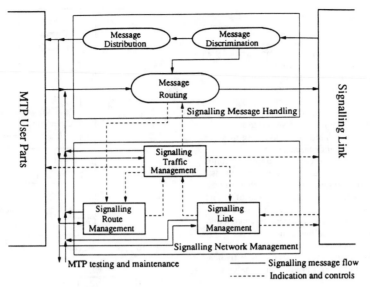

Fig. 8. Signalling network functions [4, fig. 1./Q.704].

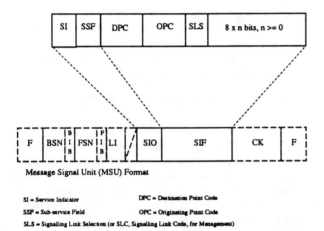

Message Signal Unit (MSU) Format

SI = Service Indicator   DPC = Destination Point Code

SSF = Sub-service Field   OPC = Originating Point Code

SLS = Signalling Link Selection (or SLC, Signalling Link Code, for Management)

Fig. 9. Signalling network message structure.

Addresses of the signalling points are unique binary codes. The standard routing label is 32 bits, comprised of 14 bits for DPC, 14 bits for OPC, and 4 bits for SLS. The international signalling networks should conform to this specification. However, the national networks may be different. For example, in North America, the national routing label is 56 bits. The DPC and OPC are each 24 bits comprised of 3 fields. These are network cluster member, network cluster and network identifier, each 8 bits long.

To send a message on a particular signalling link, the originating signalling point assembles a routing label by using a routing table. This routing table provides information on possible outgoing signalling links for each destination point code. The SLS field provides the capability to distribute the load over the possible outgoing links. Therefore, when the sequence of transmission of a transaction is required to be preserved, the same SLS should be used.

Message discrimination and distribution involves a received message, where it examines its DPC to determine whether the message is destined for the receiving signal point. If so, the SIO is examined by the message distribution function to identify the user part. Otherwise, if the receiving point has STP capability, it directs the message to the routing function. In case the routing function cannot deliver the message, it would generate a signal-

ling network management message (in this case, a transfer-prohibited message).

2) Signalling Network Management: The signalling network management is comprised of *signalling traffic management*, *signalling link management*, and *signalling route management*. These functions perform the internal network management of the signalling network and traffic in the case of failure or congestion. Failure may involve the signalling points, signalling transfer points, and links. Specific procedures have been defined to change the network configuration or restore the normal configuration upon availability of the faulty links or signalling points. General conditions that change the status of the network components have been presented in Table 1 and the procedures for signalling traffic

Table 1   Signalling Network Management Status

Signalling point	Available	Unavailable	
Signalling link	Available	Unavailable	
	Activated	Deactivated	
	Restored	Failed	
	Unblocked	Blocked	
	Uninhibited	Inhibited	
Signalling route	Available	Unavailable	Restricted
Signalling route set	Congested	Uncongested	

management, signalling link management, and signalling route management have been given in Tables 2–4, respectively.

IV. SIGNALLING CONNECTION CONTROL PART

Signalling Connection Control Part (SCCP) enhances the functionality of the MTP in several areas. These areas include connection-oriented services (logical signalling connections), connectionless control, routing, and management. The SCCP functions are used for the transfer of circuit related and noncircuit related information. Network Service Part (NSP), which includes the SCCP and MTP, provides the OSI layer 3 functionality. Figure 10 presents the basic structure of SCCP. SCCP provides the following services: basic connectionless class, sequenced MTP connectionless class, basic connection-oriented class, flow control connection-oriented class.

Table 2 Signalling Traffic Management Procedures

Procedure	Function
Changeover	Ensures that signalling traffic carried by a link that becomes unavailable is directed to alternative links while avoiding loss, duplication or missequencing
Changeback	Ensures that signalling traffic carried by alternative links is diverted to the link made available, while avoiding loss, duplication or missequencing
Forced rerouting	Ensures restoration of signalling capability between two signalling points towards a particular destination, in such a way as to minimize the consequences of failure
Controlled rerouting	Restores the optimal signalling routing and minimizes message missequencing
Signalling point restart	Restarts a signalling point when it becomes available by using Traffic Restart Allowed message and activates all signalling links of that signalling point
Management inhibiting	Is requested by management for maintenance and testing of a signalling link
Signalling traffic flow control	Limits signalling traffic when the signalling network cannot transfer all signalling traffic offered by the user due to network failures or congestion

Table 3 Signalling Link Management Procedures

Procedure	Function
Signalling Link activation restoration, and deactivation	Either signalling initial alignment, or deactivation process applies
Link set activation	To activate a specified number of signalling links for the link
Automatic Allocation of signalling terminals and signalling data links	Signalling terminals may be allocated automatically to a signalling link

Table 4 Signalling Route Management Procedures

Procedure	Function
Transfer controlled	Performed at an STP for messages relating to a given destination, when it has to inform one or more originating SP's to restrict or no longer send messages of given priority or lower.
Transfer prohibited	Performed at a signalling point acting as an STP for messages relating to a given destination, when it has to notify one or more adjacent SP's that they no longer route via the affected STP.
Transfer allowed	Performed at an SP, acting as an STP when it has to notify other adjacent SP's, that they may reroute to it.
Transfer restricted	Performed at the STP for messages relating to a given destination, when it has to notify one or more adjacent signalling points that they should, if possible, no longer route via that STP.
Signalling-route-set-test	Used at an SP to test whether or not signalling traffic towards a certain destination may be routed via adjacent STP.
Signalling-route-set-congestion test	Used at an originating SP to update the congestion status associated with a route set towards a certain destination.

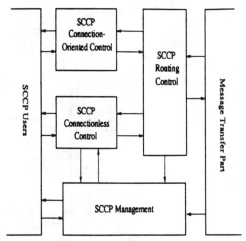

Fig. 10. Basic structure of SCCP [4].

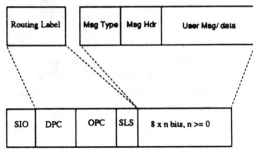

Fig. 11. SCCP message structure.

The format of SCCP is presented in Fig. 11. In the SIO field the designation of the SCCP use is given (0011 as the code). The SIF part includes the following: the routing label, the message type codes, the mandatory fixed part, the mandatory variable part, and the optional part. Figure 12 presents the detailed format of the SCCP messages.

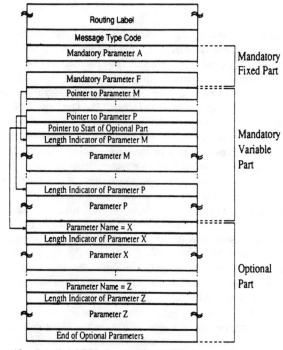

Fig. 12. Detailed SCCP message format [4].

The connection-oriented services (virtual circuit capability) of the signalling connection control include the three phases of connection establishment, data transfer, and connection release. The connection establishment involves the SCCP routing function, in addition to MTP routing. An important characteristic of SCCP is the global title routing. The SCCP routing, in both connectionless and connection-oriented service, includes a translation function which maps the SCCP address parameter from a global title (i.e., global title translation (GTT)), (e.g., dialed digits) to, for example, a point code and a subsystem number. (Subsystem Number (SSN) is a subaddress which identifies an SCCP user function.) This function in the OSI model is equivalent to the network-service-access-point (NSAP).

The global address routing is used when the originating node does not have the network address of the destination point. This function is needed in a variety of applications (for example 800 number). For example, in global title routing, the signalling message comprised of a DPC and a global title is routed to an STP, designated by its DPC. At the STP the global title address is translated into a DPC and an SSN where, subsequently, this DPC is used for network routing (i.e., the signalling point) and the SSN to identify the service at the signalling point. There are four types of global title routing designated by the global title indicator of the address indicator. They deal with aspects such as numbering plan and encoding scheme.

The SCCP management provides procedures for rerouting or throttling traffic when there is failure or congestion of the network. These functions are based on either signalling point status management or subsystem status management. The SCCP management procedures apply to both the connection-oriented and the correctionless services of the SCCP. These procedures use the information provided in the primitives or in SCCP management messages on failure, recovery, and congestion associated with MTP or subsystem, respectively. The management information messages make use of SCCP connectionless services for transfer.

V. ISDN USER PART

A. Protocol

The ISDN User Part (ISDN-UP) protocol [24] provides call-related services in support of ISDN. The protocol supports the basic bearer service and supplementary services. The basic bearer support includes the establishment of circuit-switched network connections between exchanges, as well as supervision and release of these conditions. Examples of the supplementary services include *calling line identification* (presenting or restricting calling party's number to the called party), *call forwarding*, and *user-to-user signalling* (transfer of signalling information within ISDN-UP message during call set up and clearing).

The ISDN-UP accesses the MTP directly or via the SCCP to transfer the signalling information between the user parts. When using the MTP directly (the message handling function of the MTP), which is normally the case for simple call setup and release and some supplementary services, the SIO field will indicate the ISDN-UP (coded as 0101), and the SIF will contain the routing label (DPC, OPC, and SLS) and ISDN-UP message. The ISDN-UP message consists of a Circuit Identification Code (CIC) field (for referencing a particular circuit), message type, and the parameters. The format of the ISDN-UP message is given in Fig. 13. When the interfacing of the ISDN-UP is with the SCCP, the SIO, the routing label, and the CIC are not included in the SCCP user data parameter passed between the two.

The message type code is a one octet field which uniquely

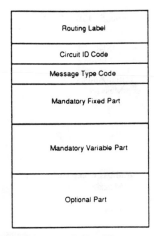

Fig. 13. The ISDN-UP message format [5].

defines the function and format of each ISDN-UP message. For example, the Initial Address Message (IAM) type is coded as 00000001, and the Address Complete Message (ACM) and Answer Message (ANM) types are coded 00000110 and 00001001, respectively. These messages are defined later.

The *mandatory fixed part* refers to a set of predefined fixed-length parameters for a particular message type. The *mandatory variable part* refers to a set of predefined variable-length parameters with pointers for a particular message type. The pointers (one octet) indicate the beginning of each parameter and all are sent successively at the beginning of the mandatory variable part (including a pointer indicating the beginning of the optional part). The length of each parameter is included in itself as the parameter length indicator prior to the contents of the parameter. However, the number of mandatory parameters is uniquely defined for each message type. The *optional part* consists of name (one octet), length indicator (one octet), and the content of a set of parameters, fixed length and variable length, that may or may not be present in any particular message type.

B. ISDN-UP Messages

The ISDN-UP functions at two exchanges communicate with each other using the ISDN-UP message format described above. There is a large set of predefined message types where each message type performs a specific function. Table 5 provides a sample list of the messages used in call setup and release. Only fixed and variable mandatory parameters have been specified. However, each message type may include fixed, variable, and optional parameters. For example, Fig. 14 presents the IAM with mandatory fixed and variable parameters.

C. Call Setup and Clearing

Using the message definition of Table 5, we present the general call setup and clearing in Fig. 15. The calling party initiates a call which generates an ISDN-UP message at the originating exchange. (As we are concerned with the backbone network, we assume that somehow the appropriate messages are sent and received at the two ends of the exchange office to or from their corresponding subscriber parties. For example, using ISDN access signalling, which is the recommended access signalling[5], the call initiation is performed by sending a *setup* message.) The signal-

---

[5]In the ANSI standards, this is not constrained to the ISDN access signalling.

Table 5 ISDN-UP Messages

ISDN-UP Message	ABR	Direction	Purpose	Parameters (Mandatory) Fixed or Variable (Octet)
Initial Address Message	IAM	Forward	To initiate call setup by reserving an outgoing trunk, and to carry the trunk code, number, and other information about routing and handling of the call	Message type, Nature of connection indicators, Forward call indicators, Calling party's category, Transmission medium requirement, Called party number (10-17)
Address Complete Message	ACM	Reverse	To indicate the complete receipt of the called party address at the final destination exchange	Message type, Backward call indicator, (3)
Answer Message	ANM	Reverse	To indicate the call has been answered	Message Type (1)
Continuity Message	COT	Forward	To verify the successful completion of a continuity-check of the communication path between the exchanges	Message type, Continuity indicators (2)
Release Message	REL	Either	To indicate that the circuit is being released	Message type, Cause indicators (4-X)
Release Complete	RLC	Either	To respond to REL and indicate ready for reseizure	Message type (1)

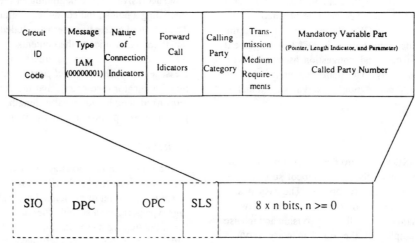

Fig. 14. An example of the IAM message with mandatory fixed and variable parameters.

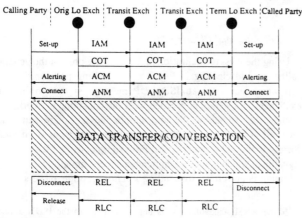

Fig. 15. Message flow for ISDN-UP basic setup and release.

ling normally takes place by transmitting an IAM to transit exchanges and finally to the destination exchange in a tandem fashion. In this case, each IAM from one exchange to the next one carries the necessary information regarding the call and the selected trunk. However, there is also a possibility for an end-to-end basis for exchange of information, particularly when the originating exchange needs to obtain information regarding the availability of the called party or available trunks to complete the call at the other end. The message flow in Fig. 15 is followed until a communication path is established between the two subscribers (when the call is successful). Normally, between three and five messages are used (at each originating, transit or destination exchange) for setting up a path. After the data transfer phase (conversation) is completed, the circuit is released by one of the exchanges sending a REL message. Normally two messages are used for clearing a call.

VI. TRANSACTION CAPABILITIES

The Transaction Capabilities (TC) protocol provides control and transfer of noncircuit-related information between two nodes in a network. For example, using TC, the signalling information can be exchanged between two exchanges, or an exchange can access a database for number translation. Additionally, a wide range of applications have been identified as TC users. These include applications in mobile telephony services (for example location of mobile roamers), ISDN supplementary services, and operation and maintenance. Transaction capabilities consist of Transaction Capability Application Part (TCAP) and Intermediate Service Part (ISP). The TCAP layer functions correspond to those residing in the OSI layer 7, whereas the ISP will provide the OSI functionality corresponding to layers 4 through 6. Figure 16 shows the services provided by the SCCP for use by the TCAP.

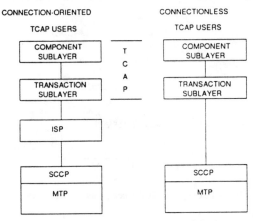

Fig. 16. Connectionless and connection-oriented TCAP structures.

Both connectionless and connection-oriented services are represented in this diagram. The former directly uses SCCP services while the latter uses the ISP services. The TC-users are categorized as either interactive or bulk data applications. The interactive applications (delay sensitive short size data) use connectionless services of TC, whereas the bulk interactive applications (delay tolerant large volume of data) use connection-oriented services of TC.

A. Transaction Capability Application Part

The TCAP[6] is the highest layer based on the SS No. 7 protocol. Examples of applications that use TCAP include toll-free service requiring database access and translation, calling card and credit card validations, directory services, and any other service that may require a query/response type of interaction or bulk data transfer. The generic services to applications that TCAP is expected to provide are independent of these applications.

In the OSI model, the communication between the Application Processes (AP's) (an AP is defined as a range of functions and features in support of particular network requirements) takes place by interactions between the Application Entities (AE's). The AE is a part of the application layer representing the communication function of the AP. An AP may be represented by one or more

AE's whereas an AE may represent only one AP. An AE consists of one or more Application Service Elements (ASE) which are used for interactions between AE's. TCAP is essentially an ASE and it is possible to have other ASE's using the service provided by TCAP.

The Association Control Service Element (ACSE) provides interactions between two application entities (AE's) communicating by means of presentation connection using at least the presentation service kernel unit. The interactive applications in the OSI model are defined under the Recommendations X.219 [21] which include the CCITT OSI applications for remote operations. In X.219, remote operations are carried out within the context of an application association built over a presentation connection.[7] In TCAP the remote operations are carried out in the context of a connectionless network layer service. The transaction sublayer serves the purpose of the ACSE and establishes a pseudo association by directly using the connectionless network layer service provided by the SCCP.

B. TCAP Message Structure

The TCAP is composed of two sublayers: the Component sublayer and the Transaction sublayer (see Fig. 17). Units of infor-

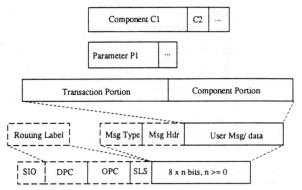

Fig. 17. TCAP message structure.

mation may be found in both sublayers. The Component sublayer provides facilities to request an *operation* (an action to be performed by the remote end), request a *reply* or establish a *dialogue*.[8] The Transaction sublayer provides the capability for the exchange of components between two TC-users. Each unit of information, within the TCAP message has the same general structure. This unit is further divided into three basic subunits: an Identifier field, a Length of Contents field, and a field containing the Contents itself.

The Identifier identifies what information is about to follow. The Length of Contents field is coded to indicate how many octets of useful data is about to follow in the Contents field. It obviously does not include the Identifier or itself. Finally, the information/data is included in the Contents field. The Contents field of each unit of information may be categorized as either *constructor* or *primitive*. If the Contents field is a constructor, its Contents field can contain further "triplets" or information units. TCAP allows unlimited nesting capability. If the Contents field contains no more "triplets," it is referred to as a primitive, i.e., it contains only one value of information.

---

[6]The ANSI standards defined under T.114.4 [28] include minor variations in several areas (the Transaction sublayer, the Component sublayer and the encoding of messages) from those defined by the CCITT in the Blue Books [6].

[7]Unless an application context definition includes Reliable Transfer Service Element (RTSE).

[8]In the ANSI standards, Query, Conversation, and Response are used.

The TCAP message structure does not make use of pointers. This type of message architecture has a high degree of overhead but has the advantage of allowing distributed processing. Thus in forming a TCAP message, each unit of information can be constructed or assembled separately. When several units are assembled, they may be housed together in a constructor and finally, the entire TCAP message would be assembled in one constructor. The Identifier and Length of Contents field can comprise more than one octet each. The TCAP formatting allows for an extended format to overcome the limitation of the SS No. 7 messages (the maximum SIF size of 272 octets).

The TCAP message, structured as a single constructor information unit, can be divided into portions—a Transaction Portion that contains information units sent by the Transaction sublayer and a Component Portion that contains information used by the Component sublayer. The Component Portion is nothing but the Contents field of an information unit housed in the Transaction Portion. The Component Portion can contain more than one Component and each of these is a constructor information unit as shown in Fig. 18. The blocking of components in TCAP messages (i.e., remote operations) does not exist in the OSI model [21], [25].

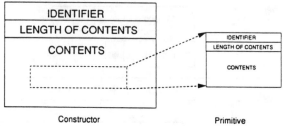

Fig. 18. Structure of TCAP information unit.

The various message types that are supported under the umbrella of the Transaction Portion are Unidirectional, Begin, End, Continue, Abort (by service Provider), and Abort (by service User). The Component types that are supported under the umbrella of the Component Portion are Invoke, Return Result (Last and Not Last), Return Error, and Reject. The use of Transaction Portion and Component Portion fields within the context of a TCAP message, the flow of TCAP messages and the exchange of components are described as follows.

Figure 19 presents an example of the flow of TCAP messages, identified by the TCAP Message Type. Node A could begin a

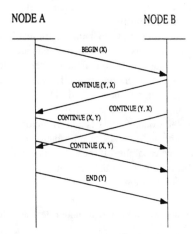

Fig. 19. An example of the flow of TCAP messages.

Message with a BEGIN (Originating Transaction ID = X). Node B could respond with a CONTINUE (Originating Transaction ID = Y, Destination Transaction ID = X). Note that in a CONTINUE Message, the Destination Transaction ID is in fact a reflection of the received Originating Transaction ID. If node B could formulate a repiy for the TCAP message received from node A without requiring further information from node A, it could respond with an END (Originating Transaction ID = X). Exchange of information, and in fact Return Result Component Types, could continue between the nodes until all Invoke Components have been replied to. The final message that ends the TCAP dialogue is an END Message Type and the result contained in it will be final by nature. In this case, the TCAP dialogue has terminated with node A responding to an Invoke Component received in a CONTINUE Message from node B.

Figure 20 presents an example of the flow to TCAP Components, identified by the Component Types. Node A has initiated

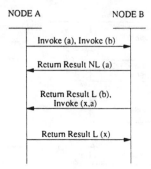

Fig. 20. An example of TCAP component flows.

a TCAP message with two Invoke Components (with two distinct Invoke ID's, ''a'' and ''b''). Node B then responds with a CONTINUE message with a Return Result—Not Last Component (Invoke ID = a, which is a reflection of the Invoke ID in the received TCAP message). Node B also sends another CONTINUE Message, two Components, Return Result L (Invoke ID = b, reflecting the ID in the received Invoke) and an Invoke (Invoke ID = x, Linked ID = a) indicating that this is a Linked Invoke or Child Invoke to a previous Invoke Component. Node A finally responds to an END. The only Component contained in it is the Return Result—Last (Invoke ID = x).

VII. TC Users

The TC users reside above TCAP, The application layer protocols include AE's and ASE's. The AE's provide the communication function of an application process where the ASE's are their components. The Operations, Maintenance and Administration Part (OMAP) is one example of a TC user with one ASE in addition to TCAP.

VIII. Performance

The performance objectives for SS No. 7 have been specified, taking into account meeting the requirements of various supported users, signalling traffic features and the transmission media characteristics. The performance requirements have been defined by a number of parameters for each SS No. 7 functional component. These include the performance specification for MTP [4, Q.706], SCCP [4, Q.716], applications using TUP [5, Q.725], and applications using ISDN-UP [5, Q.766]. In the following, we elaborate on the performance of the MTP further, as it provides the basis for transport of both call control and distributed processing applications, therefore a determining factor in their performance objectives. The MTP performance includes availability, message error loss and missequencing, message transfer times, and traffic throughput.

The availability objective is defined as the unavailability of a signaling route set which in a year should not exceed 10 min. A partitioning of this requirement can be an unavailability of no more than 3 min per year for each of the two user interface segments, an unavailability of no more than 2 min per year for each of the two network access segments, and a negligible amount for the backbone network segment. The backbone performance requirement is normally achieved by replication of the nodes and links.

The message error, loss, and missequencing requirements have been defined based on the signalling data link bit error rates of less than 10^{-6} and 10^{-4} for long term and medium term, respectively [32]. These include an undetected signal unit error rate of less than 10^{-10}, out-of-sequence and duplication of message rate of less than 10^{-10}, and loss message rate of less than 10^{-7}. There are other parameters for example resulting from management functions which have impact on the performance of MTP. However, they are not specified as strict requirements. For instance, changeover will be initiated when burst signal unit errors of approximately 128 msec occur (which results in loss of alignment). Similarly, changeover will be initiated when random signal unit errors occur at a rate exceeding 4×10^{-4} [4, Q.704 and Q.703].

The message transfer time components include propagation times of the signalling data links, queueing delays and retransmission delays, and message handling times. The queueing delay is incurred due to buffering of messages prior to sending them over the signalling links. The queuing delay depends on the selected retransmission method (basic or preventive cyclic retransmission method). Figure 21 shows the mean total queueing delay for basic error correction as a function of MSU traffic loading with mean MSU length of 15 octets over a signalling data link of 64 Kbps and a round trip propagation delay of 30 ms [4]. The

message handling time at the signalling points consists of MTP sending time at the originating signalling point (MTP transmit processing delay), MTP receiving time at the destination signalling point (MTP receive processing delay), and may include message transfer delay at the signalling transfer points. The MTP overall transfer time consists of the MTP send time, MTP receive time, overall propagation time, message transfer times of the STP's involved, and any additional queueing delay due to errors.[9]

The traffic throughput depends on the traffic characteristics presented at the signalling channel and therefore there are no specific recommendations. In practice, the links are normally engineered to handle the peak traffic load and, in the case of failure, to maintain the incurring message delays within the predefined allocation.

IX. STP IMPLEMENTATION

In this section, we present some sample implementations of STP's. In comparing the STP's with packet switches based on other protocols, one can notice the significantly higher switching rate for the STP's. This high rate is achieved by the hardware architectures to reduce the time for passing messages. Furthermore, these switches are designed to meet a high availability and reliability objective.

The DSC Communication's STP [29] referred to as MegaHub STP implements the MTP and the SCCP. Figure 22 presents a

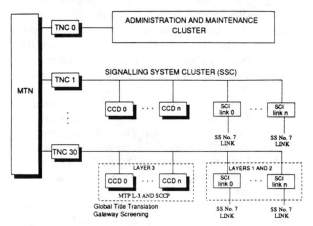

Fig. 22. Functional block diagram of DSC's STP.

functional block diagram of this STP which is comprised of the three major building elements of Message Transport Network, Administration and Maintenance Cluster, and Signalling System Clusters. Up to 30 Signalling System Clusters can communicate over a very high-speed bus called Message Transport Network. Each Signalling System Cluster can be configured with a maximum of 24 links. Each Signalling System Cluster consists of the Serial Communications Interface (SCI), the Common Channel Distribution (CCD) Processors, and a Transport Node Controller. The Serial Communications Interface performs MTP level 1 and 2 functions. The CCD Processors serve as a pooled resource (up to 8) to perform MTP routing and distribution, SCCP connectionless message routing and control, SCCP GTT, and gateway message screening. The Transport Node Controller (TNC) performs exchange of messages among processors within a Signal-

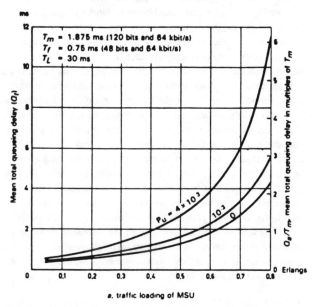

Fig. 21. Mean total queueing delay for basic error correction as a function of MSU traffic loading (signaling data link is 64 kbps, mean MSU length is 15 octets and round trip propagation delay is 30 ms. [4,] fig. 4/Q.706).

[9]The queueing delays when there are no disturbances are included in the message handling times at the signalling points and the signalling transfer points.

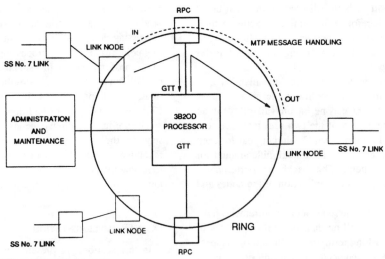

Fig. 23. Functional block diagram of AT&T's 2A STP.

ling System Cluster or between other TNC's, and maintenance functions for a cluster. The Administration and Maintenance Cluster performs a number of functions relative to system operation and management of STP. These include interface to support system, man–machine interface, and collection of measured data and statistics.

AT&T's STP [30] known as 2A STP is shown in Fig. 23. Unlike the DSC's STP, AT&T's implementation is based on a dual ring. The 2A STP consists of four major functional parts: Link Nodes, Ring Peripheral Controller (RPC), Token ring, and Central Processing Unit. The Link Nodes provide the SS No. 7 link interface to the ring. Messages arriving on a signalling link are routed over the ring to another signalling link using the Link Nodes. That is, the routing function is provided without messages reaching the central processor. For global title translation, the path is via the central processor. The RPC nodes provide interface to the 3B20D Processor. The message routing to and from the 3B20D Processor is performed by RPC nodes. The administration and maintenance support is provided through the 3B20D via a number of interfaces.

The Northern Telecom's STP (DMS-STP) has an architecture close to the DSC's. Figure 24 presents the DMS-STP [31], [33]

which is also known as part of the Supernode. This STP consists of the following major functional parts: DMS-CORE, a DMS-BUS, and a number of SS No. 7 Link Interface Units (LIU7's). The DMS-CORE provides MTP and SCCP management functions, operations support system, and maintenance system. The DMS-BUS is a high speed communication bus which interconnects a number of clusters and performs switching of messages among clusters. LIU7's provide interface to SS No. 7 links and perform MTP routing, SCCP routing, global title translation, and gateway screening. Up to 24 LIU's interconnected via a local message switch make up a Link Interface Module (LIM). Routing and global title translation of messages arriving at an LIU7 of a LIM and destined to a signalling link on a different LIM are performed at the arriving LIU 7 and are sent over the DMS-BUS.

X. Conclusion

Signalling networks based on common channel signalling system number 7 are emerging rapidly as they provide transport vehicles for intelligent network services in addition to basic call processing in the existing backbone networks or the transit networks of the ISDN. Here our focus was to provide a conceptual framework in order to describe a large number of functions performed by this protocol and consider in some detail the elements of this protocol and its unique attributes. Signalling networks are finding their own place in the local or long-haul telecommunications networks, as they could integrate a variety of control services including billing and administration of the networks. Furthermore, developments of transaction-based services will introduce a spectrum of new applications and may change the initial characteristics of the common channel signalling networks. It is expected that not very far in the future, the majority of calls made will require at least one database access before the call is delivered. The protocol has been designed with two objectives in mind, the ability to provide high performance as well as reliability. The well defined capabilities of the protocol to respond to possible processor or link failures and congestion have made common channel signalling system number 7 well accepted in the telecommunications industry.

Acknowledgment

The author would like to thank Bur Goode and Ray Piplani of IBM, Per Dahlman of Infonet Technologies, and reviewers at Bellcore for their comments.

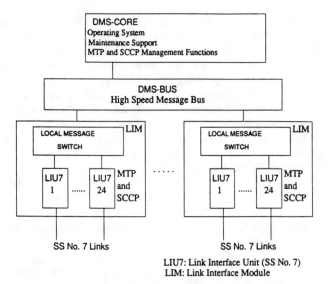

LIU7: Link Interface Unit (SS No. 7)
LIM: Link Interface Module

Fig. 24. Functional block diagram of Northern Telecom's STP.

REFERENCES

[1] Amos E. Joel, Jr., "Switching technology from Strowger switch to SPC," The Plenary Session of ISS'90 Stockholm, Sweden, May 1990.

[2] W. C. Roehr, Jr., "Inside SS no. 7: A detailed look at ISDN's signalling system plan," *Data Commun.*, pp. 120–128, Oct. 1985.

[3] G. G. Schlanger, "An overview of signaling system no. 7," *IEEE J. Select. Areas in Commun.*, vol. SAC-4, May 1986.

[4] CCITT Blue Book Recommendation Q.700-716, vol. VI, Fascicle VI.7, Specifications of Signalling System Number 7, 1989, Geneva.

[5] CCITT Blue Book Recommendation Q.721-766, vol. VI, Fascicle VI.8, Specifications of Signalling System Number 7, 1989, Geneva.

[6] CCITT Blue Book Recommendation Q.771-Q.795, vol. VI, Fascicle VI.9, Specification of Signalling System Number 7, 1989, Geneva.

[7] A. Modarressi, R. Skoog, and S. Boyles, Guest Eds. "The role of signaling system no. 7 in the global information age network," *IEEE Commun. Mag.*, (Special Issue), vol. 28, July 1990.

[8] R. Betts, R. Drignath, and M. Langenbach-Belz, "What makes a network intelligent?," in *Proc. First Int. Conf. Intelligent Networks*, Bordeaux, France, Mar. 1989, pp. 1–6.

[9] P. Ralph and V. Stoss, "The evolution of Intelligent Networks," in *Proc. First Int. Conf. Intelligent Networks*, Bordeaux, France, Mar. 1989, pp. 39–43.

[10] B. Goode, "Intelligent Network Evolution," in *Proc. IEEE Workshop on Networks*, George Mason University, Fairfax, VA, Apr. 1989.

[11] Advance Intelligent Network (AIN) Release 1 Baseline Architecture, Bellcore SR-NPL-001555, issue 1, Mar. 1990.

[11] Advance Intelligent Network (AIN) Release 1 Baseline Architecture, Bellcore SR-NPL-001555, issue 1, Mar. 1990.

[12] "Operator services systems generic requirements," Bellcore TR-TSY-000271: LIDB & LSDB Sec. 10.6, 22.3, 22.4, OSSGR, issue 1, Dec. 1985, revision 3, Mar. 1988.

[13] H. Lindqvist, "The future of roaming services and cellular networking," in *Proc. Nat. Commun. Forum*, vol. XXXXI, Sept. 1987, pp. 923–926.

[14] "Broadband aspects of ISDN, baseline document," T1S1 Tech. Subcommittee Rep. T1S1.1/89-395, Sept. 1989.

[15] S. Minzer, "Broadband ISDN and asynchronous transfer mode (ATM)," *IEEE Commun. Mag.*, vol. 27, pp. 17–24, Sept. 1989.

[16] "Database Services," Bellcore TR-TSY-000533, LSSGR, Issue 2, July 1987.

[17] CCITT Recommendation G.703, Physical/electrical characteristics of hierarchical digital interfaces, vol. III.

[18] CCITT Recommendation G.704, Functional characteristics of interfaces associated with network nodes, vol. III.

[19] CCITT Recommendation G.733, Characteristics of primary PCM multiplex equipment operating at 1544 kbit/s, vol. III.

[20] CCITT Recommendation G.736, Characteristics of digital multiplex equipment operating at 1544 kbit/s, vol. III.

[21] CCITT Blue Book Recommendations X.200 Series, vol. VIII, Fascicle VIII.4, Data communications network: Open systems interconnection (OSI)—Model and notation, service definition. Recommendation X.200-X.219, 1989, Geneva.

[22] M. Schwartz, *Telecommunication Networks*. Reading, MA: Addison-Wesley, 1988, ch. 4, pp. 127–156.

[23] B. Jabbari, "Routing and congestion control in signalling networks," Network Performance Lab., George Mason Univ., Tech. Rep., to be published.

[24] H. R. Appenzeller, "Signaling system no. 7 ISDN user part," *IEEE J. Select. Areas Commun.*, vol. SAC-4, p. 366, May 1986.

[25] B. Jabbari, A. Merchant, and R. Piplani, "Comparison of CCITT application layer protocols: X.219 and Q.771-775," Network Performance Lab., George Mason Univ., Tech. Rep., Mar. 1990.

[26] P. Distler, "Le système signalisation par canal sémaphore CCITT no. 7-premier bilan et perspective," *L' Ècho des Recherches*, no. 134, 1988.

[27] L. Bower, and F. Tanaka, "Intelligent network control of private virtual network service using the service control point," in *Proc. First Int. Conf. Intelligent Networks*, Bordeaux, France, Mar. 1989, pp. 31–33.

[28] ANSI for Telecommunications Signalling System Number 7, Transaction Capability Application Part (TSCAP), ANSI T1.114, 1988.

[29] MEGAHUB STP-Signal Transfer Point System Description, DSC Communications, 1990.

[30] D. C. Donohoe, G. H. Johannessen, and R. E. Stone, "Realization of a signaling system no. 7 network for AT&T," *IEEE J. Select. Areas Commun.*, vol. SAC-4, p. 1257, Nov. 1986.

[31] M. Langlois and B. Sembi, "DMS supermode: Cornerstone of a CCS7 network," BNR telesis, 1988-Two.

[32] CCITT Recommendation G.821, Error Performance on an international digital connection forming part of an ISDN, vol. III.

[33] BNR Miscellany, "DMS-100 family common channel signalling," July 1987.

Bijan Jabbari (Senior Member, IEEE) received the B.S. degree from Arya-Mehr University, Tehran, Iran in 1974, the M.S. and Ph.D. degrees in electrical engineering from Stanford University, Stanford, CA in 1977 and 1981, and the M.S. degree in engineering-economic systems, also from Stanford University, in 1979.

From 1979 to 1981 he was with Hewlett-Packard. From 1981 to 1983 he was an Assistant Professor at Southern Illinois University, Carbondale, IL. From 1983 to 1985 he was with Satellite Business Systems (now MCI Telecommunications), McLean, VA, where he managed programs on systems requirements definition, system specification, and architecture of the SBS next generation communications system. In 1985, he became Director at M/A-COM Telecommunications for development of Advanced Data Communications Networks. In 1988, he joined the School of Information Technology and Engineering at George Mason University, Fairfax, VA, where he is currently Associate Professor of electrical and computer engineering. His research activities include architecture and protocols for high speed packet communications, signalling protocols for telecommunication networks, broadband communications, and modeling and performance evaluation of computer networks. He is the former chairman of the IEEE Information Theory Group in Washington, DC and Northern Virginia. He is also the coeditor of the special issue on Architectures and Protocols for Integrated Broadband Switching of the IEEE Journal on Selected Areas in Communications.

Dr. Jabbari is the recipient of the 1983 Engineering Foundation's Research Initiation Grant, awarded to the best proposal written by the starting faculties. He is also a member of Eta Kappa Nu and the Association for Computing Machinery.

Chapter 3: Frame Relay

ISDN data link standards

The CCITT ISDN documents referenced four important data link control protocols: LAPD, LAPB, I.465/V.120, and frame relay. These data control link protocols are discussed below.

Initially, the principal emphasis by the CCITT was to define a data link control protocol for the D channel. This protocol, known as LAPD, is used for communication between the subscriber and the network. All D-channel traffic employs the LAPD protocol. This single protocol carries higher layer (layer 3 and above) protocol information for control signaling (Recommendation I.451/Q.931) and for X.25 packet switching. LAPD is based on LAPB, which is part of the X.25 standard, with modifications to the address field.

For B-channel traffic, the choice of data link control protocol may differ for different connections. For a packet-switched connection, LAPB is used to connect the subscriber to a packet-switching node. LAPB constitutes layer 2 of the X.25 packet-switching interface standard. It is used in conjunction with X.25 layer 3 on B channels to provide packet-switching support for ISDN users.

For a circuit-switched connection, there is an end-to-end circuit between two subscribers, and they are free to use any protocol at the link level for end-to-end data link control. However, two ISDN-related data link control protocols have been standardized: I.465/V.120 and frame relay.

I.465/V.120 is a 1988 recommendation on terminal adaptation that is based on the use of a data link control protocol similar to LAPD. This protocol, known as I.465/V.120, allows the multiplexing of multiple logical connections over a single B- or H-channel circuit between two end users.

Frame relay is a capability that takes the concept of I.465/V.120 a step further. Since the publication of the 1988 standards, the CCITT has been at work on this capability. Frame relay is based on a data link control protocol that allows multiplexing of multiple logical connections over a single B channel, but allows these connections to link with different end users. In effect, frame relay provides a packet-switching service that operates at the data link layer. Because of the importance of frame relay, this chapter is devoted to this facility.

Background

The 1988 Recommendation I.122, entitled "Framework for Providing Additional Packet Mode Bearer Services," introduced a new technique for packet transmission that has become one of the most significant contributions of the ISDN work reflected in the 1988 standards. This new technique is now generally referred to as "frame mode bearer service (FMBS)" or "frame relay." The former term emphasizes the service being offered to the user, while the latter emphasizes the protocol that implements the service. Since 1988, significant progress has been made on frame relay. In 1990, the CCITT published the following two interim recommendations:

- Recommendation I.2xy, entitled "ISDN Frame Mode Bearer Service (FMBS)," and
- Recommendation I.3xx, entitled "Congestion Management for the Frame-Relaying Bearer Service."

Work on frame relay is more advanced in the United States than in the CCITT as a whole. In 1990 and 1991, the American National Standards Institute (ANSI) issued the following three standards:

- ANSI T1.606-1990, entitled "Architectural Framework and Service Description for Frame-Relaying Bearer Service,"
- Draft ANSI T1.618-1991, entitled "Signaling Specification for Frame Relay Bearer Service," and
- Draft ANSI T1.617-1991, entitled "Core Aspects of Frame Protocol for Use with Frame Relay Bearer Service."

It is anticipated that the final CCITT recommendations will be closely aligned with the current ANSI standards.

Motivation

The traditional approach to packet switching is X.25. Several key features of the X.25 approach are

- Call control packets are used for setting up and clearing virtual circuits; these packets are carried on the same channel and same virtual circuit as data packets. In effect, inband signaling is used.
- Multiplexing of virtual circuits takes place at layer 3.
- Both layer 2 and layer 3 include flow control and error control mechanisms.

The X.25 approach results in considerable overhead. Figure 3-1(a) indicates the flow of data link frames required for the transmission of a single data packet from source end system to destination end system, and the return of an acknowledgment packet. The numbers in the figure indicate the order in which events occur. At each hop through the network, the data link control protocol involves the exchange of a data frame and an acknowledgment frame. Furthermore, to deal with the call management and flow control/error control aspects of the X.25 protocol, each intermediate node must maintain state tables for each virtual circuit.

All of this overhead may be justified when there is a significant probability of error on any of the links in the network. However, X.25 may not be the most appropriate approach for ISDN. On the one hand, ISDN employs reliable digital-transmission technology over high-quality, reliable transmission links, many of which are optical fiber. On the other hand, high data rates can be achieved with ISDN, especially when H channels are used. In this environment, the overhead of X.25 is not only unnecessary, but degrades the effective utilization of the high data rates available with ISDN.

Figure 3-1(b) indicates the operation of frame relay: A single user data frame is sent from source to destination, and an acknowledgement, generated at a higher layer, is carried back in a frame. Frame relaying is designed to eliminate as much as possible of the overhead of X.25. The key differences between a conventional X.25 packet-switching service and frame relaying are that, in frame relaying,

- Call control signaling is carried on a separate logical connection from user data; therefore, intermediate nodes need not maintain state tables or process messages relating to call control on an individual, per-connection basis.
- Multiplexing and switching of logical connections takes place at layer 2 instead of layer 3, eliminating one entire layer of processing.
- There is no hop-by-hop flow control and error control. End-to-end flow control and error control is the responsibility of a higher layer, if it is employed at all.

Let us consider the disadvantages and advantages of the frame-relaying approach. The principal potential disadvantage of frame relaying, compared to X.25, is that the ability to do link-by-link flow control and error control is lost. (Although frame relay does not provide end-to-end flow control and error control, this is easily provided at a higher layer.) In X.25, multiple virtual circuits are carried on a single physical link, and LAPB is available at the link level for providing reliable transmission from the source to the packet-switching network and from the packet-switching network to the destination. In addition, at each hop through the network, the link control protocol can be used for reliability. With the use of frame relaying, this hop-by-hop link control is lost. However, with the increasing reliability of transmission and switching facilities, this loss is not a major disadvantage.

The advantage of frame relaying is that the communications process is streamlined. The protocol functionality required at the user-network interface is reduced, as is the internal network processing. As a result, lower delay and higher throughput can be expected. Preliminary results indicate a reduction in frame-processing time of an order of magnitude, and the CCITT recommendation (Recommendation I.2xy) indicates that frame relay is to be used at access speeds of up to 2 Mbps. Thus, it is expected that frame relaying will supplant X.25 as ISDN matures.

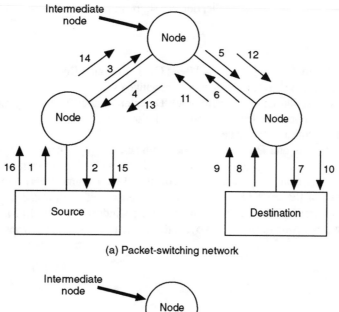

(a) Packet-switching network

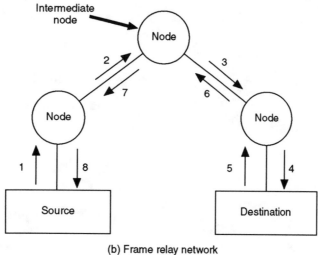

(b) Frame relay network

Figure 3-1. Packet switching versus frame relay: Source sending, destination responding.

The ANSI standard T1.606 lists four examples of applications that would benefit from the frame relay service used over a high-speed H channel, as follows:

(1) Block-interactive data. An example of a block-interactive data application would be high-resolution graphics (for example, high-resolution videotex and CAD/CAM). The pertinent characteristics of this type of application are low delays and high throughput.

(2) File transfer. The file transfer application is intended to cater to large file transfer requirements. Transit delay is not as critical in this application as it is, for example, in block-interactive data applications. High throughput might be necessary in order to produce reasonable transfer times for large files.

(3) Multiplexed low-bit rate. The multiplexed low-bit-rate application exploits the multiplexing capability of the frame-relaying service in order to provide an economical access arrangement for a large group of low-bit-rate applications. An example of one such low-bit-rate application is text editing, which is also given as an example in item (4) below. The low-bit-rate sources may be multiplexed onto a channel by a network-terminating (NT) function.

(4) Character-interactive traffic. An example of a character-interactive traffic application is text editing. The main characteristics of this type of application are short frames, low delays, and low throughput.

Paper summary

The first paper included in this chapter, "A User's Guide to Frame Relay," by Bhushan, provides a brief functional overview of frame relay and discusses its advantages.

"The Frame Relay Solution Update: Technology Description and Technology Comparison," by Sprint International, provides a more detailed technical description of frame relay and compares it with X.25 and other wide-area data networking techniques.

"Frame Relay: Protocols and Private Network Applications," by Cherukuri and Derby, looks at the protocol mechanisms of frame relay and examines non-ISDN applications of frame relay.

The final paper in this chapter, "Congestion Control in ISDN Frame-Relay Networks," by Doshi and Nguyen, examines one of the key technical design issues associated with frame relay: congestion control. Since the frame relay protocol does not include a sliding-window flow control mechanism, some other means of controlling congestion must be employed; this paper presents this other means.

A User's Guide to Frame Relay

Frame relay is an ISDN spin-off technology that significantly enhances packet performance on X.25 networks. Here's what's in it for you!

Brij Bhushan

As an Integrated Services Digital Network (ISDN) spin-off, frame relay is a high-speed packet-switching technology that achieves approximately 10 times the packet throughput of existing X.25 packet-switching networks. This has been accomplished by eliminating two-thirds of the state tables of X.25 and adding out-of-band signaling. Frame relay uses a bare minimum of routing functions in what is essentially a Layer 2 protocol derived from International Telegraph and Telephone Consultative Committee's (CCITT's) link access protocol for the ISDN D-channel (LAPD). LAPD has begun to emerge as a keystone for future high-speed packet networks.

Frame relay provides faster but much the same communications functions as standard X.25 packet switching by letting information move across a network guided and checked by seven core functions of LAPD. These functions are flag recognition, address translation, transparency, FCS checking/generation, recognition of invalid frames, discard incorrect frames, and fill interframe time.

X.25 is a protocol occupying the lower three layers of the International Organization for Standardization (ISO) Open Systems Interconnect (OSI) model. Signaling between end points, as well as the transmission of data, is multiplexed over the same link. Errors detected in the link are corrected by retransmission. X.25 virtually guarantees transmission of a "clean" data stream and enables an effective and compatible network interface for applications.

Great strides have taken place in the modern day transmission plants of the telecom services companies. Even analog transmission performance has improved tremendously using advanced modem techniques like Trellis encoding, which has reduced transmission error rates by an order of magnitude. Processing and switching functions are being implemented in hard-wired logic or Reduced Instruction Set architecture (RISC) microprocessors that have proven to increase the speed of packetization and multiplexing.

Because of major improvements in hardware technologies in transmission, processing, and switching, frame relay technology can, in a sense, be characterized as "back to the future" conceptually — getting closer to circuit switching. We now have fiber transmission or other forms of digital transmission available between almost any two locations. One consequence

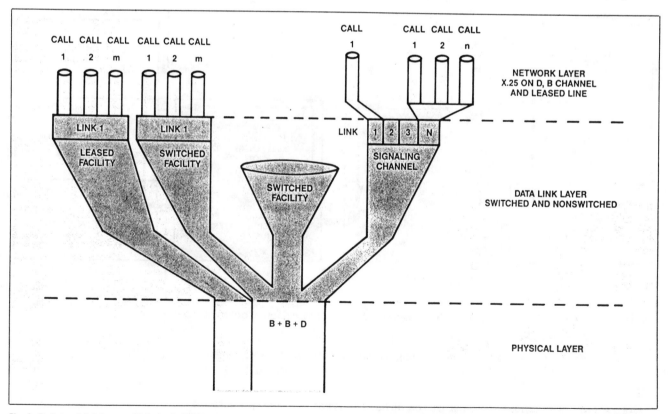

Fig. 1 Packet and link layer multiplexing in ISDN.

of this is that one of the characteristics of this "new" frame relay transmission scheme is its relatively clean performance. Error rates on the order of 1 x 10⁹ are achieved with relative ease. Gone are the days when noise in the circuits, cross talk, etc., would affect the performance of the circuit in question.

To fully appreciate frame relay, refer to the articles on packet switching by the pioneers in the field. Their studies showed that processing and multiplexing user data into X.25 frames contributed to tremendous transmission efficiencies, far in excess of overcoming the processing cost overhead. These ideas were new at the time, but the success of packet switching to date has proven them true. Now that the transmission costs are coming down remarkably, the pendulum is swinging the other way with faster throughput requirements.

The birth of frame relay has been stimulated by standards taking advantage of the low error rate digital transmission medium and a network-layering concept. Under this concept, the network backbone should offer core services and the higher-level intelligence should be migrated towards the access layer of the network.

TECHNOLOGY FACTORS

The concepts of frame relay, fiber optics, and advances in microprocessing technology almost seem preordained in time. Increased processing power and transmission capacity is essential to successful implementation of frame relay. Computing power has become so inexpensive that we have 10-30 MIPS at our desk — something that was available only in the mainframe in the 1970s. This power is thus better utilized for error detection and correction at higher layers of the protocol. The processing power can be directed to achieve specific micro- and macrolevel tasks. The natural solution is to go for RISC to perform these tasks efficiently. I do believe, though, that research must be done in the theoretical computational complexity area to determine sets that are best suited for designing the RISC processors for frame relay implementation.

Frame relay is sometimes referred to as asynchronous transfer mode (ATM) since the transfer of information is not synchronized between end points. This is possible because there is no correcting protocol between end points as in the LAPB protocol of X.25.

FUNCTIONAL EVOLUTION

Traditionally, X.25 has offered multiplexing functions via the packet layer (Layer 3) and error-free transmission between nodes via the link layer (Layer 2). There is no multiplexing done at the link layer as shown in **Figure 1**. X.25 packets at the third layer are designed to carry signaling information regarding that logical channel.

With the definition of the CCITT X.31 recommendation offering packet services in the ISDN arena, the packet protocol has been restructured and link level multiplexing is now offered (see **Figure 1**). This is accomplished via the LAPD procedures (CCITT recommendation Q.921/I.441). This, however, does not

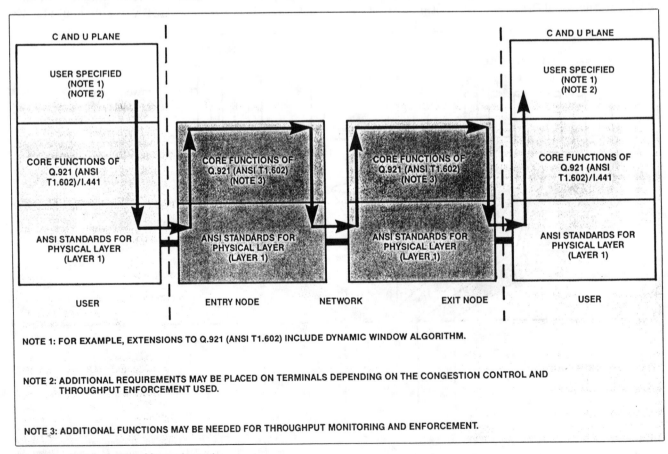

NOTE 1: FOR EXAMPLE, EXTENSIONS TO Q.921 (ANSI T1.602) INCLUDE DYNAMIC WINDOW ALGORITHM.

NOTE 2: ADDITIONAL REQUIREMENTS MAY BE PLACED ON TERMINALS DEPENDING ON THE CONGESTION CONTROL AND THROUGHPUT ENFORCEMENT USED.

NOTE 3: ADDITIONAL FUNCTIONS MAY BE NEEDED FOR THROUGHPUT MONITORING AND ENFORCEMENT.

Fig. 2 Network implementation of frame relay service.

affect the procedures of LAPB in a bearer channel, which continues to be aligned with X.25, offering no multiplexing functions.

Frame relay operates completely within the link layer. Based on LAPD protocol, it statistically multiplexes different user data streams. These data streams are called data link connections (DLCs) and are assigned an identifier (named DLCI) at call establishment time. Subsequent to call establishment, data frames carry this DLCI in all data streams. This address information is unique at the physical channel and, hence, is purely of local significance between nodes and has no consequence in the global sense.

This multiplexing function has been relegated to the lowest possible protocol layer. The network periphery thus gains more and more intelligence and leaves the network with core functions. Users will benefit from this as they will be able to add functions on top of those offered by the network and also because basic core services will be offered at attractive prices. This approach is in concert with ISDN definitions and network evolutions, in general, where there are a limited number of connection types and multipurpose user network interfaces offering increased throughput and fewer network delays (because the network has to do less functions). **Figure 2** shows a pictorial represen-

tation of frame relay protocol layers and their functional definitions.

NETWORK AND SERVICE CONCEPTS

In frame relay, the following core functions are offered by the data network:
- frame delimiting
- frame alignment
- frame transparency
- frame multiplexing/demultiplexing using DLCI
- checking a frame to assure it has an integer number of bytes
- checking the frame for its total length (neither too long nor too short)
- detection of transmission errors (no correction by retransmission).

There is no flow control service nor is there error control. Error control is expected to be implemented by end-user devices and the network nodes simply discard frames with errors. This is significant in that the designers of these protocols have assumed the presence of clean digital transmission media (like fiber optics), requiring no retransmission of errored frames.

Frame relay, when implemented in networks, will be a connection-oriented service that preserves the order of frames, does not duplicate frames, and has a very small probability of frame loss. **Table 1** shows the quality of service (QOS) parameters that are defined for frame relay services. The above list of core functions and the QOS parameters are primarily intended to monitor and make sure that the network performs as required by taking corrective maintenance and preventive actions, rather than making real-time recovery. Real-time recovery actions are delegated to the peripheral or user equipment. Other standards that are applicable to frame relay are shown in **Table 2**.

Some of the benefits of frame relay are:
- higher network throughput capacity
- better, more economical hardware implementations in silicon chips
- protocol transparency
- reduced network delay
- bandwidth savings.

Applications that may use the frame relay technique include higher capacity backbone for X.25 access networks (shown in **Figure 3**) and local area network (LAN) interconnectivity. Advantages of such interconnectivity are:

- high-speed interconnectivity at lower cost
- minimal delays since the network does not terminate protocols
- no significant new software by bridges, routers, and gateways
- network visibility to all bridges
- full logical connectivity
- an evolution path for higher-speed LAN interconnection services.

WHAT TO EXPECT

Public packet networks and private networks based on X.25 LANs, IBM SNA, or DECnet are the most suitable candidates for introducing frame relay and I

TABLE 1
QUALITY OF SERVICE PARAMETERS

Performance Parameters

Throughput
Transit Delay
Information Integrity
Residual Error Rate

Frame Errors

Delivered Errored Frames
Delivered Duplicated Frames
Delivered Out-Of-Sequence Frames
Lost Frames
Misdelivered Frames

VC Performance Parameters

Switched VC Establishment Delay
Switched VC Call Establishment Failure
Premature Disconnect
Switched VC Clearing Failure

TABLE 2
FRAME RELAY STANDARDS

Main Standards

CCITT I.122/ANSI T1S1/88-224R — architectural framework and service description

CCITT Q.921/I.441/ANSI T1.602 (1988) — ISDN user-network interface data link layer specification

ANSI T1.601 (1988) — Basic access interface for use on metallic loops for NT-Layer 1

Other Standards

CCITT I.320 (1988)	CCITT X.31 (1988)/I.462
CCITT I.430 (1988)	CCITT X.134 — X.137 (1988)
CCITT I.431 (1988)	CCITT X.213 (1988)
CCITT Q.931 (1988)/I.451	CCITT X.300 (1988)
CCITT X.25 (1988)	

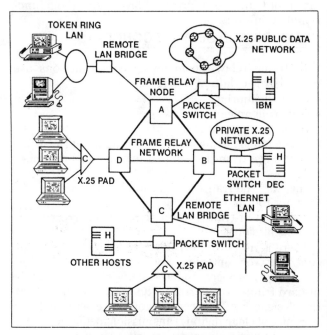

Fig. 3 Frame relay backbone with X.25 access network.

believe this will happen soon. The task for these vendors is mostly software-intensive and, therefore, the progress will be fast after frame relay services are introduced by carrier networks. These vendors are geared to develop such software as part of their main business. Thus, there are market forces in the wings ready to provide the impetus needed. Therefore, the leader will have close followers.

On the standards front, issues that need further study both at the CCITT and at the ANSI level include congestion control, internetworking requirements, further refinements of C and U Plane protocols, and QOS parameters. Other topics that can have a bearing on future products exploring frame relay include traffic priorities for host-to-host communication, broadcast of data for a variety of applications, fixed length vs. variable length packet sizes, and hierarchical encoding.

Frame relay is a technology that is still being defined. As information exchange needs increase, the volume of each data set increases due to the inclusion of graphics in the data sets. Document sizes also keep increasing with wider applications of E-Mail, which is being used for document exchange as well as evolving mail applications. The need, therefore, is for higher throughput transport mechanisms. Frame relay provides substantial improvement over the existing digital services and evolving ISDN basic and primary rate interfaces for communications in a metro area network (MAN) or wide area network (WAN) environment. □

Brij Bhushan *is the founder of the Washington, DC-based Reston Consulting Group, Inc., a company specializing in telecommunications planning, networking, voice/data integration, and applications. Bhushan has been active in CCITT standards work on X.25 and ISDN. This article was prepared for, and submitted by, Telematics International Inc. of Fort Lauderdale, FL.*

The Frame Relay Solution Update

3. TECHNOLOGY DESCRIPTION

"The Frame Relay Solution Update: Technology Description and Technology Comparison." Excerpts taken from *Telenotes*, Volume 2, Number 1, September 1991, pages 11-34, published by Sprint International Communications Corporation. Complete manuscripts available by writing *Telenotes* editor, 12490 Sunrise Valley Drive, Mailstop VARESF0101, Reston, VA 22096.

Thus far, we have discussed the trends which led to the development of frame relay. We will now turn our attention to a description of how frame relay technology actually works; the characteristics of a frame relay network; how frame relay relates to ISDN; its benefits and limitations; and a few typical scenarios in which frame relay can be deployed.

Frame Relay as a Switching Technique. One of the easiest ways to describe frame relay, which is a signalling and data transfer mechanism between intelligent endpoints and an intelligent communications network, is in comparison to a technology, like X.25, that is well-known and understood. **Figure 2** is a graphic representation of how X.25 networks accomplish data switching. What is meant by switching here is the ability to examine incoming data in order to determine its destination and to route the data accordingly. In packet-mode technologies, this is usually done on a packet-by-packet (or frame-by-frame) basis. In circuit-mode technologies, it is done on a call-by-call basis.

As shown, X.25 networks use three levels of the International Standards Organization (ISO) seven-layer network model to achieve switching. The first layer is simply a **physical layer** which provides physical and electrical connectivity of a user device to the network, or between two network nodes. The second layer is the **data link layer**, which is responsible for ensuring data integrity across a physical link. The third layer, the **network layer** (sometimes called the packet layer in the X.25 world), is tasked with end-to-end data integrity and with ensuring that the data reaches the correct destination.

In X.25, data is taken from the source device (in this example, a terminal) and is stored for processing and to make retransmission possible. This is indicated by the file cabinet in **Figure 2**. A "packet envelope" is then placed around the data. The envelope contains information about the data inside it. This information is used at the other end of the network to determine if the data arrived without errors, and to request retransmission in the event that errors are detected. There is also information in the envelope which is used to guide the data through the network to the proper destination.

Based on the packet envelope information, the network makes a determination as to where the data should now be sent. At this point, a "frame envelope" is placed around the packet envelope. This new envelope is responsible for ensuring data integrity across a single physical line. The data is then sent, via the physical layer, over the appropriate copper or fiber (or satellite, etc.) facility to the next node in the network.

When the data arrives at the next node, it is once again stored, and is then examined for errors (as indicated by the pencil and eraser). If an error is found, the faulty data can be retransmitted from the previous node, where it was stored before transmission. If no error is found, the network will strip off the frame envelope and look at the packet within the frame to determine the ultimate destination of this piece of data. If necessary it will then route it to yet another node. This process will continue until the ultimate destination node is reached, where all envelopes are examined, then removed, and the data is delivered to the endpoint user device.

It is clear from the complicated manner in which X.25 accomplishes switch-

ing that it evolved in an environment where the endpoints were not particularly intelligent and where high quality transmission lines were not necessarily available. That is why X.25 goes to great lengths to ensure that transmission errors are corrected on a link-by-link basis.

Figure 3 illustrates that, in contrast to X.25, frame relay accomplishes switching in only two layers as opposed to X.25's three layers. In frame relay technology, an intelligent endpoint, such as a LAN, sends its data to the link layer where, just as in X.25, an envelope (specifically, a Q.922A frame) is added. Alternatively, the intelligent endpoint may send the data to the network already encapsulated in the frame. In either case, this frame

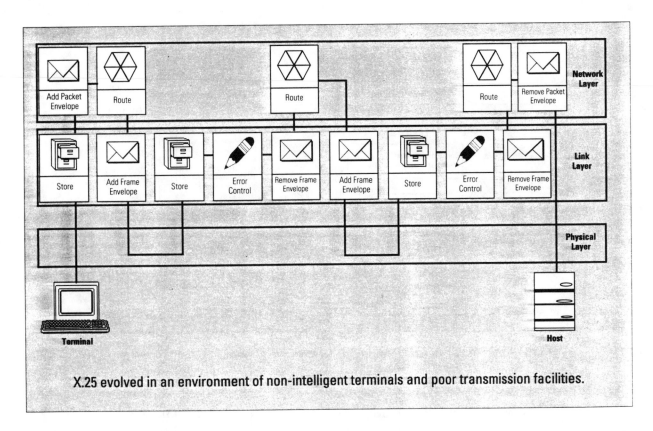

X.25 evolved in an environment of non-intelligent terminals and poor transmission facilities.

FIGURE 2.
X.25
SWITCHES
DATA IN
THREE
LAYERS

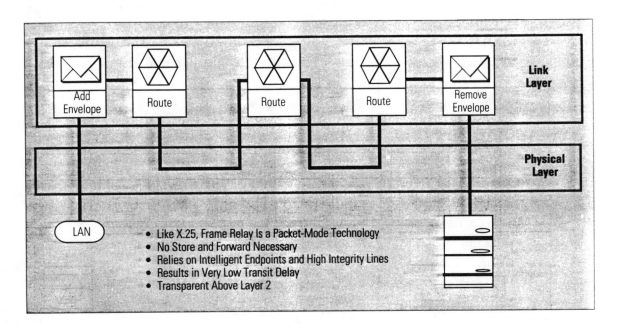

- Like X.25, Frame Relay Is a Packet-Mode Technology
- No Store and Forward Necessary
- Relies on Intelligent Endpoints and High Integrity Lines
- Results in Very Low Transit Delay
- Transparent Above Layer 2

FIGURE 3. FRAME RELAY
SWITCHES DATA IN TWO
LAYERS

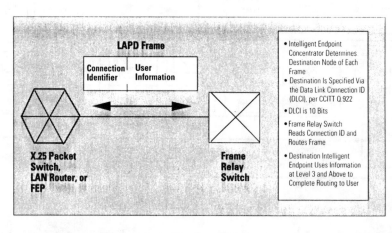

FIGURE 4.
PRINCIPLE OF
FRAME RELAY

LAPD Frame

| Connection Identifier | User Information |

X.25 Packet Switch, LAN Router, or FEP

Frame Relay Switch

- Intelligent Endpoint Concentrator Determines Destination Node of Each Frame
- Destination Is Specified Via the Data Link Connection ID (DLCI), per CCITT Q.922
- DLCI is 10 Bits
- Frame Relay Switch Reads Connection ID and Routes Frame
- Destination Intelligent Endpoint Uses Information at Level 3 and Above to Complete Routing to User

contains routing information not previously found in layer two, eliminating the need for the network to examine level three, the packet level. Instead, the frame itself is examined for a destination and the routing takes place at the network's frame layer.

Compared to X.25, frame relay performs some additional functions in layer two of the network model; notably the switching we have discussed. Yet, there is also a conspicuous absence of certain functions. For instance, there is no error correction in the frame relay nodes. This is because frame relay relies on low bit-error-rate lines to minimize errors, and on intelligent endpoints running

an end-to-end protocol across the network to recover from the few errors that do occur. The frame relay network can detect errored frames and will, in fact, discard such frames. The endpoints, and their associated end-to-end protocol, are responsible for detecting and recovering from such frame losses. By moving the error recovery process to the endpoints the network itself gains tremendous efficiencies.

Frame relay gains an additional speed advantage because there is no layer three processing taking place at layer three. Some layer three processes, such as flow control, are left to the intelligent endpoints. Others, like PAD (Packet As-

sembler/Disassembler) control, are not relevant to the intelligent endpoint environment. Since there is less complexity to the processing required of each node, there is less delay through the node itself: about 5-20 milliseconds for X.25 versus less than two milliseconds for frame relay. This reduction in delay at each node directly improves network response time.

The next question is, "How does frame relay accomplish this switching in layer two when prior to now it has only been possible by having three layers?" The answer is shown in **Figure 4**.

An intelligent endpoint such as an X.25 packet

switch, a LAN with a router, or a front end processor specifies the destination of each frame. Intelligent endpoint devices such as these know the destination of each frame from the application, and place such information in the packet layer of the protocol. With frame relay, however, an abbreviated destination is also placed in the frame layer.

For example, a LAN may need to send data to ten other LANs in a network. It is not necessary to specify at the frame layer the exact terminal or workstation for which the data is destined. That information is in the packet being carried within the frame envelope. All that is necessary for frame relay is that the first LAN specify that this data is destined for, say, LAN #7. This

destination endpoint is specified in the actual frame via a "connection identifier." In the example given above, there simply might be a connection identifier that says "7." In more formal terms the connection identifier is known as a Data Link Connection Identifier (DLCI).

In order for this process to take place, the frame must

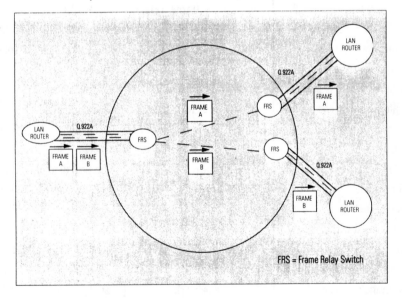

FIGURE 5. A FRAME RELAY NETWORK

FIGURE 6.
Q.922
(ANNEX A)
FRAME
FORMAT

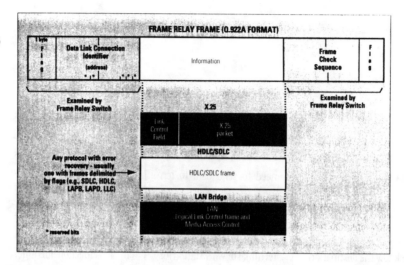

FRAME RELAY FRAME (Q.922A FORMAT)

1 byte F | Data Link Connection Identifier (address) | Information | Frame Check Sequence | F

Examined by Frame Relay Switch

Examined by Frame Relay Switch

X.25

Link Control Field | X.25 packet

Any protocol with error recovery - usually one with frames delimited by flags (e.g., SDLC, HDLC, LAPB, LAPD, LLC)

HDLC/SDLC

HDLC/SDLC frame

LAN Bridge

LAN Logical Link Control frame and Media Access Control

* reserved bits

conform to the format which is given by CCITT Q.922 Annex A (Q.922A). This protocol is a subset of the full Q.922 protocol, but does not require the network to implement the error recovery and control procedures of Q.922. Q.922A was chosen for frame relay because virtually every data protocol likely to be sent across a WAN conforms to, or can easily be made to conform to, the Q.922A frame format. SNA, X.25, TCP/IP and virtually all proprietary vendor protocols, such as DECNET, can be used with Q.922A. This makes frame relay compatible with a tremendous variety of higher level protocols.

After the intelligent endpoint has determined the destination address and placed this in the DLCI within the frame, it sends the frame out the transmission facility to the first switching node, which we will call a frame relay switch. The frame relay switch then reads the DLCI and routes the frame accordingly to the next node along the way to the destination. See **Figure 5** for an illustration of this process. Note that the routing takes place without the frame relay switch ever having to look at any higher level protocol; all of the routing decisions are made at layer two of the network.

The frame continues to be routed in this way through the network until it ultimately reaches the destination node. Only at the destination node, in this case at LAN #7, are the higher layers of the protocol examined to determine the actual user who is to receive this particular frame of information. The destination endpoint node then delivers the frame to that ultimate user. Level three and above are still needed, but are now used primarily at the endpoints. There is no need for the network in the middle to look at this information, since it can accomplish its switching function at a lower layer of the architecture.

Network Characteristics. A frame relay network is protocol transparent above layer two. It can carry any protocol so long as the frame format is using Q.922A at layer two. Existing protocols which use other than Q.922A at layer 2 can be enveloped in a Q.922A frame (See **Figure 6**). This gives frame relay tremendous flexibility in terms of the types of devices connected to the network. Most existing IBM, DEC, and LAN networks can ride over a frame relay network and the endpoints will not even realize that frame relay is there. To them, the frame relay network appears as an array of full period, high-speed circuits, which is exactly what they would like.

Another characteristic is that traffic to and from multiple destinations can be supported via a single, high-speed link between the intelligent endpoint and the network. This is similar to X.25, except that the frame relay link can function at a higher speed.

A frame relay network provides what is known in the X.25 world as a permanent virtual circuit (PVC) type of service, meaning that whenever an endpoint needs to send data, there is a pre-established path through the network for that data to reach its destination. Note that the path does not reserve any bandwidth, but it is pre-established and ready to go. The frame relay switch merely waits for a connection identifier to signal which path is to be used for a particular frame.

Frame relay service in its first implementation pro-

vides a capability similar to another X.25 concept, that of the closed user group (CUG). In the frame relay technology that we have described, it is *not* the case that any endpoint can arbitrarily talk to any other endpoint on the network. Rather, there must be a connection identifier associated with the destination endpoint that the sender is trying to reach or the data will have no way to get there. Thus, in effect, there are one or more "user groups." Within each group, devices may communicate at will. These groups are established by the network manager using configuration tools. Of course, the configuration can be modified at any time, but essentially the network will consist of several "closed user groups." In practice, this is not particularly limiting since most endpoints do talk only to a fixed set of destinations.

However, there is a future enhancement to frame relay being finalized in the standards organizations which involves the use of a new protocol called Q.933. Q.933 is derived from Q.931, the layer three signalling protocol for ISDN networks. Q.933 will allow an endpoint to dynamically specify a destination address for a frame, even if that destination address had never been specified before and was never pre-established with its own connection identifier. This will enable frame relay networks to have unrestricted connectivity, without the prior establishment of permanent virtual circuits.

Relationship to ISDN. When ISDN was originally conceived about a decade ago, it was anticipated that it would be the transport mechanism for several different types of traffic. This would be accomplished by providing specialized transport capabilities known as bearer services. One type, **circuit-mode** services, would be used for voice and transparent data. Another service anticipated was **packet-mode**, intended to support X.25 traffic. Subsequently, a third type of service, **frame relay mode**, was incorporated into ISDN planning. It was thought that there would be some types of data that would not be X.25, but would not be efficient for a circuit-mode service. Frame relay would fit the bill as a service in between circuit-mode and packet-

mode, being packet-oriented like X.25, yet protocol transparent above layer two (but still not fully transparent) like circuit mode.

The essential point is that frame relay traffic can travel easily over an ISDN network. However, it is important to note that one does not *need* an ISDN network to take advantage of the benefits of frame relay. Frame relay is perfectly well suited to any private line network and to non-ISDN public data networks.

Benefits and Limitations. Among the benefits gained by using frame relay technology is the very low delay through a frame relay switching node. The overall delay of the network itself is also reduced because high speed access lines are used and because the full bandwidth of the backbone lines is available to the data as it traverses the network. Together these two benefits combine to reduce the time users must wait for the network to complete a transaction; thus, productivity is increased.

Further benefits are derived because a single access line between an endpoint and the frame relay network can support traffic going to many destinations. Ports are saved on the endpoint device as well as on the switch itself. Another benefit of frame relay is its protocol transparency above layer 2. Frame relay allows switching of X.25, SNA, TCP/IP, or any other HDLC-like protocols, with equal ease.

Finally, because frame relay performs data switching, the network achieves mesh connectivity of endpoints; that is, any endpoint can communicate with any other endpoint so long as there is a pre-established connection identifier. Even better, this full connectivity is achieved without any penalty whatsoever in terms of number of ports, number of access lines or capacity required on the backbone trunks. Frame relay can also coexist with ISDN, but does not require ISDN. It will be compatible with future implementations of ISDN, such as B-ISDN. In summary, frame relay effectively meets the modern requirement for a high-speed, packet-mode network.

Still, there are several limitations to frame relay technology which must also be considered. As has been consistently pointed out, frame relay will not work well unless it is used in an environment where the endpoints are intelligent and the transmission facilities are of high speed and quality. Also, frame relay does not support voice. The reason is that voice traffic is highly sensitive to variations in the transmission delay introduced by the networks, while such small variations are usually not as critical to data traffic. In order for voice to be supported satisfactorily in a packet-mode environment, each packet must have a time-stamp which is monitored by the network. Frame relay lacks such a mechanism.

An additional limitation is that access links to a frame relay network are currently limited to T1 or E1 rates,

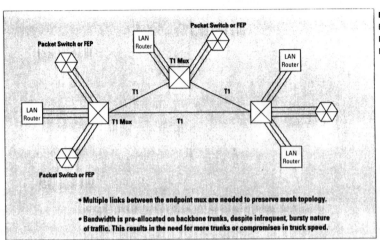

• Multiple links between the endpoint mux are needed to preserve mesh topology.

• Bandwidth is pre-allocated on backbone trunks, despite infrequent, bursty nature of traffic. This results in the need for more trunks or compromises in truck speed.

though it is important to note that there is no such limitation on trunk speeds. This is a short-term limitation of current technology and its ability to process at the link layer. Future implementations of frame relay will support access speeds up to T3 (45 million bits per second) rates.

Another limitation involves to the standard congestion control process defined for frame relay. If all the LANs connected to a frame relay node had bursts of data to send at the exact same instant in time, and if these bursts were long enough to exhaust the node's buffering queues, the network would overflow and some of those frames would be dropped. However, these congestion situations are rare if the network is engineered properly, and when they do occur the intelligent endpoints' end-to-end protocol will realize that data did not get through. The endpoints will then recover by retransmitting the missing frames.

Nonetheless, it would be advantageous for the frame relay network to be able to notify endpoint devices that were sending data when there was no capacity available in the network. Such a mechanism would avoid the possibility of clogging the network with retransmitted frames. A feature has actually been built into frame relay to enable the network to inform endpoints of network congestion. (**Please see the "Frame Relay Update," Chapter 6.**)

Lastly, due to its streamlined nature, frame relay is limited in the value-added functions it supports compared to X.25. Some of these functions may be important to certain applications. Examples include security and protocol conversion. If a user requires these value-added capabilities in a frame relay environment, one approach would be to use an X.25 device as the intelligent endpoint. This endpoint can in turn be connected to user terminal and host devices. In such a configuration, one achieves the

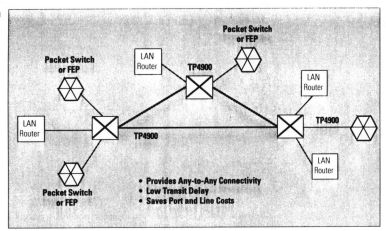

FIGURE 8. WITH FRAME RELAY

Packet Switch or FEP

LAN Router

TP4900

Packet Switch or FEP

LAN Router

Packet Switch or FEP

LAN Router

TP4900

TP4900

LAN Router

Packet Switch or FEP

• Provides Any-to-Any Connectivity
• Low Transit Delay
• Saves Port and Line Costs

additional value-added capabilities of X.25, with the efficiency of a frame relay transit switching fabric.

Deployment Scenarios. Now let us look at some deployment scenarios which involve frame relay. **Figure 7** depicts a typical corporate backbone network without frame relay. In the center are three T1 multiplexers which are being used to interconnect a variety of LAN routers and packet switches or front end processors over a shared T1 backbone. Because T1 multiplexers are indeed strictly multiplexers, and not switches, notice that multiple links between each endpoint and the multiplexer itself are needed to

create a mesh connectivity. If there were only one link between a LAN router and its associated T1 mux, for example, the mux would have no way to determine where each incoming frame was destined since a mux does not examine data but merely passes it to a fixed destination. The LAN router on the far left, for instance, requires three links to the associated T1 mux. Each link is to serve traffic that goes to each of the other three possible destination LAN routers. As a network grows, this connection requirement becomes increasingly burdensome in terms of port requirements on both the endpoint and the T1 mux.

Also, since most T1 multiplexers are circuit-mode in nature, the bandwidth on the backbone trunks will be pre-allocated for each of these connections, despite the fact that the traffic will be bursty in nature and the bandwidth will be idle much of the time. This results in the need for more trunks in order to provide the speed that is required by modern applications, or fewer trunks with associated compromises in the speeds that can be delivered to the end user. Most users, constrained by budgets, elect the latter option and allocate some small portion of the T1 backbone to each application. Thus, although physically there are T1 trunk lines, the *ef-*

fective transmission speed between endpoint devices will be only that portion of the trunk which has been allocated to the application; typically, on the order of one DS0. That means the customer's investment in a T1 network, while yielding some economies through consolidation, will *not* deliver the high-speed transmission rates called for by modern applications and PC users.

Figure 8 depicts the same network with frame relay. The T1 muxes in the middle have been replaced with frame relay switches; in this particular example, Sprint's TP4900™ frame relay switch. The multiple access links between endpoints and the T1 backbone have been replaced by a single, frame-multiplexed link. Because the frame relay switch will indeed examine and route each frame to whatever destination is specified, this network still offers full mesh connectivity. Every device can talk to every like device, just as in the previous network. However, a considerable amount has been saved in terms of ports on the endpoint devices, and ports on the T1 resource manager. Further, transit delay is reduced because each application receives the entire T1 backbone bandwidth on demand, rather than being allocated some subset of that bandwidth as in the circuit-mode environment.

4. TECHNOLOGY COMPARISON

Now let us turn to a comparison of frame relay with other technologies that are available to today's communications managers. One way to accomplish this is to take a look at a number of network characteristics, then compare available technologies against that set of characteristics.

Network Switching. The first network characteristic we will discuss is switching. Given the distributed nature of today's data networks, it is often advantageous for the network to enable any-to-any connectivity of user devices. But how does one actually accomplish such connectivity over a wide area network? One possible approach is simply to physically connect every pair of devices with point-to-point leased lines. In such a case there is no network-based switching. Instead, a LAN router, FEP or packet switch is relied upon to switch the traffic to the proper line. For a three-node network, this would require only three lines. In a four-node network, however, mesh connectivity would require six lines—double the number of lines in order to support a single additional node.

As can be seen, with this multiple point-to-point leased line approach, the number of lines required for full connectivity does not rise linearly with the number of nodes. In fact, the line requirement rises in proportion to the square of the number of nodes, as given by the following formula: to fully interconnect N nodes requires $N \times (N-1)/2$ lines. For example, a six-node network would need $6 \times (5)/2 = 15$ lines. Clearly, this is an extremely expensive approach to full connectivity for networks of any size.

An alternative to full connectivity is partial connectivity. Six LANs or front end processors (FEPs) can, in fact, be interconnected using only six lines in a "ring" configuration. As we have pointed out, the LAN router or FEP does, after all, have the ability to switch traffic, so this configuration will deliver the sought-after any-to-any connectivity, and at a substantially lower cost than the prior approach. Indeed, this particular topology is in widespread use today.

The drawback to partial connectivity is that since there is often no direct path between two endpoints, there is the necessity of a large amount of "transit" traffic. Transit traffic is data which passes through a node—called a transit node— but neither originates nor terminates on that node. Transit traffic robs a transit node of processor cycles which would otherwise be used to support traffic which originated or terminated at that node. Because any intelligent node has a finite number of such cycles, transit traffic inevitably leads to the need for larger or additional

nodes–at additional cost. Moreover, since every "hop" along the path from source to destination adds delay, a partially interconnected network has inherently more delay than a full mesh topology network. Thus, although one reduces line requirements through partial connection, there are indirect costs in terms of transit node hardware and delay.

A third alternative to which users have turned is the deployment of a T1 backbone and associated bandwidth managers (muxes). This scheme enables a logical, though not a physical, full mesh topology over a consolidated, high-speed backbone. **Figure 7**, previously discussed in a different context, depicts just such a topology. Unfortunately, this approach also

contains all of the drawbacks previously noted. For N nodes to interconnect, there must be N-1 links between each endpoint and the nearest T1 mux. If the endpoint and T1 mux are not co-located, this will constitute a major expense in access lines. And even if they are co-located, there will be high physical port costs on both the endpoints and the mux.

Fortunately, there is a fourth alternative. This alternative shall be referred to as "network switching." If the *network itself*, in addition to the intelligent endpoints, can switch traffic, then any-to-any connectivity is easily and economically achieved. Under this scenario, an endpoint requires only a single link into the network, as in **Figure 8**. That link can carry all of the traffic from one endpoint into the network. The network then actively examines and routes traffic to the proper destination. Since only a single link is needed, only one port per endpoint is required, though a second may be desired for redundancy. Because the network itself provides any-to-any connectivity and handles all required transit traffic, no customer endpoint need handle any transit traffic. In summary, a switching network facilitates full connectivity without the detrimental side-effects of alternative approaches.

There are several technologies available which offer network switching, including the good old public dial telephone network (a telephone has only one connection to the network, but can connect with any other phone). These technologies will be compared to each other, and to other technologies, below. However, there are several characteristics besides network switching which must also be compared.

Additional Network Characteristics. Ideally, a network will have very rapid call set-up, especially given that entire transactions can now last only a matter of seconds, or milliseconds at T1 rates. It would not be very appropriate for a network to take 10-20 seconds to establish a call that is only going to last a half-second!

Also desirable is the flexibility to handle a wide variety of protocols, particularly given the recent proliferation of "standard" protocols.

Some network offerings allow network management by the actual user or customer, while others do not. Likewise, some networking technologies increase overall network availability through the ability to route traffic around failures in the network. The latter characteristic is known as alternate routing.

Finally, because of the trends discussed earlier, we will discuss the ability of each networking option to be economical for high-speed, bursty traffic, since that is the nature of most of the traffic the network will carry.

Dial Service. Dial service is a switched service whereby the user specifies where traffic is to go by dialing a specific telephone number. Yet while dial service is

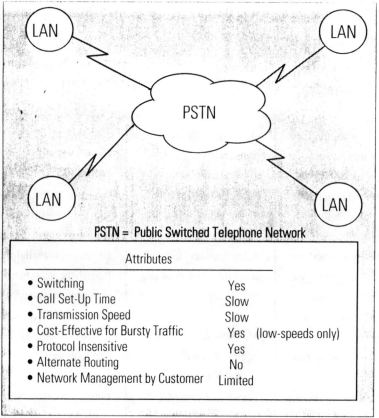

FIGURE 9.
DDD

PSTN = Public Switched Telephone Network

Attributes	
• Switching	Yes
• Call Set-Up Time	Slow
• Transmission Speed	Slow
• Cost-Effective for Bursty Traffic	Yes (low-speeds only)
• Protocol Insensitive	Yes
• Alternate Routing	No
• Network Management by Customer	Limited

switched in nature, it differs from other switched services (which we will discuss) in that it is not statistically multiplexed. That is, one dials a number to specify a destination but for the duration of the call, the transmission channel is dedicated to reach *only* that destination. Conversely, while such a call is in place, no one else can call either of the connected parties over the same lines. This contrasts with other switched services, such as X.25, which permit not only switching but simultaneous access to multiple destinations over the same transmission channel. This latter capability, known as statistical multiplexing, is independent of switching but is most powerful when both are present.

Call set-up time, ranging from a few seconds to over 10 seconds, is relatively slow in a dial network. This is acceptable for voice conversations, but is unacceptably long for those data transaction that will only last a second or less. Transmission speeds over the telephone network are also relatively slow. There is ubiquitous access today at speeds of up to 9.6 kbps, and there are now islands of access to 56 and 64 kbps dial services. A forthcoming service, currently termed "N x 64" dial service will become available in the

FIGURE 10.
LEASED LINES

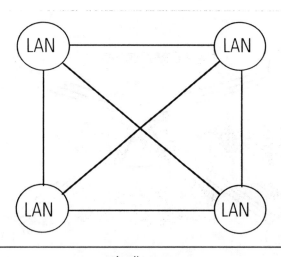

Attributes	
• Switching	No
• Call Set-Up Time	Fast
• Transmission Speed	Slow to Fast
• Cost-Effective for Bursty Traffic	No
• Protocol Insensitive	Yes
• Alternate Routing	No
• Network Management by Customer	Limited

next two years.

Dial service can be cost-effective for some bursty traffic. This is because the user does not have to have a call in place unless there is actual data to send. One can hang up when there is no more data to send. However, dial service is not cost-effective for response-time-sensitive bursty traffic because of limitations in transmission speeds and call set-up times.

In order to have the desired protocol flexibility, a protocol insensitive network is needed. The dial network, often called the Direct Distance Dialing network, or DDD network, provides a protocol insensitive service. However, there is no automatic alternate routing if there is a failure on the line. Such failures usually will result in the call being dropped, a familiar phenomenon. Finally, the user has only an extremely lim-

ited ability to manage or monitor a dial network. All of these characteristics are summarized in **Figure 9**.

Leased Lines. Leased lines are a very common and popular method of connectivity, particularly for LANs (**Figure 10**). Leased lines provide a point-to-point or multipoint-to-point (known as "multidrop") service, offering no network switching. Still, leased lines have essentially no call set-

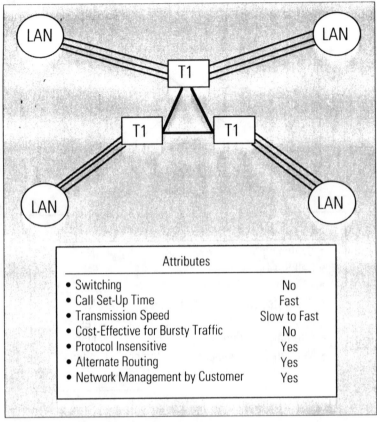

FIGURE 11.
T1 MUX
NETWORKS

Attributes	
• Switching	No
• Call Set-Up Time	Fast
• Transmission Speed	Slow to Fast
• Cost-Effective for Bursty Traffic	No
• Protocol Insensitive	Yes
• Alternate Routing	Yes
• Network Management by Customer	Yes

up time, and very high transmission speeds are readily available. However, leased lines are not cost-effective for bursty traffic because once they are in place the user must pay for each line 100 percent of the time, whether or not there is traffic present. Leased lines are protocol insensitive, but in and of themselves offer no automatic alternate routing and limited network management by

the user.

T1/E1 Networks. One strategy frequently employed to overcome some of the cost and limitations of leased lines is to deploy a T1 multiplexer network. However, it is important to understand that a T1 multiplexer network essentially emulates leased lines. Thus, most of the characteristics of the T1 mux network are very similar to those of

leased lines. There is no network switching, so the number of ports and lines emanating from each intelligent endpoint (e.g.-LAN or X.25 switch) is exactly the same as it would be with leased lines. Call set-up time is again fast, and transmission speeds can be fast or slow. Bursty traffic is not cost effective unless the T1 mux being used is packet-mode in nature, but this introduces delays. T1 cir-

FIGURE 12.
X.25

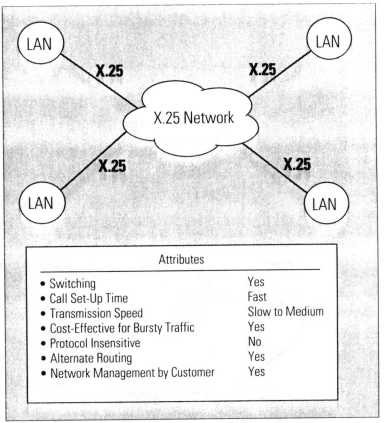

X.25 Network

Attributes	
• Switching	Yes
• Call Set-Up Time	Fast
• Transmission Speed	Slow to Medium
• Cost-Effective for Bursty Traffic	Yes
• Protocol Insensitive	No
• Alternate Routing	Yes
• Network Management by Customer	Yes

cuits, like leased lines, are protocol-insensitive. However, as shown in **Figure 11**, two differences between T1 muxes and leased lines are that T1 muxes perform automatic alternate routing around failed components, and that they allow for comprehensive network management by the customer.

X.25 Networks. X.25, as we have already discussed, provides a switched com-munications service, and call set-up times are rela-tively fast—typically less than a second (see **Figure 12**). Transmission speeds can be from 1.2 kbps to E1 rates, but are typically on the order of 64 kbps. As a packet-mode technology, X.25 is highly cost effective for bursty traffic up to the speeds supported by this technology. In addition, X.25 provides alternative routing and customer net-work management capabil-ities.

X.25, though, is not proto-col insensitive. All protocols that traverse an X.25 net-work must first be convert-ed to X.25. This requires software or hardware known as a PAD (Packet Assembler and Disassembler.) PADs are typically available for the most common protocols, but there are several proto-cols which cannot currently be supported by X.25.

Frame Relay Networks. As we have seen, frame relay is a switched technology. It therefore allows any-to-any connectivity without any additional access lines, trunk lines, or transit hops (**Figure 13**). It offers sub-second call set-up time, and the transmission speeds themselves can be very fast: up to T3. Frame relay is extremely cost effective for bursty traffic because it is a packet-mode service. It is protocol insensitive, as long as HDLC-like protocols are being employed. It also provides for alternate routing and for full network management by the user.

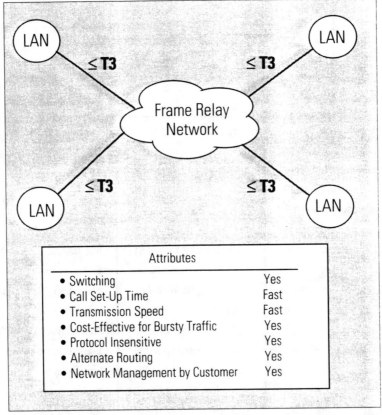

FIGURE 13.
FRAME RELAY
NETWORK

Attributes	
• Switching	Yes
• Call Set-Up Time	Fast
• Transmission Speed	Fast
• Cost-Effective for Bursty Traffic	Yes
• Protocol Insensitive	Yes
• Alternate Routing	Yes
• Network Management by Customer	Yes

Frame Relay: Protocols and Private Network Applications

Rao J. Cherukuri and Jeffrey H. Derby

IBM Corporation
PO Box 12195
Research Triangle Park, NC 27709

ABSTRACT

The Integrated Services Digital Network (ISDN) environment will be characterized by widespread availability of end-to-end digital connectivity together with a standard, highly flexible, message-oriented interface for connection control. *Frame relay* is a packet-switching technique that takes advantage of the characteristics of the ISDN environment as well as the capability of the frame structure employed by the ISDN D-channel Link Access Protocol (LAPD) to support multiplexing within layer 2. In frame relay, only the lower sub-layer of layer 2, consisting of functions such as frame delimiting, multiplexing, and error detection that are associated with the LAPD frame structure, are terminated within network nodes. The upper, procedural sub-layer, including such functions as error recovery and flow control, operates end-to-end between terminal endpoints.

This paper discusses possible protocols for both data transfer and connection control in frame relay and also describes the application of frame relay in private ISDN-based networks. First, the functions and frame structure associated with the frame sub-layer and the operation of the frame-relaying process are reviewed. We then examine the Q.931 procedures for control of frame-relay connections at user-network interfaces, as well as the transport of the associated Q.931 messages across these interfaces, for several scenarios. Finally, we describe the use of frame relay as a transport mechanism for all forms of packet-oriented traffic in private networks, focusing in particular on the synergy between the use of Q.931 procedures with appropriate extensions for inter-node signaling and the use of frame-relay to transport Q.931 messages within the network; we also briefly suggest possibilities for the evolution of private networks with frame relay into integrated packet networks.

1. INTRODUCTION

The Integrated Services Digital Network (ISDN) environment will be characterized by widespread availability of end-to-end digital connectivity together with a standard, highly flexible, message-oriented interface for connection control. *Frame relay* is a packet-switching technique that takes advantage of the characteristics of the ISDN environment as well as the capability of the frame structure employed by the ISDN D-channel Link Access Protocol (LAPD) to support multiplexing within layer 2. Frame relay is one of several so-called "additional packet-mode bearer services" defined in CCITT Recommendation I.122 [1]. Standards for frame relay are being developed by the CCITT, ANSI [2],[3] and ECMA [4]. As is the case for existing ISDN bearer services, there is for the frame-relay service a logical separation between channels carrying users' information (e.g., voice, data) and signaling channels carrying messages for control of ISDN connections; the former are said to lie in the *U-plane* (user plane) and the latter in *C-plane* (control plane). The procedures that operate in the C-plane for control of frame-relay connections are those defined in CCITT Recommendation Q.931 (I.451) [5] for control of circuit-switched connections in ISDN, with extensions as proposed by ANSI T1S1.2 in [3].

Frame relay is based on a partition of the link layer into a frame-level sub-layer, consisting of the so-called "core functions" such as frame delimiting and error detection that are associated with the LAPD frame structure, and an upper, procedural sub-layer consisting of the data link control (DLC) ele-

ments of procedure including such functions as error recovery and flow control. As defined by the CCITT in [1], "frame relaying 1" service allows users to select the DLC procedures, while "frame relaying 2" service specifies that the DLC procedures be those of LAPD with appropriate extensions. In the sequel, the term "frame relay" will refer to "frame relaying 1" unless stated otherwise.

The services provided by an ISDN are defined at the interface between the user and the network. As shown in Fig. 1, in providing a frame-relay service, the network terminates only the frame-level sub-layer, so that only the core functions are performed in frame-relay network nodes. The procedural sub-layer operates end-to-end between terminal endpoints. Several studies, including those reported in [7]-[10], have demonstrated the effectiveness of end-to-end recovery and flow control in the ISDN environment, with physical channel speeds of 64 kbits/s and up and end-to-end bit-error rates better than 1 in 10^5.

Because frame-relay network nodes do no processing above the frame-level sub-layer, frame-relay networks can be expected to provide significantly higher throughput and lower delay than networks in which processing of DLC elements of procedure (and perhaps of higher layer protocols as well) is performed in each node [11]. For the same reason, frame-relay networks provide a degree of transparency that permits users to select protocols for the DLC procedural sub-layer and higher layers that are most appropriate for the traffic carried by any particular connection; such selection would be on a per-connection basis using Q.931 procedures for negotiation of low-layer compatibility

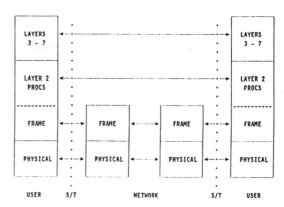

Fig. 1. The Frame-Relaying Service. The frame sub-layer is labeled "I.441 Core" in CCITT Rec. I.122. The user-network interface is shown at the ISDN S/T reference point.

0-8186-2797-2/92 $3.00 © 1989 IEEE

between terminal endpoints ([5], Annex M) and need not involve the network nodes in any way.

This paper discusses both the U-plane and C-plane protocols for frame relay and also describes the application of frame relay in private ISDN-based networks. In Section 2, we review the functions and protocols of the layer 2 sub-layers as well as the operation of the frame-relaying process. Section 3 examines the Q.931 procedures for control of frame-relay connections at user-network interfaces, as well as the transport of the associated Q.931 messages across these interfaces, for several scenarios, including the case of circuit-switched access to a frame-relay network. Finally, Section 4 describes the use of frame relay as a transport mechanism for all forms of packet-oriented traffic in private networks, focusing in particular on the synergy between the use of Q.931 procedures with appropriate extensions for inter-node signaling and the use of frame-relay to transport Q.931 messages within the network; we also briefly suggest possibilities for the evolution of private networks with frame relay into integrated packet networks.

2. DATA TRANSFER IN FRAME RELAY

CCITT Recommendation Q.921 (I.441) [6] defines a link access protocol, called LAPD, to be used at layer 2 on D-channels; D-channels are physical channels whose primary function is to transport connection-control messages across ISDN user-network interfaces. LAPD is a version of asynchronous-balanced mode HDLC. Its definition includes elements of procedure, an HDLC frame format including a two-octet address field, a mechanism for dynamic assignment of layer 2 addresses, and the capability for several independent logical links to be multiplexed within a single physical channel using layer 2 addresses.

The service definition for frame relay [1] formalizes the partition of layer 2 into a frame sub-layer and a procedural sub-layer that is implied in Q.921. As shown in Fig. 1, only the frame sub-layer is terminated by the frame-relay network. Frame relay also takes advantage of the capability of LAPD for multiplexing at the frame sub-layer. However, the procedures in Q.921 for dynamic assignment of layer 2 addresses are specific to the D-channel and are not generally applicable for frame-relay connections; the assignment of layer 2 addresses for frame-relay connections is discussed in the context of control of these connections in Section 3 below.

In this section, we review the functions and protocols of frame and procedural sub-layers of layer 2, and we also describe the frame-relaying process.

2.1 The Frame Sub-Layer

The functions associated with the frame sub-layer, referred to as *core functions* in CCITT Recommendation I.122 [1], are :

- Frame delimiting, alignment, and transparency
- Frame multiplexing/demultiplexing using the address field
- Inspection of the frame to ensure that it consists of an integer number of octets
- Inspection of the frame to ensure that it is not too long or too short
- Detection of transmission errors

Since the frame-relay network terminates the frame sub-layer, the frame structure associated with this sub-layer is defined at the user-network interface. This frame structure, which is essentially identical to that defined for LAPD in CCITT Recommen-

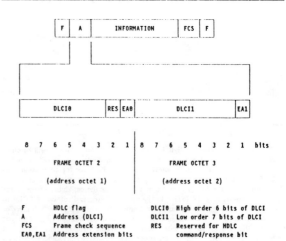

Fig. 2. Frame Format for LAPD Core Services. The field labeled "information" is ordinarily partitioned into the DLC control field and layer 2 information field.

dation Q.921 [6], is shown in Fig. 2. It is distinguished by a two-octet address field, called the *Data Link Connection Identifier (DLCI)*, sometimes referred to as the *Logical Link Identifier (LLI)*, whose contents can be assigned dynamically for any given frame-relay connection. As shown in Fig. 2, it is split into a six-bit segment and a seven-bit segment; the resulting 13-bit DLCI can take on values in the range 0 to 8191. Each possible DLCI value defines a *logical channel* within the underlying physical channel. All frames carried in a given physical channel that contain a particular DLCI value, say $DLCI = n$, will be said to flow in logical channel n within the given physical channel. Thus all frames in logical channel n within any physical channel can be identified by detecting $DLCI = n$ in their layer 2 address field.

The frame format in Fig. 2 is employed on B-channels and H-channels, when these channels carry frame-relay connections. On D-channels, which may carry frame-relay communication in addition to messages for connection control, the frame format in Fig. 2 is employed by definition. However, on D-channels the DLCI field is taken not as a single 13-bit field but rather as a 6-bit *Service Access Point Identifier (SAPI)* (the part labeled "DLCI0" in Fig. 2) and a 7-bit *Terminal Endpoint Identifier (TEI)* (the part labeled "DLCI1" in Fig. 2). Thus, a logical channel within a D-channel is identified by a (*SAPI,TEI*) pair. The SAPI value is used to indicate the nature of the logical channel (e.g. $SAPI = 0$ for signaling, $SAPI = 1$ for frame relay, $SAPI = 16$ for X.25), and the TEI value indicates the particular logical entity on the user side of the interface that terminates the logical channel. In the sequel, the acronym "DLCI" will refer to B-channels and H-channels, and "(*SAPI,TEI*)" will be used in reference to D-channels.

With regard to DLCI values for the two directions of transmission on B-channels and H-channels, the view that currently prevails within the standards community is that a logical channel is bidirectional, i.e. that the same DLCI value is used in both directions of transmission for any given logical channel; this is consistent with the use of (*SAPI,TEI*) on D-channels. The possibility of using different DLCI values in the two di-

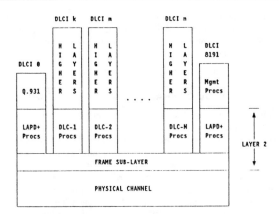

Fig. 3. Multiplexing at the Frame Sub-Layer. Logical channels 0 and 8191 are assumed to carry LAPD+ (extended LAPD) at the procedural sub-layer.

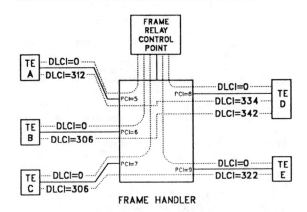

Fig. 4. An Example of Frame Relay Operation. The solid lines are physical channels; the dotted lines represent logical connections.

rections of transmission for the same frame-relay connection has been suggested in [14]; this is equivalent to viewing logical channels as being unidirectional, with the correlation between the DLCI values for the pair of logical channels that is necessary for full-duplex communication being established when the frame-relay connection is set up. In this paper, we will follow the prevalent view and assume that the same DLCI value is used in both directions of transmission for any given logical channel, except in the discussion in Section 4.

Clearly, the frame sub-layer "occupies" the entire physical channel. Logical channels are delineated within the frame sub-layer and are effectively independent above the frame sub-layer. Thus, within any physical channel, each logical channel has its own DLC elements of procedure, as well as its own set of protocols at layer 3 and above. A view of this multiplexing at the frame sub-layer is shown in Fig. 3. Referring to the figure, it is possible for the DLC elements of procedure used in logical channel n to be different from those used in logical channel m.

Within any physical channel carrying frame-relay traffic, the logical channel with $DLCI = 0$ is reserved for in-channel signaling, and that with $DLCI = 8191$ is reserved for in-channel management. All other logical channels are available for frame-relay bearer connections, with DLCI values assigned using Q.931 procedures as described below in Section 3.

2.2 The Procedural Sub-Layer

The procedural sub-layer consists of the DLC elements of procedure, which may include:

- Mode selection
- Maintaining sequence counts
- Acknowledgments
- Error recovery
- Flow control
- XID exchange

Since a frame-relay network is transparent to the procedural sub-layer, users may select protocols for this sub-layer that are most appropriate for the traffic to be carried by any particular connection, so long as they are compatible with the frame structure in Fig. 2. Such protocols include various forms of HDLC, for which the field labeled "information" in Fig. 2 would be

subdivided into the HDLC control and information fields. It is also possible to operate with a null protocol at the procedural sub-layer, if none of the functions it provides are necessary; in this case, the information field in Fig. 2 would simply contain user data.

Among the HDLC protocols that are usable at the procedural sub-layer are LAPB, LAPD, and the IEEE 802.2 logical-link control. There is also an extended version of LAPD being studied by ANSI and the CCITT for "non-D-channel applications" [12]. This extended LAPD may include a dynamic window algorithm [9],[19] for end-to-end flow control and alleviation of network congestion when frame-relay transport is used [17]. Additionally, we have described in [13] how an extended LAPD can be constructed that will inter-operate directly with IEEE 802.2 as well as with ordinary LAPD and will therefore be extremely useful for LAN-ISDN connections using frame relay and the "extended bridge" concept [16].

2.3 The Frame-Relaying Process

The frame-relaying process essentially consists of the routing of frames having the format shown in Fig. 2, based on their DLCI values. The entity that performs frame relaying will be referred to as a *frame handler (FH)*, which operates under the control of a *frame-relay control point (CP)*.

The frame-relaying process will be described in the context of the example shown in Fig. 4. Connected to the FH in the figure are a number of incoming and outgoing physical channels, each of which carries a frame sub-layer with frames having the structure shown in Fig. 2, and with multiplexing of logical channels at this frame sub-layer as described above. The physical channels, which may be 64 kbits/s B-channels, higher speed H-channels, or D-channels, are individually identifiable internally by the FH using some physical address, referred to here as a *physical channel identifier (PCI)*. The purpose of the PCI is to allow any received frame to be appropriately routed by the FH based on the DLCI value it contains and the PCI value associated with the physical channel on which it was received. A particular PCI value may be associated with a single channel or a group of channels connected to a FH; the nature of the PCIs for any given implementation will depend on the FH hardware structure and configuration mechanisms. It is sufficient to note that a given FH will have some means of identifying all the physical channels that it terminates, and that the corresponding identifiers (PCIs) may have significance that is local to within the given FH.

In general, routing of frames is controlled by entries in a connection table. It is sufficient for purposes of the present discussion to state that such a table (or its logical equivalent) exists within the FH; the implementation of the table, its relation to the FH switch fabric, as well as the structure of the switch fabric are not immediately relevant. The construction of table entries, i.e. the setup of logical connections, is described below in Section 3.

In the example shown in Fig. 4, several terminal devices (TEs) are interconnected through the FH. We assume for simplicity in this example that the FH has a different PCI for each physical channel that it terminates; in this case, DLCI values need to be unique only within individual physical channels. Referring to the figure, the FH terminates physical channels from TE C and TE E, which it identifies by physical addresses $PCI = 7$ and $PCI = 9$, respectively; from the point of view of the FH, these can be called simply physical channels 7 and 9. A logical connection exists through the FH between TEs C and E such that incoming frames from logical channel 306 on physical channel 7 are to be forwarded on logical channel 322 within physical channel 9, as follows: any incoming frame from physical channel 7 will have its layer 2 address decoded; if its DLCI value is 306, then the layer 2 address field is overwritten using the outbound DLCI value of 322, a new FCS is computed and written in the FCS field, and the modified frame is enqueued for transmission on physical channel 9. Fig. 4 also shows the possibility of establishing several logical connections to a TE over a single physical channel. In the figure, TE D has logical connections with TEs A and B. The corresponding logical channels ($DLCI = 334$ and $DLCI = 342$) within the physical channel between TE D and the FH are multiplexed at the frame level.

A final point with respect to Fig. 4 is its inclusion of logical channels between each TE and the CP, all having $DLCI = 0$. As noted above, these channels are reserved for in-channel signaling; they may be used for communication between the TEs and the CP for control of frame-relay connections. Of course, if there is a D-channel between a TE and the FH, then the logical channel within the D-channel having $SAPI = 0$ and the TEI of the TE would be used for signaling. These issues are discussed in Section 3.

As part of the frame-relay procedure, the FCS of each incoming frame is checked to insure that the frame is error-free. Assuming that the FH always buffers an incoming frame completely before beginning to transmit it on an outbound channel, then frames with FCS errors can simply be discarded by the FH. If the FH can operate in cut-through mode [15], with the capability to begin outbound transmission of a frame before the frame has been completely received, and has begun transmission of a frame with a bad FCS, it appends an abort sequence (at least seven consecutive 1s) to the frame. In either case, recovery from the error condition operates end-to-end between the communicating TEs, with no involvement of the FH in the recovery process. In addition, if the FH is congested and no buffer space is available for a frame, then the frame is simply discarded. Once again, recovery is end-to-end between the communicating TEs.

Finally, it is important to note that there may be different priority classes for connections. For example, connections hav-

ing real-time constraints, for which minimized end-to-end delay is important, may have their frames given priority over all other frames. The priority mechanism could be implemented by having a separate transmit queue for each priority class feeding each of the outbound physical channels. The priority class for any given connection would be established as part of the connection-setup procedures.

3. CONTROL OF FRAME-RELAY CONNECTIONS

The procedures of CCITT Recommendation Q.931 are employed at ISDN user-network interfaces to control frame-relay connections [3] in much the same way they are used to control circuit-switched connections. In this section, we first examine the transport between the user (TE) and the network of Q.931 messages for control of frame-relay connections. We then describe the Q.931 procedures and messages themselves.

A TE is connected to an ISDN through a *serving switch*, which is a central office, PBX, communication controller, or some similar device. A TE and its serving switch communicate for connection-control purposes via a signaling channel, using the procedures defined in Q.931. For ISDN basic access, which has a 2B + D physical channel structure, the signaling channel is a logical channel within the D-channel; signaling flows are physically out-of-band with regard to the B-channels and logically out-of-band with regard to other logical channels within the D-channel that can carry X.25 and frame-relay user data [6]. Circuit-switched connections are controlled by Q.931 message flows within the D-channel. Use of the D-channel for control of frame-relay connections depends on the nature of the serving switch and the link between the TE and the FH. We consider here three scenarios:

1. A TE's serving switch has frame-relay capability. In this case, Q.931 message flows on the D-channel can be used to control frame-relay connections as well as circuit-switched connections.

2. A TE's serving switch has no frame-relay capability, but the TE has circuit-switched access through its serving switch to a frame-relay network, as shown in Fig. 5. In this case, there is no D-channel connectivity between the TE and the frame-relay network, since the D-channel is terminated by the serving switch. In addition, it seems overly constraining for a TE to have to rely on a switch with no frame-relay capability having a mechanism for transferring D-channel messages for frame-relay connection control to a remote frame-relay network.

3. A TE has a leased connection to a frame-relay network. In this scenario, the FH to which the TE is permanently connected appears to be the TE's serving switch. However, it appears likely that for the leased equivalent of basic access the facility will not include a useful D-channel.

In scenarios 2 and 3, some mechanism other than the D-channel is needed to support communication between a TE and FH for control of frame-relay connections. Clearly, even in these cases, it is always possible to establish a physical link between TE and FH. For example, in case 2, the D-channel can be used to establish a circuit-switched connection between TE and FH, with the FH having an appropriate ISDN address; in case 3, the physical link is always present by definition. Communication between TE and FH for connection-control purposes can thus always use the physical link between them. In

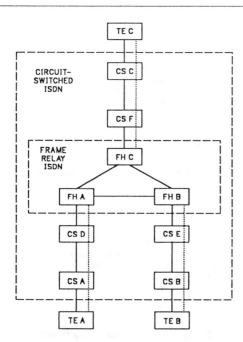

Fig. 5. Circuit-Switched Connection into a Frame-Relay Network. The boxes labeled 'CS' are circuit switches. The dotted lines show circuit-switched connections between TEs and FHs within which frame-relay connections may be set up.

particular, given that the physical link will carry frame-relay connections and will therefore be structured using the frame sub-layer as in Fig. 3, a logical separation is easily created between a signaling channel and user channels within the physical link. As described above in Section 2, the logical channel for signaling is that with $DLCI = 0$. For every physical channel terminating on a FH, logical channel 0 is routed by default within the FH to the CP; thus in scenario 2, for example, communication between a TE and the FH is possible in logical channel 0 as soon as the circuit-switched connection between the TE and the FH is established. Furthermore, this logical separation between signaling and user channels within a B-channel or H-channel is completely consistent with the view of logical separation between control and user planes taken by the CCITT [1].

Having shown that there are always appropriate paths available for communication between a TE and FH for control of frame-relay connections, we now consider the messages and procedures employed. Among the key Q.931 messages employed in establishing a connection are [5],[3]:

- SETUP, which is sent by the user to request that an outgoing connection be set up and is sent by the network to offer an incoming connection request to a user.

- CALL PROCEEDING, which is a response to the SETUP message indicating that the connection request is being processed.

- CONNECT, which is sent by the user to indicate that the incoming connection request is accepted and is sent by the network to indicate that the user's outgoing connection request has been accepted by the called user.

The messages employed during the take-down of a connection include DISCONNECT, RELEASE, and RELEASE COMPLETE.

Information elements in the SETUP message are used to indicate properties of the connection to be set up including the called user's address and subaddress, the desired transfer mode (i.e., circuit or packet), the *bearer capability* (i.e., characteristics of those layers 1-3 terminated by the network), the *low-layer compatibility* (i.e., characteristics of layers 1-3 associated with end-to-end compatibility), and the physical channel to be used. For frame-relay connections, desired values of peak and average information-transfer rates as well as the allowable value of end-to-end delay and the DLCI value to be used may also be specified in the SETUP message. Note that assignment of the physical channel and DLCI value is generally under the control of the network side and so may also be included in the network's response (such as CALL PROCEEDING) to a SETUP sent by a user.

A user requests a frame-relay connection by sending a SETUP message containing the ISDN address of the target TE, indicating that frame-relay service is desired by specifying the transfer mode as "packet-mode" and the layer 2 protocol as "Q.921 (I.441) core aspects" in the Bearer capability (BC) information element [3]. Additionally, so that the network can properly allocate bandwidth for the logical connection, the user either explicitly or implicitly specifies measures of the average and peak information-transfer rates desired [17]. Finally, the user codes the desired end-to-end layer 2 and layer 3 protocols in the Low layer compatibility (LLC) information element, for purposes of negotiation with the target TE. The DLCI value to be used on the segment of the logical connection between the calling TE and the network is provided by the network in its response to the SETUP; the DLCI value to be used on the segment of the logical connection between the network and the called TE is provided by the network in forwarding the SETUP to the called TE. A simple example of the message flows for setting up a frame-relay connection is shown in Fig. 6.

In scenario 1, the Q.931 messages flow in the D-channel associated with physical channel that will carry the logical connection being set up, in the logical channel identified by $SAPI = 0$ and the TEI of the TE involved. In addition to what is described above, the setup procedures include physical-channel selection through use of the Channel identification information element in the appropriate Q.931 messages. It should be noted that in this scenario, the frame-relay connection can be set up on the D-channel. When the D-channel is selected, there is no DLCI assignment; instead, the logical channel within the D-channel that carries the frame-relay connection is that having $SAPI = 1$ and the TEI of the TE involved.

In scenario 3, the Q.931 messages flow in logical channel 0 within the physical channel that will carry the logical connection being set up, and there is no physical-channel selection as part of the connection-control procedures.

In scenario 2, the messages for control of the frame-relay connection flow between the TE and FH in logical channel 0 within the physical channel that will carry the logical connection. However, there may first be Q.931 message flows in the D-channel between a TE and its serving switch, and between a FH and its serving switch, to set up circuit-switched connections that will underlie the logical connection.

An example of the connection-control message flows for scenario 2 is given in Fig. 7, corresponding to the configuration

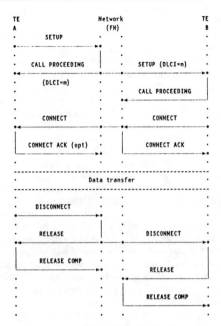

Fig. 6. **Messages Flows for Frame-Relay Connection Setup — A Simple Example.** The example assumes that B-channels or H-channels are to be used for the connection.

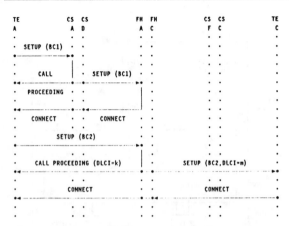

Fig. 7. **Message Flows for Frame-Relay Connection Setup — A Second Example.** This example is for scenario 2, corresponding to the configuration in Fig. 5. 'BC1' indicates circuit-switched bearer capability; 'BC2' indicates frame-relay bearer capability. For simplicity only the essential Q.931 messages are shown.

shown in Fig. 5. In the example, TE B has an existing frame-relay connection with TE C, with underlying circuit-switched connections established between TE B and FH B, and between TE C and FH C, respectively. TE A now initiates the setting up of a frame-relay connection to TE C by first requesting a circuit-switched connection to FH A from its serving switch. The SETUP sent by TE A on the D-channel is forwarded by the circuit-switched network to FH A on a D-channel, with the FH appearing on the "user side" of a user-network interface. Once the circuit-switched connection is established, TE A sends a SETUP message directly to FH A requesting a frame-relay connection to TE C. Assuming the availability of appropriate routing mechanisms within the frame-relay network, the call request is forwarded within this network to FH C. Assuming that sufficient bandwidth for the new logical connection is available on the physical connection already in existence between FH C and TE C, the call is offered by FH C to TE C on this connection by a SETUP message sent on logical channel 0 within this physical link. If sufficient bandwidth were not available, or if there were no physical connection already in existence, then FH C would request a circuit-switched connection to TE C from its serving switch prior to offering the frame-relay call request to TE C.

In all scenarios, the procedures for taking down a frame-relay connection are the same as for a circuit-switched connection, using the DISCONNECT, RELEASE, and RELEASE COMPLETE messages [5], as shown in Fig. 6. The logical channel in which the messages are sent depends on the scenario as described above. Also, in scenario 2, the user may choose to take down an underlying circuit-switched connection when there are no longer any frame-relay connections being supported by it.

4. FRAME RELAY IN PRIVATE ISDNS

A private network is a set of switching and transmission facilities provided for use by a single multi-location organization or enterprise and may include application processors for services such as voice and text messaging, route optimization, and network management functions. The switching nodes in a private network may be user-provided equipment such as PBXs, add-drop multiplexers (ADMs), so-called transmission resource managers (TRMs), or data communication controllers; alternatively, they may consist of Centrex, tandem switching, or ADM equipment imbedded in a carrier's network. The transmission facilities may be privately owned, leased from a carrier on a dedicated basis between the user's locations, or imbedded within a carrier's public network. Finally, private network services and applications may be provided either by the user's application processors or by a carrier's equipment.

A *private ISDN* is a private network based on the use of ISDN interfaces and protocols [18]. In a private ISDN, all switching nodes have ISDN capabilities, all transmission links between nodes are digital, most likely at primary rate (1.5 to 2 Mbits/s) or above, and ISDN protocols are used between nodes for control of connections within the network.

Frame relay provides highly efficient transport for heterogeneous packet-oriented data in private ISDNs just as it does in the public ISDN. However, there are several factors that make the application of frame relay in private ISDNs based on user-provided switching equipment particularly interesting. Such networks are less constrained by the need to have new equipment coexist with old equipment and new transport mechanisms, capabilities, and services supported by slowly evolving inter-node signaling protocols that must also support existing public-network transport.

In this section, we focus in particular on inter-node signaling, describing the use of Q.931 procedures with appropriate extensions for inter-node signaling and also the use of frame-relay to transport Q.931 messages within the network. We also briefly consider possibilities for the evolution of private ISDNs into integrated, fast-packet networks providing frame-relay service.

We will assume in the discussion that follows that the private network provides both frame-relay and circuit-switched service, and that all nodes in the private network have frame-relay capability.

4.1 Inter-node Signaling Using Q.931

There have been proposals in the CCITT [21] and in ANSI [22] to employ Q.931 with appropriate extensions for inter-node signaling in private ISDNs. The extended Q.931 procedures would be used to control both circuit-switched and packet-switched connections, the latter including frame-relay connections. We consider here specifically the use of these procedures to control frame-relay connections.

Any set of procedures for control of connections within a network requires some routing mechanism. The discussion that follows assumes the use of what was referred to as "source-based routing" in [18]; that is:

- Each node in the network has access to address translation and routing applications, which may be implemented on a centralized or distributed basis. Nodes obtain routing information from these applications and may inform these applications of changes in the network's effective topology due, for example, to link failures or significant changes in link utilization. We do not concern ourselves here with the protocols used for communication between nodes and these applications; they may, for example, be similar to those described in [20]. We do note, however, that any network connections required to support such communication may clearly be frame-relay connections.

- Upon receiving a call request from a TE, a node may obtain from the routing application complete routing information to the called TE, including identifiers of all nodes through which the connection is to be set up; the routing information may also include PCIs associated with the physical channels that should carry the connection. Note that the routing applications can learn about PCIs in the same way that they learn about network topology.

- The routing information obtained by the originating node may be included, perhaps using a new information element, in a Q.931 SETUP message that it forwards to the next node to be involved in the connection. With this mechanism, only the originating node needs to query a routing application for any connection to be set up.

With regard to DLCI assignment and usage, we assume that operation at user-network interfaces is consistent with what has been described above, i.e. DLCI assignment controlled by the network side and the same DLCI value for both directions of transmission. For intra-network links, however, the entities at each end are peer network nodes. We therefore assume symmetric DLCI assignment procedures, with different DLCI values in the two directions of transmission, for intra-network links; for reasons discussed in [14], a node assigns the DLCI value for all frames it is to *receive* on any given logical connection.

We illustrate these concepts with a connection-setup example, in the context of the simple network configuration in Fig. 8. The figure shows four nodes and those physical channels or links between nodes that are being used for frame-relay connections. Referring to the figure, let TE A, served by node 1, request a frame-relay connection to TE B, served by node 2.

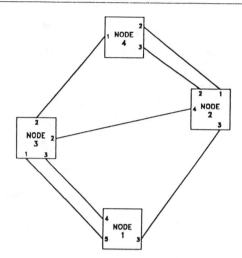

Fig. 8. A Private ISDN Network Example. The inter-node links shown are those physical channels that are carrying frame-relay connections. The numbers adjacent to these links are the PCIs associated with them by the individual nodes.

The simplified Q.931 message flows are shown in Fig. 9. The steps numbered in this figure are as follows:

1. TE A sends a SETUP message to node 1, specifying the ISDN address of TE B and the appropriate parameters as described above in Section 3.

2. Node 1 queries the routing application, which may be local or remote. In this example, current network conditions and the bandwidth requested for the new connection by TE A result in a route through node 3 to node 2. If the routing application has knowledge of PCIs, its response to node 1 may include information such as "$PCI = 5$ to node 3, $PCI = 2$ to node 2; return by $PCI = 4$ to node 3, $PCI = 1$ to node 1."

3. Node 1 sends CALL PROCEEDING to TE A, indicating that it is processing the connection request; this message specifies the physical channel and DLCI value to be used by TE A for the logical connection being set up. Node 1 also forwards to node 3 the SETUP it received from TE A, including within this message the routing information and also the DLCI value to be used in frames sent to it by node 3 on the connection being set up.

4. Node 3 forwards the SETUP message to node 2, including within this message the routing information and also the DLCI value to be used in frames sent to it by node 2 on the connection being set up.

5. Node 2 forwards the SETUP message to TE B, specifying the physical channel and also the DLCI value to be used in both directions of transmission between it and TE B for the connection being set up. Note that node 2 is aware from the routing information in the SETUP message it has received that it serves TE B directly, and it resolves locally the ISDN address of TE B that is contained in the Called party address information element in the SETUP.

6. TE B accepts the call request by sending CONNECT to node 2.

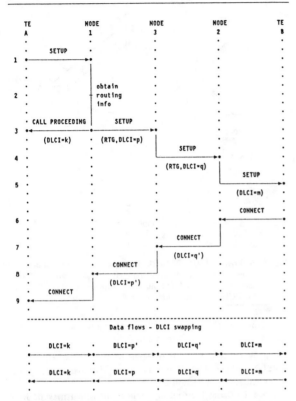

Fig. 9. Messages Flows for Frame-Relay Connection Setup in a Private ISDN. This example corresponds to the network configuration in Fig. 8. 'RTG' indicates the routing information as described in the text.

7. Node 2 forwards the CONNECT message to node 3, including within this message the DLCI value to be used in frames sent to it by node 3 on the connection being set up.

8. Node 3 forwards the CONNECT message to node 1, including within this message the DLCI value to be used in frames sent to it by node 1 on the connection being set up.

9. Node 1 forwards the CONNECT to TE A, effectively completing the setup of the logical connection.

Finally, at the bottom of Fig. 9 are highlighted the DLCI values used for data flow in each direction on each segment of the logical connection.

It will be seen that assignment of physical channels for the inter-node segments of the connection has been ignored in the example above. If PCIs are included in the routing information and there is an appropriate association defined between physical channels and PCIs, (for example, with "$PCI = 5$ to node 3" uniquely identifying for node 2 a particular physical channel to node 3), then the assignment of physical channels is implicit in the routing information. If such is not the case, then the explicit procedures for negotiating assignment of physical channels between network nodes for circuit-switched connections would be incorporated in the flows described above. Note that in either case the number of physical channels carrying frame-relay traffic between any pair of nodes is likely to be small, since frame-relay bandwidth will tend to be aggregated into a small number of

high-speed channels rather than a large number of lower-speed channels for performance reasons.

4.2 Frame-Relay Connections for Signaling

Having described the Q.931 message flows between nodes for control of frame-relay connections, we now consider how these flows are transported. Following the discussion in Sections 2 and 3, each physical channel carrying frame-relay traffic between a pair of nodes contains a logical channel ($DLCI = 0$) that is routed by default within each node to the node control point. Thus in the example given above, the Q.931 messages between nodes 1, 2, and 3 in Fig. 9 may be carried in logical channel 0 within the physical channels that will carry the connection being set up. These $DLCI = 0$ logical channels, which provide point-to-point logical connections between control points in adjacent nodes, may also carry Q.931 messages for control of circuit-switched connections.

Although the use of $DLCI = 0$ logical channels for inter-node signaling will be adequate in some cases, a mechanism with greater flexibility may be needed to meet general objectives for private ISDN capabilities [18]. In particular, we consider the ability to employ *non-associated signaling*, in which messages for controlling a connection may follow a different route through the network than that taken by the connection itself, and the ability to dynamically set up and take down connections that carry signaling flows between non-adjacent network nodes. Among the applications that demonstrate the value of these abilities are:

- The availability of back-up signaling connections, perhaps with different routes for reliability reasons, and the ability to set up such connections dynamically on an as-needed basis.
- The capability to add bandwidth for signaling between a pair of nodes or reroute the existing signaling bandwidth due to changing network conditions.
- The capability for direct communication between the originating and terminating nodes of a user connection, e.g. for control of some supplementary services that do not involve intermediate nodes, or to determine if a call request can be offered to a called user before initiating set up procedures for the connection through the network.

We find that frame relay can provide logical connections for signaling between non-adjacent nodes, and further that these connections for signaling can be set up and taken down in the same way as any other frame-relay connection. Consider that the communicating entities at each end of such a connection are node control points. These control points are processors that have access to facilities for communication with other processors (e.g., other control points, mainframes). They may in fact be viewed as TEs having the special function of controlling the operation of switching nodes and that attach to the network via the switching nodes they control, with their own ISDN addresses. A node control point, acting in the guise of such a TE, can request (from itself, acting in the guise of serving switch) a frame-relay connection to the control point of any other node. That such a connection is to be used for signaling would be indicated by using the "Q.931" code point for the layer 3 protocol parameter in the BC information element of the SETUP message; the connection would be assigned a high priority accordingly. As an example, consider that the control point of node 2 desires a logical connection to the control point of node 3, other than provided by logical channel 0 in the point-to-point physical channel between nodes 2 and 3, perhaps as a back-up connection or for additional bandwidth as determined by a network management entity. Node 2 obtains routing information as for any connection request, which we will assume for this example is via node 4, perhaps specified as "$PCI = 1$ to node 4, $PCI = 1$ to node 3; return by $PCI = 2$ to node 4, $PCI = 2$ to node 2." Node 2 then sends SETUP to node 4 via its existing logical signaling connection with node 4, specifying the ISDN address of node 3's control point as the called-party address and frame-relay bearer capability with Q.931 given as the layer 3 protocol. Node 4 forwards the SETUP message to node 3 via its existing logical signaling connection with node 3, and the CONNECT messages flow back from node 3 to node 4 and thence to node 2. The DLCI values to be used for the connection being set up are contained in the SETUP and CONNECT messages, just as they are in the flows shown in Fig. 9. The resulting logical connection could be used for the flows between nodes 2 and 3 in Fig. 9, instead of the $DLCI = 0$ logical channel in the physical link between these nodes.

In proposing the use of frame-relay for connections that carry signaling information, it is important to consider performance requirements for such connections, including robustness and low end-to-end delay. Frame-relay connections, with a set of link-layer procedures such as extended LAPD operating end-to-end, should meet these requirements. The capability to set up such connections, some of which may be used as back-ups, further enhances the robustness of frame relay for transporting signaling information.

We thus have the possibility of frame relay being employed in the private ISDN for all packet-oriented traffic, with the same transmission and switching facilities being shared by signaling flows and user data, and the same Q.931 procedures being employed to control connections for signaling flows as well as connections for user data. In addition, a common network architecture, including directory and routing applications, topology management, use of back-up connections, and general network management could be shared by signaling and user data. There remains, of course, the logical separation between U-plane and C-plane throughout the network based on multiplexing of logical channels at the frame sub-layer.

4.3 Frame Relay and Integrated Packet Networks

The concept of an ISDN employing packet transport for both voice and data, relying on hardware-based "fast packet switching" and high-speed digital transmission, has been developed by Turner in several papers, beginning with [23]. Frame relay is clearly a fast-packet-switching mechanism. It therefore seems natural to consider the evolution of private ISDNs with frame-relay capability into integrated packet networks in which voice connections are realized using packet-speech techniques and frame relay rather than circuit switching. A detailed performance analysis demonstrating the feasibility of packet speech in frame-relay networks, including such factors as susceptibility to packet loss, variability of end-to-end delay, the possible need for time stamps, and appropriate playout mechanisms is beyond the scope of this paper. We note, however, that the packet-speech protocol proposed for integrated packet networks in [24] is directly applicable to frame relay. That is, the only function of the procedural sub-layer for packet-speech connections would be to provide time stamps on an end-to-end basis, if they are deemed necessary; neither recovery nor flow control would be employed. It should also be noted that frame-relay voice connections could be placed in a higher priority class than data connections to obtain better control over end-to-end delay.

A further evolution of private ISDNs to networks with fully self-routing capabilities becomes reasonable once links with speeds of tens of megabits per second become prevalent between network nodes. In the architecture described in [25], each frame carries a routing header that completely specifies the path it is to take through the network. This technique reduces the per-frame processing required below that for standard frame relay in that table look-ups for DLCI swapping are no longer necessary in intermediate nodes. In addition, there is no longer any need for explicit action by an intermediate node in setting up a connection through it. Of course, the frame format employed within the network will no longer be that of Fig. 2. Instead, the frame format may be that of Fig. 2 modified by the insertion of a self-routing header between the frame delimiter (flag) and the DLCI field. The function of originating and terminating nodes would be such that the frames at user-network interfaces for frame-relay connections still have the standard format of Fig. 2. Thus the self-routing network can provide frame-relay service, and TEs that obtain frame-relay service from standard frame-relay networks as described in this paper can obtain the service in the same way from the self-routing network.

5. SUMMARY

This paper has discussed several aspects of frame relay, a packet-switching technique that takes advantage of the high-speed digital transmission and standardized protocols whose widespread availability characterize the ISDN environment. The partition of layer 2 into a frame sub-layer and a procedural sub-layer and the operation of frame relay with only the frame sub-layer being terminated by the network were reviewed. Q.931 procedures for control of frame-relay connections at user-network interfaces, as well as the transport of the associated Q.931 messages across these interfaces, were examined for several scenarios. Finally, we discussed the use of frame relay as a transport mechanism for all forms of packet-oriented traffic in private networks, focusing on the use of Q.931 procedures with appropriate extensions for inter-node signaling and the use of frame-relay to transport Q.931 messages within the network, and also briefly indicating possibilities for evolution of private networks with frame relay into integrated packet networks.

REFERENCES

[1] CCITT, *Recommendation I.122: Framework for providing additional packet mode bearer services.* Melbourne, CCITT Blue Book, 1988.

[2] ANSI T1S1, *Frame Relaying Bearer Service: Architectural framework and service description.* ANSI document T1S1/88-185, Dec. 1988.

[3] ANSI T1S1, *Signaling specification for frame relay (Rev. 6).* ANSI document T1S1.2/88-440, Dec. 1988.

[4] ECMA TC32, *Packetized Data Transfer in Private Switching Networks.* Draft Technical Report TR/PMA, ECMA/TC32/87/237, Nov. 1987.

[5] CCITT, *Recommendation Q.931 (I.451): ISDN user-network interface layer 3 specifications for basic call control.* Melbourne, CCITT Blue Book, 1988.

[6] CCITT, *Recommendation Q.921 (I.441): ISDN user-network interface data link layer specification.* Melbourne, CCITT Ble Book, 1988.

[7] N. T. Batis, *Load increase under link-by-link and end-to-end error recovery.* ANSI document T1D1.1/87-02, Source: AT&T Technologies, 5-9 Jan. 1987.

[8] A. Bhargava, J. F. Kurose, D. Towsley, and G. Van Leemput, "Performance comparison of error control schemes in high speed computer communication networks," *Proc. INFOCOM'88*, New Orleans, pp. 694-703, April 1988.

[9] M. Nassehi, "Flow control in frame relay networks," *Proc. GLOBECOM'88*, Hollywood, FL, pp. 1784-1790, Nov. 1988.

[10] D. T. D. Luan and D. M. Lucantoni, "Throughput analysis of a window-based flow control subject to bandwidth management," *Proc. INFOCOM'88*, New Orleans, pp. 411-417, April 1988.

[11] N. T. Batis, *Delay and throughput in a frame-relaying network.* ANSI document T1D1.1/87-04, Source: AT&T Technologies, 5-9 Jan. 1987.

[12] CCITT SG XI, *Revised draft for "ISDN data link layer specification for non D channel application".* Geneva, WP XI/6, Temp. Doc. 116, May 1988.

[13] R. J. Cherukuri, J. H. Derby, and D. Jäpel, "Harmonization of the ISDN D-channel link-access protocol with the IEEE 802.2 logical-link control," *Proc. GLOBECOM'88*, Hollywood, FL, pp. 711-715, Nov. 1988.

[14] J. H. Derby and R. J. Cherukuri, *Symmetric DLCI assignment procedures for frame relay.* ANSI document T1S1.2/88-157, Source: IBM, April 1988.

[15] P. Kermani and L. Kleinrock, "Virtual cut-through: A new computer communication switching technique," *Computer Networks*, vol. 3, pp. 267-286, 1979.

[16] D. Jäpel and E. Port, "LAN/ISDN interconnect via frame relay," *Proc. GLOBECOM'88*, Hollywood, FL, pp. 1791-1797, Nov. 1988.

[17] R. M. Amy and J. H. Derby, *Congestion control in frame-relay networks.* ANSI document T1S1.1/88-206, Source: IBM, May 1988.

[18] J. H. Derby and R. C. Kunzelman, "Private ISDNs — Beyond software defined networks," *Proc. ICC'87*, Seattle, pp. 1230-1234, June 1987.

[19] R. J. Cherukuri and J. H. Derby, *A congestion control method for layer 2.* ANSI document T1S1.2/88-092, Source: IBM, April 1988.

[20] A. E. Baratz, J. P. Gray, P. E. Green, Jr., J. M. Jaffe, and D. P. Pozefsky, "SNA networks of small systems," *IEEE J. Sel. Areas Commun.*, vol. SAC-3 no. 3, pp. 416-426, May 1985.

[21] CCITT SG XI, *Meeting report: Ad hoc private network signaling.* Geneva, WP XI/6, Temp. Doc. 607, Aug. 1987.

[22] ANSI T1D1, *Report of the ad hoc group on PBX-PBX/private networking.* ANSI document T1D1.1/87-173, March 1987.

[23] J. S. Turner and L. F. Wyatt, "A packet network architecture for integrated services," *Proc. GLOBECOM'83*, San Diego, pp. 45-50, Nov. 1983.

[24] W. L. Hoberecht, "A layered network protocol for packet voice and data integration," *IEEE J. Sel. Areas Commun.*, vol. SAC-1 no. 6, pp. 1006-1013, Dec. 1983.

[25] I. Cidon and I. Gopal, "PARIS: An approach to integrated high-speed private networks," *Int. J. Digital & Analog Cabled Systems*, to appear.

CONGESTION CONTROL IN ISDN FRAME-RELAY NETWORKS

Bharat T. Doshi and Han Q. Nguyen

Bharat T. Doshi is a
supervisor in the Per-
formance Analysis
Department at AT&T
Bell Laboratories in
Holmdel, New Jersey.
Work in his group
involves performance
analysis and traffic
engineering for
switching, data com-
munication, computer,
and production sys-
tems. His research
interests include
queueing theory and
stochastic processes
and their applications
to performance analy-
sis. He received a
B.Tech. degree in
mechanical engineer-
ing from the India
Institute of Technol-
ogy, Bombay, and a
Ph.D. in operations
research from Cornell
University. He joined
AT&T in 1979. **Han Q.
Nguyen** is a supervi-
sor in the Data
Architecture Planning
Department at AT&T
Bell Laboratories in
Holmdel, New Jersey.
His group is responsi-
ble for overall
architecture and pro-
tocol planning for (continued on page 132)

Like X.25 packet networks, ISDN frame-relay networks require effective congestion control mechanisms
to cope with unanticipated network component failures
and overloads. Unlike X.25 packet networks, ISDN
frame-relay networks perform the requisite packet-
switching function *without* terminating the link and network layer data-transfer protocols. They therefore
cannot use delayed acknowledgment and/or receiver-
not-ready indications embedded in these protocols for
congestion control. This paper reviews the measures
that can be used to control congestion effectively in
ISDN frame-relay networks.

Introduction

In ISDN frame-relay virtual-circuit networking, to take advantage of the higher speed and quality of digital transmission facilities, the
network's protocol processing function in the virtual-circuit data-
transfer phase is streamlined to minimize transit delay and maximize
throughput. At each network node, only the core procedures of LAPD
are performed in the relay process. That is, incoming LAPD frames are
checked only for valid frame-check-sequence (FCS) and address fields;
invalid frames are simply discarded, while valid frames are switched
("relayed") toward their destination on the basis of their virtual-circuit
identity as indicated in the frame address. The remaining LAPD protocol procedures and the layer 3 protocol—including, in particular, error-
correction (via retransmission) and flow-control procedures—are left to
operate between the LAPD end points on an end-to-end basis.

Thus, unlike today's X.25 packet networks, ISDN frame-relay
networks cannot make use of delayed acknowledgment and receiver-not-
ready (RNR) indication for congestion control. Consequently, formulating effective and efficient alternative congestion controls is particularly
important in the architectural design of ISDN frame-relay networks.

In this article, we review design considerations and discuss
control techniques for ISDN frame-relay networks that use a virtual-
circuit-based edge-to-edge internodal relay architecture. Some of

the techniques are common to all virtual-circuit networks and thus will be described only briefly. Others have been developed for the particular constraints and flexibility of ISDN frame-relay networks; these will be discussed in greater detail.

Congestion Control Objectives

Network component (node, trunk) failures and unanticipated high traffic demand are potential causes for congestion in packet networks in general and in frame-relay networks in particular. When a network component fails, retransmissions initiated by the end points increase traffic levels on the network paths that lead to the failed component. Excessively high traffic levels, whether due to failure recovery attempts or network component service oversubscription, can cause network transit delays to exceed the end-to-end acknowledgment time-out values, and/or frames to be discarded by the network nodes because of buffer overflow. (The term *oversubscription* is used loosely to refer to the condition when too many virtual circuits have been set up or when a moderately large number of virtual circuits transmit simultaneously—a rare occurrence.) Acknowledgment time-outs and frame loss (and out-of-sequence errors) in turn increase the frequency of retransmission, further aggravating congestion and potentially causing it to spread.

Without some form of congestion control, as first pointed out by Kleinrock[1] for packet networks and demonstrated by Rege and Chen[2] for ISDN frame-relay networks, the network's *useful* throughput would greatly decrease while the network transit delay would grow unacceptably large. This performance degradation is not discriminatory. All users will suffer service degradation even if the congestion is caused by a few "overactive" users, unless special control measures are taken to ensure fairness.

The objectives of an overall control strategy are:

1. The probability of congestion during the data-transfer phase must be kept low. If congestion does develop, the adverse effects on the network and user-perceived performance should be minimized.
2. The network must not have to rely on cooperation (i.e., voluntary flow-rate reductions) from the end points to protect itself against congestion collapse, although such cooperation would enhance performance.
3. The controls should be effective over a wide range of network speeds [e.g., 56/64 kilobits per second (kb/s), T1.5, T45] and traffic characteristics.
4. The controls should not interfere with the natural data-transfer operations in the absence of congestion, and should incur only negligible overhead.

Elements of an Overall Control Plan

A comprehensive congestion avoidance and control plan consists of distributed real-time controls, centralized network-management (near real-time) controls, and long-term network engineering procedures and practices.

Distributed real-time controls are exercised by the network nodes and the end points. These controls can be characterized by their roles (preventive controls versus reactive controls) and their operating time scales (slow-acting versus fast-acting), both of which directly depend on the operational traffic units (virtual circuit versus frame).

At the high end of the operating time scale (seconds to minutes), the network will attempt to prevent congestion by spreading traffic load for each given source-destination node pair among a set of multiple alternate paths in setting up new virtual calls. (For permanent virtual circuits, load balancing is done as part of the engineering and provisioning process.) If all alternate paths for a source-destination node pair already are loaded sufficiently in comparison with the available bandwidth and buffer resources, then new call-setup requests between that node pair will be denied. In the event that severe congestion develops and persists at some network component, the network may attempt to reroute selected existing virtual calls locally around the congested component or onto completely different alternate paths. If the rerouting cannot be done (e.g., in case of global overload) then some existing virtual calls may be disconnected.

At the low end of the operating time scale (milliseconds to seconds), control techniques are applied by the network to minimize "hogging" of resources by any particular virtual circuit and to maximize useful throughput if a network component becomes overloaded. The control techniques include throughput enforcement, buffer management, internodal trunk service discipline, and frame discarding, all of which are discussed later in this paper.

Because no distributed control scheme can be expected to deal flawlessly (or even adequately) with each and every unanticipated network event, it is necessary to supplement the distributed controls with centralized network management's override capabilities (i.e., to change the distributed nodal controls' parameter values and/or block or unblock their actions). The override capabilities are invoked according to global network status to fine-tune the distributed controls to the particular network situation as necessary. For example, automatic controls such as virtual-circuit rerouting and virtual-call disconnecting are initiated under centralized network management's close supervision and control, since these controls can have severe impact on existing traffic. Because of their centralized and global nature, override controls have a latency of several minutes.

With these controls, a network should be able to protect itself adequately against congestion. Of course, if the end points cooperate by shedding their loads when the network becomes congested, performance will be improved even more.

Note that, together, the above control mecha-

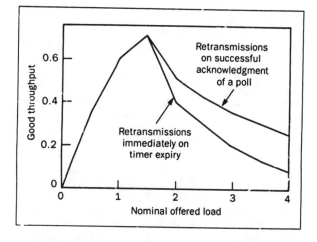

Figure 1. Good throughput with and without polling.

nisms can only optimize traffic performance within the confines of the available network resources. Whenever the available network resources fall short of the service demand level, traffic performance (e.g., virtual call-setup blocking rate) would still be unavoidably degraded. Consequently, long-term network engineering procedures, usually done on a weekly or monthly basis, must be relied upon to ensure that network resources are adequate to keep the probability of traffic overload (from unanticipated failures or statistical surge in service demand) as low as possible without making the network service uneconomical.

Overall, network engineering procedures, network management, and routing-related controls used for today's packet-switched, virtual-circuit networks, such as X.25 networks, can be applied directly to ISDN frame-relay networks. However, X.25 networks rely on the flow-control mechanisms made available through layer 2 and 3 protocol termination to effect real-time congestion control. For ISDN frame-relay networks, alternative real-time control mechanisms must be designed and evaluated. We now focus on these alternative real-time controls.

Real-Time Controls

The purpose of prudent engineering, intelligent routing algorithms, and call-setup controls is to keep the probability of congestion low during the data-transfer phase. When low activity per virtual circuit (very bursty traffic) requires some degree of concentration (i.e., the sum of the access-line speeds of the virtual circuits set up on a trunk exceeds the trunk's available bandwidth), the probability of short-term congestion is not zero. The effects of such congestion in ISDN frame-relay networks are characterized in Reference 2.

The simulation model used in that study closely mimics the essence of the LAPD protocol, including end-to-end protocol operations such as window rotation, rejects, time-outs, polls [i.e., receiver-ready (RR) frames with poll-bit set]. The model uses a mix of character-interactive, block-interactive, and file-transfer types of traffic. The study presents two cases. In the first, a LAPD acknowledgment timer expiry (T200 = 1 second) initiates retransmission of all unacknowledged frames. In the second, a poll is sent every time the T200 timer expires, and retransmissions are initiated only when acknowledgment for the poll frame is received. The results, illustrated in Figure 1, show that, without any additional control measures, the good throughput on the congested trunk drops dramatically as the congestion level increases. The throughput drop for the second scheme is much less severe than in the first scheme but is still not acceptable. This suggests two things:

- Polling on the expiry of T200 timer is strongly recommended for all end points and should be made mandatory, if possible.
- If the congestion-level and buffer-size scenarios studied in Reference 2 are likely, a real-time congestion control mechanism is necessary to maintain high useful throughput during periods of congestion.

Other effects of short-term congestion demonstrated in Reference 2 and in other studies of similar networks[1,3-5] include violation of delay requirements for delay-critical applications (e.g., echoplexing), throughput and delay

degradation for all virtual circuits although only a few over-active virtual circuits are responsible for congestion, spread of congestion to initially uncongested components because of excessive retransmissions, and session disconnections caused by T200 timers running out too many times.

In light of these potential effects on the network and user-perceived performance, real-time congestion controls should have the following objectives:

1. Maintain a high level of useful throughput by minimizing time-outs and out-of-sequence deliveries.
2. Prevent spread of congestion.
3. Protect well-behaved users from the misbehaved ones. In the event of a general overload, divide the "pain" equitably. This is what is generally referred to as *fairness*. The issue of fairness has been the focus of many studies of flow and congestion control problems.[6] However, its definition remains vague. Thus, it is defined practically as *preventing hogging of resources by a small number of users*.
4. To the extent possible, provide delays consistent with the service objectives (especially for very delay-sensitive applications).
5. Prevent session disconnections unless desired for congestion control.

In addition, real-time controls should foster network self-reliance, robustness, and efficiency.

We will now discuss a set of congestion control mechanisms and their effectiveness in meeting the above objectives during the data-transfer phase. These schemes can be broadly categorized as follows:

- Controls that reduce load, maintain delay objectives, and ensure a degree of fairness through the natural elasticity in window-based end-to-end protocol, adequate buffer provisioning, and queue management.
- Controls that (1) involve explicit or implicit detection of congestion by the congested component or by the end points and (2) take actions to reduce the load offered to the congested component, to minimize retransmissions, and to preserve a degree of fairness. The control

Table I. Buffer Size and Maximum Delay

| Access speed C_a (b/s) | Trunk speed C_L (b/s) | Per-virtual-circuit activity level α | | | | | | | |
| | | 0.01 | | 0.05 | | 0.25 | | 0.50 | |
		Buffer (kB)	D_{max} (s)	Buffer (kB)	D_{max} (s)	Buffer (kB)	D_{max} (s)	Buffer (kB)	D_{max} (s)
16 k	64 k	113	14.1	22.5	2.81	4.5	0.56	2.25	0.28
16 k	1.544 M	2020	10.5	404	2.11	81	0.42	40	0.21
64 k	1.544 M	960	5.0	192	1.0	38	0.20	1!	0.10
64 k	64 k	68	8.5	14	1.7	2.7	0.34	1.35	0.17
1.544 M	1.544 M	620	3.23	124	0.65	25	0.13	12.4	0.07
1.544 M	45 M	14,207	3.08	2841	0.62	568	0.12	284	0.06

Round-trip propagation delay = 60 ms; LAPD frame size = 136 bytes; Links in the connection = 6; kB = kilobytes; s = seconds

Table II. Buffer Size and Overflow Probability with Dedicated and Shared Buffers

| Access speed C_a | | Trunk speed C_L (Mb/s) | Buffer size, kilobytes | | | Probability, HP overflow | |
HP (kb/s)	LP (Mb/s)		Fully dedicated	Hybrid HP	Hybrid LP	Normal (0.5)	Overload (2.0)
16	1.544	1.544	1716	15	58	7.4×10^{-23}	2.8×10^{-6}
64	1.544	1.544	887	25	58	3.4×10^{-22}	2.5×10^{-6}

HP = high priority; LP = low priority

actions may be in the congested component, in the end points, or in both.

Assumptions. The design of a network's distributed controls is highly dependent on the particular network's *internodal* relay architecture, i.e., the procedure by which user-data frames are relayed from one node to the next between the network edges. Just as with today's packet networks, frame-relay networks' internodal relay architectures are likely to be vendor-proprietary and vary significantly from one vendor's network to another. Plausible architectures could range from a quasi-datagram-based approach with sufficient built-in procedural precaution to ensure a negligible probability of virtual-circuit frames arriving out of sequence, to a virtual-route-based approach, to a virtual-circuit-based approach.

In this article, we assume that the network uses a straightforward virtual-circuit-based internodal relay architecture. At each node, the incoming line/trunk identity (ID) and logical-link address (in the LAPD address field) of an incoming frame are used to map into the frame's outgoing line/trunk ID and logical-link address. The outgoing logical-link address is substituted for the incoming logical-link address in the frame's LAPD address field before the frame is sent out. This procedure requires each switch (including, in particular, tandem switches) to maintain *per-virtual-circuit* translation records for all of its virtual circuits in order to perform the frame-relay operations during the data-transfer phase. With this type of internodal relay architecture, the transmitting and receiving protocol handlers at each network node can identify the virtual circuit to which a particular frame belongs and, therefore, can apply appropriate control measures with the degree of selectivity required to maintain fairness.

For other internal protocols in which the internal network nodes do not have access to the identity of the virtual circuit sending a given frame, some aspects of congestion control (especially the actions in the end points) remain similar. Others are different in the sense that some actions are taken at the network edge rather than at the congested component.[7]

The other assumption we make is that the end points use a window-based protocol (the LAPD I-frame procedures or similar procedures) above the LAPD core procedures. For ease of discussion, we choose to use the LAPD I-frame procedures as an example.

Implicit Controls. For any window-based protocol, the delays caused by higher occupancy of trunk transmit buffers during congestion automatically slow down window rotation, reducing the offered load. If each trunk buffer is sized to hold the entire window's worth of frames for each virtual circuit that the call setup control allows, then, as long as the T200 timers do not run out, no frames will be dropped and the natural elasticity of the protocol will achieve the desired load shedding. Also, since no frames are dropped due to buffer overflow, no bandwidth is wasted for retransmissions and the ideal network throughput objective is achieved.

Two factors affect the feasibility of full buffer dedication: (1) the size, cost, and management complexity of the buffer and (2) the delay induced by a large buffer under congestion and the resulting T200 timer expiries, which may cause retransmissions and/or session disconnects. In addition, unless the buffers are managed with a sophisticated selective service strategy, the resulting delays will not be acceptable for delay-sensitive applications.

Table I shows the total buffer size and worst-case frame delay [under first-in, first-out (FIFO) discipline] for various access-line speeds, trunk speeds, and activity levels. We assume that the call-setup control limits the number of virtual circuits so that the trunk is busy no more than 50 percent of the time in the long run. It seems that when the ratio of the trunk speed C_L to the access-line speed C_a is not very large and the activity level α is high enough, full buffer dedication is indeed possible. At higher values of C_L/C_a and lower activity levels, the required buffer size is large and the worst-case delay is much bigger than the default value of the T200 timer (1 second). If polling on timer expiry is made mandatory, timer expiry may not result in immediate retransmissions. However, frequent expiry of timers may result in a LAPD end point disconnecting the session. Finally, the delays shown in Table I for large C_L/C_a and small α may not be acceptable for the application mix even if priorities are used to provide better service to some applications at the expense of others.

Suppose the traffic mix consists of a large number of virtual circuits having high values of C_L/C_a and short bursts of data, coupled with a small number of virtual circuits having small values of C_L/C_a and longer bursts of data. For example, the former may be interactive and low-speed file-transfer traffic and the latter may be very high speed file transfers and LAN bridge traffic. Then the above discussion suggests the following strategy: For the former type of virtual circuits (type I), provide a shared buffer sized to keep the probability of overflow small. For the latter (type II), dedicate a full window's worth of buffer for each virtual circuit set up on the trunk. Serve type I traffic with nonpreemptive priority over type II traffic. Higher priority allows a small shared buffer without causing a high probability of overflow. Lower priority to type II traffic magnifies the natural elasticity and slows down the truly high-speed virtual circuits for which the possibility of a buffer overflow has been eliminated. Although there is a small probability that the type I buffer can overflow, the large number of virtual circuits involved makes the event statistically less likely. In addition, since type I virtual circuits are assumed to send short bursts of data, congestions caused

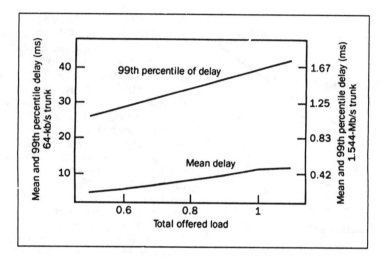

Figure 2. Mean and 99th percentile delay for a 10-byte frame in high-priority queue. The high-priority traffic mix is 90 percent 10-byte frames and 10 percent 136-byte frames.

by statistical fluctuations will be of short duration and will not have significant detrimental effects if they remain infrequent. Table II illustrates the saving in buffer size possible using this scheme. (Rege and Chen[8] give details of the model and more extensive results.) If the primary danger of congestion comes from relatively few high-speed virtual circuits (access line speed close to the trunk speed), then this scheme is very attractive.

If a sizable fraction of traffic comes from high-speed virtual circuits with relatively low activity level, then the above scheme does not help to reduce the buffer requirement. Also, even if most of the virtual circuits are of type I, unusual events may cause unpredictably high (in a statistical sense) type I traffic. This results in extended periods of congestion, buffer overflow, and retransmissions. Some form of additional real-time control is then necessary. We will discuss those controls under "Explicit Real-Time Controls."

Even when full buffer dedication is economically feasible and typical delays can be maintained below the T200 timer value, the delays may not be acceptable for some applications. Moreover, with the full buffer dedication, a few overactive virtual circuits can cause high buffer content, higher delays for all virtual circuits, and smaller throughput even for well behaved virtual circuits. These considerations are important even under moderate to heavy load and remain important when the offered load reaches true congestion levels. Additional buffer management and service strategies are necessary to protect delay-sensitive applications and maintain fairness. The former objective can be achieved by serving delay-sensitive applications at higher priority than the others. As long as the load in the high-priority queue is kept at moderate level, the delay there will remain small even if the overall load is high. Two types of priority mechanisms are possible: *explicit* and *implicit*.

If, as discussed earlier, the primary danger of high load and congestion comes from virtual circuits that require very high speed data transfer (high-speed file transfer, LAN traffic, etc.), they can be identified at virtual-circuit setup and served at low priority during the data-transfer phase. This gives an explicit priority to the frames from other virtual circuits (type I traffic). Figure 2 shows the mean and 99th percentile of the delay seen by a 10-byte frame in the high-priority queue as functions of the total load for the trunk speeds of 6₄ kb/s and 1.544 mega-

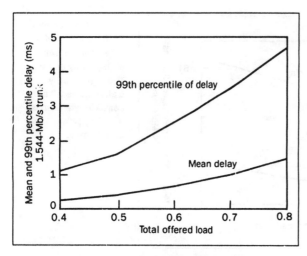

Figure 3. Mean and 99th percentile delay for a 10-byte frame over two trunks. The traffic mix is 87 percent 10-byte frames, 9 percent 48-byte frames, and 4 percent 136-byte frames.

bits per second (Mb/s) when the frame size in the low-priority queue is 136 bytes. (The mean and 99th percentile are obtained through analytical modeling and by inverting the Laplace transforms.[9]) Other parameters are specified in the figure. Clearly, excellent low-delay performance is possible for the high-priority traffic even at high overall load.

Many type I virtual circuits, however, may have mixed delay requirements. For example, a terminal may be in editing mode, requiring very short echoplexing delay; or it may be receiving a screen full of data from the host. In this latter mode, a much longer delay can be tolerated. Treating all this type I traffic in a single high-priority queue may result in high load in the high-priority queue and defeat the purpose of the priority treatment; as Figure 2 shows, this is more crucial at lower trunk speeds.

This suggests additional discriminatory treatment even within the type I traffic. Typically, low delays are

required when short frames are sent infrequently, while longer bursts of full LAPD frames can tolerate somewhat longer delays. This fact can be exploited to provide an additional implicit priority to the delay-sensitive short frames within type I traffic. Two queues are maintained for the type I traffic. When a frame arrives at the trunk buffer, the buffer is checked to see if any frame belonging to the same virtual circuit is present. If there is, the new frame is put in the lower-priority queue. Otherwise, the frame length is checked. If it is below a threshold, the frame is sent to the higher-priority queue. If it is above the threshold, it is put in the lower-priority queue. The type II traffic can be served in a third, even lower-priority, queue. Variations of this implicit priority mechanism have ensured low delay for character interactive traffic in AT&T data switches.[10] For analysis of such schemes, see References 10-12. While the analysis in References 10 and 11 refers to a byte-stream protocol, extension to a LAPD-based protocol is immediate.

The need for this implicit priority scheme depends on the aggregate type I traffic and the trunk speed and becomes less crucial at higher trunk speeds. Suppose, for example, that the type I traffic is limited to 80 percent of the trunk capacity even under congestion. Then, as shown in Figure 3, the 99th percentile of the delay over two trunks with FIFO service for type I traffic is under 5 milliseconds (ms) for 1.544-Mb/s trunks. This delay for 64-kb/s trunks would be about 120 ms and very sensitive to the load in the queue, as well as to the traffic mix and the frame lengths. Additional implicit priority at lower trunk speeds can maintain the load in the highest priority well below 80 percent and provide robust delay performance.

While priority queueing gives excellent service to delay-sensitive applications even under overall congestion, it does not protect some overactive virtual circuits from degrading delay and throughput performance of other virtual circuits in the low-priority queue. If all virtual circuits (other than those sending very delay-sensitive traffic) are equally important (e.g., if they have the same throughput class), serving the low-priority queue in a round-robin manner will allow roughly equal throughput to all virtual circuits under heavy congestion.[13]

This is demonstrated in Table III, which shows the throughput allocation among four hypothetical virtual circuits, two of which offer more load than the others, under various total traffic-load levels. If the virtual circuits have different legitimate throughput requirements, the round-robin service can be modified so that more than one frame (depending on the throughput class of the virtual circuit) can be transmitted from a virtual circuit during each shot at the service. Another suitable mechanism for protecting well-behaved virtual circuits and ensuring a degree of fairness is to monitor the buffer occupancy (and/or bandwidth usage) by virtual circuit and serve the recently overactive virtual circuits from a third, lowest-priority queue. Since this allows all the queues to be served FIFO, the queue management is simplified. This may make it more attractive at higher trunk speeds.

Overall, when a full window's worth of buffer dedication is economically feasible and does not cause T200 timer expiry problems, it is possible to maintain high overall throughput even under congestion. In addition, with appropriate priority structure and service discipline, it is possible to protect delay-sensitive applications effectively and maintain a degree of fairness under congestion. In fact, in this case the congestion control mechanism is built directly into the call-setup controls and buffer-management strategies. No explicit actions are needed during periods of short-term congestion.

Explicit Real-Time Controls. As mentioned earlier, it is not always feasible to dedicate a full window's worth of buffers for every virtual circuit and achieve all congestion-control objectives automatically. When the sum of the windows for the virtual circuits set up on a trunk exceeds the trunk transmit-buffer size, the buffer can overflow during periods when the sum of the access-line speeds of active virtual circuits exceeds the trunk bandwidth. A frame dropped due to buffer overflow may cause the following frames on the same virtual circuit to be received out of

Table III. Throughput Equity under Round-Robin Discipline

Case	Nominal peak offered load from VCs			Trunk utilization due to VCs		
	1 and 2	3 and 4	Total	1 and 2	3 and 4	Total
1	0.06	0.41	0.47	0.06	0.41	0.47
2	0.47	0.823	1.293	0.41	0.588	0.998
3	0.615	1.273	1.888	0.454	0.546	1.000
4	0.889	1.556	2.445	0.487	0.513	1.000
5	1.2	2.0	3.2	0.500	0.500	1.000

Note: Four VCs; VCs 1 and 2 offer less load than VCs 3 and 4. (VC = virtual circuit.)

sequence, resulting in a REJECT and retransmission of up to a whole window's worth of frames. If a whole window's worth of data gets dropped, the T200 timer will expire and a poll will be sent. If this succeeds, the whole window will be retransmitted. These retransmissions result in a dramatic drop in good throughput, as observed in Reference 2. Schemes are necessary to detect congestion and minimize its adverse effects. The following observations suggest some effective control mechanisms:

- During congestion, the effective throughput on the trunk drops because it uses some of its bandwidth to transmit frames which will be received out of sequence and will have to be retransmitted in any case. A strategy which identifies such frames and discards them, even if they do not cause buffer overflow, will reduce the throughput degradation. The frames received on a virtual circuit immediately after a frame is dropped for that virtual circuit because of buffer overflow are candidates for dropping. Such a selective discard strategy can be enhanced further to monitor buffer occupancy or bandwidth usage of virtual circuits and to penalize overactive virtual circuits by initiating discards at a lower threshold for them.
- Buffer overflow, frame losses, and retransmissions

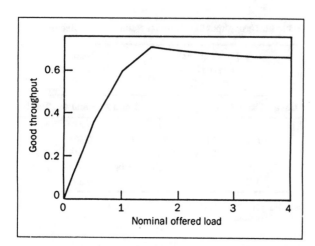

Figure 4. Good throughput with a selective discard control. Scheme ensures fair treatment.

occur because the sum of the window sizes for the currently active virtual circuits exceeds the available buffer size. Frame losses can be minimized if the effective window can be reduced for each virtual circuit and/or the number of virtual circuits simultaneously transmitting data to the trunk can be reduced. Reducing the window also reduces the number of frames to be retransmitted in the event of a frame loss.

Network-based control. A selective discarding scheme of the type discussed above was included in the simulation mentioned earlier.[2] The results, illustrated in Figure 4, show excellent good-throughput performance. As mentioned above, this scheme also permits throughput enforcement and hence fair treatment under congestion. In addition, this type of control is network-based and does not rely on cooperation from the end point. On the other hand, frames are not dropped until they reach the congested component. This may affect the load on preceding trunks in the connections and degrade their delay performance. This potential for the spread of congestion can be

reduced if the end points cooperate and reduce the load they offer to the network under congestion.

End-point-based controls. When a frame is dropped because of buffer overflow in the network, the following frame will generate a REJECT from the receiving end point. If a whole window's worth of frames is lost, the sending end point will time-out. In either case, the sending end point may assume the existence of congestion along the connection and reduce the load it is offering to the network.

One mechanism is to lower the end point's effective window size. Various window-reduction schemes have been proposed.[3-5] Typical schemes are:
- Reduce window size by 1 to W_{min}, the minimum window size.
- Reduce to W_{min}.
- Reduce to max $\{W_{min}, \alpha W\}$, where W is the current effective window size and α is a fraction, $0 < \alpha < 1$.

Successful transmissions (and acknowledgments) may indicate that the congestion has gone away and window size should be increased. Once again, various window-relaxation schemes have been proposed. For example:
- Increase by 1 up to W_{max}, the maximum window size, after N consecutive successful transmissions.
- Increase by 1 (up to W_{max}) after W successful transmissions, where W is the current effective window size.

Many of these combinations have been analyzed under a variety of traffic patterns and network parameters by B. Barbour, K.-J. Chen, and K. M. Rege at Bell Laboratories. Chen et al. report on some of this work in Reference 14. Overall, a scheme that reduces W to W_{min} (typically 1) and increases it by 1 after a fixed number of successive successful transmissions performs best when the nominal window size is small (3 or 4). Close to this scheme in performance is a scheme that reduces the window to half its current value instead of to W_{min}. When the nominal window size is large (10 or more), however, the latter scheme outperforms the former except under very heavy congestion. Both schemes achieve very good overall throughput performance.

Table IV. Good Throughput with and without Fairness Enforcement

Nominal offered load	Good throughput under various control strategies		
	A	B	C
1.5	0.68	0.53	0.69
3.0	0.66	0.50	0.68
4.5	0.64	0.45	0.65

A: All VCs adapt windows, no network control
B: Half the VCs adapt windows, no network control
C: Half the VCs adapt windows, fairness enforced at congested component

Another mechanism to reduce the offered load is to stop transmitting for a fixed or random duration on receiving a REJECT, or on T200 timer expiry. With enough randomness, this will reduce the number of virtual circuits simultaneously sending data to the same trunks. When the voluntary stop period expires, the virtual circuit may begin with window size 1 and change the size in increments as in the scheme discussed above.

Adaptive schemes in the end points and selective discard schemes at the congested trunk can work together synergistically to achieve all the objectives of congestion control. Endpoints reduce the offered load at the source. The actions by the congested component guarantee high good throughput, even if some end points do not adapt, and enforce fair treatment of all virtual circuits. For example, Table IV shows the throughput performance under three scenarios: A—all virtual circuits adapt their windows with no network control; B—only half of the virtual circuits adapt their windows with no network control; C—only half of the virtual circuits adapt their windows, and the network nodes employ a discard strategy in which the discard threshold for a virtual circuit depends on the number of frames it has in the transmit buffer. The effectiveness of the throughput enforcement mechanism is obvious from the results. In addition, the priority queueing and service discipline (round-robin, for example) can protect delay-sensitive applications and provide a fairer delay/throughput performance.

Controls with network—end-point interaction. In previous sections, we discussed controls in which both congestion detection and control action are at the same place (at the congested component or in the end point). Usually, congestion detection is more accurate in the congested component (for example, a frame received out of sequence does not mean that congestion has been encountered, even if it results in a REJECT). On the other hand,

load shedding is more effective in the end points (it cuts the traffic at the source before any of the network resources are used on a frame that will be dropped eventually). This suggests that improved performance is possible if the congested component detects the congestion (high buffer or trunk occupancy) and communicates to the end points via advisory "messages," and the end points react to these "messages" by load-shedding actions. Load can be shed by adapting windows or stopping for a duration. The results in References 2 and 14 indicate excellent throughput performance from such schemes. However, such schemes involve additional complexity and overhead and need "message" standardization; the amount of complexity and overhead depend on the particular "message" conveyance mechanism chosen. These should be considered in deciding whether to use advisory "messages" for short-term real-time control. In the event of longer-term, more widely spread congestion, a slower-acting control involving advisory "messages" may be very effective as part of the overall network management.

Summary

Congestion is always a possibility in any data communications network (in any service system, for that matter) that allows some degree of sharing for economic reasons. Prudent engineering, path diversity, adaptive routing, and call-setup controls can minimize but cannot, in general, eliminate the potential for congestion during the data-transfer phase. Also, these long-term and near-real-time preventive controls (as well as reactive network-management-type controls) are similar, in general, for all virtual-circuit networks (e.g., X.25). It is during the data-transfer phase, where a real-time reactive control is needed to minimize the adverse effects of congestion, that the differences between ISDN frame-relay and X.25-based networks are more important. Thus, we have concentrated our discussion on real-time controls. Unlike X.25-based networks, ISDN frame-relay networks do not terminate level 2 or 3 in any network node and thus cannot use delayed acknowledgments and/or RNR for real-time congestion control. Our discussion shows that controls that, together, maintain high effective throughput, protect delay-sensitive applications, and ensure a degree of fairness under congestion can be provided for ISDN frame-relay networks.

Acknowledgment

Special acknowledgments are due to K.-J. Chen, K. Rege, and B. Barbour for their analysis of many of the controls discussed in this article. In addition, we have benefited from technical discussions with A. E. Eckberg, A. G. Fraser, D. T. Luan, D. M. Lucantoni, and D. Sheng.

References

1. L. Kleinrock, "On Flow Control in Computer Networks," *International Conference on Communications*, Toronto, June 1978.
2. K. M. Rege and K.-J. Chen, "A Performance Study of LAPD Frame-Relay Protocols for Packetized Data Transfer over ISDN Networks," *Fifth International Teletraffic Conference Seminar*, Lake Como, Italy, 1987.
3. W. Bux and D. Grillo, "Flow Control in Local-Area Networks of Interconnected Token Rings," *IEEE Transactions on Communications*, Vol. COM-33, No. 10, October 1985.
4. R. Jain, "A Timeout-Based Congestion Control Scheme for Window Flow-Controlled Networks," *IEEE Journal on Selected Areas in Communications*, Vol. SAC-4, No. 7, October 1986.
5. R. Jain, K. K. Ramakrishnan, and D. Chiu, "Congestion Avoidance in Computer Networks with a Connectionless Network Layer," *Tenth Data Communications Symposium*, October 1987.
6. M. Gerla, H. W. Chan, and J. R. B. deMarca, "Fairness in Computer Networks," *International Conference on Communications*, Chicago, June 1985.
7. D. M. Lucantoni and D. T. Luan, "Throughput Analysis of an Adaptive Window Based Flow-Control Subject to Bandwidth Management," *International Teletraffic Conference*, Turin, Italy, June 1988.
8. K. M. Rege and K.-J. Chen, "An Analytical Model for Buffer and Trunk Sizing and Severe Congestion Avoidance in LAPD Frame-Relay Networks," *Record of the International Conference on Communications*, Philadelphia, June 1988.
9. D. L. Jagerman, "An Inversion Technique for the Laplace Transform with Application to Approximation," *Bell System Technical Journal*, Vol. 57, No. 3, March 1978, pp. 669-710.
10. B. T. Doshi and K. M. Rege, "Analysis of a Multistage Queue," *The Bell System Technical Journal*, Vol. 57, No. 3, March 1978, pp. 669-710.
11. A. G. Fraser and S. P. Morgan, "Queueing and Framing Disciplines for a Mixture of Data Traffic Types," *AT&T Technical Journal*, Vol. 63, No. 6, July-August 1984, pp. 1061-1087.
12. C. Y. Lo, "Performance Analysis of a Two Priority Packet Queue," *AT&T Technical Journal*, Vol. 66, No. 3, May-June 1987.
13. E. L. Hahne and R. G. Gallager, "Round Robin Scheduling for Fairness Flow Control in Data Communication Networks," International Conference on Communications, June 1986.
14. K.-J. Chen et al., "Performance of LAPD Frame-Relay Networks: Transmission Error Effects and Congestion Control," *International Teletraffic Conference*, Turin, Italy, June 1988.

Biographies (continued)

advanced, wide-area data networks. He received a B.S. in industrial and systems engineering from Ohio University and an M.S. in operations research from Virginia Polytechnic Institute. He joined AT&T in 1978.

(Manuscript received September 29, 1988)

Chapter 4: Broadband ISDN (B-ISDN)

Background

Planning for ISDN began as far back as 1976. Only now is ISDN moving from the planning stage to the development of prototypes and actual implementations. It will be many years before the full spectrum of ISDN services becomes widely available, and refinements and improvements to ISDN services and network facilities will continue during this time. However, much of the planning and design effort is now directed toward a network concept that will be far more revolutionary than ISDN itself. This new concept is referred to as "broadband ISDN (B-ISDN)."

In one of its first working documents on B-ISDN, the CCITT modestly defined B-ISDN as "a service requiring transmission channels capable of supporting rates greater than the primary rate." Behind this innocuous statement lie plans for a network and set of services that will have far more impact on business and residential customers than ISDN. With B-ISDN, services — especially video services — requiring data rates that are orders of magnitudes beyond those that can be delivered by ISDN will become available. To contrast the concept of B-ISDN, with its new network and new services, with the original concept of ISDN, the original concept is now being referred to as "narrowband ISDN."

The evolution toward B-ISDN was triggered primarily by an increasing demand for high-bit-rate services, especially image and video services, and developments in the technology that supports these services. The key developments in this technology are as follows:

• Optical-fiber transmission systems that can offer low-cost high-data-rate transmission channels for network trunks and for subscriber lines;
• Microelectronic circuits that can offer low-cost high-speed building blocks for switching, transmission, and subscriber equipment; and
• High-quality video monitors and cameras that can, with sufficient production quantities, be offered at low cost.

These advances in technology will result in the integration of a wide range of communications facilities and the support of, in effect, universal communications with the following key characteristics:

• Worldwide exchange between any two subscribers in any medium or combination of media;
• Retrieval and sharing of massive amounts of information from multiple sources, in multiple media, among people in a shared electronic environment; and
• Distribution — including switched distribution — of a wide variety of cultural, entertainment, and educational materials to home or office, virtually on demand.

B-ISDN services

The driving force behind B-ISDN is to provide services. The services that B-ISDN will provide form the set of requirements that the network must satisfy. The CCITT classifies the services that could be provided by a B-ISDN into

• Interactive services, in which there is a two-way exchange of information (other than control-signaling information) between two subscribers or between a subscriber and a service provider, and
• Distribution services, in which the information transfer is primarily one way, from service provider to B-ISDN subscriber.

These two types of services are discussed in more detail below.

Interactive services. Interactive services are further classified as conversational, messaging, and retrieval services.

Conversational services. Conversational services provide for real-time dialogue between a user and an application or a user and a server. This category of interactive services encompasses a wide range of applications and data types, including the transmission of video, data, and documents. An example of a conversational service that would require higher capacity than that narrowband ISDN can provide is a remote image application, such as CAD/CAM or the review and manipulation of medical images from a hospital image database server. Another such example is video teleconferencing. Compared to the other two types of interactive services, conversational services place the greatest demand on the network, requiring high throughput and short response time.

Messaging services. Messaging services offer user-to-user communication between individual users via storage units with store-and-forward mailbox and/or message-handling functions that include information editing, processing, and conversion. In contrast to conversational services, messaging services are not in real time. Hence, they place lesser demands on the network and do not require that both users be available at the same time. Analogous narrowband services are X.400 and Teletex. One new form of messaging service that could be supported by ISDN is video mail, which is analogous to today's electronic mail (text/graphic mail) and voice mail.

Retrieval services. Retrieval services enable users to retrieve information stored in information centers, databases, or libraries of television and film. With this service, a user could order full-length films or videos from a film/video library facility.

Of greater interest to business, educational, and medical organizations, the envisioned broadband retrieval service would also allow the retrieval of high-resolution images such as X-ray or computerized axial tomography (CAT) scans, mixed-media documents, and large data files. This service could also be used for remote education and training.

Distribution services. B-ISDN distribution services are further classified into those without and those with user presentation control.

Distribution services without user presentation control. These distribution services are also referred to as "broadcast services." They provide a continuous flow of information, which is distributed from a central source to an unlimited number of authorized receivers connected to the network. Each user can access the flow of information, but has no control over the flow. In particular, the user cannot control the starting time or the order of the presentation of the broadcast information. All users simply tap into the information flow.

The most common example of these services is broadcast television. Currently, broadcast television is available through network broadcast via radio waves and through cable television distribution systems. With the capacities planned for B-ISDN, distribution services without user presentation control could be integrated with the other telecommunications services. In addition, television resolutions higher than those currently used for broadcast television can now be achieved, and it is anticipated that these higher quality services will also be available via B-ISDN.

Distribution services with user presentation control. These distribution services also distribute information from a central source to a large number of users. However, the information is provided as a sequence of information entities (for example, frames) with cyclical repetition. So, each user individually can access the cyclically distributed information and can control both the starting time and the order of presentation of the information. Because of the cyclical repetition, the information entities, selected by the user, are always presented from the beginning.

Standards

In 1988, the CCITT issued — as part of its I-series of recommendations on ISDN — the first two recommendations relating to B-ISDN, as follows:

- Recommendation I.113, entitled "Vocabulary of Terms for Broadband Aspects of ISDN," and
- Recommendation I.121, entitled "Broadband Aspects of ISDN."

Recommendations I.113 and I.121 represent the level of consensus reached as of late 1988 within the CCITT concerning the nature of the future B-ISDN. These documents provided a preliminary description of and a basis for future standardization and development work. Table 4-1 presents some of the important statements made in these documents.

Table 4-1. Noteworthy statements in Recommendations I.113 and I.121.

Broadband: A service or system requiring transmission channels capable of supporting rates greater than the primary rate.
The term B-ISDN is used for convenience in order to refer to and emphasize the broadband aspects of ISDN. The intent, however, is that there be one comprehensive notion of an ISDN which provides broadband and other ISDN services.
Asynchronous transfer mode (ATM) is the target transfer mode solution for implementing a B-ISDN. It will influence the standardization of digital hierarchies and multiplexing structures, switching and interfaces for broadband signals.
B-ISDN will be based on the concepts developed for ISDN and may evolve by progressively incorporating additional functions and services (e.g., high quality video applications).
The reference configuration defined in I.411 is considered sufficiently general to be applicable not only for a basic access and a primary rate access but also to a broadband access. Both reference points S and T are valid for broadband accesses.

Table 4-2 lists the factors that are guiding CCITT work on B-ISDN.

Table 4-2. Factors guiding CCITT work on B-ISDN.

• The emerging demand for broadband services
• The availability of high-speed transmission, switching, and signal-processing technologies
• The improved data- and image-processing capabilities available to the user
• The advances in software application processing in the computer and telecommunications industries
• The need to integrate both interactive and distribution services
• The need to integrate both circuit and packet transfer mode into one universal broadband network
• The need to provide flexibility in satisfying the requirements of both user and operator
• The need to cover broadband aspects of ISDN in CCITT recommendations

With both demand (user interest) and supply (the technology for high-speed networking) evolving rapidly, the usual practice of issuing recommendations every four years would be fatal to hopes of developing a standardized high-speed network utility. To head off the possibility of a fragmentation of effort and a proliferation of nonstandard products and services, the CCITT issued a 1990 set of interim recommendations on B-ISDN. This set of 14 documents provided, for the first time, a detailed and specific master plan for the broadband revolution. Table 4-3 lists these recommendations, giving the title and description of each. The rest of this chapter provides an overview of this master plan.

B-ISDN protocol architecture

Figure 4-1 presents a reference model of B-ISDN protocol architecture. The protocol architecture for B-ISDN introduces some new elements not found in the ISDN architecture. For B-ISDN, the transfer of information across the user-network interface will use asynchronous transfer mode (ATM).

Both X.25 and ATM are forms of packet transmission across the user-network interface. In this respect, X.25 and ATM are similar; however, ATM is much faster. Significant differences between X.25 and ATM are that

- X.25 includes control signaling on the same channel as data transfer, whereas ATM makes use of common-channel signaling.
- X.25 packets may be of varying length, whereas ATM packets are of fixed size: 53 eight-bit bytes long, to be precise. These fixed-size packets are also referred to as "cells."

Two layers of the B-ISDN protocol architecture relate to ATM functions: the ATM layer, which is common to all services and provides packet transfer capabilities, and the ATM adaptation layer (AAL), which is service dependent. (See Figure 4-1.) The AAL maps higher layer information into ATM cells to be transported over B-ISDN, then collects information from ATM cells for delivery to higher layers.

The 1988 Recommendation I.121, which contains the protocol reference model depicted in Figure 4-1, provided virtually no detail on the functions to be performed at each layer. The 1990 documents included a more detailed description of functions to be performed, as presented in Table 4-4.

ATM adaptation layer (AAL)

The use of ATM creates the need for an adaptation layer to support information transfer protocols not based on ATM. Two examples listed in the 1988 recommendations were pulse-code modulation (PCM) voice and LAPD, the standard data link control protocol for ISDN.

PCM voice is an application that produces a stream of bits from a voice signal. For this application to be used over ATM, PCM bits must be assembled into cells for transmission and read out on reception in such a way as to produce a smooth, constant flow of bits to the receiver.

For LAPD signaling to be carried across the network, LAPD frames must be mapped into ATM cells. This procedure will probably involve segmenting one LAPD frame into a number of cells on transmission and reassembling the frame from cells on reception. If the use of LAPD over ATM is allowed, all of the existing ISDN applications and control-signaling protocols can be used on B-ISDN.

The 1988 recommendations briefly mentioned AAL and pointed out its functions of mapping information into cells and performing segmentation and reassembly. The 1990 documents provided greater detail on the functions and services of this layer. In the area of services, four classes of service were defined: classes A, B, C, and D (see Table 4-5). This classification was based on whether or not a timing relationship must be maintained between source and destination, whether or not the application requires a constant bit rate, and whether the transfer is connection-oriented or connectionless.

An example of a class A service is circuit emulation. In circuit emulation, a constant bit rate — which requires the maintenance of a timing relation — is used and the transfer is connection oriented. An example of a class B service is variable-bit-rate video, such as might be used in a teleconference. Here, the application is connection oriented and timing is important, but the bit rate varies depending on the amount of activity in the scene. Classes C and D correspond to data transfer applications. In both classes, the bit rate may vary and no particular timing relationship is required; differences in data rate are handled by the end systems using buffers. The data transfer may be either connection oriented (class C) or connectionless (class D).

Table 4-3. 1990 Interim CCITT recommendations on B-ISDN.

Number	Title	Description
I.113	Vocabulary of Terms for Broadband Aspects of ISDN	Defines terms considered essential to the understanding and application of the principles of B-ISDN
I.121	Broadband Aspects of ISDN	States the basic principles of B-ISDN and indicates the evolution of ISDN required to support advanced services and applications
I.150	B-ISDN ATM Functional Characteristics	Summarizes the functions of the ATM layer
I.211	B-ISDN Service Aspects	Serves as a guideline for evolving Recommendations on B-ISDN services; includes a classification of B-ISDN services and a consideration of necessary network aspects
I.311	B-ISDN General Network Aspects	Describes networking techniques, signaling principles, traffic control, and resources management for B-ISDN; introduces concepts of transmission path, virtual path, and virtual channel
I.321	B-ISDN Protocol Reference Model and Its Application	Describes additions to the ISDN protocol reference model needed to accommodate B-ISDN services and functions
I.327	B-ISDN Functional Architecture	Describes additions to the ISDN functional architecture needed to accommodate B-ISDN services and functions
I.35b	Broadband ISDN Performance	Defines the performance parameters and performance objectives for the ATM layer of a broadband ISDN
I.361	B-ISDN ATM Layer Specification	Describes the ATM layer, including cell structure, cell coding, and ATM protocol
I.362	B-ISDN ATM Adaptation Layer (AAL) Functional Description	Provides a service classification for AAL and indicates the relationship between AAL services and AAL protocols
I.363	B-ISDN ATM Adaptation Layer (AAL) Specification	Describes the interactions between the AAL and the next higher layer, the AAL and the ATM layer, and AAL peer-to-peer operations
I.413	B-ISDN User-Network Interface	Gives the reference configuration for the B-ISDN user-network interface and examples of physical realizations
I.432	B-ISDN User-Network Interface Physical Layer Specification	Defines the physical layer interface for B-ISDN; includes physical medium specification, timing and framing aspects, and header error control
I.610	OAM Principles of B-ISDN Access	Describes the minimum functions required to maintain the physical layer and the ATM layer of the customer access

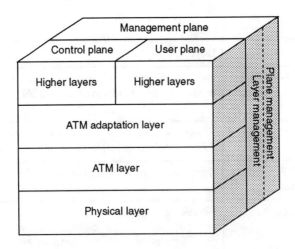

Figure 4-1. B-ISDN protocol reference model (Recommendation I.121).

Table 4-4. Functions of the B-ISDN layers.

	Higher layer functions	Higher layers	
	Convergence	CS	AAL
	Segmentation and reassembly	SAR	
Layer management	Generic flow control Cell header generation/extraction Cell VPI/VCI translation Cell multiplex and demultiplex	ATM	
	Cell rate decoupling HEC header sequence generation/verification Cell delineation Transmission frame adaptation Transmission frame generation/recovery	TC	Physical layer
	Bit timing Physical medium	PM	

CS =	Convergence sublayer
SAR =	Segmentation and reassembly sublayer
AAL =	ATM adaptation layer
VPI/VCI =	Virtual path identifier/virtual channel identifier
ATM =	Asynchronous transfer mode
HEC =	Header error control
TC =	Transmission control sublayer
PM =	Physical medium sublayer

Table 4-5. Service classification for ATM adaptation layer (Recommendation I.362).

	Class A	Class B	Class C	Class D
Timing relationship between source and destination	Required		Not required	
Bit rate	Constant	Variable		
Connection mode	Connection-oriented			Connectionless

To support these various classes of service, a set of protocols at the AAL level is defined. The 1990 recommendations provide a preliminary definition of AAL that is primarily functional. However, the recommendations do include some detail concerning header formats and procedures. The details of the AAL protocols remain to be worked out.

ATM

As noted, B-ISDN will use ATM, making it a packet-based network at the user interface and almost certainly a packet-based network in terms of its internal switching as well. Although the basic nature of B-ISDN is packet switching, the CCITT recommendations state that B-ISDN will support circuit-mode applications. Thus, ISDN — which began as an evolution from the circuit-switching telephone networks — will transform itself into a packet-switching network as it takes on broadband services.

ATM is similar in concept to frame relay, which is a packet interface technique planned to be used in narrowband ISDN and available today in some products that transmit over dedicated T1 circuits. Both ATM and frame relay use a streamlined set of functions to provide maximum throughput, taking advantage of the reliability and fidelity of modern digital networks to provide high-speed packet switching by avoiding repeated error checking and other protocol functions. ATM takes this streamlining process much further than frame relay to be able to exploit transmission channels in the tens and hundreds of megabits per second.

In ATM, transmission capacity is assigned to a connection based on subscriber requirements and available capacity. Data transfer is connection oriented, using concepts similar to those of the virtual circuit in X.25. ATM uses two connection concepts: virtual channel and virtual path. A virtual channel, much like an X.25 virtual circuit, provides a logical packet connection between two users. A virtual path defines a route from source to destination through a network. Multiple virtual channels may be bundled together to use the same virtual path.

The use of two connection concepts has certain advantages. For one thing, much of the work of setting up connections is done when a virtual path is first established. The addition of a new virtual channel to an existing virtual path requires little overhead. In addition, a number of data transport functions, such as flow control, can be done at the virtual-path level, simplifying the network architecture.

Each ATM cell consists of a five-octet header and a 48-octet information field. The format for the header at the user-network interface includes the following fields:

• Generic flow control. This field is to be used for end-to-end flow control between ATM users. Its specific use is not defined, but is left for further study.

• Virtual path identifier. This field identifies the path or route between source and destination.

• Virtual channel identifier. This field defines a logical connection between two ATM users.

• Payload type. In this field, a value of 00 is for user information; that is, for information from the next higher layer. Other values are not defined, but are left for further study. Presumably, network management and maintenance values will be assigned.

• Cell loss priority. In this field, a value of one means that this cell is subject to discard, whereas a value of zero indicates a higher priority application for which discard is inappropriate. Discard might occur in the case of high network congestion.

• Header error control. In this field, an 8-bit error code can be used to correct single-bit errors in the header and to detect double-bit errors.

All of the details just described were new to the 1990 interim recommendations. In the 1988 document, the header fields and header size were undefined, and whether or not to use fixed-size cells had not yet been decided.

Physical layer

The physical layer of B-ISDN covers the details of data rates to be supported, the nature of the physical medium, and the multiplex structure for transmitting cells. In terms of data rates available to B-ISDN subscribers, the physical layer defines three new transmission services. The first of these, which has been discussed in a number of papers, consists of a full-duplex 155.52-Mbps service. However, this is by no means all that B-ISDN would provide. The second service defined is asymmetrical, providing transmission from the subscriber to the network at 155.52 Mbps and in the other direction at 622.08 Mbps. The highest capacity service yet defined is a full-duplex 622.08-Mbps service.

A data rate of 155.52 Mbps can certainly support all of the narrowband ISDN services; that is, it can readily support one or more basic- or primary-rate interfaces. In addition, it can support most of the B-ISDN services. At the rate of 155.52 Mbps, one or several video channels can be supported, depending on the video resolution and the coding technique used. Thus, the full-duplex 155.52-Mbps service will probably be the most common B-ISDN service.

The higher data rate of 622.08 Mbps is needed to handle multiple video distribution, such as might be required when a business conducts multiple simultaneous videoconferences. This data rate makes sense in the network-to-subscriber direction. The typical subscriber, who would not initiate distribution services, would thus still be able to use the lower (155.52-Mbps) service. The full-duplex 622.08-Mbps service would be appropriate for a video distribution provider.

The 1988 document discussed the need for a 150-Mbps and 600-Mbps data rate service. The specific rates for the 1990 documents were chosen to be compatible with defined digital-transmission services. Also, the 1988 document included a list of specific channel data rates to be supported within these services. The 1990 documents dropped all reference to channel rates; thus, the user and the network are allowed to negotiate any channel capacity that can fit in the available capacity provided by the network. Therefore, B-ISDN became considerably more flexible and could be tailored precisely to a wide variety of applications. The 1988 document did not address the issue of the physical medium on the subscriber's premises. In contrast, the latest documents provided preliminary specifications of the medium for the interface between the user and B-ISDN.

For the full-duplex 155.52-Mbps service, either coaxial cable or optical fiber may be used. The coaxial cable is to support connections up to a maximum distance of 100 to 200 meters, with one cable being used for transmission in each direction. The parameters defined in the 1988 Recommendation G.703 are to be used. Optical fiber is to support connections up to a maximum distance of 800 to 2000 meters. The details of the optical media (for example, single mode versus multimode and single full-duplex fiber versus dual fiber) have been postponed for further study. For a service that includes the 622.08-Mbps rate in one or both directions, optical fiber is to be used. Again, the details of the fiber parameters are left for further study.

A final important issue at the physical layer is the transmission structure to be used to multiplex cells from various virtual channels. The 1988 document discussed this issue in general terms and proposed three alternatives. For the 155.52-Mbps data rate, the 1990 documents reduced the number of options to two and provided more detail. For the 622.08-Mbps data rate, the multiplex structure is left for further study.

The first of the two options for the 155.52-Mbps data rate is the use of a continuous stream of cells, with no multiplex frame structure imposed at the interface. Synchronization is on a cell-by-cell basis; that is, the receiver is responsible for properly delineating cells on the 53-octet cell boundaries. This task is accomplished using the header error control (HEC) field. As long as the HEC calculation is indicating no errors, it is assumed that cell alignment is being properly maintained. An occasional error does not change this assumption; however, a string of error detections would indicate that the receiver is out of alignment, at which point the receiver performs a hunting procedure to recover alignment.

The second option is the placement of the cells in a synchronous time-division multiplex envelope. In this case, the bit stream at the interface has an external frame based on the synchronous digital hierarchy (SDH) defined in Recommendation G.709. In the United States, this frame structure is referred to as the synchronous optical network (SONET). The SDH frame may be used exclusively for ATM cells or may also carry other bit streams not yet defined in B-ISDN.

The SDH standard defines a hierarchy of data rates, all of which are multiples of 51.84 Mbps, including 155.52 Mbps and 622.08 Mbps. Therefore, the SDH scheme could also be used to support the higher B-ISDN data rate. However, the 1990 specification did not address this possibility.

The future direction of ISDN

Since the publication of the 1988 Blue Book, the central focus of the CCITT has been the development of specifications for B-ISDN. B-ISDN is based on ATM — a fast packet-switching technology. ATM specifies the manner in which data are to be structured for transmission over virtual channels. To accommodate a variety of applications, the AAL provides a mapping from various application transfer techniques to ATM. The physical medium to be used on the subscriber's premises can be either coaxial cable or optical fiber, depending on the data rate and distance requirements.

Although many issues remain to be resolved, the network architecture and supported services for B-ISDN are beginning to solidify since the publication of the 1990 interim recommendations on B-ISDN. Sufficient detail now exists for both providers and users to begin to plan for the arrival of this exciting new network facility.

The role of B-ISDN

As the details of B-ISDN, as defined by the CCITT, are filled in, will the specifications drive the industry and the marketplace? Probably not, or at least not exclusively. The same forces that have thwarted efforts to confer universality on ISDN will be in play. With the increasing use of image-processing and high-performance workstations, the need for high data rates has arrived now, instead of in the late 1990s, when it was predicted to arrive. Vendors and customers are seeking high-data-rate solutions now, and these are not always compatible with the B-ISDN direction or even with its general philosophy.

For data transport, much of the design-and-implementation effort today is being driven by the need to support LANs of ever-greater capacity. Indeed, this trend toward higher capacity highlights difficulties in other standards areas. For example, the Fiber Distributed Data Interface (FDDI) set of standards for a 100-Mbps LAN is still not finally nailed down, yet is already considered inadequate for a number of applications. LAN products already exist that operate at much greater speeds than 100 Mbps and that are not compatible with FDDI. As these LANs come on line, users and vendors are finding ways to lash them together into high-speed wide-area networks (WANs). One family of approaches makes use of high-performance bridges and routers linked by high-speed private or leased lines. These approaches do not use ATM or the B-ISDN reference configurations.

It is important to keep in mind that B-ISDN is, and will be, nothing more than a collection of technical standards that describe how to put together a high-speed network. Specifically, B-ISDN describes a particular network that is embedded in — and is an extension of — an ISDN approach to networking. This B-ISDN strategy is only one way to design a facility to support the high-data-rate services that are, and will be, required. Other ways are already being deployed, and other approaches will emerge in the 1990s. As with ISDN, B-ISDN will be one particular solution offered by some vendors; however, again as with ISDN, it will not enjoy the status of universality.

Paper summary

The first paper included in this chapter, "International Standardization of BISDN," by Day, summarizes the current status and direction of CCITT standards for B-ISDN.

"ISDN — The Path to Broadband Networks," by Kleinrock, evaluates the effect of ISDN on the field of data networks and discusses the evolution to B-ISDN that is being driven by technology and applications.

"Broadband Communications: The Commercial Impact," by Timms, projects the introduction of B-ISDN services. This paper looks at the infrastructure that is developing to support B-ISDN and at scenarios for B-ISDN introduction.

"Implications of New Network Services on BISDN Capabilities," by Amin-Salehi, Flinchbaugh, and Pate, discusses some of the new broadband services and the implications that these services have on the capabilities and functions required for the B-ISDN architecture, switching, transport, and signaling.

The final paper in this chapter, "The Role of the Broadband Integrated Services Digital Network," by White, provides an overview of the services and networking technologies under consideration for B-ISDN.

International Standardization of BISDN

Andrew Day

International standardization of Broadband Integrated Services Digital Network (BISDN) has extended over a period of six years, and is currently being studied across several International Consultative Committee for Telephone and Telegraph (CCITT) Study Groups (SGs) and impacting activities within the Joint CCITT/CCIR SG (CMTT) and International Radio Consultative Committee (CCIR).[1]

During this time, the main concentration of BISDN standardization has been within CCITT SGXVII, which commenced BISDN studies in January 1985, even while the basic details of the 64 kb/s ISDN were still being elaborated. The first four years of BISDN activity resulted in the approval in 1988 of the first CCITT Recommendation (I.121), providing an initial framework for BISDN development and standardization. In many ways the progress in this early period appeared slow with the framework recommendation leaving open many fundamental technical decisions and concepts.

In restrospect, however, the directions in I.121 were so new and different as to represent a major shift in the technical base and service opportunities available through public telecommunications networks. Although initially it was envisaged that BISDN would follow the circuit switching philosophy of the Narrowband ISDN (NISDN), the use of Asynchronous Transfer Mode (ATM) transport has pushed BISDN into a new generation of telecommunications, as novel and significant as the initial ISDN concept. The adoption of the ATM switching and transfer mechanism as the backbone of the BISDN will not only provide the next generation switching technology to ISDN, but provides BISDN with the capability to meet technology and market uncertainties with a flexibility unavailable in NISDN. In addition, the ATM technique will allow BISDN to technically compete in the market areas of high-speed data services (providing local and network wide transport [Local Area Network—LANs/Metropolitan Area Networks—MANs]) and the potentially enormous and high growth video sector.

[1]CCITT, CCIR, and CMTT are the main standardization bodies of the International Telecommunications Union (ITU) based in Geneva, Switzerland.

Reprinted from *IEEE LTS — The Magazine of Lightwave Telecommunication Systems*, August 1991, pages 13-20. Copyright © 1991 by The Institute of Electrical and Electronics Engineers, Inc. All rights reserved.

Table I. CCITT 1990 BISDN Recommendations

Area	Recommendation
General	I.113 Vocabulary of Terms I.121 General Broadband Aspects I.610 Operations and Maintenance
Services	I.211 Service Aspects
Network	I.311 General Network Aspects I.321 Protocol Reference Model I.327 Functional Architecture
Adaptation	I.362 Adaptation Principles I.363 Adaptation Specification
ATM Layer	I.150 ATM Functional Characteristics I.361 ATM Specification
Physical Layer	I.413 UNI Reference Configurations I.432 UNI Specification

Since the approval of I.121 in 1988, CCITT SGXVII has achieved unparalleled progress in establishing BISDN principles and initial specifications. At the November 1990 SGXVII meeting in Japan, CCITT unanimously approved 13 BISDN Recommendations (see Table I) using the recently adopted CCITT Accelerated Approval Procedures. From the starting point of I.121 two years ago, these 13 1990 BISDN Recommendations not only outlined the fundamental principles of the next generation of telecommunications, but made substantial in-roads to the specification of the BISDN sufficient to allow field trials in the next two years, and BISDN commercial services before 1995.

Already further progress has occurred towards an enhanced set of 1992 recommendations, with major breakthroughs achieved at the recent June 1991 SGXVII meeting in Geneva.

The purpose of this article is to outline the status and characteristics of BISDN as they are currently being defined in CCITT, to outline the broad scope and impact in other areas of the ITU, and identify the new service opportunities that BISDN will bring to public telecommunications networks in the 1990s and beyond.

143

Table II. Possible Broadband Services In ISDN

Service Classes	Type of Information	Examples of Broadband Services
Conversational Services	Moving Pictures (Video) and Sound	Broadband Video Telephony Broadband Videoconference Video Surveillance Video/Audio Information Transmission Service
	Sound	Multiple Sound Program Signals
	Data	High-Speed Unrestricted Digital Information Transmission Service (e.g., LAN and MAN) High-Volume File Transfer Service High-Speed Teleaction
	Document	High-Speed Telefax High-Resolution Image Communication Service Document Communication Service
Messaging Services	Moving Pictures (Video) and Sound	Video Mail Service
	Document	Document Mail Service
Retrieval Services	Text, Data, Graphics, Sound, Still Images, and Moving Pictures	Broadband Videotex Video Retrieval Service High-Resolution Image Retrieval Document Retrieval Service Data Retrieval Service
Distribution Services Without User Individual Presentation Control	Video	Existing Quality Distribution Service (PAL, SECAM, and NTSC) Extended Quality TV Distribution Service – Enhanced Definition TV – High Quality TV High-Definition TV Distribution Service Pay TV (Pay-Per-View and Pay-Per-Channel)
	Text, Graphics, and Still Images	Document Distribution Service
	Data	High-Speed Unrestricted Digital Information Distribution Service
	Moving Pictures and Sound	Video Information Distribution Service
Distribution Services With User Individual Presentation Control	Text, Graphics, Sound, and Still Images	Full Channel Broadcast Videography

PROFILE OF BISDN DEVELOPMENTS

The drive for BISDN standardization follows essentially the same philosophy as that of the NISDN or 64 kb/s ISDN—to provide a public telecommunications network that can support a range of integrated services over a unique customer interface, with common customer control and management, rather than through separate, service specific networks with multiple interfaces, control, and management.

Recognizing the service limits of NISDN from the outset, BISDN has been developed for a highly expansive scope of new services, the delivery of which will require several new and different technologies. In addition to supporting the services of the NISDN, high-speed data services and the complete range of video services have been targetted for BISDN. These new service areas placed three fundamental demands on BISDN standardization, namely the need for:

- Increased end-to-end service capacity, necessitating high capacity transmission and switching
- Increased network efficiency to allow the economic support of the different characteristics of high-speed data services
- Greatly enhanced flexibility to meet both the very different characteristics of the range of services and lessen the network impact of future technology and market uncertainties

These demands have resulted in the following technology platforms for BISDN:

- The use of Synchronous Digital Hierarchy (SDH) facilities (primarily over optical fiber links) to achieve customer network interface capacities of 155 Mb/s and 622 Mb/s
- The use of ATM switching facilities to provide significant flexibility and efficiency in the support of BISDN services. This is achieved through the variable bit rate switching capabilities available through ATM, which allows BISDN to both emulate the capabilities of LANs and MANs and the different rates required for different qualities of video services.

The service capabilities that arise from these technologies and BISDN standardization are discussed later in this article.

In addition to a change in service scope and technology base for BISDN, there has also been a major philosophical shift in the approach to BISDN standardization. For BISDN there has been a clear commercial drive for the direction of standardization, with the priority of work closely linked to facilities required to meet emerging market demands. At the same time, increased emphasis has been placed on the practical issues of operations, maintenance, and performance for BISDN and the need to closely tie together related standardization developments in other CCITT groups (e.g., signaling in CCITT SGXI). The use of the new CCITT accelerated approval procedures, which allow recommendations to be approved within a four year study period rather than only at the end, has also advanced the rate of agreements and in part, the methodology used in CCITT. The last three years of BISDN standardization in CCITT SGXVIII has been marked by a clear international

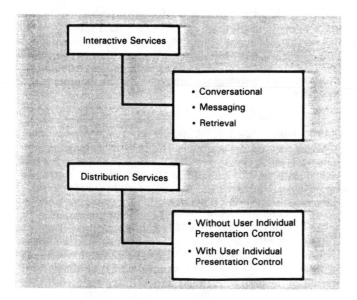

Fig. 1. Classification of broadband services.

willingness for cooperation and compromise to produce timely international recommendations.

TECHNICAL CHARACTERISTICS OF BISDN
Introduction

Characterizing the key elements of BISDN may be logically outlined by considering four main aspects, viz:

- The services supported by BISDN, including their impact on end-to-end network requirements (*BISDN Services*)
- The different protocol layers necessary to build a BISDN capable of supporting the services outlined above (*ATM Technique, Protocol Aspects of BISDN,* and *ATM Adaptation Layer*)
- The nature of the User-Network Interface (UNI) including the features necessary to support different customer premises' configurations (*User-Network Interface*)
- The network control aspects necessary to allow the protocols and UNI to support BISDN services. These include signaling, resource management, performance and operations, and maintenance (*BISDN Network Issues*)

BISDN Services (Rec I.211)

The service aspects of BISDN have been jointly considered by CCITT SGI and SGXVIII. As shown in Table II, a wide range of voice, text, image, data, and video services may be supported by BISDN. To simplify these services, CCITT has also classified services into different types as shown in Figure 1. In addition to the normal type of two-way interactive services available on telecommunications networks today, BISDN will also support a wide range of distributive services. For example, for video type services this would allow BISDN to support video services typically carried by cable television networks today.

To determine the association with network capabilities, CCITT has defined two categories of BISDN bearer services, using the characteristics of four different classes of services (see Figure 2).

Connection-Oriented Bearer Services

These services have characteristics that require a connection to be established before communication commences. Service classes A, B, and C will use this bearer service (e.g., voice, variable bit rate video, and X.25 data services/signaling).

Connectionless Bearer Service

The nature of these services allows the connection between users to be established and disconnected at the same time the information is transferred. Service Class D will use this bearer service (e.g., LAN interconnect).

These different ways of classifying and characterizing services indicate the vast scope of services that can be supported by BISDN, and the different impacts they have on establishing the necessary network standards.

ATM Technique (Rec I.150, I.361)

ATM has emerged over the last six years as the next generation switching system and fundamental transport basis for BISDN and telecommunications in the decade ahead. ATM represents convergence of two switch concepts developed in the 1980s—Asynchronous Time Division (ATD) multiplexing and Fast Packet Switching (FPS). The first of these was developed to increase the flexibility of circuit switching and the second from technology and protocol enhancements arising from packet switching techniques.

The basis of ATM is a 53-octet fixed length cell (or packet) consisting of a 48-octet information field to carry the user or network information and a 5-octet header that contains information used to route the cell to the destination. ATM standardization details the method of multiplexing and transferring information and leaves open the switching technology used to support it.

The nature of ATM allows the use of virtual connections rather than the fixed connections that are used in the circuit switched NISDN. This results in many changes to the network structure and support protocols for BISDN and as outlined later in this article, provides a new range of service opportunities previously unavailable on public telecommunication networks.

A key element in the standardization of ATM is the header functionalities associated with each cell. CCITT Recommendation I.361 details the following main header functions (see Figure 3) each reflecting an ATM layer protocol function:

- A routing or address field to carry the Virtual Channel (VC) or Virtual Path (VP) identification of each ATM cell
- A Generic Flow Control (GFC) field that may be used at the UNI to control the flow of user information within the customer premises network to the public network
- A payload type field
- A Cell Loss Priority (CLP) indicator

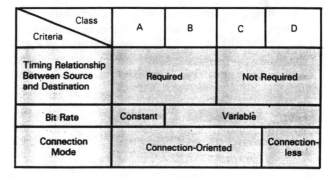

Key:

Voice: Class A Service
Variable Bit Rate Video: Class B Service
X.25 Packet Services
Signalling Service } Class C Service
LAN Interconnect: Class D Service

Fig. 2. Service classes in the BISDN.

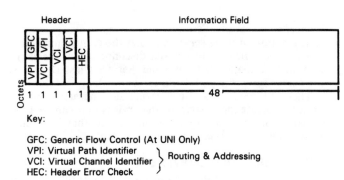

Key:

GFC: Generic Flow Control (At UNI Only)
VPI: Virtual Path Identifier ⎫
VCI: Virtual Channel Identifier ⎬ Routing & Addressing
HEC: Header Error Check   ⎭

Fig. 3. BISDN ATM cell structure.

- A Header Error Control (HEC) field to protect the integrity of the header information

ATM cells may be transferred from one user to the other in different ways. For example, at the UNI, ATM cells may be carried in an externally framed transmission system (such as SDH) or in a cell-based transmission structure. Within the network, ATM cells will also be mapped into the payload of existing plesiochronous transmission systems as well as SDH.

Protocol Aspects of BISDN (I.321)

The Protocol Reference Model (PRM) for the BISDN has evolved through several phases during the standardization process. Unlike the NISDN, for which the user plane contains generally only a Layer 1 physical layer functionality, with higher layer network functions contained only in the control plane, BISDN has a significantly richer protocol stack for the support of all services. The layers of the BISDN PRM are shown in Figure 4. The three layers shown are physical, ATM, and adaptation.

Physical Layer

This layer consists of two sublayers:

- The physical medium sublayer provides bit transmission capability and includes functions that are dependent on the physical medium used.
- The transmission convergence sublayer transfers the flow of bits available from the physical medium sublayer into a flow of valid cells that can be used by the ATM layer above. This includes transmission frame generation, recovery and adaptation, cell delineation, cell HEC sequence generation and verification, and cell rate decoupling (insertion of idle cells when necessary).

The physical layer has several different options within it to allow either the use of the SDH physical layer or a cell-based physical layer to exist at the UNI. This layer is further discussed in *User-Network Interface.*

ATM Layer

The ATM layer is a unique layer that provides the carriage of all services on the BISDN using small fixed size cells. The cell consists of a user information field and a header, the primary role of the header being to identify cells belonging to the same information stream. Each information stream uses a separate VC. The ATM layer is common to all services, but varies in header functionality between the UNI and the Network Node Interface. The ATM layer supports the Adaptation Layer (AAL) which provides different functionality to accommodate various services.

The Adaptation Layer

The AAL provides the link between the services to be carried on BISDN and the generic ATM cells used by the

BISDN. As such it provides a functionality that will generally be different for the four service classes shown in Figure 2, necessitating four different AAL types. The AAL consists of a sublayer which provides cell segmentation and reassembly to interface to the ATM layer and also a more service-specific convergence function to interface to the bearer services being carried.

Higher Layers

In some cases, the AAL will also have to support higher network layers. For example, in the case of signaling, the AAL must be able to support the necessary Layer 3 signaling protocols, while for the support of Class D (connectionless) services, the AAL should support a higher layer that contains addressing and routing functionality.

The exact alignment between the layers of the OSI Model and the BISDN PRM is still not clear, and requires further detailed analysis in CCITT. The distinction between protocols used in the user and control planes becomes blurred in the case where the same AAL type is used to support connection-oriented data services and signaling.

ATM Adaptation Layer (Rec I.362, I.363)

The ATM adaptation functionality is a key element in BISDN standardization as it represents the link between the many services that BISDN supports and the generic, service independent ATM technique. To support the four service classes A–D (and the associated bearer services), four AAL types are being standardized.

- Type 1 AAL—used for the support of constant bit rate, connection-oriented services that have a timing requirement between source and destination (Service Class A.) Type 1 AAL will be used to support existing voice services, new constant bit rate video services, and provide circuit emulation when required. This AAL allows the full flexibility of ATM to be used, but does not utilize the potential ATM efficiencies.

- Type 2 AAL—used to support variable bit rate, connection-oriented services that also have a timing requirement between source and destination. (Service Class B.) The nature of these services is less well known, as they are currently not available. Examples include variable bit rate video for interactive or distributive services. This Type 2 AAL allows the full flexibility and efficiency of ATM to be utilized.

- Type 3 AAL—used to support connection-oriented variable bit rate services with no timing relationship. This includes data services such as X.25 and Frame Mode Bear-

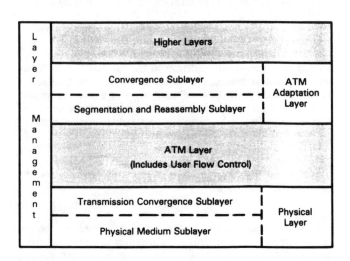

Fig. 4. BISDN protocol reference model.

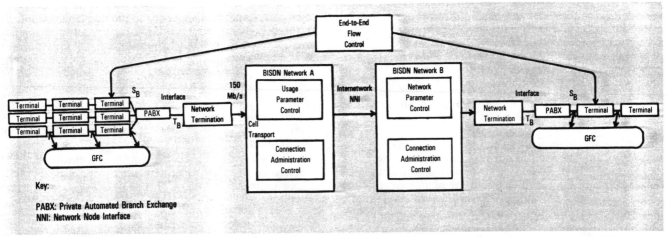

Fig. 5. Reference configuration for traffic control and resource management.

er Services (FMBSs), signaling, and future high-speed data services.

• Type 4 AAL—used to support connectionless data services such as those supported by LANs and MANs.

In addition to supporting the carriage of different services, the AAL has a key role in the interworking of BISDN with different networks and services. For example, the interworking of telephony services would use AAL Type 1, interworking of X.25 services and FMBS would use AAL Type 3, and the interconnection of LANs or MANs, AAL Type 4.

User-Network Interface (Rec I.413, I.432)

The reference configuration at the UNI used for NISDN is considered general enough to also be applicable to BISDN. However, the physical configurations that may exist represent an increased emphasis on the use of shared medium applications using bus or ring topologies. This has specific implications at the ATM layer at the UNI.

At the physical layer, interfaces have been standardized at 155 Mb/s and 622 Mb/s. Two options exist for these interfaces—SDH-based and cell-based physical layers. These options may exist at both the T_B and S_B reference points.

For the 155 Mb/s, the transfer capacity available to the ATM layer is the same for both options and is 149.760 Mb/s. The exact rate available for user information depends on ATM and AAL header sizes, signaling, and Operations, Administration, and Maintenance (OAM) requirements. Further information on the physical layer is contained in a companion article in this edition.

The use of shared medium applications at the UNI also places demands on the ATM layer, to ensure the fair and equitable support of different services and terminals on the UNI. Four bits of the ATM header have been assigned for a GFC mechanism to facilitate the control of information transfer in the event of short term overload conditions. The GFC mechanism is independent of the physical layer. Further information on GFC and related issues is contained in a companion article in this edition.

BISDN Network Issues

Several initiatives are occurring under the umbrella of BISDN networking. These include BISDN signaling, BISDN resource management, operations and maintenance, performance, and networking techniques.

BISDN Signaling (I.311)

CCITT SGXI and SGXVII are jointly addressing the requirements and specification of signaling to be used for BISDN. The nature of ATM and the increasing requirements of service control will realize significant changes to signaling over the next decade. First, signaling information will be carried on ATM virtual connections that appear as *signaling VCs* at the UNI. In order to set up user network signaling VCs that may be required, a meta signaling function operating at the ATM layer is required to resolve contention, allocate capacity, and establish, clear, and check the status of signaling channels.

Once established, the protocols used on the signaling VC will be different from those used in the NISDN. The presence of the ATM layer and the AAL Type 3 require changes to both Layers 2 and 3 signaling.

For Layer 3, it has been agreed that a two stage standardization process should be adopted. In the first stage, Layer 3 will be incrementally evolved from NISDN to allow basic call control of ATM circuits. The second stage addresses the longer term situation in which it is expected that ISDN signaling will be separated into new bearer and call control signaling components, the latter within the umbrella of the ISDN Signaling Control Part (ISCP). The time-frame for ISCP is linked with the timetable for BISDN developments.

BISDN Resource Management (I.311, I.trf [Draft])

The support of a variety of new and different services on a single network structure, and the utilizing of constant and variable bit rate, real time and nonreal time, and connection-oriented and connectionless services raises many new questions as to how the available network resources are used and managed to deliver the required service qualities to customers. A reference configuration for traffic control and resource management has been agreed within CCITT (see Figure 5) which indicates the following main elements are used:

• Connection Admission Control (CAC)—This function controls the access of services to the network to ensure that sufficient resources are available to support the service at its required quality of service.

• Usage Parameter Control (UPC)—This function monitors and controls the user's traffic characteristics to ensure they are consistent with the characteristics requested by the user at connection time. This is used to protect the network resources from malicious and/or unintentional behavior which may affect the quality of service of other services already established on the network.

• Network Parameter Control (NPC)—This function may be used to control resources when different networks are interworked, again to protect the use of network resources from increases in the volume of traffic from other networks.

In addition to these network related control functions, the user may allow different priority traffic flows by using the CLP function contained in the ATM cell header and may use an error control protocol between end systems.

These functions are generally referred to as congestion control capabilities. Congestion control and resource management issues are further discussed in a companion article in this edition.

Operations and Maintenance (Rec I.610)

A key component in the commercial support of services is the standardization of associated operations and maintenance capabilities. Rec I.610 covers the maintenance of the BISDN UNI and the subscriber access controlled by the network, across both the physical and ATM layers. Maintenance functions are layered consistent with the BISDN PRM, and allocated to the PRM management plane. As such, maintenance functions are independent from maintenance capabilities of other layers and must be processed at each level to obtain information concerning the OAM quality and status.

Three OAM information flows have been agreed at the physical layer and two at the ATM layer.

Performance (Rec I.35B [Draft])

CCITT has also commenced work on the general performance capabilities of BISDN, with emphasis on the parameters to be defined, their measurability, and acceptable values. Clearly a close, iterative link exists between these performance issues and the type of resource management capabilities that should be standardized. CCITT expects to approve the first BISDN Performance Recommendation (currently I.35B) in 1992.

Networking Techniques (I.311.327)

The network architectures and structure for BISDN are also being studied in CCITT to determine efficient service support structures for BISDN. Initial analysis has included the use of VPs (groupings of VCs) as key elements to simplify ATM structures, service delivery, and resource management. The role of different VC/VP switch and crossconnect elements and their impact/relationship with SDH crossconnect elements are currently being assessed in CCITT. These issues are discussed in a companion article in this edition.

CCITT is also examining the impact that network evolution issues may have on BISDN standardization, without actually standardizing it. Information on BISDN standardization issues is discussed in a companion article in this edition.

BISDN SERVICE IMPLICATIONS AND OPPORTUNITIES
Introduction

The technical capabilities of ATM will bring a range of new service opportunities to public telecommunications networks, to facilitate the BISDN objectives of service integration across voice, text, image, data, and video services. The purpose of this section is to outline how the technical capabilities of ATM allow this full service range to be commercially supported, and to outline the broader implications. By addressing this link between ATM's capabilities and the service integration objectives of BISDN, a logical analysis of these objectives can be realized.

Service Opportunities Through ATM

In addition to supporting the newer type of services outlined above, ATM must also be able to support today's telecommunication services such as telephony, which are essentially constant bit rate services. In this case, ATM matches the characteristics of these services by ensuring an end-to-end capacity capability necessary to provide circuit emulation throughout the duration of a call, rather than trying to achieve transport efficiencies. In this case, ATM allows enhancement beyond circuit switching both in the service capacity that can be supported and the flexibility it offers. ATM allows as much capacity to be used as may be required for a particular service, by using only the number of ATM cells necessary to provide the required capacity. This flexibility in end-to-end service capacity may be realized in the following different ways:

- To vary the total capacity available to a customer as their telecommunications requirements change over time (e.g., as a business expands)
- To allow the customer to select different service capacities at the time of establishing a call, perhaps to vary the quality of a video service being used
- To allow the customer to vary the service capacity during a call, for example either to invoke a higher video quality or add a new service in addition to the one being used. This will be particularly important for the support of multimedia services which are discussed below.
- To allow connections to be characterized by statistical parameters and allow instantaneous changes to the service capacity during the call. Using the variable bit rate capabilities of ATM, this may maximize efficiency gains.

To achieve the full service advantages of ATM, the variable bit rate characteristics of ATM can be used to closely match the characteristics of a new range of services, in particular, data and video services. Data services are characterized by highly bursty traffic characteristics, quick response times, and requiring at times a high level of multiple terminal usage. ATM provides the capability to match these bursty traffic characteristics by using as many cells as required to achieve the fast response times. Additional capabilities such as the use of the UNI in shared media applications, and the availability of the GFC ATM contention and flow control mechanisms, means that ATM can economically and commercially emulate both LANs as well as network wide LAN interconnection (i.e., MANs).

The use of ATM variable bit rate capabilities also raises some interesting opportunities for the support and interworking of video services, and the coding used for the different video signals. In particular, ATM offers the potential to integrate the coding capabilities for two-way video (video telephony/video conferencing), retrieval video services, and one-way distributive video services, by using a unique family of related video coders-decoders (codecs). The implications of these developments are elaborated below.

Coupling these network services capabilities together has highlighted the potential for a new range of multimedia services, in which a customer's terminal will have the capability to send, receive, process, and display multiple types of information across voice, text, image, graphics, data, and video services. The network capabilities for these services are currently being addressed in SGXVII, to guide the services work in CCITT SG I and the signaling capabilities in CCITT SG XI to allow the support of BISDN multimedia services.

Implications of ATM—Integrated Video Services (IVS)

The potential of BISDN to support a wide range of video qualities (Rec H.261, PAL/NTSC, Rec 611, HDTV) and video types (interactive and distributive) provides opportunities for high network efficiencies in the support of video services. However, for the user, these efficiencies may not be realized if the current trend of using different video codecs and displays for different video services continue. Advantages available through a multiservice BISDN can

Table III. Timetable of Network and Service Results From CCITT Study Group XVIII

Release 1—1990/1992	Release 2—Enhancements to Release 1	Release 3—Enhancements to Release 2
BISDN Bearer Services • Connection-Oriented Circuits at 64 kb/s and Above (AAL Type 1) • Connectionless Data Service (AAL Type4) • ATM Service (User Specified AAL)	**BISDN Bearer Services** • Variable Rate Services Delivered "real time" End-to-End (AAL Type 2) • Variable Rate Data Services (AAL Type 3) (These Services May Use Priority ATM Cells for Critical Information)	**BISDN Bearer Services** • Multimedia Services • Distributive Services • Selection of Quality of Service
Network Architecture and Capabilities • Switched VC Connections (ATM Switching) • Semipermanent VP Connections • Connectionless Servers Accessed Using Semipermanent Connections	**Network Architecture and Capabilities** • Switched (Dial-Up) Access to Connectionless Servers • Enhanced Resource Management and Standard Operations Management Systems for VPs • Intelligent Network Access • Ability to Change Connection Bandwidth During Call	**Network Architecture and Capabilities** • Configuration of VPs with Integrated Operations, Management, and Switching Systems
Traffic Characteristics • Bandwidth Specified as Peak Requirements Only	**Traffic Characteristics** • Bandwidth Specified as Traffic Characteristic Parameters (e.g., Average, Burstiness, and Peak Duration)	
Connection Configurations • Point-to-Point, Unidirectional, and Bidirectional Connections • Point-to-Multipoint and Broadcast Connections for Signaling at the UNI • Symmetrical or Asymmetrical Bandwidth • One Connection Per Call	**Connection Configurations** • Simple Point-to-Multipoint Connections, Including Ability to Add/Drop Connection Branches • More Than One Connection per Call and the Ability to Add/Drop Connections During the Call	**Connection Configurations** • Broadcast Connections
Interworking • With Existing ISDN 64 kb/s Bearers • With Connectionless Networks		
Other Features • Common Channel Signaling • AAL Type 3 for Signaling • Meta-signaling Channel at the UNI • Basic Supplementary Services (e.g., Calling Line Identification)	**Other Features** • Enhanced Set of Supplementary Services	

also be extended to the end user by minimizing the number of video terminals needed to access a range of interactive and distributive video and still image based services. To achieve these advantages, CCITT has the objective of achieving the highest level of video service integration, by maximizing the commonality of video codecs, display, and control across the full range of video services. From a customer viewpoint, the integrated support of video services should offer lowered costs and enhanced flexibility.

The technical characteristics of ATM greatly assist these objectives. To achieve the commonality of coding and display outlined above, a layered approach to video coding represents the most promising approach. In this approach, different layers of information are coded, so the lowest layer of information relates to the most basic picture quality, with each additional layer adding more information to build up different levels of video service quality. When layered video coding is coupled with variable bit rate video coding, significant advantages concerning efficient video service commonality and service integration and interworking arise. The use of multiple ATM VCs, and the variable bit rate nature of ATM provide a close link between BISDN developments and the objectives behind integrated video services.

To achieve this flexibility and provide integrated service support, alignment and consistency is required between the different ITU standards bodies. This includes CCITT SGXV (ATM video coding), CMTT (distributive video coding), and CCIR (High Definition Television (HDTV) and studio video), as well as a variety of other ITU bodies.

This coordination is actively being facilitated through a current video coordination activity organized by CCITT SGXVII, to ensure consistency and commonality across the range of video services and their links with network development.

STATUS OF BISDN STANDARDS DEVELOPMENT IN CCITT

The 1990 CCITT Recommendations have significantly stabilized the platform for international BISDN development. In particular, these recommendations provide sufficient detail and stability to allow the production of prototype BISDN systems and telephone company (telco) involvement in initial BISDN field trials. Details of one of these field trials is outlined in a companion article in this issue.

For 1992 CCITT has the objective to enhance these 1990 Recommendations to allow the initial support of commercial BISDN services. Although it is premature to fully outline possible 1992 Recommendations, the following provides the status of CCITT agreements to the middle of 1991, which may be expected to form the basis of the 1992 Recommendations.

• The physical layer of the 155 Mb/s SDH option of the UNI should be largely specified by 1992. Structures for the cell-based option for the 155 Mb/s UNI and the SDH 622 Mb/s interface have recently been agreed upon.

• The ATM layer should be largely specified by 1992, although it is unclear as to the extent of GFC specification that will be available, as several options are currently being analyzed in CCITT.

- The AAL will be largely specified for Types 1, 3, and 4, which will allow the support of some areas of Service Classes A, C, and D. In particular, Types 1 and 4 should be specified sufficiently to support initial basic services. Little work has been done on the AAL Type 2 to support Service Class B.
- The timetable for the first stage of BISDN signaling is unclear, although enhancements to the existing signaling to support basic call control should be available in 1992/1993.
- Resource management standardization is likely to be limited to peak rate control of services, sufficient to provide some basic network service support only. A new recommendation (I.trf) is scheduled for 1992.
- Agreements have been made in the OAM information flows for BISDN physical and ATM layers, but the full specification of OAM mechanism will occur post 1992.

Together these capabilities are expected to allow the initial basic support of commercial BISDN services, with ATM connections primarily on a semipermanent, peak rate managed basis.

Table III provides a more detailed projection of the priority of work in CCITT SGXVII on BISDN, including the likely packaging of network capabilities. Standardization post 1992 will provide further enhancements to these issues with particular emphasis on control issues such as signaling and resource management, and the support issues of OAM, performance, etc.

CONCLUSION

The 1990 BISDN Recommendations represent a significant platform for the establishment of a public broadband telecommunications infrastructure to satisfy global requirements for telecommunications services in the 1990s and beyond. Study in CCITT is continuing to provide further enhancements of these recommendations in 1992 to allow the initial introduction of BISDN services in the 1993–1995 timeframe. The full opportunities available from ATM's capabilities will only be realized towards the end of this decade once these network capabilities are matched by a broad base of terminal and application processes. Within this longer timeframe the service support base of a BISDN-based public telecommunications infrastructure will be significantly enhanced to that which exists today.

Bibliography

CCITT Recommendation I.113, "Vocabulary of Terms for Broadband Aspects of ISDN," 1990.
CCITT Recommendation I.121, "Broadband Aspects of ISDN," 1990.
CCITT Recommendation I.150, "BISDN ATM Functional Characteristics," 1990.
CCITT Recommendation I.211, "BISDN Service Aspects," 1990.
CCITT Recommendation I.311, "BISDN General Network Aspects," 1990.
CCITT Recommendation I.321, "BISDN Protocol Reference Model and Its Application," 1990.
CCITT Recommendation I.327, "BISDN Functional Architecture," 1990.
CCITT Recommendation I.361, "BISDN ATM Layer Specification," 1990.
CCITT Recommendation I.362, "BISDN ATM Adaptation Layer (AAL) Functional Discription," 1990.
CCITT Recommendation I.413, "BISDN User-Network Interface," 1990.
CCITT Recommendation I.432, "BISDN User-Network Interface Physical Layer Specification," 1990.
CCITT Recommendation I.610, "OAM Principles of BISDN Access," 1990.

Biography

Andrew Day is responsible for the development of network strategies across the complete range of Telecom Australia's network development.

ISDN—The Path to Broadband Networks

LEONARD KLEINROCK, FELLOW, IEEE

Invited Paper

We are in the midst of revolutionary improvements in data communications. The need for connectivity has never been as great as it is today due to the rapid growth of desktop processing machines which must communicate among themselves as well as with centralized computing and database facilities. Alas, in the midst of this progress, we find ourselves burdened by the curse of incompatibility among vendor-specific products, protocols, procedures, and interfaces.

At the same time, the national and international bodies have been hard at work attempting to provide some stability by introducing standards for connectivity. The problem, of course, is one of timing; a premature standard stifles the development of mature technology, while a tardy standard is in danger of being rejected by a community that is locked into irreversible commitments to cumbersome ad hoc solutions. ISDN is an emerging standard which represents an international effort to solve some of our connectivity problems. If it rolls out in a timely fashion and addresses real needs to the end user community, it has a chance for success in the networking world.

The carriers are committed to ISDN and have a clear motivation and potential for succeeding in its development. Narrowband ISDN is a ho-hum service for which some important applications have been identified, but which has not sparked a stampede of acceptance. On the other hand, broadband ISDN (BISDN) is a service that has identified capabilities that are truly exciting and could very well dominate data networking in this decade. The success of BISDN will depend strongly on the rollout of products, the ubiquity of its presence, and the tarriffing of its services.

I. INTRODUCTION

Telecommunications is currently a huge industry approaching an annual revenue of $200 000 000 000; it has one of the fastest growth rates of all industries today. Moreover, it is based on some of the most exciting technologies available, changing rapidly, and influencing almost every aspect of business, commerce, education, health, government, and entertainment. Its products are visible to everyone, and yet, the full impact of this juggernaut is not yet appreciated by most observers.

What has caused this enormous growth has been the explosion of digital technology (which itself was fueled by semiconductor electronics, namely, integrated circuits of very large scale, as well as the development of the unbelievable capabilities of fiber-optic communication). This digital technology appeared first as data-processing machines and soon had its impact on data communications. This impact emerged as data communication networks, principally in the form of packet switching in the 1970's [1]. Since then, the data-processing industry and the data communication

Manuscript received April 30, 1990; revised September 17, 1990. This work was sponsored by the Defense Advanced Research Projects Agency of the U.S. Department of Defense under Contract MDA 903-87-C-0663.

The author is with the Computer Science Department, University of California, Los Angeles, CA 90024-1956.

IEEE Log Number 9041451.

industry have converged in a fashion that will never again let them separate. You can no longer discuss one without the other.

The product rollout has been staggering and we have been provided a broad range of advanced services, but not without a price. We have now reached a stage of uncontrolled chaos in the marketplace of data processing and data communications. Multivendor systems are almost universal, and the inability of the elements in this heterogeneous environment to interwork is legion. There have been international efforts to bring some order to this chaos through the introduction of standards. Such efforts are almost always slow, laborious, political, petty, boring, ponderous, thankless, and of the utmost criticality. The International Standards Organization has developed the seven-layer Open Systems Interconnection (OSI) reference model for communications. The IEEE 802.X series of standards for communications is growing. We have seen the Consultative Committee for International Telephony and Telegraphy (CCITT) recommendations for their X series of standards proliferate. Moreover, and of most interest to this paper, CCITT has been developing the Integrated Services Digital Network (ISDN) standard since the mid-1970's. The definition and details of this standard are covered elsewhere in these Proceedings.

It is the purpose of this paper to evaluate the effect of ISDN on the field of data networks, to anticipate future directions for this technology, and to discuss how the user should view these developments.

Whereas this paper discusses such issues, the fact is that the underlying issue is really one of *infrastructure*, rather than of ISDN networking by itself. Network technology provides us the capability to install a powerful communications and information technology infrastructure that will enable untold growth and access in the years to come. ISDN is one cornerstone of that technology.

II. CURRENT STATUS

There are more than 200 000 ISDN access lines installed today, and that number will likely grow to three-quarters of a billion by 1995 [2]. Its use in public networks is clear, and it is beginning to penetrate the private network market as well. It has taken 29 years from the first digital T1 system to today's ISDN developments. 1988 was a critical year, for it was in that year that Signalling System Seven (SS7) installations increased enormously, providing the out-of-band common channel signaling capability on which ISDN is based [3]. We have seen a very rapid rollout from the availability of the basic rate interface (BRI) at 144 kb/s

0-8186-2797-2/92 $3.00 © 1991 IEEE

(2 B + D) and the primary rate interface (PRI) at 23 × 64 kb/s to today's beginning of BISDN at 155 Mb/s and growing to over 13 Gb/s speeds. Indeed, we have already seen the early demonstrations of the 802.6 Metropolitan Area Network (MAN) standard based on the distributed queue dual bus (DQDB) access method; this demonstation was part of the switched multimegabit data service (SMDS) offered at 45 Mb/s. Things are moving quickly.

A. The Barriers

Indeed, it is remarkable that ISDN is here at all, given the large number of compelling barriers that it has had to overcome. Primarily, the problem has been that ISDN is a technology developed and desired by the carriers, and not one that was initiated by user demand. As a result, a deadlock persisted that took the following form. First, the carriers were unwilling to deploy a central office ISDN switch until they could estimate the market that would justify the huge expenditures involved. The market could not be estimated until the users judged their likely use of the technology; but the users could not make this judgement until they could be given cost and timing of the ISDN products. To provide this product cost and timing information, the system suppliers needed the chip set cost. But the chip manufacturers were unwilling to tool up until they could see the market that could not develop until the central office switches were in place. This deadlock could only be broken by the carriers who did indeed take the first step and got the process moving.

As we unwind from this deadlock, users are concerned that if they buy now and ISDN is a failure, then they will be left stranded with an obsolete technology whereas if ISDN is successful, then costs will drop due to the usual economies of scale. In both cases, the user is motivated to wait; the user is clearly unclear as to when he should jump on the ISDN bandwagon. Further, the real attraction of ISDN will come when the service is ubiquitous and becomes available in all of the locations in which he is interested; but networking technology expands at a slow rate due largely to the enormous cost of providing broad coverage. We have seen this curse of distributed services many times in the past; for example, it occurred with the introduction of telephones, of Federal Express overnight mail, of public packet switched networks, of FAX, of electronic mail, and more.

The problem is further exacerbated by the fact that not all implementations of ISDN products are interoperable; for example, it is the usual case that ISDN adapters from different manufacturers cannot communicate with each other. The average price of an ISDN adapter for a PC today is $1500, whereas adapters for LAN interconnection of PC's sell for less than $800 (and include a microprocessor as well). The full ISDN standard has not yet been finalized by the CCITT. The fact that there is no equivalent of the Corporation for Open Systems (COS) for ISDN leads to the problem of vendor products that are incompatible. The existence of more than one version of a standard is an oxymoron. And the specter of possible changes in the standard or in the unofficial portions of the standard many well cause today's purchased equipment to become obsolete.

B. The Enablers

In spite of the barriers seen by the carriers, the suppliers, and the users to the introduction and deployment of ISDN, these same groups see significant advantages to ISDN that have been hastening its introduction.

The carriers have passed through a number of years of equal access since divestiture, which has produced a highly competitive marketplace. They have been energized to offer more than just transport and to extend their offerings to central-office based services of various types, most of which are dependent upon the introduction of ISDN. Moreover, the flattening demand of PBX equipment has produced a marketplace in which one vendor's gain is the other vendor's loss (i.e., a zero-sum game). Consequently, a carrier must add value to its offerings to differentiate it and to expand the size of its market; ISDN is the vehicle for this added value. The chip manufacturers have long since recognized that the mass-produced memory chip marketplace has been lost to the Japanese. These manufacturers need other markets, and the ISDN chip market is an attractive one for them.

Major corporate users have seen the cost of their separate voice and data networks rise. These users have begun to recognize that an advanced, integrated corporate network offers them a critical competitive edge as well as lower network costs. The additional function being offered by advanced networks is becoming very attractive to them and their top management is being convinced of these facts. ISDN offers a migration path to achieve these goals. The first customers of the ISDN services have been very large organizations with growing networking needs; the large consumer contact firms (e.g., American Express) are quickly moving in this direction.

The success of ISDN depends critically upon the success of the applications that take advantage of its capabilities. Indeed, it is the identification and development of a rich set of applications that will hasten the growth of ISDN more than any other factor. We have seen this phenomenon at work in a number of other network related systems in the past. Packet switching succeeded in the commercial environment largely because of the electronic mail application that it supported. SNA took hold because of the support it provided for transaction processing. PC LAN's have proliferated because of the need to share peripherals and data.

We have yet to identify the hot new application(s) that will drive ISDN steeply up the demand curve. Some of the applications that have been identified so far include automatic number identification (ANI) as well as the ability to turn off ANI, reduced call setup time from 20 s to less than 3 s, the availability of a single access point for digital services (thus eliminating multiple dedicated access lines), the ability to provide video-based telephony, voice–data applications, desktop ISDN links, etc. So far, none of these have sparked a rush to the ISDN market.

Nevertheless, the carriers are overwhelmingly behind ISDN and they will do all in their power to promote it. It is in their interest to do so. In the long run, it will be in the user's interest as well, for the carriers are the ones who will provide the networking infrastructure that is called for. Today's networks are disorganized, expensive, not integrated, slow, complex, difficult to manage, and unable to interoperate with each other; an international standard interface such as ISDN is badly needed. To their credit, the Europeans have been much more aggressive than the North Americans in implementing ISDN. And if you still doubt that the case for ISDN is justified, consider the fact that the less-developed and under-developed regions of the world are anxious to connect to the world standard network. There is no way that each of them can or should establish their own standard. There absolutely must be an available world standard to which they can attach.

ISDN is a technology that allows those who have not kept pace with the growth in networking technology to catch up immediately.

III. NARROWBAND ISDN IS NOT ENOUGH

The BRI and PRI ISDN offerings are often collectively referred to as *narrowband* ISDN (NISDN) to distinguish them from BISDN. The data rates associated with NISDN are inadequate for many applications of interest. On the one hand, the BRI providing 64 kb/s channels is not a large improvement over today's modems, which provide data service at 9.6 kb/s and 19.3 kb/s and which are widely available. It is also the case that 64 kb/s is a nonstarter for the data transmission speeds to which today's users have become accustomed (e.g., local area networks running at 10 Mb/s and more). The PRI running at 1.54 Mb/s is a clear improvement over BRI, but is no different in available speed than is the popular T1 offerings in use by the community today (so why abandon T1 and introduce new equipment interfaces for PRI?). Add to that the nasty incompatibilities faced by multinational corporations when they find that PRI in Europe is 2.05 Mb/s rather than 1.54 Mb/s in North America; of course, this problem already exists in today's T1 offerings. The PRI rate is still a significant step away from the bandwidth needs of the data processing community; it takes almost 5 min to move a 50-megabyte file at T1 transmission speeds.

From the viewpoint of data networks, the real excitement of ISDN comes about when one discusses the capabilities of BISDN. 155 Mb/s is a real improvement over today's speeds. The 50-megabyte file can now be moved in 2.5 s! The precursor to BISDN is the growing use of the T3 service (45 Mb/s). Indeed, the huge popularity of T1 and the growing popularity of T3 are setting the stage for the introduction of BISDN at 155 Mb/s and 620 Mb/s.

The need for broadband speeds comes from a number of applications. The existence of today's high bandwidth customer premises networks (i.e., local area networks (LAN's) require long distance broadband to interconnect them; LAN interconnetion using switched broadband data service is a clear and current application. The emerging field of teleradiology in which one transmits medical imagery among hospitals, physicians, and patients requires large bandwidths due to the enormous data files; the typical pair of chest X-rays we all get in a routine medical examination requires as much storage as four volumes of the Encyclopedia Britannica. A similar need comes from the field of telepathology, i.e., the transmission of optical images of biological samples. On-line access to supercomputer output showing real-time rotation of complex molecules in three dimensions in full color can be a real bandwidth hog. File server access to rapid scanning of visual and textual data is another application. The growth of CAD applications will be one source of rapid development and deployment of customized ISDN chips.

Indeed, the first applications of BISDN will be in the commercial and scientific sectors. However, following that, a real drive for broadband will be in the residential sector in order to provide entertainment. For example, CATV cable service passes by 86% of American homes, 55% of homes subscribe to CATV cable services, 30% of homes purchase more than one premium movie channel, 10% buy pay-per-view services, and the average home consumes 7 hours of television per day [4]. HDTV will increase the demand for sevices and will place enormous bandwidth requirements on our communication plant. If the FCC allows CATV services to be offered by the telephone companies, it would be a tremendous pull from the demand side for the installation of broadband capability to the subscriber base. Of course, optical fiber will be the medium providing these large bandwidths, and the economies that support fiber installation are already here.

Currently, there are well over a million miles of installed fiber in the U.S. It is now less expensive to install fiber than it is to install copper for large office buildings. Fiber to the curb (FTTC) is becoming competitive for new installations, and fiber to the home (FTTH) is under serious consideration already. The appropriate strategy is to begin the FTTC and FTTH installations now, while NISDN is deploying.

Thus the real payoff in the data networks world for ISDN is the promise of BISDN and all the services and capabilities it will bring.

IV. CURRENT NETS ARE INADEQUATE

It is clear that the data networks we inherited from the 1980's are inadequate to handle the applications and capabilities required by the 1990's. Today's packet switched data networks have a number of problems with them: They are high cost, they are low speed, they introduce large switching delays, they have relatively high error rates, the switches require too much intelligence, the switches are electronic, there is too much storage in the network, the protocols are too heavyweight, and too much processing is done in the network.

For example, X.25 packet switching networks are serving a real need as they currently exist. However, they are based essentially on 64-kb/s speeds and use heavyweight protocols (they process up to layer 3 at every hop). As an alternate to X.25 packet switching, frame relay is currently being considered for the interim version of fast packet switching, whereby the LAPD link level protocol will be used to perform switching functions at layer 2 without the layer 3 processing overhead [5], [6].

Tomorrow's broadband networks require new architectures to handle the changing requirements. The move from megabits per second to gigabits per second requires dramatic changes in thinking and in structure. In Table 1 we list some of these contrasts.

Table 1 Packet Network Characteristics: Present Versus Future

	Today	Broadband
Packets/s	Thousands	Millions
Bandwidth	64 kb/s	150 M/-620 Mb/s
Bandwidth allocation	Fixed	Dynamic
Services	Voice, data	Integrated voice, data and image
Switch delay	50–100 ms	10 ms
Propagation delay	Insignificant	Dominant
Error control	Link-to-link	End-to-end
Protocols	Heavyweight	Lightweight
Bottleneck	Link bandwidth	Switch bandwidth

The path from today's data networks to those of tomorrow is being paved right now. T3 offerings at 44.7 Mb/s are beginning to penetrate the private networking marketplace. The synchronous optical network (SONET) standard for optical transmission was agreed upon by the CCITT in 1988 [7] and has promoted BISDN product development. The operations, administration, and maintenance (OA&M) portions of the SONET standard should be completed by the end of 1990 and will only require software updates to implement. SONET has laid out a hierarchy of transmission speeds from 51.8 Mb/s up to 13.27 Gb/s and higher. These enormous speeds are fine for point to point communications (assuming the end points can gobble up gigabits per second), but certainly place some outrageous demands on the internal switches in the network.

These very large communication bandwidths have caused a wealth of research and experimentation to take place in the research laboratories in the advanced area of fast packet switching [8]. Fast packet switching will likely use parallel processing architectures in the switch to handle the millions of packets per second mentioned above. There is a number of competing architectures being proposed for the interconnection networks within these switches and many of them use the Banyan switch in one form or another [9]. The advantage of these architectures is that many packets can be switched simultaneously through the switching fabric using the concurrent processing capability of the parallel processors.

A new multiplexing scheme known as asynchronous transfer mode (ATM) [10] has been adopted for BISDN which uses fixed length packets (called cells) of length 53 bytes (48 bytes of data and 5 bytes of header), has highly simplified protocols (no windowing and no processor-intensive work), incorporates no error detection on the data (only on the header), and implements only layer 1 and basic layer 2 functions in the 7-layer OSI standard. ATM provides connection-oriented virtual circuits, handles continuous and bursty data, eliminates the need for multiple TDM channel rates, provides separate signal and information channels, and is independent of the transmission medium. ATM differs from packet switching in the following ways: ATM has fixed length cells (instead of variable length packets); ATM uses highly simplified protocols (instead of processor-intensive protocols); ATM does not do error correction on the data on a link-by-link basis; and ATM does not do any layer 3 operations.

In addition, the IEEE 802.6 committtee has recently approved a protocol for use in MAN's based on the Distributed Queue Dual Bus (DQDB) [11]. This 802.6 MAN standard is compatible with ATM/BISDN and provides a natural addition to the emerging world of Broadband. The common format shared among this MAN standard, ATM, and BISDN greatly simplifies the internetworking problems of the forthcoming broadband era. Meanwhile, the fiber distributed data interface (FDDI) has met with some success as a 100-Mb/s offering [12].

The carriers are beginning to offer their switched multimegabit data service (SMDS) [13] which will probably be the first manifestation of the 802.6 MAN. SMDS has already been demonstrated at 45 Mb/s and will soon be offered on a tariffed basis. SMDS differs from ISDN in that it is a connectionless data service that includes broadcast and multicast features. ISDN, on the other hand, is an integrated voice and data service offering both circuit-switched and packet switched features.

A near-term problem we foresee for the carriers who are to offer these services is the issue of establishing a tariff that will satisfy the end user in matching his patterns of use in the emerging applications.

In the next five years, we can anticipate that X.25 packet switching will migrate to frame relay, to FDDI and then to the 802.6 DQDB via SMDS, finally bringing us to the ATM/BISDN offerings.

As these brave new broadband capabilities develop, it must be understood that our current networks are ill-suited to provide services using these increased bandwidths. We must re-engineer the architecture of our networks to accommodate these bandwidths, a topic we address in the next section.

V. High Bandwidth Networking

Broadband ISDN is the proposed foundation for wide area networks (WAN's) that are capable of supporting applications needing high speed, low latency, rich functionality, and support of mixed media (i.e., voice, data, image, video, graphics, fax, etc.). The market demand for these advanced applications is clearly growing. Furthermore, the core technologies to provide these services are emerging: high-speed switches are being designed, high-speed fiber access networks are being deployed, the SONET hierarchy has been defined, ATM multiplexing techniques are agreed upon, etc. Indeed, technology is solving most of the performance problems we can foresee (link speeds, processor speeds, and memory sizes are increasing on their own).

As we move into gigabit networks, however, we must take a "clean sheet" approach to many of the systems issues [14], [15]. The critical areas to be considered include switching technology, processor interfaces, protocols, connection-oriented communications, routing, layered architectures, and coexistence with carrier environments. We must be prepared to allow different switch technologies to work in the future broadband networks; these include the BISDN fast packet switching techniques, photonic switches, and wave-length division multiplexing (WLDM). The architecture we select must not depend upon which of these happens to be implemented.

As for switching, tomorrow's networks must be prepared to handle packet, circuit, and hybrid switches. Large packets or groups of packets will have to be switched simultaneously; at gigabit bandwidths, one cannot afford the overhead of switching small blocks independently. Sophisticated dynamic bandwidth reservation algorithms must be developed. Multicast algorithms and capabilities must be developed (fiber is point-to-point, whereas satellite and ground-based radio are broadcast and multicast).

Beyond all of these, the question of the network management system is extremely important. Today's nets are reactive, not proactive. We must introduce proactive diagnosis and service restoral before users sense a problem. We need proactive resource management. Since huge volumes of raw data will be flowing into the management control center, we must use thresholds, filters and alerts, and even expert systems, for early problem detection and resolution. These management functions must operate in a distributed fashion for fault containment, privilege definition, and localization of security failures. Multiple classes of service must be supported. Adaptive protocols and error recovery mechanisms must be developed. Indeed, the management of the emerging internetwork is turning out to be the ultimate challenge in distributed systems.

As we consider these problems, it is clear that the carriers have been facing large network problems for most of this century. They understand management, billing, accountability, security, availability, introduction of new technology on a large scale, etc. However, over the last twenty years, the innovations in data networking have come from the data-processing industry, and not from the carriers. (This in spite of the fact that the data-processing solutions have used the underlying carrier plant to establish their data networks). As we move into the broadband era, it is essential that these two (merged) industries cooperate in providing service to the user community. BISDN holds much promise for advanced networking, and the technological and managerial hurdles that must be overcome are best solved jointly by these two industries.

VI. Conclusions

The concept of ISDN was generated from the carriers. Its early growth was much slower than had been promised due to a number of reasons, key among them being the lack of real user demand for the service. However, in the past two years, the narrowband ISDN (NISDN) penetration has accelerated faster than the skeptics had been predicting.

ISDN is the means by which the less advanced users can quickly catch up to today's technology. However, the real payoff will come with BISDN. The data network services and capacity offered by BISDN are truly exciting and advanced. But we must proceed with NISDN before we can achieve BISDN.

The carriers have an enormous investment in ISDN and they are highly motivated to bring about its success. The carriers are the key to the future networking infrastructure for the U.S. and the rest of the world. The data-processing industry cannot "go it alone" in this endeavor; they must cooperate and encourage the carriers. Both groups must agree on common standards for both private and public networking as this infrastructure grows. ISDN is one important step in this direction. Beyond that, however, it must be recognized that a revolutionary approach must be taken in providing the gigabit/second services about which we are talking. The fundamental architecture of our plant must be overhauled significantly; that overhaul is already well underway.

It is perhaps worthwhile to review some of the economic factors that have, and will, affect the architecture of our communication networks. The cost of moving data across a network consists of two important components; the cost of the channels and the cost of the switches. In the early days of communications, the channel was the expensive component (copper wires strung up on telephone poles) and the switch was a poorly paid human operator. As a result, one could afford to waste switch capacity to save on the expensive communications component. Then, a revolution occurred in communications: microwave radio was introduced and this dramatically dropped the cost of the communications component. At the same time, the switch cost dropped (automatic switches in the form of relays and vacuum tubes appeared), but not as dramatically as the channel. Consequently, a reversal occurred where the switch was now more expensive than the communication channel. Now it was sensible to waste communications capacity in order to save on the switch. Thus circuit switching was introduced. In the 1970's, another reversal occurred when integrated electronics (VLSI) appeared, which dramatically dropped the switch cost relative to the communications cost. Once again, we could afford to waste switching capacity in order to save yet more on the communications costs. Thus packet switching was introduced.

That was the past. Let us now peek into the future. Is there anything out there in the near term that will dramatically drop the cost of the switch? Gallium arsenide components will help, but they do not represent a revolutionary change. On the other hand, warm superconductivity, if it comes, would indeed be a dramatic improvement in switch technology. It would allow the wires to be thinner (and still not generate much heat) thereby allowing smaller dimensions (i.e., reduced latency due to the speed of light) and tighter packing. However, warm superconductivity is not a near-term likelihood. Further, photonic switching would be a revolutionary improvement in switch technology. Here, too, we are talking about a laboratory experiment and not a near-term development. So the answer is "no"; we cannot foresee a dramatic improvement in switch technology near term. But how about a revolution in communications? Is there a technology out there that will dramatically reduce the cost of communications? The answer is a resounding "YES"! Indeed it is already taking place, and it is called fiber optics. As stated above, we have well over a million miles of fiber optics in place in the U.S. alone. We are in the midst of the next reversal, which leads us to a situation where communications are plentiful and the bottleneck has once again become the switch. Our networking architectures are undergoing a massive revamping as we move into this environment. Our 1980's architectures are inadequate for the economics and applications of the 1990's.

In response to this current reversal, we see BISDN services coming along, we see fast packet switching architectures, we see ATM, we see the 802.6 MAN, we see LAN developments, we see FDDI, etc. And, once we get all that wonderful technology in place, is it possible that either warm superconductivity and/or photonic switching will come along so as to cause yet a further reversal and thus another reshuffling of the cards? It seems there will be a need for continual improvement of architectures and systems as new technological developments spawn new possibilities and new applications.

As we begin to move through the 1990's we forsee that broadband ISDN will play an important role in bringing about some of the exciting networking developments. A great deal of research has gone into broadband networking in the last few years. The next few years will see development of products and growth in demand. There is no question but that this technology will provide the basis for a ubiquitous communications infrastructure of enormous capacity.

Let us conclude this paper by listing some of the components that we are likely to see in this time frame:

- Worldwide Data Networks
- Advanced Network Machines
- Optical Fiber Networks
- Gigabit/second Networks
- Megapacket/s Superswitches
- Optical Switches
- Pervasive Local Area Networks
- LAN-MAN-WAN Hierarchy
- Processing Satellites
- Intelligent Network Directories
- Continuous Speech Recognition
- Image Communication Mode
- Digital Signal Compression
- Massively Parallel Systems
- Massively Connected Systems
- Neural Networks
- Pervasive Expert Systems.

It is clear from this list that the convergence of data processing and data communications is virtually complete. Distributed information networks are poised to provide the many services required for the emerging information society. ISDN will serve to hasten access to these information networks, eventually providing a major thrust when BISDN products and services begin to roll out.

References

[1] L. Kleinrock, *Queueing Systems, Volume II: Computer Applications.* New York: Wiley, 1976.

[2] IDC White Paper, "ISDN integrated services digital networks," *Computer World*, CW Publishing, Jan. 22, 1990.

[3] W. Stallings, *ISDN: An Introduction.* New York: Macmillan, 1989.

[4] M. Frame, "Broadband service needs," *IEEE Commun. Mag.*, pp. 59–62, Apr. 1990.

[5] S. J. Lowe, "Plugging into frame relay for speed and flexibility," *Data Commun. Mag.*, pp. 54–62, Apr. 1990.

[6] E. E. Mier, "New signs of life for packet switching," *Data Commun.*, pp. 90–106, Dec. 1989.

[7] R. Ballart and Y. C. Ching, "SONET: Now it's the standard optical network," *IEEE Commun. Mag.*, pp. 8–15, Mar. 1989.

[8] J. S. Turner, "Design of an integrated services packet network," *IEEE J. Select. Areas Commun.*, vol. 4, pp. 1373–1380, Nov. 1986.

[9] L. R. Goke and G. J. Lipovski, "Banyan networks for partitioning multiprocessor systems," in *Proc. 1st Annual Symp. on Computer*

Architecture, G. J. Lipovski and S. A. Szgenda, Eds. Gainesville, FL: ACM, pp. 21–28, 1973.

[10] R. Handel, "Evolution of ISDN towards broadband ISDN," *IEEE Network Mag.*, pp. 7–13, Jan. 1989.

[11] G. C. Kessler, "IEEE 802.6 MAN," *LAN Mag.*, pp. 102–116, Apr. 1990.

[12] K. J. Thurber, "Getting a handle on FDDI," *Data Commun. Mag.*, pp. 28–32, June 21, 1989.

[13] "Generic system requirements in support of switched multi-megabit data service," Bellcore Tech. Advisory, TA-TSY-000772, Issue 3, Oct. 1989.

[14] L. Kleinrock *et al.*, "Toward a national research network," Washington, DC: National Academic Press, 1988.

[15] B. Leiner, Ed., "Critical issues in high bandwidth networking," Research Institute for Advanced Computer Science report, Oct. 1988.

Leonard Kleinrock (Fellow, IEEE) received the B.S. degree in electrical engineering from the City College of New York in 1957 and the M.S.E.E. and Ph.D.E.E. degrees from the Massachusetts Institute of Technology in 1959 and 1963, respectively.

While at M.I.T., he worked at the Research Laboratory for Electronics, as well as with the computer research group of Lincoln Laboratory in advanced technology. He joined the faculty at UCLA in 1963, where he is now a Professor of computer science. His research interests focus on performance evaluation of high speed networks and parallel and distributed systems. He has had over 160 papers published and is the author of five books—*Communications Nets: Stochastic Message Flow and Delay*, 1964; *Queueing Systems, Volume I: Theory*, 1975; *Queueing Systems, Volume II: Computer Applications*, 1976; *Solutions Manual for Queueing Systems, Volume I*, 1982, and most recently, *Solutions Manual for Queueing Systems, Volume II*, 1986. He is a well-known lecturer in the computer industry. He is the principal investigator for the DARPA Parallel Systems Laboratory contract at UCLA. He was a cofounder of Linkabit Corporation. He is also the founder and CEO of Technology Transfer Institute, a computer/communications seminar and consulting organization located in Santa Monica, CA.

Dr. Kleinrock is a member of the National Academy of Engineering, is a Guggenheim Fellow, and a member of the Computer Science and Technology Board of the National Research Council. He has received numerous best paper and teaching awards, including the ICC 1978 Prize Winning Paper Award, the 1976 Lanchester Prize for outstanding work in Operations Research, and the Communications Society 1975 Leonard G. Abraham Prize Paper Award. In 1982, as well as having been selected to receive the C.C.N.Y. Townsend Harris Medal, he was cowinner of the L. M. Ericsson Prize, presented by His Majesty King Carl Gustaf of Sweden, for his outstanding contribution in packet switching technology. In July of 1986, he received the 12th Marconi International Fellowship Award, presented by His Royal Highness Prince Albert, brother of King Baudoin of Belgium, for his pioneering work in the field of computer networks. In the same year, he received the UCLA Outstanding Teacher Award.

Broadband Communications: The Commercial Impact

Stephen Timms

The Dawn of Broadband
The Broadband Phenomenon

Reprinted from *IEEE Network Magazine*, July 1989, pages 10-15.
Copyright © 1989 by The Institute of Electrical and Electronics Engineers, Inc. All rights reserved.

Broadband is no longer just a pipedream. Its introduction does not depend on implausible technological leaps nor on enormous demand for hitherto unknown services. A clear market-led pathway to broadband is identified in this paper, and the first steps along it have already been taken.

The key point is that an optical fiber infrastructure is already taking shape. There are already business customers enjoying end-to-end fiber in the U.S. and Europe.

That is not to say that switched broadband services are appearing. So far, there is very little sign of them. But the biggest obstacle to their introduction has always been regarded as the need to replace the existing copper infrastructure with optical fiber. The conclusion of our research is that the replacement has already started, because under some conditions it already makes economic sense to use fiber, just for conventional services.

The reasons for using fiber are not hard to find. In many city center commercial areas, there is a chronic shortage of circuit capacity. The financial services sector is making increasing demands for telecommunications services. The copper wire infrastructure is being stretched to its limits; laying more copper is expensive, particularly since duct space to put it into is not always available.

Fiber, by contrast, offers a far greater capacity for a given thickness of cable, and much better potential for expansion. It is more expensive than copper, but not much, and the margin is decreasing all the time. In the United States, we expect over 3 million business sites to be equipped with fiber access to carrier networks by the year 2000, and 2 million homes. Fiber has the extra benefit of better quality transmission—and the attraction that it could be used in the future for new services, bringing in extra revenue to the carrier.

The picture emerging in the four countries studied in this paper (the United States, United Kingdom, France, and Germany) is one of islands of fiber in major commercial centers. Once these are in place, it will not be too costly to introduce broadband switches, supporting niche applications on an overlay basis.

Thus, switched broadband communications will start to appear, initially in the commercial centers where a fiber infrastructure is already available. By the mid-1990s, these services will be becoming widespread—and by the end of the 1990s, when residential subscribers start to be connected in large numbers, broadband will account for a similar proportion of carrier service revenues (around 7%) to that accounted for by non-voice communications today. (A different pattern is developing in France, where half a million fiber residential subscriber connections are already on order for cable TV networks, and much quicker residential penetration is envisaged.)

Three observations will serve to illustrate the scale of the phenomenon:

- In the US, the use of T1 or DS1 1.5-Mb/s digital leased circuits for networking has emerged as the major topic in corporate communications, and there is now a rapid growth in the use of DS3 45-Mb/s circuits.

- The work of the CCITT study group on Integrated Services Digital Network (ISDN) has been increasingly concerned with topics in broadband since finalization of ISDN standards at the end of 1984;

- Over 40 major European equipment manufacturers collaborated in the first phase of the RACE program, supported by the inter-government European Commission, which has as one of its main aims the establishment, by 1995, of a Europe-wide integrated broadband communications network.

What is Broadband?

Figure 1 puts broadband in the context of other forms of communication. It represents a major step forward in telecommunications, but certainly does not exhaust the theoretically conceivable possibilities for information transfer.

The term broadband is used in a wide variety of different ways. We set out here the definitions we use throughout this paper. We distinguish between two uses of the term, broadband access and broadband applications.

Broadband access is digital access from a subscriber's premises to a telephone company's (telco's) switch via an optical fiber connection, supporting a data rate greater than 2 Mb/s. Subscriber access, particularly for business users, will be provided increasingly by means of optical fiber. We use the term Integrated Broadband Access (IBA) to signify broadband access over a single optical fiber to a range of telecommunications networks, including narrowband networks. IBA is likely to work initially at a data rate of around 150 Mb/s.

Broadband applications are applications that are implemented through broadband access and require a data rate greater than is generally available in a typical, narrowband ISDN (i.e., greater than 128 kb/s). The leading applications will include high-speed links between Local Area Networks (LANs) and most implementations of video communication.

The Infrastructure for Broadband

A central conclusion from our research is that the infrastructure for broadband transmission is already being set up. Optical fiber has increasingly dominated interexchange networks in the past 3 to 4 years. The U.S. now has several nationwide networks largely based on fiber. In the U.K., British Telecom's long distance network is over 60% fiber and the network of its much smaller rival, Mercury, is mostly optical al-

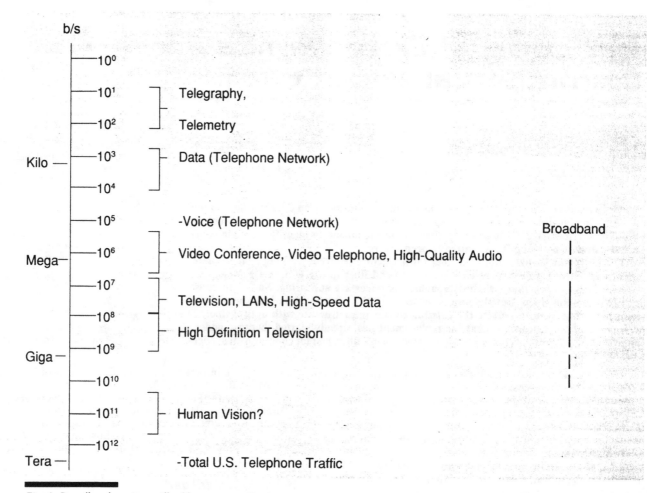

b/s

- 10^0
- 10^1 — Telegraphy,
- 10^2 — Telemetry
- Kilo — 10^3 — Data (Telephone Network)
- 10^4
- 10^5 — -Voice (Telephone Network)
- Mega — 10^6 — Video Conference, Video Telephone, High-Quality Audio
- 10^7 — Television, LANs, High-Speed Data
- 10^8 — High Definition Television
- Giga — 10^9
- 10^{10}
- 10^{11} — Human Vision?
- 10^{12}
- Tera — -Total U.S. Telephone Traffic

Broadband

Fig. 1. Broadband services will address new application areas.

ready. The Federal Post Office in Germany also has an ambitious program of fiber deployment.

But fiber is no longer confined to long distance networks. Regional Bell Operating Companies in the U.S. have laid as much optical fiber as the long distance carriers. And the fiber is gradually moving further out from the local exchange and closer to the subscriber. It is, for example, common in new installations for the link between a street cabinet and local exchange to be fiber, while the tails to the individual subscribers are still copper.

Even in the last mile to the subscriber, fiber is beginning to make its appearance. In France, half a million residential fiber connections have already been ordered for local video communication networks. Initially, these are for cable TV only, but it is intended to use them for switched telephony too, when French standards for ISDN have been finalized. In the U.S. and U.K., business subscribers in major centers are being converted to fiber access, because it makes economic sense as a way to provide existing narrowband services. Rapid availability of additional circuits is especially attractive when, as in London, long delays for new circuits have been common. The trend is being given a further boost in the U.S. by the establishment of fiber metropolitan networks in the biggest cities, to compete with the local telephone companies.

On the customer premises too, the use of LANs operating at data rates above 2 Mb/s is already common; and the growing use of fiber networks promises much higher speeds. It will only be a matter of time until the general business communications picture is of major sites using high-speed LANs for their internal needs, connected to carriers by optical fiber.

Two Scenarios for Broadband

Two alternative routes can be envisaged for the introduction of broadband services in a country: the market-driven route and the investment-led route.

The difference is in objectives. The market-driven route entails carriers responding to the demands currently being made of them. In the investment-led route, carriers aim to lead the market and create new demands by substantial investment in fiber residential networks.

The Market-Driven Route

Commercial pressures are already forcing optical fiber into the local loop for business subscribers. As the fiber infrastructure comes into place, so the opportunity will arise for carriers to introduce broadband switching on an overlay basis to subscribers with fiber access, at a relatively modest cost.

The key application for early switched broadband services will be high-speed data communication. Continuing rapid improvements in the price-performance of computing equipment, supporting new applications such as desktop publishing, will fuel substantial demand for high-speed data services. LANs will need to be interconnected at 10 Mb/s or more. Switched services supporting these applications for business users will be available from about 1992. The new services will be used to support video conferencing too, though this will be on a smaller scale than high-speed data.

An alternative view arose from a study commissioned by the European Commission and completed as Ovum's report was published. (See the account in *Telecommunications*, international edition, July 1988.) It suggests, on the basis of an extensive interview program, that video telephony will be as important as high-speed data communications in attracting users to broadband services by 1995. We regard this as unrealistic, in view of the limited interest among users in video telephony.

By the end of the 1990s, broadband switch costs will have fallen to a level not very much more than the cost of typical digital switches today, and it will start to be commercially attractive for carriers to extend IBA to residential subscribers. The main attraction for users at home will be the potential for using the fiber infrastructure for receiving entertainment TV services. The application will be similar to current advanced cable TV services, except that:

- High definition television broadcasts will be available, offering greatly improved picture and sound quality compared with today's off-air and cable broadcasts.
- Subscribers will be able to choose broadcasts from huge video libraries, instead of being restricted to the programs being broadcast at any particular time.

Video telephony will start to make an appearance by the end of the 1990s as well. By that time, broadband services will account for a similar proportion (around 7%) of carrier service revenues to that accounted for by non-voice services today.

The Investment-Led Route

Some carriers, though, will choose a more ambitious path to broadband, investing heavily in the early 1990s, in order to provide switched broadband services to residential subscribers and small businesses at the same time as or even before users in major commercial centers. These investments will have a long payback period. In Europe, France is the most committed to following this route. Major benefits are anticipated in equipment suppliers having an early domestic market in wide area broadband technology, with its enormous worldwide potential. The competitive advantage to small and medium-sized businesses in international markets, able to work more effectively through access to advanced services, will also be an important factor.

In the U.S., Southern Bell is also poised to pursue a bold approach to broadband, and a handful of other telephone companies are considering this option. The attraction lies in securing new revenue streams for long-term growth, particularly in entertainment TV markets.

Carrier Costs and Rewards

The introduction of broadband services will incur heavy costs for carriers: new local subscriber connections, new local exchanges, and new facilities in the trunk network. The cost of putting fiber into subscriber connections is very substantial, and will become of increasing relative significance as the costs of the electronics fall. Subscriber equipment will also be much more expensive than it is now.

The rewards will also be very considerable, with the promise of substantial new revenues that cannot be earned from narrowband services. In summary, we believe that carriers will be able to cost-justify the provision of overlay switched broadband services for business customers by the early 1990s, but that switched broadband services for residential subscribers will not be financially attractive to carriers until the end of the 1990s.

Local Subscriber Connections

The costs of optical fiber connections are falling rapidly, and will soon be little more than their copper equivalents for new installations. Optimistic commentators believe that the cost differential will have disappeared by 1990; certainly, there should be little to choose between them by 1992. The bulk of the cost of installing optical fiber local connections—around

two-thirds of it—is accounted for, however, by the construction work, which will not become any less expensive than it is at present.

A typical cost per subscriber for installing a fiber local loop is around $1,000. In some places, the replacement of subscriber connections with fiber can be justified already, and it is starting to happen. Elsewhere—that is, outside the main business centers—the need for a new fiber infrastructure will continue to be an obstacle to the introduction of broadband services, until there is clearer evidence that additional revenues will be generated.

Switching

By 1995, a local exchange capable of switching 140-Mb/s signals will cost 3 to 4 times as much as a comparable narrowband digital exchange costs today: $1,500 to $2,000 per subscriber. After that, the price will fall, perhaps by as much as 20% per year, so that by the end of the century it will not be much more in real terms than a modern local exchange today.

Long Distance Network

The introduction of broadband services will also require upgrading the interexchange network, though the cost per subscriber will be much less than for either the local loop or local exchange.

The Rewards

To offset these costs, Ovum believes that broadband offers the best prospects for entirely new carrier revenues in the period from now to the year 2000. Unlike ISDN, where the new services offered represent only a modest addition to what is already in place, broadband will support dramatically new services:

- Switched data communication several orders of magnitude faster than now possible
- Rapid transmission of high resolution images
- Video communication

Revenue per subscriber with broadband could be twice as much as at present, if video communication were to become widespread.

A Schedule for Broadband Services

Figure 2 shows how broadband will develop in the period from now to the year 2000. IBA will appear on a substantial scale, starting with major business centers, from 1988 onwards. Switched broadband services will become available from 1992–3.

Market Growth

Figure 3 shows how we expect the deployment of IBA and broadband applications to develop in the period from now to the year 2000. By 1995, 3% of all business sites in the U.S., U.K., France, and Germany will have IBA. In most cases, the fiber access will be used exclusively for narrowband services, but 0.1% of sites will be using it for video communication, and 0.3% (about one IBA site in ten) for high-speed data communications. By the year 2000, IBA will extend to 16% of business sites in the four countries, and nearly half of the IBA sites will be making use of high-speed data communications. Only 1.3% of business sites will be using IBA for access to video services.

Among the conclusions about the four countries arising from Ovum's broadband market model are:

- Broadband will account for some 7% of total carrier service revenues overall by the year 2000. In 1995, the proportion will be around 1%.
- The split of broadband service revenue between residential and business video services and business data services will

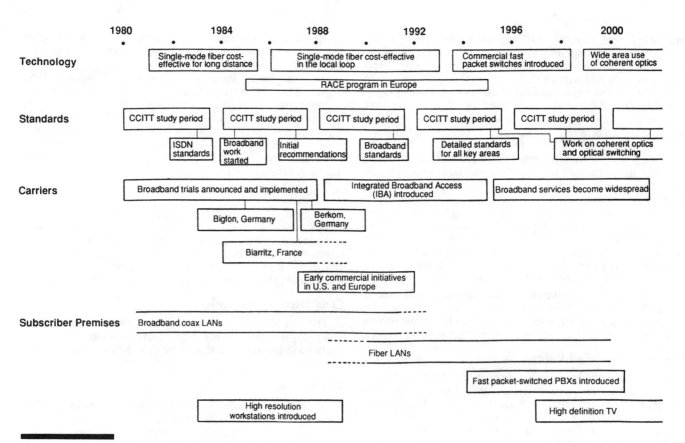

Fig. 2. The development timetable for broadband.

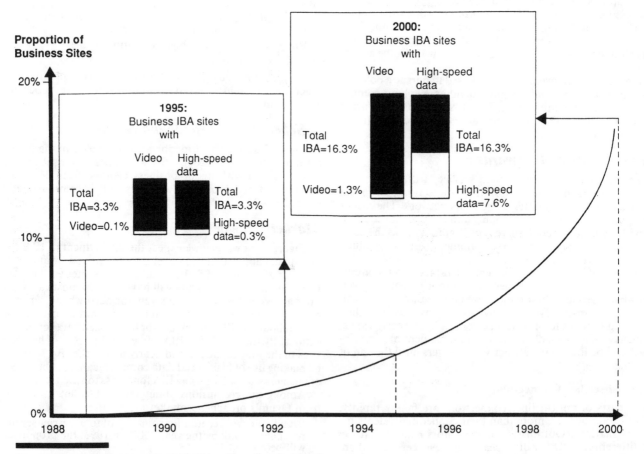

Fig. 3. Proportion of business sites with IBA and broadband applications
(U.S., U.K., France, and Germany).

still vary widely between the countries in the year 2000. High-speed data services for business will generate over 80% of broadband service revenue in the U.S. and U.K., 65% of the total in Germany, and 40% in France.

- Business video services will be relatively most important in Germany, accounting for about 30% of broadband service revenues, compared with 10–15% in the other countries.
- In 1995, some 600,000 business terminals in the four countries will be accessing broadband services—90% of them will be for high-speed data communication, and 10% for video. By the year 2000, there will be nearly 9 million terminals, and 94% of them will be for high-speed data.

Broadband: Ends and Means

What For and How?

Broadband will represent a major leap forward in the power available to communications users, potentially a step-up of several orders of magnitude. But the transition to broadband raises a host of commercial questions:

- What are the applications it will be used for?
- Who will the customers be?
- Will the market be able to support the investment needed?
- What technology will be adopted?
- What will be the migration path from today's networks?

Ends: Applications and Users

The potential for much greater communications throughput—more information conveyed in the same time, or the same information conveyed much faster—brings a vast new array of applications within reach: high-speed data for business, high resolution image for professional and entertainment use, and interactive video communications.

The first part of this article described how broadband will emerge where an optical fiber infrastructure is already in place in the local loop, justified on the basis of access to existing narrowband services. These fiber networks are being introduced mainly in large commercial centers, and the first applications to drive the introduction of broadband will, correspondingly, be in business.

We see three applications playing a key role in generating the early demand for broadband:

- High-speed data communication
- LAN interconnection
- Video conferencing

High-Speed Data Communication

There is a growing mismatch between the computing power and communications functionality available to business users. Narrowband data services will be severely strained in meeting the developing needs of growing numbers of computer users in the coming decade. By 1995, switched 50-Mb/s data services will be needed to bring communications performance back in line with the increase in desktop computing power since 1975.

Niche applications for high-speed data communications are already appearing. For example:

- Bulk File Transfer.

Banks are making extensive use of high-speed links between data processing centers—for example, to operate main and back-up computer centers in tandem. Audi AG operates a 50-Mb/s optical fiber link over 1,100 meters between two data centers at its vehicle manufacturing plant in Southern Germany.

- Workstation Communications.

Ford in Detroit is using links operating at 10 Mb/s and above for workstation communications, such as swapping CAD information between engineering workstations; sending maintenance and repair information stored on optical disk to workstations on the manufacturing plant floor; and downloading software for local execution of specific applications.

- Mainframe Channel Extenders.

Citibank in New York uses optical fiber for a link operating at 45 Mb/s between a mainframe and a printer located in a different building.

High-speed data links also offer great potential for communicating still images. Examples of application areas include the medical market (for X-ray and other images) and the burgeoning use of desktop publishing systems and high resolution computerized graphics.

LAN Interconnection

An application of high-speed data communications that stands out as particularly important in its own right is the interconnection of LANs. Today's LANs typically operate at data rates of 10 Mb/s. Bridge techniques allow them to be interconnected at much lower speeds, such as 1.5 Mb/s, but full-speed links give better functionality and are already being deployed. Citibank is using its network in New York to link LANs at 10 Mb/s, and ICC in Washington offers a 10 Mb/s inter-LAN service over its fiber metropolitan network. The introduction of fiber LANs operating at up to 100 Mb/s will generate a demand for even higher speeds.

The need for LAN interconnection arises when, for example:

- Teams working at split sites on technical projects require access to common data
- Part of a department is relocated away from the main office
- Computing resources have to be shared between different college or university departments

We expect that, by 1995, inter-LAN traffic will account for up to half of all switched high-speed data traffic.

Video Conferencing

The feasibility of broadband switching at a reasonable price will greatly enhance the attractiveness of video conferencing, particularly when low-cost video equipment becomes available. We expect video conferencing to account for 10–15% of the carrier revenue generated by broadband services during the 1990s.

At present, video conferencing services use data rates below 1.5 Mb/s for the video signal, and there are efforts to reduce the rate still further by using better compression techniques. In the future, the data rate used is likely to increase gradually, to improve the picture quality and reduce the cost of the compression equipment needed.

An interesting approach is being taken in the new German forerunner broadband overlay network, where switched video conferencing is expected to account for a substantial proportion of usage: access to the network will be by fiber at 140 Mb/s, but within the network, transmission will be at 2 Mb/s when 140 Mb/s links are not available. This arrangement allows the costs of compression equipment to be shared among users.

The Importance of Video

The discussion of video conferencing raises an important question: what will the role of video communications be in creating demand for broadband services? Broadband is sometimes characterized as primarily the medium for interactive video. Our view, however, is that, at least until the end of the century, high-speed data will be a much more important driver.

We have already suggested that video conferencing will be an important broadband application, but on a relatively modest scale. There are two other potentially enormous markets for video: video telephony and TV distribution.

Video Telephony

Video telephony is personal video communication from a desktop terminal—in contrast to video conferencing, where a studio is involved. There are two major barriers to video telephony:

- There is very little sign of market demand for it.

Its feasibility is well known, but few users have problems that video telephony would solve. AT&T's Picturephone trials in the 1960s were a well-publicized failure. German researchers have shown that video does enhance the effectiveness of business communications, but we believe that it will be a long time before this message is accepted by users.

- It will be expensive.

Studies in France and Germany have suggested that video telephony could cost at least ten times as much as voice telephony. The price differential will undoubtedly decrease, but it will still be a factor of at least four by the end of the century, and market research indicates that it will have to fall to at most two before the service becomes widely accepted.

In France, it is suggested that low-speed, low-quality video telephony will be introduced first, leading to a higher-quality broadband service by about 1995. This is a plausible scenario; at any rate, video telephony will not have a major role in broadband until at least the late 1990s.

TV Distribution

The market for wired TV distribution is potentially huge, opening up the prospect of pushing fiber broadband access into the residential sector. A number of factors will delay this, however:

- Fiber is not essential for a good cable TV service. Coaxial cable-based systems are still cheaper. Teletronic Communications of Canada, for example, offers a hybrid coax system combining analog TV with digital voice and data, and this can satisfy most residential requirements.
- There are various regulatory obstacles to the delivery of voice and cable TV services over the same physical connection.
- Cable TV ventures, especially in Europe, are in any case having difficulty in achieving financial success. There is little incentive for anyone to try technologically adventurous experiments.

The first two factors will gradually diminish in importance; fiber will become increasingly competitive with coax. The third will start to disappear when high definition television becomes available around 1995, offering a premium quality service that will not be available off-air. Fiber will compete here with direct broadcasting by satellite.

The distribution of entertainment TV is therefore unlikely to justify the introduction of fiber into the residential sector—on strict rate of return criteria—until the late 1990s. There are already projects, though, in the U.S. and France, justified on strategic grounds, in which fiber is being introduced into residential networks for TV. These will continue to be developed where an investment-led strategy is being adopted, making an important contribution to progress with broadband.

Means: How Will it be Achieved?

Key decisions about the future shape of broadband communications are being made now. A consensus is forming that the first broadband services will be accessed over fiber links, with a channel rate around 150–160 Mb/s. This will be the basic access rate; higher-speed access will probably be around 600 Mb/s. The following two sections describe the technology that will pro-vide the transmission and switching for broadband. The third component of the network, the terminal equipment, remains much less well defined.

A new technology, which will probably be ready in time for second-generation broadband systems in the late 1990s, is coherent optics. This will allow the development of tunable receivers for optical signals, using similar principles to those of radio engineering, and will greatly increase both the sensitivity and the capacity of fiber systems.

Transmission: Optical Fiber

Optical fiber, invented barely twenty years ago, is now clearly established as the transmission medium of choice for telecommunications. It is already the major medium for long distance transmission in the U.S., U.K., and Germany, and fiber access is beginning to appear in local loops as well. End-to-end single-mode fiber will be a feature of much high-value wide area communications in the next ten years. It will be the key element in making broadband a practical proposition, offering far greater transmission capacity and higher communication quality than copper.

Fiber design has evolved to maximize transmission capacity. The major constraints on silica fiber capacity, in the order in which fiber design has addressed them since the late 1960s, are:

- Power loss, through the absorption of light in the fiber
- Interference between the different light modes transmitted along the fiber
- Signal dispersion caused by two effects: the light at different wavelengths in the transmitted beam has different refractive indices (material dispersion); and some of the light travels in the cladding, rather than in the fiber core (waveguide dispersion)

Power loss problems have been minimized by choosing light wavelengths for which absorption is minimized. The first wavelength used was $0.8\,\mu$. Later, it was found that $1.3\,\mu$ light had even lower absorption characteristics, and $1.5\,\mu$ light lower still. The three windows for fiber optic transmission are the small wavelength ranges around these values, all of which are used in current fiber systems.

Interference between different modes was initially tackled by introducing graded index fiber, having a refractive index that varied across its breadth, to equalize the transmission speeds of the modes. Graded index fiber is expensive to produce, and in many applications has been superseded by a simpler solution: single-mode fiber, which is so slender that only one mode can propagate along it. Single-mode fiber has considerably greater capacity than graded index fiber, and, in volume, is cheaper to produce. Its small size means, however, that more expensive light sources have to be used to send light along it, and also that joining strands together is more difficult and costly. These drawbacks favor graded index fiber for short-distance links, such as those used in LANs. In wide area networks, even for the subscriber loop, single-mode fiber is favored increasingly.

The two forms of dispersion can be made to counteract one another by careful design of the refractive index profile of a single-mode fiber. The newest high-performance fiber systems use this effect to create very low loss characteristics over a wide range of wavelengths.

Switching: Fast Packet Technology

The first integrated narrowband and broadband switches will be deployed in the early 1990s, and will make use of packet-switching techniques. While packet-switching has had a disappointing level of take-up in the past, the flexibility it offers will be indispensable for handling the wide range of user demands that a broadband network will have to cope with.

Without it, user access connections will have to be divided up into fixed channels, with one channel for each desired speed, and this will impose an unacceptable degree of inflexibility and of inefficient network usage.

Realizing the importance of this new topic, switch suppliers all over the developed world have been turning their attention to it. CCITT standards discussions initially used the term "new transfer modes" for it, but now refer to "asynchronous transfer modes." AT&T uses the term "wideband packet technology" while others in the U.S. speak simply of "fast packet-switching"; in Europe, asynchronous time division switching has been a key element in the RACE program of collaborative research, and differs only slightly from the techniques being developed in the U.S.

Simpler circuit-switched equipment will be used for early services, dedicated to a small range of high-speed applications and staying totally separate from voice and low-speed data communications. IBA, however, will require the use of packet switches, or hybrid circuit-/packet-switched exchanges. Some suppliers believe that it will be possible to upgrade their ISDN exchanges for broadband adding a broadband module, but existing non-digital exchanges will have to be replaced altogether before broadband services can be offered.

Biography

Stephen Timms studied at Cambridge University, England, where he was awarded a senior scholarship and the degrees of MA in mathematics and MPhil in control engineering and operational research. He has ten years experience of consultancy in telecommunications markets, focusing on the provision of advice to European and U.S. telcos and equipment suppliers.

Mr. Timms has been a Principal Consultant at Ovum since 1986, and was the lead author for the Ovum reports, "Broadband Communications: The Commercial Impact," 1987, and "ISDN: Customer Premises Equipment," 1988. He is at present working on a major study of user migration routes to ISDN, which has been commissioned from Ovum by the Eurodata Foundation on behalf of ten European PTTs.

Implications of New Network Services on BISDN Capabilities

B. Amin-Salehi   G.D. Flinchbaugh   L.R. Pate

Bell Communications Research
331 Newman Springs Road
Red Bank, New Jersey 07701, USA

ABSTRACT

BISDN is the target network for supporting interactive and distributive services in the 1990s and beyond. BISDN capabilities are expected to be introduced in the early to mid-1990s, and will use single-mode fiber for transmission and SONET/ATM for multiplexing and switching. User applications in the next decade will undergo a dramatic change, evolving from medium to high-speed communication requirements, and from single-media applications to applications requiring a vast range of bandwidths as well as integration of different types of media. These factors place special demands on future networks and pose a challenge to network designers. This paper discusses some of the new broadband services that emerging user applications will rely on, and the implications that these services have on the capabilities and functions required for the BISDN architecture, switching, transport and signaling.

1. INTRODUCTION

Rapid advances in optical transmission and VLSI electronic technologies and progress in standardization efforts have brought the realization of the broadband ISDN (BISDN) closer to reality. BISDN has the promise of enabling network providers to offer many new services in the next decade. It delivers:

- The flexibility to transport and switch a diverse range of services with bandwidth requirements from a few kb/s to several hundred Mb/s;

- The capability to support voice, wide-bandwidth video and high-speed data services; and

- The versatility to become a unified transport network supporting the above services, thus bringing cost savings to the network provider by avoiding the deployment and maintenance of service-specific networks.

The number of local area networks (LANs) has been growing at an average rate of 29 percent per year [1], representing a tremendous market potential for providing LAN interconnectivity. This demand arises both from geographical dispersion of the customers' locations and the desire for inter-customer computer communications. The operating speeds of these networks today range from 10 Mb/s to 100 Mb/s. The 64-kb/s-based ISDN may not meet the delay requirements expected by the LAN customers. Moreover, the

LAN to ISDN access protocol adaptation necessary for supporting LAN interconnectivity by 64-kb/s-based ISDN is complex and presents a severe performance bottleneck. Switched Multi-megabit Data Service (SMDS) is a high-speed, connectionless data service that provides both high transmission speed (up to 155 Mb/s), low delay and a simple, efficient protocol adaptation for LAN interconnection.

The network penetration of optical transmission facilities with huge amounts of transmission capacity coupled with the introduction of broadband switching has brought the possibility of network providers offering residential video services. Advancements in the computer industry have stimulated interest and led to experimentation with premises-based multimedia applications. To enable interconnectivity between islands supporting these services, BISDN needs to provide transport, switching and control functions required by these applications.

This paper discusses three categories of emerging services that are expected to be supported by the BISDN, namely: SMDS, video distribution services, and multimedia services. Section 2 of this paper is devoted to motivation and definition of SMDS, telecommunications network-provided video services and multimedia applications. This is followed by a discussion of transport, switching, signaling and control requirements of these services in Section 3. Section 4 then describes the BISDN architecture that may be deployed in the early to mid-1990s. This section also assesses the capabilities of the BISDN to meet the functional requirements of the broadband services detailed in Section 3. The conclusion of this paper summarizes the capabilities of the BISDN to support broadband services and lists some issues requiring further investigation.

2. BROADBAND SERVICES

The services to be offered by telecommunications networks are becoming increasingly diversified. New service opportunities that address this trend in both residential and business environments extend beyond voice and low-speed data applications. This section describes three new categories of services that can be provided by the BISDN.

2.1 Switched Multi-megabit Data Service

2.1.1 Motivation: High-speed data communications has rapidly entered the office environment due to two synergistic technological trends:

- The availability of LAN technology with high-capacity, low-delay performance at a low per-port interconnection cost, and

0-8186-2797-2/92 $3.00 © 1990 IEEE

- A dramatic improvement in the ratio of processing power-to-cost of computing equipment.

The combination of powerful desktop workstations and very high-speed local networking has led to the development of sophisticated "distributed processing" techniques which are used to integrate distributed computers and other resources into a unified system. Such a system can provide users with real-time access to shared files and executable software. Moreover, the growth of distributed applications is likely to continue as they bring users increases in productivity, management and control.

As more clusters of hosts and workstations interconnected by high-speed local networks appear, the need to bridge together these islands of high-performance computing arises. In the past, low speed links were used; however, many important applications could not be extended to remote locations due to their delay requirements. Recently, customers have begun to use T1 facilities to interconnect their islands of computing into a geographically distributed, high-speed environment. But customers are still demanding higher transmission rates than can be provided by the public network. Clearly, an opportunity exists for an economical, high-speed data service which will integrate easily into the customer's current and evolving data communication environment while providing high performance and high reliability.

2.1.2 Service Definition: Bellcore has defined a high-speed, connectionless, public packet-switched data service called Switched Multi-megabit Data Service (SMDS) [2]. Many of the service features of SMDS are similar to the functions performed by LAN equipment. This allows subscribers who are experienced in the use of LAN technology to use SMDS without significant changes to their communication architecture. SMDS is a connectionless service based on the exchange of variable-length customer data packets[1].

SMDS uses the North American Telephone Numbering Plan which is consistent with the 15 digit CCITT E.164 ISDN addressing standard. An extension is included to allow for group addressing. Group addressing permits a number of Subscriber-Network Interfaces (SNIs) to be indicated by a single group address. Also, customers may have multiple addresses per SNI. For security reasons, the source address within every packet is verified as being legitimately assigned to the SNI. SMDS customers may limit their own degree of connectivity by means of source and destination address screening. By appropriately combining address screening options, a subscriber can form a "logical private network."

Since customer throughput requirements and CPE capabilities vary widely, "access classes" have been defined for SMDS. Each access class supports a particular rate of information flow by restricting the average bit rate in each direction across the SNI while supporting the high peak bit rates needed for low delay. Separate access classes may be used for sending and receiving information across the SNI. Access classes are achieved by means of a "credit manager" mechanism within the SMDS Interface Protocol (SIP).

As currently defined, SMDS will not provide real-time monitoring of error conditions or network management

information to subscribers. In the future, however, such information may be offered to subscribers as an optional service. Such optional services would take advantage of the network provider's operations capabilities to collect and analyze error and performance information. This information can be useful to subscribers for their own network management systems.

Of the three types of broadband services examined in this paper, SMDS is the most well defined and will be the first introduced in a public offering. Current operating telephone company plans are to roll out an early availability SMDS in 1991. The line interfaces will be DS1 and DS3 with several access classes that are yet to be determined. Later, as technology matures and market demand evolves, SONET access interfaces will be offered in addition to DS1 and DS3.

2.2 Video Services

Two types of video services with promising market potential in the coming years are entertainment distribution services and retrieval services. The former are targeted at residential customers while the latter are of use to both residential and business customers.

2.2.1 Switched Access Television: Since the introduction of Community Antenna Television (CATV) in the 1960s, many service providers have been using this medium to provide services in the fields of education, sports and entertainment. One common characteristic of these services separating them from public TV broadcast is that unlike ordinary television, the TV signal is transmitted by cable or microwave to a predetermined community of interest, thereby allowing the service providers to charge premiums for their service.

In the USA, CATV systems are based on NTSC coded analog video signals, frequency division multiplexed into 6 MHz bands. The NTSC signal uses a 3.5 MHz color subcarrier. The color and richness in color of the reproduced signal depend on the phase and amplitude values of the color subcarrier. Transmission impairments such as crosstalk, phase and amplitude distortion can cause degradation of the signal quality. Some coding schemes exist that compensate for many of the degradations of the NTSC video, producing an extended quality television (EQTV) [3]. High definition television (HDTV) further increases the resolution of the TV signal which becomes important for larger size screen television sets. Both EQTV and HDTV require more bandwidth than NTSC video. Thus, providing higher quality video signals entails using higher transmission capacity. Also, increasing the number of television channels results in the increase of the transmission capacity required for CATV systems.

BISDN allows for switched access television. Switched access television has several advantages over the traditional distribution networks. First, it provides customers with both higher quality signals and increased selectivity without increasing the transmission capacity of the distribution network. Second, it removes the requirement for scrambling at the source and descrambling of the signal at the receiver which are utilized by the CATV service vendors to bar unauthorized users from programming reception. The need for scrambling stems from the fact that all channels are broadcast to all users. Switched access television also

---

1. At the present time, the maximum SMDS packet size is specified to be 9188 octets.

introduces the possibility for more flexible billing such as *pay per viewing* in addition to the monthly billing option. Figure 1 shows the distribution of CATV via traditional coaxial cable distribution networks and via BISDN.

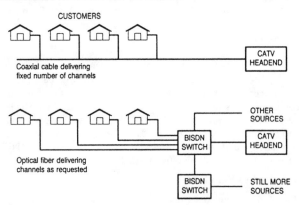

Figure 1. Coaxial Cable and BISDN Distribution of CATV.

2.2.2 Video on Demand: In recent years, the widespread use of video cassette recorders coupled with the growing abundance of video vendors that rent video cassettes and equipment has demonstrated an increasing desire on the part of residential users to have control over timing and selection of entertainment program viewing. With BISDN, the users can call a video information center or a service vendor via a low-speed data or signaling channel and select a particular still image or live video segment from the library or the vendor's archives. Once the required video file is selected, the video signal is switched via BISDN to the user, as shown in Figure 2.

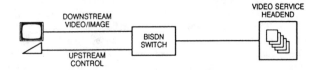

Figure 2. Video-On-Demand Service.

With this service, the users are no longer required to buy or rent video cassettes and VCRs. Besides residential entertainment, there are many more applications for this service in the fields of business, real-estate, education and medicine.

At the present time, compressed teleconference quality video is available using a DS3 interface. By the early 1990s, entertainment quality video (NTSC) should be available using SONET virtual tributary capabilities. A wide range of video services with flexible means of control will be possible when ATM/SONET multiplexing and switching equipment is introduced in the early to mid-1990s.

2.3 Multimedia Services and Applications

Multimedia services and applications are rapidly emerging as a result of some important developments in the computer industry including:

- Faster processing and more memory to handle high-resolution, bit-mapped displays,
- Distributed processing,
- Multi-tasking operating systems,
- Windowing systems,
- Sophisticated graphics processing,
- Support of video on a workstation[2], and
- Stereo audio support.

With the advent of these and other supporting technologies, the applications of today's computer user have evolved from text-based applications to highly sophisticated graphics and image based applications. While the needs of the simpler applications were met by low-speed connections (1200 b/s - 2400 b/s), the more complex applications require direct high-speed connections to a computer or access to a local area network. In response to the evolution of applications and the growing prevalence of distributed processing and expensive specialized resources, users want to be able to run these applications over a distance. Currently, however, unless a private network is installed, they are almost entirely limited to communication within the same floor or building. The evolving broadband network has the potential to provide the wide ranging, sophisticated, and ubiquitous support that these multimedia services require.

2.3.1 Some Representative Applications: A multimedia application is one that can include several different types of media such as audio, video, encoded text, raster and vector graphics, image data, and control data. Some major areas where multimedia applications are useful and growing in demand are:

Medicine	Investment Banking
Architecture	Graphic Arts
Entertainment	Engineering
Education	Scientific Visualization
Consulting	On-job Training
Desktop Publishing	Advertising
Video Editing	Research

To give the reader an idea of typical multimedia applications, four core applications useful in all of these areas are described briefly.

Multimedia Call and Conference

Perhaps the most basic multimedia application is the multimedia call or conference that allows multiple parties to communicate using audio, video, graphics, text, or some other medium that is most convenient. A multimedia conference can be much more than just an audio and video link between users. The participants can co-edit or annotate documents and images, demonstrate techniques or procedures using a video window, and take "meeting notes" simply by saving on-screen snapshots of the contents of different windows (video, graphics, or text) as the meeting progresses. Audio processing and special video hardware can allow side conferences for two or more users who want to talk privately during an ongoing conference. The main conference is still audible to the side conferees, but the audio level is mixed lower than the side conference. An important issue for consideration is the floor control policies to be implemented. Control of who can be seen, who can control cameras, audio mix, volume, and effects must be decided and may vary with each conference group.

---

2 Video support is becoming very prevalent. Major workstation vendors support or are planning to support it in their upcoming product lines. Various PCs also support video, and in fact a video board is available that will fit any PC with a 386 bus.

Small, intimate groups may choose to let all participants have control relying on social protocols to prevent anarchy. Larger groups probably would want to impose a policy limiting the number of people with control to a small group or an individual moderator. There is no set limit on the size of a multimedia conference, however human factors issues, such as the number of conferees that can be simultaneously presented to a user, and control policy may restrict the number of active participants before technology does.

Multimedia Mail

Multimedia mail is an extension of the text-based electronic mail model. It allows the user to incorporate audio, video, graphics, images, and text into a message. The range of the available media enables the user to send information in the most natural format. Separate information streams can be synchronized so that, for example, a specified frame in the video can trigger a graphics overlay or an additional audio track. This feature can be used to create a tutorial, an advertisement, or to provide cues for the user to perform some action.

Multimedia Database

The emergence of convenient optical mass storage and hypertext or hypermedia [4] user interfaces combine to provide a very suitable platform for a networked reference service with information available on a wide range of topics including art, history, science, and music. In addition, tutorials and demonstrations can be recorded on optical disc and used for educational and training purposes. Home users can browse through shopping catalogs stored in an optical disc database accessed through the network.

Other Multimedia Applications Based on Shared Resources

Many of the sophisticated resources used in multimedia applications offer strong motivation for sharing them as a network resource among many users. Examples include specialized processors for graphics processing, image processing, media conversion, audio enhancement, and video editing. Often the resources are expensive, based on rapidly changing underlying technology, require complicated or expensive maintenance, or are used infrequently. Other resources such as conference bridges have functional reasons for centralization.

2.3.2 Network Support of Multimedia Applications: Multimedia applications are based on multimedia services. Frequently these services will be very basic components that can be combined to form other, more complex services. No assumption is made in this paper about who owns these services or where they reside on the network. It is assumed that as services develop and as the economic and regulatory environments evolve, the lines of ownership and placement within the network will change. For this reason, flexibility of the network and uniformity of service interfaces become very important.

Figure 3 shows an example of a multimedia workstation connected to an integrated digital network that offers access to shared resources and multimedia services.

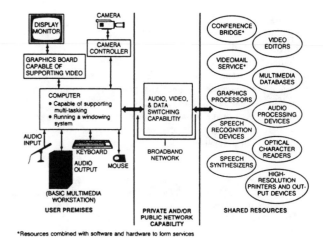

*Resources combined with software and hardware to form services

Figure 3. Multimedia Network Environment.

Many permutations of the workstation are possible. The audio input and output could be replaced with a telephone or the graphics/video board for the computer could be replaced with a second monitor for display of video. Some workstations might not support video at all. Today's implementations of this multimedia environment typically have separate networks and switching for audio, video, and data and use analog video. In the future, with an integrated broadband network and digital video, all information can be handled on the same network and the switching capability can be handled in the same manner. The shared resources can be owned by the network provider, the user, or another private company. The resources can be combined with each other directly or augmented by dedicated software and hardware to form a new service as in the case of the conference bridge and the video mail services.

3. SERVICE REQUIREMENTS

Emerging broadband services will exhibit diversity in many respects. Differences include bandwidth allocation, control overhead, and traffic statistics among others. In order for the broadband network to effectively support the new services, it is essential that network designers fully understand the capabilities and functions that these services will require from the network. This section is devoted to a description of these service requirements.

3.1 SMDS

Below is a discussion that identifies some of the requirements that SMDS places on the broadband network in terms of performance, control, switching and processing, and operations support.

3.1.1 Performance: One of the primary objectives of SMDS is to provide LAN-like capabilities over a large geographical area. Such a goal will certainly push the limits of existing technology and place stringent requirements on the performance of the supporting broadband network. In order to become a useful communication medium for distributed processing applications, the network supporting SMDS needs to meet tight end-to-end delay and error requirements. Such performance requirements exist not only for point-to-point applications, but also for point-to-multipoint ones. Studies of typical applications have led to the formulation of performance requirements which are documented in Technical Advisories published by Bellcore [5]. Since SMDS is scheduled to be introduced as the first public broadband service, early implementations of the broadband network can be dedicated to supporting the service. As such, the network can be specifically engineered to meet the performance requirements of SMDS. Eventually, however, the network will be called upon to support other broadband services which will share the transport, switching and processing resources with SMDS. These additional services will complicate the task of meeting SMDS performance objectives.

3.1.2 Control: Although SMDS has been defined as a connectionless service with no signaling or call processing overhead, the network will be required to implement access control mechanisms to limit the average rate at which SMDS customers can send and receive information. This type of control is essential since customer throughput requirements are likely to be quite diverse. Central to SMDS access control is the credit manager algorithm. In effect, the credit manager algorithm maintains an information unit balance. Withdrawals are made from the balance when information is transferred, while deposits are made at regular intervals in time. When the balance drops below a specified threshold, customer data is discarded. The discarding of data continues until the balance rises back above the threshold. The network must implement this functionality for traffic both entering and leaving the network. In addition to access control, the network is also required to have rate internal controls to limit congestion within the network.

3.1.3 Switching and Processing: The SMDS functions of switching, multicasting, address verification and screening, and routing will place challenging demands on the switching and processing entities within the network. Since SMDS subscribers may transmit at rates up to 155 Mb/s, the switching and processing entities must be capable of high throughput. And, since SMDS is defined with stringent end-to-end delay requirements, switching and processing delay must be carefully controlled.

3.1.4 Operations Support: Many corporations are finding it increasingly burdensome to perform operations or management tasks on their own private data networks. Thus, a particular advantage of having the operating telephone companies provide a high-speed data communications service such as SMDS is their tremendous operations experience in planning, engineering, provisioning, managing, administering, and maintaining large networks. It is critical that the operations aspects of SMDS be addressed early in its development cycle. Currently, two of the more difficult and important operations issues of SMDS are billing and feedback of customer usage information. Several approaches for billing of SMDS are under study at this time. Among these approaches are flat rate and usage sensitive billing. Usage sensitive billing, which tracks the aggregate amount of information a customer transmits, may be particularly difficult given the high bandwidth and burstiness of SMDS traffic. Although not currently part of the SMDS service definition, feedback of customer usage information may be a valuable additional service to provide to customers. It could be used by subscribers for better control and management of their own networks. Such an added feature requires that selected characteristics of customer traffic be measured and recorded. The operations systems supporting SMDS are a

convenient way to collect, process, store and disseminate the customer usage information. The type of data collected and the manner in which it is fed back to the customer are currently being investigated.

3.2 Video Services

In the following section the network requirements for switched access television and video on demand service are discussed separately.

3.2.1 Switched Access Television: The bandwidth requirements to carry NTSC, EQTV and HDTV video are respectively: 115 Mb/s, 243 Mb/s and 1.2 Gb/s. With low bit rate coding and other compression schemes, however, the NTSC video signal rate can be reduced to the 44.7 Mb/s (DS3) rate while EQTV and HDTV channels are reduced to 150 Mb/s. Thus, switching at the maximum rate of 150 Mb/s would suffice for supporting all the entertainment video services reviewed in Section 2. It may be desirable for a customer to simultaneously receive a number of video channels. Thus, the customer access facilities may require a transmission capacity of several 150 Mb/s channels. When several customers access the same video channel simultaneously, multicast switching and remote switching capabilities help in reducing the transmission capacity required for the facilities between the headend video station, the switch, and the interoffice facilities.

Traditional voice networks have a typical call arrival rate of a few calls/hr per line during busy hour. In switched access television, changing TV channels requires a call request. With short TV programming intervals, call arrival rates during network peak loading conditions may become as frequent as a few calls/min [6]. This phenomenon imposes a much higher processing capacity requirement on the switch than voice services.

Switched access television also requires significantly shorter setup delays than telephony. Compared with the maximum voice setup delays of 3 seconds, the tolerable delay for the user in changing a TV channel is about 100 ms [7]. Another parameter for contrast between voice and entertainment video services is call holding time. Whereas holding time for a voice call is on the average 3 minutes, the duration of a video call, for both switched access TV and video on demand may range from 15 minutes to 3 hours.

3.2.2 Video on Demand: Due to the entertainment nature of many video on demand applications, there are many similarities in the service characteristics of video on demand and switched access television (*e.g.,* bandwidth and call holding time). On the other hand, there are some important differences. In particular, by definition video on demand services have a point-to-point nature. This removes the requirement of point-to-multipoint switching from the BISDN switch while demanding more capacity for the transmission facilities. Since video on demand is a new service, it is reasonable to expect that initially, it will have lower volume and call arrival rates than switched access television. Less stringent response times may also be tolerated by the users for video on demand than those for switched access television.

3.3 Multimedia Services

Multimedia applications have a wide range of traffic characteristics and network requirements that make them a special challenge for network designers. The requirements are broken down into the categories of performance, signaling and control, transport and switching, and operations support.

3.3.1 Performance: The performance required for multimedia applications and services depends greatly on the particular application. Highly interactive applications such as using the mouse to draw on the screen require fraction of a second response times or the user quickly becomes annoyed. Other applications such as typing text into a file are much more tolerant since some delay can be hidden while the user thinks. In both of these cases, the variance of the delay is almost more important than the delay itself. If the user expects to wait a certain amount of time, then he or she can better adjust to work around the delay.

The media involved is also an important consideration. Spurious errors in audio or video transmission may be annoying, but usually the basic information content is preserved. Our eyes and ears are able to integrate over some erroneous information and concentrate on the message being sent. In contrast, spurious errors in data transmission can destroy the meaning of the information entirely. Audio or video services can often handle a low level of errors, but delay, and variance of delay may be intolerable. HDTV, in particular, may have very strict delay requirements. Conversely, for data services, delay may be acceptable in some cases.

Multimedia services will be more complex and require more processing to establish and control connections, but may still require fast setup times. Users, however, may not be tolerant of longer setup times just because the service is more complex. Long setup times decrease the revenue-producing utilization of shared resources and may lead users to counterproductive behavior. For example, users may stay connected to a resource just in case it will be needed in the future. This has far-reaching implications for resource sizing, traffic engineering, and pricing of the service.

3.3.2 Signaling and Control: Multimedia applications need multiple connections each with individual bandwidth and performance requirements. However, the signaling procedures specified to date for 64-kb/s-based ISDN bearer connections allow establishment of single connection calls for voice or data at the fixed rate of 64 kb/s. Discussions regarding capabilities to setup and control multimedia calls are just now starting in Committee T1 and CCITT. Signaling and control procedures are needed that allow for several connections that are part of a single call or application to be bundled and treated as a single logical unit by the network. Synchronization of each of these connections is also an important requirement so that the individual information arrives in the proper sequence at the appropriate time. Synchronization of information streams of two different media types would be needed, for example, for a tutorial application in which a graphics overlay must be synchronized with a video segment.

It is necessary to have signaling protocols that can support user to machine connections as well as connections in which the originator of the call is not one of the endpoints of the connection. For example, a database request might require one database to connect to another for additional information.

The network would have to provide for this remote connection setup. Signaling capability is also needed to separate call control from connection control [8] so that:

- Multimedia calls would require only one call setup (as opposed to one setup per connection),
- Connections for different media or processes could be easily added or removed from the call when a multimedia call is established.

The existing 64-kb/s-based ISDN signaling does not provide the capabilities needed for multi-point (where all of the endpoints need not be a person) call establishment or for conferencing. Today, conference calls are established through reservation of a network-based resource such as a conference bridge; at a previously agreed time, all the parties call the conference bridge to interconnect. With multicast call setup signaling, no scheduling will be required; the user would be able to request and establish a conference call with other parties in real time. The protocols needed for this signaling feature need to be developed and incorporated into the BISDN signaling procedures. A desirable feature for multiparty call control would be the capability to establish *private sub-channels* to support consultation among a subset of the participants in an ongoing conference call.

Network congestion control must also be considered. BISDN supports services with both constant bit rate (CBR) and variable bit rate (VBR) characteristics. CBR services require a fixed amount of bandwidth. For these services, bandwidth is allocated to each channel at call setup or through service order. The network can control congestion for these services rather easily by denying the user the requested bandwidth through signaling (*e.g.,* fast-busy signal). VBR services however have a random bandwidth demand, making congestion control a more difficult task.

3.3.3 Transport and Switching: Multimedia services need reliable, flexible, and integrated switching for the wide range of channel types that are required to support different media types (*e.g.,* audio, video, graphics, and data). Multimedia services also require channels of a range of bandwidths. Some services such as those involving live video and wideband graphics have very high bandwidth needs (hundreds of Mb/s), yet low-bandwidth, low-delay channels are also necessary for control. The bandwidth ranges for the different media are the result of differences in complexity of the application, sophistication of the hardware, and the format of the information. The level of interactivity for the application contributes to the range of bandwidth needed for control.

3.3.4 Operations Support: An effective operations system is imperative if network supported multimedia services are to be successfully deployed. Systems to handle billing, maintenance, testing, and provisioning must be designed to conform to new call models emerging as a result of multimedia applications that are different from those existing in the telephony model.

New billing models may be based on new parameters in addition to time or distance of a connection. Even though one part of a call may be unsuccessful, the remaining part of the call, billed on a prorated basis, may still be of value to the user.

Maintenance and testing systems are deeply affected by the potential complexity of multimedia calls. The impacts of individual component failures are high because many points of failure for services exist. Maintenance systems must try to consider all the possible configurations for testing and maintenance. Furthermore, since partitioning a service so as to isolate a fault becomes quite complex, regular and frequent maintenance and testing is imperative. High reliability and/or real-time failure identification and recovery are needed. An important tool for designing and fine tuning all of these systems will be detailed records showing such information as:

- Connection attempts,
- Connection failures,
- Resource failure or unavailability,
- Network actions involved,
- Endpoints involved,
- Time of each connection,
- Bandwidth (*e.g.*, peak, average) for each connection.

This information can be pared down or modified for customer billing and maintenance and support crews.

4. BROADBAND NETWORK ARCHITECTURE

This section describes the early to mid-1990s view of the BISDN architecture adopted by the Standards Committee T1. It describes some of the driving technologies behind the BISDN concept as well as the target architecture being used as a reference by network designers. The capabilities of the BISDN architecture are then examined in light of the service requirements which were presented in Section 3.

4.1 Properties of the BISDN Architecture

The BISDN architecture is based on

- Single-mode fiber transmission systems,

- SONET (Synchronous Optical Network) signal format at the physical layer of transmission, and

- ATM (Asynchronous Transfer Mode) for multiplexing and switching.

Optical fibers provide very large (up to a few Gb/s) transmission capacity, are immune to electromagnetic interference, and incur low operations costs. They have been proven to be a very reliable transmission medium surpassing the bit error rate (BER) of 10^{-9} for which broadband systems are currently being designed. A factor contributing to the cost efficiency of optical fiber systems is their long repeater spacing. Compared with the nominal requirement of 1.6 km for T-Carrier (1.5 Mb/s) systems, the repeater spacing for optical fiber systems operating at transmission speeds of 1.7 Gb/s has been reported [9] to be about 40 km.

At the physical layer of transmission, information will be carried in the SONET format. SONET is a byte-interleaved Synchronous Digital Hierarchy (SDH) which comprises a family of standard electrical synchronous transport signals (STS). STS signals may be converted to a family of standard optical carriers (OC). Through STS and OC interfaces, SONET provides a set of standard transmission interfaces for customer premises equipment, switches, distribution and interoffice transport systems.

ATM is the standard technique for multiplexing and switching in the target BISDN and is under intense study both in the USA and internationally. Information is carried in fixed-length cells within the payload of a SONET STS signal. Each cell is identified by an explicit Virtual Path/Virtual Channel Identifier (VPI/VCI) contained in the header of the cell. The explicit channel identification of ATM is expected to simplify multiplexing and switching of digital information. Different channels with different bandwidths are supported in the same transmission stream without requiring a transmission hierarchy for the channel rates. With synchronous transfer mode (STM) switching channels of different rates may require multiple switching fabrics, each designed to switch channels at one specific rate. This can entail additional equipment costs and increased complexity associated with multiple fabric control and operations support. With ATM cell switching, a single fabric can support multi-rate switching.

ATM also provides for flexible bandwidth allocation. Since the bandwidth of an ATM channel is determined by the rate at which the channel places cells into the transmission stream, the bandwidth of the channel is not limited to certain discrete values, such as 1.5 Mb/s and 45 Mb/s. Finally, ATM is planned to support bursty as well as fixed-rate CBR services.

4.2 The Target BISDN Architecture

Figure 4 shows a physical representation of the target BISDN.

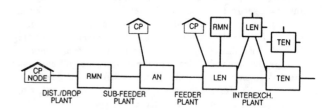

Figure 4. BISDN Architecture.

The transmission medium for the interoffice, feeder and distribution plant is single mode fiber. The user-network interface operates at the SONET rates of 155 Mb/s or 622 Mb/s. At the feeder and subfeeder plant, SONET rates of 622 Mb/s and 2.4 Gb/s are supported, and the inter-exchange facilities may have a transmission speed of 2.4 Gb/s or higher. SONET provides multiplexing of the subscriber channels with the minimum modularity of 155 Mb/s. Multiplexing of lower-rate channels is achieved by ATM through interleaving cells within the SONET payload. Other aspects of the BISDN architecture such as signaling and congestion control are currently under study.

4.3 Capabilities of the Target Architecture

A critical part of planning any network is to evaluate the capabilities of the architecture to provide the services for which the network was intended. In this paper, we have attempted to present several new broadband services, along with their requirements, and a view of the target network architecture. Below, the planned capabilities of that target architecture are assessed for supporting the services and their requirements.

4.3.1 Capabilities to Support SMDS: The transport protocol architecture of a broadband network supporting SMDS is shown in Figure 5 [10].

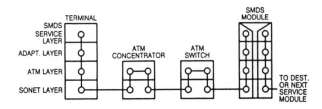

Figure 5. Protocol Architecture of the BISDN Supporting SMDS.

The SMDS service layer provides the functions required by SMDS using ATM for transfer of information. As mentioned earlier some of the functions required by SMDS include group addressing, address screening and verification, and routing. The SMDS handler in the Local Exchange Node (LEN) processes the SMDS packets. The service adaptation layer provides a segmentation and reassembly (SAR) function for SMDS by mapping the SMDS packets into the payload of ATM cells. Multiplexing and switching functions are provided by the ATM layer. SONET provides the physical layer functions.

The OC-3 (155 Mb/s) user-network interface will be sufficient to allow the transport of a customer's SMDS traffic. Since SMDS is a connectionless service and is designed to handle bursty sources, it can statistically share the access transport facilities with other services. Switching functions will be performed by ATM switches within the LENs. Most processing functions, including address verification and screening and routing, will be performed by the SMDS handler. Broadband network elements will have standard interfaces to operations systems, however the manner in which SMDS-specific operations tasks are performed is an area currently under study.

4.3.2 Capabilities to Support Video Services: For video services, the OC-12 (622 Mb/s) user-network interfaces allow the transport of up to 4 EQTV/HDTV channels. For lower-rate video signals (*e.g.*, NTSC video), more than four channels can be carried over OC-12 interfaces. OC-3 (155 Mb/s) interfaces may be sufficient for video on demand, since with this service the user would access only one channel at a time. Multicasting may be supported by the ATM cell switch or by SONET circuit switching in the target architecture. Due to the long holding times of video services, initially the video channels may be circuit switched. Signaling messages and protocols for video services have not been specified yet, but may be much simpler than those defined for interactive services (*e.g.*, telephony).

4.3.3 Capabilities to Support Multimedia Services: The major transmission, multiplexing, and switching needs for multimedia services are addressed in the planned BISDN architecture by single mode fiber, SONET, and ATM. As discussed in Section 3.3.2, the signaling and control issues raised by multimedia calls are just beginning to be addressed by committee T1 and CCITT. The areas of performance and operations are still under study.

5. CONCLUSION

Three representative services that are intended to be supported by the broadband network were presented: a connectionless data service, switched and on-demand video service, and multiparty/multimedia services. A brief description of each service's motivation and definition was followed by a discussion of the general requirements that these services would place on the broadband network. This was followed by a presentation of the current industry view of the emerging BISDN architecture. Based on this view, an assessment was made of the architecture's capabilities to meet the service requirements discussed earlier.

The current plan for the BISDN architecture addresses the service requirements for switching, transmission and multiplexing. Issues requiring further study include signaling, congestion control and performance. It is not yet possible to project with precision which broadband services will be in high demand during the next decade. What can be stated however is that a versatile and flexible BISDN will be well positioned to support the more complex services of the 1990s.

ACKNOWLEDGEMENTS
The authors acknowledge the helpful comments of their colleagues at Bellcore, including B-R. Chen, G. Dobrowski, J. Fleck, F. Gratzer, L. Linnell, L. Ludwig, R. Schnitzler, H. Sherry, D. Spears, and S. Walters.

REFERENCES

[1] "1987 Market Survey", *Data Communication Magazine*, January 1987, pp.85-93.

[2] C.F. Hemrick, R.W. Klessig, and J.M. McRoberts, "Switched Multi-megabit Data Service and Early Availability via MAN Technology," *IEEE Communications Magazine*, April 1988, Vol. 26, No. 4, pp. 9-14.

[3] D.R. Spears, "Broadband ISDN - Service Visions and Technological Realities," *International Journal of Digital and Analog Cabled Systems*, 1988, Vol. 1, pp. 3-18.

[4] J.B. Smith, S.F. Weiss, "Special Section on Hypertext: An Overview," *Communications of the ACM*, July 1988, Vol. 31, pp. 816-819.

[5] "Generic System Requirements in Support of Switched Multi-megabit Data Service," Bellcore Technical Advisory TA-TSY-000772, Issue 3, Oct. 1989.

[6] D.R. Spears, "Broadband ISDN Switching Capabilities from a Services Perspective," *IEEE Journal on Selected Areas of Communications*, Vol. SAC-5, No.8, October 1987, pp.1222-1230.

[7] Leonard Kleinrock, "Networks in the Nineties" Course Material, June 2, 1989.

[8] S.E. Minzer, D.R. Spears, "New Directions in Signaling for Broadband ISDN," *IEEE Communications Magazine*, February 1989, Vol. 27, No. 2, pp. 6-14.

[9] P. Kaiser, "Status and Future Trends in Terrestrial Optical Fiber Systems in North America," *IEEE Communications Magazine*, October 1987, Vol. 25, No. 10, pp. 8-21.

[10] B. Amin-Salehi, D.R. Spears, "Transport Example of a Connectionless Service," T1S1.1/88-426, October 10, 1988.

The Role of the Broadband Integrated Services Digital Network

Patrick E. White

THE BROADBAND INTEGRATED SERVICES Digital Network (BISDN) is commonly viewed as the next major step in the evolution of the switched telephone network. It is based on an infrastructure consisting of optical fiber transmission and high-speed electronic switching systems, at least in the early stages. The BISDN is designed to handle a wide variety of services ranging from voice to data and, ultimately, the distribution of high-quality entertainment video signals. BISDN is also expected to support multimedia services such as conferencing, which have subelements consisting of voice, data, and video.

In addition to supporting new services, the BISDN can reduce the costs of operating the network. This is accomplished by extending the integration provided by the narrowband ISDN on the loop to include the switching, signaling, and transport facilities in the rest of the network. For example, BISDN provides the capability to integrate the 56 or 64 kb/s network and the X.25 packet network, as well as the broad spectrum of providing networks that operate at 64 kb/s to 45 Mb/s. This latter capability is particularly important, since it enables the BISDN network operator to handle special services in a more standardized switched manner. Thus, the BISDN can minimize the need to build service-specific transmission and switching systems to support a broad mix of services, and it can effectively integrate network signaling with user information to reduce costs further.

This article provides an overview of the services and networking technologies under consideration for BISDN. It outlines future directions and challenges for broadband research and development, and discusses some of the key technology issues, particularly those concerned with the administration and control of broadband networks.

Broadband Services

Figure 1 illustrates some of the services being considered for the BISDN. As indicated in the previous section, some examples of these services include telemetry signals for remote meter reading, voice at a variety of bit rates and quality levels, low- to moderate-speed data for terminal/computer interactions, and higher-speed data for workstations and/or LAN interconnection. In addition to these services, consideration is also given to supporting various forms of high-quality graphical images and full-motion video signals on broadband networks [1].

Reprinted from *IEEE Communications Magazine*, March 1991, pages 116-119. Copyright © 1991 by The Institute of Electrical and Electronics Engineers, Inc. All rights reserved.

BISDN services are expected to have widely varying bandwidth, burstiness, and session length requirements. Thus, in comparison with the existing telephone network, which is optimized to carry voice (which has relatively fixed characteristics—bandwidth, attempts per busy hour, and session length), the BISDN must have considerably more flexibility in its design to meet its more diverse service requirements.

Bandwidth, burstiness, and session length variations are not the only figures of merit for future broadband services. In particular, some services, such as the distribution of entertainment video to the home, may have asymmetrical transmission requirements. For example, for the delivery of entertainment video signals to the home, a high-speed connection is required in the downstream direction, and a much-lower-speed connection is required in the upstream direction to the network, to carry channel-change requests and other supervisory signals.

Other services (for example, voice and data) can also have asymmetrical transmission characteristics. Voice information services, such as the familiar 976 services in the United States, are typically one way. Terminal/computer and computer/computer interactions are rarely symmetrical, but the direction of high-speed transmission may vary over the course of the session.

In response to this range of service requirements, the BISDN design is based on high-speed packet techniques, which

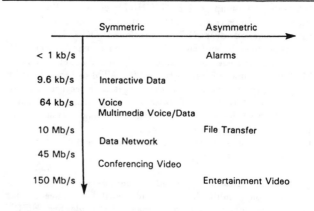

Fig. 1. Potential BISDN services.

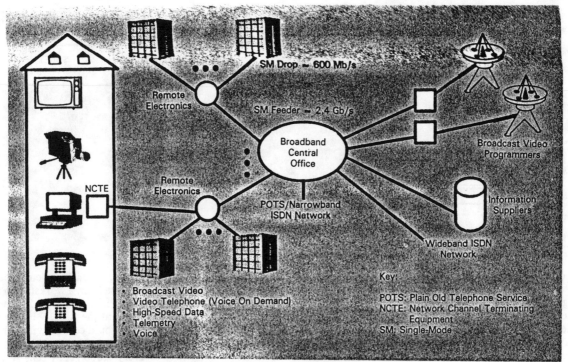

Fig. 2. Future broadband system.

will be discussed later. The basic concept is that high-speed packet networking can provide bandwidth flexibility in addition to handling asymmetrical communication streams in a single integrated network platform.

Broadband Architectures

Video Distribution

The architectures and technologies considered for broadband networks have evolved considerably since broadband systems research began in the middle to late 1970's. In the early planning, it was believed that the distribution of entertainment video signals to the home was the only broadband service worthy of consideration. Thus, there was a major emphasis on low-cost video delivery, in a manner compatible with existing Cable Television (CATV) systems, if at all possible. Key features of the early designs included analog video transmission over multimode fiber driven by Light-Emitting Diodes (LEDs) operating in the 850 nm region. Later, as digital delivery became more accepted, an important area of research for the early systems was the feasibility of using LEDs coupled with single-mode fiber to improve reliability and reduce costs [2].

Today, low-cost entertainment video delivery is still an important consideration, and analog modulation methods are not completely ruled out. However, as indicated in the discussion of potential broadband services, it is now recognized that broadband networks should be capable of handling a broad range of services, and that they should not be restricted to video distribution.

Figure 2 shows one of the architectures under consideration for video distribution. The major elements of the architecture include the central office, the remote electronics, and the fiber cable to each living unit. Entertainment video signals from a variety of sources—motion picture studios, broadcasters, and information suppliers (e.g., video-on-demand vendors)—terminate at the central office. From there, the signals are routed to the remote electronics sites, where they are made available to end-user customers on an as-needed basis. That is, in response to program change requests from the customer, the

remote electronics are capable of switching to any channel available from the broadband central office [3].

Due to the relatively high costs of providing fiber directly to the living unit, this architecture is commonly viewed as more long-term. The near-term alternative is to provide fiber to the "curb," or distribution pedestal serving a cluster of living units (typically four to eight). This approach permits the sharing of optoelectronic components at the terminating end of the fiber to reduce costs [4]. In other alternative architectures, "passive" optical multiplexing replaces the active electronic multiplexing/demultiplexing (mux/demux) capabilities in the remote electronics to reduce costs further [5]. Indeed, as illustrated in Figure 3, a passive fiber-to-the-curb architecture is economically competitive with copper loops for ISDN voice services and provides an important transition step towards full fiber-to-the-home deployment [6].

Asynchronous Transfer Mode

In recognition of the fact that the BISDN must support a range of services, a new transmission and switching technique termed Asynchronous Transfer Mode (ATM) was proposed.

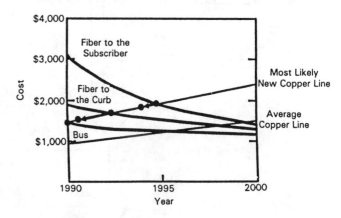

Fig. 3. Installed first costs.

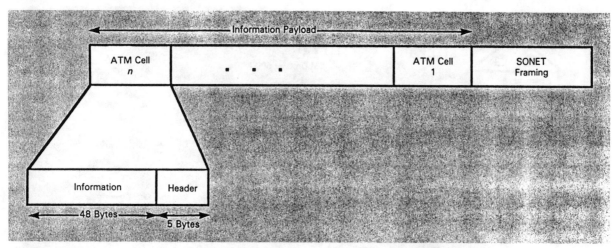

Fig. 4. ATM.

ATM combines the capabilities of Time-Division Multiplexing (TDM) to permit the efficient transport and switching of the wide variation in information services characteristics envisioned for the BISDN.

Two forms of ATM have been proposed to the International Consultative Committee for Telephone and Telegraph (CCITT). In one approach, ATM cells are embedded in a synchronous time multiplexed bit stream, the Synchronous Optical Network (SONET); in the other, they are not. The remaining discussion assumes the case where the cells are embedded in SONET [7].

Figure 4 provides an overview of this structure. Each ATM cell is 48 bytes long and has a 5-byte header. They occur at fixed intervals in the SONET frame. This makes ATM similar to TDM in the multiplexing and switching of real-time information streams. However, unlike TDM, the position of a particular ATM cell in the SONET frame is not necessarily unique to a particular customer's "call," and therefore it cannot be used for routing. Instead, the ATM header, which contains a destination address, must always be examined for routing, as in today's packet networks.

This combination of the properties of packet and TDM enables ATM to efficiently transport real-time information such as voice and video, while at the same time providing the flexibility to handle information at a variety of rates. This is illustrated in Fig. 5. In this picture, the end-user customer wishes to multiplex voice at 64 kb/s, data from a workstation at 10 Mb/s, and video at 45 Mb/s onto the BISDN network. If it is assumed that the network will operate at the BISDN H4 rate of 155.52 Mb/s, every third ATM cell would contain video information, 1 of every 15 ATM cells would contain data from the workstation, and 1 of every 2,000 ATM cells would contain voice. Thus, bandwidth variation is handled by the frequency of appearance of the associated cell in the network. Furthermore, since all cells are of the same size, both switch fabric and multiplexer designs are simplified.

Future Directions and Challenges

Congestion control in ATM networks is widely cited as one of the more important technical problems that need to be resolved before BISDN can be introduced on a large scale. There are several issues. First, there is little hard information available on the characteristics of the traffic that will be offered to the BISDN network. Second, there is no agreement on the procedures that will be used to efficiently mix traffic with widely varying characteristics on a single integrated network. Indeed, congestion control in broadband networks is currently an area of active research.

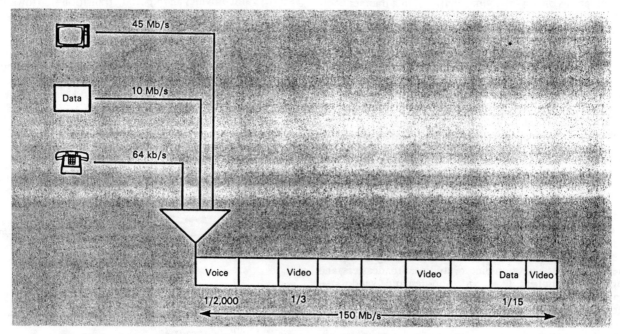

Fig. 5. Mapping services into ATM.

Other important problems include the selection and definition of which BISDN services are likely to have high customer demand and which should become the focus for network optimization efforts. Along the same lines, the development of more cost-competitive architectures to reduce the entry costs of BISDN, particularly for today's services, is critical for driving early large-scale deployment.

Excellent progress has been made in proposing low-cost fiber-to-the-curb architectures for voice services. However, an important issue for these plans is how to evolve them to support high-speed services, specifically the delivery of entertainment video services to the home.

For the longer term, continued research efforts should be maintained on high-speed optical delivery technology, dense wavelength-division multiplexing, and coherent detection. Continued effort should also be placed on switching technology for Terabit capacities. These efforts are needed to support the expected development of higher-bandwidth information services, as well as to provide the network architect with more flexibility to optimize the overall network.

References

[1] P. E. White, "The Broadband ISDN, The Next Generation Switching System," *ICC '86 Proc.*

[2] J. L. Gimlet *et al.*, "Transmission Experiments at 560 Mb/S and 150 Mb/s Using Single Mode Fiber and 1300 nm LEDs," *Proc. 11th Euro. Conf. on Opt. Commun.*, Oct. 1985.

[3] L. R. Linnell, "A Wideband Local Access Architecture Using Emerging Technology Components," *IEEE J. on Sel. Areas in Commun.*, vol. JSAC-4, pp. 612–618, July 1986.

[4] "Fiber in the Loop Architecture Summary Report," Bellcore, SR-TSY-001681, issue 1, June 1990.

[5] D. W. Faulkner, D. B. Payne, and J. R. Stern, "Passive Optical Telephony Networks and Broadband Evolution," *Proc. Globecom '88*, Nov. 1988.

[6] P. W. Shumate, "Cost Projections for Fiber in the Loop," *IEEE LCS*, vol. 1, no. 1, pp. 73–76, Feb. 1990.

[7] S. E. Minzer, "Broadband ISDN and Asynchronous Transfer Mode (ATM)," *IEEE Commun. Mag.*, pp. 17–24 and 57, Sept. 1989.

Biography

Patrick E. White is Assistant Vice President of Network Transmission Technology at Bell Communications Research (Bellcore) in Morristown, New Jersey. This organization formulates and verifies national and international network transmission standards and requirements for Bellcore client companies. Specific areas of current interest include SONET, Asymmetric Digital Subscriber Line/High-bit-rate Digital Subscriber Line (ADSL/HDSL) technology, microwave and radio transmission, and end-user perception of transmission quality.

He began his professional career in 1973 at Bell Laboratories in Naperville, Illinois. He developed software for the first 1AESS™ telephone switching system. He was promoted to Supervisor in 1978, with responsibility for ensuring the quality of new software releases for the 2, 2B, and 3ESS telephone switching systems. He later supervised a team of engineers developing software for the Voice Storage System, a network-based computer system capable of recording busy and unanswered calls, and recording messages for later delivery. As Supervisor, he also led groups conducting exploratory studies of integrated voice/data services in the telephone network, later called Integrated Services Digital Network (ISDN). In this capacity, he was a member of the AT&T team that participated in international discussions leading to the development of standards recommendations for the ISDN. He was promoted to Department Head in 1983, with responsibility for conducting exploratory studies of high-speed fiber-optic-based telephone networks capable of transporting entertainment video signals together with voice and data.

He was transferred to Bellcore on January 1, 1984, in conjunction with the divestiture of AT&T. As Division Manager of Network Architecture Research, he had similar responsibilities for research in high-speed networks. His research team developed one of the first prototype communications networks capable of transporting 150 Mb/s video signals simultaneously with 56 Mb/s packet-switched voice and data. In January 1988, he was promoted to Assistant Vice President of New Architecture and Service Concepts Planning, with responsibility for formulating network architecture plans and developing new services concepts. His center developed Bellcore's Information Networking Architecture (INA), a new network architecture for the Information Age. In January 1990, he assumed his current position.

Dr. White holds a Ph.D. degree in electrical engineering/computer science from Northwestern University, Evanston, Illinois, and is a member of the Eta Kappa Nu and Tau Beta Pi national engineering honor societies. He is a member of the IEEE and the Association of Computer Manufacturers (ACM). He edits articles on telephone switching systems for *IEEE Communications Magazine* and has guest edited a special issue of the *IEEE Journal on Selected Areas in Communications* on broadband switching systems. He has authored numerous papers on topics ranging from software engineering and ISDN to high-speed communications systems.

™ESS is a trademark of AT&T.

Chapter 5: Asynchronous Transfer Mode (ATM) and Synchronous Optical Network/Synchronous Digital Hierarchy (SONET/SDH)

Synchronous versus asynchronous transfer

When the standards work on B-ISDN began in the mid-1980s, most CCITT participants generally assumed that some form of synchronous TDM technique would be used, as is the case with the basic- and primary-rate-access methods for ISDN. Under this assumption, the interface structure that was proposed was

$$j \times H4 + k \times H2 + l \times H1 + m \times H0 + n \times B + D,$$

where D, B, H0, and H1 (H11 or H12) are narrowband ISDN channels; H2 and H4 are new B-ISDN fixed-rate channels; and j, k, l, m, and n are constants that depend on the particular service offered. H2 was proposed to be in the range of 30 to 45 Mbps and H4 was proposed to be in the range of 120 to 140 Mbps.

Although the synchronous TDM approach is a natural extension of narrowband ISDN, it does not provide the best model for B-ISDN. Two basic disadvantages of the synchronous approach for high-speed transmission are the following:

(1) The synchronous TDM approach does not provide a flexible interface for meeting a variety of needs. At the high data rates offered by B-ISDN, a wide variety of applications — and many different data rates — might need to be switched. One or two fixed-rate channel types do not provide a structure that can easily accommodate this need. Furthermore, many data (as opposed to voice or video) applications are bursty in nature (that is, data transmission occurs in intermittent bursts) and can be more efficiently handled with some sort of packet-switching approach.

(2) The use of multiple high data rates (for example, a number of H2 and H4 channels) complicates the switching system. The synchronous TDM approach would require switches that can handle data streams of multiple high data rates, in contrast to narrowband ISDN, which has only the 64-Kbps data stream to switch.

Thus, synchronous TDM has been rejected. However, it is still possible to multiplex several ATM streams using synchronous TDM techniques to achieve transmission interfaces that exceed the rate of operation of ATM switches and multiplexers.

ATM overview

ATM is similar in concept to frame relay. Both ATM and frame relay take advantage of the reliability and fidelity of modern digital facilities to provide faster packet switching than X.25. ATM, at its higher data rate, is even more streamlined in its functionality than frame relay, as we shall see.

ATM is a packet-oriented transfer mode. Like frame relay and X.25, it allows multiple logical connections to be multiplexed over a single physical interface. The information flow on each logical connection is organized into fixed-size packets called "cells." As with frame relay, there is no link-by-link error control or flow control.

Figure 5-1 shows the overall hierarchy of transport in an ATM-based network. This hierarchy is seen from the point of view of the internal network functions needed to support ATM, as well as from the point of view of the user-network functions. The ATM layer consists of the virtual channel level and the virtual path level; these are discussed in the next subsection. The physical layer can be divided into the following three functional levels:

(1) Transmission path level. This level extends between network elements that assemble and disassemble the payload of a transmission system. For end-to-end communication, the payload is end-user

information. For user-to-network communication, the payload may be signaling information. Cell delineation and header error control functions are required at the endpoints of each transmission path.

(2) Digital section level. This level extends between network elements that assemble and disassemble a continuous bit or byte stream. These network elements are the exchanges or signal transfer points in a network that are involved in switching data streams.

(3) Regenerator section level. This level is a portion of a digital section. An example of this level is a repeater that is used to simply regenerate the digital signal along a transmission path that is too long to be used without such regeneration; no switching is involved.

Higher layers		
ATM layer	Virtual channel level	
	Virtual path level	
Physical layer	Transmission path level	
	Digital section level	
	Regenerator section level	

Figure 5-1. ATM transport hierarchy.

Virtual channels and virtual paths

Virtual channels. Logical connections in ATM are referred to as "virtual channels." A virtual channel is analogous to a virtual circuit in X.25 or a frame relay logical connection. It is the basic unit of switching in B-ISDN. A virtual channel is set up between two end users through the network, and a variable-rate, full-duplex flow of fixed-size cells is exchanged over the connection. Virtual channels are also used for user-network exchange (control signaling) and network-network exchange (network management and routing).

Virtual paths. For ATM, a second sublayer of processing has been introduced that deals with the concept of virtual paths (Figure 5-2). A virtual path is a bundle of virtual channels that have the same endpoints. Thus, all of the cells flowing over all of the virtual channels in a single virtual path are switched together. Several advantages of the use of virtual paths are

• Simplified network architecture. Network transport functions can be separated into those related to an individual logical connection (virtual channel) and those related to a group of logical connections (virtual path).

• Increased network performance and reliability. The network deals with fewer, aggregated entities.

• Reduced processing and short connection setup time. Much of the work is done when the virtual path is set up. The addition of new virtual channels to an existing virtual path involves minimal processing.

• Enhanced network services. Although the use of the virtual path is internal to the network, the virtual path is visible to the end user. Thus, the user may define closed user groups or closed networks of virtual-channel bundles.

SONET/SDH overview

SONET is an optical-transmission interface originally proposed by BellCore and standardized by ANSI. A compatible version of this interface — SDH — was published by the CCITT in Recommendations G.707, G.708, and G.709. SONET is intended to provide a specification for taking advantage of the high-speed digital-transmission capability of optical fiber. The SONET standard does the following:

• Establishes a standard multiplexing format using any number of 51.84-Mbps signals as building blocks. Because each building block can carry a DS3 signal, a standard rate is defined for any high-bandwidth transmission system that might be developed.

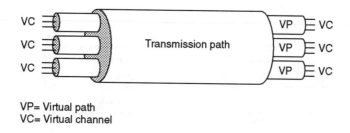

VP= Virtual path
VC= Virtual channel

Figure 5-2. ATM connection relationships.

• Establishes an optical-signal standard for interconnecting equipment from different suppliers.

• Establishes extensive operations, administration, and maintenance (OAM) capabilities as part of the standard.

• Defines a synchronous multiplexing format for carrying lower level digital signals (for example, DS1, DS2, and CCITT standards). The synchronous structure greatly simplifies the interface to digital switches, digital cross-connect switches, and add-drop multiplexers.

• Establishes a flexible architecture capable of accommodating future applications — such as broadband ISDN — that have a variety of transmission rates.

Three key needs have driven the development of SONET, as follows:

(1) The need to push multiplexing standards beyond the existing DS3 (44.736-Mbps) level. With the increasing use of optical-transmission systems, a number of vendors have introduced their own proprietary schemes of combining anywhere from two to 12 DS3s into an optical signal. In addition, the European schemes, based on the CCITT hierarchy, are incompatible with North American schemes. SONET provides a standardized hierarchy of multiplexed digital-transmission rates that accommodates existing North American and CCITT rates.

(2) The need to provide economic access to small amounts of traffic within the bulk payload of an optical signal. For this purpose, SONET introduces a new approach to TDM.

(3) The need to prepare for future sophisticated service offerings, such as virtual private networking, time-of-day bandwidth allocation, and support of the broadband ISDN ATM transmission technique. To meet this need, network management capabilities within the synchronous time-division signal were increased substantially.

Signal hierarchy

The SONET specification defines a hierarchy of standardized digital data rates (Table 5-1). The data rate at the lowest level, STS-1 (synchronous transport signal — level 1), is 51.84 Mbps. This rate can be used to carry a single DS3 signal or a group of lower rate signals — such as DS1, DS1C, or DS2 — plus CCITT rates (for example, 2.048 Mbps). Multiple STS-1 signals can be combined to form an STS-N signal. The signal is created by interleaving bytes from N STS-1 signals that are mutually synchronized. For the CCITT SDH, the lowest rate is 155.52 Mbps, which is designated STM-1. STM-1 corresponds to SONET STS-3.

System hierarchy

SONET capabilities have been mapped into a four-layer logical hierarchy [Figure 5-3(a)], as follows:

• Path layer. This layer is responsible for end-to-end transport of data at the appropriate signaling speed.

• Line layer. This layer is responsible for synchronization, multiplexing of data onto the SONET frames, and protection switching.

Table 5-1. SONET/SDH signal hierarchy.

SONET designation	CCITT designation	Data rate (Mbps)	Payload rate (Mbps)
STS-1		51.84	50.112
STS-3	STM-1	155.52	150.336
STS-9	STM-3	466.56	451.008
STS-12	STM-4	622.08	601.344
STS-18	STM-6	933.12	902.016
STS-24	STM-8	1244.16	1202.688
STS-36	STM-12	1866.24	1804.032
STS-48	STM-16	2488.32	2405.376

• Section layer. This layer creates the basic SONET frames, converts electronic signals to photonic ones, and has some monitoring capabilities.

• Photonic layer. This is the physical layer. It specifies the type of optical fiber that may be used. In addition, it includes details such as the required minimum powers and dispersion characteristics of the transmitting lasers and the required sensitivity of the receivers.

Figure 5-3(b) shows the physical realization of the logical layers. A section is the basic physical building block and represents a single run of optical cable between two optical-fiber transmitter/receivers. For shorter runs, the cable may run directly between two end units. For longer distances, regenerating repeaters are needed. The repeater is a simple device that accepts a digital stream of data on one side and regenerates and repeats each bit out the other side. Issues of synchronization and timing are addressed by the repeater. A line is a sequence of one or more sections such that the internal signal or channel structure of the signal remains constant. Endpoints and intermediate switches/multiplexers that may add or drop channels terminate a line. Finally, a path connects two end terminals; it corresponds to an end-to-end circuit. Data are assembled at the beginning of a path and are not accessed or modified until they ares disassembled at the other end of the path.

SONET and B-ISDN

SONET has been developed as a synchronous transmission service for very high-speed facilities. It is a follow-on to today's services, such as T1 and T3 and, in addition, can be used to multiplex lower speed synchronous traffic over a higher speed line. Thus, the transition to SONET will be natural. Users of existing T1 and T3 services will find SONET attractive as their requirements grow and as high-speed fiber-based facilities become available.

The other role for SONET is in support of broadband ISDN. B-ISDN is based on the use of an asynchronous cell transmission scheme. But SONET facilities can be used to carry B-ISDN cells as payload. The growing use of SONET in the coming years will thus help smooth the way to broadband ISDN.

Paper summary

The first paper included in this chapter, "SONET: Now It's the Standard Optical Network," by Ballart and Ching, describes the 1988 version of SONET/SDH, which is the basis for short-term planning.

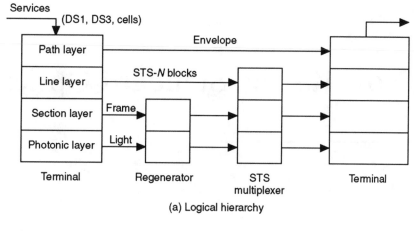

(a) Logical hierarchy

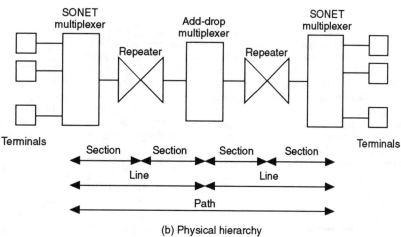

(b) Physical hierarchy

Figure 5-3. SONET system hierarchy.

"Progress in Standardization of SONET," by Boehm, describes current and future directions for SONET/SDH.

"Synchronous Optical Network and Broadband ISDN Protocols," by Hac and Mutlu, is a survey of SONET and ATM, with a discussion of how SONET can be used as the cell transport mechanism for ATM in B-ISDN.

"Broad-Band ATM Network Architecture Based on Virtual Paths," by Sato, Ohta, and Tokizawa, examines the various technical issues surrounding the use of virtual paths.

The final paper in this chapter, "Survey of Traffic Control Schemes and Protocols in ATM Networks," by Bai and Suda, provides a detailed look at traffic control techniques for ATM. This paper also examines the ATM protocol and formats in some detail and examines the use of SONET/SDH for the transmission of ATM cells.

SONET: Now It's the Standard Optical Network

Ralph Ballart
Yau-Chau Ching

SONET (SYNCHRONOUS OPTICAL NETWORK) IS the name of a newly adopted standard, originally proposed by Bellcore (Bell Communications Research) for a family of interfaces for use in Operating Telephone Company (OTC) optical networks. With single-mode fiber becoming the medium of choice for high-speed digital transport, the lack of signal standards for optical networks inevitably led to a proliferation of proprietary interfaces. Thus, the fiber optics transmission systems of one manufacturer cannot optically interconnect with those of any other manufacturer, and the ability to mix and match different equipment is restricted. SONET defines standard optical signals, a synchronous frame structure for the multiplexed digital traffic, and operations procedures.

> *SONET defines standard optical signals, a synchronous frame structure for the multiplexed digital traffic, and operations procedures.*

SONET standardization began during 1985 in the T1X1 subcommittee of the ANSI-accredited Committee T1 to standardize carrier-to-carrier (e.g., NYNEX-to-MCI) optical interfaces. Clearly, such a standard would also have an impact on intra-carrier networks, and for that reason has been a subject of great interest for many carriers, manufacturers, and others. Initial T1 standards for SONET rates and formats and optical parameters have now been completed. The history and technical highlights of the SONET standard and its applications are the subject of this paper.

Since it began in the post-divestiture environment, SONET standardization can be thought of as a paradigm for the development of new transmission signal standards. Bellcore's original SONET proposal was not fully detailed because all the technical questions were not yet answered. However, some aspects of the proposal have been carried through the entire process and are now part of the final standards. These include:

Reprinted from *IEEE Communications Magazine*, March 1989, pages 8-15. Copyright © 1989 by The Institute of Electrical and Electronics Engineers, Inc. All rights reserved.

- The need for a family of digital signal interfaces, since the march of technology is going to continually increase optical interface bit rates
- The use of a base rate SONET signal near 50 Mb/s to accommodate the DS3 electrical signal at 44.736 Mb/s
- The use of synchronous multiplexing to simplify multiplexing and demultiplexing of SONET component signals, to obtain easy access to SONET payloads and to exploit the increasing synchronization of the network
- Support for the transport of broadband (> 50 Mb/s) payloads
- Specification of enough overhead channels and functions to fully support facility maintenance

As standardization progressed, two key challenges emerged, the solution of which gave SONET universal application. The first was to make SONET work in a plesiochronous[1] environment and still retain its synchronous nature; the solution was the development of payload pointers to indicate the phase of SONET payloads with respect to the overall frame structure (see "SONET Signal Standard—Technical Highlights"). The second was to extend SONET to become an international transmission standard, and thereby begin to resolve the incompatibilities between the European signal hierarchy (based on 2.048 Mb/s) and the North American hierarchy (based on 1.544 Mb/s). Toward the latter goal, the International Telegraph and Telephone Consultative Committee (CCITT) standardization of SONET concepts began in 1986 and the first Recommendations (standards) were completed in June 1988.

This paper will not present a full technical picture of the national and international SONET standards. Instead, we will concentrate on those aspects of the standards and standardization process that are of particular interest. In the next section, a brief and instructional history of the SONET standard is presented. As philosopher George Santayana said, "Those who cannot remember the past are condemned to repeat it." We will then discuss key technical aspects of the SONET standard. Finally, an outline of future work is given in the final section.

---

[1] As defined in CCITT, corresponding signals are plesiochronous if their significant instants occur at nominally the same rate, any variation in rate being constrained within specified limits.

A History of SONET in T1 and CCITT

The standardization of SONET in T1 started in two different directions and in three areas. First, the Interexchange Carrier Compatibility Forum (ICCF), at the urging of MCI in 1984, requested T1 to work on standards that would allow the interconnection of multi-owner, multi-manufacturer fiber optic transmission terminals (also known as the mid-fiber meet capability). Of several ambitious tasks that ICCF wanted addressed to ensure a full mid-fiber meet capability, two were submitted to T1. A proposal on optical interface parameters (e.g., wavelength, optical power levels, etc.) was submitted to T1X1 in August 1984 and, after three and a half years of intensive work, resulted in a draft standard on single-mode optical interface specifications [1]. The ICCF proposal on long-term operations was submitted to T1M1 and resulted in a draft standard on fiber optic systems maintenance [2].

In February 1985, Bellcore proposed to T1X1 a network approach to fiber system standardization that would allow not only the interconnection of multi-owner, multi-manufacturer fiber optic transmission terminals, but also the interconnection of fiber optic network elements of varying functionalities. For example, the standard would allow the direct interconnection between several optical line terminating multiplexers, manufactured and owned by different entities, and a digital cross-connect system. In addition, the proposal suggested a hierarchical family of digital signals whose rates are integer multiples of a basic module signal, and suggested a simple synchronous bit-interleaving multiplexing technique that would allow economical implementations. Thus, the term Synchronous Optical NETwork (SONET) was coined. This proposal eventually led to a draft standard on optical rates and formats [3]. For the remainder of this paper, the focal points are the history and highlights of the rates and formats document. However, one should always be reminded that this document is only one part of the inseparable triplet: optical interface specifications, rates and formats specifications, and operations specifications.

As it turned out, the notions of a network approach and simple synchronous multiplexing had been independently investigated by many manufacturers. Some of them were already developing product plans, thus complicating the standards process. With the desire of the network providers (i.e., the OTCs) for expedited standards, SONET quickly gained support and momentum. By August 1985, T1X1 approved a project proposal based on the SONET principle. Because the issues on rates and formats were complex and required diligent but timely technical analyses, a steady stream of contributions poured into T1X1. Several ad hoc groups were formed and interim meetings were called to address them. The contributions came from over thirty entities, representing the manufacturers and the network providers alike.

In the early stage, the main topic of contention was the rate of the basic module. From two original proposals of 50.688 Mb/s (from Bellcore) and 146.432 Mb/s (from AT&T), a new rate of 49.920 Mb/s was derived and agreed on. In addition, the notion of a Virtual Tributary (VT) was introduced and accepted as the cornerstone for transporting DS1 services. By the beginning of 1987, substantial details had been agreed upon and a draft document was almost ready for voting. Then came CCITT.

The SONET standards were first developed in T1X1 to serve the U.S. telecommunications networks. When CCITT first expressed its interest in SONET in the summer of 1986, major procedural difficulties appeared. According to the established protocol, only contributions that had consensus in T1X1 were forwarded, through U.S. Study Group C, to CCITT. As a result, some aspects of U.S. positions in CCITT appeared to lack flexibility without input from T1X1. Addi-

TABLE I. CCITT Rec. G.702 Asynchronous Digital Hierarchies (in Mb/s)

Level	North America	Europe	Japan
1	1.544 (DS1)	2.048	1.544
2	6.312 (DS2)	8.448	6.312
3	44.736 (DS3)	34.368	32.064
4	—	139.264	97.728

tionally, the views of other administrations in CCITT were not thoroughly understood in T1X1. There were also differences in schedule and perceived urgency. CCITT runs by a four-year plenary period and their meetings are six to nine months apart, while T1 approves standards whenever they are ready and its technical subcommittees meet at least four times a year. While T1X1 saw the SONET standard as a way to stop the proliferation of incompatible fiber optic transmission terminals, no such need was perceived by many other nations whose networks were still fully regulated and non-competitive.

The procedural difficulties were partially resolved when representatives from the Japanese and British delegations started to participate in T1X1 meetings in April 1987. These representatives not only gave to T1X1 the perspectives of two important supporters of an international SONET standard, they also served as a conduit between T1X1 and CEPT, the European telecommunications organization.

Separately, interests in an international SONET standard also gained support in the US. Spearheaded by Bellcore, informal discussions in search of an acceptable solution took place in a variety of forums, and contributions in support of this standard were submitted to both T1 and CCITT. Many of these informal discussions had the highest level of corporate support from several U.S. companies, including manufacturers and network providers.

In July 1986, CCITT Study Group XVIII began the study of a new synchronous signal hierarchy and its associated Network Node Interface (NNI). The NNI is a non-media-specific network interface and is distinct from the user-network interface associated with Broadband ISDN. The interaction between T1X1 and CCITT on SONET and the new synchronous hierarchy was fascinating to the participants and will probably alter the way international standards are made in the future. The U.S. wanted an international standard, but not at the price of scrapping SONET or seriously delaying an American national standard upon which OTC networks were planned. The CCITT was not used to working so quickly on so complicated an issue, but was concerned about being supplanted by the T1 committee in the development of new standards.

The U.S. first formally proposed SONET to CCITT for use in the NNI at the February 1987 Brasilia meeting; this proposal had a base signal level (rate) near 50 Mb/s. Table I shows that the European signal hierarchy has no level near 50 Mb/s, and therefore CEPT wanted the new synchronous hierarchy to have a base signal near 150 Mb/s to transport their 139.264 Mb/s signal.

Thus, the informal European response was that the U.S. must change from bit interleave to byte interleave multiplexing to provide a byte organized frame structure at 150 Mb/s. However, there was still no indication from many administrations that an international standard was either desirable or achievable. It took T1X1 three months and three meetings to agree to byte-interleaving and the results were submitted to CCITT as a new T1X1 draft standard document. Thus, T1X1 never gave up the responsibility of developing a SONET standard for the U.S. and, while conceding changes to CCITT wishes, progress was made in other areas of the U.S. standard.

After CCITT met again in Hamburg in July 1987, a formal request was made to all administrations to consider two alternative proposals for an NNI specification near 150 Mb/s. The U.S. proposal was based on the SONET STS-3 frame structure; the STS-3 frame could be drawn as a rectangle with 13 rows and 180 columns of bytes. CEPT proposed, instead, a new STS-3 frame with 9 rows and 270 columns. (Commonly referred to as the 9-row/13-row debate, this prompted one amateur poet to chide that neither conforms to the correct SON(N)ET format of 14 lines.) An NNI near 150 Mb/s received unanimous support because it was assumed that future broadband payloads would be about that size. A North American basic module near 50 Mb/s could be easily derived in both proposals, with a frame structure of either 13 rows and 60 columns or 9 rows and 90 columns.

The Europeans wanted a 9-row frame structure to accommodate their 2.048 Mb/s primary rate signal. This signal has 32 bytes per 125 μs, but in the 13-row proposal could only be accommodated in the most straightforward way using three 13-byte columns, or 39 bytes. The Europeans decried this waste of bandwidth, and refused to consider any alternative (and more efficient) mapping of the 2.048 Mb/s signal into the 13-row structure. Their 9-row frame structure could carry the U.S. 1,544 Mb/s primary rate signal (requiring about 24 bytes/125 μs) in 3 columns of 9 bytes and the 2.048 Mb/s signal in 4 columns of 9 bytes.

The CEPT 9-row proposal called for changes in both the rate and format in the U.S., just as T1X1 was about to complete the SONET standard. However, the request also carried an attractive incentive from a CEPT subcommittee, who stated in a letter that these were the only changes necessary for an international agreement. In addition, the text of the CEPT proposal was based largely on the T1X1 draft document, so that it was complete. Therefore, after the Hamburg meeting, there was tremendous international pressure on the U.S. to accept the 9-row proposal. After some intense debates in T1X1, the U.S. agreed to change.

Unfortunately, the CEPT proposal did not have unanimous support from all CEPT administrations. While some administrations were anxious to get an international standard, a few became concerned that the 9-row proposal favored the U.S. DS3 signal over the CEPT 34.368 Mb/s signal. A CEPT contribution to the November 1987 CCITT meeting stated that it was too early to draft Recommendations on a new synchronous hierarchy. Little progress was made at that meeting and the international SONET standard was in serious jeopardy.

Many T1X1 participants were upset at the apparent change in CEPT's position. Since there were no alternative proposals from CCITT at its November meeting, T1X1 decided to approve the two SONET documents for T1 letter balloting. However, the balloting schedule was deliberately set such that it fell between the CCITT meeting at the beginning of February 1988 and the T1X1 meeting at the end of February 1988. This scheduling allowed a last ditch attempt for an international agreement. In CCITT, a mad rush to rescue the international standard also took place. In addition to a series of informal discussions, a pre-CCITT meeting was held in Tokyo to search for a compromise. Under the skillful helmsmanship of Mr. K. Okimi of Japan, the CCITT meeting in Seoul proposed one additional change to the U.S. draft standards. The new proposal called for a change in the order that 50 Mb/s tributaries are byte-multiplexed to higher SONET signal levels. It also put more emphasis on the NNI as a 150 Mb/s signal by including optional payload structures to better accommodate the European 34.368 Mb/s signal. The U.S. CCITT delegates eventually viewed this proposal as a minor change to the U.S. standard (minor to the extent that equipment under development would probably not require modification) and agreed to accept it. An

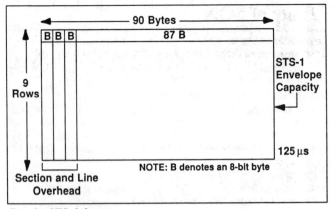

Fig. 1. *STS-1 frame.*

extensive set of three CCITT Recommendations was drafted and approved by the working party plenary. The U.S. acceptance of these changes was predicated on the understanding that no additional changes of substance would be considered in approving the final versions of the Recommendations.

In February 1988, T1X1 accepted the new changes at its meeting in Phoenix. T1 default balloting based on the change was completed in May and the final passage of the American national standard is expected this summer. Editorial corrections to the CCITT Recommendations [4–6] were completed in June during the Study Group XVIII meeting and with their final approval later this year, the international SONET standard will be born!

SONET Signal Standard—Technical Highlights

In this section, we describe the technical highlights of the American national standards related to SONET. We use U.S. rather than CCITT terminology, although everything described is consistent with both the American national standards and the CCITT Recommendations.

SONET Signal Hierarchy

The basic building block and first level of the SONET signal hierarchy is called the Synchronous Transport Signal—Level 1 (STS-1). The STS-1 has a bit rate of 51.84 Mb/s and is assumed to be synchronous with an appropriate network synchronization source. The STS-1 frame structure can be drawn as 90 columns and 9-rows of 8 bit bytes (Figure 1). The order of transmission of the bytes is row by row, from left to right, with one entire frame being transmitted every 125 μs. (125 μs frame period supports digital voice signal transport, since these signals are encoded using 1 byte/125 μs = 64 kb/s.) The first three columns of the STS-1 contain section and line overhead bytes (see the following subsection). The remaining 87 columns and 9-rows are used to carry the STS-1 Synchronous Payload Envelope (SPE); the SPE is used to carry SONET payloads including 9 bytes of path overhead (see next section). The STS-1 can carry a clear channel DS3 signal (44.736 Mb/s) or, alternatively, a variety of lower-rate signals such as DS1, DS1C, and DS2.

No physical interface for the STS-1 signal has been defined as yet; the Optical Carrier—Level 1 (OC-1) is obtained from the STS-1 after scrambling (to avoid long strings of ones and zeros and allow clock recovery at receivers) and electrical-to-optical conversion. The OC-1 is the lowest-level optical signal to be used at SONET equipment and network interfaces.

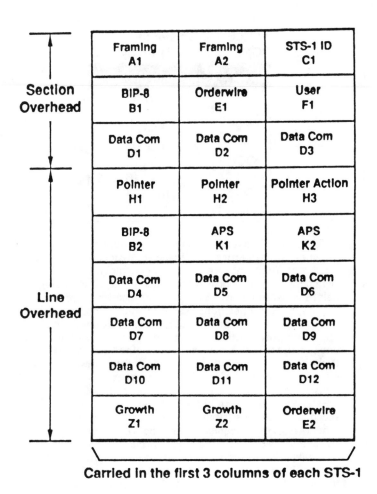

Section Overhead	Framing A1	Framing A2	STS-1 ID C1
	BIP-8 B1	Orderwire E1	User F1
	Data Com D1	Data Com D2	Data Com D3
Line Overhead	Pointer H1	Pointer H2	Pointer Action H3
	BIP-8 B2	APS K1	APS K2
	Data Com D4	Data Com D5	Data Com D6
	Data Com D7	Data Com D8	Data Com D9
	Data Com D10	Data Com D11	Data Com D12
	Growth Z1	Growth Z2	Orderwire E2

Carried in the first 3 columns of each STS-1

Path Layer Overhead (carried as part of SONET payloads)
Trace J1
BIP-8 B3
Signal Label C2
Path Status G1
User Channel F2
Multiframe H4
Growth Z3
Growth Z4
Growth Z5

Fig. 2. SONET overhead bytes.

SONET Overhead Channels

The SONET overhead is divided into section, line, and path layers; Figure 2 shows the overhead bytes and their relative positions in the SONET frame structure. This division clearly reflects the segregation of processing functions in network elements (equipment) and promotes understanding of the overhead functions. The section layer contains those overhead channels that are processed by all SONET equipment including regenerators. The section overhead channels for an STS-1 include two framing bytes that show the start of each STS-1 frame, an STS-1 identification byte, an 8-bit Bit-Interleaved Parity (BIP-8) check for section error monitoring, an orderwire channel for craft (network maintenance personnel) communications, a channel for unspecified network user (operator) applications, and three bytes for a section level data communications channel to carry maintenance and provisioning information. When a SONET signal is scrambled, the only bytes left unscrambled are the section layer framing bytes and the STS-1 identification bytes. The second (link) layer of the section data communications channel protocol is LAPD while ISO 8473 is under study for the third (network) layer; higher layers of the protocol will be defined in future updates of the standard.

The line overhead is processed at all SONET equipment except regenerators. It includes the STS-1 pointer bytes (discussed below), an additional BIP-8 for line error monitoring, a two-byte Automatic Protection Switching (APS) message channel (both *1 + 1* and *1 by N* protection are supported), a nine-byte line data communications channel, bytes reserved for future growth, and a line orderwire channel. The higher lay-

ers of the line data communications channel are not specified in the current version of the SONET standard.

The path overhead bytes are processed at SONET STS-1 payload terminating equipment; that is, the path overhead is part of the SONET STS-1 payload and travels with it. The path overhead includes a path BIP-8 for end-to-end payload error monitoring, a signal label byte to identify the type of payload being carried, a path status byte to carry maintenance signals, a multiframe alignment byte to show DSO signaling bit phase, and others.

Multiplexing

Higher rate SONET signals are obtained by first byte-interleaving *N* frame-aligned STS-1s to form an STS-*N* (Figure 3). Byte-interleaving and frame alignment are used primarily to obtain a byte-organized frame format at the 150 Mb/s level that is acceptable to the CCITT; as discussed below, frame alignment and byte-interleaving also help an STS-*N* to carry broadband payloads of about 150 or 600 Mb/s. All the section and line overhead channels in STS-1 #1 of an STS-*N* are used; however, many of the overhead channels in the remaining STS-1s are unused. (Only the section overhead framing, STS-1 ID, and BIP-8 channels and the line overhead pointer and BIP-8 channels are used in all STS-1s in an STS-*N*.) The STS-*N* is then scrambled and converted to an Optical Carrier—Level *N* (OC-*N*) signal. The OC-*N* will have a line rate exactly *N* times that of an OC-1. Table II shows the OC-*N* levels allowed by the American national standard.

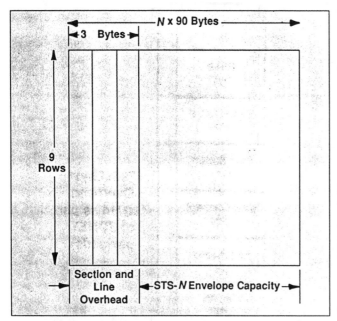

Fig. 3. STS-N frame

Level	Line Rate (Mb/s)
OC-1	51.84
OC-3	155.52
OC-9	466.56
OC-12	622.08
OC-18	933.12
OC-24	1244.16
OC-36	1866.24
OC-48	2488.32

TABLE II. Levels of the SONET Signal Hierarchy

SONET STS-1 Payload Pointer

Each SONET STS-1 signal carries a payload pointer in its line overhead. The STS-1 payload pointer is a key innovation of SONET, and it is used for multiplexing synchronization in a plesiochronous environment and also to frame align STS-N signals.

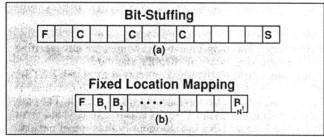

Fig. 4. Payload multiplexing methods.

Pointers and Multiplexing Synchronization

There are two conventional ways to multiplex payloads into higher-rate signals. The first is to use positive bit-stuffing to increase the bit rate of a tributary signal to match the available payload capacity in a higher-rate signal. As shown in Figure 4a, bit-stuffing indicators (labeled C) are located in fixed positions with respect to signal frame F and indicate whether the stuffing bit S carries real or dummy data in each higher-level signal frame. Examples of bit stuffing are the multiplexing of four DS1 signals into the DS2 signal and the multiplexing of seven DS2 signals into the asynchronous DS3 signal. Bit-stuffing can accommodate large (asynchronous) frequency variations of the multiplexed payloads. However, access to those payloads from the higher-level multiplexed signal is conceptually difficult, since the tributary signal must first be destuffed (real bits separated from the dummy bits) and then the framing pattern of the payload must be identified if complete payload access is required.

The second conventional method is the use of fixed location mapping of tributaries into higher-rate signals. As network synchronization increases with the deployment of digital switches, it becomes possible to synchronize transmission signals to the overall network clock. Fixed location mapping is the use of specific bit positions in a higher-rate synchronous signal to carry lower-rate synchronous signals; for example, in Figure 4b, frame position B2 would always carry information from one specific tributary payload. This method allows easy access to the transported tributary payloads, since no destuffing is required. The SYNTRAN DS3 signal is an example of a synchronous signal that uses fixed location mapping of its tributary DS1 signals. However, there is no guarantee that the high-speed signal and its tributary will be phase-aligned with each other. Also, small frequency differences between the transport signal and its tributary signal may occur, due to synchronization network failures or at plesiochronous boundaries. Therefore, multiplexing equipment interfaces require 125-μs buffers to phase-align and slip (repeat or delete a frame of information to correct frequency differences) the tributary signal. These buffers are undesirable because of the signal delay that they impose and the signal impairment that slipping causes.

In SONET, payload pointers represent a novel technique that allows easy access to synchronous payloads while avoiding the need for 125-μs buffers and associated slips at multiplexing equipment interfaces. The payload pointer is a number carried in each STS-1 line overhead (bytes H1, H2 in Figure 2) that indicates the starting byte location of the STS-1 SPE payload within the STS-1 frame (Figure 5). Thus, the payload is not locked to the STS-1 frame structure as it would be if fixed location mapping was used but instead floats with respect to the STS-1 frame. (The STS-1 section and line overhead byte positions determine the STS-1 frame structure; note in Figure 5 that the 9-row-by-87-column SPE payload maps into an irregular shape across two 125-μs STS-1 frames.)

Any small frequency variations of the STS-1 payload can be accommodated by either increasing or decreasing the pointer value; however, the pointers cannot adjust to asynchronous frequency differences. For example, if the STS-1 payload data rate is high with respect to the STS-1 frame rate, the payload pointer is decremented by one and the H3 overhead byte is used to carry data for one frame (Figure 6). If the payload data rate is slow with respect to the STS-1 frame rate, the data byte immediately following the H3 byte is nulled for one frame and the pointer is incremented by one (Figure 7). Thus, slips and their associated data loss are avoided while the phase of the STS-1 synchronous payload is immediately known by simply reading the pointer value. Thus, SONET pointers combine the best features of the positive bit-stuffing and fixed location mapping methods. Of course, these advantages come at the cost of having to process the pointers; however, pointer processing appears readily implementable in today's Very Large Scale Integration (VLSI) technologies.

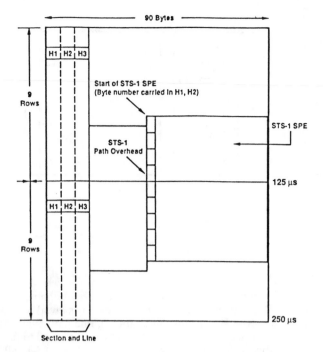

Fig. 5. STS-1 SPE in interior of STS-1 frame.

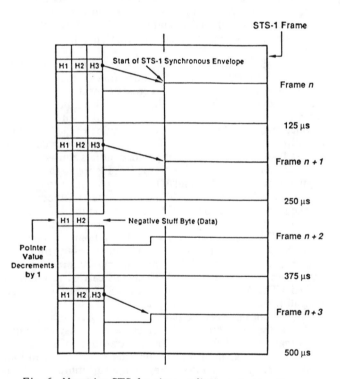

Fig. 6. Negative STS-1 pointer adjustment operation.

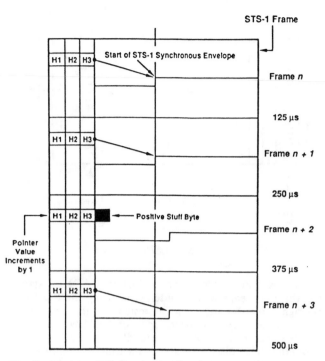

Fig. 7. Positive STS-1 pointer adjustment operation.

and line overhead bytes, two phase-aligned signals (A and B) are formed. A and B can then be byte-interleaved to form a higher level STS-N signal. As shown, this can be done with minimum payload buffering and signal delay.

With frame alignment, the STS-1 pointers in an STS-N are grouped together for easy access at an OC-N receiver using a single STS-N framing circuit. If it is desired to carry a broadband payload requiring, for example, three STS-1 payloads, the phase and frequency of the three STS-1 payloads must be locked together as the broadband payload is transported through the network. This is easily done by using a "concatenation indication" in the second and third STS-1 pointers. The concatenation indication is a pointer value that indicates to an STS-1 pointer processor that this pointer should have the same value as the previous STS-1 pointer. Thus, by frame aligning STS-N signals and using pointer concatenation, multiple STS-1 payloads can be created. The STS-N signal that is locked together in this way is called an STS-Nc, where the "c" stands for concatenated. Allowed values of STS-Nc are STS-2c, STS-3c, STS-6c, STS-9c, etc. For broadband User Network Interfaces (UNI), STS-3c and STS-12c are of particular interest.

Broadband Payload Transport with Payload Pointers

As discussed above, STS-1 payload pointers can be used to adjust the frequencies of several STS-1 payloads in multiplexing to the STS-N signal level. As this is done, the various STS-1 section and line overhead bytes are frame-aligned. In Figure 8, two hypothetical and simplified SONET frames (A and B) are out of phase with respect to the arbitrary, outgoing (multiplexed) SONET signal phase. By recalculating the SONET pointer values and regenerating the SONET section

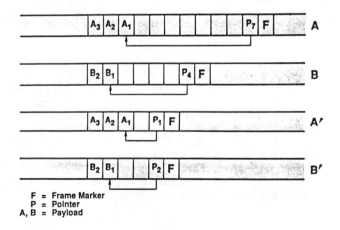

F = Frame Marker
P = Pointer
A, B = Payload

Fig. 8. Frame alignment using pointers.

187

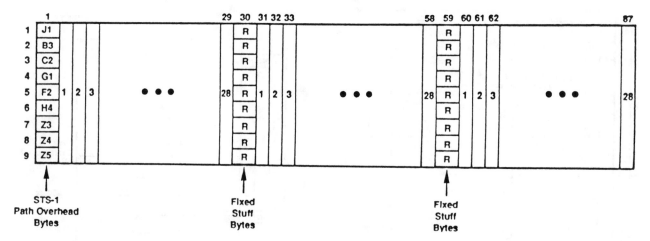

Fig. 9. VT-structured STS-1 SPE: all VT1.5.

As discussed in the section on the history of SONET standards, the Europeans had no interest in using the SONET STS-1 signal. Instead, they were interested in using a base signal of about 150 Mb/s to allow transport of their 139.264 Mb/s electrical signal and for possible Broadband ISDN applications. As the above discussion shows, the technical solution to this problem is the use of the STS-3c signal. In the U.S., we can continue to think of this signal as three concatenated STS-1 signals. In Europe and the CCITT, the STS-3c is considered as the basic building block of the new synchronous hierarchy and is referred to as the Synchronous Transport Module—Level 1 (STM-1).

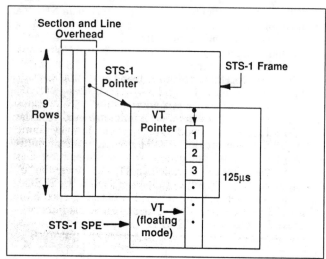

Fig. 10. Pointers and VT payload access.

Sub-STS-1 Payloads

To transport payloads requiring less than an STS-1 payload capacity, the STS-1 SPE is divided into payload structures called virtual tributaries (VTs). There are four sizes of VTs: VT1.5, VT2, VT3, and VT6, where each VT has enough bandwidth to carry a DS1, CEPT-1 (2.048 Mb/s), DS1C, and DS2 signal, respectively. Each VT occupies several 9-row columns within the SPE. The VT1.5 is carried in three columns (27 bytes), the VT2 in 4 columns (36 bytes), the VT3 in six columns (54 bytes), and the VT6 in twelve columns (108 bytes).

A VT group is defined to be a 9-row-by-12-column payload structure that can carry four VT1.5s, three VT2s, two VT3s, or one VT6. Seven VT groups (84 columns), one path overhead column, and two unused columns are byte-interleaved to fully occupy the STS-1 SPE. Figure 9 shows the STS-1 SPE configured to carry 28 VT1.5s. VT groups carrying different VT types can be mixed within one STS-1. As discussed in the section on history, the ability of the 9-row format structure to flexibly carry both the 1.544 and the 2.048 Mb/s signals was a necessary step in reaching an international agreement on SONET.

Two different modes have been adopted for transporting payloads within a VT. The VT operating in the "floating" mode improves the transport and cross-connection of VT payloads. A floating VT is so called because a VT pointer is used to show the starting byte position of the VT SPE within the VT payload structure. In this sense, the operation of the VT pointer is directly analogous to that of the STS-1 pointer, and has the same advantages of minimizing payload buffers and associated delay when mapping signals into the VT. Figure 10 shows conceptually how the STS-1 and VT pointers are used to locate a particular VT payload in an STS-1. The other VT mode is the "locked" mode. The locked VT does not use the VT pointer, but instead locks the VT payload structure directly to the STS-1 SPE. (Of course, the STS-1 SPE still floats with respect to the STS-1 frame.) The locked mode improves the transport and cross-connection of DS0 signals by maintaining the relative phase and frequency of DS0 signals carried in multiple locked VT's. When VT-organized, each STS-1 SPE carries either all floating or all locked VTs.

More than one specific payload mapping is possible with each of the VT modes described above. Asynchronous mappings are used for clear channel transport of nominally asynchronous signals using the floating mode of operation; conventional positive bit-stuffing is used to multiplex these signals into the VT SPE. "Byte synchronous" mappings have been defined in both the locked and floating modes for the efficient, synchronous transport of DS0 signals and their associated signaling; conventional fixed position mappings are used to carry the DS0's in the VT SPE (floating mode) or VT (locked mode). "Bit synchronous" mappings are used in both the locked and floating modes for the clear channel transport of unframed, synchronous signals. The VT mappings that have been defined in the current version of the American national standard are given in Table III.

TABLE III. Sub-STS-1 Mappings

Mappings	VT (Virtual Tributary) Modes	
	Floating	Locked
Asynchronous	DS1 CEPT-1 DS1C, DS2	—
Byte Synchronous	DS1 CEP-1	DS1 CEP-1 SYNTRAN
Bit Synchronous	DS1 CEP-1	DS1 CEP-1

Optical Parameters

The SONET optical interface parameters were developed in parallel with the SONET rates and formats. The optical parameters specified in the American national standard include spectral characteristics, line rate, power levels, and pulse shapes; jitter specifications will be developed in the next phase of the standard. The current optical specifications extend up to OC-48 (see Table II). It is expected that as more experience is gained with high data rate systems, the optical parameters associated with OC-18, OC-24, OC-36, and OC-48 will be updated.

The intent of this first optical interface standard is to provide specifications for "long reach" fiber transmission systems, i.e., systems using lasers. The second phase of SONET standardization in T1 will address "short reach" specifications for fiber transmission systems based on LEDs and low-power, loop lasers.

Conclusion and Future Work

The Synchronous Optical Network concept was developed to promulgate standard optical transmission signal interfaces to allow mid-section meets of fiber systems, easy access to tributary signals, and direct optical interfaces on terminals, and to provide new network features. The basic SONET signal format can transport all signals of the North American hierarchy up to and including DS3, and also future broadband signals. SONET will soon be an American national standard and a CCITT transmission signal hierarchy standard. The second phase of SONET T1 standardization will fully specify the data communications channel protocols, specify short-reach SONET optical interfaces for use in intra-office applications, and update SONET optical parameters for selected levels above OC-12.

SONET represents a successful test case for standards-making in the post-divestiture environment. Of course, the ultimate test for any standard is the development of products and services that are compliant with the new standard. For specific implementations, requirements beyond those contained in the standard are often needed. For example, Bellcore has issued a series of Technical Advisories giving additional requirements for SONET multiplexes, digital cross-connect systems, and digital switch interfaces. The first field trials of SONET equipment are expected in 1989.

References

[1] ANSI T1.106-1988, "American National Standard for Telecommunications—Digital Hierarchy Optical Interface Specifications, Single Mode," to be issued.

[2] T1M1.2/87-37R2 "Functional Requirements for Fiber Optic Terminating Equipment."

[3] ANSI T1.105-1988 "American National Standard for Telecommunication—Digital Hierarchy Optical Rates and Formats Specification," to be issued.

[4] CCITT Recommendation G.707, "Synchronous Digital Hierarchy Bit Rates," to be issued.

[5] CCITT Recommendation G.708, "Network Node Interface for the Synchronous Digital Hierarchy," to be issued.

[6] CCITT Recommendation G.709, "Synchronous Multiplexing Structure," to be issued.

Biography

Ralph Ballart is District Manager of Network Node Equipment Requirements at Bell Communications Research, Inc. (Bellcore), responsible for the development of requirements for SONET digital cross-connect systems and trunk side digital switch interfaces. Ralph is also Chairman of the T1X1.5 U.S. CCITT Drafting Sub-working Group that has responsibility for drafting contributions related to SONET to CCITT Study Group XVIII.

He received his B.S. degree in physics from the then Polytechnic Institute of Brooklyn in 1973 and his Ph.D. in physics from the University of Arizona in 1980. He joined Bell Telephone Laboratories in 1980 and worked on fundamental network planning tools and network applications for digital cross-connect systems. In 1984, he joined Bellcore and worked on requirements for SYNTRAN equipment. He was promoted to District Manager in 1985; his district participated in the technical development of SONET and its international standardization in CCITT. Dr. Ballart is a member of IEEE Communications Society.

Yau-Chau Ching is District Manager of SONET Interface Standards, responsible for strategic planning to support the SONET project in its initial applications as well as its later extension to Broadband ISDN. He is the Co-Chairman of T1X1.5 Working Group (Optical Hierarchy), where much of the SONET standardization work takes place. Before the inception of T1X1.5, he was the Co-Chairman of T1X1.4 Subworking Group on Optical Rates and Formats and an active member of T1X1.4 Subworking Group on Optical Interface. These latter groups were the predecessors of T1X1.5.

He received his B.E.E.E. degree from City College of New York in 1966 and his Ph.D. from New York University in 1969 under a National Science Foundation fellowship. From 1969 to 1984, he was with Bell Laboratories, where he did a series of exploratory development work in data compression, such as interframe video coding, digital speech interpolation, embedded ADPCM coding, and Fast Packet Network. From 1980 to 1983, he supervised a group responsible for the implementation of the Access Interface to the Fast Packet Network.

Since the divestiture of the Bell System, he has been with Bellcore, where his district was responsible for the generic requirements of fiber optic transmission systems. His district was also the originator of the SONET concept in Bellcore and its strong advocate in T1X1. Dr. Ching is a member of IEEE, Tau Beta Pi, and Eta Kappa Nu, and he holds 11 patents.

Progress in Standardization of SONET

Rodney J. Boehm

Before the North American telecommunications industry went through divestiture, most standards for telecommunication were developed by AT&T and distributed to other vendors interested in building equipment to those specifications. When the Bell System was broken up into the corporations we know today, this standardization process needed to change. To fill the place of a single organization setting standards, a committee in the Exchange Carriers' Standards Association (ECSA) was established. This is known today as Committee T1 (T1 referring to the fact that this was the first standardizations committee for telecommunications established in ECSA).

At the same time, a new company was being formed to provide the Regional Bell Operating Companies (RBOCs) the same support Bell Laboratories had supplied them before divestiture. This company is known as Bell Communications Research (Bellcore). One of its major jobs, but by no means the only one, was to establish Technical Requirements for equipment needed by the RBOCs and aid in the standardization process. Since many of the existing specifications were generated by AT&T and had not formally been standardized, Bellcore had a great deal of work to accomplish in a very short time.

Even though existing interfaces needed to be standardized, some people were attempting to establish specifications for interfaces not yet dreamed of. One of the interexchange companies approached some of the RBOCs and asked to establish an interface optically. Since, at that time, all optical systems had proprietary frame formats and optical parameters, there was not a standard manner in which to accomplish this. Two methods were finally agreed to, one short-term and the other longer-term. The short-term method, definitely less preferable to the companies involved, was to agree to purchase the same system on both ends of the fiber. The other was to start a standards project in the newly formed T1 committee to specify a standardized optical interface.

The RBOCs sought help from Bellcore (referred to as the Central Services Organization at the time while Judge Green decided whether this new company could use the Bell name) to initiate the standardization effort. Mr. Yau Ching and I were assigned the task of getting the optical interface project started. We knew some form of a proposal needed to be developed; therefore we established and documented the basic concepts behind the Synchronous Optical Network (SONET).

This was the skeleton of a proposal and did not contain all of the details necessary for a supplier to build a system with a standardized interface. We knew that establishment of an optical interface in the telecommunications network would have far-ranging effects and would be with us for many years. We also knew that many people were working on optical systems and could provide valuable input to this project. Therefore, we decided to bring the framework of a proposal to the standards body and work out the details of the interface in open forums to enlist the support and intelligence contained in our industry.

After three years of very hard work, over 400 contributions by numerous corporations, many compromises, gallons of coffee, hundreds of thousands of airline miles, and much personal time spent away from families, we developed an optical interface specification that not only accomplished our initial goals, but also went beyond this and became an interface specification that will allow us to build today's networks and transition easily to tomorrow's networks. As will be shown later, this interface was also adopted as an international telecommunication standard that can be used in all countries. This project illustrates the standardization process at its best because dedicated people helped to take an idea and develop it into a specification that goes beyond its initial application into something that will affect the telecommunications network for years to come.

Project Goals

Initially, we established very simple goals for this project, that is, to be able to specify an optical interface that would allow optical midspan meets between different suppliers' equipment. This would be analogous to the DS3 or DS1 interfaces so prevalent in the network today. We quickly realized that selecting a single interface rate would be impossible because so many different applications exist-

Reprinted from *IEEE LCS — The Magazine of Lightwave Communication Systems*, May 1990, pages 8-16. Copyright © 1990 by The Institute of Electrical and Electronics Engineers, Inc. All rights reserved.

0-8186-2797-2/92 $3.00 © 1990 IEEE

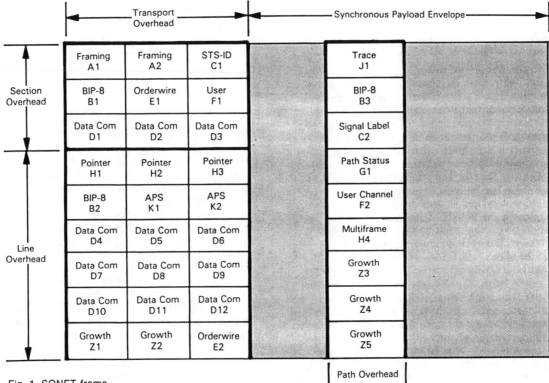

Fig. 1. SONET frame.

ed. In addition, we recognized that it would be a difficult and time-consuming process to establish even a single interface. Therefore, a method was needed to allow the establishment of a family of interfaces at the same time. In this manner, a number of interfaces would be established simultaneously, thus avoiding the time-consuming process of defining them one at a time.

We chose to specify a base signal, complete with a format, and a multiplexing method that would allow us to create a number of interfaces from the base signal. After a compromise was reached with the Consultative Committee for International Telephone and Telegraph (CCITT), a base signal with a rate of 51.84 Mb/s and the frame format shown in Figure 1 was chosen. The multiplexing method chosen was to synchronously byte interleave the basic signals together to form higher-rate interfaces. Using this technique, a simple one-step multiplex and demultiplex process can be designed to provide direct access to the desired basic signal in a higher-rate interface. An analogy of stacking blocks on top of each other to make a taller tower is a very appropriate one. The term "synchronous" in SONET came from this multiplexing technique. Now that we had a base signal and a multiplexing technique, we could create a family of interfaces that could satisfy all information transport needs. Algorithms were established to allow us to multiplex up to 256 base signals together, which would create interfaces from 51.84 Mb/s to 13.27 Gb/s.

Accomplishments in the Initial Document Release

We accomplished most of the goals with the release of the initial SONET specifications, American National Standards Institute (ANSI) T1.105-1988 [1] and ANSI T1.106-1988 [2]. While the numbers are somewhat confusing, the specifications are actually simple. ANSI T1.105-1988 contains specifications for the rate and format of the SONET interface. This is analogous to other format specifications for other interfaces, such as the DS1 or DS3 format. A SONET interface, however, is different in some very important ways, which will be covered in more detail later. Also

contained in this document are instructions for mapping different payloads into the interface, multiplexing techniques, and overhead specifications.

ANSI T1.106-1988 contains the optical parameter specification needed to complete the interface specification. This is analogous to the electrical parameter specification for a DS1 or DS3 signal. These specifications were released in this manner to allow different optical parameters to be specified for different rate signals in different applications. ANSI T1.106-1988 specifies parameters for longer distance spans in single-mode fiber. This was given the highest priority by the committee. Another specification under development, described later in more detail, will specify a much shorter distance interface that can use significantly less expensive optical components.

As mentioned before, most of the goals were met by these two standards. One of the major items not specified but under very active development is the specification of the embedded operations channels, called Data Communication Channels (DCC). Two channels are currently allocated bandwidth in the overhead. One is the section DCC and the other is the line DCC. These will be covered in further detail in another section.

Because these channels will be used to communicate operations support information from one Network Element (NE) to another, some people have maintained the basic goal of defining a midspan meet interface has not been achieved. In fact, all of the necessary specifications for reliable information transfer have been completed.

It is the protocol stack and messages necessary to trade operations information that are not complete. This situation is analogous to connecting one vendor's M13 to another. Transport of DS1s can take place reliably; however, commands to loop back a DS1 or notify the other multiplexer that the far end has an alarm cannot be accomplished because no standard method has been established to perform this function.

Therefore, while a midspan meet can be accomplished, many of the features in transmission equipment used by network providers are not present. This situation was to be corrected by the SONET Phase II document scheduled for release in December of 1989. After a great deal of work, only the protocol specification for the DCCs was released. This will be covered in more detail in a subsequent section.

Decision to Phase the Standard

One could legitimately ask questions concerning the wisdom in releasing the SONET specification in phases. The reason this approach was taken can be seen by looking at the normal development cycle needed to design telecommunication equipment. Since signals must be processed at very high speeds and cost is a primary consideration, most multiplexing and demultiplexing functions must be accomplished in Application Specific Integrated Circuits (ASICs). Design time for these can be quite lengthy.

In order to allow suppliers to start developing the needed ASICs, we released the SONET specification that detailed the multiplexing and demultiplexing functions first. For the same reason, the optical parameter specification was released in the same time frame. We left specification of the DCCs until later phases because most of the changes to equipment would be in software, which could be updated much more easily than hardware changes. In addition, we determined that specification of these channels would take a couple of years beyond the time when the initial rate, format, and optical specifications were available.

By phasing the standard, manufacturers could start designing equipment and network providers could start deploying equipment knowing that as the standard was completed for the DCCs, only software, or at most a processor card, would need to be updated.

Differences In The SONET Standard And Other Interface Specifications

Most transmission signals have been designed to carry only a limited set of payloads. For instance, the DS1 was designed to carry 24 voice signals at 64 kb/s. Other types of payloads are now being mapped into the basic DS1 format, but they must maintain some of the signal structure inherent in the DS1 format. We knew the SONET interface must be able to carry all of the North American and Conference of European Postal and Telecommunications administrations (CEPT) signals; however, we also knew the signal structure must allow transport of signals and services not defined, with characteristics not known.

The concept of layering the basic signal was introduced in the standards body to allow the SONET interface to be structured properly. Figure 1 illustrates this by showing the major layers. A SONET interface is basically broken into two parts, with divisions within each of these parts. The two major parts are the Synchronous Payload Envelope (SPE) and transport overhead. An SPE is the portion of the signal that can be structured to efficiently carry signals with different characteristics and formats. For instance, the SPE is structured one way to directly carry DS1s and another way to carry DS3s. Included within the SPE is Path overhead, which is used to carry information about the signal (such as performance checks, a signal structure indication, etc) from end to end through the entire transmission system. This allows complete end-to-end checks.

Transport overhead is the other major division within the basic signal. This is overhead necessary for transport through the network. It is broken into two parts, section overhead and line overhead. Section overhead is that overhead necessary for reliable communication between NEs such as terminals and regenerators. A minimum amount of overhead is placed here to allow regenerators to be constructed as cost effectively as possible. Some of the functions contained here are framing, high-level performance monitoring, a DCC, and an orderwire channel. More will

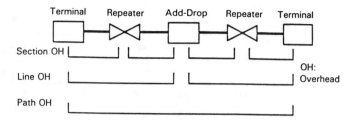

Fig. 2. Section, line, and path overhead usage.

be presented about the DCC in later sections.

Line overhead was established to allow reliable communication of necessary information between more complicated NEs such as terminals, digital cross-connects, multiplexers, and switches. Some of the functions contained in this layer include pointers for frequency justification, automatic protection switching channels, a much larger DCC, a lower-level performance monitoring check, and an express orderwire.

By structuring the overhead in this manner, NEs need only access the information necessary and, thus, cost can be avoided in some NEs because not all of the overhead must be processed. Figure 2 illustrates the layers different NEs need to process. For a complete discussion of the overhead and functions of each byte, see [1].

In addition to layering the interface to allow signals to be transported with different characteristics, we established a method of linking several basic signals together to form a transport channel with greater than 50 Mb/s carrying capacity. This capability became very important in the establishment of an international optical specification which is described in more detail in a later section. Establishing this procedure will allow the SONET interface to transport Broadband Integrated Services Digital Network (BISDN), Fiber Distributed Data Interface (FDDI), IEEE 802.6, and other signals that have not been defined, which will require a larger bandwidth channel than 50 Mb/s.

Subsequent Standards Work

The rest of this article will concentrate on other related standards work involving the SONET interface. First, we will cover the international standardization effort that took place in CCITT and some of the different terms used in this standard that have counterparts in the ANSI document. Next, we will concentrate on the SONET Phase II effort, the short-reach optical parameter specification, other related standards efforts, what is going on currently in SONET standardization, and some of the network impact of a standard that will be released in phases.

CCITT STANDARDIZATION EFFORT

In the summer of 1986, CCITT expressed an interest in defining an optical interface similar to the work going on in the United States. We proposed the same signal structure developed in the US. Because international compatibility was not one of the initial project goals in the US, the signal structure was not particularly suited to transport of a CEPT hierarchy. We had based our interface on signals with granularity of 50 Mb/s, which the rest of CCITT did not favor. Instead, granularity of 150 Mb/s was preferred. In addition to this, the original format was not well suited to transport 2.048-Mb/s signals.

Everyone very much wanted an international standard that would finally provide a common hierarchy for the three hierarchies—North American, Japanese, and CEPT. After numerous compromises on both sides, a Synchronous Digital Hierarchy (SDH) was defined that would satisfy all of the needs of countries with different hierarchies. One of

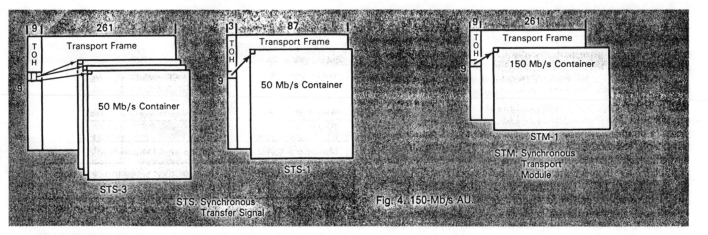

Fig. 3. 50-Mb/s AUs.

the compromises involved changing a number of terms from the North American SONET specification to ones recognized by CCITT SDH recommendations. Both specify the same signal; however, it is sometimes difficult to tell because of terminology. Here, we will explain some of the different terms and how they are related to each other. For a complete definition of all the terms and how they are used, please see [3–5].

Administrative Units

We made very little progress in international standards until the concept of Administrative Units (AUs) was introduced. Basically, an AU is a bundle of bandwidth used to manage a telecommunications network. In the US, most networks are managed in DS1s and DS3s. In other words, most transmission networks are managed at the DS1 and DS3 level. This is the reason digital cross-connect systems are being introduced to switch signals at these rates.

In order for a network provider to manage a network at an AU, the transmission signal must be capable of being broken into these size bandwidth bundles very economically. This is the reason the original SONET signal was optimized at approximately 50 Mb/s (DS3 size bundles) and why such careful work was put into the concept of virtual tributaries (DS1 size bundles).

CEPT countries do not manage their networks at DS1s and DS3s. Instead, their networks were managed at 2.048 Mb/s and 34 Mb/s or 139 Mb/s. Clearly, a 50 Mb/s signal would not accommodate management at these levels.

Fortunately, we had developed an algorithm that allowed us to link a number of the basic signals together to form a concatenated signal. The basic signal in North America is called an STS-1 (Synchronous Transport Signal—level 1). When three are multiplexed together, it is called an STS-3; and when three are concatenated, it is called an STS-3c. Concatenation specifies that these signals are to be considered as a single signal and transported that way through the network. The algorithm established actually allows any number of STS-1s to be concatenated. When these signals are linked together, it forms a transport channel in multiples of 50 Mb/s. Using the STS-3c signal as a base allowed CCITT and the US to reach a compromise that satisfied everyone.

Figure 3 illustrates a 50-Mb/s administrative unit and how an STS-3 is formed from this. Notice pointers are used to indicate the beginning of the SPE. A good pointer description can be found in [6]. Figure 4 illustrates a 150-Mb/s AU. Note that because of the concatenation algorithm, establishing a 50-Mb/s AU with pointers also establishes a 150-Mb/s AU. Figure 5 illustrates 34-Mb/s AU containers. Note that CCITT has established only a 150-Mb/s base interface; therefore, the 34-Mb/s AU is administered by de-

coding four pointers located in a special location in a 150-Mb/s frame. Because of this, choosing 34-Mb/s AUs also establishes a 150-Mb/s AU. CCITT has established the name of the basic signal at 150 Mb/s as a Synchronous Transport Module—level 1 (STM-1), which is completely equivalent to the STS-3c established in the US.

By observing the needs of different countries and different hierarchies, we were able to establish base signals that would allow network providers the ability to administer the SONET network in the same manner as their existing network, saving untold network management system investment dollars. In addition, we were able to establish a common meeting point at which both hierarchies could join and above which there would be common interfaces.

The final concept incorporated into AUs is the ability to carry one type of AU in a country optimized for the other type. Figure 6 illustrates nested signals. A nested signal is a set of AUs contained within a 150-Mb/s AU, which is transported through a network. Using nested signals, a CEPT Hierarchy country can carry three AU-3s through their network using a 150-Mb/s AU without constructing a special network to manage it. A North American Hierarchy-based country can transport four 34-Mb/s signals in the same manner. Nested signals are to be used to transport bulk traffic (e.g., DS3s or 34-Mb/s) through the network because lower-level traffic (DS1s, 2.048-Mb/s, etc.) would be transported in virtual tributaries.

Virtual Tributaries

Mentioned before, North American Hierarchy networks are managed at DS1 and DS3 rates. We established AUs to manage a DS3 but we needed to define another easily manageable container for DS1s. In SONET, these are called Virtual Tributaries (VTs). Basically, a VT is a container into which one can place a sub-DS3 signal for efficient management. There are several different types for different-

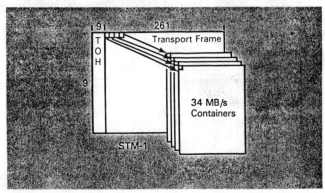

Fig. 5. 34-Mb/s AUs.

size signals: VT1.5, VT2, VT3, and VT6 for DS1, 2.048-Mb/s, DS1C, and DS2 signals. In addition to this, we have established an algorithm that will allow VTs to be concatenated together to create a variable-size transport pipe.

A VT Group is a set of VTs that has been grouped together to carry like VTs. VT groups were established because it was recognized that four DS1s or three 2.048-Mb/s signals could be contained in a VT6. By establishing VT groups, a single VT-mapped STS-1 signal can transport a mixture of DS1 and 2.048 Mb/s signals—something no other hierarchy can accomplish easily.

CCITT established a signal identical to a VT called a Tributary Unit (TU). In addition, a TUG (or Tributary Unit Group) was established to correspond to a VT group. Even though their terms are different, they refer to the same signal format. For further information on CCITT definitions, see [4], and for SONET, see [1].

Results

The most significant outcome of this work is that now one transmission interface hierarchy can be established throughout the world. Starting at 150 Mb/s, the hierarchy of the world telecommunication networks becomes common. Because they still need to transport the existing asynchronous hierarchies, payload structures will be different; but at least the transmission and cross-connecting equipment can be common.

SONET PHASE II

We achieved many of our initial goals for SONET standardization when the first specifications were published. However, we still did not have a standard for communicating operations support information across the DCCs. Operations support information includes commands (such as DS1 loop backs), alarm information, provisioning information (such as what options to set in a particular interface card), surveillance information (such as performance monitoring data), and other information needed to maintain an NE. We had established the bandwidth allocated for the DCCs (192 kb/s for the section DCC and 576 kb/s in the line DCC) but there was insufficient time to reach consensus on the protocol and messages to be used over these channels. To many, one of the significant advantages of a SONET interface was the availability of the DCC channels, which would be used to construct an operation support network at the same time as the transport network would be constructed. Therefore, standardization of the DCC became the primary goal of the SONET Phase II effort.

T1M1 has primary responsibility in developing protocols and messages for use in operation support networks in telecommunications interfaces. We requested that they develop a standard for SONET, and a joint ad hoc group was formed to aid in standardization. T1M1 at the time was

Table I. SONET Supplement Contents

Item	Description
Text Changes	Editorial in nature
Timing and Synchronization	Clarifications and requirement relaxation
APS	Clarification
Mapping Additions	Added an ATM and DS4NA mapping
Overhead Usage	Specification when to use certain overhead
DCC Protocol	Specifies the protocol used on the Line and Section DCC

completely involved in the development of generic interfaces for all Operating Support (OS)-to-NE and NE-to-NE interfaces, and was organized to accomplish this. When our request to develop a specification for a single interface arrived, it caused a massive redirection of resources and involved many of the acting working groups in T1M1. The effort and time dedicated to our request was very significant and a great deal of credit goes to T1M1 for responding to our request with the specifications developed.

Because the work was fragmented across several working groups and many people interested in only the SONET interface had to attend numerous meetings where only a portion of the time could be dedicated to SONET, a decision was made to complete the specification of the protocol in T1M1 and move the final message specification back to T1X1.5, where all of the time could be dedicated to this task. Obviously, a great deal of coordination is necessary between these groups to ensure that standards for the SONET-specific messages and generic standards do not diverge. This recent change is significant because it will allow us to dedicate the time and resources necessary to complete the specification in a timely manner.

Even though specification of the DCCs was the primary goal of the SONET Phase II effort, there were a number of other items that needed to be cleaned up. A document has been produced (T1X1/89-075) that contains all of the additions and substitutions for SONET Phase II. It should complete the final voting process some time in the Summer of 1990; however, few changes during this process are anticipated. Table I summarizes the contents of the supplement.

Results

The supplement (T1X1/89-075) contains a great deal of information, and it is not known at this time if ANSI will choose to issue the supplement as a separate document or reissue the ANSI TI.105-1988 document. However, it is important to understand some of the major changes contained in this document.

Probably the changes that will have the least effect on equipment designs are the minor editorial and text changes One significant addition was the inclusion of the term SONET in the standard. Until this point in time, the term SONET had been avoided for a variety of reasons. When most of these reasons were found to be unjustifiable, we included the term to allow someone to more easily identify the standard in a search. Another change included relaxing the synchronization requirements for NEs. After careful examination of pointer justification movements, stuffing techniques, and desynchronizer phase lock loop characteristics, it was found that the specification could be relaxed somewhat while maintaining required jitter performance.

Changes were made to the automatic protection section, which clarified many points and provided a method of

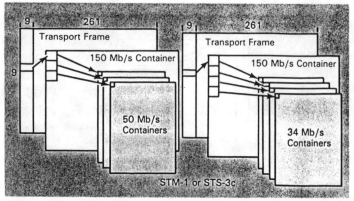

Fig. 6. Nested signals.

Table II. Overhead Specification

Signal	Drop Side		Line Side (Optical)		
	Electrical	Optical	Protection	Line 1	Line 2-*N*
A_1-A_2	R	R	R	R	R
B_1	NA	NA	R	R	R
D_1 - D_3	NA	NA	R	R	NA
C_1	R	R	R	R	R
E_1	NA	NA	OPT	OPT	NA
F_1	NA	NA	OPT	OPT	NA
B_2	R	R	R	R	R
D_4 - D_{12}	NA	NA	OPT	OPT	NA
E_2	NA	NA	OPT	OPT	NA
H_1 - H_3	R	R	R	R	R
K_1, K_2 (APS)	NA	Note 1	R	NA	NA
K_2(6-8) Line AIS	NA	NA	R	R	R
K_2(6-8) Line FERF	R	R	R	R	R
H_1, H_2 (Path AIS)	R	R	R	R	R

Note 1: For Further Study

communicating switch status (such as lock out) via a standard means. Part of this included requiring the section DCC to be present in the line side interface or providing an alternate method of communicating information through the OS network.

Two new mappings were added and clarifications to the byte synchronous mappings were included. The new mappings include a DS4NA (139.264 Mb/s) mapping and an Asynchronous Transfer Mode (ATM) mapping for BISDN. An ATM mapping is significant because the details concerning cell size in CCITT have settled sufficiently to allow an ATM mapping to be generated. Additionally, this mapping will also be used with very slight modifications for the IEEE 802.6 mapping. This can be accomplished because the cell size for BISDN and IEEE 802.6 are the same.

Another clarification added to the document is a table describing the usage of various overhead bytes in different situations. Table II lists line side and drop side interfaces and specifies which overhead bytes are to be present at the interface. Notice that there are both electrical and optical drop side interfaces, which corresponds to the electrical interface parameters recently agreed to by T1X1.4 and the short-reach optical parameter specification currently under letter ballot in T1X1.5. One of the main drivers behind this table was to restrict the use of DCCs on the drop side interface. Recent contributions to T1M1 have indicated that communication of operation support information within an office or location can be much more cost effectively accomplished with a Local Communication Network (LCN). This will be described in the section on future standards work.

DCC Specification

In previous sections, we have discussed the goals of completely specifying the DCCs and the method used to accomplish this. Because of underestimation of the effort required and the organization of the work, we were only able to specify the protocol stack used on the DCCs. This means we can now transfer data reliably over these channels, but we do not yet have a common language that will allow us to communicate. The protocol stack is contained in Figure 7 and more information about choices made within each layer is contained in T1X1/89-075.

Is it useful to have the protocol specified without message? The answer is yes, because now hardware can be built that will implement the protocol. When the messages are specified, then software can be updated to include the messages. The only risk lies in ensuring that sufficient memory or processing power is included when the hardware is developed.

SHORT-REACH OPTICAL INTERFACE SPECIFICATION

So much emphasis has been placed on the standardization of the DCCs that it is easy to overlook other very important work. One example is the issuance of the Short-Reach Optical Parameter Standard (T1X1/89-076). Work on this specification started at the same time as the DCC specification. The goal for this document was to assign optical parameters to an interface that is optimized for shorter distances (somewhere around two kilometers). By restricting the distance, lower-cost components can be used, which will allow a lower-cost interface to be established.

Main uses for this specification include interfaces between different NEs inside a central office and short interfaces to customers. If these interfaces are used inside an office (drop side), then certain overhead need not be present (e.g., section and line DCCs, order wire, etc.). The reason is to minimize the cost of providing an optical interface between equipment inside an office by using only those overhead bytes necessary. See Table II for compete specification.

If, on the other hand, the short-reach parameters are applied to an interface to a customer, then it is a line side interface, and most of the overhead must be present to ensure reliable data transfer. These two cases illustrate the need to keep the optical parameter and format specifications separate.

OTHER RELATED STANDARDS ACTIVITIES

Because we have specified SONET to be a transport signal in the public network that is capable of transporting many different services of varying capacity and structure, a great deal of interest has been generated in developing mappings for new services. Local area networks can be built or a data network can be constructed inside a single location or campus to satisfy a particular need. When these networks must be connected through the public network, often some type of conversion from the data format or rate must be performed to meet the existing public network standards. When SONET equipment is deployed, it can allow us to create bandwidth channels through the public network more easily and structure the SPE to more efficiently transport the service.

BISDN is one service that will require a large bandwidth channel through the public network. A great deal of effort is being made in the final definition of BISDN service. Several issues are already resolved. Two of the most important are the ATM cell size, 5-byte header and 48-byte information field, and how it will be transported in the public network. An STS-3c was chosen to carry the BISDN signal because it offers a 150-Mb/s channel and is identical to the international interface at STM-1. Mentioned in a previous section, the BISDN ATM mapping is included in the

Layer	Name	Protocol
7	Application	ISO 9595-2, 9596-2 (CMISE) X.217, X.227 (ACSE) X.219, X.229 (ROSE)
6	Presentation	X.216, X.226 X.209, (ASN.1 Basic Encoding Rules)
5	Session	X.215, X.225
4	Transport	ISO 8073, 8073-PDAD2 (TP4)
3	Network	ISO 8473 (ISO IP)
2	Data Link	LAPD or LAPD FR
1	Physical	DCC

Fig. 7. DCC protocol stack.

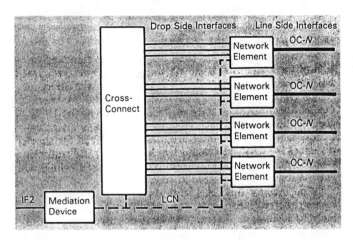

Fig. 8. LCN deployment.

SONET Phase II supplement. By carrying the BISDN signal as a SONET payload, we can allow ATM to perform the functions it does best (supplying variable bandwidth to a customer) and the synchronous frame of the SONET signal to perform the functions it does best (providing a large bandwidth channel that is maintainable in the network).

A related activity is the IEEE 802.6 standardization effort. A great deal of work by numerous people have ensured that the important characteristics of the IEEE 802.6 standard are identical to the BISDN standard. Because of this, the IEEE 802.6 signal can be carried in a SONET STS-3c payload in much the same manner as is the BISDN signal. In fact, only a very minor modification to the mapping, involving allocation additional bandwidth for a control channel needed in the IEEE 802.6 signal, is necessary. Therefore, a method of transport for this signal in the public network will exist when SONET equipment is deployed.

The X3T9 Committee has undertaken a project to map the FDDI interface into a SONET payload. Again, the reason for this is to provide a method of easily transporting this signal through the public network. The mapping is under consideration currently but will most likely map the 125-Mb/s FDDI signal into the 150-Mb/s payload of an STS-3c. More analysis must be performed to ensure this method is the proper approach; however, we will most likely see results within the year.

These are some examples of what is currently going on in related standards bodies to utilize some of the capabilities available in a SONET signal. Others will surely follow as more people look at methods of obtaining bandwidth channels through the network and more SONET equipment is deployed. There are several capabilities included in the SONET format to facilitate this, including the ability to link VTs together to create bandwidth channels in multiples of 1.5 Mb/s and the ability to link STSs together to form channels in multiples of 50 Mb/s. This, coupled with payload transparency through SONET equipment and extensive performance monitoring, will ensure that additional applications of the interface will be found.

SONET STANDARDS IN THE FUTURE

As we have shown, not all of the goals of Phase II were met and other work must be accomplished. The standard, in fact, will have numerous other phases, both here and in CCITT. Their phases will involve mostly software changes and can be implemented by updating software contained in the NEs.

North American Activities

The main activities in North America will involve standardization of the DCCs and related NE-to-OS interfaces.

As we saw in previous sections, we were able to standardize the protocol stack for the DCC but not the messages. Actually, two steps are involved in standardizing the messages. The first is to specify an information model. In its simplest terms, an information model is an agreement about the characteristics of an NE that one wants to communicate to another party. This is how many parameters will be communicated, how one can describe performance monitoring, and so on. After this agreement is reached, the actual message that will transfer the information can be constructed. This work is being developed in the T1X1.5 Operations, Administration, Maintenance, and Provisioning (OAM&P) Sub-Working Groups. (One thing you can say about standards bodies is that they really know how to pick group names!) When this is finally specified, common information can be communicated across the DCC.

Because of the complexity of the problem, message sets will most likely be released in several phases. The first set will accomplish surveillance and alarm functions. Other sets will include provisioning, etc. This is the reason it is so important to deploy an NE that can have the software updated as the standard evolves, and why we specified the hardware affecting portions of the interface first. Most commercial software packages require updating every couple of years and the SONET equipment will most likely follow the same course.

A related but separate standards activity has recently been started in T1M1. This is to define an LCN to communicate DCC information inside a central office or on the drop side of equipment. It was recognized that the DCCs provided a great deal of data transport capability, but that currently no interfaces existed between NEs and OSs that allow full benefit to be gained from this capability. Therefore, an LCN protocol has been suggested that uses an IEEE 802.3 Ethernet Connection over twisted-pair wire for the lower layers and the same upper layers as the DCCs. Figure 8 illustrates a situation where an LCN can be used for NE-to-NE and NE-to-mediation-device communication. Current recommendations for this link are either 1 Mb/s or 10 Mb/s.

The purpose for defining an LCN in this manner is to allow a multidrop data network to be created that could transfer a large amount of operations data over a short time. In addition, because the upper layers are the same as the DCC, the software necessary to implement the DCC and messages standardized for the DCC can be used for the LCN.

While this is not yet a standard and is not part of the Phase II recommendation, it is gaining a great deal of support and should become a standard within the year.

In addition to concentrating on OS and DCC issues, future work will include additional optical parameters for interfacing above 600 Mb/s, additional mappings for new services, and add/drop and ring automatic protection systems.

NETWORK IMPACT OF STANDARDS EVOLUTION

We have seen in the previous sections that the SONET standard will evolve over a number of years. A natural concern for organizations deploying equipment is the matter of when the standard is complete enough to start deployment. Actually, we have developed this standard in a method that minimizes the impact of evolution, and deployment can start today. In fact, SONET equipment can be considered just another generation of equipment available for deployment. In this section, we will examine some of the situations that will occur with SONET deployment and how these can be planned for. In addition, we will look at the developing Operations Support System (OSS) interfaces and how these will affect deployment of some of the important capabilities embedded in SONET equipment.

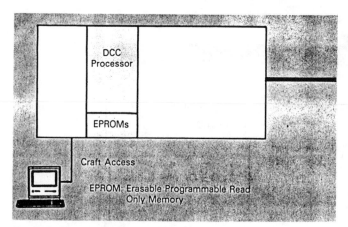

Fig. 9. Software update possibilities.

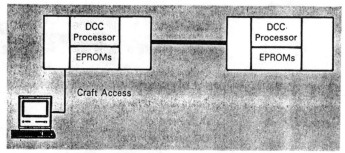

Fig. 10. Point-to-point system update.

DCC Evolution

Other sections in this paper have pointed out the fact that the SONET Phase I standard specified the interface in sufficient detail to allow reliable information transport from one point to another. This includes all of the North American hierarchy as well as the CCITT-specified hierarchy. What was left for Phase II was the completion of specification of the DCC channel. We wanted to completely specify the protocol and message set to be used over these channels. As we have seen, we were only able to complete the protocol specification, and the standardized message sets will need to be added to the equipment at a later date. The reason for releasing the specification in this manner was to allow hardware development to be completed and update the necessary software when the messages become available.

As illustrated in Figure 9, most NEs are constructed with a microprocessor to process messages on the DCC. Since the protocol is now specified to allow these processors to communicate reliably over the DCCs, when a new message set is defined, the software must be updated to include this message set if this interface requires it.[1] This is analogous to obtaining updates or new releases of software for a word processor or spreadsheet routine. In both cases, care must be taken to ensure backward compatibility. How the update is accomplished depends largely on the hardware architecture chosen by the equipment supplier. One could replace Erasable Programmable Read Only Memories (EPROMs), or load the new software into memory via a craft terminal. As will be illustrated later, eventually we will download software to NEs from central OSSs. Until a message set is standardized, vendor-specific messages can be used to allow the equipment to function as needed. It is in the best interest of all parties to complete the standardization of messages in order to reduce reliance on vendor-specific messages.

Figure 10 illustrates the situation when two NEs are connected in a link. Here again, software can be updated by replacing EPROMs or by downloading software into one element and using the DCC to load it into the other end.

Figure 11 illustrates the procedure we would like to arrive at in the future. In this case, many SONET NEs are connected in a network, and they are not all from a single supplier. In fact, not all of the elements are the same type of equipment. Some of them are terminals, hubs, add/drop elements, and Distributed Communication System (DCS) elements. This network has been connected with the LCN, which can be used to facilitate downloading message sets and software updates from a central location. When a vendor supplies an update, it can be loaded into the mediation device and addressed to the appropriate NE. This way a

number of elements can be updated, some of them not from the same supplier, when new generics of software are released.

As can be seen in these examples, networks can be built with SONET equipment and then updated with messages as they are developed. Of course, the actual method of furnishing and implementing the update will be dependent on the supplier of the equipment, but the standard can be constructed to allow this to happen. It is important to realize that some of this capability, specifically the messages to allow dowloading updates to other NEs, must be standardized first, but this should be a task of high priority in the committee because it greatly eases deployment of the equipment into the network.

Operations Support Interfaces

One of the most common difficulties facing an NE supplier, as well as NE buyers, is selection of the OSS interfaces that need to be supplied. The most common interface in use today is parallel contact closures. These will only supply alarm information from the element. Because microprocessors have become so inexpensive and NEs have become so intelligent, furnishing an NE of today's generation with a parallel alarm interface is like having a stock ticker that tells you only if the Dow Jones Average is up or down. Useful information if you need this to invest, but all of the detail is lost.

Other interfaces are standardized or are in the process of being standardized (e.g., TBOS, TABS, IF2, IF4, and LCN). Because most of the currently available interfaces cannot supply the detailed information network management systems require, many vendor-specific interfaces have been deployed as well. The question quickly becomes one of the chicken and the egg. Since we are building SONET equipment with a very sophisticated DCC interface that will allow us to perform many needed functions and allow us access to a great deal of information about that element, which interface should be designed? The answer is very clear but not always satisfying: One must build all of them, because network management systems are already in place to manage the equipment currently in the network, and it is

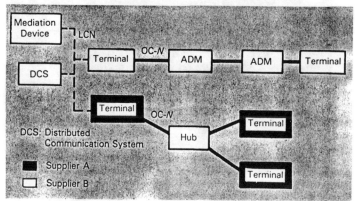

Fig. 11. SONET network.

[1]If the equipment is functioning reliably and adequately without the new message set, then it may not be necessary to include the new set unless other circumstances require it.

Table III. SONET Standard Status

	Approved	In Process
Optical Parameters (Long Reach)	ANSI T1.106-1988	
Rates And Formats	ANSI T1.105-1988	T1X1/89-075
DCC Protocol	–	T1X1/89-075
OS Interface Protocol	T1.204-1988 - Lower Layers T1.205-1988 - Upper Layers	
DCC Message Sets	–	T1X1.5 OAM&P Group
Optical Parameters (Short Reach)	T1X1/89-076	
LCN	–	T1M1
STS Electrical Interfaces	–	T1X1.4

very expensive to change them. However, many of these interfaces are implemented using polling protocols, and the SONET DCC protocol stack is non-polling. There is a link between the DCC implementation and the chosen OSS interface. A rational migration plan must be developed.

It is true that many of the embedded systems are in the process of being migrated to OSSs that will allow some of the more sophisticated interfaces to be used, but this will happen slowly and equipment must be deployed into the network before OSSs can be migrated. This is the same situation as if another generation of optical transport equipment was developed that did not have a standardized interface.

This point is very important. The specification of DCC messages and protocol is dependent on the interface to the OSS. When SONET equipment is deployed that contains a DCC implemented according to the standard, the NE must supply needed information through an OSS capable of accepting it.

A mediation device, as shown in Figure 12, will also aid in migration from one type of OSS interface to another. It can be used to gather information from a variety of interfaces in older-generation equipment that is not economical to migrate to the newer OSS interfaces. In this manner, the high-level OSS can still gather information from the entire network in a common manner. The mediation device can be used as a protocol converter and an OSS network manager.

SONET NEs can and will exist in any of these environments. It is up to the network builder to decide what is the best OSS interface to be deployed. It is up to the suppliers of the equipment to ensure that these interfaces are supplied cost effectively.

CONCLUSIONS

As we have seen in this article, the SONET standard has been divided into phases in order to allow equipment suppliers to deliver, and network builders to deploy, hardware in the network. Because the standard has been developed in phases, it makes the job a little more difficult. However, sufficient detail exists in the standards to allow graceful migration as more of the standard is developed. This is because the later phases of the standard will affect only the messages used to communicate network management information from one NE to another, and these can be supplied by software updates. A summary of the status of SONET standards can be seen in Table III.

Additionally, we have shown how this interface can be used to build networks that can efficiently transport services today and tomorrow without knowing the structure of these future signals. Many other applications will be found for this interface in the future. We have only started to scratch the surface of what is possible.

References

[1] ANSI T1.105-1988, "American National Standard for Telecommunications—Digital Hierarchy Optical Rates and Formats Specification," 1988.

[2] ANSI T1.106-1988, "American National Standard for Telecommunications—Digital Hierarchy Optical Interface Specifications, Single Mode," 1988.

[3] CCITT Recommendations G.707, "Synchronous Digital Hierarchy Bit Rates," to be issued.

[4] CCITT Recommendation G.708, "Network Node Interface for the Synchronous Digital Hierarchy," to be issued.

[5] CCITT Recommendation G.709, "Synchronous Multiplexing Structure," to be issued.

[6] R. Ballart and Y. C. Ching, "SONET: Now It's the Standard Optical Network." *IEEE Commun. Mag.*, Mar. 1989.

Biography

Rodney J. Boehm is the Director of Technology Planning at Fujitsu America Inc., and is responsible for standards and strategic planning. Rodney is also Co-Chariman of the T1X1.5 Working Group, which is responsible for SONET standardization.

He received his B.S.E.E. and M.E.E.E. from Texas A&M University in May 1978 and December 1979, respectively. Then he joined Bell Laboratories, where he was a High-Speed Logic Designer for digital radio products. At the time of divestiture, Mr. Boehm joined Bellcore, where he and Mr. Y. C. Ching originated the SONET specification.

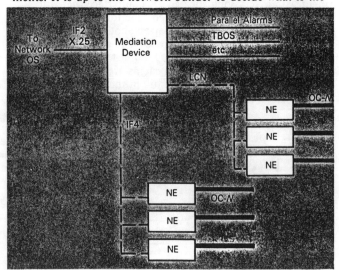

Fig. 12. Mediation-device interfaces.

Synchronous Optical Network and Broadband ISDN Protocols

Anna Hać and Hasan B. Mutlu

AT&T Bell Laboratories

Future transmission systems will be based heavily on fiber optics technology.[1] Fiber optic networks — the newest technology in data transfer — support the high-speed, low-delay data transfer needed to meet the increasing demand for high-bit-rate applications, particularly image and video services. Fiber optic networks offer not only the speed and capability for tomorrow's network customers, but they also provide the performance demanded for broadband services.

A broadband service requires an information transfer rate exceeding the capacity of a primary-rate interface. Two data rates have been defined for the primary interface: 1.544 megabits per second and 2.048 megabits per second.[2] The interface at 1.544 megabits per second is based on the North American DS-1 transmission structure, which is used for the transmission service. The interface at 2.048 megabits per second, however, is based on the European transmission structure of the same data rate.

The B-ISDN (Broadband Integrated Services Digital Network) is a network that can be used for services requiring

> The increasing demand for high-performance voice, data, video, and image communication networks has challenged researchers to design some innovative network architectures and protocol and interface structures.

high-speed packet switching. It is based on existing ISDN principles, and work to define and standardize B-ISDN is already under way in the International Telegraph and Telephone Consultative Committee (CCITT).[3] The proposed B-ISDN uses a flexible multiplexing format called ATM (asynchronous transfer mode). In the US proposal, Sonet (synchronous optical network) is specified as a physical layer of B-ISDN.[4]

The proposed B-ISDN supports a wide range of audio, video, and data applications in the same network. The service classes of B-ISDN are interactive and distribution services. The interactive services consist of conversational, messaging, and retrieval services involving two-way information exchange between two subscribers. The distribution services are represented by services with and without user individual presentation control. These services include broadcast services and provide a one-way flow of information distributed from a central source to an unlimited number of authorized receivers connected to the network. Examples of broadband services are

- broadband bearer services,
- high-quality broadband video telephony,
- high-quality broadband video conferencing,

Reprinted from *Computer*, November 1989, pages 26-34.

- existing-quality and high-definition TV distribution, and
- broadband videotex.

The primary objective of this article is to provide high-level technical information on Sonet, B-ISDN protocols, and interface structures. Since the B-ISDN protocol standards to be used in the Broadband Reference Model are currently being discussed in the CCITT, most of the standards are not yet available. For example, although CCITT has agreed that ATM will be based on fixed-length cells[1] (a fixed-size packet is called a cell), the length of the cells and the content or length of the cell headers have not been agreed on. Therefore, some of the protocols described here are not based on agreements reached in national and international standards bodies.

B-ISDN architecture and ISO model

A computer network can be defined as a collection of host computers that are interconnected (information exchange is possible), autonomous (the computers control themselves), and independently suspicious (they question their input). In any network there are hosts that run application programs. These hosts communicate with each other through the communications subnet. The communications subnet may consist of a set of point-to-point channels connecting switching elements known as nodes, or a single broadcast channel (for example, bus, ring, loop, star, or satellite/radio).

Most networks are designed as a set of layers, each offering a class of transparent services to the layer above. Each layer on a given host establishes a virtual communication with the associated layer on another host. An individual layer within a host receives a message from the next higher level and envelops the message with required information for the corresponding layer in the next host. The expanded message is subsequently passed to the next lower layer. Finally, at the lowest layer, the message is physically transmitted. In the targeted host, each layer strips off the information transmitted by its counterpart and sends the remainder up to the next layer. At the lowest layer, physical communication is established with the corresponding host, but the higher layers use virtual communication.

The set of layers and the associated set of protocols that implement the communication function are called a computer communication architecture. The architecture does not include the interfaces in its definition, since network users have little concern for how a particular system determines its interface structure. The methods for the implementation of a protocol (that is, hardware or software implementation of a specific function) are not characterized by the architecture. As long as correct usage of a protocol is satisfied, the means by which it is implemented does not affect the architecture.

Glossary of acronyms

ATM	Asynchronous transfer mode
B-ISDN	Broadband Integrated Services Digital Network
CCITT	International Telegraph and Telephone Consultative Committee
DS-1	A digital signal in the Bell system digital transmission hierarchy with a specific frame format at 1.544 megabits per second
DS-3	A digital signal in the Bell system digital transmission hierarchy with a specific frame format at 44.736 megabits per second
HCS	Header check sequence
ISDN	Integrated Services Digital Network — planned foundation for telecommunication service using digital transmission and switching technology to provide voice and data communications
ISO	International Standards Organization
MAC	Medium access control
NNI	Network node interface
OA&M	Operation, administration, and maintenance
OC-1	Optical carrier at level 1
OC-N	Optical carrier at level N
OSI	Open Systems Interconnection — a concept that will permit different vendors' products to work together
PBX	Private branch exchange — a telephone exchange on the user's premises that provides a circuit-switching capability for telephones on extension lines within the building and access to the public network
Sonet	Synchronous optical network
STS-1	Synchronous transport signal at level 1
STS-N	Synchronous transport signal at level N
STS-Nc	Concatenated synchronous transport signal at level Nc
UNI	User network interface
VCI	Virtual circuit identifier

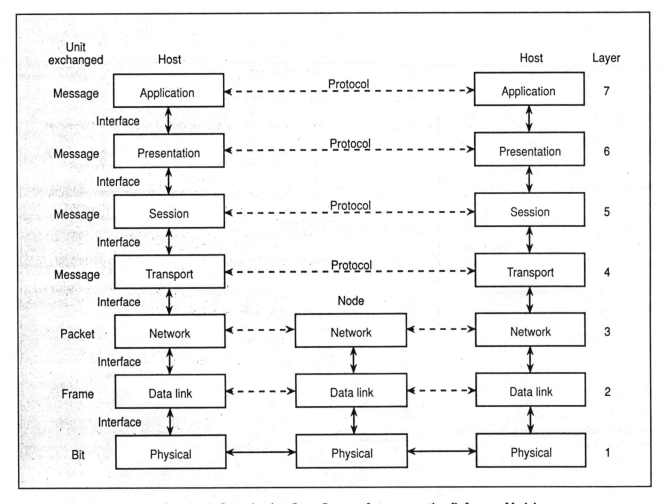

Figure 1. The International Standards Organization Open Systems Interconnection Reference Model.

Figure 1 shows a specific layered communications architecture reference model of OSI (Open Systems Interconnection) approved in 1983 as an international standard by both the ISO[5] and the CCITT.[6]

The bottom three layers (1, 2, and 3) of this model provide the networking capability — that is, the agreements between hosts and nodes or between nodes and nodes — and they address issues concerning the communications subnet. (These layers of protocol are called "chained," since the corresponding headers and trailers are removed, tested, and regenerated at every step of the pass across the network.) The upper four layers (4 through 7) administer the processing — at both ends — needed to transmit the information to the end user in a proper and identifiable format. The information associated with these layers is not tested by the nodes. (These layers of protocol are called "end-to-end" protocols.)

This article focuses on the chained lay-ers and defines associated protocols and interface structures to be used by B-ISDN.

Sonet

In the US proposal to the CCITT, Sonet (synchronous optical network) is recommended as a physical protocol for broadband services. A transmission system for a broadband interface at the physical layer uses framing techniques to transport information. Figure 2 shows the Sonet structure.

Sonet frames allow for both voice channels and broadband services, and they carry framing overhead that is not embedded in the cell structure. Transport overhead is distributed throughout the frame. Each frame consists of 9 bytes of section overhead, 18 bytes of line overhead, 9 bytes of path overhead, and 774 bytes of payload transmitted in a pattern of 3 bytes of section/line overhead followed by 87 bytes of payload plus path overhead. Section over-head is processed at each repeater. Line overhead is passed transparently through repeaters and is processed by terminal equipment at the ends of each span processed by a repeater. Path overhead is passed transparently from the point where the STS-1 (synchronous transport signal at level 1) payload is constructed to the point where it is decomposed. The STS-1 building block consists of transport overhead, path overhead, and the payload. The higher speed STS-N (synchronous transport signal at level N) is also built of transport overhead, payload, and the path overhead. Transport overhead is replicated in each Sonet STS-N frame.

An STS-N signal contains N copies of the section, line, and path overheads. If an STS-N signal is sent between two multiplexers with no intervening demultiplexing, it is permitted to send only one copy of the path overhead. This is an STS-N concatenated (STS-Nc) signal. Since any intervening transmission equipment ex-

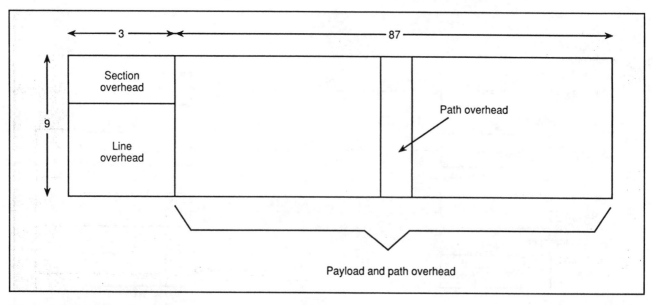

Figure 2. Sonet structure.

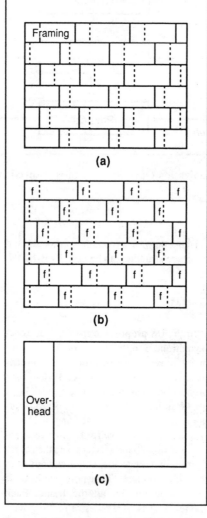

Figure 3. Formats for framing broadband interfaces: (a) periodic framing, (b) framing pattern in each cell header, (c) no framing in the cell structure.

pects to see the individual section and line overheads embedded in the signal, N copies of the section and line overheads are required in the STS-Nc signal. For B-ISDN the payload is divided into a number of fixed-length ATM cells, described later.

Broadband interfaces can be framed by using the following techniques (see Figure 3):

(1) A framing pattern is inserted every 125 microseconds (periodic framing, Figure 3a). Customer terminals can derive 125-microsecond timing from the network. Positioned channels based on the 125-microsecond periodic rate can be supported in an ATM-based hybrid interface structure. Synchronous multiplexing is also easier at a higher-than-normal (narrowband) interface rate.

(2) The framing pattern is carried in each cell header (Figure 3b). This allows for lower overhead than in the periodic framing format, if larger cell sizes are selected. An empty cell is not needed to carry the framing pattern. Synchronous multiplexing is also easier at a higher-than-normal (narrowband) interface rate.

(3) Framing overhead is not embedded within the cell structure (Figure 3c). This frame format is used by Sonet, which can carry ATM-based interface structures. When ATM is carried within a Sonet frame, a framing pattern within the cell structure is not required.

Sonet can be used for optical transmission for both the UNI (user network interface) and the NNI (network node interface). At the UNI many of the Sonet overhead bytes are not defined. B-ISDN proposals involving Sonet usually use the STS-3c frame. Sonet bit rates are integer multiples of 51.730 megabits per second. The base bit stream is made up of 125-microsecond frames of 810 bytes, where the bit rate is the integer part of the calculated bit rate. The B-ISDN user network interfaces will use two bit rates: 150 megabits per second and 600 megabits per second. Each of these interfaces will support broadband services and 64-kilobit-per-second-based ISDN services. The US proposes that the 600-megabit-per-second B-ISDN interface be structured either as four byte-interleaved STS-3c signals or as a single STS-12c.[7] Because of the path overhead, the payload of the STS-12c is slightly greater than the payload of four STS-3c signals.

Sonet is based on a layered architecture; Figure 4 shows its hierarchical structure. (The STS-Nc is a concatenated synchronous transport signal at level N. DS1 and DS3 are the digital signals in the North American digital transmission hierarchy with specific frame formats at 1.544 megabits per second and 44.736 megabits per second, respectively.)

The photonic layer is used for a fiber optic connection of light transfer. The section layer is used for frame transport. The line layer allows for transport of STS-1 through STS-Nc blocks between STS-level multiplexers. This layer uses line layer overhead and maps synchronous

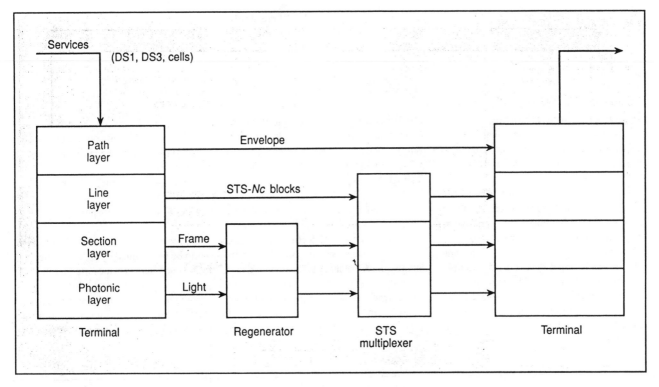

Figure 4. Sonet hierarchical structure.

payload envelopes into a transmission frame. The path layer uses path overhead and maps services into the format of the synchronous payload envelope.

In the US proposals to the CCITT, the B-ISDN transport architecture is based on the Sonet protocol.

The interoffice transport network connects service nodes via transport nodes and high-capacity fiber optic links. The links integrate the transport of voice, data, and video.

In the current architecture proposal for B-ISDN, the main components of the B-ISDN interoffice transport architecture are[8]

(1) *Interoffice facilities*. These are composed of single-mode optical fiber using the Sonet transmission format. The rates for interoffice transport are usually OC-M (OC-24 or higher) and could possibly increase to 2.49 gigabits per second (OC-48) or higher. These rates support the $n \times$ 155.52-megabit-per-second B-ISDN interface rate.

(2) *Sonet OC-M lightwave terminal*. The low- and high-speed interfaces are for the 155.52-megabit-per-second and OC-M optical signals, respectively. Line generation and termination functions include framing, synchronization, line and section overhead processing, and conversion of

optical and electrical signals.

(3) *Sonet facility restoration switch*. This switch provides facility protection and restoration rates at Sonet OC-M line rates.

(4) *Transport node controller*. This controller provides control and timing functions for each of the transport node components.

B-ISDN configuration

A functional reference architecture model for the broadband network is a conceptual division of functions that must be performed in transporting information through the network. It is a useful tool for analyzing and comparing various network architecture alternatives. Figure 5 provides a conceptual model for a B-ISDN reference configuration consisting of functional groupings partitioned by reference points R, S_B, and T_B. (Functional groupings are certain finite arrangements of physical equipment or combinations of equipment. Reference points are conceptual points used to separate groups of functions.) The subscript B indicates broadband reference points.

The reference points can also be viewed as physical interface units. Each functional

grouping has a different set of functions to perform. The TE (terminal equipment) functions, which include the lowest three layers of the OSI Reference Model, are usually performed by digital telephones, data terminals, and integrated workstations. The TE1 functions follow ISDN recommendations. The TE2 functions do not follow ISDN recommendations; they use the TA (terminal adaptor) converter to connect to a broadband network, since these devices run their own protocols and do not have B-ISDN interfaces (for example, IEEE 802.3 Local Area Network).

The R reference point is for non-ISDN physical interfaces, which require TAs to convert the protocol of the TE2 to the ATM-supported S_B/T_B interface of the NT (network termination). User equipment complying with ISDN standards can be connected at the S_B and T_B reference points (dependent on the primary versus basic ISDN rate). The S_B/T_B interface is based on ATM and has the same capacity as the U_B (loop interface). The interfaces at these reference points support 64-kilobit-per-second-based ISDN and B-ISDN services.

The NT2 functions are performed by PBXs (private branch exchanges) and terminal controllers. These functions contain local switching between the S_B interfaces, an S_B interface with the T_B interface, multiplexing of several S_B interfaces at layers 2 and 3, and concentration functions. Note that the NT2 functional grouping can be removed from Figure 5 for a specific configuration. In this case a single interface would bring the S_B and T_B reference points together (hybrid interface), and the NT would then perform all routing functions and switching between terminals on the customer premises. The NT can also multiplex several end-user terminals onto the U_B interface.

NT1 functions terminate the transmission line from the central office. The function of this grouping is to provide the physical layer interworking of the T_B and U_B interfaces. Although only one broadband T_B input is supported, multiple U_B interfaces can also be supported to increase reliability. The U_B interface is the designation for the physical interface between the NT and the local exchange. The functions of the NT1 and NT2 are similar for 64-kilobit-per-second-based ISDN and B-ISDN.

ATM

B-ISDN is based on a new multiplexing architecture called ATM (asynchronous transfer mode), which associates calls with cells by a label in the header.[4] In a labeled channel, data is put into cells prefixed with a header. The header contains at least one VCI (virtual circuit identifier) that identifies the virtual circuit a cell is associated with, and an error detection field. The information field is transported transparently by the ATM layer of the network, and no processing (for example, error control) is performed on the information field at the ATM layer.[3] The ATM provides great flexibility in supporting both continuous and "bursty" traffic streams by integrating services in common switching and transmission facilities.

Channel rates. Narrowband channel rates are defined as follows:

- B — 64 kilobits per second
- H0 — 384 kilobits per second (=6B)
- H11 — 1.536 megabits per second (=24B)
- H12 — 1.920 megabits per second (=30B)
- D — 16/64 kilobits per second

Although the broadband channels are yet to be determined by CCITT, video and high-speed data services are identified as principal applications to be taken into account in determining broadband channel rates. Broadband channels refer to virtual channels with appropriate channel bit

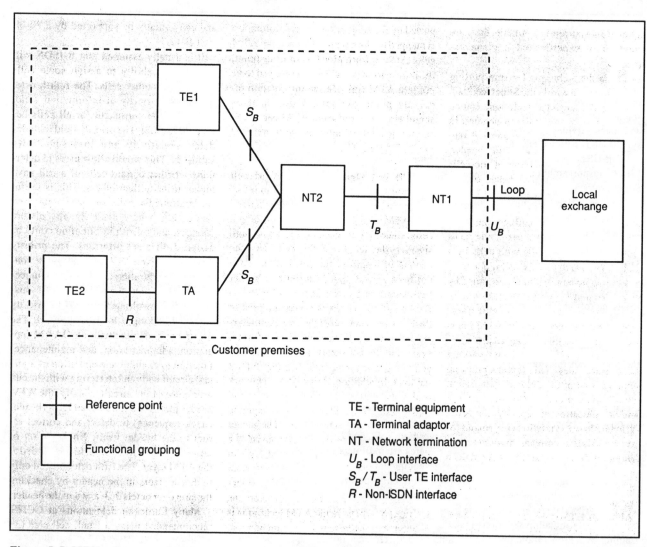

Figure 5. B-ISDN reference points.

rates. In addition to B, H0, and H1 narrowband channels, B-ISDN will support broadband channels H2 and H4 with the following bit rates:[3]

- H21 — 32.768 megabits per second
- H22 — 44.160 megabits per second
- H3 — 60-70 megabits per second (not identified)
- H4 — 132.480-138.240 megabits per second (an integer multiple of B channel)

The ATM cell should be designed so that the B-ISDN interface has sufficient payload capacity to carry one H4 channel (for example, applications such as bulk data transfer of text, facsimile, enhanced video information), plus signaling and a small number of narrowband services.[9]

ATM protocol structure. The CCITT agreed that B-ISDN will be based on a packetlike ATM structure.[4] Although commercial products using ATM techniques are not currently available, there are a number of experimental implementations.[10]

ATM is the technique for transporting user information within the Sonet payload. Conceptually, the ATM technique can be thought of as a multiplexing scheme in which user information is organized into blocks and each is appended with a header, forming a cell. Multiplexing of the cells onto the Sonet payload is based on the contents of the cell header. Unlike the STM (synchronous transfer mode) technique, which identifies calls by the position of a time slot within a frame, the ATM technique associates calls with cells by a label in the header. This technique also ensures that no bandwidth is consumed by the connection's using a virtual circuit unless information is actually being transported. One advantage of the ATM interface structure is that it can easily carry different types of services with varying data transfer rates. This feature plays an important role in the network integration enhancement process. Because of the dynamic allocation of capacity, the ATM is also sensitive to variations in demand for service and is thus convenient for bursty or continuous data services. Since ATM does not use fixed-rate connections, it can provide higher flexibility in network synchronization.

Although ATM provides many advantages, it also presents several challenges.[11] One is voice delay, since considerable delay could be introduced during creation of the cell. Another challenge is congestion control; momentary overloads could cause buffers in the switches to overflow and cells to be lost.

Figure 6 shows the layers of ATM functions in the ATM protocol model. Two specific layers related to ATM functions are an ATM layer common to all services and providing cell transfer capabilities, and an adaptation layer that is service dependent.[3]

Since the B-ISDN will be used to transfer information from different sources, this information should be adapted into ATM cells to be transported over the B-ISDN network. Transferring information by means of a stream of cells is the basic concept of ATM. The boundary between the ATM layer and the service adaptation layer corresponds to the differences between functions applied to the header and functions applied to the information field. The higher layer functions of the user and control planes and the connections between ATM and non-ATM interfaces are supported by the adaptation layer. Information is mapped by the adaptation layer into ATM cells. At the information transmitting point, the information is divided or collected to be put into ATM cells. At the information receiving point, the information is reassembled or read out from ATM cells. The service adaptation layer can be terminated in NT, TA, and TE.

ATM cell structure. The ATM cell structure consists of a header and an information field. Although CCITT has agreed that ATM will be based on fixed-length cells (since they are easier to process at high speeds), the length of the cells and the content or length of the cell headers have not been agreed upon. Currently a header field length of 5 octets and an information field length of 64 octets appear favored in the US. Confirmation of the cell parameters at a header size of 5 octets with an information field of 64 octets is contingent on achieving a mapping into a Sonet STS-3 payload. In addition, voice delay, network delay, header-processing capacity, and transmission efficiency should be studied to determine the exact field size. The header and the information field each consist of a fixed integer number of octets at a given reference point. In addition, the information field length is the same for all connections at all reference points (for example, UNI and NNI) where the ATM technique is applied. According to the recommendation, each ATM cell includes a VCI that associates the information field of the cell with a

specific virtual circuit. The Sonet payload available for ATM is 149.760 megabits per second. Usable bandwidth provided by the ATM depends on header and information field size and the manner in which cells are mapped into the Sonet frame.

Figure 7 presents the format of a 5-octet ATM header, which is currently under study.[3] The first octet of the ATM header provides MAC (medium access control) to the physical media, thus providing a contention resolution scheme when multiple terminals are on the same T_B interface. The MAC should be able to support shared access to the media for the B-ISDN services. This first octet can also be used for congestion control. The following two octets and half of the fourth octet include the VCI field, which identifies a particular connection over a UNI or NNI. Although this would allow for more than a million simultaneous connections, only 65,000 simultaneous connections are expected to be used at the UNI. These 65,000 simultaneous connections appear to be adequate and can actually be supported by a 20-bit VCI field.

It is usually assumed that B-ISDN will have the capability to assign some cells priority over other cells. The fourth octet carries the priority-of-information field, which will be consistent for all cells belonging to a call. The priority field includes delay sensitivity and loss sensitivity subfields. This would allow users to determine whether certain cells of a call have higher priority than others. This is useful for multimedia calls or for compressed video calls where sync signals, picture changes, and refresh information could be assigned different priorities. The priority level for a given VCI should remain constant for the duration of the virtual connection to eliminate the possibility of missequencing resulting from a high-priority cell's overtaking a low-priority cell. The fourth octet also includes an OA&M (operation, administration, and maintenance) function to examine the operation of a virtual circuit without interfering with the end user's use of the circuit. Finally, the ATM header includes a field called HCS (header check sequence) to detect and correct errors in the header itself. No detection of errors in the information field is provided at the ATM layer. The fifth octet is used only to detect errors in the header by checking the sum over octets 2, 3, and 4 in the header.

Many European delegations at CCITT recommended using a small cell size (34 octets) with a 2-octet header. The Europeans claim that a larger information field (greater than 32 octets) increases buffering in the network, introduces high voice packetization delay, and causes breakage inefficiencies. However, a longer cell size with larger headers is favored by the majority of delegates.[3]

The important criteria for selection of the ATM information field size are voice delay, efficiency, and cell arrival rate. According to a study conducted by Bell Communications Research, for a typical combination of data services optimum efficiency is satisfied with ATM cells between 50 and 100 octets long, which is much larger than what European administrations propose.[12] Bell Communications Research also demonstrated that to ensure real-time performance, an ATM cell must be processed in the same amount of time it takes to be transmitted.

Traffic classification for B-ISDN. The ATM is expected to handle a wide variety of traffic types ranging from circuitlike connections of fixed sized and guaranteed bandwidth to highly bursty data services. Integrating the various traffic types is important for B-ISDN. Therefore, the schemes for packet multiplexing, bandwidth allocation, and congestion control should be investigated to ensure fairness and efficient resource usage. Several studies have already been conducted to address some of the issues of integrating different traffic sources.[13] Although investigating various aspects of traffic integration is beyond the scope of this article, it is important to identify and understand some of the traffic types likely to be integrated in B-ISDN. They may have differences in tolerance to queueing delay, buffering, and bandwidth requirements. Therefore, it is useful to characterize the following B-ISDN traffic types:

(1) *Delay-sensitive high-bandwidth services*. This traffic type requires a fixed high bandwidth for the duration of a call and demands real-time service. Examples of this traffic type are conference video, real-time image and document retrieval, and local area network interconnects.

(2) *Delay-insensitive high-bandwidth services*. This traffic type includes bulk information transport services. The user can designate the extent of delay that is tolerable (specified, for example, as minutes, hours, or overnight). Examples of this traffic type are delay-tolerant document, image, and video delivery services.

(3) *Delay-sensitive low-bandwidth statistically multiplexed services*. This traffic

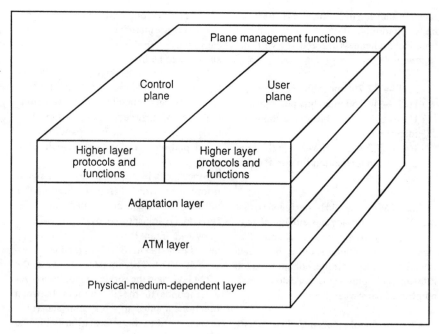

Figure 6. B-ISDN asynchronous transfer mode (ATM) protocol model.

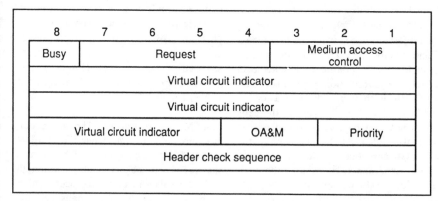

Figure 7. Asynchronous transfer mode header format.

type includes calls that are delay sensitive with end-to-end delay requirements ranging from a few tens to a few hundreds of milliseconds. Examples of such traffic are packetized voice, interactive data, and enquiry-response messages.

B-ISDN is the proposed basis for wide-area networks that will support high-speed, low-delay, functionally rich voice, data, and video applications. ATM is the target information transfer mode solution for broadband networks, and it allows the B-ISDN interfaces to carry thousands of simultaneous data, voice, and video conversations. The US position calls for the interface structures of a broadband interface to be based on ATM and to be built on emerging Sonet-framed interfaces. ATM provides the technology to integrate a wide variety of information into multimedia services by supporting voice, video, and data services separately with varying bandwidth and service requirements. In ATM the information is placed into cells prefixed with a header that includes a label for channel identification.

In the US, Sonet is intended to be the physical layer for B-ISDN. Sonet frames allow for both voice channels and broadband services. The frames carry framing overhead that is not embedded in the cell structure. Transport overhead is distributed throughout the frame. Sonet is based on a layered architecture and can be used for optical transmission for both the UNI and the NNI.

The B-ISDN is based on existing ISDN principles and can evolve by identifying additional functions and services. There is already an increasing demand for high-performance voice, data, video, and image communication networks, and B-ISDN is believed to be capable of meeting these needs once the networks are available and deployed. The B-ISDN protocol standards to be used in the Broadband Reference Model are currently being discussed in the CCITT, and most of the standards are not available yet. Therefore, some of the protocols described here are not based on agreements reached in national and international standards bodies.☐

Acknowledgments

We wish to thank Elizabeth Dunham, Gary Henry, Hank Kafka, Matt Merges, Marianne Paker, and Niel Ransom for their comments on the manuscript.

References

1. V.C. Marney-Petix, *Networking and Data Communications*, Reston Publishing Co., Reston, Va., 1986.

2. W. Stallings, *ISDN: An Introduction*, Macmillan, New York, 1989.

3. National Standards Organization, T1S1 Technical Subcommittee, "Broadband Aspects of ISDN," Dec. 1988.

4. International Telegraph and Telephone Consultative Committee SG VIII Draft Recommendation I.121, 1988.

5. *ISO International Standard 7498, Information Processing Systems — Open Systems Interconnection — Basic Reference Model*, Geneva, Oct. 1983.

6. *CCITT Draft Recommendation X.200, Reference Model of Open Systems Interconnection for CCITT Applications*, Geneva, June 1983.

7. "Broadband User-Network Interface Frame Format and Overhead Structure," Bell Communications Research, Tech. Report T1D1.1/87-494, 1987.

8. D.-P. Hsing and S. Minzer, "Preliminary Special Report on Broadband ISDN Access," *Bell Communications Research Special Report*, SR-TSY-000857, Issue 1, Dec. 1987.

9. "Fundamental Parameters for the Broadband User-Network Interface," Bell Communications Research, Tech. Report T1D1.1/87-491, 1987.

10. J.S. Turner, "New Directions in Communications," *IEEE Comm. Magazine*, Oct. 1986, pp. 8-15.

11. W.R. Byrne, A. Papanicolaou, and M.N. Ransom, "Worldwide Standardization of Broadband ISDN," *Int'l J. Digital and Analog Cabled Systems*, Dec. 1988, pp. 181-192.

12. "Some Considerations in Selecting a Cell Information Field Size," Bell Communications Research, Tech. Report T1D1.1/87-493, 1987.

13. K. Sriram and R.S. Dighe, "On Methodologies for Packet Multiplexing, Bandwidth Allocation, and Congestion Control in Broadband ISDN," in preparation.

Anna Hać is a member of the technical staff in the Advanced Software Technology Department at AT&T Bell Laboratories in Naperville, Illinois. She works on performance analysis and design of object-oriented systems, distributed architectures for software-switching applications, and congestion control in computer communication networks. Her research is in system and work-load modeling, performance analysis, reliability, modeling process synchronization mechanisms for distributed systems, distributed file systems, and distributed algorithms. She has published more than 40 papers in archival journals and international conference proceedings.

Hać received MS and PhD degrees in computer science from the Technical University of Warsaw, Poland, in 1977 and 1982, respectively. She has been a visiting scientist at the University of London, a postdoctoral fellow at the University of California at Berkeley, and an assistant professor of computer science at Johns Hopkins University. She is a member of IEEE, ACM, SIGOps, SIGComm, and SIGMetrics.

Hasan B. Mutlu, a member of the technical staff in the Computing Technology Department at AT&T Bell Laboratories in Naperville, Illinois, develops analytical models for measuring the performance of computing systems and computer networks. He worked in several research and development groups responsible for modeling and analysis of computing systems and computer networks. He also belongs to a group responsible for identifying and gathering needed information for validation of the developed models. He proposes improvement plans for the analyzed systems and develops objectives, modeling concepts, and plans to evaluate alternative systems and formulate system plans.

The authors can be contacted at AT&T Bell Laboratories, Room IHP 1F-224, 200 Park Plaza, Naperville, IL 60566-7050.

Broad-Band ATM Network Architecture Based on Virtual Paths

KEN-ICHI SATO, MEMBER, IEEE, SATORU OHTA, MEMBER, IEEE, AND IKUO TOKIZAWA, MEMBER, IEEE

Reprinted from *IEEE Transactions on Communications*, Volume 38, Number 8, August 1990, pages 1212-1222. Copyright © 1990 by The Institute of Electrical and Electronics Engineers, Inc. All rights reserved.

Abstract—This paper explores broad-band transport techniques and network architectures based on the virtual path concept. ATM (asynchronous transfer mode) techniques, when coupled with recent technological innovations, are expected to pave the way for future universal transport networks. The multiplexing and transport benefits of the ATM have a great impact on network architecture. The virtual path concept, which exploits the ATM's capabilities, is proposed to construct an efficient and economic network. The concept matches well current and anticipated technological trends. First, this paper discusses characteristics and implementation techniques of virtual paths. Advantages of the virtual path concept and its impact on transport network architecture are then demonstrated. The virtual path strategy is also shown to provide efficiently for networks with dynamic reconfiguration capability, which we will enhance network performance. Finally, some basic analytical results on the dynamic control effects of virtual paths are provided.

I. INTRODUCTION

THE need for broad-band ISDN has been recognized, and great effort is currently being focused on the development of broad-band transport technology, including information transport techniques, transport systems architecture, user–network and network–node interfaces (UNI and NNI) [1], [2], and network introduction strategies. The future telecommunications network should provide various information services in the most efficient and economical way possible [3]–[6]. The information bit rates transported in the network will range from thousands to hundreds of millions of bits per second, and the statistical nature of each type of service will differ. This wide range of bit rates and different statistical natures have to be handled efficiently by the network. The network should also be able to evolve to meet unknown future demands for increased flexibility, capacity, and reliability.

Transport techniques based on the ATM (asynchronous transfer mode [7]) are being recognized as effective in constructing a network which reflects the features mentioned above [8]. ATM systems have become possible through recent technological innovations such as fiber optics, VLSI's, and microprocessors. In the ATM, information is organized into short fixed-length blocks to which are attached short flow-identification labels (prefixes). The blocks with the labels (called cells [9]) are transported to their destination according to their labels [10], [11]. By making the most of the burstiness of information flows and by employing the store-and-forward process for transportation (which introduces variable delay into the network), the ATM can economically provide integrated transport capability at virtually any bit rate. In the ATM-based network, hierarchical structures of channel/path [12] (bundles of circuits) and the resulting rather complicated TDM frame structure of the interfaces [13], [14]

Paper approved by the Editor for CATV of the IEEE Communications Society. Manuscript received December 14, 1988; revised August 17, 1989. This paper was presented in part at the IEEE International Symposium on Subscriber Loops and Services (ISSLS'88), Boston, MA, September 1988 and the IEEE Global Communications Conference (GLOBECOM'88), Ft. Lauderdale, FL, November 1988.

The authors are with the NTT Transmission Systems Laboratories, Yokosuka-shi, Kanagawa-ken, 238 Japan.

IEEE Log Number 9037480.

can be eliminated. Therefore, multiplexing and transport aspects of the ATM are expected to have a great impact on network architecture.

Recently, very large capacity optical transmission systems [15] such as F-1.6G systems [16] have been developed and are now in practical use. These fiber-optic transmission technologies have significantly reduced the transmission cost portion of total network cost. The trend toward reduced transmission cost is expected to continue into the future, thus making the node cost relatively high. This leads to the conclusion that the total network cost would be reduced most effectively by node cost reduction, which could be achieved by simplification of both node functions and transport network architecture. However, this simplification may slightly decrease the efficiency of utilizing transmission line capacity.

Considering the inherent characteristics of the ATM and the network cost trend, this paper explores an effective transport technique and network architecture based on the virtual path concept [17]–[21]. First, problems in the existing STM (synchronous transfer mode)-based transport techniques are described. These become more and more obvious when a wide variety of services with different information transfer rates have to be supported. Next, a virtual path concept is described, which exploits ATM features and is expected to play a significant role in constructing a simplified network architecture. The characteristics and implementation techniques of the virtual path are then discussed. The advantages of virtual paths and their impact on the transport network architecture are demonstrated. The overall network performance will be enhanced by the adaptive reconfiguration capability of the network. The benefits of and possible strategies for implementing dynamic reconfiguration capability are described next. It is also shown that the dynamic reconfiguration capability will be effectively provided in the network by the virtual path strategy. Finally, some analytical results on the dynamical control effects of virtual path bandwidth are demonstrated.

II. CURRENT STM-BASED TRANSPORT TECHNIQUES

Current network systems are dedicated to a specific service, such as a plain old telephone service, circuit- and packet-switching services for low-speed data (less than 64 kb/s), narrow-band ISDN services, broad-band switching services for video communication, and different kinds of leased line services. This is because our current communications technologies have been designed around specific applications, and are difficult to adapt to new services. Current network systems are schematically illustrated in Fig. 1. The inherent problems of the STM-based networks have been recognized [21]. Here, some of the problems are described from the viewpoint of information transport techniques.

In STM-based networks, TDM frame structures were developed to efficiently multiplex transmission channels and paths with hierarchical capacities, with the least overhead. Increasing demands for a variety of services with different information transfer rates, and a hierarchical scheme of transmission capacities, have imposed a rather complicated and inflexible TDM frame structure of interfaces [13], [14] among component systems and among equipment within the networks. This increases network node cost. For multiplexing/demultiplexing service channels into/out of the transmission lines, existing facilities require multiple processing stages, which deteriorates the utilization of transmission line capacity [12] and necessitates a rather complicated design for accommodating traffic net-

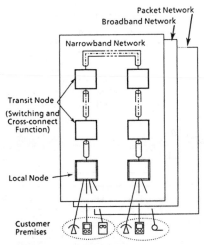

Fig. 1. Schematic illustration of current transport networks.

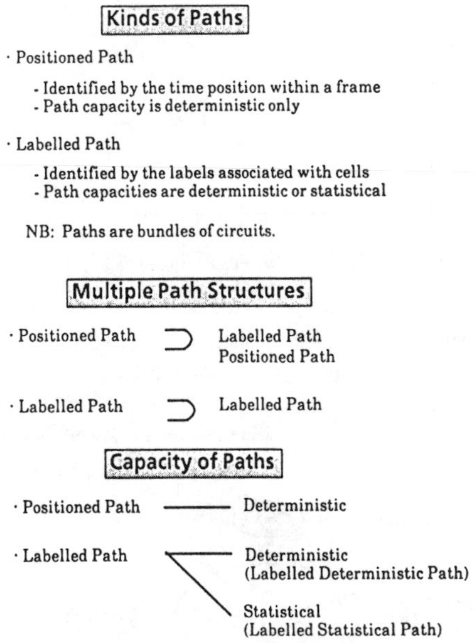

Kinds of Paths

· Positioned Path

    - Identified by the time position within a frame
    - Path capacity is deterministic only

· Labelled Path

    - Identified by the labels associated with cells
    - Path capacities are deterministic or statistical

NB: Paths are bundles of circuits.

Multiple Path Structures

· Positioned Path ⊃ Labelled Path
                  Positioned Path

· Labelled Path ⊃ Labelled Path

Capacity of Paths

· Positioned Path ———— Deterministic

· Labelled Path ⟨ Deterministic (Labelled Deterministic Path)

                Statistical (Labelled Statistical Path)

Fig. 2. Description of paths.

works within the transmission facilities network [12], [22]. For example, even if the multiplexing efficiency of service channels is 0.8 for each stage of multiplexing, five stages of multiplexing results in the final link utilization of only 0.33 ($=0.8^5$). These problems become more and more obvious as demand increases for a variety of services with a wide range of information transfer rates. Furthermore, these multiple multiplexing/demultiplexing stages and the hierarchical path structure prevent flexible logical network reconfiguration such as dynamic path routing and dynamic path bandwidth allocation. Because of this, only limited protection is provided to the network against network failures. This also imposes significant restrictions on the end customers' ability to control their closed networks.

III. ATM FEATURES

The outstanding features of ATM techniques in view of transport network development are briefly summarized below.

Inherent Rate Adaption and Flexible Interface Structure: The ATM provides an integrated communication capability employing deterministic and statistical channels at virtually any bit rate. This is provided without a complicated interface structure which carries a multiplicity of channel rates. Customers can dynamically fashion labeled channels (see Section IV) to meet their immediate service needs within a simple interface structure. No modifications of the interface structure are required to provide new services. Thus, the ATM provides basic communication capabilities in an application-independent fashion, and can be used as a foundation on which a variety of applications are supported.

Nonhierarchical Multiplexing: The uniqueness of the information unit (cell) which is transported in the network, independent of specific channel rates, enables direct multiplexing/demultiplexing of service channels that have a variety of bit rates into/out of the transmission lines while employing simplified hardware and software [21]. Thus, multiple stages of multiplexers/demultiplexers as in the existing facilities are eliminated. Capitalizing on this nonhierarchical multiplexing capability of channel/path, logical reconfiguration of the network, such as dynamic bandwidth allocation and routing of paths, can be implemented in a very effective way, as will be described in Section V.

IV. VIRTUAL PATH CONCEPT

As mentioned earlier, simplification of network architecture coupled with simplification of node processing is the key to developing a cost-effective, flexible network. This will be made possible by implementing the virtual path concept. Introduction of the virtual path concept into an ATM-based network allows management of virtual circuits by grouping them into bundles. Consequently, the virtual circuits can be transported, processed, and managed in bundles, which permits significant advantages. These include greatly reduced node costs and simplification of both the transport network architec-

ture and required OAM (operation, administration, and maintenance) functions. Details are described in the following.

A. General Description of Path

In STM-based networks, only positioned paths carried within a framed interface are possible. Specific time slots within the frame are assigned to each path. Positioned paths are identified by their time position within a frame, and the capacity of the path is deterministic only. On the other hand, in ATM networks, labeled paths can be implemented which are identified by the labels associated with the transmitted cells. The capacities of labeled paths are either deterministic (LDP: labeled deterministic path) or statistical (LSP: labeled statistical path). Each path can accommodate other paths to form a multilevel path structure. Generally, a positioned path can accommodate both labeled paths and positioned paths. Labeled paths can, however, accommodate only labeled paths. Features of each kind of path are summarized in Fig. 2.

An example of a multilevel path structure is illustrated schematically in Fig. 3, reflecting path capacity and the kinds of paths. The statistical capacity of an LSP can be characterized in terms of a set of parameters. Those parameters can be a peak value (the maximum number of cells that can be transmitted per time unit), an average value (the average number of cells per time unit), peak duration (the maximum time at peak level), etc. [23]. What set of parameters works best to define the statistical path capacity has not yet been identified. Even when the specific capacity of an LSP is given by a set of parameters, the number of cells transported "through" the path within the transmission line varies with time. Only statistical values are defined by the set of parameters.

B. Virtual Path

Definition of Virtual Path: A virtual path is broadly defined as a labeled path (bundles of multiplexed circuits) which is defined between virtual path terminators. Here, a virtual path is defined in a more limited sense as a labeled path which is terminated by virtual path terminators which can identify each connection from or to the network elements (terminals) included in the segment network to which the virtual path terminators belong (see Fig. 4). The segment networks can be, for example, local switching networks, LAN's (local area networks), or private networks. Virtual path terminators can be switching systems, LAN gateways, or private network gateways. The capacity of a virtual path can be deterministic or statistical according to the requirements. Thus, a virtual path provides a logical direct link between virtual path terminators.

Multilevel Structure of Virtual Path Network: Virtual path net-

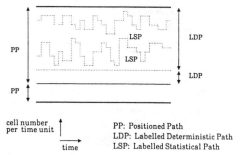

cell number
per time unit ↑

time →

PP: Positioned Path
LDP: Labelled Deterministic Path
LSP: Labelled Statistical Path

Fig. 3. Schematic illustration of multilevel path structure reflecting path capacity and kinds of paths.

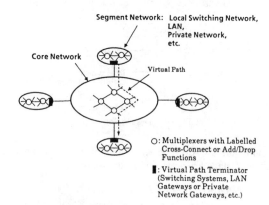

Segment Network: Local Switching Network,
LAN,
Private Network,
etc.

Core Network

Virtual Path

○ : Multiplexers with Labelled
Cross-Connect or Add/Drop
Functions

■ : Virtual Path Terminator
(Switching Systems, LAN
Gateways or Private
Network Gateways, etc.)

Core Network: Connecting segment networks, in which all the cells are
identified by their VCIs at the VP terminator.

Fig. 4. Virtual path concept.

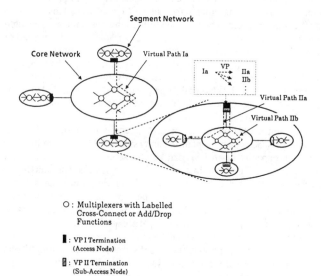

Segment Network

Core Network

Virtual Path Ia

Virtual Path IIa

Virtual Path IIb

○ : Multiplexers with Labelled
Cross-Connect or Add/Drop
Functions

■ : VP I Termination
(Access Node)

▨ : VP II Termination
(Sub-Access Node)

Fig. 5. Multilevel structure of virtual path network.

works can form a multilevel structure as shown in Fig. 5. In the figure, virtual path Ia (VP Ia) is terminated at the destination node virtual path terminator. The virtual channels accommodated in the VP Ia are identified and some of them can be switched into another virtual path (VP IIa, for example) defined in the segment network, thus forming a multilevel structure of virtual path networks. An example of this is given in Section IV-D.

Virtual Path Identifier: The identification of a virtual path can be carried out using a virtual path identifier (VPI) which is associated with a cell. A VPI can be attached to each cell or can be collectively placed in the overheat (OH) region of an STM/ATM frame [20] if these frame structures are adopted. These frame structures accommodate a fixed number of cells within their payloads. Moreover, the VPI can be attached to concatenated cells which belong to the same

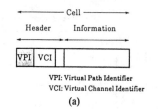

← Cell →

Header   Information

| VPI | VCI | |

VPI: Virtual Path Identifier
VCI: Virtual Channel Identifier

(a)

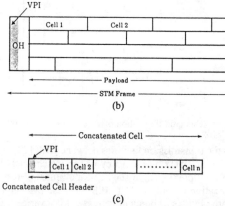

VPI

OH

Cell 1   Cell 2

Payload

STM Frame

(b)

← Concatenated Cell →

VPI

Cell 1 | Cell 2 | | ·········· | Cell n

Concatenated Cell Header

(c)

Fig. 6. Illustration of VPI placement in (a) each cell header, (b) OH of STM frame, and (c) header of a concatenated cell consisting of cells belonging to the same virtual path.

virtual path, in a way similar to the composite packet scheme [24], [25].

Possible placements of VPI are illustrated in Fig. 6. When VPI's associated with each cell are placed collectively in the overhead region of an STM/ATM frame [Fig. 6(b)], the required node memory increases so as to allocate the payload capacity to each virtual path and to accommodate VPI's in the OH. Consequently, processing delay increases. If the VPI is attached to concatenated cells [Fig. 6(c)], processing is required for the concatenation of cells belonging to the same path. Processing is also required to launch concatenated cells within the specified time so as to restrict the delay at the node, even if the number of cells does not reach the fixed value of the concatenated cell. To perform these processes, both the required memory size and delay are increased. Although this scheme decreases the frequencies of cell switching at transport nodes because of the cell concatenation, the store-and-forward delay (waiting time plus service time) increases because of the longer concatenated cell length [26]. Furthermore, if multiple lengths of concatenated cells are defined, the complexity of the switching fabric increases. Considering the above, it was concluded that the VPI should be attached to each cell, as shown in Fig. 6(a).

Header Organization: Two opposing cell header organization techniques for virtual path and virtual channel identification are possible—the implicit and explicit schemes [23]. In the implicit scheme, the virtual path and virtual channel are translated from a logical number which implicitly represents them. On the other hand, in the explicit scheme, dedicated fields are defined for virtual path and virtual channel identification. These fields are used selectively by the switch in the exchange and cross-connect nodes according to the function necessary for cell handling. The implicit and explicit schemes are compared as follows.

In the explicit scheme, routing table renewal at transit nodes, at which paths can be cross connected according to the VPI's without referring to the VCI's (virtual channel identifiers), are necessary only when paths are set up, released, or rerouted (see Section IV-C). This eliminates processing on a call-by-call basis at each transit node during call establishment and release, and consequently, the call setup time is greatly reduced.

On the other hand, in the implicit scheme, routing table renewals on a call-by-call basis at transit nodes are necessary, which requires longer call setup times. In the explicit scheme, generally, longer

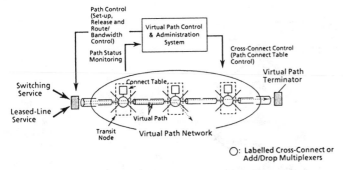

Fig. 7. Schematic illustration of virtual path implementation.

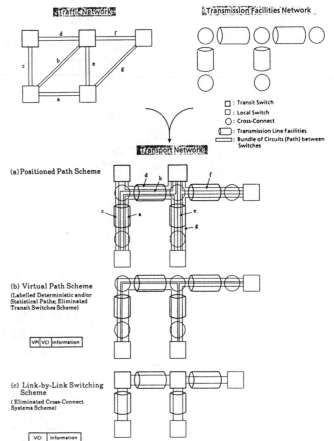

Fig. 8. Transport network configurations based on different circuit handling strategies.

headers are needed to carry both the VPI and VCI, while only the dedicated field, VPI or VCI, is identified at nodes according to the node functions necessary. On the other hand, in the implicit scheme, shorter headers are needed, while all the numbers must be identified at each node to perform the same functions. Thus, the explicit scheme requires less memory for the path connection table at transit nodes. Considering all of the above, the explicit scheme is essential in order to fully utilize the advantages of the virtual path strategy (see Section IV-E).

Logical Path Number: A large number of virtual paths can exist at the same time in the network, while only a limited number of virtual paths is multiplexed in each transmission link. Thus, it is advantageous to adopt the logical path numbers associated with each link as VPI's instead of adopting numbers with global significance in the network. This is similar to the way in which logical channel numbers (LCN's) are used as VCI's. The adoption of a logical path number scheme can not only save the bits needed for a VPI, but also separate the VPI header from the physical structure of the network. Therefore, this scheme implies no constraints due to the header size on the expansion of the network.

C. Virtual Path Implementation

Virtual paths are implemented by employing virtual path terminators and labeled cross-connect and/or add/drop multiplexers. This is schematically illustrated in Fig. 7. Virtual path routes are established or released by setting the path connect tables of the labeled cross-connect and/or add/drop multiplexers on the path, and the transmission capacity is reserved or cleared along the path at the same time.

Virtual paths are established or released dynamically, based on long-term service provisioning, short-term demand, or even immediate demand for alternate routings in case of network failures. Call setup is performed at an access node. During the call setup process, the access node identifies the appropriate path or establishes a path if necessary, and makes the decision whether to accept or reject the call based on the current path usage status. Thus, transit nodes in the transport network are free from call-by-call based processing during call setup, which considerably reduces transit node cost.

Once a call is set up, the access node writes the appropriate VPI number in the header of each cell which has a specific VCI corresponding to the call. The cells are transported through the transport network, and at transit nodes, only the VPI needs to be identified. At the access node on the other end, the virtual path is terminated and cells are switched according to their VCI's to a virtual circuit or to another virtual path (multilevel virtual path structure), as was explained in Section IV-B.

D. Network Configuration Based on Virtual Path Concept

In the ATM-based networks, two basic types of transport techniques can be employed to provide end-to-end connection. One is to apply link-by-link switching, and the other is to utilize a path concept. Fig. 8 shows how end-to-end connection can be provided by demonstrating how a traffic network can be accommodated by the transmission facilities network. In the figure, three ways are compared for accommodating the traffic network. These are (a) the po-

sitioned path scheme that is used for existing STM-based networks, (b) the virtual path scheme, in which transit switches are eliminated and virtual paths are defined between local switches, and (c) the link-by-link switching scheme. These can be applied to the network at the same time in combination. For example, in case (b), multiple stages of switching hierarchy and the positioned path scheme can also be implemented at the same time if necessary.

If virtual paths are applied between any access nodes (local switches in local access networks), they can be logically connected in a mesh configuration. In STM-based networks, it is not practical to develop an equivalent mesh path configuration. This is because of the following. 1) The hierarchical structure of the positioned paths prevents the efficient use of transmission capacity [12], [22] and necessitates the use of multistage multi/demultiplexers. In addition, it is very difficult to directly multi/demultiplex service channels with a variety of channel rates into/out of positioned paths while employing simple hardware and software. 2) Dividing the transmission line's capacity among several positioned paths with small capacities greatly reduces the statistical effects of calls. To achieve sufficient statistical effects for efficiently utilizing transmission link capacities, a multistage switching hierarchy is required.

In contrast, in ATM-based networks, the following characteristics can be exploited to construct a simple network such as one employing a mesh path configuration. 1) Direct multi/demultiplexing of each service channel with a variety of bit rates becomes possible while employing simple hardware and software [21]. A nonhierarchical labeled path structure results in efficient use of transmission capacity. 2) Statistical bandwidth allocation capability for the calls (statistical cell multiplexing) allows the efficient use of transmission capacity. The statistical multiplexing effects of the traffic can be based on the total capacity of labeled statistical paths multiplexed on the link, instead of individual labeled statistical path capacity defined between the switches. This is made possible by employing a labeled path structure.

211

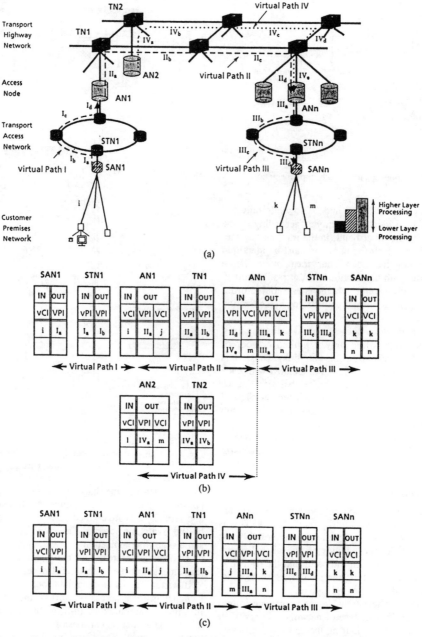

In the call connect tables shown above, only the parts identified and changed in the routing header are shown. In the figure, node equipment is divided according to its function, however, some can be practically implemented in an integrated fashion.

Fig. 9. (a) Possible network configuration applying virtual path concept. (b) Call connect table when LCN associated with VP II is provided to each cell. (c) Call connect table when LCN associated with incoming link to ANn is provided to each call at AN1.

Thus, by applying the virtual path concept in an ATM-based network, switching stages could be reduced and the circuit spans could be made longer. This will materially reduce network costs (node costs) and also simplify the traffic flow. Thereby, both the transport network architecture and required OAM functions can be simplified.

Possible Network Configuration: A possible network configuration that fully utilizes the virtual path concept is shown in Fig. 9(a). The network consists of:

- a transport highway network which consists of transport nodes (TN's) and high-speed optical transmission lines, and accommodates virtual paths logically connecting access nodes;
- access nodes (AN's) which control and manage each call, and terminate virtual paths;
- transport access networks, which carry information from sub-

scribers to access nodes through subtransport nodes (STN's) and high-speed optical transmission lines in which a large number of calls are concentrated and multiplexed by subaccess nodes (SAN's).

In this network model, single-switching-stage architecture is adopted. However, multiple-switching stages can also be applied according to the transmission/processing cost ratio. The TN's and STN's are ATM cross connects or add/drop multiplexers. More than one virtual path will be defined between AN's or between AN's and SAN's, according to the configuration of the transmission facilities network, for increased network reliability. Generally, a transport highway network which accommodates virtual paths will exhibit a hierarchical structure, such as a backbone network with regional networks [21] (not shown here), in order to restrict the maximum number of nodes traversed along the path and to facilitate network OAM.

In the model, virtual paths are also defined in the transport access network (for example, Virtual Path I: between SAN1 and AN1), thus forming a multilevel structure of virtual path networks, as explained in Section IV-B (Fig. 5). Virtual Path II is defined between AN1 and ANn. However, it can also be defined between AN1 and SANn, eliminating the termination at ANn. Other variations for defining virtual paths are possible.

In Fig. 9, two different ways of defining VCI's are shown. These are explained below, taking Virtual Path II as an example. In the call connect table presented in Fig. 9, only the parts identified and changed in the cell routing header are shown.

At AN1, one of the ways is to base the VCI of each cell of a particular call on the LCN associated with each virtual path (in this case, VP II) going out from AN1 [see Fig. 9(b)]. By this technique, at the VP II terminator of the destination node (ANn), each call multiplexed on the link coming into ANn is identified by mapping both the VPI and VCI of each cell. This is because cells belonging to different virtual paths terminated at the node may have the same VCI's. This means that the require maximum address space of the call connect table of the virtual path terminator at ANn should be 2^{m+n} (m = VPI [bit], n = VCI [bit]). On the other hand, the maximum number of calls multiplexed on a link is limited due to the link capacity, regardless of the length of the VPI and VCI. Therefore, the maximum address space needed in practice is limited, and is usually less than 2^{m+n}.

The other way is to base the VCI on the LCN associated with the incoming link to the virtual path terminator in ANn (destination node) which accommodates Virtual Path II [see Fig. 9(c)]. This is possible by sending the LCN to AN1 at the call setup process. By this technique, at the virtual path terminator in ANn, each call multiplexed on the incoming link to ANn is identified only by the VCI of each cell; thus, the necessary address space of the call connect table should be 2^n (n = VCI [bit]). This memory size is equivalent to that for the link-by-link switching technique.

E. Advantages of Virtual Path

The implementation of the virtual path concept provides the network with many desirable characteristics. The advantages of the virtual path technique when compared to the link-by-link switching technique and positioned path technique are summarized in the following.

Simplified Network Architecture: The network transport functions can be separated into individual-circuit related and grouped-circuits related functions. This reduces such processing at transit nodes along a path as call-by-call routing, bandwidth allocation, and routing table renewal, as shown in Fig. 10(a). There are many levels of virtual path strategies related to the management of paths, as shown in the figure. The figure includes virtual path strategies for dynamic network reconfiguration, to be described in Section V. The processing required depends on the level, as does the utilization of transmission link capacities. A schematic illustration of the transmission capacities utilization is shown in Fig. 10(b). The increase of the utilization efficiency is paid for by an increase in necessary processing.

The reduced processing made possible by applying the virtual path strategy and the direct multi/demultiplexing capability of service channels results in simplified hardware and software for node facilities. Furthermore, by using the virtual path strategy, the switching stages can be reduced and the spans of circuits can be increased. Thus, traffic flows are simplified, and consequently, the routing processing and the required OAM will be simplified. The virtual path strategy is made more and more feasible with advancements in low-cost communications capabilities by optical technology. Thus, network architecture can be simplified.

Increased Network Performance and Reliability: Virtual paths provide the network with another level of virtual circuit handling in addition to the circuit level and link levels [27], [28]. The virtual path capacities are nonhierarchical, and no processing is necessary at nodes along the path between virtual path terminators when the path capacity is allocated/cleared or altered. Conversely, in STM-based networks, processing of time slot reallocation within TDM frames is necessary. Routing alterations of virtual paths are possible simply by changing information in the path connection tables at nodes along the path. Therefore, no specific equipment [29] in addition to the labeled cross-connect systems is required for the path routing alterations to protect against network failures. Thus, dynamic path routing and dynamic path bandwidth allocation are more easily implemented than in STM-based networks. This feature also increases the adaptability of a network to varying network traffic and to unexpected sudden increases in network traffic, as will be described in Section V. Virtual paths also provide the network with the flexibility needed for network reconfiguration in case of network failure. The performance and the reliability of the network will consequently be enhanced and increased network OAM capabilities will be provided.

Reduced Processing and Short Connection Time: As mentioned earlier, call establishment processing on a call-by-call basis is eliminated at nodes along a path between the virtual path terminators. This produces short connection time.

Enhanced Network Services: Virtual paths can be applied not only to transport highway networks, but also to transport access networks, as shown in Fig. 9. Furthermore, customers may directly access virtual paths. This provides the effective means to construct closed networks which end-customers can control (see Section V). The VPI field of a cell header can be utilized for other purposes in parts of the network where virtual paths are not defined. For example, VPI fields can be utilized to implement center-to-end distribution services such as CATV services in transport access networks.

Most of the advantages mentioned above are partly offset by the reduced utilization of link capacity when compared to link-by-link switching [see Fig. 10(b)]. However, this offset is expected to become more and more insignificant due to the continuing transmission cost reduction attained by the development of optical transmission technologies [16].

V. DYNAMIC CONTROL OF VIRTUAL PATH

The effectiveness of virtual paths can be extended by dynamic path controls such as dynamic path routing and dynamic path bandwidth allocation, which provides a network with dynamic reconfiguration capability. Adaptive reconfiguration capability of the network produces many enhancements of network performance [30].

- Adaptability to unexpected traffic variations and network failures will be enhanced, thus increasing the reliability of the network.
- The amount of traffic which can be carried in the network will increase.
- The network operating companies can improve the quality of the services they offer, such as in greater responsiveness to changing customer demands, and can offer new services at reduced cost. Network operation costs will also be reduced.
- Customers will be able to control their own closed networks on a real-time basis, to reconfigure the number of circuits among different locations, for example.

In STM-based networks, the means to create adaptable and flexible networks have been studied from the viewpoints of 1) the reconfiguration of circuit connections, mainly in relation to traffic networks (this method is known as group transit switching [31] or the variable communication network [32]), and 2) the reconfiguration of path networks employing cross-connect functions in relation to both traffic and facilities networks (known as dynamic network architecture [33]). A comparison of these is shown schematically in Fig. 11. The relation between a traffic network and a facilities network is depicted in Fig. 8, and explanations are given in Fig. 12 of (i) the dynamic connection arrangement of bundles of circuits employing switches, and (ii) dynamic path bandwidth allocation employing cross-connect functions. Dynamic route arrangement schemes of circuits and paths are not illustrated in the figure.

In an ATM network, dynamic control of virtual paths employing the labeled cross-connect function [Fig. 12 (ii), (b) and (ii), (c)]

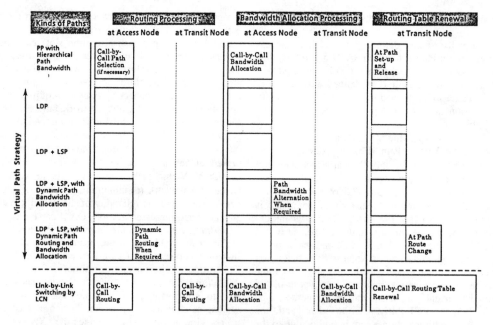

(a) Processing Required at Call Set-up

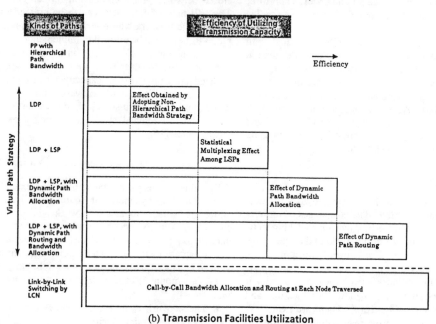

(b) Transmission Facilities Utilization

Fig. 10. Required processing and transmission facilities utilization for different levels of path management compared to link-by-link switching scheme.

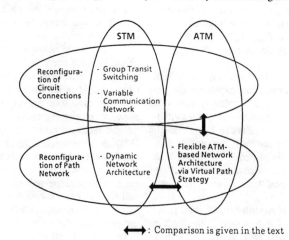

⟷ : Comparison is given in the text

Fig. 11. Logical network reconfiguration scheme.

214

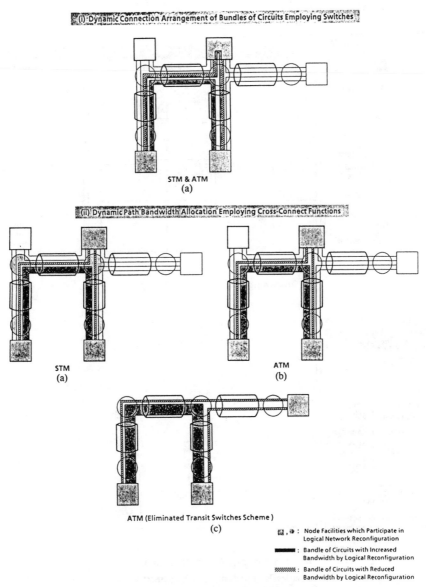

STM & ATM
(a)

STM
(a)

ATM
(b)

ATM (Eliminated Transit Switches Scheme)
(c)

▨ , ⊕ : Node Facilities which Participate in Logical Network Reconfiguration

▬▬▬ : Bandle of Circuits with Increased Bandwidth by Logical Reconfiguration

▨▨▨ : Bandle of Circuits with Reduced Bandwidth by Logical Reconfiguration

Fig. 12.   Logical network reconfiguration strategies.

has significant advantages over dynamic connection arrangement of circuits employing switches [Fig. 12 (i), (a)].

• No connection arrangements at the circuit level are required; thus, routing table renewal regarding virtual circuits or VCI reservation for semi-deterministic connections is not required at cross connects. Furthermore, in dynamic virtual path bandwidth allocation, routing table renewal on virtual paths in the nodes along paths is not required either.

• Substantial flexibility is retained when the numbers of hierarchical switching stages are reduced and the numbers of transit switches are decreased [21] [see Fig. 12 (ii), (c)].

The virtual path strategy greatly facilitates dynamic control of paths compared to the positioned path strategy in STM-based networks. This is because of the following.

• Virtual path bandwidth is determined nonhierarchically, which enables optimized or improved path routing and bandwidth control, and results in more efficient use of transmission capacity in the network.

• Direct multiplexing/demultiplexing of each virtual path with a different bandwidth becomes possible while employing simple hardware and software. This also greatly simplifies the design for accommodating traffic networks within the transmission facilities network [12], [22].

• Statistical bandwidth allocation capability for calls (statistical cell multiplexing) allows efficient use of transmission capacity, even if the path bandwidth is small. The statistical multiplexing effects of the traffic can be based on the total capacity of the multiplexed virtual path with statistical bandwidth, instead of on individual path capacity defined between switches.

• No processing is necessary at nodes along the paths between virtual path terminators when the path bandwidth is allocated/cleared or altered, eliminating time slot reallocation within a TDM frame as in STM-based networks. The alteration of path routing is possible simply by changing routing information in the path connection tables at nodes along the path.

Considering the above, dynamic control of virtual paths is expected to provide an effective means for constructing dynamically reconfigurable ATM-based networks. As described before, the dynamic control enhances adaptability and flexibility of the network or improves the transmission link capacity utilization, while it increases necessary processing (see Fig. 10). In the dynamic control of virtual paths, different levels of path management are identified as shown in Fig. 13. The processing required depends on the level as does the utilization of transmission link capacities, which is schematically illustrated in Fig. 13. The increase in the link utilization efficiency is paid for by the increase in necessary processing.

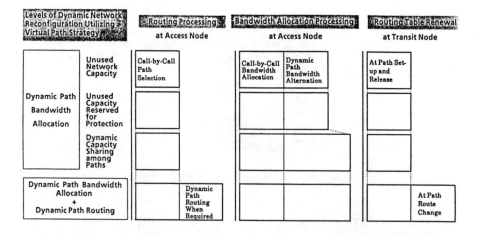

(a) Processing Required at Call Set-up

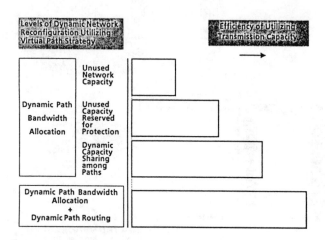

(b) Transmission Facilities Utilization

Fig. 13. Different levels of virtual path management for dynamic network reconfiguration.

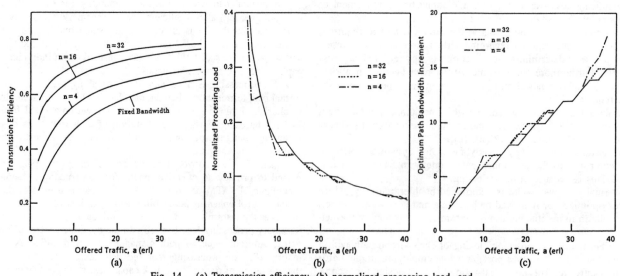

Fig. 14. (a) Transmission efficiency, (b) normalized processing load, and (c) optimum path bandwidth increment size versus offered traffic to each virtual path.

A. Dynamic Bandwidth Allocation of Virtual Path

Which level of virtual path management (see Fig. 13) is to be applied is decided after the processing/transmission cost ratio has been determined. This paper, as the first step, demonstrates some basic analytical results on dynamic path bandwidth control effects. The tradeoffs between transmission link utilization and required processing are evaluated for a simplified model as described in [33]. In the model, the bandwidth of each virtual path accommodated in a link is increased or decreased in increments of "S" according to the amount of calls offered to each path where every call is assumed to have the same bandwidth "1." Other assumptions adopted to make the evaluation easier are as follows.

- The bandwidths of each call and path are deterministic only (no statistical effect on the bandwidth is considered).
- The average traffic offered to each virtual path is identical, and the call arrival process is a Poisson process.

Under these assumptions, one of the links in the network was analyzed [34]. The detailed analytical development will be provided elsewhere.

Fig. 14 shows (a) transmission efficiency, and (b) normalized processing load versus offered traffic to each virtual path, in which the number of paths n multiplexed on the link is altered. In the calculation, the path bandwidth increment S is optimized for maximum transmission efficiency. The optimum increment size of S is shown in Fig. 14(c). The transmission efficiency is defined as the ratio of carried traffic to the minimum link capacity required to satisfy a specific call blocking probability. The normalized processing load is defined as the ratio of the frequency of the virtual path bandwidth change request and that of call setup. In this evaluation, the upper limit of each virtual path bandwidth was set at $4S$ to make the analysis easier, and the call blocking probability was 10^{-3}. In Fig. 14(a), transmission efficiency without dynamic bandwidth control is also presented, which was obtained by using the Erlang B equation. Fig. 14 shows that by the dynamic bandwidth allocation of virtual paths, transmission efficiency is considerably improved, while the increase in processing load is insignificant. The increase in processing load is less than 15% when the traffic offered to each virtual path is more than 10 Erlangs.

VI. Conclusions

Broad-band transport techniques and network architecture were explored. Multiplexing and transport aspects of ATM were shown to have a great and beneficial impact on network architecture. The virtual path concept, which makes the best of ATM features, has been proposed and was investigated. It is a critical issue to determine on which technique—the positioned path scheme or the virtual path scheme—future ATM-based networks should be based to accommodate traffic networks within transmission facilities networks. The attainable performance and capabilities of future networks are strongly influenced by the technique adopted. The virtual path concept and its implementation techniques were investigated from various points of view. It was demonstrated that by implementing the virtual path concept, the network is provided with many desirable features necessary for future communication networks. Furthermore, by dynamic control of the virtual path, adaptive reconfiguration capability of the network was shown to be effectively provided, and network performance enhanced.

The virtual path concept presented here will be implemented in the laboratory and tested in the near future. The analytical challenge remains for precisely determining the advantages created by dynamic control of virtual paths. The information transport technique based on the virtual path concept matches well the current trend toward transmission cost reduction achieved by using optical technologies. It is expected to be implemented in the mid-1990's, revolutionizing existing networks. Customers who access the network will be on the leading edge of communication technology, and will reap the benefits of an advanced information society through enhanced transport capability and integrated standard access.

References

[1] Y. Inoue, I. Tokizawa, and N. Terada, "Basic consideration to define broadband network interfaces," in *Proc. GLOBECOM'87*, Tokyo, Japan, Nov. 1987, pp. 13.2.1–13.2.5.

[2] M. W. Becker, T. T. Lee, and S. E. Minzer, "A protocol and prototype for broadband subscriber access to ISDN's," in *Proc. ISS*, Pheonix, AZ, Mar. 1987.

[3] J. K. Kultzer and W. A. Montgomery, "Statistical switching architecture for future services," in *Proc. ISS'84*, Florence, Italy, May 1984, session 43 A, paper 1, pp. 1–6.

[4] J. S. Turner, "New directions in communication," in *Proc. Int. Zurich Seminar Digital Commun.*, Zurich, Switzerland, Mar. 1986, pp. A3.1–A3.7.

[5] T. Miki, S. Kano, Y. Inoue, and H. Yamaguchi, "Lightwave-based intelligent transport network," in *Proc. ISSLS'86*, Tokyo, Japan, Sept. 1986, pp. 47–52.

[6] K. Sato, H. Nakada, and Y. Sato, "Variable rate speech coding and network delay analysis for universal transport network," in *Proc. INFOCOM'88*, New Orleans, LA, Mar. 1988, pp. 8A.2.1–8A.2.10.

[7] "Report of the Brasilia meeting of broadband task group—Part B," TD130, CCITT SG XVIII, ISDN Expert Meeting, Brasilia, Feb. 1987 (source: Chairman, Broadband Task Group of SG XVIII).

[8] K. Sato and I. Tokizawa, "Flexible asynchronous transfer mode networks utilizing virtual paths," in *Proc. ICC'90*, Atlanta, GA, Apr. 1990, pp. 318.4.1–318.4.8.

[9] "Part C.9 of the report of working party XVIII 15: Proposed draft recommendation I.113—Vocabulary of terms for broadband ISDNs," TD no. 35, CCITT SG XVIII, Hamburg Meeting, July 1987 (source: Special Rapporteur for Question 19/VXIII).

[10] A. Thomas, J. P. Coudreuse, and M. Servel, "Asynchronous time-division techniques: An experimental packet network integrating video communication," in *Proc. ISS'84*, Florence, Italy, May 1984, session 32C, paper 2, pp. 1–7.

[11] P. Gonet, P. Adam, and J. P. Coudreuse, "Asynchronous time-division switching: The way to flexible broadband communication networks," in *Proc. Int. Zurich Seminar Digital Commun.*, Zurich, Switzerland, Mar. 1986, pp. D5.1–D5.7.

[12] Y. Okano, T. Kawata, and T. Miki, "Designing digital paths in transmission networks," in *Proc. GLOBECOM'86*, Houston, TX, 1986, pp. 25.2.1–25.2.5.

[13] "Requirements for interfacing digital terminal equipment to services employing the extended superframe format," Pub. 54010, AT&T, Oct. 1984.

[14] Y. Maeda, M. Tokunaga, and I. Tokizawa, "An advanced multimedia TDM system for closed network," in *Proc. ICC'87*, Seattle, WA, 1987, pp. 30A.3.1–30A.3.5.

[15] K. Ogawa, S. S. Austin, and S. R. Johnson, "High capacity single mode system—Its performance and maintenance features," in *Proc. GLOBECOM'87*, Tokyo, Japan, Nov. 1987, pp. 22.3.1–22.3.5.

[16] K. Nakagawa, K. Aoyama, J. Yamada, and N. Yoshikai, "Field experiments on the F-1.6G optical fiber trunk transmission system," in *Proc. GLOBECOM'86*, Houston, TX, Dec. 1986, p. 34.1.

[17] K. Sato and M. Hoshi, "Digital integrated transport network—II," NTT R&D Document 697, in Japanese, May 1987.

[18] T. Kanada, K. Sato, and T. Tsuboi, "An ATM based transport network architecture," presented at IEEE ComSoc Int. Workshop on Future Prospects of Burst/Packetized Multimedia Commun., Osaka, Japan, Nov. 1987, p. 2.2.

[19] K. Sato, T. Kanada, and I. Tokizawa, "High-speed burst transport system architecture" (in Japanese), IEICE Tech. Rep., Vol. 87, no. 320, p. IN87-84, Dec. 1987.

[20] "Some key features on UNI and NNI considering ATM (a framework for discussion)," Delayed Contribution D.1566/XVIII, CCITT SG XVIII, Seoul Meeting, Jan. 1988 (source: NTT).

[21] I. Tokizawa, T. Kanada, and K. Sato, "A new transport network architecture based on asynchronous transfer mode techniques," in *Proc. ISSLS'88*, Boston, MA, Sept. 1988, pp. 11.2.1–11.2.5.

[22] Y. Okano, S. Ohta, and T. Kawata, "Assessment of cross-connect systems in transmission networks," in *Proc. GLOBECOM'87*, Tokyo, Japan, Nov. 1987.

[23] "Part B of the report of the Hamburg meeting of the BBTG," Rep. R 46(B), CCITT SG XVIII, Hamburg Meeting, July 1987 (source: BBTG of Study Group VXIII).

[24] G. J. Coviello, "Comparative discussion of circuit- versus packet-switched voice," *IEEE Trans. Commun.*, vol. COM-27, pp. 1153–1160, Aug. 1979.

[25] J. G. Gruber, "Delay related issues in integrated voice and data networks," *IEEE Trans. Commun.*, vol. COM-29, pp. 786–800, June 1981.

[26] L. Kleinrock, *Queueing Systems, Vol. I: Theory.* New York: Wiley, 1975.

[27] R. G. Addie and R. E. Warfield, "Bandwidth switching and new network architectures," in *Proc. ITC 12*, Torino, Italy, June 1988, pp. 2.3iiA.1.1–2.3iiA.1.7.

[28] J. L. Burgin, R. G. Addie, and S. L. Sutherland, "Information transfer protocols for the broadband ISDN," presented at the Workshop on Asynchronous Transfer Mode, Geneva Switzerland, June 1988.

[29] S. Aoe, M. Ishikawa, and S. Okada, "Mastergroup switching systems for high reliability toll transmission," *Japan Telecommun. Rev.*, pp. 40–48, 1969.

[30] K. Sato, S. Ohta, and I. Tokizawa, "Dynamic reconfiguration of ATM-based network via virtual path strategy," in *Proc. 2nd IEEE ComSoc Int. Multimedia Commun. Workshop*, Ottawa, Ont., Canada, Apr. 1989, p. 3.3.

[31] N. Shimasaki, A. Okada, and T. Yamaguchi, "Group transit switching—A new operational approach to be applicable to switched communication network," in *Proc. ICC'74*, June 1974, p. 11D.

[32] M. Akiyama, "Variable communication network design," in *Proc. 9th Int. Teletraffic Congr.*, 1979.

[33] M. Blauer, M. Methiwalla, J. Miceli, and J. Yan, "Transport services management," *Telesis*, vol. 1, pp. 39–43, 1986.

[34] S. Ohta, K. Sato, and I. Tokizawa, "A dynamically controllable ATM transport network based on the virtual path concept," in *Proc. GLOBECOM'88*, Ft. Lauderdale, FL, Nov. 1988, pp. 39.2.1–39.2.5.

Dr. Sato is a member of the Institute of Electronics, Information, and Communication Engineers (IEICE) of Japan and of the IEEE Communications Society and Computer Society.

Satoru Ohta (M'89) received the B.E. and M.E. degrees in electronics engineering from the Tokyo Institute of Technology, Tokyo, Japan, in 1981 and 1983, respectively.

In 1983 he joined the Electrical Communications Laboratories, NTT, Yokosuka, Japan. He worked on research and development of digital cross-connect systems, transmission synthesis, and broad-band ISDN. Recently, he has been engaged in research on information theory at NTT Transmission Systems Laboratories.

Mr. Ohta is a member of the Institute of Electronics, Information, and Communication Engineers of Japan.

Ken-Ichi Sato (M'86) was born in Tokyo, Japan, in September 1953. He received the B.S., M.S., and Ph.D. degrees in electronics engineering from the University of Tokyo, Tokyo, Japan, in 1976, 1978, and 1986, respectively.

In 1978 he joined Yokosuka Electrical Communication Laboratories, NTT. During 1978–1984 he was engaged in research and development of optical fiber transmission. His R&D experiences cover fiber optic video transmission systems for CATV distribution systems and subscriber loop systems, and noise characterization in optical transmission systems. Since 1985 he has been active in the development of broad-band ISDN based on ATM techniques. His main research interests include information transport network architecture, variable network architecture, broad-band transport technology, and network delay analysis. He has over 30 technical publications in his field, and served as a Co-Guest Editor of an issue of the IEEE JOURNAL ON SELECTED AREAS IN COMMUNICATIONS in 1989–1990.

Ikuo Tokizawa (M'87) was born in Nagano, Japan, in 1946. He received the B.E. degree from Shinshu University, Nagano, Japan, in 1969.

He joined NTT (Nippon Telegraph and Telephone Corporation) Laboratories in 1969. He initially engaged in the development of multiplexers for high-capacity FDM coaxial transmission systems. In 1975 he was active in the field of digital signal processing, and worked on research for digital filters, low bit-rate and wide-band 64 kb/s speech codecs, and signal processors. From 1984 to 1987 he was a Research Group Leader, responsible for the development of digital synchronous multiplexers, including STM-based digital cross-connect systems and the new synchronous network node interface (NNI). He is currently a Research Group Leader in the Transport Processing Laboratory of NTT Transmission Systems Laboratories. His responsibilities are in research and development of architecture, systems, and technologies for future ATM-based transport networks.

Survey of Traffic Control Schemes and Protocols in ATM Networks

JAIME JUNGOK BAE, MEMBER, IEEE, AND TATSUYA SUDA, MEMBER, IEEE

In the past few years, Broadband ISDN (B-ISDN) has received increased attention as a communication architecture capable of supporting multimedia applications. Among the techniques proposed to implement B-ISDN, Asynchronous Transfer Mode (ATM) is considered to be the most promising transfer technique because of its efficiency and flexibility.

In ATM networks, the performance bottleneck of the network, which was once the channel transmission speed, is shifted to the processing speed at the network switching nodes and the propagation delay of the channel. This shift is because the high-speed channel increases the ratio of propagation delay to cell transmission time and the ratio of processing time to cell transmission time. Due to the increased ratio of propagation delay to cell transmission time, a large number of cells can be in transit between two ATM switching nodes. In addition, the increased ratio of processing time to cell transmission time makes it difficult to implement hop-by-hop control schemes. Therefore, traffic control in ATM networks is a challenge, and new network architectures (flow control schemes, error control schemes, etc.) are required in ATM networks.

This paper surveys a number of important research topics in ATM networks. The topics covered include mathematical modeling of various types of traffic sources, congestion control and error control schemes for ATM networks, and priority schemes to support multiple classes of traffic. Standard activity for ATM networks and future research problems in ATM are also presented.

I. INTRODUCTION

Due to the increased demand for communication services of all kinds (e.g., voice, data, and video), Broadband ISDN (B-ISDN) has received increased attention in the past few years. The key to a successful B-ISDN system is the ability to support a wide variety of traffic and diverse service and performance requirements. B-ISDN is required to support traffic requiring bandwidth ranging from a few kilobits per second (e.g., a slow terminal) to several hundred megabits per second (e.g., moving image data). Some traffic, such as interactive data and video, is highly bursty; while some traffic, such as large files, is continuous. B-ISDN is also required to meet diverse service and performance requirements of multimedia traffic. Real-time voice, for instance, requires rapid transfer through a network, but the loss of small amounts of voice information is tolerable. In many data applications, real-time delivery is not of primary importance, but high throughput and

strict error control are required. Some services, such as real-time video communications, require error-free transmission as well as rapid transfer [1].

B-ISDN should also be able to facilitate expected (as well as unexpected) future services in a practical and easily expanded fashion. Examples of expected future services include high-definition TV (HDTV), broadband videotex, and video/document retrieval services [2], [3].

To meet the previously stated requirements for a successful B-ISDN, several techinques have been proposed for the switching and multiplexing schemes (''transfer mode''). These schemes include circuit-switching based Synchronous Transfer Mode (STM) and packet-switching based Asynchronous Transfer Mode (ATM).

STM, a circuit switching based technique, was initially considered an appropriate transfer mode for B-ISDN because of its compatibility with existing systems. In STM, bandwidth is organized in a periodic frame, which consists of time slots (Fig. 1(a)). A framing slot indicates the start of each frame. As in traditional circuit switching, each slot in an STM frame is assigned to a particular call, and the call is identified by the position of the slot. In STM, slots are assigned based on the peak transfer rate of the call so that the required service quality can be guaranteed even at the peak load. Because of its circuit-like nature, STM is suitable for fixed-rate services; however, STM cannot support traffic efficiently since, in STM, bandwidth is wasted during the period in which information is transported below peak rate.

ATM eliminates the inflexibility and inefficiency found in STM. In ATM, information flow is organized into fixed-size blocks called ''cells,'' each consisting of a header and an information field. Cells are transmitted over a virtual circuit, and routing is performed based on the Virtual Circuit Identifier (VCI) contained in the cell header. The cell transmission time is equal to a slot length, and slots are allocated to a call on demand (Fig. 1(b)). ATM's fundamental difference from STM is that slot assignments are not fixed; instead, the time slots are assigned in an asynchronous (demand-based) manner. In ATM, therefore, no bandwidth is consumed unless information is actually being transported.

Between ATM and STM, ATM is considered to be most promising because of its efficiency and flexibility. Because slots are allocated to services on demand, ATM can easily accommodate variable bit rate services. Moreover, in ATM, no bandwidth is consumed unless information is actually being transmitted. ATM can also gain bandwidth efficiency by statistically multiplexing

Manuscript received March 10, 1990; revised August 16, 1990. This work was supported in part by the National Science Foundation under Grant NCR-8907909 and by the University of California MICRO Program.

The authors are with the Department of Information and Computer Science, University of California, Irvine, CA 92717.

IEEE Log Number 9040850.

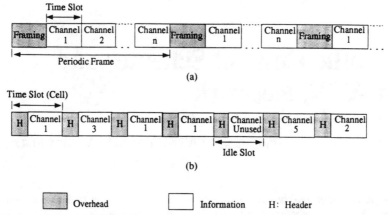

Fig. 1. STM and ATM principles. (a) STM Multiplexing. (b) ATM Multiplexing.

bursty traffic sources. Since bursty traffic does not require continuous allocation of the bandwidth at its peak rate, a large number of bursty traffic sources can share the bandwidth. ATM can also support circuit-oriented and continuous bit-rate services by allocating bandwidth based on the peak rate (given that sufficient resources are available). Because of these advantages, ATM is considered more suitable for B-ISDN. This paper therefore focuses on ATM and surveys a number of important research topics related to ATM networks.

The organization of this paper is as follows. In Section II, various mathematical models proposed for data, voice and video are surveyed. In Section III, congestion control schemes suitable for ATM networks are examined. In Section IV, effective error control schemes for ATM networks are examined. In Section V, various priority schemes proposed to support multiple service classes are discussed. In Section VI, ATM standardization activities are presented. In Section VII, a summary of this paper is given, and possible future research problems are discussed. Finally, in Section VIII, brief concluding remarks are given.

II. MODELING OF TRAFFIC SOURCES

As mentioned earlier, ATM networks must support various communications services, such as data, voice, and video, each having different traffic characteristics. To evaluate the performance of such networks, accurate source modeling is required. The purpose of this section is to examine several traffic models proposed for data, voice, and video sources. The various mathematical models described below have been examined against actual measured data, and their accuracy has been validated.

A. Input Traffic Models for Data Sources

It is well-known that generation of data from a single data source is well characterized by a Poisson arrival process (continuous time case) or by a geometric interarrival process (discrete time case). For interactive data transmission, a single cell may be generated at a time. For a bulk data transmission, such as a file transfer, a large number of cells may be generated at a time (batch arrivals).

In existing packet networks, packets could be either of variable or constant length. In ATM networks, however, the cell size is fixed. Furthermore, because the size of a cell is relatively short compared to the length of a packet in existing networks, multiple cells may be created from one data packet.

B. Input Traffic Models for Voice Sources

An arrival process of cells from a voice source (and a video source) is fairly complex due to the strong correlation among arrivals. In this subsection, input traffic models proposed for a voice source are examined.

The arrival process of new voice calls and the distribution of their durations can be characterized by a Poisson process and by an exponential distribution, respectively. Within a call, talkspurts and silent periods alternate. During talkspurts, voice cells are generated periodically; during silent periods, no cells are generated. The correlated generation of voice cells within a call can be modeled by an Interrupted Poisson Process (IPP) [4]-[8]. In an IPP model, each voice source is characterized by ON (corresponding to talkspurt) and OFF (corresponding to silence duration) periods, which appear in turn. The transition from ON to OFF occurs with the probability β, and the transition from OFF to ON occurs with the probability α. In a discrete time case, ON and OFF periods are geometrically distributed with the mean $1/\beta$ and $1/\alpha$, respectively. Cells are generated during the ON period according to a Bernoulli distribution with the rate λ; no cell is generated during the OFF period (Fig. 2). (The continuous time analog is an exponential distribution using a Poisson process.)

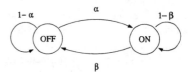

Fig. 2. IPP model.

When N independent voice sources are multiplexed, aggregated cell arrivals are governed by the number of voice sources in the ON state. Assuming a discrete time system, the probability P_n that n out of N voice sources are in the ON state (n voice cell arrivals in a slot) is given by

$$P_n = \binom{N}{n} \left(\frac{\alpha}{\alpha + \beta}\right)^n \left(\frac{\beta}{\alpha + \beta}\right)^{N-n}, \quad \text{for } 0 \leq n \leq N. \quad (1)$$

The continuous time analog represents the number of voice sources in the ON state as a birth–death process with birth rate $\lambda(n)$ and death rate $\mu(n)$, where

$$\lambda(n) = (N - n)\alpha, \quad \mu(n) = n\beta, \quad \text{for } 0 \leq n \leq N. \quad (2)$$

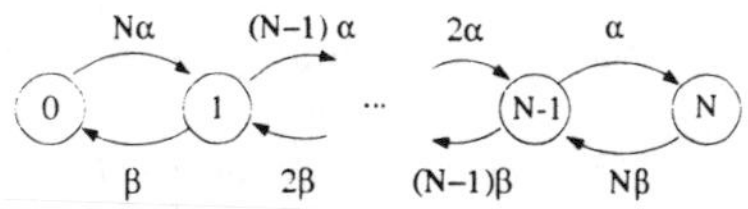

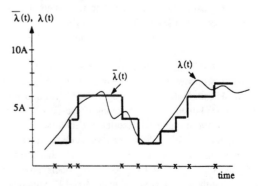

Fig. 3. Birth–death model for the number of active voice sources.

Figure 3 shows the birth–death model. For this continuous time case, the probability P_n that n out of N voice sources are in the ON state is also given by (1) [6].

Another common approach for modeling aggregate arrivals from N voice sources is to use a two-state Markov Modulated Poisson Process (MMPP) [9], [10]. The MMPP is a doubly stochastic Poisson process where the rate process is determined by the state of a continuous-time Markov chain [9]. In the two-state MMPP model, an aggregate arrival process is characterized by two alternating states. It is usually assumed that the duration of each state follows a geometrical (discrete time case) or an exponential (continuous time case) distribution, and cell arrivals in each state follow a Bernoulli (or a Poisson) distribution with different rates. Therefore, four parameters are necessary to describe an MMPP: the mean duration of each state and the arrival rate in each state. Note that an IPP, a process used to describe a single voice source, is a special case of the MMPP in which no cell arrives during an OFF period.

To determine the value of these four parameters, the following MMPP statistical characteristics are matched with the measured data [9]:

1) the mean arrival rate;
2) the variance-to-mean ratio of the number of arrivals in a time interval $(0, t_1)$;
3) the long term variance-to-mean ratio of the number of arrivals;
4) the third moment of the number of arrivals in $(0, t_2)$.

Note that the analytical models described in Sections II-A and II-B can model only constant bit rate traffic. Analytical models which can adequately model variable bit rate traffic are not yet available.

C. Input Traffic Models for Video Sources

Video traffic requires large bandwidth. For instance, in TV applications a frame of 512×512 resolution is transmitted every $1/30$ second, generating $512 \times 512 \times 8 \times 30$ bits per second (approximately 63 Mbits/s), if a simple PCM coding scheme is used. Therefore, video sources are usually compressed by using an interframe variable-rate coding scheme which encodes only significant differences between successive frames. This introduces a strong correlation among cell arrivals from successive frames.

Like a voice source, a video source generates correlated cell arrivals; however, its statistical nature is quite different from a voice source. Two types of correlations are evident in the cell generation process of a video source: short-term correlation and long-term correlation. Short-term correlation corresponds to uniform activity levels (i.e., small fluctuations in bit rates), and its effects last for a very short period of time (on the order of a few hundred milliseconds). Long-term correlation corresponds to sudden scene changes, which cause a large rate of arrivals, and its effects last for a relatively long period of time (on the order of a few seconds) [11]. In Section II-C-1), models which consider only short-term correlation (i.e., models for video sources without scene changes) are examined. In Section II-C-2), models which

consider both short-term and long-term correlation (i.e., models for video sources with scene changes) are examined.

1) Models for Video Sources Without Scene Changes: In this section, models proposed for video sources *without* scene changes are examined. These models are applicable to video scenes with relatively uniform activity levels such as videotelephone scenes showing a person talking. Two models have been proposed. The first model approximates a video source by an autoregressive (AR) process [12], [13]. This model describes the cell generation process of a video source quite accurately. However, because of its complexity, queueing analysis based on this model is very complicated and may not be tractable. This model is more suitable for use in simulations. The second model approximates a video source (or video sources) by a discrete-state Markov model [13]. This model is more tractable in queueing analysis than the first model, and yet describes the cell generation process of a video source (or video sources) well.

a) Model A: Continuous-state AR Markov Model [13]: Here, a single video source is approximated by an autoregressive (AR) process. The definition of an AR process is as follows:

$$\lambda(n) = \sum_{m=1}^{M} a_m \lambda(n - m) + bw(n) \qquad (3)$$

where $\lambda(n)$ represents the source bit rate during the nth frame; M is the model order; $w(n)$ is a Gaussian random process; and $a_m (m = 1, 2, \cdots, M)$ and b are coefficients. It is shown that the first-order autoregressive Markov model

$$\lambda(n) = a_1 \lambda(n - 1) + bw(n) \qquad (4)$$

is sufficient for engineering purposes. Assuming that $w(n)$ has the mean η and the variance 1, and that $|a_1|$ is less than 1, the values of coefficients a_1 and b are determined by matching the steady-state average $E(\lambda)$ and discrete autocovariance $C(n)$ of the AR process with the measured data. $E(\lambda)$ and $C(n)$ of the AR process in (4) are given by [14]

$$E(\lambda) = \frac{b}{1 - a_1} \eta, \qquad C(n) = \frac{b^2}{1 - a_1^2} a_1^n, \qquad n \geq 0. \qquad (5)$$

This model provides a rather accurate approximation of the bit rate of a single video source without scene changes. However, as stated above, analysis of a queueing model with the above arrival process can be very complex and may not be tractable; therefore, this model is suitable for use in simulations.

b) Model B: Discrete-state, continuous-time Markov Process [13]: The process $\lambda(t)$ describing the bit rate of a video source at time t is a continuous-time, continuous-state process. In this model, process $\lambda(t)$ is sampled at random Poisson time instances and the states are quantized at these points (Fig. 4). In

Fig. 4. Poisson sampling and quantization of the source rate.

other words, the process $\lambda(t)$ is approximated by a continuous-time process $\overline{\lambda}(t)$ with discrete jumps at random Poisson times. This approximation can be improved by decreasing the quantization step A and increasing the sampling rate.

The state transition diagram $\overline{\lambda}(t)$ is shown in Fig. 5. The pro-

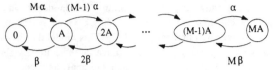

Fig. 5. State transition diagram—Model B.

cess $\overline{\lambda}(t)$ can be used to describe a single source, as well as an aggregation of several sources. The aggregated arrival process from N video sources can transit between $M + 1$ levels. The label in each state indicates the data rate in that state (A is a constant). To determine values of the quantization step A and the transition rates α and β, the steady-state mean $E(\overline{\lambda}_N)$, variance $\overline{C}_N(0)$ and autocovariance function $\overline{C}_N(\tau)$ of the process $\overline{\lambda}(t)$ (describing an aggregate of N independent sources) are matched with the measured data. (τ is a time parameter.) $E(\overline{\lambda}_N)$, $\overline{C}_N(0)$ and $\overline{C}_N(\tau)$ are given by

$$E(\overline{\lambda}_N) = MA \frac{\alpha}{\alpha + \beta}, \qquad \overline{C}_N(0) = MA^2 \frac{\alpha}{\alpha + \beta} \left(1 - \frac{\beta}{\alpha + \beta} \right)$$

$$\overline{C}_N(\tau) = \overline{C}_N(0) e^{-(\alpha + \beta)\tau} . \tag{6}$$

The number of quantization levels M is chosen arbitrarily, but it should be large enough to cover all likely bit rates.

The process in Fig. 5 can be decomposed into a superposition of simpler processes. It can be thought of as a superposition of M independent identical ON–OFF minisources, each being modeled as in Fig. 6. Each minisource alternates between ON and OFF

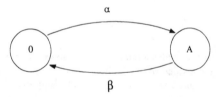

Fig. 6. Minisource model.

states. The transition from ON to OFF state occurs with the rate β, and the transition from OFF to ON state occurs with rate α. (Thus both ON and OFF periods are exponentially distributed.) The data rate of a minisource in the ON state is A; a minisource does not generate bits during the OFF state (data rate is 0). (Note that in Fig. 5, a label associated with the state represents the data rate of a minisource in the state.) The state of the aggregated arrival process can thus be represented by the number of minisources which are in the ON state.

2) Models for Video Sources with Scene Changes: In this section, models proposed for video sources *with* scene changes are examined. These models capture both short-term and long-term correlations explained at the beginning of Section II-C and thus these models are suitable to describe a cell generation process from video scenes with sudden changes, such as videotelephone scenes showing changes between listener and talker modes, or scene changes in broadcast TV [11]. Two models have been proposed: the first model is an extension of Model B explained above; the second model approximates a video source by the discrete-

state continuous-time Markov process (Model B) with batch arrivals.

a) Model C: An extension of Model B [11]: The state transition diagram of the cell generation process from an aggregation of N video sources is shown in Fig. 7. (This process can also be

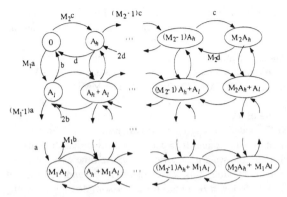

Fig. 7. State transition rate diagram for the aggregate source model (with scene changes).

used to describe a single video source with scene changes.) The label in each state indicates the data rate in the state. There are two basic data rate levels: a high data rate A_h, which represents a sudden scene change, and a low data rate A_l, which represents a uniform activity level. If scene changes do not exist (i.e., if we delete the states which contain a high rate A_h), the process in Fig. 7 reduces to the one used in Model B. The aggregated process of N video sources can transit between $(M_1 + 1)(M_2 + 1)$ levels, where $M_1 = NM$, $M_2 = N$. Here, M is chosen arbitrarily.

To determine the values of system parameters c and d (the transition probabilities between uniform activity level and high activity level), the fraction of the time spent in the high activity level ($c/(c + d)$) and the average time spent in the high activity level ($1/d$) are equated with the actual measured data. To determine the rest of the parameters in the model, i.e., the transition probabilities within the uniform activity level (a and b), and the two basic data rates (A_l and A_h), the first and second order statistics are matched with the actual measured data.

As in Model B, the process described in Fig. 7 can be decomposed into a superposition of simpler processes. This process can be thought of as a superposition of M_1 independent identical ON–OFF minisources of the type shown in Fig. 8(a) and M_2 of the type

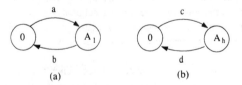

Fig. 8. Miniprocess models.

shown in Fig. 8(b). The state of the aggregated arrival process can thus be described as the number of each type minisource which is in the ON state.

b) Model D: Discrete-state continuous-time Markov Process with batch arrivals [15, 16]: In this model, the cell arrival process from a single video source *with* scene changes is modeled as a discrete-state continuous-time Markov process with batch arrivals. The uniform activity level is represented by a discrete-state continuous-time Markov process as in Model B. This M-state

Markov process can be decomposed into M independent identical ON-OFF minisources. Scene changes (high activity levels) are represented by a batch arrival process. The interarrival times between scene changes (between batches) are assumed to be exponentially distributed, and the batch size is assumed to be constant.

III. CONGESTION CONTROL IN ATM NETWORKS

In an ATM network, most traffic sources are bursty. A bursty source may generate cells at a near-peak rate for a very short period of time and immediately afterwards it may become inactive, generating no cells. Such a bursty traffic source will not require continuous allocation of bandwidth at its peak rate. Since an ATM network supports a large number of such bursty traffic sources, statistical multiplexing can be used to gain bandwidth efficiency, allowing more traffic sources to share the bandwidth. But notice, if a large number of traffic sources become active simultaneously, severe network congestion can result.

Due to the effects of high-speed channels, congestion control is a challenge for an ATM network. High-speed channels significantly limit the congestion control schemes applicable. As an example, consider two adjacent switching nodes, A and B, linked by a 100-km cable. Assume 500-bit long cells and the typical propagation delay time of 5 μs per 1 km of a cable. (The exact cell size is 424 bits (53 octets) according to the CCITT standards [17], [18]. However, the cell size of 500 bits is used in this example for simplicity.) Consider the following scenario. Assume a 1 Mbits/s channel speed. One cell transmission time becomes (500 bits)/(1 Mbits/s) = 0.5 ms. Node A starts transmitting a cell. It takes 500 μsec for the electric signal to propagate to node B. Thus when the first bit of the cell reaches B, A is transmitting the last bit of the same cell. Let's replace the channel with a 1 Gbits/s fiber optic cable. The cell transmission time reduces to (500 bits)/(1 Gbits) = 0.5 μs, while the propagation delay time remains the same. Again, A starts transmitting a packet. This time, when the first bit of the packet arrives at B, A is transmitting the 1000th cell. 1000 cells are already on the channel propagating towards B. This example shows that in high-speed networks such as ATM networks, overhead due to propagation delay time becomes significant. Thus control schemes, such as those which adjust A's input rate based on feedback from B, may not work in ATM networks. As clearly shown in this example, having high-speed channels changes the network situation dramatically; thus some of the congestion schemes developed for existing networks may no longer be applicable in such high-speed networks.

Another factor which makes congestion control in ATM challenging is the simplicity of the protocols used in high-speed networks. Simple, possibly hardwired protocols are preferred in ATM networks in order to match the high speed of the network channels. As shown in the above example, replacing 1 Mbits/s channel with 1 Gbits/s channel reduces the cell transmission time from 0.5 ms to 0.5 μs. On the other hand, the time required to process a protocol remains the same. As a result, in a high-speed network environment protocol processing time can be a bottleneck. In order to avoid such a bottleneck, ATM networks use simplified protocols, pushing most of the link-by-link layer protocols to higher edge-to-edge layers. This makes it difficult to implement link-by-link congestion control schemes.

For these reasons, many of the congestion schemes developed for existing networks may not be applicable to ATM networks. Many of the congestion control schemes developed for existing networks fall in the class of reactive control. Reactive control reacts to the congestion after it happens and tries to bring the degree of network congestion to an acceptable level. However, reactive control is not suitable for use in ATM networks.

A new concept is therefore required for congestion control in an ATM environment. Various congestion control approaches have been proposed for ATM networks, most of which fall in the class of preventive control. Preventive control tries to prevent congestion before it happens. The objective of preventive control is to ensure *a priori* that network traffic will not reach the level which causes unacceptable congestion. In the following, we first explain the reasons that reactive control does not perform well in ATM networks (Section III-A), and then examine various preventive control schemes proposed for ATM networks (Section III-B).

A. Reactive Control

At the onset of congestion, reactive control instructs the source nodes to throttle their traffic flow by giving feedback to them. A major problem with reactive control in high-speed networks is slow feedback. As shown in the example given above, the effects of high-speed channels make the overhead due to propagation delay significant; therefore, by the time that feedback reaches the source nodes and the control is triggered, it may be too late to react effectively.

There is a possible improvement technique to overcome the difficulty caused by slow feedback. If reactive control is performed between network users and the edge of the network as in [19], the effect of propagation delay may not be significant since the distance feedback information propagates is short. However, this limits the reactive control to the edge of the network.

Reactive flow control, in general, may not be effective in an ATM environment because of the previously discussed problem. Preventive control, however, tries to overcome this problem with reactive control and controls congestion more effectively in ATM networks. Preventive control schemes are examined in Section III-B.

B. Preventive Control

Unlike reactive control where control is invoked upon the detection of congestion, preventive control does not wait until congestion actually occurs, but rather tries to prevent the network from reaching an unacceptable level of congestion. The most common and effective approach is to control traffic flow at entry points to the network (i.e., at the access nodes). This approach is especially effective in ATM networks because of its connection-oriented transport. With connection-oriented transport, a decision to admit new traffic can be made based on knowledge of the state of the route which the traffic would follow [20].

Preventive control for ATM can be performed in two ways: admission control and bandwidth enforcement. Admission control determines whether to accept or reject a new connection at the time of call setup. This decision is based on traffic characteristics of the new connection and the current network load. The bandwidth enforcement monitors individual connections to ensure that the actual traffic flow conforms with that reported at call establishment. In Section III-B-1) and III-B-2) admission control and bandwidth enforcement are discussed in detail.

Holtzman has proposed a new and very different approach to preventive control [21] and has applied his approach to admission control. In admission control, the decision to accept a new connection is made based on the predicted network performance. If there is some uncertainty in the parameter values of the incoming traffic, the network may underestimate the impact of accepting a new call and congestion may result. Holtzman's approach tries to prevent the network congestion by taking uncertainties in traffic parameter values into account. Holtzman's approach is described in Section III-B-3).

1) Admission Control: Admission control decides whether to accept or reject a new connection based on whether the required performance can be maintained. When a new connection is requested, the network examines its service requirements (e.g., acceptable cell transmission delay and loss probability) and traffic characteristics (e.g., peak rate, average rate, etc.) The network then examines the current load and decides whether or not to accept the new connection.

Three major research issues in admission control are listed as follows.

- What traffic parameters (traffic descriptors) are required to accurately predict network performance?
- What criteria should the network use to decide whether or not to accept a new connection?
- How does network performance depend on various traffic parameters?

In the following, these three issues are discussed.

a) Traffic descriptors: When a new connection is requested, the network needs to know the traffic characteristics of the new connection in order to accurately predict its ability to maintain a certain performance level. A set of traffic descriptors given from a user to a network should include sufficient parameters so that the network can accurately determine the user's traffic characteristics. However, for simplicity's sake a set of traffic descriptors should include the fewest possible parameters.

The peak bit rate, the average bit rate, and a measure of burstiness are the most commonly used parameters for traffic descriptors. Among them, ''burstiness'' is the most important parameter, especially in an ATM network where most traffic sources are highly bursty. Burstiness is a parameter which describes how densely or sparsely cell arrivals occur. It is well-known that burstiness plays a critical role in determining network performance; however, consensus is yet to be reached concerning an appropriate way to describe the burstiness of a traffic source. Possible definitions of burstiness proposed include:

1) the ratio of peak bit rate to average bit rate [22]–[25];
2) the average burst length, i.e., the mean duration of the time interval during which the traffic source transmits at the peak rate [26];
3) burst factor defined as the average number of bits accumulated in a buffer during a burst, namely, (peak bit rate − average service bit rate) × average burst length [27];
4) cell jitter ratio defined as the variance-to-mean ratio of the cell interarrival times, namely, Var [cell interarrival times]$/E$ [cell interarrival times] [28];
5) the squared coefficient of variation of the interarrival times, namely, Var [cell interarrival times]$/E^2$ [cell interarrival time] [29];
6) peakedness defined as the variance-to-mean ratio of the number of busy servers in a fictitious infinite server group [30].

Deciding the best way to describe the burstiness is a very difficult task which needs to be studied further. The authors of this paper believe that the burst length should somehow be taken into account since it significantly affects the performance. In [5], [22], [26], [27], [31], it is shown that the longer the burst length, the worse the network performance becomes; namely, the cell loss probability becomes larger and the cell transmission delay becomes longer. The effect of the average burst length is also examined in [25]. It is shown that with longer bursts, statistical multiplexing becomes less effective, and thus fewer active sources can be supported for a given amount of bandwidth. The authors also believe that more than one parameter may be necessary to describe burstiness.

In [32], a new traffic descriptor is proposed. In this paper, the difficulty of using the peak bit rate or the average bit rate as a traffic descriptor uniformly across the different types of traffic is realized. If the peak bit rate is used regardless of the type of traffic, a large portion of bandwidth will be wasted, especially when the network traffic is bursty. On the other hand, if the average bit rate is used regardless of the type of traffic, the continuous-bit-oriented (CBO) traffic will suffer severe performance degradation. In [32], a new bit rate, called the effective bit rate, is proposed. An effective bit rate is defined as a fraction of the peak bit rate, namely, effective bit rate = (peak bit rate) × a, where a is a constant. The value of a is determined based on the traffic characteristics of the source. By changing the value of a, we can improve the network resource utilization. Further study is required to determine an appropriate value of a for different types of traffic.

b) Decision criteria: The cell transmission delays and the cell loss probabilities, because they are good indications of the degree of network congestion, are the most commonly used decision criteria in admission control. When transmission delays and cell loss probabilities are applied in admission control, their long-term time-averaged values have been used in the past [22], [24], [26], [31]–[33]. Using a long-term time-averaged value, however, may not be sufficient in an ATM network because here the network traffic can change rapidly and dynamically, forcing the network to move from one degree of congestion to another. Fig. 9 [4] sketches how the cell loss probability changes in an ATM

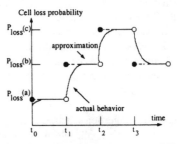

Fig. 9. Time dependent behavior of cell loss probability.

network as a function of time. In this figure, the number of active calls jumps from a at time t_0 to b at time t_1, and to c at time t_2. At time t_3, the number of active calls decreases to b. The solid curve in the figure shows the time-dependent behavior of the cell loss probability. For instance, when the number of active calls increase to b at time t_1, the network responds to the change and starts losing a large number of cells; gradually, the network goes up to the next level of congestion and reaches the value of the cell loss probability in steady state $P_{loss}(b)$. When another increase occurs at time t_2, the network responds again, gradually reaching the steady state, and so on. When the network traffic is highly bursty and changes dynamically, temporal network congestion can occur, and it is possible that a large number of cells are lost during congestion periods, even when the long-term time-averaged value of loss rate is kept small. In voice communication, for example, this burst loss of voice cells may cause noticeable performance degradation (clicks) at a destination user. Therefore, some decision criteria which take the temporal behavior of the network into account may be needed.

In [4], an instantaneous cell loss probability is proposed and used as a decision criterion to consider the temporal behavior of a network. An instantaneous cell loss probability is a time-dependent cell loss probability (function of slot position or time), not the value averaged over a long period of time. The solid curve in Fig. 9 shows the instantaneous cell loss probability. In [4], the instantaneous cell loss probability is approximated by its steady-state value (dashed lines in Fig. 9), and an approximate analysis is developed. A new connection is accepted by the network only when the instantaneous cell loss rate is kept below a threshold value at each switching node for longer than a predetermined percentage of time.

In [4], the ineffectiveness of using the long-term time-averaged cell loss probability as a decision criterion is demonstrated through numerical examples using realistic parameter values. It is shown that network congestion can last for a length of time on the order of a hundred milliseconds even when the long-term time-averaged cell loss probability is kept small. In voice conversation, this congestion period is comparable to a burst (talkspurt) length, and thus a whole talkspurt can be lost during congestion. It is also shown that this burst cell loss can be avoided by using the instantaneous cell loss probability as a decision criterion in admission control.

In [6], the insufficiency of measuring only the long-term time-averaged cell loss probability is discussed further, and the temporal behavior of voice cell loss probability is studied. Under the realistic parameter values, it is found that the cell loss rate changes slowly and remains at zero most of the time. However, once congestion occurs and the cell loss probability becomes large, the cell loss probability may remain large for a long period, causing voice distortion perceptible at the receiver. It is shown that the average cell loss probability within a blocking period (i.e., the time period during which the buffer is full, and thus cells are blocked) is much larger than the long-term time-averaged cell loss rate. Therefore, the long-term time-averaged cell loss probability does not reflect the temporal behavior of voice cell loss, and it is not sufficient to measure voice distortion incurred.

c) Effects of traffic parameters on ATM network performance: One of the important research issues in admission control is to investigate the effect of various traffic parameters on network performance.

In [4], [22], [26], [27], [31], the effects of statistical multiplexing of bursty sources in an ATM network are investigated. They investigate how the performance (the cell loss probability and the average delay time) varies as a function of various parameters, such as the number of sources, the peak bit rate, and the burstiness of the sources. Some of the common observations made in these papers are listed as follows.

• The average burst length is a very important parameter. As the average burst length increases, the performance degrades, i.e., the cell loss probability and delay time increase significantly [22], [26], [27], [31].

• As the peak rate of each source is increased, the cell loss probability increases [26], [27]. This should be intuitively clear.

• In the case where homogeneous sources are multiplexed, if the offered load (i.e., the number of sources × mean bit of each source) is kept constant, the cell loss probability decreases as the number of sources multiplexed increases. The reason for this is that when the number of sources multiplexed increases (keeping the offered load constant), the mean bit rate of each source decreases. The mean bit rate is a product of peak bit rate and the fraction of time in which a source is in the active-state (i.e., the state in which a source is transmitting at the peak rate). Therefore, the reduction in the mean bit rate means the reduction in either the peak bit rate or the burst length (or both). In either case, the cell loss probability decreases [22], [27].

• In the case where heterogeneous sources are multiplexed, high bit rate sources dominate the performance; an increase in high bit rate traffic causes more significant increases in the cell loss probability than does an increase in low bit rate traffic [31]. A similar observation is made in the case where homogeneous sources are multiplexed; when high bit rate sources are multiplexed, the fluctuation in the cell loss is larger than when low bit rate sources are multiplexed [4]. This is due to the fact that because of the high bit rate, the number of traffic sources which can be multiplexed on one link is rather limited and not large enough to smooth out the bursty nature of each cell.

• The cell loss probability decreases as the offered load decreases [22], [31]. Thus a very efficient way to lower the cell loss probability is to decrease the offered load by providing larger bandwidth. This is only possible, however, if one can assume that bandwidth is negligibly cheap.

In [25], the effects of traffic parameters on the network performance are investigated and a method is proposed to calculate the bandwidth required to satisfy a given performance requirement. Two different cases are considered: the case where homogeneous traffic sources are multiplexed and the case where heterogeneous sources are multiplexed. In both cases, the peak bit rate (Bp), a measure of burstiness (b) defined as the peak-to-mean bit rate ratio (Bp/Bm, where Bm is the mean bit rate), and the mean number of cells (L) generated from a burst are used as traffic descriptors. In the following, we summarize the bandwidth assignment rule proposed for the homogeneous traffic case.

In the case where homogeneous traffic sources are multiplexed, the bandwidth required to satisfy a given cell loss requirement is calculated by

$$W = n\frac{Bp}{b}R(b, n, L) \qquad (7)$$

where n is the number of active traffic sources; $n(Bp/b)$ ($= nBm$) is the offered traffic; and $R(b, n, L)$ is a coefficient whose value depends on the triplet (b, n, L). $R(b, n, L)$ is called an expansion factor, and its value is obtained by performing a single simulation for each triplet (b, n, L) for a given cell loss requirement. In this paper, a cell loss requirement of 10^{-5} is assumed. This cell loss probability is rather large to be used in a real system; this cell loss probability is used because the simulation run time prohibits the choice of a more realistic cell loss probability of 10^{-9}.

Using (7), if the offered traffic ($n(Bp/b)$) and the expansion factor $R(b, n, L)$ are given, required bandwidth W can be determined. The remaining question is whether the expansion factor is a function of a triplet (b, n, L), or a function of a quadruplet (Bp, Bm, n, L). In [25], it is claimed that a triplet (b, n, L) is sufficient to determine the expansion factor, and it is supported by examining simulation results for two cases: $Bp = 10$ Mbits/s or 2 Mbits/s. To determine that this approach is truly valid, more cases should be examined.

The approach proposed in this paper considers the burstiness of the traffic and uses the peak-to-mean bit rate ratio ($b = Bp/Bm$) and the mean number of cells generated in a burst (L) to determine required bandwidth (W). Even though the approach of using $R(b, n, L)$ to calculate required bandwidth is simpler than the approach in which the quadruplet (Bp, Bm, n, L) is used, it has the following problem. To implement this approach, the values of $R(b, n, L)$ need to be precomputed through the simulation and stored in each node. Therefore, the number of possible combinations of (b, n, L) needs to be tractably small. This may limit the size of the network to which this approach can apply.

2) Bandwidth Enforcement:[1] Since users may deliberately exceed the traffic volume declared at the call setup (i.e., values of their traffic descriptors), and thus easily overload the network, admission control alone is not sufficient. After a connection is accepted, traffic flow of the connection must be monitored to ensure that the actual traffic flow conforms with that specified at call establishment. For this purpose, the bandwidth enforcement mechanism is implemented at the edges of the network. Once a violation is detected, the traffic flow is enforced by discarding and/or buffering violating cells.

A Leaky Bucket method [27], [34]–[36] is one of the typical bandwidth enforcement mechanisms used for ATM networks; this method can enforce the average bandwidth and the burst factor of a traffic source. One possible implementation of a Leaky Bucket method is to control the traffic flow by means of tokens. A queueing model for the Leaky Bucket method is illustrated in Fig. 10 [37]. An arriving cell first enters a queue. If the queue is full,

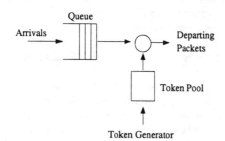

Fig. 10. A queueing model for a leaky bucket method.

cells are simply discarded. To enter the network, a cell must first obtain a token from a token-pool; if there is no token, a cell must wait in the queue until a new token is generated. Tokens are generated at a fixed rate corresponding to the average rate of the connection. If the number of tokens in the token pool exceeds some prefined threshold value, the process of token generation stops. This threshold value corresponds to the burstiness of the transmission; the larger the threshold value, the bigger the burstiness. This method enforces the average input rate while allowing for a certain degree of burstiness. The Leaky Bucket method can also enforce the peak bandwidth by generating tokens at the rate corresponding to the peak rate.

In the original Leaky Bucket method proposed in [34], the input buffer is not provided. In [36], the input buffer is suggested to provide better control of the trade-off between the cell waiting times and the cell loss probabilities. In an extreme case where no input buffer is provided, incoming cells do not have to wait in the buffer, but a large number of cells may be lost since all the violating cells are discarded. In the other extreme case (where an infinite input buffer is provided), no incoming cell will be lost, but cells may suffer a long waiting time. By choosing an appropriate input queue size, the trade-off between these two extremes can be controlled. In [37], an exact analysis of Leaky Bucket

methods with and without an input queue is presented, providing the Laplace transforms for the waiting times and the interdeparture times of cells from the system (i.e., interdeparture times of tokens from a token pool). The expected waiting time, the cell loss probability, and the variance of the interdeparture times are also obtained. In this paper, a Poisson process is assumed for the cell arrival process. A Poisson process, however, may not accurately describe bursty traffic found in ATM networks.

In the Leaky Bucket method, violating cells are either discarded or stored in a buffer even when the network load is light, and thus network resources are wasted. The total network throughput can be improved by using the marking method[2] presented in [25], [26], [38]. In this scheme, violating cells, rather than being discarded, are permitted to enter the network with violation tags in their cell headers. These violating cells are discarded only when they arrive at a congested node. If there are no congested nodes along the routes, the violating cells are transmitted without being discarded. This marking method can easily be implemented using the Leaky Bucket method described above. When the queue length exceeds a threshold, cells are marked as "droppable" instead of being discarded. Through simulations it is shown that by choosing an appropriate threshold value, the marking method can guarantee a performance level required by nonviolating cells and at the same time, can improve the network throughput. One possible disadvantage of this marking scheme is that processing time in each node is increased slightly because each node has to distinguish tagged cells from nonviolating cells when the node is in a congested state. Each node must also monitor its state to determine if it is in congestion. (For instance, each node may check its queue length to detect the congested state.) However, this extra processing can be done quickly and easily and the overall merits of the marking method far exceed its slight disadvantages.

An ideal bandwidth enforcement scheme should be able to correctly identify all the violating cells and discard or tag only violating cells. It should also be able to detect violation rapidly once it occurs. However, the bursty nature of the traffic carried in ATM networks makes it difficult to implement such an ideal scheme. When the traffic is bursty, a large number of cells may be generated in a short period of time, yet conform to the traffic descriptor values claimed at the time of call establishment. For instance, the average cell arrival rate can be kept constant if cells do not arrive for a while, even if there is a burst of cell arrivals in a short time period. In this case, none of these cells should be considered violating cells. If a small value is used for a threshold, some of the cells will be falsely identified as violating cells; therefore, a relatively large threshold value must be used to avoid discarding or tagging nonviolating cells. However, this large threshold value makes it harder to distinguish truly violating transmissions from temporary burst transmissions; thus the time required to detect violations is increased. As a result, in an ATM environment it may be more desirable to apply a marking method in order to avoid undesired enforcement actions by the network.

Bandwidth enforcement schemes may also be used with traffic shaping.[3] The purpose of traffic shaping is to throttle cell inputs into a network to avoid the bursty cell transmissions. Burst cell transmissions are avoided, for example, by separating successive ATM cells by idle times. The shaping function could be performed by the access control either at a user-network interface or

---

[1]Referred to also as policing.

[2]Referred to also as a Virtual Leaky Bucket Method.

[3]Referred to also as traffic smoothing.

at a data source by buffering and injecting cells into the network at a slower speed. Since traffic shaping reduces network congestion by suppressing inputs to the network, it may be able to support a greater number of calls than a network without the shaping function. With traffic shaping, the entire transmission of traffic may be unnecessarily slowed since cells are injected into a network at a slower speed even when the network load is light. However, with traffic shaping this degradation in the service quality is achieved in a more graceful way.

3) Coping with Traffic Uncertainties: In the previous sections, admission control and bandwidth enforcement schemes are examined. In admission control, the network performance is predicted based on the traffic descriptor values provided by the network users, and then a decision is made as to whether a new connection is accepted or not. In bandwidth enforcement, each connection is monitored, and the traffic flow is forced to conform with the traffic descriptor values provided by the network users. However, the exact traffic characteristics may not be available to the network users, and therefore, the values of traffic descriptors provided by the users may involve large uncertainty. In such a case, a network may underestimate the impact of accepting a new connection and congestion may result.

Very little attention has been paid to the problem of uncertainty in traffic descriptor values. Holtzman addressed this issue in [21], examining three approaches which were originally proposed in other contexts, and considering their application to the problem of traffic uncertainty in ATM networks. The three approaches examined by Holtzman are the approach using random variables [39], the fuzzy set approach [40], and the neural net approach to learn about the uncertain environment [41]. In this section, the first approach, which is the most promising and widely applicable, is discussed.

In the first approach discussed by Holtzman, the uncertainty in the traffic descriptor values is quantified by using a random variable for each uncertain parameter in the traffic model. Assume that the cell arrival process to the network is characterized by a point process parameterized by k traffic parameters, $x_1, \cdots, x_k$. Further, assume that the delay incurred by cells through the network in question is a function of the k traffic descriptors and is given by $D(x_1, \cdots, x_k)$. Assume that the performance requirement is given, and it is to keep the delay (mean or percentile) less than a given threshold value D^* (i.e., $D(x_1, \cdots, x_k) < D^*$). Since it is assumed that the delay function $D(x_1, \cdots, x_k)$ is known, we can determine the feasible parameter region Ω to satisfy the performance requirement $D(x_1, \cdots, x_k) < D^*$. Ω is a range of possible values of the traffic descriptors which satisfy a given performance requirement.

Let us denote $Y^j = (Y_1^j, \cdots, Y_k^j)$ as a set of random variables which parameterize the arrival stream for the jth network user. Using $Y^j (j = 1, \cdots, n)$, the aggregated cell arrival process from n users can be obtained. Let us denote this aggregated arrival process as $X^{(n)} = (X_1^{(n)}, \cdots, X_k^{(n)})$. In general, $X^{(n)} = f(Y^1, \cdots, Y^n)$. $X^{(n)}$ is a set of random variables which parameterize the cell arrival process from the superposition of n users.

From $X^{(n)}$, the number of users n^*, which can be supported by the network satisfying the performance requirement $D(x_1, \cdots, x_k) < D^*$ with high probability, can be determined. n^* is given by $n^* = \max_n \{ n: P[X^{(n)} \in \Omega] > 1 - \delta \}$, where δ is a predefined tolerance level. (For nonhomogeneous superpositions, the traffic mix should be specified.)

In obtaining the aggregated arrival process $X^{(n)}$, traffic uncertainties are considered. The process of obtaining $X^{(n)}$ can be bet-

ter illustrated using an example. Assume that the traffic generated by the jth user is characterized by the mean cell arrival rate and the squared coefficient of variation of the time between cell arrivals. Further, assume that these two parameters have uncertainties. For the traffic generated by the jth user the following can be assumed.

- The mean cell arrival rate is modeled by a normally distributed random variable Y_1^j, with mean λ_j and variance $\sigma_{\lambda j}^2$.
- The squared coefficient of variation of the time between cell arrivals is modeled by a normally distributed random variable Y_2^j, with mean c_j^2 and variance $\sigma_{c_j^2}^2$.
- The random variables Y_1^j and Y_2^j are mutually independent.

As previously stated, the uncertainties in the mean cell arrival rate and the squared coefficient of variation of the time between arrivals are quantified by using random variables Y_1^j and Y_2^j, respectively. Then for the superposed arrival process $X^{(n)} = (X_1^{(n)}, X_2^{(n)})$, $X_1^{(n)}$ (the mean arrival rate) and $X_2^{(n)}$ (the squared coefficient of variation of the time between arrivals) need to be calculated. They are calculated using the QNA approximation [42]. That is,

$$X_1^{(n)} = \sum_{j=1}^{n} Y_1^j, \qquad X_2^{(n)} = W^{(n)}(Z^{(n)} - 1) + 1 \qquad (8)$$

where

$$Z^{(n)} = \frac{\sum_{j=1}^{n} Y_1^j Y_2^j}{\sum_{j=1}^{n} Y_1^j}, \qquad W^{(n)} = \frac{1}{1 + 4(1 - P^{(n)})(V^{(n)} - 1)}.$$

$$(9)$$

$P^{(n)}$ and $V^{(n)}$ are given by

$$P^{(n)} = s \sum_{i=1}^{n} Y_1^i, \qquad V^{(n)} = \frac{\left(\sum_{i=1}^{n} Y_1^i \right)^2}{\sum_{i=1}^{n} (Y_1^i)^2} \qquad (10)$$

where s is the mean service time.

Finally, the joint distribution of $X_1^{(n)}$ and $X_2^{(n)}$ needs to be computed. It is found that a bivariate normal distribution is a good approximation. The means and variances of random variables $X_1^{(n)}$ and $X_2^{(n)}$, and the correlation between $X_1^{(n)}$ and $X_2^{(n)}$ are approximated using a Taylor series expansion technique.

Note that although this approach allows uncertainty in parameter values, it must have *a priori* knowledge about the system model (e.g., knowledge about the arrival process and the service process).

IV. Error Control in ATM Networks

Due to the use of optical fibers, the ratio of propagation delay to cell transmission time and the ratio of processing time to cell transmission time have increased in ATM networks. The use of optical fibers has also resulted in significant reduction in the channel error rate. These changes make it necessary to reexamine the error control schemes used in existing networks.

Before examining error control schemes, it should be noted that flow control (which is conventionally coupled with error control as a form of window flow control) must be independent of error control in high-speed networks such as ATM networks [43]. The use of windows for both flow control and error control leads to a conflict. In a high-speed network, where the ratio of propagation delay to cell transmission time is large, a large window must be used to achieve high throughput; however, a large window imposes little control effect. In the worst case, an entire window may be transmitted at once, possibly leading to network congestion. Therefore, some form of rate-based flow control schemes such as the Leaky Bucket method discussed in Section III-B-2) must be used independently of error control as a flow control scheme. In this section, various error control schemes are examined under a high-speed environment.

Error control schemes can be implemented on a link-by-link basis or an edge-to-edge basis. In a link-by-link scheme, retransmission of lost or erred cells takes place only between adjacent switching nodes, whereas in an edge-to-edge scheme, retransmission takes place only between the source and destination nodes. The suitability of link-by-link and edge-to-edge schemes in high-speed networks is discussed in Section IV-A.

Error control schemes can be placed into two classes depending on the retransmission protocols (Automatic Repeat Request (ARQ) protocols) for erred/lost cells: go-back-n and selective-repeat protocols. In both go-back-n and selective-repeat protocols, the transmitter sends cells continuously without waiting for an acknowledgement from the receiver. Upon receipt of a negative acknowledgement (NAK) or when timeout occurs, a go-back-n protocol retransmits all the cells starting with the lost cell, whereas a selective-repeat protocol retransmits only the lost cell. In Section IV-B these schemes are further discussed with possible improvements under a high-speed environment.

A. Link-by-Link versus Edge-to-Edge Schemes

In traditional packet networks (e.g., X.25/X.75), error control is done on a link-by-link basis. Link-by-link error control, however, may not be appropriate in high-speed networks such as an ATM network. Link-by-link schemes involve heavy protocol processing because cells are manipulated and processed at each node in the network. The overhead of protocol processing is very significant in high-speed networks, while in existing networks, this overhead is considered to be negligible (a packet length and a channel speed are the bottleneck in determining the packet transmission delay). Therefore, in high-speed networks, edge-to-edge schemes may become more attractive, despite the fact that it "wastes" the successful transmissions over all earlier links if error or loss happens later on the path [44]. In edge-to-edge schemes, an erred or lost cell is retransmitted from the source, and thus if errors/losses occur on a link far from the source, edge-to-edge retransmisson wastes the successful transmissions over all earlier links.

Some papers investigate the issue of link-by-link versus edge-to-edge schemes [44]–[47]. In [44], the performance of these two schemes are investigated and compared. The network is modeled as a tandem queueing network, where each queue represents a single switching node along a virtual circuit. Finite buffers are assumed except at the source node (infinite buffers are assumed at the source). Blocked cells due to buffer overflow are considered lost and have to be retransmitted. The effects of propagation delay are considered, while the processing times required in an error recovery protocol are assumed to be negligible. From a mathematical analysis and simulations, they concluded the following:

• For small virtual circuit (VC) throughput values, there is no significant performance difference between the link-by-link and the edge-to-edge schemes.

• As the VC throughput increases, the edge-to-edge scheme performs better than the link-by-link scheme. The edge-to-edge scheme experiences smaller delays and reaches the saturation point at a higher throughput value than the link-by-link scheme. This is because the edge-to-edge scheme buffers a copy of a cell only at the source and releases the buffer immediately upon completion of cell transmission at the intermediate nodes, whereas the link-by-link scheme buffers each cell until it is acknowledged. Therefore, for high throughput values, blocking due to buffer overflow happens less frequently in the edge-to-edge scheme, yielding lower delays and a higher maximal throughput.

• When the error probability is increased, the link-by-link scheme performs marginally better than the edge-to-edge scheme at lower throughput values. This is because when an error occurs, link-by-link recovers faster than edge-to-edge since the link-by-link scheme receives feedback earlier than the edge-to-edge scheme. However, as the throughput increases, blocking due to buffer overflow becomes significant, and thus the edge-to-edge scheme eventually achieves better performance.

• When the propagation delay is decreased, the relative performance of a link-by-link scheme improves. (The opposite holds when the propagation delay is increased, or equivalently, when the channel speed is increased.) This is because when the propagation delay is decreased, the intermediate nodes need to buffer a copy of a cell for a shorter time, and thus the blocking probabilities for the link-by-link case decreases.

• As the number of hops increases, the relative difference in the performance of the two schemes decreases. This is due to the disadvantage of edge-to-edge schemes discussed earlier: if errors/losses occur on a link far from the source, edge-to-edge schemes waste the successful transmissions over all earlier links. It is conjectured that, as the number of hops increases, the performance of link-by-link schemes will eventually become better than that of edge-to-edge, but this crossover occurs when the number of hops becomes unrealistically large.

In summary, the authors conclude that even under assumptions that favor the link-by-link scheme (e.g., no node processing time is considered, and an analytic model which overestimates the delay for the edge-to-edge schemes is used), the edge-to-edge scheme performs better than the link-by-link scheme, requiring fewer network resources such as buffers and computation time.

The performance of link-by-link and edge-to-edge schemes in a high-speed environment is also investigated in [45]. Here, the effects of processing time required for error recovery are considered, while the effects of propagation delay are assumed to be negligible. The network is modeled as a tandem queueing network with feedback loops between adjacent nodes (for a link-by-link scheme), and the source and destination nodes (for an edge-to-edge scheme). Each queue represents a protocol layer within a switching node, rather than a switching node as a whole. Infinite buffers are assumed at each switching node. It is concluded that for a network with very high-speed and low-error-rate channels, the edge-to-edge scheme gives better performance (i.e., gives the smaller cell transmission delay and cell loss probability) than the link-by-link scheme. The analytic models used in this paper are validated in [46] through simulations.

In [47], link-by-link and edge-to-edge schemes are studied through simulated for existing X.25 packet networks. The propagation delays and processing times are considered, although they are relatively small (on the same order as a packet transmission time). It is concluded that the edge-to-edge protocol alone can yield good performance if the value for the edge-to-edge timeout is large enough to avoid unnecessary timeouts (i.e., timeouts under heavy loads on error-free transmissions). It is also shown that the addition of a link-by-link control significantly improves the network performance under light loads. The improvement gained by adding link-by-link control is reduced as the load increases. This is because under a light load, the link-by-link control causes little queueing since there is not much traffic, and thus very few edge-to-edge timeouts occur. On the contrary, when traffic load is heavy, the additional link processing causes queues to build up, which in turn causes edge-to-edge timeouts.

In conclusion, in ATM networks, where the effects of propagation delay and processing time are significant, the edge-to-edge scheme gives better performance than the link-to-link scheme.

B. Go-Back-N versus Selective-Repeat Protocols

The channel propagation delay has a strong effect on the performance of ARQ protocols. As the ratio of propagation delay to cell transmission time increases, the go-back-n protocol suffers from the reduced throughput because of the large number of cell retransmissions required. The selective-repeat protocol achieves better throughputs than the go-back-n protocol since it retransmits only those cells that are negatively acknowledged or whose timeouts have expired. However, in the selective-repeat protocol, a reordering buffer is required at the receiver since cells need to be buffered until all preceding cells are received correctly.

In existing networks such as X.25 networks, the go-back-n protocol is the most commonly used protocol since it eliminates the need for reordering buffers and is easy to implement. Furthermore, this protocol provides reasonably good performance when the propagation delay is comparable to the packet transmission time [48]. However, in ATM networks where the channel speed is very high and the ratio of propagation delay to cell transmission time is very large, the number of cells in transit can be very large, and the go-back-n protocol may not perform well. For example, as we saw in the example given at the beginning of Section III, if we use 500-bit long cells, 5 μs/km propagation delay and 1 Gbits/s channel, and if the transmitter and the receiver are 100 km apart, there are 1000 cells in transit from the transmitter to the receiver. Therefore, if a go-back-n protocol is used, upon receipt of a NAK, the transmitter may need to retransmit 2000 cells. This can cause significant reduction in throughput. Thus the go-back-n protocol becomes less attractive, and the selective-repeat becomes more attractive in a high-speed network environment.

In [48], a throughput analysis of a selective repeat protocol in high-speed network environments is presented. Through numerical examples it is shown that as the ratio of propagation delay to cell transmission time increases, the selective-repeat achieves significantly better throughput performance than a go-back-n protocol. However, at the same time, the buffers required for reordering cells become large. This effect is studied in [49], and the upper bound on the mean buffer occupancy is derived.

The trade-off between the throughput and the buffer requirement should be carefully weighed to determine which ARQ protocol is more effective in a high-speed environment. However, with the advancement in VLSI technology, cost-effective reordering buffers are in fact coming to the marketplace [50], and the implementation of selective-repeat is believed to be simple as long as the cell size is constant [51]. Therefore, the current trend is to favor the selective-repeat procotol over the go-back-n protocol.

In the above, the effects of propagation delay on the performance of ARQ protocols are examined. Another important factor which needs to be addressed is the use of optical fiber and its extremely low error rate. The effects of low error rate on the performance of ARQ protocols also need to be considered. As the error rate decreases, errors rarely happen, and thus the inefficiency of the go-back-n protocol becomes less significant since retransmissions are rarely required. Even though the selective-repeat protocol always achieves better throughput, the performance difference between the selective-repeat and go-back-n protocols becomes smaller as the error rate on the channel decreases. The effects of large propagation delay and low error rate need to be carefully examined to determine the best ARQ scheme for ATM networks.

Finally, it should be noted that to improve selective-repeat protocols a "block" concept can be introduced. A block is a group of cells, and a single acknowledgement message is used to acknowledge a block of cells, not an individual cell. Selective-repeat is performed on a block basis, and either block can be retransmitted or, if an acknowledgement contains the list of cells to be retransmitted, only the erred/lost cells can be retransmitted.

Several forms of block acknowledgement schemes have been proposed in [43], [51]–[53]. All the block acknowledgement schemes share a common advantage over a per-cell acknowledgement scheme: they reduce the large overhead incurred by sending a separate acknowledgement for each cell. Furthermore, the number of bits required to address the erred/lost cells is reduced if the entire block is retransmitted, even when one cell in a block is delivered incorrectly [53]. This reduction in the address field results in a reduction in processing time by reducing the size of tables which have to be searched to determine which blocks have to be retransmitted. This effect of reduced processing time is more significant in high-speed networks since minimum processing is required to match the rapid channel speed.

In conclusion, the authors of this paper believe that a block acknowledgement scheme in conjunction with a block-based selective-repeat retransmission protocol executed on an edge-to-edge basis is the most appropriate error control scheme in very high-speed networks such as ATM.

V. Multiple Traffic Classes

As mentioned earlier, ATM networks must support diversity of service and performance requirements. For instance, real-time voice and video have strict delay requirements, whereas in many data applications, real-time delivery is not a primary concern. Even within delay-sensitive traffic (e.g., voice or video), different traffic streams may have different delay requirements; some data may contain more urgent information than others. Some traffic (e.g., data) is loss-sensitive and thus must be received without any errors, whereas the inherent structure of speech allows for some loss of information without significant quality degradation. Ideally, uniform control mechanisms should be applied across all the media; however, this is extremely difficult. As an alternative, the notion of multiple traffic classes or grade of service (GOS) can be introduced and different control mechanisms can be applied to different traffic classes.

To support multiple classes of traffic in ATM networks, priority mechanisms can be used. Multiple priority levels are provided, and different priority levels are given to different classes of traffic. There are two ways to use priorities: one is to use a priority mechanism as a scheduling method (i.e., queueing discipline). In this way, different delay requirements can be satisfied by scheduling (serving) delay-sensitive or urgent traffic first. The second way is to use a priority scheme to control congestion. In this case, when network congestion occurs, different cell loss requirements can be satisfied by selectively discarding (low priority) cells. In the following sections, priority schemes are examined in more detail.

A. Priority Scheme as a Scheduling Method

Various priority schemes can be used as a scheduling method at a switching node in an ATM network. The simplest priority scheme is a static (or fixed) priority scheme. In this scheme, priority is always given to the delay-sensitive class, and the delay-sensitive class is always scheduled for service before the loss-sensitive traffic. This scheme causes relatively high losses for the loss-sensitive traffic while providing relatively low delays for the delay-sensitive traffic.

Since the static priority scheme always schedules the high priority traffic first, if a large portion of the network traffic consists of high priority traffic, the performance for the low priority traffic will be severely degraded. Two dynamic priority schemes, Minimum Laxity Threshold (MLT) and Queue Length Threshold (QLT) [54], try to reduce the performance degradation for the low priority traffic. In these dynamic priority schemes, priority level changes with time.

In the MLT scheme, the laxity of a cell is defined as the number of slots remaining before its deadline expires. A cell remains in the queue until either the cell is transmitted or the laxity reaches zero; when the laxity reaches zero, the cell is discarded and considered lost. In this scheme, priority is given to the delay-sensitive traffic if there are any delay-sensitive cells in the queue whose laxity is less than some threshold value; otherwise priority is given to the loss-sensitive traffic. In the QLT scheme, priority is given to the loss-sensitive traffic when the number of loss-sensitive cells in the queue exceeds some threshold value; otherwise priority is given to the delay-sensitive traffic.

In both the MLT and QLT schemes, a desired performance level for each of the high and low priority classes can be achieved by choosing an appropriate value for the threshold. The MLT discipline, however, may involve heavy processing at each switching node because the laxity of each real-time cell needs to be updated in every time slot, and each queue needs to be searched to find the minimum laxity cell. Therefore, unless the number of queued cells at each switching node is small, the MLT discipline may not work well in an ATM network, where processing time becomes a bottleneck. In [54], the performance of MLT and QLT disciplines are examined and the analytical models for the two disciplines are developed. Here, little difference in the performance trade-offs is observed in the MLT and the QLT disciplines, and it is concluded that QLT is more practical than MLT due to its simpler implementation.

The above priority schemes differentiate between delay-sensitive and loss-sensitive data in order to meet the performance requirement of each traffic type. As mentioned earlier, even within delay-sensitive traffic, there may be multiple classes, each having a different delay requirement. Head-of-the-Line with Priority Jumps (HOL-PJ) is proposed in [55] to satisfy different delay requirements within delay-sensitive traffic. In this scheme, higher priority is given to the class of traffic with stricter delay requirements. It is assumed that each priority class forms its own queue. Within the same priority class, cells are served FCFS, while higher priority queues have nonpreemptive priority over lower priority queues. A limit is imposed on the maximum queueing delay of cells within each queue; when the waiting time of a cell exceeds the maximum delay limit, that cell jumps to the end of the next higher priority queue. Thus the queueing delay of a cell before it joins the highest priority queue is bounded by the sum of the delay limits at all the queues with priorities equal to higher than the cell's original class. The performance for different classes can be controlled by adjusting the values of the delay limit. A possible disadvantage of this scheme is the processing overhead required for monitoring cells for time-out and moving cells to the next level priority queue. Also, each arriving cell needs to be time-stamped. It is claimed in [55] that these tasks are simple, and the processing overhead is relatively small.

There are other priority schemes proposed to satisfy different delay requirements within the delay-sensitive traffic. For instance, refer to [56]–[61] for the Minimum-Laxity-First (MLF) (or Earliest-Due-Date (EDD)) scheme and [62] for the Earliest-Deadline-First (EDF) scheme.

B. Priority Scheme as a Local Congestion Control Scheme

Priority schemes can be used as local congestion control schemes to satisfy different cell loss requirements of different classes of traffic. For instance, data traffic is loss-sensitive whereas voice traffic can tolerate some loss of information. With a priority scheme, when congestion is detected, priority is given to loss-sensitive traffic (e.g., data) over loss-insensitive traffic (e.g., voice), and cells from lower priority classes are discarded first. This priority scheme recognizes the different cell loss requirements of different classes of traffic. In [63], the impact of discarding voice cells on data traffic is studied. It is shown that the mean waiting time for data can be significantly reduced by discarding voice cells during congestion periods.

In discarding voice information, an improvement can be obtained by selectively discarding voice cells containing less important information. For example, in coded speech, active speech usually carries more important information than background noise during pauses. By discarding cells containing less important information (e.g., background noise), the quality of the reconstructed voice can be maintained. In [63]–[66], priority is given to voice cells containing important information and low priority voice packets are dropped first when congestion occurs. Congestion is controlled locally by selectively discarding voice cells whose loss will have the least effect on the quality of the reconstructed voice signal. It is shown that such a prioritized system is capable of achieving better performance than nonprioritized systems [66].

In the above scheme, a priority level is assigned to each voice cell at the transmitter. The priority level of a cell can be determined by the following methods [66].

• In the embedded coding method [67], the encoded information is divided into more significant bits and less significant bits. More significant bits form high priority cells, and less significant bits form low priority cells.

• In the even/odd sample method [68], speech samples are identified as either even or odd. Even samples form high priority voice cells, and odd samples form low priority voice cells (or vice versa).

• In the multiple energy level detection method, voice cells (from talkspurts) are classified as "semisilence" or "active" according to their energy level. (No cells are generated from silent periods.) Priority is placed on "active" voice cells.

Once the cell priority is determined using one of the above methods, low priority cells are discarded at the onset of congestion.

Slightly different techniques to control voice traffic have been proposed. In [69]–[72], priority is assigned to more important (significant) bits, not to cells. Each cell consists of high priority bits (more significant bits) and low priority bits (less significant bits), and cell size is reduced in response to overload by dropping low priority bits. This technique has a major disadvantage: it requires network nodes to know the internal structure of a voice cell in order to distinguish high priority bits from low priority bits and to manipulate the cell contents [64]. This will increase cell processing at each switching node; thus this technique may not be suitable for ATM networks. Furthermore, since the cell size is constant in ATM networks, it is not clear how this technique can be applied in ATM networks.

Discarding cells based on the importance of their contents can also be applied to video traffic. If an embedded coding technique[4] [73]–[75] is used for the image then coded information is separated into two bit streams: a stream containing essential information and a stream containing picture enhancement information. Cells containing essential information are given higher priority than those containing the picture enhancements. When congestion occurs, only low priority cells are discarded. With this scheme, even when networks become congested, the essential parts of coded information are transmitted, thus it is expected that cell loss will have only a small influence on picture quality [74].

VI. STANDARDIZATION OF ATM

In the CCITT Recommendation I.121, a guideline for future B-ISDN standardization, ATM has been accepted as the final transfer mode for B-ISDN [76]. According to this recommendation, information flow in ATM is organized into fixed-size cells, each consisting of a header and an information field. Fixed-size cells are chosen over variable-size units because, based on the state of the existing experimental fast packet switching technology, it is believed that fixed-size cells can be switched more efficiently [77]. These cells are transmitted over a virtual circuit and cells belonging to the same virtual circuit are identified by the header.

ATM is, by definition, a connection-oriented technique. This connection-oriented mode minimizes delay variation since cells belonging to the same call follow the same route. It also minimizes the processing required to make routing decisions.

Although agreement has been reached on some aspects of ATM, a number of issues have not yet been resolved. In the CCITT Study Group XVIII meeting held in June 1989, some agreement was reached on the ATM cell format, the underlying transmission system, and the layered architecture for ATM networks. In Section VI-A the ATM cell format is discussed, and in Section VI-B standard activities on the underlying transmission structure is discussed. The layered architecture for ATM networks is discussed in Section VI-C.

A. ATM Cell Format

The size of an ATM cell should be small in order to reduce the degrading effect of the packetization delay at the source. For instance, considerable delay could be introduced during creation of a voice cell if the size of a cell is large. T1S1, a body commissioned by the American National Standards Institute (ANSI) to develop ISDN standards for North America, had proposed an ATM cell consisting of a 5-octet header and a 64-octet informa-

[4]Referred to also as a layered coding technique or a hierarchical coding technique.

tion field, while the European Telecommunications Standard Institute (ETSI), a regional organization that coordinates telecommunications policies in Europe, had proposed an ATM cell consisting of a 4-octet header and a 32-octet information field [77]. As a compromise, the CCITT has reached an international agreement on an ATM cell consisting of a 5-octet header and a 48-octet information field [17], [18]. The CCITT header formats which will be used at User-Network Interface (UNI) and Network-Node Interface (NNI) are shown in Fig. 11 [78]. For UNI, the header

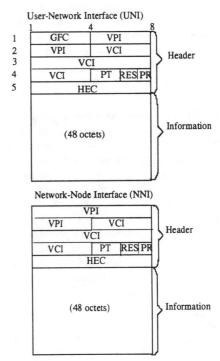

Fig. 11. ATM cell structure.

contains a 4-bit "generic flow control" (GFC) field, a 24-bit label field containing Virtual Path Identifier (VPI) and Virtual Circuit Identifier (VCI) subfields (8 bits for the VPI and 16 bits for the VCI), a 2-bit payload type (PT) field, a 1-bit reserved field, a 1-bit priority (PR) field, and an 8-bit header error check (HEC) field. For NNI, the header does not contain a GFC field, and the extra 4 bits are used for a VPI field.

The GFC field is used to assist the customer premises in controlling the flow of traffic for different qualities of service. The exact procedures for how to use this field are not agreed upon as yet. One candidate for the use of this field is a multiple priority level indicator to control the flow of information in a service-dependent manner. The GFC field appears only at the UNI.

The "Virtual Path" concept [79], [80] is adopted in a label field. The VPI provides an explicit path identification for a cell, while VCI provides an explicit circuit identification for a cell. Basically, a virtual path is a bundle of virtual circuits which is switched as a unit by defining one additional layer of multiplexing on a per-cell basis underneath the VCI. A predefined route is provided with each virtual path; thus it is not necessary to rewrite the routing table at call setup. Therefore, call-by-call processing at switching nodes is reduced and call set-up delay is decreased. Although the transmission efficiency may decrease because of the label overhead, this effect is negligible since large bandwidth will be available as high capacity optical fibers become more widely used [79].

The PT field can be used for maintenance purposes, and it indicates whether the cell contains user information or network maintenance information. This field allows for the insertion of cells on to a virtual channel without impacting the user's data.

The PR field indicates cell loss priority and is used to selectively discard cells when congestion occurs. One possible implementation is to set this field to zero for the cells which need guaranteed delivery and to set it to one for the cells which are droppable. When congestion occurs, cells whose PR field set to one are dropped first.

The HEC field provides single-bit error correction or multiple-bit error detection capabilities on the cell header. The polynomial used to generate the header error check value is $X^8 + X^2 + X + 1$. The HEC monitors errors for the entire header. One bit in the header is reserved for the future use.

B. Transmission Structure

T1S1 and ETSI disagrees on the transmission structure underlying the ATM layer. T1S1 favors the Synchronous Optical Networks (SONET) approach, whereas ETSI favors the Asynchronous Time Division (ATD) approach [77]. In the ATD approach, no frame structure is imposed on the UNI, and all of its physical bandwidth is organized as ATM cells; while in the SONET approach, ATM cells are carried within the payload of another framework, such as a SONET frame. The payload is an area used to carry the service or signal being transported.

ATD, a version of ATM originally proposed by France, is a frameless interface carrying no synchronous channels [81] (Fig. 12). It consists solely of cells, and synchronization is maintained

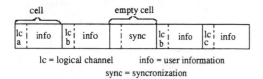

lc = logical channel   info = user information

sync = syncronization

Fig. 12. ATD structure.

by filling empty cells with a special synchronization pattern. The advantage of using ATD as a transmission structure underlying the ATM layer is the simplified interface which results when both transmission and transfer mode functions are based on a common structure. ETSI favors this approach.

The SONET approach will be further discussed in Section VI-B-1).

1) SONET: SONET (Synchronous Optical Network), originally proposed by Bellcore (Bell Communications Research), is a standard optical interface. In this section, frame structure and key features of SONET are first presented, and the approach of using SONET as the underlying transmission structure and its advantages and disadvantages are also discussed.

a) SONET STS-1 frame structure: In SONET, there is a basic building block called the synchronous transport signal level 1 (STS-1) frame. The STS-1 frame has a bit rate of 51.84 Mbits/s and repeats every 125 μ seconds. A 125-μsec frame period supports digital voice signal transport since each byte can represent a 64 kbits/s (= byte/125μsec) DS0 channel.

The STS-1 frame structure is illustrated in Fig. 13. It consists of 9 rows and 90 columns (9 × 90 bytes), and it is transmitted row by row, from left to right. The STS-1 frame is divided into two areas known as the transport overhead and the Synchronous Payload Envelope (SPE). The transport overhead is used to carry

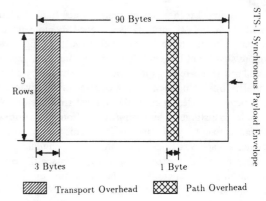

Fig. 13. STS-1 frame structure.

overhead information and the SPE is used to carry the SONET payload. Within the SPE, there is 1 column (= 9 bytes) of path overhead. A path corresponds to a logical connection between source and destination; the functions of path overhead will be discussed later (Fig. 14).

The transport overhead consists of 3 columns (= 3 × 9 bytes) and carries overhead bits for connections at the section level (connection between regenerators) and connections at the line level (connection between light-wave terminating equipments). Refer to Fig. 14 for the concept of section and line. The section overhead is processed at each regenerator. The line overhead is passed transparently through regenerators and is processed by light-wave terminating equipment. The transport overhead bits and their functions include:

- framing bytes to show the start of each STS-1 frame;
- an STS-1 identification byte;
- STS-1 pointer bytes (will be discussed later);
- parity checks for section and line error monitoring;
- signaling bits for fast, automatic protection switching or redundancy, to make optical lines fault-tolerant;
- local (section) and express (line) orderwire channels for voice communication between elements;
- data communication channels (or embedded operations channels) for alarms, maintenance, control, monitor, administration, and other communication needs between section (or line) terminating equipment such as lightwave, cross-connections, and digital loop carrier elements;
- extra bytes reserved for the future use.

Basically, the transport overhead carries information necessary for secure transmission of the SPE.

The SPE is used to carry SONET payloads including 1 column of path overhead. Path overhead is passed transparently from the point where the STS-1 payload is composed to the point where it is decomposed [2]. Some of the important functions of the path overhead are:

- end-to-end payload error monitoring;
- identification of the type of payload being carried;
- path status indication;
- a trace function which allows a user to trace a signal through the network as it goes through different elements.

The rest of the SPE is used to carry service or signal being transported. The SONET SPE can be used to carry either ATM-based or STM-based payloads.

b) Multiplexing of STS-1 frames: Higher rate SONET signals (STS-N) are obtained by synchronously byte multiplexing N

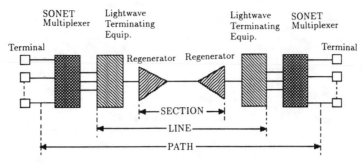

Fig. 14. Concept of section, line, and path.

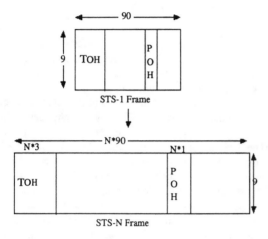

TOH: Transport Overhead   POH: Path Overhead

Fig. 15. STS-N frame structure.

STS-1 frames. The STS-N frame structure is depicted in Fig. 15. It consists of 9 rows and $N \times 90$ columns. The transport overhead consists of $N \times 3$ columns, and there are $N \times 1$ columns of path overhead. The aggregated bit rate of an STS-N signal is exactly N times the basic rate of 51.84 Mbits/s. For example, a STS-3 carries three byte-interleaved STS-1 signals in an aggregated bit rate of 155.52 Mbits/s. Currently, the only values of N allowed are 1, 3, 9, 12, 18, 24, 36, and 48. The optical signals can be obtained by passing the electrical STS-N signal through an electro-optic conversion. The optical signal of STS-N is called an Optical Carrier Level N (OC-N). The OC-N will have a line rate exactly same as the STS-N. Table 1 shows the SONET digital interface rates.

Table 1   SONET Digital Interface Rates

Level	Line Rate (Mb/s)
OC-1	51.84
OC-3	155.52
OC-9	466.56
OC-12	622.08
OC-18	933.12
OC-24	1244.16
OC-36	1866.24
OC-48	2488.32

If all the STS-1 signals in the STS-N go to the same destination, they can be concatenated. The STS-N signal that is concatenated is called an STS-Nc, where the letter ''c'' stands for con-

catenation. In this format, the payload is treated as a single unit, and thus only one column of path overhead is needed. This is not the case in the unconcatenated STS-N signals. However, N copies of the section and line overheads are still required in the STS-Nc signal since any intervening transmission equipment expects to see the individual section and line overheads [2].

c) Virtual tributaries: One of the key features in SONET is payload structures called virtual tributaries (VT's). Virtual tributaries function as separate containers within the STS-1 frame structure and are used to carry a variety of lower rate signals such as DS1, DS1C, DS2 within an STS-1. In order to efficiently accommodate the North American and European digital hierarchy, these containers come with four different sizes: VT1.5, VT2, VT3, and VT6. A VT1.5 can be used to carry a North American DS1 signal (1.544 Mbits/s), a VT2 for a European CEPT-1 signal (2.048 Mbits/s), a VT3 for a DS1C signal (3.152 Mbits/s), and a VT6 for a DS2 signal (6.312 Mbits/s). A DS3 signal (44.736 Mbits/s) is carried in an STS-1 SPE.

d) SONET pointers: SONET uses payload pointers to allow easy access to the payload. As mentioned earlier, the STS-1 frame is divided into the transport overhead and STS-1 SPE. The payload is easily accessed since the STS-1 payload pointer, contained in the transport overhead, indicates the starting byte location of the STS-1 SPE within the STS-1 frame. The STS-1 payload pointer also avoids the need for the slip buffers and eliminates associated payload corruption and delay. In conventional methods, such as fixed location mapping, slip buffers are needed at the multiplexing equipment interfaces to take care of frequency differences by either repeating or deleting a frame of information. This increases delay and may cause signal impairment due to slipping. The STS-1 payload pointer avoids the need for slip buffers since small frequency variations of the STS-1 payload can be accommodated by adjusting the pointer value. Detailed discussion of pointer operation can be found in [82].

SONET can also have VT pointers. The VT pointers follow the same principle as the STS-1 payload pointers, except at the VT level. The VT pointer indicates the position of the starting byte of the VT SPE within the VT payload structure. The pointer adjustment rules are analogous to that of the STS-1 pointer, and the VT pointer has the same advantages as the STS-1 pointer, i.e., dynamic alignment between the STS-1 SPE and the VT SPE, minimal delay, etc.

e) ATM within SONET: Figure 16 shows ATM carried within SONET. In the figure, it is assumed that the UNI is SONET-based and uses the STS-3c format with a gross bit rate of 155.520 Mbits/s. B-ISDN proposals using SONET usually use the STS-3c frame [2]. SONET overhead is not embedded within the cell structure, and the SONET payload carries ATM cells multiplexed using ATM techniques. T1S1 favors SONET over ATD because of the following reasons [77].

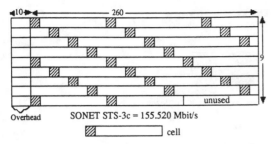

Fig. 16. ATM within SONET (150 Mbit/s).

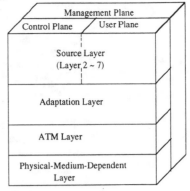

Fig. 17. B-ISDN ATM protocol mode.

• SONET is more compatible with the existing circuit-switched networks than a new structure such as ATD. Furthermore, SONET SPE can be used to carry ATM-based payloads as well as STM-based payloads. Therefore, SONET makes the transition from the existing networks to ATM networks more smoothly than ATD.

• Some specific connection can be circuit switched using a SONET channel. For example, a connection carrying video traffic can be mapped into its own exclusive payload envelope of the SONET STS-3c signal, which can be circuit switched.

• Using SONET synchronous multiplexing capabilities, several ATM streams can be combined to build interfaces with higher bit rates than those supported by the ATM layer. For example, four separate ATM streams, each having bit rate of 155 Mbits/s (STS-3c), can be combined to build a 622 Mbits/s (STS-12) interface, even though the ATM layer supports interfaces with bit rate of only 155 Mbits/s. This may be more cost effective than making the ATM layer to support interfaces with bit rates of 622 Mbits/s.

A possible disadvantage of using SONET is that existing equipment may not be SONET-compatible. For example, equipment not designed for SONET may not be easily adapted to the VT-1.5 (1.728 Mbits/s) payload rate of SONET [83].

CCITT will standardize two physical interfaces to B-ISDN, one based on SONET and the other based on a variation of ATD [17]. The UNI interface rate for both of these is set at 155.520 Mbits/s [17].

C. Layered Architecture for ATM Networks

Significant changes have taken place in ATM networks. ATM networks provide huge bandwidth with low error rates using optical fiber. In such a high-speed network environment, processing time becomes a bottleneck. The conventional OSI 7 layer protocol architecture may be too heavy, i.e., it involves too much processing, and thus a new protocol architecture is needed.

Layered architectures for ATM networks have been studied in [2], [84]–[87], and some agreement has been made in the CCITT Study Group XVIII meeting held in June 1989. Figure 17 [88] depicts a B-ISDN ATM protocol model. In this figure, the protocol hierarchy consists of the physical-medium-dependent (PMD) layer, the ATM layer, the adaptation layer, and the higher service layer. Note that functional layering in the B-ISDN protocol model does not follow the OSI model [89].

The physical-medium-dependent (PMD) layer[5] underlies the ATM layer. As mentioned previously CCITT will standardize two physical interfaces to B-ISDN, one based on SONET and the other based on a variation of ATD. This layer is responsible for the

[5]Referred to also as transmission layer.

proper bit transmission and performs functions which are necessary to insert/extract the cell flow into/out-of a transmission frame. This layer is also responsible for electro-optical conversion since in B-ISDN, the physical medium is optical fiber.

The ATM layer contains all the details of the ATM technique, and it is common to all services. This layer is physical medium independent, and thus it is independent of the underlying PMD layer. The data unit of this layer is an ATM cell, and the ATM layer performs the cell header functions. As discussed in Section VI-A, major functions of the header include cell routing based on VCI/VPI and error detection on the header based on HEC. This layer also performs cell-based multiplexing/demultiplexing and cell delineation. The information field of an ATM cell is passed transparently through the ATM layer, and no processing, including error control, is performed on the information field at the ATM layer.

The adaptation layer and the higher layers of the ATM protocol model are service-dependent. The boundary between the ATM layer and the adaptation layer corresponds to the differences between functions applied to the cell header and functions applied to the information field [2]. The adaptation layer provides the higher service layer with the necessary functions which are not provided by the ATM layer, for instance, preserving timing, data frame boundaries and source clock. Functions of the adaptation layer are further described in the following.

Four service classes are defined at the adaptation layer (Table 2 [78]). Class 1 services corresponds to constant bit rate (CBR)

Table 2 Service Classes

	Class 1	Class 2	Class 3	Class 4
Timing between source and destination	related		not related	
Bit rate	constant		variable	
Connection mode	connection-oriented			connectionless

services. CBR audio and video belong to this class. Class 2 services corresponds to variable bit rate (VBR), connection-oriented services. Examples of class 2 services are variable bit rate audio and video. For class 1 and 2 services, timing between source and destination needs to be related. Class 3 services also correspond to VBR connection-oriented services, but the timing between source and destination need not be related. Connection-oriented data and signaling data are examples of class 3 services. Class 4 services correspond to VBR connectionless services, and connectionless data belong to this class.

The adaptation layer is divided into two sublayers, the Segmentation and Reassembly (SAR) Sublayer and the Convergence (CS) Sublayer; these two sublayers provide different functions for each of the four service classes. The following description gives a possible implementation of the adaptation layer for class 3 and 4 services. Two modes of adaptation service are provided for class 3 and 4 services: Message Mode and Streaming Mode. Message Mode service is used for framed data, whereas Streaming Mode service is used for low-speed continuous data with low delay requirements. For Message Mode service (Fig. 18 [78]), the CS Sublayer accepts a Service Data Unit (SDU) from the higher service layer. A SDU is a service-specific, higher layer information unit. It then prepends a 4-octet header (CS_PDU Header) to the SDU, pads the SDU (0 to 3-octet PAD) to make it an integral multiple of 32-bits, and appends a 4-octet trailer (CS_PDU Trailer). The functions of the header and trailer fields include service indication and cell loss detection. The CS_PDU Header, SDU, PAD, and CS_PDU Trailer structure is referred to as a CS_PDU (Convergence Sublayer Protocol Data Units). After the trailer is appended, the CS_PDU is passed to the next sublayer, SAR Sublayer, for segmentation. The SAR Sublayer accepts a CS_PDU from the CS Sublayer and segments it into N 44-octet SAR Sublayer SDU (SAR_SDU) Payloads; thus the last SAR_SDU Payload may have some unused portion. It then prepends a 2-octet header (SAR_SDU Header) to the SAR_SDU Payload and appends a 2-octet trailer (SAR_SDU Trailer) to the SAR_SDU Payload. The functions of the header and trailer fields include:

- segmentation/reassembly;
- identification of segment type (e.g., a beginning of a message (BOM), a continuation of a message (COM), an end of a message (EOM), or a single SAR_SDU message (SSM));
- identification of a message;
- indication of partially filled segment;
- bit error detection for the entire contents of the SAR_SDU.

The SAR_SDU Header, SAR_SDU Payload, and SAR_SDU Trailer structure is referred to as a SAR_SDU. After the trailer is appended, the SAR_SDU is passed to the ATM layer.

For Streaming Mode service (Fig. 19 [78]), unlike in Message Mode service where one CS_PDU consists of one SDU, a CS_PDU may consist of several SDU's. As in Message Mode service, a CS_PDU Header (4 octets), a PAD (0-3 octets) and a CS_PDU Trailer (4 octets) are added to complete a CS_PDU. Then, the SAR sublayer segment the CS_PDU into N 44-octet SAR_SDU Payloads such that each SDU is contained in a separate SAR_SDU. Therefore, unlike in Message Mode service where only the last segment may contain some unused portion, in Streaming Mode service any segment can have some unused portion. As in Message Mode service, the SAR Sublayer adds a 2-octet header and a 2-octet trailer to a SAR_SDU Payload. The functions of each field are identical to those of the Message Mode service.

The possible CBR service (Class 1 service) adaptation func-

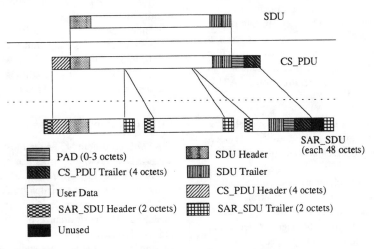

Fig. 18. Message mode service.

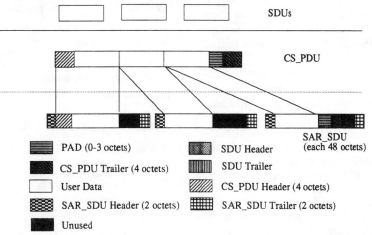

Fig. 19. Streaming mode service.

tions include:

- source clock frequency recovery;
- forward error correction;
- time stamping;
- sequence number processing;
- handling of lost or misdelivered cells.

Adaptation layer functions for Class 2 services are not well defined. For further discussion, refer to [78].

The higher service layer provides separate functions for the User Plane and the Control Plane, whereas lower layers (i.e., PDM layer, ATM layer, and adaptation layer) provide functions common for those two planes. The Control Plane is responsible for signaling, whereas the User Plane is responsible for the transfer of user information. In the Control Plane, much of the structure of existing N-ISDN (Narrowband ISDN) is maintained with some future enhancements. For example, an error detection/correction and flow control protocol in case of overload can be derived from the ISDN LAP-D protocol, and the call control (call establishment/release) mechanism is compatible to the N-ISDN protocol I.451. However, for the User Plane, most of the link-by-link layer protocols are removed or pushed to higher edge-to-edge layers. For example, no link-by-link error control is provided.

VII. Summary and Future Research Problems

Among the techniques proposed for B-ISDN transfer mode, the ATM concept is considered to be the most promising transfer technique because of its flexibility and efficiency. In this paper, a number of topics related to ATM networks are surveyed and reviewed. The topics covered are modeling of various traffic sources, congestion control, error control, priority schemes to support multiple classes of traffic and standardization of ATM. The following conclusions are made.

- The cell arrival process for data sources can be modeled by a simple Poisson process. However, voice sources or video sources require more complex processes because of the correlation among cell arrivals.
- Due to the effects of high-speed channels, preventive control is more effective in ATM networks than reactive control.
- Due to the use of optical fibers, in ATM networks, the channel error rate is very small. The effects of propagation delay and processing time become significant in such high-speed networks. These fundamental changes trigger the necessity to reexamine the error control schemes used in existing networks. A block acknowledgment scheme in conjunction with a block-based selective-repeat retransmission protocol executed on an edge-to-edge basis seems to be the most promising approach for error control in ATM networks.
- Due to the diversity of service and performance requirements, the notion of multiple traffic classes is required, and separate control mechanisms should be used according to the traffic classes. An effective method to support multiple classes of traffic is the priority scheme.
- In CCITT Recommendation I.121, ATM is accepted as the final transfer mode for B-ISDN. Although some consensus has been made on some aspects of ATM, a number of issues related to ATM still need further study for standardization.

Finally, it should be noted that there are still a number of unsolved research problems in the area of ATM networks. The following presents some of the future research problems.

- In most of the past analytic work, homogeneous traffic sources are assumed. Quantitative performance analysis assuming heterogeneous traffic sources needs to be studied further.
- In most of the past analysis, Poisson arrivals are assumed. Poisson processes, however, do not adequately describe many of the traffic sources found in ATM networks. Performance analyses of ATM networks assuming more accurate arrival processes need to be studied.
- Accurate source modeling for video is still an open research area.
- In most of the past work, congestion is measured through the queue length. In other words, if the queue length exceeds some threshold value, the network is considered to be in congestion. This mechanism of detecting congestion may not reflect the status of the network accurately in an ATM network, where the bursty traffic may cause rapid and dynamic fluctuations in the buffer occupancy. This mechanism, thus, may lead to false detection of network congestion. More accurate ways to detect congestion need to be investigated.
- The cell loss probability has been analyzed only on the multiplexed link, and not for each connection. The cell loss probability for an individual connection needs to be analyzed to obtain the performance seen by the end users.
- When a large portion of traffic consists of the high priority traffic, the performance for the low priority traffic will be severely degraded. In such a case, segregation schemes (i.e., partitioning network resources according to the given quality class) may work better than the priority schemes. Performance comparison between priority and segregation schemes needs to be done.
- Block acknowledgment schemes need to be analyzed considering the effects of propagation delay and processing time.
- In most of the past analytic work, performance of a single switching node is investigated. The performance of a more general network topology needs to be investigated.

VIII. Concluding Remarks

ATM is considered to be the most promising transfer technique for B-ISDN. ATM networks use optical fiber and provide huge bandwidth with low error rates. Due to the effects of high-speed channels, the ratio of propagation delay to cell transmission time and the ratio of processing time to cell transmission time are increased. The performance bottleneck of the ATM network is therefore shifted from the channel transmission speed to the processing speed at the network switching nodes and the propagation delay of the channel. Due to these fundamental changes, new network architectures are required for ATM.

Acknowledgment

The authors would like to thank Dr. Takashi Kamitake of Toshiba and Dr. Masayuki Murata of Osaka University for their continuous encouragement and help.

References

[1] H. Ichikawa, M. Aoki, and T. Uchiyama, "High-speed packet switching systems for multimedia communications," *IEEE J. Select. Areas Commun.*, vol. SAC-5, pp. 1336–1345, Oct. 1987.

[2] A. Hac and H. B. Mutlu, "Synchronous optical network and broadband ISDN protocols," *Computer*, vol. 22, no. 11, pp. 26–34, Nov. 1989.

[3] R. Handel, "Evolution of ISDN towards broadband ISDN," *IEEE Network*, pp. 7–13, Jan. 1989.

[4] T. Kamitake and T. Suda, "Evaluation of an admission control

scheme for an ATM network considering fluctuations in cell loss rate," in *Proc. IEEE GLOBECOM '89*, pp. 49.4.1–49.4.7.

[5] M. Murata, Y. Oie, T. Suda, and H. Miyahara, "Analysis of a discrete-time single-server queue with bursty inputs for traffic control in ATM networks," in *Proc. IEEE GLOBECOM '89*, pp. 49.5.1–49.5.7.

[6] S-Q. Li, "Study of information loss in packet voice systems," *IEEE Trans. Commun.*, vol. 37, pp. 1192–1202, Nov. 1989.

[7] J. N. Daigle and J. D. Langford, "Models for analysis of packet voice communications systems," *IEEE J. Select. Areas Commun.*, vol. SAC-4, pp. 847–855, Sept. 1986.

[8] I. Ide, "Superposition of interrupted Poisson processes and its application to packetized voice multiplexers," in *Proc. 12th Int. Teletraffic Congress*, Torino, Italy, 1988.

[9] H. Heffes and D. M. Lucantoni, "A Markov modulated characterization of packetized voice and data traffic and related statistical multiplexer performance," *IEEE J. Select. Areas Commun.*, vol. SAC-4, pp. 856–868, Sept. 1986.

[10] K. Q. Liao and L. G. Mason, "A discrete-time single server queue with a two-level modulated input and its applications," in *Proc. IEEE GLOBECOM '89* pp. 26.1.1–26.1.6.

[11] P. Sen, B. Maglaris, N. E. Rikli, and D. Anastassiou, "Models for packet switching of variable-bit-rate video sources," *IEEE J. Select. Areas Commun.*, vol. 7, pp. 865–869, June 1989.

[12] M. Nomura, T. Fujii, and N. Ohta, "Basic characteristics of variable rate video coding in ATM environment," *IEEE J. Select. Areas Commun.*, vol. 7, pp. 752–760, June 1989.

[13] B. Maglaris, D. Anastassiou, P. Sen, G. Karlsson, and J. D. Robbins, "Performance models of statistical multiplexing in packet video communications," *IEEE Trans. Commun.*, vol. 36, pp. 834–844, July 1988.

[14] A. Papoulis, *Probability, Random Variables, and Stochastic Processes*. New York, NY: McGraw Hill, 1984.

[15] Y. Yasuda, H. Yasuda, N. Ohta, and F. Kishino, "Packet video transmission through ATM networks," in *Proc. IEEE GLOBECOM '89*, pp. 25.1.1–25.1.5.

[16] H. Yamada, K. Miyake, F. Kishino, and K. Manabe, "Modeling of arrival process of packetized video and related statistical multiplexer performance," in *Proc. IECEJ National Conf.*, 1989.

[17] CCITT Study Group XVIII, "WP XVIII/8—Report of meeting," Temporary Document no. 16 (Plenary), Geneva, Switzerland, June 1989.

[18] CCITT Study Group XVIII, "Meeting Report of Sub-Working Party 8/1 ATM," Temporary Document No. 14-E (Plenary), Geneva, Switzerland, June 1989.

[19] A. Gersht and K. J. Lee, "A congestion control framework for ATM networks," in *Proc. IEEE INFOCOM '89*, pp. 701–710.

[20] G. M. Woodruff, R. G. Rogers, and P. S. Richards, "A congestion control framework for high-speed intergrated packetized transport," in *Proc. IEEE GLOBECOM '88*, pp. 7.1.1.–7.1.5.

[21] J. M. Holtzman, "Coping with broadband traffic uncertainties: Statistical uncertainty, fuzziness, neural networks," presented at *IEEE Workshop on Computer Commun.*, Data Point, CA, Oct. 1989.

[22] L. Dittmann and S. B. Jacobsen, "Statistical multiplexing of identical bursty sources in an ATM network," in *Proc. IEEE GLOBECOM '88*, pp. 39.6.1–39.6.5.

[23] J. Kulzer and W. Montgomery, "Statistical switching architecture for future services," in *Proc. ISS '84*, pp. 43A.1.1–43A.1.6.

[24] T. Y. Choi, "Statistical multiplexing of bursty sources in an ATM network," *Multimedia '89*.

[25] G. Gallassi, G. Rigolio, and L. Fratta, "ATM: Bandwidth assignment and bandwidth enforcement policies," in *Proc. IEEE GLOBECOM '89*, pp. 49.6.1–49.6.6.

[26] M. Hirano and N. Watanabe, "Characteristics of a cell multiplexer for bursty ATM traffic," in *Proc. IEEE ICC '89*, pp. 13.2.1–13.2.5.

[27] S. Akhtar, "Congestion control in a fast packet switching network," master's thesis, Washington University, St. Louis, MD, Dec. 1987.

[28] J. Y. Hui and E. Arthurs, "A broadband packet switch for integrated transport," *IEEE J. Select. Areas Commun.*, vol. SAC-5, pp. 1264–1273, Oct. 1987.

[29] K. Sriram and W. Whitt, "Characterizing superposition arrival processes in packet multiplexers for voice and data," *IEEE J. Select. Areas Commun.*, vol. SAC-4, pp. 833–846, Sept. 1986.

[30] A. E. Eckberg, "Generalized peakedness of teletraffic processes," in *Proc. 10th Int. Teletraffic Congress*, Montreal, P. Q. 1983.

[31] S. B. Jacobsen, K. Moth, L. Dittmann, and K. Sallberg, "Load control in ATM networks," *ISS '90*, to be published.

[32] K. Nakamaki, M. Kawakatsu, and A. Notoya, "Traffic control for ATM networks," in *Proc. IEEE ICC '89*, pp. 22.5.1–22.5.5.

[33] H. Esaki, Y. Katsube, K. Iwamura, and T. Kodama, "A study on connection admission control for an ATM network," R & D Center, Toshiba Corp., Tech. Rep., 1989.

[34] J. S. Turner, "New directions in communications (or which way to the information age?)," *IEEE Commun. Mag.*, vol. 25, pp. 8–15, Oct. 1986.

[35] M. W. Beckner, T. T. Lee, and S. E. Minzer, "A protocol and prototype for broadband subscriber access to ISDN's," in *Proc. ISS '87*, pp. B6.3.1–B6.3.8.

[36] I. Cidon and I. S. Gopal, "PARIS: An approach to integrated high-speed private networks," *Int. J. Digital & Analog Cabled Systems*, vol. 1, pp. 77–86, Apr.-June, 1988.

[37] M. Sidi, W. Z. Liu, I. Cidon, and I. Gopal, "Congestion control through input rate regulation," in *Proc. IEEE GLOBECOM '89*, pp. 49.2.1–49.2.5.

[38] A. E. Eckberg, Jr., D. T. Luan, and D. M Lucantoni, "Meeting the challenge: Congestion and flow control strategies for broadband information transport," in *Proc. IEEE GLOBECOM '89*, pp. 49.3.1–49.3.5.

[39] K. S. Meier-Hellstern and P. E. Wirth, "Packet switch provisioning accounting for uncertainty in the forecasting of customer characteristics," presented at *Proc. 7th Int. Teletraffic Congress Specialists Seminar*, Adelaide, Australia, Sept. 1989.

[40] R-J. Li and E. S. Lee, "Analysis of a fuzzy queue," *Comput. Math Appl.*, vol. 17, no. 7, pp. 1143–1147, 1989.

[41] A. Hiramatsu, "ATM communication network control by neural network," *Int. Joint Conf. on Neural Networks '89*, Washington, DC, June 1989.

[42] W. Whitt, "The queueing network analyzer," *Bell Syst. Tech. J.*, pt. 1, vol. 62, no. 9, pp. 2779–2815, 1983.

[43] D. D. Clark, M. L. Lambert, and L. Zhang, "NETBLT: A high throughput transport protocol," in *Proc. ACM SIGCOMM '87*, pp. 353–359.

[44] A. Bhargava, J. F. Kurose, D. Towsley, and G. Vanleemput, "Performance comparison of error control schemes in high-speed computer communication networks," *IEEE J. Select. Areas Commun.*, vol. 6, pp. 1565–1575, Dec. 1988.

[45] T. Suda and N. Watanabe, "Evaluation of error recovery schemes for a high-speed packet switched network: Link-by-link versus edge-to-edge schemes," in *Proc. IEEE INFOCOM '88*, pp. 722–731.

[46] T. Bradley and T. Suda, "Performance of error recovery schemes in a fast packet switching network," in *Proc. IEEE ICC '90*, pp. 308.2.1–308.2.6.

[47] P. Brady, "Performance of an edge-to-edge protocol in a simulated X.25/X.75 packet network," *IEEE J. Select. Areas Commun.*, vol. 6, pp. 190–196, Jan. 1988.

[48] H. Ahmadi, P. Kermani, and P. Tran-gia, "Throughput analysis of a class of selective repeat protocols in high-speed environments," in *Proc. IEEE GLOBECOM '89*, pp. 26.4.1–26.4.9.

[49] N. Shacham, "Queueing analysis of a selective-repeat ARQ receiver," in *Proc. IEEE INFOCOM '87*, pp. 512–520.

[50] M. Schwartz, *Telecommunication Networks: Protocols, Modeling and Analysis*. Reading, MA: Addison-Wesley p. 124, 1987.

[51] W. Zwaenepoel, "Protocol for large data transfers over local networks," in *Proc. ACM SIGCOMM '85*, pp. 22–32.

[52] G. M. Brown, M. G. Gouda, and R. E. Miller, "Block acknowledgement: Redesigning the window protocol," in *Proc. ACM SIGCOMM '89*, pp. 128–135.

[53] K. Sabnani and A. Netravali, "A high speed transport protocol for datagram/virtual circuit networks," in *Proc. ACM SIGCOMM '89*, pp. 146–157.

[54] R. Chipalkatti, J. F. Kurose, and D. Towsley, "Scheduling policies for real-time and nonreal-time traffic in a statistical multiplexer," in *Proc. IEEE INFOCOM '89*, pp. 774–783.

[55] Y. Lin and J. Kobza, "Analysis of a delay-dependent priority discipline in a multiclass traffic packet switching node," in *Proc. IEEE INFOCOM '88*, pp. 9A.4.1–9A.4.1.10.

[56] J. R. Jackson, "Some problems in queueing with dynamic priorities," *Naval Res. Logist. Quart.*, vol. 7, no. 3, 1960.

[57] J. R. Jackson, "Queues with dynamic priority discipline," *Management Sci.*, vol. 8, no. 1, 1961.

[58] J. R. Jackson, "Waiting time distributions for queues with dynamics priorities," *Naval Res. Logist. Quart.*, vol. 9, no. 1, 1962.

[59] P. Bhattacharya and A. Ephremides, "Optimal scheduling with strict deadlines," *IEEE Trans. Automat. Contr.*, vol. 34, pp. 721–728, July 1989.

[60] H. Goldberg, "Analysis of the earliest due date scheduling rule in queueing systems," *Math. Oper. Res.*, vol. 2, no. 2, pp. 145–154, May 1977.

[61] S. Panwar, D. Towsley and J. Wolf, "Optimal scheduling policies for a class of queues with customer deadlines to the beginning of service," *J. Ass. Comput. Mach.*, vol. 35, no. 4, pp. 832–844, Oct. 1988.

[62] T. M. Chen, J. Walrand, and D. G. Messerschmitt, "Dynamic priority protocols for packet voice," *IEEE J. Select. Areas Commun.*, vol. 7, June 1989.

[63] N. Yin, S-Q. Li, and T. E. Stern, "Data performance in an integrated packet voice/data system using voice congestion control," in *Proc. IEEE GLOBECOM '88*, pp. 16.4.1–16.4.5.

[64] D. W. Petr, L. A. DaSilva, Jr., and V. S. Frost, "Priority discarding of speech in integrated packet networks," *IEEE J. Select. Areas Commun.*, vol. 7, pp. 644–659, June 1989.

[65] N. Yin, T. E. Stern, and S-Q. Li, "Performance analysis of a priority-oriented packet voice system," in *Proc. IEEE INFOCOM '87*, pp. 856–863.

[66] N. Yin, S-Q. Li, and T. E. Stern, "Congestion control for packet voice by selective packet discarding," in *Proc. IEEE GLOBECOM '87*, pp. 45.3.1–45.3.4.

[67] D. J. Goodman, "Embedded DPCM for variable bit rate transmission," *IEEE Trans. Commun.*, vol. COM-28, pp. 1040–1046, July 1980.

[68] N. S. Jayant and S. W. Christensen, "Effects of packet losses in waveform codded speech and improvements due to an odd-even sample-interpolation procedure," *IEEE Trans. Commun.*, vol. COM-29, pp. 101–109, Feb. 1981.

[69] K. Sriram and D. M. Lucantoni, "Traffic smoothing effects of bit dropping in a packet voice multiplexer," in *Proc. IEEE INFOCOM '88*, pp. 8A.1.1–8A.1.12.

[70] V. R. karanam, K. Sriram, and D. O. Bowker, "Performance evaluation of variable-bit-rate voice in packet-switched networks," *AT&T Tech. J.*, pp. 57–69, Sept./Oct. 1988.

[71] S. Dravida and K. Sriram, "End-to-end performance models for variable bit rate voice over Tandem links in packet networks," in *Proc. IEEE INFOCOM '89*, pp. 1089–1095.

[72] R. W. Muise, T. J. Schoenfeld, and G. H. Zimmerman, "Experiments with wideband packet technology," presented at *Proc. 1986 Int. Zurich Seminar Digital Commun.*, paper D4, Mar. 1986.

[73] W. Verbiest, L. Pinnoo, and B. Voeten, "The impact of the ATM concept on video coding," *IEEE J. Select. Areas Commun.*, vol. 6, pp. 1623–1632, Dec. 1988.

[74] F. Kishino, K. Manabe, Y. Hayashih, and H. Yasuda, "Variable bit-rate coding of video signals for ATM networks," *IEEE J. Select. Areas Commun.*, vol. 7, pp. 801–806, June 1989.

[75] M. Ghanbari, "Two-layer coding of video signals for VBR networks," *IEEE J. Select. Areas Commun.*, vol. 7, pp. 771–781, June 1989.

[76] CCITT, "Draft recommendation I.121-broadband aspects of ISDN," CCITT, TD49 (PLEN), Seoul, Korea, Feb. 1988.

[77] S. E. Minzer, "Broadband ISDN and asynchronous transfer mode (ATM)," *IEEE Commun. Mag.*, vol. 27, pp. 17–24, Sept. 1989.

[78] R. Vickers, Broadband ISDN Tutorial #3, *IEEE INFOCOM '90*.

[79] S. Ohta, K. Sato, and I. Tokizawa, "A dynamically controllable ATM transport network based on the virtual path concept," in *Proc. IEEE GLOBECOM '88*, pp. 39.2.1–39.2.5.

[80] K. Toyoshima, M. Sasagawa, and I. Tokizawa, "Flexible surveillance capabilities for ATM-based transmission systems," in *Proc. IEEE ICC '89*, pp. 22.3.1–22.3.6.

[81] S. E. Minzer, "Broadband user-network interfaces to ISDN," in *Proc. IEEE ICC '87*, pp. 11.2.1–11.2.6.

[82] R. Ballart and Y-C. Ching, "SONET: Now it's the standard optical network," *IEEE Commun. Mag.*, pp. 8–15, Mar. 1989.

[83] G. L. Pringle, "SONET: problem or opportunity?," *Telephony Mag.*, pp. 61–65, Aug. 1989.

[84] B. Eklundh, I. Gard, and G. Leijonhufvud, "A layered architecture for ATM networks," in *Proc. IEEE GLOBECOM '88*, pp. 13.1.1–13.1.6.

[85] M. J. Rider, "Protocols for ATM access networks," in *Proc. IEEE GLOBECOM '88*, pp. 4.4.1–4.4.6.

[86] J. P. Vorstermans and A. P. De Vleeschouwer, "Layered ATM systems and architectural concepts for subscribers' premises networks," *IEEE J. Select. Areas Commun.*, vol. 6, pp. 1545–1555, Dec. 1988.

[87] V. Frantzen, "Trends in the development of public telecommunication networks," *Comput. Networks and ISDN Syst.*, vol. 14, pp. 339–358, 1987.

[88] CCITT Study Group XVIII, "Report of SWP-8/4 network spects," Temporary Document No. 18 (Plenary), Geneva, Switzerland, June 1989.

[89] CCITT Study Group XVIII, Draft Recommendation, May 1990.

Jaime Jungok Bae (Member, IEEE) received the B.S. and M.S. degrees in information and computer science from the University of California, Irvine, in 1987 and 1989, respectively. She is currently working towards the Ph.D. degree in information and computer science at the University of California, Irvine.

Her research interests include the design and performance analysis of computer communication networks, high speed networks, and B-ISDN systems. She is currently investigating congestion control and error control schemes in ATM networks.

Ms. Bae is a member of ACM and Phi Beta Kappa.

Tatsuya Suda (Member, IEEE) received the B.E., M.E., and Dr.E. degrees in applied mathematics and physics from Kyoto University, Kyoto, Japan, in 1977, 1979, and 1982, respectively.

From 1982 to 1984, he was with the Department of Computer Science, Columbia University, New York, as a postdoctoral research associate. Since 1984 he has been with the Department of Information and Computer Science, University of California, Irvine, CA, as an Assistant Professor and as an Associate Professor.

He received an IBM postdoctoral fellowship in 1983. He served as a representative of the IEEE Technical Committee on Computer Communications to the ICC 89 Conference. He is currently a conference coordinator of the IEEE Technical Committee on Computer Communications. He has also been engaged in research in the fields of computer communications, high speed networks, distributed systems, and performance modeling and evaluation.

Dr. Suda is a member of ACM.

Glossary

Definitions for terms marked by an asterisk (*) are taken from *U.S. Federal Standard 1037A, Glossary of Telecommunication Terms* (1986). Those for terms marked by a dagger (†) are taken from CCITT Recommendation I.112, entitled "Vocabulary of Terms for ISDN" (1988).

Access protocol.† A defined set of procedures that is adopted at an interface at a specified reference point between a user and a network to enable the user to employ the services and/or facilities of that network.

Analog data.* Data represented by a physical quantity that is considered to be continuously variable and whose magnitude is made directly proportional to the data or to a suitable function of the data.

Analog signal. A continuously varying electromagnetic wave that may be propagated over a variety of media.

Analog transmission. The transmission of analog signals without regard to content. The signal may be amplified, but there is no intermediate attempt to recover the data from the signal.

Application layer. Layer 7 of the open systems interconnection (OSI) model. This layer defines the interface of the system with the user and provides useful application-oriented services.

Asynchronous transfer mode (ATM). A form of packet transmission using fixed-size packets called "cells." ATM is the data transfer interface for broadband ISDN. Unlike X.25, ATM does not provide error control and flow control mechanisms.

ATM adaptation layer (AAL). The layer that maps information transfer protocols onto the asynchronous transfer mode (ATM).

Bandwidth.* The difference between the limiting frequencies of a continuous frequency band.

Basic access.† A term used to describe a simple standardized combination of access channels that together constitute the access arrangements for the majority of ISDN users.

Bell Operating Company (BOC). One of 22 AT&T subsidiaries that — before the divestiture of AT&T — built, operated, and maintained the local and intrastate networks and provided most of the day-to-day service for customers. After divestiture, the BOCs retained their identities within seven regional BOCs (RBOCs); today, the BOCs are responsible for local service, as defined by local access and transport areas (LATAs).

Bit stuffing. The insertion of extra bits into a data stream to avoid the appearance of unintended control sequences.

Broadband ISDN (B-ISDN). A second generation of ISDN. The key characteristic of broadband ISDN is that it provides transmission channels capable of supporting rates greater than the primary ISDN rate.

Cell relay. The packet-switching mechanism used for the fixed-size packets called "cells." Asynchronous transfer mode (ATM) is based on cell relay technology.

Centrex.† A service offered by operating telephone companies that provides, from the telephone company office, functions and features comparable to those provided by a private branch exchange (PBX).

Circuit switching. A method of communicating in which a dedicated communications path is established between two devices through one or more intermediate switching nodes. Unlike packet switching, digital data are sent as a continuous stream of bits. Data rate is guaranteed and delay is limited essentially to propagation time.

Codec. A device that transforms analog data into a digital bit stream (coder) and digital signals into analog data (decoder).

Common carrier. In the United States, companies that furnish long-distance telecommunications services to the public. Common carriers are subject to regulation by federal and state regulatory commissions.

Common-channel signaling.† A method of signaling in which signaling information relating to a multiplicity of circuits, or function or for network management, is conveyed over a single channel by addressed messages.

Communications architecture. The hardware and software structure that implements the communications function.

Cyclic redundancy check (CRC). An error-detecting code in which the code is the remainder resulting from dividing the bits to be checked by a predetermined binary number.

Data circuit-terminating equipment (DCE). In a data station, the equipment that provides the signal conversion and coding between the data terminal equipment (DTE) and the line. The DCE may be separate equipment or an integral part of the DTE or of intermediate equipment such as a switching mode. The DCE may perform other functions that are normally performed at the network end of the line.

Datagram. In packet switching, a self-contained packet, independent of other packets, that does not require acknowledgment and that carries information sufficient for routing from the originating data terminal equipment (DTE), without relying on earlier exchanges between the DTEs and the network.

Data link layer. Layer 2 of the open systems interconnection (OSI) model. This layer converts an unreliable transmission channel into a reliable one.

Data terminal equipment (DTE).* Equipment consisting of digital end instruments that convert the user information into data signals for transmission or reconvert the received data signals into user information.

Digital data.* Data represented by discrete values or conditions.

Digital PBX. A private branch exchange (PBX) that operates internally on digital signals. Thus, voice signals must be digitized for use in the PBX.

Digital signal. A discrete or discontinuous signal, such as a sequence of voltage pulses.

Digital transmission. The transmission of digital data, or analog data that have been digitized, using either an analog or digital signal, in which the digital content is recovered and repeated at intermediate points to reduce the effects of impairments such as noise, distortion, and attenuation.

Digitize.* To convert an analog signal to a digital signal.

Encapsulation. The addition of control information by a protocol entity to data obtained form a protocol user.

Error-detecting code.* A code in which each data signal conforms to specific rules of construction, so that departures from this construction in the received signal can be automatically detected.

Error rate.* The ratio of the number of data units that are in error to the total number of data units.

Exchange area. A geographical area within which there is a single uniform set of charges for telephone service. A call between any two points within an exchange area is a local call.

Facsimile. A system for the transmission of images. At the transmitter, the image is scanned; at the receiving station, the image is reconstructed and duplicated on some form of paper.

Fast packet switching. An approach to packet switching that attempts to exploit the high capacity of current digital-transmission services. Formats and procedures are designed to minimize packet-processing time.

Flow control. A function performed by a receiving entity to limit the amount or rate of data sent by a transmitting entity.

Frame mode bearer service (FMBS). A service by which data are transferred in variable-size packets, called "frames," at the data link layer. This service is provided in ISDN for use over the B channel as an alternative to X.25. Unlike X.25, FMBS does not provide error control and flow control mechanisms.

Frame relay. The packet-switching mechanism used for the frames of the frame mode bearer service.

Frequency-division multiplexing (FDM). Division of a transmission facility into two or more channels by splitting the frequency band transmitted by the facility into narrower bands, each of which is used to constitute a distinct channel.

Full-duplex transmission. Transmission of data in both directions at the same time.

Functional group.† A set of functions that may be performed by a single equipment.

Half-duplex transmission. Data transmitted in either direction, one direction at a time.

Header. System-defined control information that precedes user data.

Inchannel signaling. A technique in which the same channel is used to carry network control signals as that used to carry the call to which the control signals relate.

Integrated digital network (IDN). A circuit-switched telecommunications network that uses digital technology to integrate transmission and switching functions.

Integrated services digital network (ISDN). Planned worldwide telecommunications service that will use digital-transmission and switching technology to support voice and digital data communications.

Layer.† A conceptual region that embodies one or more functions between an upper logical boundary and a lower logical boundary.

Local access and transport area (LATA). A geographic area generally equivalent to a Standard Metropolitan Statistical Area. The territory served by the Bell system was divided at divestiture into approximately 160 LATAs. Intra-LATA services are provided by the Bell Operating Companies (BOCs).

Local loop. A transmission path, generally twisted pair, between the individual subscriber and the nearest switching center of a public telecommunications network. Also referred to as a "subscriber loop."

Modem. A device that transforms a digital bit stream into an analog signal (modulator) and an analog signal into a digital bit stream (demodulator).

Multiplexing.* In data transmission, a function that permits two or more data sources to share a common transmission medium, such that each data source has its own channel.

Network layer. Layer 3 of the open systems interconnection (OSI) model. This layer is responsible for routing data through a communications network.

Network terminating equipment (NTE). A grouping of ISDN functions at the boundary between ISDN and the subscriber.

Open systems interconnection (OSI) reference model. A model of communications between cooperating devices. It defines a seven-layer architecture of communication functions.

Packet switching. A method of transmitting messages through a communications network in which long messages are subdivided into short packets. Each packet is passed from source to destination through intermediate nodes. At each node, the entire message is received, stored briefly, and then passed on to the next node.

Physical layer. Layer 1 of the open systems interconnection (OSI) model. This layer is concerned with the electrical, mechanical, and timing aspects of signal transmission over a medium.

Picture element (pel).* The smallest discrete scanning-line sample of a facsimile system that contains only black/white information (that is, no gray shading information is used in the sample).

Piggybacking. The inclusion of an acknowledgment of a previously received protocol data unit in an outgoing protocol data unit.

Ping-pong transmission technique. See **Time-compression multiplexing (TCM).**

Point-to-point. A term that describes a configuration in which two stations share a transmission path.

Postal, Telegraph, and Telephone (PTT). A government organization that operates a nationalized public telecommunications network.

Presentation layer. Layer 6 of the open systems interconnection (OSI) model. This layer is concerned with data format and display.

Private branch exchange (PBX). A telephone exchange on the user's premises. PBX provides a circuit-switching facility for telephones on extension lines within the user's building and access to the public telephone network.

Private network. A facility in which the customer leases circuits and, sometimes, switching capacity for the customer's exclusive use. Access may be provided to a public switched telecommunications service.

Protocol.† A formal statement of the procedures that are adopted to ensure communication between two or more functions within the same layer of a hierarchy of functions.

Protocol data unit (PDU).* Information that is delivered as a unit between peer entities of a network and may contain control information, address information, or data.

Pseudoternary coding. A form of digital signaling in which three signal levels are used to encode binary data. In ISDN, the form of pseudoternary is one in which binary one is represented by no line signal and binary zero is represented, alternately, by positive and negative voltage pulses.

Public data network (PDN). A packet-switched network that is publicly available to subscribers. Usually, the term connotes government control or national monopoly.

Pulse-code modulation (PCM). A process in which a signal is sampled, and the magnitude of each sample — with respect to a fixed reference — is quantized and converted by coding to a digital signal.

Recognized private operating agency (RPOA). A private or government-controlled corporation that provides telecommunications services (for example, AT&T). RPOAs participate as nonvoting members of the CCITT.

Reference configuration.† A combination of functional groups and reference points that shows possible network arrangements.

Reference point.† A conceptual point at the conjunction of two nonoverlapping functional groupings.

Regional Bell Operating Company (RBOC). One of seven corporations that were formed from AT&T to provide local telephone service. The seven RBOCs have roughly equivalent assets and financial strengths. Each RBOC comprises from one to seven Bell Operating Companies (BOCs), each of which provides telephone service for a local area.

Service access point (SAP). An address that identifies a user of the services of a protocol entity. A protocol entity provides one or more SAPs, for use by higher level entities.

Session layer. Layer 5 of the open systems interconnection (OSI) model. This layer manages a logical connection (or "session") between two communicating processes or applications.

Signaling.† The exchange of information that is specifically concerned with the establishment and control of connections and with management in a telecommunications network.

Signaling System Number 7 (SS7). A CCITT-defined interface to digital telephone networks. SS7 provides the control functionality required for the operation of the network.

Sliding-window technique. A method of flow control in which a transmitting station may send numbered protocol data units (PDUs) within a window of numbers. The window changes dynamically to allow additional PDUs to be sent.

Software-defined network (SDN). A facility based on a public circuit-switched network that gives to the user the appearance of a private network. The network is "software defined" in the sense that the user provides the service supplier with entries to a database used by the supplier to configure, manage, monitor, and report on the operation of the network.

Space-division switching. A circuit-switching technique in which each connection through the switch takes a physically separate and dedicated path.

Specialized common carrier. In the United States, a telecommunications common carrier — other than AT&T and the Bell Operating Companies (BOCs) — authorized to provide a variety of transmission services.

Spectrum. An absolute, contiguous range of frequencies.

Subscriber loop. See **Local loop.**

Synchronous digital hierarchy (SDH). A hierarchy of high-speed synchronous time-division multiplexing (TDM) facilities defined by a CCITT specification of frame structure and transmission protocols.

Synchronous optical network (SONET). An American National Standards Institute (ANSI) specification that is compatible with the SDH specification. SONET covers one more data rate than does SDH.

Synchronous time-division multiplexing. A method of time-division multiplexing (TDM) in which time slots on a shared transmission line are assigned to devices on a fixed, predetermined basis.

Teleaction service.† Telemetry service. A type of telecommunications service that uses short messages, which require a very low transmission rate, between the user and the network.

Telecommunications service.† Service that is offered by an administration or RPOA to its customers in order to satisfy a specific telecommunications requirement. Bearer service, teleservice, and teleaction service are types of telecommunications services.

Telematics. User-oriented information transfer services, including Teletex, videotex, and facsimile.

Teleservice.† A type of telecommunications service that provides the complete capability, including terminal equipment functions, for communication between users according to protocols established by agreement between administrations and/or RPOAs.

Teletex. A text communications service that provides message preparation and transmission facilities.

Teletext. A one-way information-retrieval service. A fixed number of information pages are repetitively broadcast on unused portions of a TV channel bandwidth. A decoder at the television set is used to select and display pages.

Time-compression multiplexing (TCM). A means for providing full-duplex digital data transmission over a single twisted pair. Data are buffered at each end and are sent across the line at approximately double the subscriber data rate, with the two ends taking turns. TCM is also referred to as "Ping-pong transmission technique."

Time-division multiplexing (TDM). A means for dividing a transmission facility into multiple channels by allotting the facility to different channels, one at a time.

Time-division multiplexing (TDM) bus switching. A form of time-division switching in which time slots are used to transfer data over a shared bus between transmitter and receiver.

Time-division switching. A circuit-switching technique in which time slots in a time-multiplexed stream of data are manipulated to pass data from an input to an output.

Transport layer. Layer 4 of the open systems interconnection (OSI) model. This layer provides the reliable, sequenced transfer of data between endpoints.

User-user protocol.† A protocol that is adopted between two or more users in order to ensure communication between them.

Value-added network (VAN). A privately owned packet-switched network whose services are sold to the public.

Videotex. A two-way information-retrieval service accessible to terminals and television sets equipped with a special decoder. Pages of information at a central resource are retrieved interactively over a switched telephone line connection.

Virtual channel. A logical connection between two stations that is established at the start of transmission by an ATM network.

Virtual circuit. A logical connection between two stations that is established at the start of transmission by a packet-switching mechanism. All packets follow the same route, need not carry a complete address, and arrive in sequence.

Virtual path. A set of virtual channels that have the same endpoints and that share the same transmission characteristics.

List of Acronyms

AAL	Asynchronous transfer mode (ATM) adaptation layer
ANSI	American National Standards Institute
ATM	Asynchronous transfer mode
B-ISDN	Broadband ISDN
BOC	Bell Operating Company
CCITT	Comité Consultatif International Télégraphique et Téléphonique (International Telegraphy and Telephony Consultative Committee)
CPE	Customer premises equipment
CRC	Cyclic redundancy check
DCE	Data circuit-terminating equipment
DTE	Data terminal equipment
FDDI	Fiber Distributed Data Interface
FDM	Frequency-division multiplexing
FMBS	Frame mode bearer service
HDLC	High-level data link control
HEC	Header error control
IDN	Integrated digital network
ISDN	Integrated services digital network
ISO	International Organization for Standardization
LAN	Local area network
LAPB	Link access protocol-balanced
LAPD	Link access protocol-D channel
LATA	Local access and transport area
LEC	Local-exchange carrier
LLC	Logical link control
MAC	Medium access control

MAN	Metropolitan area network
NT	Networking terminating
NTE	Network terminating equipment
OAM	Operations, administration, and maintenance
OSI	Open systems interconnection
PBX	Private branch exchange
PCM	Pulse-code modulation
PDN	Public data network
PDU	Protocol data unit
PTT	Postal, Telegraph, and Telephone
RBOC	Regional Bell Operating Company (BOC)
RPOA	Recognized private operating agency
SAP	Service access point
SDH	Synchronous digital hierarchy
SDN	Software-defined network
SMDS	Switched Multimegabit Data Service
SONET	Synchronous optical network
SS7	Signaling System Number 7
STS	Synchronous transport signal
TCM	Time-compression multiplexing
TDM	Time-division multiplexing
VAN	Value-added network
VPC	Very personal computer
WAN	Wide-area network

Annotated Bibliography

Chapter 1: Integrated Services Digital Network (ISDN) Overview

E. Carr, "The Message-Makers," *The Economist*, Mar. 10, 1990. Surveys the state of the telephone network industry. Highlights the shortcomings of ISDN and the ways in which it has failed to live up to its expectations.

K. Grillo et al., "CCITT E.700 Recommendation Series — A Framework for Traffic Engineering of ISDN," *IEEE J. Selected Areas Comm.*, Jan. 1991. Reports on the first recommendations formalized in a dedicated series on ISDN traffic engineering; covers traffic modeling, ISDN grade of service, and the mobile service extension to the E.700 series.

G. Held, "Is ISDN an Obsolete Data Network?," *Data Comm.*, Nov. 1989. Provides a useful balance to the hoopla surrounding ISDN. Examines a number of applications that might be better served by alternatives to ISDN.

D. Morgan, M. Lach, and R. Bushnell, "ISDN as an Enabler for Enterprise Integration," *IEEE Comm. Magazine*, Apr. 1990. Looks at the use of ISDN features to meet requirements for computer-integrated manufacturing applications.

D. Wolf and S. King, "Making the Most of ISDN Now," *Data Comm.*, Aug. 1989. Discusses terminal adapters. Looks in detail at the types of parameters that should be provided by the adapter and at the parameter values that are useful for various devices and applications.

D. Wright and M. To, "A Characterization of Telecommunication Services in the 1990s," *Proc. IEEE Infocom '89*, IEEE Computer Society Press, Los Alamitos, Calif., 1989. Lists voice, data, facsimile, image, audio, and video services that will require ISDN and B-ISDN support. Discusses the implications for the use of ATM.

T. Yokoi and K. Kodaira, "Grade of Service in the ISDN Era," *IEEE Comm. Magazine*, Apr. 1989. Focuses on the specification method for ISDN grade of service.

Chapter 2: ISDN Protocols and Network Architecture

I. Brodsky, "Tapping into ISDN," *Data Comm.*, Apr. 1990. Surveys types of ISDN terminal adapters from a user's point of view.

M. Fujioka, Y. Ikeda, and M. Norigoe, "Error Control Criteria in the Message Transfer Part of CCITT Signaling System No. 7," *IEEE Trans. Comm.*, Sept. 1990. Analyzes the alternative error control mechanisms defined in the data link layer of SS7. Indicates by a performance analysis which mechanism to choose based on expected traffic characteristics.

N. Iorio, "Integrating ISDN and OSI: An Example," *IEEE Network Magazine*, Jan. 1991. Reports on a successful multivendor trial, sponsored by the National Institute of Standards and Technology, demonstrating the integration of OSI and ISDN architectures.

H. Ishii, "ISDN User-Network Interface Management Protocol," *IEEE Network Magazine*, Sept. 1989. Reviews the current status of CCITT standardization efforts for a network management protocol at the user-network interface; then discusses requirements not met in the current version, together with suggestions for improvement.

T. Kearns and M. Mellon, "The Role of ISDN Signaling in Global Networks," *IEEE Comm. Magazine*, July 1990. Provides an overview of Recommendation I.451/Q.931 user-network signaling protocol and SS7, and shows the relationship between the two.

R. Koenig, "How to Make the PBX-to-ISDN Connection," *Data Comm.*, May 1989. Examines alternative means for interfacing a PBX to an ISDN.

H. Lassers, "ISDN Terminal Portability in the RBOC Networks," *IEEE Network Magazine*, Sept. 1989. Addresses the fact that differences in ISDN switch implementations lead to the inability to use a telephone designed for one switch with another switch. Proposes several alternative techniques for providing telephone portability.

K. Lee and Y. Lim, "Performance Analysis of the Congestion Control Scheme in Signaling System No. 7," *Proc. IEEE Infocom '89*, IEEE Computer Society Press, Los Alamitos, Calif., 1989. Examines the congestion control scheme used in the signaling network level of SS7. Discusses the algorithm in detail and then presents a performance analysis.

N. Mitra and S. Usiskin, "Relationship of Signaling System No. 7 Protocol Architecture to the OSI Reference Model," *IEEE Network Magazine*, Jan. 1991. Maps SS7 components into OSI layers. Also, deals with network layer services and the relationship between OSI and SS7 addressing.

A. Modarressi and R. Skoog, "Signaling System No. 7: A Tutorial," *IEEE Comm. Magazine*, July 1990. Surveys in detail the various components of SS7. Provides a good complement to the paper on SS7 in this tutorial.

W. Roehr, "Knocking on Users' Doors: Signaling System 7," *Data Comm.*, Feb. 1989. Provides a brief overview of SS7.

D. Seligman, "Mastering SS7 Takes a Special Vocabulary," *Data Comm.*, Feb. 1989. Introduces briefly some of the fundamental principles of SS7.

D. Su and L. Collica, "ISDN Conformance Testing," *Proc. IEEE*, Feb. 1991. Surveys the theory, practice, and standardization activities of conformance testing of the protocols for ISDN.

R. Urquhart, "Maintenance of Common-Channel Signaling Networks," *Telecommunications*, Aug. 1989. Discusses the difficulties of installing and maintaining an SS7 network as part of a telecommunications network.

S. Wakid and K. Roberts, "Application Profile for ISDN," *Proc. IEEE*, Feb. 1991. Presents the protocol structure for the use of ISDN to support application level services. Then examines transaction processing and electronic data exchange in more detail.

A. Weissberger, "The Evolving Versions of ISDN's Terminal Adapter," *Data Comm.*, Mar. 1989. Provides a detailed examination of the CCITT recommendations dealing with protocol conversion between existing terminal equipment and the ISDN user-network interface standard.

G. Willman and P. Kuhn, "Performance Modeling of Signaling System No. 7," *IEEE Comm. Magazine*, July 1990. Presents an analysis methodology for SS7. At the same time, provides insight into the functioning of the various components of SS7.

Chapter 3: Frame Relay

K. Chen and K. Rege, "A Comparative Performance Study of Various Congestion Controls for ISDN Frame-Relay Networks," *Proc. IEEE Infocom '89*, IEEE Computer Society Press, Los Alamitos, Calif., 1989. Reports on the results of a study of alternative approaches to providing congestion control for frame relay networks.

K. Chen, K. Ho, and V. Saksena, "Analysis and Design of a Highly Reliable Transport Architecture for ISDN Frame-Relay Networks," *IEEE J. Selected Areas Comm.*, Oct. 1989. Looks at alternative strategies for congestion control, virtual-circuit routing, and failure detection by frame relay nodes.

F. Henderson and J. McCoy, "Less Is Faster," *LAN Magazine*, July 1991. Provides a good technical overview of frame relay from the point of view of its use for LAN-WAN interconnection.

W. Lai, "Frame Relaying Service: An Overview," *Proc. IEEE Infocom '89*, IEEE Computer Society Press, Los Alamitos, Calif., 1989. Provides an informative overview that looks at key functional characteristics, including multiplexing, call control, congestion control, and internetworking.

W. Lai, "Network and Nodal Architectures for the Interworking between Frame Relaying Services," *Computer Comm. Rev.*, Jan. 1989. Looks at different architectures for the provision of frame relay service across multiple networks. Concludes that an internodal strategy is superior to an internetwork strategy.

J. Lamont and M. Hui, "Some Experience with LAN Interconnection via Frame Relaying," *IEEE Network Magazine*, Sept. 1989. Examines the use of frame relaying for connecting remote bridges for LAN interconnection.

N. Lippis, "Frame Relay Redraws the Map for Wide-Area Networks," *Data Comm.*, July 1990. Surveys the non-ISDN uses of frame relay that are already coming to market for various wide-area networking applications.

P. Marsden, "Interworking IEEE 802/FDDI LANs via the ISDN Frame Relay Bearer Service," *Proc. IEEE*, Feb. 1991. Shows how MAC-level bridges can be designed to exploit the power of frame relay for internetworking.

A. Miller, "The Role of LAPD and Frame Relay in ISDN and Private Networks," *Telecommunications*, Nov. 1990. Provides a brief overview of frame relay and its use to support LAPD.

Chapter 4: Broadband ISDN (B-ISDN)

H. Bauch, "Transmission Systems for the BISDN," *IEEE LTS — Magazine Lightwave Telecommunication Systems*, Aug. 1991. Discusses suggested transmission systems and transmission systems already implemented that can support B-ISDN.

B. Butscher, G. Goldacker, and P. Todorova, "A Protocol Architecture for Transport Services in B-ISDN," *Proc. Future Trends '90, Second IEEE Workshop Future Trends Distributed Computing Systems*, IEEE Computer Society Press, Los Alamitos, Calif., 1990. Proposes a protocol architecture for B-ISDN transport services. Also, addresses issues of control signaling.

W. Byrne et al., "Evolution of Metropolitan Area Networks to Broadband ISDN," *IEEE Comm. Magazine*, Jan. 1991. Describes the possible convergence of broadband ISDN standards with the IEEE 802.6 MAN standards. Shows how 802.6 MANs can support B-ISDN ATM switching, leading to an evolution of MAN and B-ISDN that is mutually supporting.

J. Coudresuse, "Network Evolution towards BISDN," *IEEE LTS — Magazine Lightwave Telecommunication Systems*, Aug. 1991. Summarizes requirements that B-ISDN is intended to meet and comments on how the technical solutions standardized by B-ISDN meet those requirements.

D. Eigen, "Narrowband and Broadband ISDN CPE Directions," *IEEE Comm. Magazine*, Apr. 1990. Surveys types of customer premises equipment (CPE) that are needed to exploit the features of narrowband and broadband ISDN.

R. Foldvik, "The Evolutionary Path to Broadband ISDN," *Proc. Ninth Ann. Int'l Phoenix Conf. Computers and Comm.*, IEEE Computer Society Press, Los Alamitos, Calif., 1990. Looks at the way in which current and forthcoming high-speed networking capabilities — including FDDI, IEEE 802.6, and Switched Multimegabit Data Service (SMDS) — may lead to a natural evolution to B-ISDN.

M. Frame, "Broadband Service Needs," *IEEE Comm. Magazine*, Apr. 1990. Examines both residential and business broadband services. Describes service requirements, a first residential application of broadband technology, and a future all-fiber network architecture.

R. Handel, "Evolution of ISDN towards Broadband ISDN," *IEEE Network Magazine*, Jan. 1989. Addresses the impact of ATM and broadband ISDN architecture on network scenarios and network evolution.

S. Kano, K. Kitami, and M. Kawarasake, "ISDN Standardization," *Proc. IEEE*, Feb. 1991. Focuses on ISDN basic and supplementary services and broadband ISDN recommendations.

S. Minzer, "New Directions in Signaling for Broadband ISDN," *IEEE Comm. Magazine*, Feb. 1989. Analyzes the new requirements for call control signaling introduced by B-ISDN. Presents a conceptual model for representing ISDN calls as the basis for structuring a more flexible signaling protocol to meet the needs of a broadband environment.

K. Murano et al., "Technologies towards Broadband ISDN," *IEEE Comm. Magazine*, Apr. 1990. Examines fiber local loops, SDH, and ATM.

J. Patterson and C. Egido, "Three Keys to the Broadband Future: A View of Applications," *IEEE Network Magazine*, Mar. 1990. Examines the services that B-ISDN must provide to attract support from network providers; these services include interactive applications, access to large information sources, and access to information processing systems.

S. Walters, "A New Direction for Broadband ISDN," *IEEE Comm. Magazine*, Sept. 1991. Considers the current industry strategy to introduce ISDN and discusses alternative strategies.

Chapter 5: Asynchronous Transfer Mode (ATM) and Synchronous Optical Network/Synchronous Digital Hierarchy (SONET/SDH)

J. Anderson and M. Nguyen, "ATM-Layer OAM Implementation Issues," *IEEE Comm. Magazine*, Sept. 1991. Provides a summary of the current CCITT specifications of ATM-layer operations, administration, and maintenance; then discusses fault management and performance management function implementations for ATM.

T. Aprille, "Introducing SONET into the Local Exchange Carrier Network," *IEEE Comm. Magazine*, Aug. 1990. Looks at the existing network and the target SONET-based network; then describes the transition from the one to the other.

K. Asatani, K. Harrison, and R. Ballart, "CCITT Standardization of Network Node Interface of Synchronous Digital Hierarchy," *IEEE Comm. Magazine*, Aug. 1990. Provides an overview of SDH.

B. Bhushan, "Frame Relay, Fast Packet, and Packet Switching — Convergence or Coexistence?," *Telecommunications*, Dec. 1990. Provides an insightful comparison of X.25, frame relay, and ATM.

H. Breuer, "ATM-Layer OAM: Principles and Open Issues," *IEEE Comm. Magazine*, Sept. 1991. Discusses operations, administration, and maintenance principles for the ATM layer of B-ISDN. Contrasts the approach for B-ISDN with the approaches taken for basic- and primary-rate ISDN.

J. Burgin and D. Dorman, "Broadband ISDN Resource Management: The Role of Virtual Paths," *IEEE Comm. Magazine*, Sept. 1991. Provides an overview of a hierarchy of resource management controls for B-ISDN; shows that virtual paths will be a substantial component of that hierarchy.

A. Eckberg, B. Doshi, and R. Zoccolillo, "Controlling Congestion in B-ISDN/ATM: Issues and Strategies," *IEEE Comm. Magazine*, Sept. 1991. Looks at the goals for congestion control, examines a system of interlocking congestion controls, and presents some example scenarios.

S. Fleming, "What Users Can Expect from the New Virtual Wideband Services," *Telecommunications*, Oct. 1990. Assesses the applicability of frame relay and ATM.

G. Gallassi, G. Rigolio, and L. Verri, "Resource Management and Dimensioning in ATM Networks," *IEEE Network Magazine*, May 1990. Presents a resource management strategy based on statistical multiplexing using ATM; then examines the application of this strategy in providing efficient use of an ATM network.

W. Grover and T. Moore, "Design and Characterization of an Error-Correcting Code for the SONET STS-1 Tributary," *IEEE Trans. Comm.*, Apr. 1990. Reports on the design of a single-error-correcting (SEC), double-error-detecting (DED) code applicable to the STS-1 SONET format.

R. Holter, "SONET: A Network Management Viewpoint," *IEEE LCS — Magazine Lightwave Communication Systems*, Nov. 1990. Looks at the built-in network management features of SONET, including performance monitoring.

S. Isaky and M. Ishikura, "ATM Network Architecture for Supporting the Connectionless Service," *Proc. IEEE Infocom '90*, IEEE Computer Society Press, Los Alamitos, Calif., 1990. Examines the protocol and functional architectures needed to operate the International Organization for Standardization (ISO) connectionless internetwork protocol over ATM.

K. Korostoff, "Private Networks for Uncertain Times," *Telecommunications*, Feb. 1991. Looks at the uses of frame relay and ATM in private network configurations. Highlights the design issues that must be considered in choosing one of these technologies.

H. Kroner, "Comparative Performance Study of Space Priority Mechanisms for ATM Networks," *Proc. IEEE Infocom '90*, IEEE Computer Society Press, Los Alamitos, Calif., 1990. Describes different priority strategies that can be used with an ATM user-network interface. Provides a comparative-performance analysis.

J. Lane and D. Upp, "SONET: The Next Premises Interface," *Telecommunications*, Feb. 1991. Provides a brief overview of SONET, with an examination of the frame format.

J. McQuillan, "Broadband Networks: The End of Distance?," *Data Comm.*, June 1990. Provides a nontechnical survey of the key technologies leading to high-speed networks, including B-ISDN; covers the key areas of frame relay, ATM, and SONET.

S. Minzer, "Broadband ISDN and Asynchronous Transfer Mode (ATM)," *IEEE Comm. Magazine*, Sept. 1989. Provides an overview of ATM.

T. Okada, H. Ohnishi, and N. Morita, "Traffic Control in Asynchronous Transfer Mode," *IEEE Comm. Magazine*, Sept. 1991. Examines the traffic control problem in ATM and provides a technical discussion of some solutions.

J. Roberts, "Variable-Bit Rate Traffic Control in B-ISDN," *IEEE Comm. Magazine*, Sept. 1991. Examines traffic control schemes that allow overallocation, while guaranteeing that quality-of-service standards are respected for all admitted communications. (ATM allows for overallocating of link capacity by admitting a number of variable-bit-rate sources, the sum of whose peak bit rates is greater than the link capacity.)

N. Sandesara, G. Ritchie, and B. Engel-Smith, "Plans and Considerations for SONET Deployment," *IEEE Comm. Magazine*, Aug. 1990. Provides a local-exchange carrier (LEC) perspective on the advantages of deploying SONET, the rate at which SONET will be deployed, some typical early applications and architectures, and the role SONET will play in the evolution of the LEC network of the future.

Y. Sato and K. Sato, "Virtual Path and Link Capacity Design for ATM Networks," *IEEE J. Selected Areas Comm.*, Jan. 1991. Proposes a path and link capacity design method for ATM networks. Presents both capacity design policies and analytic techniques for assessment.

K. Sato, H. Ueda, and M. Yoshikai, "The Role of Virtual Path Crossconnection," *IEEE LTS — Magazine Lightwave Telecommunication Systems*, Aug. 1991. Examines in detail the virtual path concept. Presents an overview of virtual paths, and then discusses how virtual path portions can be crossconnected to produce end-to-end logical connections.

G. Stassinopoulos, I. Venieris, and R. Carli, "ATM Adaptation Layer Protocols and IEEE LAN Interconnection," *Proc. 15th Conf. Local Computer Networks*, IEEE Computer Society Press, Los Alamitos, Calif., 1990. Describes AAL briefly; then shows how it can be used to adapt logical link control (LLC) to ATM.

F. Vakil and H. Saito, "On Congestion Control in ATM Networks," *IEEE LTS — The Magazine of Lightwave Telecommunication Systems*, Aug. 1991. Describes the congestion control problem in ATM networks, summarizes the main congestion control strategies that could be used, and looks at implementation techniques.

W. Wang, T. Saadawi, and K. Aihara, "Bandwidth Variation and Control for ATM Networks," *Proc. Future Trends '90, Second IEEE Workshop Future Trends Distributed Computing Systems*, IEEE Computer Society Press, Los Alamitos, Calif., 1990. Assesses the impact of user-initiated bandwidth variation on network performance. Presents a means for controlling congestion and evaluates its effectiveness.

S. Yoneda, "Broadband ISDN ATM Layer Management: Operations, Administration, and Maintenance Considerations," *IEEE Network Magazine*, May 1990. Discusses an ATM layer management entity and its functions.

About the Author

William Stallings is an independent consultant with nearly 20 years of experience in data and computer communications. His clients have included major corporations and government agencies in the United States and Europe. Prior to forming his own consulting firm, Comp-Comm Consulting of Brewster, Massachusetts, he was vice president of CSM Corporation, a firm specializing in data processing and data communications for the health care industry. Before this, he was director of systems analysis and design for CTEC, Inc., a firm specializing in command, control, and communications systems. He holds a PhD from MIT in computer science and a BS from the University of Notre Dame in electrical engineering.

Stallings is a frequent lecturer and the author of numerous papers and a dozen books on networking and computers, including *Data and Computer Communications*, which has become the standard in the field. Also, he is the editor of four collections of papers.

Textbooks

Business Data Communications, The Macmillan Publishing Company, New York, N.Y., 1990

Computer Organization and Architecture, second edition, The Macmillan Publishing Company, New York, N.Y., 1990

Data and Computer Communications, third edition, The Macmillan Publishing Company, New York, N.Y., 1991

ISDN and Broadband ISDN, second edition, The Macmillan Publishing Company, New York, N.Y., 1992

Operating Systems, The Macmillan Publishing Company, New York, N.Y., 1992

Local and Metropolitan Area Networks, fourth edition, The Macmillan Publishing Company, New York, N.Y., 1992

Professional/reference books

A Manager's Guide to Local Networks, Prentice-Hall Inc., Englewood Cliffs, N.J., 1983

Handbook of Computer-Communications Standards, Volume I: The Open Systems Interconnection (OSI) Reference Model and OSI-Related Standards, second edition, Howard W. Sams & Company, Inc., Indianapolis, Ind., 1990

Handbook of Computer-Communications Standards, Volume II: Local Area Network Standards, second edition, Howard W. Sams & Company, Inc., Indianapolis, Ind., 1990

Handbook of Computer-Communications Standards, Volume III: The TCP/IP Protocol Suite, second edition, Howard W. Sams & Company, Inc., Indianapolis, Ind., 1990

The Business Guide to Local Area Networks, Howard W. Sams & Company, Inc., Indianapolis, Ind., 1990

Networking Standards: The Guide to OSI, ISDN, LAN, and MAN Standards, Addison-Wesley Publishing Company, Reading, Mass., 1992

Collections of papers

Local Network Technology, third edition, IEEE Computer Society Press, Los Alamitos, Calif., 1988

Reduced Instruction Set Computers, second edition, IEEE Computer Society Press, Los Alamitos, Calif., 1989

Computer Communications: Architectures, Protocols, and Standards, third edition, IEEE Computer Society Press, Los Alamitos, Calif., 1990

Integrated Services Digital Networks and Broadband ISDN, IEEE Computer Society Press, Los Alamitos, Calif., 1990

 **IEEE Computer Society**

IEEE Computer Society Press Publications

Monographs: A monograph is an authored book consisting of 100-percent original material.

Tutorials: A tutorial is a collection of original materials prepared by the editors, and reprints of the best articles published in a subject area. Tutorials must contain at least five percent of original material (although we recommend 15 to 20 percent of original material).

Reprint collections: A reprint collection contains reprints (divided into sections) with a preface, table of contents, and section introductions discussing the reprints and why they were selected. Collections contain less than five percent of original material.

Technology series: Each technology series is a brief reprint collection — approximately 126-136 pages and containing 12 to 13 papers, each paper focusing on a subset of a specific discipline, such as networks, architecture, software, or robotics.

Submission of proposals: For guidelines on preparing CS Press books, write the Editorial Director, IEEE Computer Society Press, PO Box 3014, 10662 Los Vaqueros Circle, Los Alamitos, CA 90720-1264, or telephone (714) 821-8380.

Purpose

The IEEE Computer Society advances the theory and practice of computer science and engineering, promotes the exchange of technical information among 100,000 members worldwide, and provides a wide range of services to members and nonmembers.

Membership

All members receive the acclaimed monthly magazine *Computer*, discounts, and opportunities to serve (all activities are led by volunteer members). Membership is open to all IEEE members, affiliate society members, and others seriously interested in the computer field.

Publications and Activities

Computer magazine: An authoritative, easy-to-read magazine containing tutorials and in-depth articles on topics across the computer field, plus news, conference reports, book reviews, calendars, calls for papers, interviews, and new products.

Periodicals: The society publishes six magazines and five research transactions. For more details, refer to our membership application or request information as noted above.

Conference proceedings, tutorial texts, and standards documents: The IEEE Computer Society Press publishes more than 100 titles every year.

Standards working groups: Over 100 of these groups produce IEEE standards used throughout the industrial world.

Technical committees: Over 30 TCs publish newsletters, provide interaction with peers in specialty areas, and directly influence standards, conferences, and education.

Conferences/Education: The society holds about 100 conferences each year and sponsors many educational activities, including computing science accreditation.

Chapters: Regular and student chapters worldwide provide the opportunity to interact with colleagues, hear technical experts, and serve the local professional community.

Other IEEE Computer Society Press Titles

MONOGRAPHS

Analyzing Computer Architectures
Written by Jerome C. Huck and Michael J. Flynn
(ISBN 0-8186-8857-2); 206 pages

Branch Strategy Taxonomy and Performance Models
Written by Harvey G. Cragon
(ISBN 0-8186-9111-5); 150 pages

Desktop Publishing for the Writer:
Designing, Writing, and Developing
Written by Richard Ziegfeld and John Tarp
(ISBN 0-8186-8840-8); 380 pages

Digital Image Warping
Written by George Wolberg
(ISBN 0-8186-8944-7); 340 pages

Integrating Design and Test —
CAE Tools for ATE Programming
Written by Kenneth P. Parker
(ISBN 0-8186-8788-6); 160 pages

JSP and JSD —
The Jackson Approach to Software Development
(Second Edition)
Written by John R. Cameron
(ISBN 0-8186-8858-0); 560 pages

National Computer Policies
Written by Ben G. Matley and Thomas A. McDannold
(ISBN 0-8186-8784-3); 192 pages

Optic Flow Computation: A Unified Perspective
Written by Ajit Singh
(ISBN 0-8186-2602-X); 256 pages

Physical Level Interfaces and Protocols
Written by Uyless Black
(ISBN 0-8186-8824-2); 240 pages

Protecting Your Proprietary Rights in Computer
and High-Technology Industries
Written by Tobey B. Marzouk, Esq.
(ISBN 0-8186-8754-1); 224 pages

X.25 and Related Protocols
Written by Uyless Black
(ISBN 0-8186-8976-5); 304 pages

TUTORIALS

Advanced Computer Architecture
Edited by Dharma P. Agrawal
(ISBN 0-8186-0667-3); 400 pages

Advances in Distributed System Reliability
Edited by Suresh Rai and Dharma P. Agrawal
(ISBN 0-8186-8907-2); 352 pages

Architectural Alternatives for Exploiting Parallelism
Edited by David J. Lilja
(ISBN 0-8186-2642-9); 464 pages

Autonomous Mobile Robots:
Perception, Mapping and Navigation — Volume 1
Edited by S. S. Iyengar and A. Elfes
(ISBN 0-8186-9018-6); 425 pages

Autonomous Mobile Robots:
Control, Planning, and Architecture — Volume 2
Edited by S. S. Iyengar and A. Elfes
(ISBN 0-8186-9116-6); 425 pages

Broadband Switching:
Architectures, Protocols, Design, and Analysis
Edited by C. Dhas, V. K. Konangi, and M. Sreetharan
(ISBN 0-8186-8926-9); 528 pages

Computer and Network Security
Edited by M. D. Abrams and H. J. Podell
(ISBN 0-8186-0756-4); 448 pages

Computer Architecture
Edited by D. Gajski, V. Milutinovic, H. Siegel, and B. Furht
(ISBN 0-8186-0704-1); 602 pages

Computer Arithmetic I
Edited by Earl E. Swartzlander, Jr.
(ISBN 0-8186-8931-5); 398 pages

Computer Arithmetic II
Edited by Earl E. Swartzlander, Jr.
(ISBN 0-8186-8945-5); 412 pages

Computer Communications:
Architectures, Protocols, and Standards (Third Edition)
Edited by William Stallings
(ISBN 0-8186-2710-7); 368 pages

Computer Graphics Hardware: Image Generation and Display
Edited by H. K. Reghbati and A. Y. C. Lee
(ISBN 0-8186-0753-X); 384 pages

Computer Graphics: Image Synthesis
Edited by Kenneth Joy, Nelson Max, Charles Grant,
and Lansing Hatfield
(ISBN 0-8186-8854-8); 380 pages

Computer Vision: Principles
Edited by Rangachar Kasturi and Ramesh Jain
(ISBN 0-8186-9102-6); 700 pages

Computer Vision: Advances and Applications
Edited by Rangachar Kasturi and Ramesh Jain
(ISBN 0-8186-9103-4); 720 pages

Digital Image Processing (Second Edition)
Edited by Rama Chellappa
(ISBN 0-8186-2362-4); 400 pages

Digital Private Branch Exchanges (PBXs)
Edited by Edwin Coover
(ISBN 0-8186-0829-3); 394 pages

Distributed Computing Network Reliability
Edited by Suresh Rai and Dharma P. Agrawal
(ISBN 0-8186-8908-0); 357 pages

Distributed-Software Engineering
Edited by Sol Shatz and Jia-Ping Wang
(ISBN 0-8186-8856-4); 294 pages

Domain Analysis and Software Systems Modeling
Edited by Ruben-Prieto Diaz and Guillermo Arango
(ISBN 0-8186-8996-X); 312 pages

Formal Verification of Hardware Design
Edited by Michael Yoeli
(ISBN 0-8186-9017-8); 340 pages

Groupware:
Software for Computer-Supported Cooperative Work
Edited by David Marca and Geoffrey Bock
(ISBN 0-8186-2637-2); 500 pages

Hard Real-Time Systems
Edited by J. A. Stankovic and K. Ramamritham
(ISBN 0-8186-0819-6); 624 pages

For further information call 1-800-CS-BOOKS or write:

IEEE Computer Society Press, 10662 Los Vaqueros Circle, PO Box 3014,
Los Alamitos, California 90720-1264, USA

IEEE Computer Society, 13, avenue de l'Aquilon,
B-1200 Brussels, BELGIUM

IEEE Computer Society, Ooshima Building, 2-19-1 Minami-Aoyama,
Minato-ku, Tokyo 107, JAPAN

Integrated Services Digital Networks (ISDN)
(Second Edition)
Edited by William Stallings
(ISBN 0-8186-0823-4); 406 pages

Knowledge-Based Systems:
Fundamentals and Tools
Edited by Oscar N. Garcia and Yi-Tzuu Chien
(ISBN 0-8186-1924-4); 512 pages

Local Network Technology (Third Edition)
Edited by William Stallings
(ISBN 0-8186-0825-0); 512 pages

Microprogramming and Firmware Engineering
Edited by V. M. Milutinovic
(ISBN 0-8186-0839-0); 416 pages

Modeling and Control of Automated Manufacturing Systems
Edited by Alan A. Desrochers
(ISBN 0-8186-8916-1); 384 pages

Nearest Neighbor Pattern Classification Techniques
Edited by Belur V. Dasarathy
(ISBN 0-8186-8930-7); 464 pages

New Paradigms for Software Development
Edited by William Agresti
(ISBN 0-8186-0707-6); 304 pages

Object-Oriented Computing, Volume 1: Concepts
Edited by Gerald E. Petersen
(ISBN 0-8186-0821-8); 214 pages

Object-Oriented Computing, Volume 2: Implementations
Edited by Gerald E. Petersen
(ISBN 0-8186-0822-6); 324 pages

Parallel Architectures for Database Systems
Edited by A. R. Hurson, L. L. Miller, and S. H. Pakzad
(ISBN 0-8186-8838-6); 478 pages

Reduced Instruction Set Computers (RISC)
(Second Edition)
Edited by William Stallings
(ISBN 0-8186-8943-9); 448 pages

Software Engineering Project Management
Edited by Richard H. Thayer
(ISBN 0-8186-0751-3); 512 pages

Software Maintenance and Computers
Edited by David H. Longstreet
(ISBN 0-8186-8898-X); 304 pages

Software Quality Assurance:
A Practical Approach
Edited by T.S. Chow
(ISBN 0-8186-0569-3); 506 pages

Software Reuse — Emerging Technology
Edited by Will Tracz
(ISBN 0-8186-0846-3); 400 pages

Software Risk Management
Edited by Barry W. Boehm
(ISBN 0-8186-8906-4); 508 pages

Standards, Guidelines and Examples on System
and Software Requirements Engineering
Edited by Merlin Dorfman and Richard H. Thayer
(ISBN 0-8186-8922-6); 626 pages

System and Software Requirements Engineering
Edited by Richard H. Thayer and Merlin Dorfman
(ISBN 0-8186-8921-8); 740 pages

Test Access Port and Boundary-Scan Architecture
Edited by Colin M. Maunder and Rodham E. Tulloss
(ISBN 0-8186-9070-4); 400 pages

Visual Programming Environments: Paradigms and Systems
Edited by Ephraim Glinert
(ISBN 0-8186-8973-0); 680 pages

Visual Programming Environments: Applications and Issues
Edited by Ephraim Glinert
(ISBN 0-8186-8974-9); 704 pages

Visualization in Scientific Computing
Edited by G. M. Nielson, B. Shriver, and L. Rosenblum
(ISBN 0-8186-8979-X); 304 pages

Volume Visualization
Edited by Arie Kaufman
(ISBN 0-8186-9020-8); 494 pages

REPRINT COLLECTIONS

Distributed Computing Systems:
Concepts and Structures
Edited by A. L. Ananda and B. Srinivasan
(ISBN 0-8186-8975-0); 416 pages

Expert Systems:
A Software Methodology for Modern Applications
Edited by Peter G. Raeth
(ISBN 0-8186-8904-8); 476 pages

Milestones in Software Evolution
Edited by Paul W. Oman and Ted G. Lewis
(ISBN 0-8186-9033-X); 332 pages

Object-Oriented Databases
Edited by Ez Nahouraii and Fred Petry
(ISBN 0-8186-8929-3); 256 pages

Validating and Verifying Knowledge-Based Systems
Edited by Uma G. Gupta
(ISBN 0-8186-8995-1); 400 pages

ARTIFICIAL NEURAL NETWORKS TECHNOLOGY SERIES

Artificial Neural Networks —
Concept Learning
Edited by Joachim Diederich
(ISBN 0-8186-2015-3); 160 pages

Artificial Neural Networks —
Electronic Implementation
Edited by Nelson Morgan
(ISBN 0-8186-2029-3); 144 pages

Artificial Neural Networks —
Theoretical Concepts
Edited by V. Vemuri
(ISBN 0-8186-0855-2); 160 pages

SOFTWARE TECHNOLOGY SERIES

Computer-Aided Software Engineering (CASE)
Edited by E. J. Chikofsky
(ISBN 0-8186-1917-1); 110 pages

Software Reliability Models:
Theoretical Development, Evaluation, and Applications
Edited by Yashwant K. Malaiya and Pradip K. Srimani
(ISBN 0-8186-2110-9); 136 pages

MATHEMATICS TECHNOLOGY SERIES

Computer Algorithms
Edited by Jun-ichi Aoe
(ISBN 0-8186-2123-0); 154 pages

Multiple-Valued Logic in VLSI Design
Edited by Jon T. Butler
(ISBN 0-8186-2127-3); 128 pages

COMMUNICATIONS TECHNOLOGY SERIES

Multicast Communication in Distributed Systems
Edited by Mustaque Ahamad
(ISBN 0-8186-1970-8); 110 pages

ROBOTICS TECHNOLOGY SERIES

Multirobot Systems
Edited by Rajiv Mehrotra and Murali R. Varanasi
(ISBN 0-8186-1977-5); 122 pages

MONOGRAPHS

OPTIC FLOW COMPUTATION:
A Unified Perspective
by Ajit Singh

This monograph provides a new estimation-theoretic framework for optic flow computation and unifies and integrates the existing approaches for this framework. It examines a new framework that views the problem of recovering optic flow from time-varying imagery as a parameter-estimation problem and applies statistical estimation theory techniques to optic flow computation. It also discusses its application for recursive estimation of 3D scene geometry from optic flow using Kalman-filtering-based techniques.

The book addresses five major issues: unification: conservation and neighborhood information, integration of the three approaches, clarification of the distinction between image flow and optic flow, past research on optic flow computation from a new perspective, and incremental estimation of optic flow in real-time applications.

256 pages. January 1992. ISBN 0-8186-2602-X.
Catalog # 2602 $60.00 / $40.00 Member

X.25 AND RELATED PROTOCOLS
by Uyless Black

This monograph presents a tutorial view of X.25, discusses other protocols with which it operates, and provides a convenient reference guide to its protocols. The text contains all original material, including six appendices, over 100 illustrations, and more than 50 tables.

X.25 and Related Protocols explains X.25 operations, the advantages and disadvantages of its use, the concepts and terms of packet networks, and the role other standards play in the operation of X.25. It presents a considerable amount of detailed information about X.25 and its role in various systems such as LANs, PBXs, and ISDNs. The book covers a wide variety of subjects such as switching and routing in networks, the OSI model, physical-layer protocols and interfaces, high-level data-link control (HDLC), X.25 packet structures and types, and internetworking with SNA, DECnet, X.75, LANs, and ISDN

304 pages. 1991. Hardbound. ISBN 0-8186-8976-5.
Catalog # 1976 $70.00 / $45.00 Member

DIGITAL IMAGE WARPING
by George Wolberg

Digital image warping is a growing branch of the image processing field dealing primarily with geometric transformation techniques. Traditionally used for geometric correction in remote sensing and medical imaging, warping has recently enjoyed a new surge of interest stemming from computer graphics use in image synthesis and special effects.

This book, containing all original material, clarifies the various terminologies, motivations, and contributions of the many disciplines involved in this technology. The material is balanced between theory (proofs and formulas derived to motivate algorithms and to establish a standard of comparison) and practice (algorithms that can be implemented). It includes 36 color photographs and contains informative sections on image reconstruction, real-time texture mapping, separable algorithms, 2-pass transforms, mesh warping, and special effects.

340 pages. 1990. Hardbound. ISBN 0-8186-8944-7.
Catalog # 1944 $60.00 / $45.00 Member

BRANCH STRATEGY TAXONOMY AND PERFORMANCE MODELS
by Harvey G. Cragon

This book provides a taxonomy that classifies and describes strategies in a consistent fashion, presents analytic models that permit the evaluation of each strategy under varying work load and pipeline parameters, and describes a modeling methodology that facilitates the evaluation of new branching strategies. It interprets analytic models that give a designer the capability of evaluating branching strategies while considering the implementation of parameters such as pipeline length and the location of the branch-effective address ALU.

The monograph investigates these six branching strategies along with their subordinate strategies and performance models: baseline strategy, pipeline freeze strategies, branch prediction strategies, fetch multiple paths strategies, instruction sequence alteration strategies, and composite strategies

120 pages. February 1992. Hardbound. ISBN 0-8186-9111-5.
Catalog # 2111 $45.00 / $30.00 Member

from *IEEE COMPUTER SOCIETY PRESS*

To order any of these titles or for information on other books,
call 1-800-CS-BOOKS or order by *FAX* at (714) 821-4010

 IEEE COMPUTER SOCIETY

(in California call 714-821-8380)

 THE INSTITUTE OF ELECTRICAL AND ELECTRONICS ENGINEERS, INC.

PUBLISH WITH IEEE COMPUTER SOCIETY PRESS

TODAY'S COMPUTER SCIENCE PROFESSIONALS ARE TURNING TO US TO PUBLISH THEIR TEXTS

BENEFITS OF IEEE COMPUTER SOCIETY PRESS PUBLISHING :

- ❑ **Timely publication schedules**
- ❑ **Society's professional reputation and recognition**
- ❑ **High-quality, reasonably priced books**
- ❑ **Course classroom adoption**
- ❑ **Open options on the type and level of publication to develop**
- ❑ **Built-in mechanisms to reach a strong constituency of professionals**
- ❑ **Peer review and reference**

Enjoy the personal, professional, and financial recognition of having your name in print alongside other respected professionals in the fields of computer and engineering technology. Our rapid turnaround (from approved proposal to the published product) assures you against publication of dated technical material, and gives you the potential for additional royalties and sales from new editions. Your royalty payments are based not only on sales, but also on the amount of time and effort you expend in writing original material for your book.

Your book will be advertised to a vast audience through IEEE Computer Society Press catalogs and brochures that reach over 500,000 carefully chosen professionals in numerous disciplines. Our wide distribution also includes promotional programs through our European and Asian offices, and over-the-counter sales at 50 international computer and engineering conferences annually.

IEEE Computer Society Press books have a proven sales record, and our tutorials enjoy a unique niche in today's fast moving technical fields and help us maintain our goal to publish up-to-date, viable computer science information.

Steps for Book Submittals:

1- Submit your proposal to the Editorial Director of IEEE Computer Society Press. It should include the following data: title; your name, address, and telephone number; a detailed outline; a summary of the subject matter; a statement of the technical level of the book, the intended audience, and the potential market; a table of contents including the titles, authors, and sources for all reprints; and a biography.

2- Upon acceptance of your proposal, prepare and submit copies of the completed manuscript, including xerox copies of any reprinted papers and any other pertinent information, and mail to the Editorial Director of IEEE Computer Society Press.

3- The manuscript will then be reviewed by other respected experts in the field, and the editor-in-charge.

4- Upon publication, you will receive an initial royalty payment with additional royalties based on a percentage of the net sales and on the amount of original material included in the book.

We are searching for authors in the following computer science areas:

ADA	LOCAL AREA NETWORKS
ARCHITECTURE	OPTICAL STORAGE DATABASES
ARTIFICIAL INTELLIGENCE	PARALLEL PROCESSING
AUTOMATED TEST EQUIPMENT	PATTERN RECOGNITION
CAD / CAE	PERSONAL COMPUTING
COMPUTER GRAPHICS	RELIABILITY
COMPUTER LANGUAGES	ROBOTICS
COMPUTER MATHEMATICS	SOFTWARE ENGINEERING
COMPUTER WORKSTATIONS	SOFTWARE ENVIRONMENTS
DATABASE ENGINEERING	SOFTWARE MAINTENANCE
DIGITAL IMAGE PROCESSING	SOFTWARE TESTING AND
DISTRIBUTED PROCESSING	VALIDATION
EXPERT SYSTEMS	AND OTHER AREAS AT THE
FAULT-TOLERANT COMPUTING	FOREFRONT OF
IMAGING	COMPUTING TECHNOLOGY !

Interested ?

For more detailed guidelines please contact:

Editorial Director, c/o IEEE Computer Society Press, 10662 Los Vaqueros Circle, Los Alamitos, California 90720-1264.

IEEE COMPUTER SOCIETY

THE INSTITUTE OF ELECTRICAL AND ELECTRONICS ENGINEERS, INC.